CHINA, THE UNITED STATES, AND THE FUTURE
OF SOUTHEAST ASIA

China, the United States, and the Future of Southeast Asia

U.S.-China Relations, Volume II

Edited by David B. H. Denoon

NEW YORK UNIVERSITY PRESS
New York

NEW YORK UNIVERSITY PRESS
New York
www.nyupress.org

References to Internet websites (URLs) were accurate at the time of writing. Neither the author nor New York University Press is responsible for URLs that may have expired or changed since the manuscript was prepared.

ISBN: 978-1-4798-6630-4 (hardback)
ISBN: 978-1-4798-1032-1 (paperback)

For Library of Congress Cataloging-in-Publication data, please contact the Library of Congress.

New York University Press books are printed on acid-free paper, and their binding materials are chosen for strength and durability. We strive to use environmentally responsible suppliers and materials to the greatest extent possible in publishing our books.

Manufactured in the United States of America

10 9 8 7 6 5 4 3 2 1

Also available as an ebook

CONTENTS

PREFACE

This is the second book in a three-volume series exploring the relations between the United States and China in regions of the world where neither state is dominant. There is already a massive literature on the bilateral relations between the United States and China, but distinctly less has been published on how the countries deal with each other in parts of the globe where they have interests but not necessarily vital interests.

The first volume in the series dealt with Central Asia (Kazakhstan, Kyrgyzstan, Tajikistan, Turkmenistan, and Uzbekistan). One of the principal findings of that book was that China and the United States had very different objectives in Central Asia, and that Beijing and Washington are not directly competitive there.

The current focus of the United States in Central Asia is on security issues, while China's interests are overwhelmingly on extracting natural gas and oil. Also, to the extent that their interests overlap on security, they are compatible because both China and the United States are concerned about militant Islam.

As we will see in this volume, the situation in Southeast Asia is significantly different from patterns in Central Asia. In Southeast Asia, both China and the United States have major economic, political, and security concerns. In addition, the South China Sea, where there are hotly disputed territorial claims between China and its neighbors, is a principal waterway that touches most of the countries in the region, and affects Northeast Asia as well.

Since 2007 China has been taking a far more assertive stance toward its neighbors than it did in the 1976 to 2006 period. In the earlier period, China was recovering from the effects of the Cultural Revolution, concentrating on economic development, and taking a low-keyed position toward the rest of Southeast Asia. The earlier position included offering aid to Thailand at the time of its Financial Crisis in 1997, offering a generous set of terms for the Association of the Southeast Asian Nations—ASEAN-China Free Trade Agreement, and emphasizing negotiations as a means of resolving territorial disputes.

In the post-2007 period, China has changed its foreign policy significantly. The nation has challenged Japan over its control of the Senkaku (Diaoyu Islands), has disregarded Vietnam and Philippine claims to islets far from China shores, and has constructed airfields and artificial islands on atolls hundreds of miles from the recognized Chinese borders. In this process China has driven a wedge between the northern states in ASEAN (Myanmar, Thailand, Laos, and Cambodia), which have no claims in the South China Sea, and Vietnam, the Philippines, Malaysia, Indonesia, and Brunei, which do. The Vietnamese and the southern states are worried about China's occupation of the islands and fear that Beijing's aggressiveness is the beginning of more to come.

Thus, in Central Asia, China and the United States are on separate tracks, while in Southeast Asia, Beijing and Washington often find themselves at loggerheads. This book provides an overview of developments in the region and assesses the reactions of both the individual Southeast Asian states and the outside powers.

Two special notes regarding developments in Southeast Asia and the timing of this manuscript are important. First, on July 12, 2016, the Permanent Court of Arbitration (PCA) ruled in favor of the Philippines on all but one count in the dispute. Manuscripts for this volume were submitted before that ruling, so do not discuss it—although several chapters refer to the proceedings of the PCA at the Hague. The Chinese government has stated that it will ignore the rulings of the PCA. So the dispute between the Southeast Asian states and China remains unsettled. Second, the new president of the Philippines, Rodrigo Duarte, has made a number of very hostile statements about the United States (the Philippines' principal military ally) and has indicated that he intends to negotiate directly with China regarding the Sino-Phil territorial disputes in the South China Sea. Were president Duarte to continue to create friction in the U.S.-Philippine alliance and to reach a settlement of the Sino-Phil territorial disputes, the strategic balance in Asia would be dramatically changed. The uncertainty over whether China will eventually compromise on the PCA ruling and what final course of action the Philippines will take could continue for a sizable period of time. Thus it seems reasonable to proceed with publication now but note these important uncertainties that this book cannot resolve.

Edited books need a range of ideas, commitment by the authors, and patience from all concerned to produce an integrated volume. My thanks go to each and every author for tolerance of my assorted suggestions and making the effort to revise manuscripts to produce a volume that can be read by both specialists and the attentive public.

Special thanks also go to Ms. Dongbo Wang, who played a key administrative role in every stage of this book's development, from the planning of the conference that launched the project to the final editing. In addition, Fei Cai,

Zelong Tang, Sainan Yu, Xing Lu, and Bingxin Fa were also very helpful as research assistants.

At the launch conference, Amb. Winston Lord, Amb. J. Stapleton Roy, Amb. David Merrill, and professors Hugh Patrick and M. Ishaq Nadiri each made insightful suggestions about how the papers could be revised. Also, Amb. Richard Solomon gave an extremely useful presentation setting out the changing strategic picture in Southeast Asia.

Thanks also go to unnamed reviewers recruited by NYU Press and to the editors at NYU Press, Ms. Ilene Kalish and Ms. Caelyn Cobb, who shepherded us through the publication process.

David B. H. Denoon
New York
October 2016

Introduction

DAVID B. H. DENOON

Since World War II, Southeast Asia has gone through several cycles of optimism and pessimism. In the 1950s and 1960s, as most of the countries were trying to establish their independence and autonomy, the major challenge was from communist insurgencies (which succeeded in Vietnam, Laos, and Cambodia). Ironically, just as South Vietnam was succumbing to North Vietnam, the remaining pro-Western states in the region were beginning to move in a market-oriented direction.

The Association of Southeast Asian Nations (ASEAN) was created in 1967 by Thailand, Malaysia, Singapore, the Philippines, and Indonesia. Those five states became the modernizing and, eventually, export-oriented center of the region. The ASEAN states were transformed from "dominoes to dynamos."[1] Although all of the ASEAN countries protected a substantial state sector, they moved from an inward-looking, import-substituting industrial strategy in the 1960s to an export focus in the 1970s.[2] This led to significantly higher economic growth rates and a sense of optimism pervading the pro-Western part of Southeast Asia. It also led the authoritarian states in the region to slightly open their economies and to want to join ASEAN.

The 1990s represented the height of optimism about the future of Southeast Asia from both insiders and outside observers. Many of the largest economies were growing at 7 percent per year or faster, and the expectation was that once the region was unified, it would become a bloc with major influence.[3]

Nevertheless, 1997 proved to be a major crisis point for Southeast Asia. The region appeared to be in the middle of an economic boom, and ASEAN had just agreed to expand its membership to include the three remaining countries in the region (Myanmar, Laos, and Cambodia). Few of the region's governments anticipated the crash that started in July 1997 and was to set the area back for years to come.[4]

Also, most of the advocates of expanding ASEAN assumed that Southeast Asia would soon start acting as a cohesive group of ten nations. There were numerous comparisons made between ASEAN and the European Union; and with a population of roughly four hundred million at that time, there were many reasons to think ASEAN would be a powerhouse. Although outside observers were skeptical of how integrated the region would become, commentary *within* the ASEAN states was strongly upbeat.

If it had been known that the 1997 financial crisis would significantly lower the economic growth trajectory for the region and that Southeast Asia would, in essence, split between those states that were pro-China and those that were pro-Western, the enthusiasm for the region's prospects would have been more muted.

So, in Southeast Asia, following the pessimism of the 1960s and the optimism of the 1980s and 1990s, the major letdown of the 1997 financial crisis occurred. The first decade of the twenty-first century was, therefore, a rebuilding period for the ASEAN economies. The first priority was the recapitalization and restructuring of the banking systems—especially in Thailand and Indonesia.[5] Then attention was focused on consolidating and extending the term structure of many countries' debts.[6] The results were impressive.

Most of the countries hurt by the 1997 financial crash began to run trade surpluses and built up their foreign-exchange reserves to the point where they were financially stable and less vulnerable to speculative attack. Thus, the major economies in the region recovered, and some of the Marxist states (notably Vietnam and Cambodia) adopted many market-oriented policies, increasing their economic growth rates. Most of the Southeast Asian states are now growing steadily, so the regional economic picture is bright.

Yet, just as the economic scene in Southeast Asia has improved, critical internal political and foreign policy problems have come to the fore. Most of the ASEAN states are politically stable. However, Thailand, which has the second largest economy in the region and a vital, central location, faces major internal political turmoil. Also, China's growing assertiveness on territorial and security issues is placing most of the ASEAN governments in the uncomfortable position of having to decide if they want to become pro-Beijing or join with those states resisting Chinese policy.

Thailand's difficulties, in many ways, mirror the dilemmas facing other governments in the region that must deal with social friction within their societies. A deep split has developed between the traditional Thais, who support the monarchy and favor market-oriented policies, and the populists, who favor income redistribution and more government intervention.[7] These divisions are exacerbated by an ethnic split between the local Chinese, who favor former Prime Minister Thaksin Shinawatra, and those many Thais who hold the monarchy in high esteem.

Thaksin, and his many proxies, have been able to win national elections in the past decade and a half, but his opponents, in the middle- and upper-income groups, tenaciously oppose his populist policies and his vote-buying style of politics. This led to military intervention in the spring of 2014. At present, it is unclear how long Thailand will remain under military rule. It is also uncertain if Thailand will return to full democracy or some kind of limited system that constrains Thaksin and his followers.

At the moment, more than half of ASEAN's states have some form of authoritarian or quasi-authoritarian leadership, and these circumstances seem likely to continue for the indefinite future.[8]

The foreign policy dilemmas facing the ASEAN states are trying as well. The original five member countries of ASEAN were all anticommunist and saw China, in the 1960s, as a radical state to be avoided. The Cultural Revolution went on for a decade (from 1966 to 1976), and kept China mostly focused inward in that period. Yet, Maoist policies supported insurgencies overseas, so China was regarded warily. Then, in the first two decades after the Cultural Revolution, China's attention was overwhelmingly concentrated on improving its economy. This meant that, between 1976 and 1997, China changed from being a dangerous revolutionary state to being a calm neighbor, offering a vast, appealing market.[9]

Beijing enhanced its image in Southeast Asia by offering to establish the China-ASEAN Free Trade Agreement and not requiring the ASEAN countries to immediately lower their import tariffs. This meant that the ASEAN states got two enormous advantages in trading with China: (1) access to a booming market and (2) zero tariffs for their exports while being able to, temporarily, maintain protection for domestically produced goods. Hence, in the first five years of the new century, China became a highly appreciated neighbor.

Nevertheless, in 2007, as China began to take a harder position on territorial questions in the East and South China Sea, the Southeast Asian nations began to be more concerned about Beijing's intentions. These concerns have only grown in the past seven years as China has (1) declared the Paracel Islands (also claimed by Vietnam) to be part of the Hainan Island Administrative District; (2) blockaded a Philippine ship in the second Thomas Shoal; (3) expanded its military presence on various islands and atolls in the South China Sea; and (4) moved a massive oil rig, HS981, into Vietnam's Exclusive Economic Zone. (The Chinese subsequently moved the rig back to an area near Hainan Island, but only after violent rioting against the Vietnamese.)[10] In addition, in 2016, China began placing radar antennas and antiaircraft missiles on the northern outcroppings it occupies in the South China Sea. The Chinese military occupation of these areas directly contradicts promises President Xi Jinping made to President Obama in the fall of 2015.

As Chinese policies have grown more assertive, the entire tenor of relations between China and Southeast Asia has changed. For many years the Southeast Asians followed the jousting between China and Japan over the Senkaku/Diaoyu Islands but hoped that the same friction would not affect them and the competing claims in the South China Sea. Yet, once China claimed all the islands, atolls, and waters inside its "nine-dash line," the Southeast Asians recognized that there was going to be a basic standoff on this issue.[11] During 2013–14, debates over the South China Sea led to increasingly tense and pointed exchanges between the ASEAN claimant states and China.[12] These led the Philippine government to take its case against China to the ITLOS (International Tribunal for the Law of the Sea), where all but one of the Philippine claims were upheld (see discussion in the concluding chapter).

The Chinese government asserts it is establishing the basis for a regional security architecture by building up the Shanghai Cooperation Organization (SCO) and the Conference on Interaction and Confidence-Building Measures in Asia (CICA).[13] Yet the Chinese Foreign Ministry spokesman told reporters, "Anything that China does on any of the islands in the South China Sea is within its sovereign rights and the Philippines has nothing to do with it," which shows how rigid and aggressive Beijing's position is.[14]

Thus, the scene in Southeast Asia has mixed elements. The ASEAN country economies are performing exceptionally well, but cooperation among the ASEAN governments has stalled and there is real apprehension about what China's next moves will be. If China decides to take a more conciliatory line or even negotiates on regional territorial questions, there will be a collective sigh of relief from the ASEAN states. If, however, China pursues its current hard line, the ASEAN governments will need to decide how to buttress their security and there will likely be major fissures within ASEAN.

Themes in This Volume

There are seven principal themes that recur throughout this volume and tie the collection together:

1. Relations between the Southeast Asian states and China are mixed and deeply ambivalent. Some relations are close and supportive, others are just distant, while still others are severely strained.
2. Thailand, Cambodia, and Laos have the closest relations with China, while Myanmar has extensive trade relations but an increasingly fraught interaction over water rights and the impact of Chinese foreign direct investment (FDI). Vietnam and the Philippines have sharp differences with China on

territorial questions in the South China Sea, while Malaysia, Brunei, Singapore, and Indonesia have cordial but not close relations.

3. All of the ASEAN states trade actively with China and are happy to have Chinese FDI. Yet, Chinese FDI in ASEAN declined in 2014.

4. Relations between the Southeast Asian states and the United States are almost the converse of their relations with China. U.S. relations with Thailand include a security treaty, but since the recent military coup, a mutually circumspect attitude has held. U.S. links with Cambodia and Laos are limited—but are balanced by close working ties with the Philippines, Vietnam, Brunei, Malaysia, Singapore, and Indonesia.

5. Countries in Southeast Asia face a dilemma: as China's prominence grows, they will need to decide if they want to side with China, that is, *Bandwagon* or *Balance* (i.e., cooperate with states that are skeptical of Chinese motives like Japan, the United States, and India).

6. The geopolitical map in Southeast Asia is, with one exception (Vietnam), split between the Northern and Southern members of ASEAN. Nations in the Northern Tier (Myanmar, Thailand, Cambodia and Laos) have the best ties with China, while those in the Southern Tier have the most distant relations. China's current position on sovereignty in the South China Sea is likely to only widen these differences within ASEAN.

7. The United States has a vital interest in freedom of navigation (by air and sea) and in keeping the Southern Tier of ASEAN independent of Chinese control. In 2016, the Obama administration increased U.S. naval patrols in the South China Sea in open waters near accepted reefs that China recently occupied. The question becomes, will the Chinese government press its position now or wait to see if the Southern Tier of ASEAN loses confidence in U.S. security ties?

Structure of the Volume

This book is divided into four sections: (1) overview chapters, (2) analyses of countries within Southeast Asia, (3) analyses of how outside powers interact with Southeast Asia, and (4) the conclusion.

The overview chapters elaborate the main themes identified above. In providing a survey of the economic scene, Vikram Nehru explains why the 1997 financial crisis took such a toll on Southeast Asia. Three of the largest economies in the region (Thailand, Indonesia, and Malaysia) had open capital markets and suffered when investors withdrew their funds.[15] Thailand and Indonesia both lost more than 40 percent of the value of their currencies, which made it very difficult for local firms that had borrowed in foreign currencies to repay their debts. The resulting turmoil led to many bankruptcies and delayed many new projects for years. Yet, as Nehru illustrates, the Southeast Asian governments subsequently adopted more cautious economic policies that helped form the basis for the current impressive economic growth in the region.

In her essay on Southeast Asian foreign policy, Ann Marie Murphy demonstrates that ASEAN, as an organization, does not itself have a coherent foreign policy that the ten member states can agree upon. There are certain accepted principles of operation, such as "noninterference" and "the ASEAN Way" of consensus decision making. Yet, the ten countries are sufficiently diverse and have such different objectives that it is not feasible to form an overall, cohesive ASEAN foreign policy. What does happen periodically, however, is the recognition that, on particular issues, interests of the ten states are sufficiently aligned that they can act as a group. This happens more frequently on economic issues, like the formation of the ASEAN Free Trade Agreement and the China-ASEAN Free Trade Agreement, than it does on political topics, like seeking security guarantees from outside powers. Moreover, given the growing North-South split within ASEAN over the extent of ties to China, the chances of ASEAN consensus on major political topics are minimal.

In evaluating nontraditional security issues in Southeast Asia, Amy Freedman notes that there is virtual unanimity on the principles of improving the environment through plans to ban burning of bogs and forests. However, just as with foreign policy topics, ASEAN has no enforcement mechanism, so environmental guidelines are flouted with impunity by countries, like Indonesia, that have strong local interest groups that want to continue banned practices. Similarly, there is no enforcement mechanism to compel countries to keep their food markets open (to foreign purchasers) during droughts, which would help smooth the swings in food prices. Hence, it is fair to say that ASEAN is a voluntary association of states, not a federalist structure on the way to political union. This means that there is no group cohesion mechanism to encourage individual states to make any sacrifices for the other nine members.

Patterns of behavior within ASEAN are quite diverse. Four of the five Northern Tier states (Myanmar, Laos, Cambodia, and Thailand) have accommodations with Beijing. As Catharin Dalpino's chapter illustrates, Myanmar was much closer to China when it was under complete military rule than it is today, when the military and civilians share power. Also riots against Chinese dams and mines have made a quasi-democratic Myanmar government worried about hewing too close to Beijing's wishes. Public opinion plays a much smaller role in the calculus of the Lao and Cambodian governments, and aid from China is critical in sustaining these regimes. Thailand is a mixed case because there is a large and very influential Chinese community in Bangkok that is overwhelmingly in business and favors close ties with Beijing. Yet, matters are complicated, as discussed above, because Thaksin Shinawatra himself is Chinese, making pro-royalist Chinese ambivalent about whom to align with. Most Thais see an advantage in keeping ties with the United States, but there is no enthusiasm for any efforts to "balance against China." So, among the Northern Tier Four, China can count on a sufficient bloc within ASEAN to thwart any effort at limiting Chinese influence.

Vietnam is the pronounced exception in the Northern Tier. Hanoi has had a very complicated relationship with China for centuries. Many Vietnamese deeply resent Beijing's pressure, but at the same time the Vietnamese emulate Chinese methods for internal political control. The Vietnamese political elite is split between those who want to keep good relations with Beijing and those who want a more nationalistic stance. Vietnam's defense White Paper is a multifaceted document alluding to various threats, but also noting the importance of dealing with nontraditional security issues like climate change, illegal immigration, and health issues.[16]

China's recent violations of Vietnam's Exclusive Economic Zone have produced such a violent response, however, that there is now little to be gained in Hanoi by advocating a conciliatory line toward China. As Tran Truong Thuy points out, China has deeply hurt its chances of rapprochement with Vietnam. Circumstances are quite similar in the Philippines, where, for the decade after 1997, there was a pro-Beijing faction, but recent events have made Philippine cooperation with China highly suspect.

In the Southern Tier states in ASEAN (Brunei, Malaysia, Singapore, and Indonesia), there has been a concerted effort to avoid friction with China, but also deep skepticism about Beijing's intentions.[17]

Because of Singapore's large Chinese majority and the Lee family's pride in Chinese traditions, there was, during the 1980s and 1990s, a clear Sinophilia in Singapore's foreign policy. That has faded as the leadership in Singapore has recognized that they need U.S. ties as a counterbalance to China. As Heng Yee-Kuang explains, Singapore wants no tension with China and has no territorial disputes in the South China Sea; nevertheless, its leaders see China's assertiveness as an ominous challenge to the ASEAN states.

Brunei, Malaysia, and Indonesia form the Muslim arc in ASEAN and, as such, have little natural affinity with China. Yet, at the same time, each state in its own way is skeptical of U.S. intentions. As Zakaria Ahmad and Evan Laksmana show, Brunei avoids major foreign policy choices and both Malaysia and Indonesia have a low-keyed, somewhat jaundiced view of China's objectives. Malaysia has a significant Chinese minority (approximately 30 percent of the population); and for many years Prime Minister Mahathir courted China as a way to shore up his Malay-Chinese political coalition. Yet, Malaysian businessmen see China as a competitor in many regards, and there is an inherent limit to how far a Malaysian prime minister can go in accommodating China.[18] Similarly, Indonesians highly value their "Non-Aligned" status and have avoided formally linking with either China or the United States.[19] Nevertheless, since the beginning of the Suharto era, Indonesia and the United States have had various executive agreements that have facilitated cooperation on security matters; and in June 2014, Indonesia finally took a stand, rejecting China's nine-dash line as a basis for settlement of territorial disputes in the South China Sea. And ASEAN, as a group, strengthened its position on peaceful resolution of the dispute in the April 27, 2015, statement.[20] Moreover, Indonesia's new President Jokowi has taken a much more assertive stance in defending Indonesia's fishing rights.

Hence we see that ASEAN as an organization is split between links to China, a preferred avoidance of commitment by several states, and quiet, informal relations with the United States.

In Southeast Asia there are very substantial differences in operating style among the outside powers as well. The United States and China are the two most visible outside states, but Japan and India are significant players as well. The European Union is also a vital actor on economic and human rights issues, but not a key participant on security matters.

China's most significant economic initiative is the China-ASEAN Free Trade Agreement (discussed above). As Chen Shaofeng discusses, China got very significant political gains from its approach to the Central America Free Trade Agreement (CAFTA). Now, however, there are more Southeast Asians who worry about economic competition from China.[21]

Yet, on balance, it is China's profile on political and security matters that is most discussed in the Southeast Asian states. As Chu Shulong indicates, China has long made assorted claims in the South China Sea. Despite Chinese assertions of peaceful intent, China's recent moves to reinforce its claims have concerned many ASEAN governments.[22]

The United States has two major advantages over China in the eyes of Southeast Asians: (1) Washington provides nonthreatening sea- and air-lane protection and a broad range of security benefits, and (2) the United States has no territorial claims in the ASEAN region. So, although the U.S. government wants access to ports and airfields, periodically a source of friction with allies and cooperating states, differences between ASEAN and Washington can usually be negotiated in a low-keyed manner.[23] Because China provides no "public goods" protection in Southeast Asia and is a distinct challenger to the territorial claims of the ASEAN states, Beijing's naval and air forces are seen in a different light than those of the United States.

As McDevitt and Ott point out, the United States has long taken "no position" on the various claims to territory and exclusive economic zones in the South China Sea. The principal admonition from Washington has been that "assorted claimants should resolve their differences peacefully." An important modification of that policy was Secretary of State Clinton's comments, at the July 2010 ASEAN Regional Forum meeting, that the United States was willing to play a "facilitator's role" in helping to resolve the territorial disputes.[24] More recently, U.S. Secretary of Defense Ashton Carter directly criticized China's construction of artificial islands in the South China Sea.[25] These two interventions have irritated the leadership in Beijing, who see them as American meddling in a dispute that does not directly involve the United States. For their part, U.S. congressional and executive branch leaders have increasingly seen China's coercive tactics against Vietnam and the Philippines as endangering freedom of navigation in the South China Sea. Thus, as we will explore in this volume, the United States may not be able to stay entirely out of the South China Sea disputes if China continues its current tactics. Not only is the Philippines a formal treaty ally, but Vietnam could be a key "cooperating country" in a U.S.-led effort to strengthen links among Pacific states.

Japan and India have somewhat similar relationships to Southeast Asia. Both countries have recently had predominantly economic ties to the ASEAN region. Japan has both more trade and more investment than India, but India's interest in the region is growing rapidly. Also, leaders in Tokyo and New Delhi are in the process of sorting out what kinds of new ventures and commitments they want to make in Southeast Asia. In this context, Japan has sent ships on friendly visits to Philippine ports.

Moreover, decision makers in Tokyo recognize that they face problems comparable to those of the ASEAN leaders in deciding how to deal with China. Thus, as Lincoln notes, Japan could form a political consensus to cooperate with certain Southeast Asian governments, but it would be a major departure from post–World War II norms.[26] Japan has offered to finance coast guard ships for the Philippines, and its new flexibility on exporting some weapon systems may help it form closer links with Vietnam. Nevertheless, the Japanese public's caution about overseas commitment is a continuing brake on a more active "collective self-defense."

As Naidu and Sachdeva illustrate, India is not willing to directly challenge China in Southeast Asia, but it is taking a number of steps to solidify its links to the ASEAN states.[27] New Delhi has an explicit "Look East Policy": it sponsors major joint military exercises with ASEAN states, and it offered military hardware to Vietnam. These moves would certainly be viewed by independent observers as a rebuff to China. Also, though India's Prime Minister N. Modi is talking about closer cooperation with China, the two states have fundamentally different interests. India and China are at loggerheads over China's support for Pakistan, and there is a major territorial dispute along the Indo-Chinese border, including the entire Indian state of Arunachal Pradesh.

In the conclusion to this volume, we will explore a number of options that the countries in East and Southeast Asia may pursue if their perceived security situation deteriorates.

In sum, in Central Asia, Chinese and American interests diverge, and there is little direct competition. Yet, in Southeast Asia, China's rising profile provides a challenge to the U.S. role as the dominant outside power. During the period 1997 to 2007, when China's focus in Southeast Asia was primarily economic, there was little U.S.-China friction. However, since 2007, as China has taken a more assertive position toward Japan, Vietnam, and the Philippines over sovereignty and territorial questions, U.S. policy makers have grown increasingly concerned. The U.S. preference is to focus on freedom of navigation (for air and sea lanes); but as China has exhibited a range of new tactics in confronting states with which it has disagreements, the United States has begun to respond. Since Japan and the Philippines are both treaty allies, the Washington is sorting out how to support its friends without encouraging them to take actions that will provoke China. As this book goes to press, there are frequent disturbances in the South China Sea that bear watching.

The changing scene in the ASEAN region illustrates the basic theme of this volume: Southeast Asia is a venue where tensions and U.S.-Chinese competition are rising.

NOTES

1 J. Bresnan, *From Dominoes to Dynamos: The Transformation of Southeast Asia* (New York: Council on Foreign Relations, 1994).

2 S. Haggard and Euysong Kim, "The Sources of East Asia's Economic Growth," *Access Asia Review* 1, no. 1 (1997): 31–63.

3 S. Paribatra, "From ASEAN Six to ASEAN Ten," *Contemporary Southeast Asia* 16, no. 3 (1994): 243–58.

4 For an analysis of why the Southeast Asian countries experienced such a wrenching setback in 1997, see D. Denoon, *The Economic and Strategic Rise of China and India—Asian Realignments after the 1997 Financial Crisis* (New York: Palgrave Macmillan, 2007), chap. 2.

5 J. Boorman, et al., "Managing Financial Crises: The Experience in East Asia," *Carnegie-Rochester Conference Series on Public Policy* 53 (2000): 1–60.

6   W. Arnold, "Clearing Up Malaysia's Debts," *New York Times*, December 12, 2002, W1.

7   For analysis of how the collapse of the financial system in Thailand in 1997 laid the base for the current political groupings, see P. Phongpaichit and C. Baker, *Thailand's Crisis* (Bangkok: Silkworm Books, 2000).

8   Vietnam, Cambodia, Thailand, Myanmar, Brunei, and Singapore all have some form of restraints on civil liberties.

9   Z. Ji and Z. Ma, "China's Neighboring Diplomacy Demands Top-Level Design," *Contemporary International Relations* 23, no. 6 (2013).

10 The rioting led to the deaths of a number of Chinese working in plants in Vietnam as well the destruction of a number of Chinese and Taiwanese manufacturing facilities.

11 The nine-dash line came from earlier Kuomintang maps in 1946 (preceding the current People's Republic of China government). However, it was never codified in a treaty or accepted by other states as an indication of sovereign Chinese territory.

12 S. Simon, "The ASEAN Regional Forum: Beyond the Talk Shop?," *NBR Analysis Brief*, July 11, 2013, and S. Tiezzi, "Shangri-la Regional Dialogue Highlights Regional Tensions," *Diplomat*, May 31, 2014.

13 "SCO and CICA Join Forces in Fight to Maintain Security," *Shanghai Daily*, May 21, 2014.

14 "China Builds Artificial Islands in the S. China Sea," *Bloomberg*, June 6, 2014.

15 Malaysia took a very assertive stance during the crisis and followed policies pioneered by Chile in earlier financial downturns. The authorities in Kuala Lumpur instituted controls on short-term capital movements shortly after the 1997 crisis began, allowing investors to withdraw their funds only six months after they had been committed. This helped stabilize the Malaysian currency and avoided the catastrophic drops in currency value that Thailand and Indonesia experienced.

16 *Vietnam Defence White Paper* (Hanoi, 2009), 17–18.

17 For example, many Indonesians still believe that China played a role in the coup attempt in 1965 that led to the assassination of Jakarta's top army generals. The reaction against those murders, ultimately, brought Suharto to power.

18 M. Allagappa, "Is ASEAN the Cornerstone of Malaysia's Foreign Policy?," *Edge*, November 19, 2012.

19 D. Novoty, *Torn between America and China: Elite Perceptions in Indonesian Foreign Policy* (Singapore: Institute of Southeast Asian Studies, 2010).

20 ASEAN, "Chairman's Statement of the 26th ASEAN Summit," April 27, 2015.

21 J. Ravenhill, "Is China an Economic Threat to Southeast Asia?," *Asian Survey* 46, no. 5 (2006).

22 For an example of Chinese statements of peaceful intentions, see Yang Jiechi, "Go Along the Road of Peaceful Development," *China Daily*, December 14, 2012, 6.

23 A counterexample was the standoff between the United States and the Philippine government in 1991 that led to the U.S. withdrawal from both the Subic Bay naval facility and Clark Air Base.

24 Secretary of State Hillary Clinton, remarks, Hanoi, July 23, 2010, www.state.gov.

25 G. Lubold and T. Moss, "Defense Chiefs Clash over South China Sea," *Wall Street Journal*, May 30, 2015.

26 "Japan and Southeast Asia: Hand in Hand," *Economist*, June 1, 2013, 44.

27 For an overview of Indian ties with Southeast Asia, see *ASEAN-India Connectivity Report: India Country Study* (New Delhi: RIS, 2012).

PART I

Overview

1

Southeast Asia

Thriving in the Shadow of Giants

VIKRAM NEHRU

Introduction

At first glance, the countries of Southeast Asia appear a diverse lot. The region includes a small, rich oil kingdom (Brunei); a wealthy entrepôt economy (Singapore); a postconflict society (Cambodia); a country emerging from half a century of autarkic military rule (Myanmar); a poor, landlocked economy blessed with hydropower and minerals (Laos); a populous nation modeled on China's political structures and matching its growth potential (Vietnam); and four diverse middle-income, market-oriented economies that aspire to join the ranks of advanced countries (Indonesia, Malaysia, the Philippines, and Thailand).

But what these countries share are a strategic location sitting astride one of the world's busiest sea lanes, access to plentiful natural resources, and close proximity to the world's two giant countries—China and India. Their diversity and increasing economic integration lie at the heart of Asia's rapid and resilient economic growth. Cross-border conflicts have been few, short, and contained; and domestic political insurgencies are gradually being overcome, one by one. And a regional institutional architecture is emerging that will help develop shared solutions to common regional and global challenges.

Together, these developments have helped underpin Southeast Asia's impressive economic performance over the years and positioned it well for future economic and social progress. The two largest economies in the world—the United States and China—recognize the enormous economic and strategic potential of Southeast Asia and have made the region a core element in their regional and global plans.

At the same time, Southeast Asia confronts many challenges that could derail its continued rapid economic and institutional development. Some of these challenges emanate from outside the region, such as the region's vulnerability to global economic instability and, more recently, to the slowdown in the Chinese economy. Southeast Asia's openness to trade and financial flows has been an essential ingredient to its development success, but it has also carved channels that immediately transmit global trade and financial instability to the domestic economy, and often even amplify them. Similarly, potential friction between China's rise as a regional military power and America's rebalancing strategy toward Asia could, if poorly managed, affect Southeast Asia's long-term security and stability.

Other challenges come from within the region. Political, ethnic, and communal tensions threaten stability and development in some countries. Inadequate investment in an institutional and regulatory framework to support a range of public goods—regional peace, social mobility, infrastructure, environmental protection, good governance, and a globally competitive private sector—threatens the sustainability of the region's growth in the long term. And weak regional institutions unable to deliver regional public goods—such as further trade and financial integration, or responses to growing transborder risks that include health pandemics, nontraditional security threats, and extreme weather events related to regional and global climate change—could also undermine the region's steady economic progress.

This chapter first examines the factors behind Southeast Asia's long-term economic progress and the development of a regional institutional structure that has helped make this progress resilient over several decades. It then examines the economic outlook for the region and assesses the important risks that could slow—or even disrupt—its continued rapid and resilient growth.

Southeast Asia's Long-Term Economic Performance

Southeast Asia's ten economies have a combined GDP of US$2.3 trillion (much bigger than that of India); a population of over 600 million people (nearly twice that of the United States); and an average per capita income that is almost two-thirds of China's (see table 1.1). If Southeast Asia were one economy, it would be the world's seventh largest.[1] It would also be the most trade-dependent, with a trade-to-GDP ratio well in excess of 100 percent.

The enormous diversity of Southeast Asian economies has meant that neither policy approaches toward development nor development outcomes have been uniform. Yet, over the broad span of the past four decades, Southeast Asia has been one of the world's consistently good economic performers. Average per capita income in the region climbed faster than in any other developing region (see figure 1.1). In the 1970s, several Southeast Asian economies were singled out for their economic promise. Singapore (together with South Korea, Hong Kong, and Taiwan in Northeast Asia) was dubbed an Asian tiger, while Indonesia, Malaysia, the Philippines, and Thailand were considered tiger

TABLE 1.1. Southeast Asia: Key economic and social indicators 2014[a]

Country	Population (in millions)	GDP per capita (current US$)	Trade (% of GDP)	Gross fixed capital formation (% of GDP)	Urban population (% of total)	Population growth (annual %)	Military expenditures (% of GDP)	Infant mortality rate (per 1,000 live births)	Internet users (per 100 people)
Southeast Asian countries									
Brunei Darussalam	0.4	40,980	106.6	27.3	76.9	1.4	3.1	8.6	68.8
Cambodia	15.3	1,095	129.0	20.9	20.5	1.6	1.7	24.6	9.0
Indonesia	254.5	3,492	48.2	32.6	53.0	1.3	0.8	22.8	17.1
Lao PDR	6.7	1,793	90.1	30.1	37.6	1.6	0.2[b]	50.7	14.3
Malaysia	29.9	11,307	138.5	26.0	74.0	1.5	1.5	6.0	67.5
Myanmar	53.4	1,204	44.3[c]	NA	33.6	0.9	3.7	39.5	2.1
Philippines	99.1	2,873	61.1	20.8	44.5	1.6	1.2	22.2	39.7
Singapore	5.5	56,285	350.9	25.4	100.0	1.3	3.2	2.1	82.0
Thailand	67.7	5,977	131.8	24.6	49.2	0.4	1.4	10.5	34.9
Vietnam	90.7	2,052	90.7	23.8	33.0	1.1	2.3	17.3	48.3
Southeast Asia	623.3	4,044	116.3	27.3[d]	47.1	1.2	1.6[b]	22.0[e]	28.7
Other developing regions									
South Asia	1,721.0	1,504	46.7	26.9	32.6	1.4	2.4	41.9	16.6
Middle East and North Africa	357.3	4,313	65.7	25.6	60.0	1.9	3.8	20.8	32.7
Sub-Saharan Africa	973.4	1,776	60.3	21.1	37.2	2.7	1.0	56.3	19.2
Latin America and Caribbean	525.2	9,091	48.5	21.0	77.8	1.1	1.3	15.9	47.5
Europe and Central Asia	264.4	6,874	74.1	20.4	59.9	0.7	2.0	0	48.2

a. The data are for 2014, except where indicated.
b. Laos data for 2012.
c. Estimate for 2013/14. Data from IMF, "2015 Article IV Consultation."
d. Excludes Myanmar.
e. Data for 2015 taken from ADB, "Key Indicators for Asia and the Pacific 2015."
Sources: World Bank, World Development Indicators, http://databank.worldbank.org; IMF, "2015 Article IV Consultation and First Review under the Staff-Monitored Program," Country Report no. 15/267 (September 2015), www.imf.org; ADB, "Key Indicators for Asia and the Pacific 2015" (October 2015), www.adb.org; author's calculations.

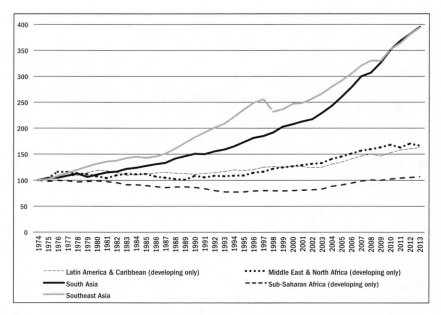

Figure 1.1. Increases in per capita income: Comparison across developing regions, 1974–2013 (1974 = 100; in 2005 prices). Sources: World Bank, World Development Indicators (available at http://databank.worldbank.org/data); author's calculations.

economies in the making. Singapore lived up to its early moniker and is now a high-income economy. But economic progress in the remaining four middle-income economies was more mixed. Growth in Indonesia, Malaysia, and Thailand, while rapid till the late 1990s, was hit badly by the Asian financial crisis in 1997–98; their growth since has not been as rapid as in the pre-crisis years (see table 1.2). The Philippines, on the other hand, suffered from weak growth through the 1980s and 1990s, earning it the unfortunate reputation of being the "sick man of Asia," but its growth picked up after 2004, and over the past few years it has been one of the better performers in Southeast Asia.

Cambodia, Laos, and Vietnam—three Southeast Asian countries that emerged from conflict only after 1975—became the fastest growing economies in the region in the first decade of the new millennium. The economies of Cambodia and Laos gained significantly from relatively open trade and investment policies and have benefited from rapidly growing neighbors (China, Vietnam, and Thailand). Vietnam adopted China's economic model and enjoyed similarly explosive growth and poverty reduction, albeit combined—again, rather like China—with episodes of overheating and economic instability.

TABLE 1.2. Growth performance of Southeast Asian economies, 1980–2014 (percentages)

	1980–90	1991–96	1997–99	2000–2014
Brunei Darussalam	−1.8	3.1	1.2	1.0
Cambodia	NA	NA	8.4	7.8
Indonesia	6.4	7.6	−6.4	5.4
Lao PDR	NA	6.7	5.6	7.4
Malaysia	6.0	9.6	−0.8	4.8
Myanmar[a]	1.3	7.3	8.4	9.5
Philippines	1.7	3.5	1.2	5.1
Singapore	7.7	8.8	1.9	5.4
Thailand	7.8	7.6	−1.7	4.1
Vietnam	NA	8.9	5.3	6.4
SE Asia[b]	6.2	7.6	−1.9	5.1

a. Myanmar for 2000–2014 calculated using IMF WOE October 2015 data.
b. Excludes Myanmar over the whole period, Cambodia before 1993, and Vietnam and Laos before 1984. Calculated using World Bank WDI.
Sources: World Bank World Development Indicators, http://databank.worldbank.org; IMF WOE, www.imf.org; author's calculations.

From the standpoint of economic performance, Myanmar was Southeast Asia's sole exception. Five decades of autarkic economic policies under repressive military rule smothered what had been a thriving economy, inhibited growth and poverty reduction, and destroyed the country's economic institutions. But unexpected political liberalization in 2012 was followed by several key economic reforms and sharp increases in foreign aid that have already helped accelerate growth and improve living standards. At the same time, however, several uncertainties cloud Myanmar's progress, including continued conflict in some ethnic states and periodic communal bloodletting against the minority Muslim Rohingya community.

An examination of Southeast Asia's economic growth over the past four decades reveals relatively long periods of uninterrupted rapid growth. But these have been punctuated by sudden and sharp growth slowdowns (see figure 1.2). Most of these growth slowdowns were the consequence of global recessions that transmitted their effects through strong trade and financial links with the global economy (discussed in the next section). But the sharpest slowdown in 1998 was not imported from abroad. It was homegrown and came to be known as the Asian financial crisis. The pebble that triggered the avalanche was the July 1997 devaluation of the Thai baht (itself the accumulated result of unsustainable macroeconomic policies), which set in motion

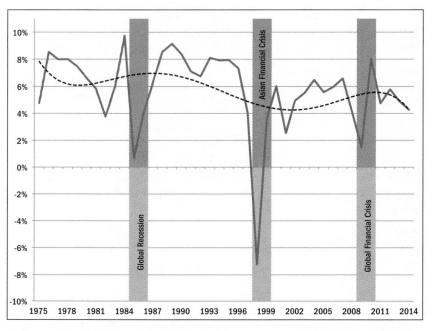

Figure 1.2. Southeast Asia: Annual GDP growth rate, 1975–2014 (weighted; percentage per year). Sources: World Bank, World Development Indicators (available at: http://databank.worldbank.org/data) data for all Southeast Asian countries with available data in a given year; author's calculations.

an economic and financial crisis that not only consumed the Thai economy and every other important Southeast Asian economy, but also spread beyond the borders of Southeast Asia to affect the entire world. The Southeast Asian economy most affected by the Asian financial crisis—Indonesia—suffered not only a catastrophic recession (GDP declined by over 13 percent in 1998) and a virtual meltdown of its financial sector, but also considerable political unrest that eventually led to the departure of President Suharto, who had presided over Indonesian politics for the previous three decades.[2]

Since the Asian financial crisis, the three Southeast Asian economies that suffered the most—Indonesia, Malaysia, and Thailand—have not quite regained their pre-crisis luster. Growth since 2000 has been significantly below the level achieved in pre-crisis years. Three factors account for this. First, post-crisis macroeconomic policies were more prudent and sustainable in light of the lessons learned from the crisis. Second, global economic growth, which was slower post-2000 than in the first half of the 1990s, inevitably affected the performance of Southeast Asian economies. And third, large banks and corporations in Southeast Asia were still deleveraging in the first few years of the new millennium, which kept investment depressed and slowed GDP growth.

But thanks to prudent macroeconomic policies since the Asian financial crisis, Southeast Asian economies entered the global financial crisis of 2009–10 from a position of strength—with adequate fiscal space to counteract the contractionary impact of the crisis, and with banks and corporations that had sufficiently robust balance sheets to absorb the sharp downturn in global trade and large exchange rate depreciations. As a result, governments were able to take appropriate countercyclical policies and economies saw their growth momentum restored in just one year after the initial shock.[3] Indeed, notwithstanding the global economic crisis, trend growth for most Southeast Asian economies remained stable from 2000 to 2010 and even registered an uptick toward the end of the decade.[4]

Southeast Asia's rapid recovery from the global financial crisis once again made it a preferred destination for foreign investors. This proved a mixed blessing. On the one hand, foreign direct investment inflows increased after 2010, helping to boost growth and productivity. On the other, like other emerging market economies, Southeast Asian economies received higher levels of short-term capital inflows and foreign-currency-denominated debt—thanks in large part to unprecedented expansionary monetary policies in the advanced economies since 2008. These portfolio and debt inflows led to a real appreciation in Southeast Asian exchange rates, drove up asset prices (stocks, bonds, real estate), increased domestic demand, raised external debt burdens of financial and nonfinancial corporations, and contributed to growing external current account deficits (or reduced surpluses).[5] These were classic signs of overheating, and once again Southeast Asian economies became vulnerable to a capital flow reversal. That reversal was eventually triggered in May 2013 by Ben Bernanke, then chairman of the U.S. Federal Reserve, warning that the U.S. quantitative-easing program would be "tapered" at some point in the future as conditions in the U.S. economy improved. Virtually overnight, Southeast Asian economies experienced a stock market sell-off, currency depreciation, and higher interest rates.[6] To make matters worse, the Chinese economy also entered a growth slowdown, affecting demand for Southeast Asian commodities and lowering global commodity prices. This time, however, Southeast Asian policy makers were more constrained in taking countercyclical measures because of earlier overheating and the attenuation of fiscal space. As a result growth has once again slowed, and the medium-term future is clouded by the prospect of an upward trend in global interest rates as the advanced economies continue to reverse their monetary policy stance.

In summary, shocks have periodically slowed growth rates in Southeast Asia, but they have not detracted from the region's economic performance over the long term, which has compared favorably with other developing regions. A key factor that contributed to Southeast Asia's economic success—its openness to foreign trade and investment—has also been the source of its macroeconomic vulnerability. But there have also been other factors that have contributed to its success, a subject to which we now turn.

The Common Factors behind Southeast Asia's Economic Performance

Given the immense diversity of Southeast Asian economies, the factors behind their relatively successful performance of the past half century cannot possibly be all the same. Indeed, the economic trajectory of each Southeast Asian economy has been different, reflecting unique policy approaches, political systems, and institutional settings. But the fact that virtually all the economies of the region enjoyed relatively rapid growth points to some common factors at work.

One of those common factors is geography. Southeast Asia sits astride the Malacca Straits, the world's second busiest shipping channel (after the English Channel) and second most popular oil tanker route (after the Strait of Hormuz). Well over half the world's merchant fleet capacity uses the channel each year, making it one of the most important shipping channels in the world (see figure 1.3). Another dimension of Southeast Asia's geography is its abundance of natural wealth. The region is replete with oil, hydro, and geothermal power, various minerals, timber, rice, palm oil, cocoa, and coffee. These resources and Southeast Asia's unique position astride the major trading route between East and West have over the centuries attracted traders, colonists, and, more recently, foreign investors. The region has become a key supplier of commodities to the global economy, most recently to resource-hungry China. And its traditional dependence on trade has given its economies some of the world's highest trade-to-GDP ratios.

Southeast Asia's blend of natural resource abundance and trade openness also provided the springboard for the region's industrialization in the 1970s and 1980s, especially in Singapore, Thailand, and Malaysia. These countries adopted export-oriented policies followed by their successful northern neighbors—Japan, South Korea, and Taiwan—and were helped by foreign direct investment from the advanced economies, especially Japan. Indonesia followed suit in 1985, Vietnam in 1986, Laos in 1989, and Cambodia in 1999.

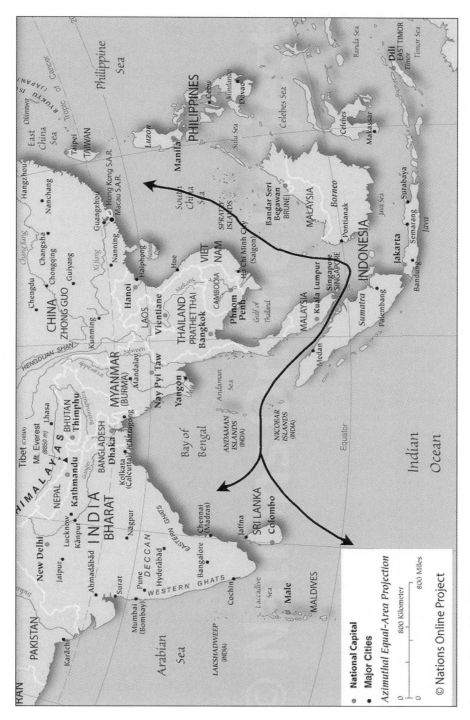

Figure 1.3. Map of the Malacca Straits.

Until the early 1990s, the globalization of Southeast Asian industry was primarily driven by multinational corporations headquartered in developed countries—many of them from Japan in response to the appreciation of the yen after the Plaza Accord in 1985. These corporations established assembly facilities and similar labor-intensive manufacturing facilities in Southeast Asia to take advantage of the region's abundant labor and strategic location. The skills and experience accumulated through this period put Southeast Asia in a strong position to take advantage of the emergence of highly competitive assembly industries in China in the late 1980s and 1990s. Southeast Asian economies now became suppliers of parts and components to the Asian production networks, which were led by the dramatic growth of assembly industries in China. The more advanced Southeast Asian economies like Singapore and Malaysia moved up the value chain to develop a comparative advantage in design and testing, while Thailand and Malaysia, and later Vietnam, acquired a comparative advantage in the fabrication of parts and components.

The incorporation of Southeast Asian economies into regional supply chains and global production networks contributed to a sharp increase in intra-industry trade.[7] There is evidence that this growth in trade took place in sectors—such as electronics—that are subject to increasing returns to scale.[8] These increasing returns are of three types: those within firms (internal economies of scale), those across firms producing similar products but located within clusters (external economies of scale), and those arising from firms producing differentiated products in an urban setting (urbanization economies). By capturing increasing returns to scale, Southeast Asian economies—especially those on the mainland—were able to improve international competitiveness, which, in turn, attracted more investment that further enhanced competitiveness. Recent research on rapid unconditional convergence in manufacturing productivity between developing and advanced economies further supports this view and is central to the rapid growth of Southeast Asian economies.[9]

Southeast Asia's success has in no small part been aided by Singapore, which has become a financing hub for the region as well as a supplier of high-end, high-tech services. Singapore's location in the Malacca Straits has made it the world's largest transshipment port, and a global center for logistics, finance, and business services. More recently, it has become a global center for biomedical sciences and is aiming to become the location of choice for headquarters of global companies, especially those focused on research and development, intellectual property rights management, and product life cycle management.

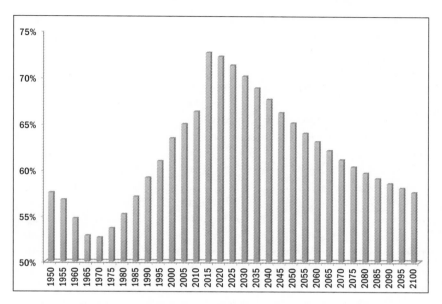

Figure 1.4. Southeast Asia: Working ratio, 1950–2100. Population between the ages of fifteen and sixty-four as a share of the total population. Projections for 2015 onward. Based on a medium variant. Source: UN Population Division, "World Population Prospects: The 2012 Revision," http://esa.un.org/wpp.

While Southeast Asia's geographic location, resource abundance, and proximity to China have been important factors in its economic success, none of these could have been exploited had it not been for supportive demographics and good development policies at home. Southeast Asian economies have reaped a demographic dividend as falling death rates preceded declining birth rates, which led to a bulge in the labor force and contributed to lower dependency ratios, higher output growth, higher savings, greater participation of women in the labor force, and better human capital outcomes (see figure 1.4).[10] Singapore and Thailand have largely exhausted their demographic dividend and already face the challenges of transitioning to an aging society. Malaysia and Vietnam are near the turning point. But the remaining Southeast Asian economies can still look forward to the benefits of a demographic dividend for a few more years. The labor force, as a share of the population in Indonesia, is expected to continue to increase till at least the 2020s, while labor force ratios in the Laos, Cambodia, and the Philippines are likely to reach their apex only near 2040.

Perhaps most importantly, the accelerated growth generated by Southeast Asia's demographic dividend gave rise to increased domestic savings, which triggered a virtuous circle of growth-saving-investment-growth.[11] This "second" demographic dividend, properly nurtured through stable financial systems, macroeconomic stability, and other development policies, can last for several decades. Other policies—for infrastructure, education, and macroeconomic management—complemented Southeast Asia's openness to foreign trade and investment. For example, the emphasis on universal primary and secondary education paid handsome dividends, especially in Indonesia, Malaysia, Thailand, and Vietnam. And Singapore is positioning itself to become a global center for high-quality tertiary education. Similarly, although infrastructure is a critical constraint in many Southeast Asian economies, Singapore has done exceptionally well in installing world-class infrastructure systems, while Malaysia and Thailand have also done relatively well compared to most developing countries. Indonesia and the Philippines, on the other hand, face the challenge of providing adequate infrastructure across sprawling archipelagos, while Vietnam, Cambodia, Laos, and Myanmar, given their lower per capita income levels, still have to catch up with their neighbors.

The Region's Institutional Architecture

A key strength of Southeast Asia is its regional institutional architecture, which in its scope and depth is unmatched by any other developing region. All ten Southeast Asian nations belong to the Association of Southeast Asian Nations (ASEAN)—a forty-seven-year-old regional organization that was founded in 1967 and has confounded its critics who periodically predicted its imminent demise. Today, ASEAN is stronger than ever. Of its three pillars—economic, security, and sociocultural—it has arguably been most active and successful in the economic sphere, pursuing economic integration within the ASEAN member community. Its most recent achievement in this regard—one it had been working toward for many years—is the creation of an ASEAN Economic Community (AEC), a single market for goods, services, investments, and skilled labor, which finally came into being at the end of 2015.

Well before the formation of the AEC, ASEAN had already lowered trade tariffs and established an ASEAN Free Trade Area (AFTA) among its members. In fact, unilateral trade liberalization by ASEAN countries has gone deeper than WTO requirements, so much so that less than 10 percent of intra-ASEAN trade avails itself of AFTA concessions.[12] The margins of preference between AFTA and most favored nation (MFN) are so low that the administrative costs of availing additional concessions under AFTA usually don't justify the additional benefits. This is not to say that most Southeast Asian economies don't employ trade barriers. They most certainly do. But these are usually WTO-consistent, behind-the-border technical barriers to trade (such as trade and investment licensing, procurement restrictions, preshipment and postshipment inspection requirements, restricted ports of entry, phyto-sanitary standards, technology transfer requirements, and so on). While the ASEAN Trade in Goods Agreement (ATIGA) requires countries to report these barriers to the ASEAN Secretariat, it requires only those that constitute barriers to trade to be eliminated by 2018.[13]

The same is true for trade in services within ASEAN. While commitments to liberalize trade in services under the ASEAN Framework Agreement on Services (AFAS) exceed the commitments under GAT, progress in services integration has been modest. Nearly all ASEAN countries—with the notable exception of Singapore—impose opaque and discretionary licensing require-ments for service providers. As a result, the World Bank's services trade restric-tiveness index for the region is 60 percent higher than the global average.[14] Transport and professional services are sectors where regulations governing foreign trade and investment tend to be the most restrictive. These behind-the-border measures are usually idiosyncratic (varying by country and sector), difficult to identify, and impossible to quantify; consequently their removal is hard to negotiate. Liberalizing services trade in line with AFAS and AEC commitments will require altering the complex web of domestic laws and regulations to make them consistent with these international obligations. In many instances, such reforms will come up against vested interests that would be prepared to block efforts at promoting competition from abroad. But if policy makers were to persevere and succeed in implementing this important agenda, not only would the contribution to trade and growth be significant, it could potentially transform ASEAN into a global services hub.

The AEC's commitment to liberalize services trade includes facilitating the cross-border flow of skilled and qualified professionals. To this end, ASEAN has created eight mutual recognition arrangements covering important pro-fessional services (engineering, nursing, architecture, surveying, tourism, medicine, dentistry, and accountancy). Work on an ASEAN Qualifications Reference Framework has also begun that would enable comparisons of pro-fessional qualifications across member states; similar efforts are ongoing to harmonize educational standards through the ASEAN University Network (AUN). None of these initiatives, however, appear to have stimulated mobil-ity of skills across borders, and invariably the reason once again is domestic laws and regulations that protect domestic service providers from foreign competition.

Perhaps more important than agreement to facilitate skills mobility across borders is ASEAN's need for a framework to deal with its 5.5 million unskilled migrant workers—most of them in Thailand, Malaysia, and Singapore. Tight immigration restrictions have encouraged illegal migration, exposing migrants to potential abuse, human trafficking, forced labor, sexual exploitation, and bodily harm. ASEAN needs to build on the ASEAN Declaration on the Protection and Promotion of the Rights of Migrant Workers and create a legal framework that facilitates the flow of temporary migrants and protects their rights.

Finally, the AEC aims to free the cross-border movement of capital among ASEAN member countries. The ASEAN Comprehensive Investment Agreement (ACIA), signed in 2009, liberalizes, promotes, facilitates, and protects foreign direct investment, but it has been preempted by market forces that already encourage the flow of capital across ASEAN borders. In fact, ASEAN governments would be better served if investor protection—currently restricted to ASEAN investors producing goods and manufacturing-related services—were extended to non-ASEAN investors and all services.

Similarly, the arrangements afforded to ASEAN-sourced FDI under ACIA need to be extended to FDI from all sources. More FDI flows into ASEAN member countries from outside the region rather than from other ASEAN countries. The modest intra-ASEAN FDI that does occur tends to be by foreign investors with investments in the region that are looking to expand and sovereign wealth funds located in Singapore or Malaysia seeking to diversify their investment portfolio.

These developments suggest that establishment of the AEC may not accelerate trade liberalization significantly, but it will play an immensely useful role in providing the private sector with policy certainty and prevent opportunistic efforts by member economies to adopt trade barriers during economic downturns. As important, now that the AEC is almost a reality, attention is already shifting to a post-2015 agenda, which will dismantle behind-the-border barriers to trade within ASEAN and harmonize legal and regulatory frameworks. The growing presence of cross-border production networks and their importance to international competitiveness of Southeast Asian firms are increasing the pressure on policy makers to remove any remaining impediments to the smooth flow of trade in goods, services, skills, and finance.

Ironically, while trade within ASEAN has grown very rapidly, averaging over 10 percent a year for the past two decades, it has grown less rapidly than ASEAN's trade with China, which has grown at more than twice that pace. Indeed, China's rapid economic growth is creating a strong gravitational force that is drawing into its orbit all the economies within close geographical proximity. In accordance with the laws of gravity, the economies of Southeast Asia that are closer to China—those on the mainland of the continent—have seen their trade grow faster than those of maritime Southeast Asia (Indonesia and the Philippines). And the China-ASEAN free trade agreement (FTA), which came into effect in the beginning of 2010, will likely continue—and perhaps even accentuate—this trend.

ASEAN-India trade is growing just as fast as ASEAN-China trade (almost 20 percent a year on average), albeit for just over a decade and from a very small base. The ASEAN-India free trade agreement, signed in 2009, will be fully operational by 2016. It foresees the phased elimination of tariffs for 80 percent of traded items and the reduction of tariffs to 5 percent for another 10 percent. An ASEAN-India Services and Investment FTA has also been negotiated and was signed in September 2014. This should help accelerate trade growth in a sector where India has demonstrated comparative advantage in international markets.

The next phase in ASEAN's integration with its major trading partners is being driven by two parallel trade initiatives. The first is the Trans-Pacific Partnership (TPP)—which includes only four of ASEAN's ten members (Brunei, Malaysia, Singapore, and Vietnam)—and is championed by the United States, which views it as a critical element in its rebalancing strategy toward Asia. The second is the Regional Comprehensive Economic Partnership (RCEP), which was launched late last year by ASEAN's ten member countries and six regional partners with which it has free trade agreements (Australia, China, India, Japan, Korea, and New Zealand). If negotiations for the RCEP are successful, it will become the largest FTA in the world.

Negotiations for the TPP—which involves twelve partner countries[15]— were concluded successfully in late 2015, and the proposal now awaits ratification in the member economies. The late entry of Japan in the negotiations added considerable weight and credibility to the proceedings but also significantly increased their complexity. In addition, the unusual scope, ambition, and complexity of the issues, and the disparate interests of the countries involved, posed significant challenges to reaching an agreement. Finally, political opposition within its biggest backer, the United States, complicated passage of the Trade Promotion Authority in the U.S. Congress, but its approval is expected to "fast-track" congressional approval of the TPP now that it has been successfully negotiated.

What makes the TPP unusual is its ambitious scope. It confronts barriers to trade and investment that operate at—and behind—national borders, not just by tackling tariff, non-tariff, and technical barriers but also by addressing intellectual property rights, the policy environment for state enterprises, investor-state dispute settlement arrangements, labor rights, and environmental protection, to name a few. The only trade agreement approaching such ambition was the one concluded by South Korea and the United States, which, no doubt, served as an important reference point for the TPP negotiators. Now that the TPP negotiations have been concluded, other Southeast Asian countries—Indonesia, Thailand, and the Philippines—have expressed an interest in joining.

Negotiations of the RCEP began in 2012, but progress in the talks has been slow and plans to complete them by end-2015 were always optimistic. The challenge here will be the merging of five ASEAN FTA agreements with its six strategic partners (Australia and New Zealand share one FTA) while at the same time increasing the ambition of the final agreement. Even after several rounds of negotiations, participants haven't yet agreed on a template for the negotiations, let alone broached the more contentious issues of trade in goods and services, investment, intellectual property competition, dispute resolution, and the environment.

While the RCEP can coexist with the TPP, the two agreements not only include a different combination of countries (most significantly, the TPP excludes China and six members of ASEAN, while the RCEP excludes the United States), but also represent different philosophies on how economic integration should be achieved. The philosophy behind the TPP is that ambitious trade agreements can be leveraged to remove behind-the-border barriers to trade and thereby drive domestic reform—and its open architecture permits new members to join. RCEP's approach to trade reform is fundamentally different. For example, it restricts membership to a preselected set of sixteen countries (all members of ASEAN and its six strategic partners)[16] and, given their diverse levels of development, incorporates "special and differential treatment" for participating members. Its in-built flexibility allows the pace of domestic reforms to drive the pace of trade liberalization, rather than the other way around, but at the same time protects against a retreat into protectionism. Although the RCEP may initially reflect the standards of the country least willing to liberalize its trade and investment, it could potentially prove more adaptable, as the India-ASEAN and the China-ASEAN free trade agreements have proved.

Completing the regional institutional architecture is APEC (Asia-Pacific Economic Cooperation)—an organization consisting of twenty-one advanced and developing economies bordering the Pacific Ocean that focuses on reaching nonbinding agreements on economic cooperation across a range of areas, including trade. Although some ASEAN members are not members of APEC (Myanmar, Laos, and Cambodia), cooperation between APEC and ASEAN, as well as ASEAN's observer status in APEC, ensures close coordination of policy approaches and objectives. An important recent APEC initiative was to launch an assessment of the feasibility of a Free Trade Agreement for the

Asia-Pacific (FTAAP) that would combine the TPP and the RCEP to form one mega free trade area. While the establishment of an FTAAP remains several years, if not decades, in the future, its introduction as an agenda item in APEC talks highlights the general acceptance that free and open international trade and investment will remain a cornerstone of development in the region.

Besides promoting economic integration, ASEAN has played a pivotal stabilizing role in the region as well as the world, mediating conflicts between neighboring Southeast Asian countries at their incipient stages and, as a result, preventing local cross-border clashes from erupting into full-fledged hostilities. A recent example is its hard work to ease tensions between member countries (such as Thailand and Cambodia) and to develop a code of conduct for the South China Sea. The organization was also a constructive force in Myanmar's recent dramatic move toward greater political and economic liberalization.

ASEAN's political and economic usefulness has drawn in other countries. In 1999, China, Japan, and Korea institutionalized their partnership with ASEAN through ASEAN+3. The expanded group's successes include institutions for economic surveillance and information sharing, a new mechanism for providing liquidity during a financial crisis (the Multilateral Chiang-Mai Initiative), and a pledge to establish a regional 720,000-ton rice reserve facility after the 2011 international food crisis. Although untested and unused, these initiatives are important building blocks for enhancing the subregion's economic stability and provide a useful platform for further collaboration. And, by including Japan and China, ASEAN+3 provides a neutral forum in which the two countries can resolve bilateral issues.

ASEAN is engaging with even more countries through the East Asia Summit (EAS), first held in 2005, which brings ASEAN+3 together with Australia, India, New Zealand, the United States, and Russia. The EAS is rapidly becoming a key regional forum for discussing regional security challenges, including ways to manage tensions in the South China Sea, as well as cooperative efforts to keep open sea lanes of communication, safety at sea, disaster relief, and nontraditional security issues (such as piracy at sea and terrorism). By bringing together leaders of ASEAN together with its eight most important international partners, the annual EAS leaders' meeting has quickly become the apex institution in the ASEAN family of institutions, providing opportunities to discuss thorny and contentious regional issues in a nonthreatening, nonbinding multilateral setting. It has also ensured an important role for ASEAN as a group capable of bringing together the large regional and global powers (especially China and the United States) to discuss issues of common concern and to fashion common cooperative approaches to complex challenges.

The high-level annual EAS summits are complemented by the ASEAN Defense Ministers Meeting Plus (ADMM+). The ADMM+ is a body that includes the same countries as the EAS, focuses on defense and security questions, and also meets annually, usually at the working level but also periodically at the ministerial level. These meetings are aimed at not only discussing important strategic and security questions of the day but also proposing cooperative approaches to deal with them. In 2011, the ADMM+ established five working groups covering humanitarian assistance and disaster relief, military medicine, counterterrorism, peacekeeping, and maritime security. These working groups meet twice annually and have prepared concrete joint programs (such as military and maritime security exercises) to ensure better cooperation and understanding among its members.

The ASEAN Regional Forum (ARF), which was established in 1994 and also meets once a year, has a mandate that largely overlaps with the ADMM+. But what distinguishes it is its membership—comprising twenty-seven nations including the EU and North Korea—making it the largest security discussion forum in the world.[17] ARF's primary purpose is to build confidence among its member countries with the possibility that over time the group could graduate to conflict prevention and even conflict resolution. For Southeast Asia, the forum is a useful institution to discuss their common security concerns and engage their partners in ensuring peace and stability in the subregion and its environs. ASEAN has also used the forum to foster dialogue between nonmember countries—such as China and the United States, Korea and Japan, and most recently, Japan and China—to encourage peaceful resolution of any differences that may bear consequences for the Southeast Asian region. Disaster management has been a key focus for the ARF, but other issues on ARF's agenda have included the South China Sea, developments in North Korea, the Syrian conflict, and regional nontraditional security concerns such as natural disasters, piracy, terrorism, the illegal drug trade, human trafficking, and cybersecurity.

Southeast Asia's Economic Outlook

Southeast Asia's relative economic success through the recent (2008–10) global economic crisis has been impressive. Owing to strong fiscal stimulus measures in many countries, increases in private capital inflows (foreign direct investment as well as portfolio flows), and greater dependence on domestic demand growth, growth was strong in 2010 (7.8 percent), but has since averaged roughly 5 percent a year (see table 1.3).

TABLE 1.3. Southeast Asia: GDP growth, 2012–14 and 2015–19 forecast (percentages)

	Actual values			OECD forecast
	2012	2013	2014	2015–19
Brunei Darussalam	0.9	−1.8	−2.3	1.6
Cambodia	7.3	7.5	7.1	7.1
Indonesia	6.0	5.6	5.0	6.0
Lao PDR	8.0	8.5	7.5	7.6
Malaysia	5.5	4.7	6.0	5.6
Myanmar	5.6	8.2	8.5	7.8
Philippines	6.7	7.1	6.1	6.2
Singapore	3.4	4.4	2.9	3.5
Thailand	7.3	2.8	0.9	4.1
Vietnam	5.2	5.4	6.0	5.7
SE Asia	6.7	5.6	5.1	5.6

Sources: Actual (for all countries except Myanmar 2012): World Bank, World Development Indicators, http://databank.worldbank.org; for Myanmar 2012: IMF, "Myanmar 2015 Article IV Consultation" (September 2015), www.imf.org. For OECD forecast: OECD, "Economic Outlook for China, India, and Southeast Asia 2015: Strengthening Institutional Capacity" (Paris: OECD Publishing, December 2014).

Looking forward, there are three ways in which Southeast Asia's future growth prospects will continue to be shaped by its economic integration with the global economy, together with the quality of its macroeconomic management. First, technological catch-up, facilitated by trade and foreign direct investment, will mean that the long-term growth trend in Southeast Asia will remain well above that of the advanced economies so that Southeast Asia's per capita incomes will continue to converge with that of advanced economies for decades to come. Second, trade and financial integration will also mean that short-term cyclical and shock-induced perturbations in advanced economies will continue to transmit themselves rapidly to Southeast Asian economies; as a consequence, growth variations around trend growth in Southeast Asia will be tightly "coupled" with cyclical growth variations in advanced countries (see figure 1.5). And finally, some Southeast Asian economies—notably Indonesia, and to a lesser extent Malaysia, Philippines, and Thailand, which have relatively open capital accounts and where nonresidents own a significant share of short-term domestic financial assets—will continue to be buffeted by monetary policy shifts in advanced economies. Given asynchronous recoveries in advanced countries and aggressive monetary policies by some central banks to reignite growth and recovery, the capital account channel is likely to

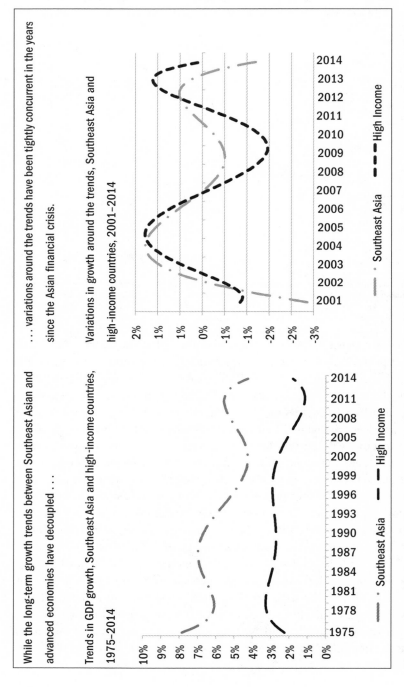

Figure 1.5. Decoupling and coupling between Southeast Asian economies and high-income economies (1975–2014; 2001–13). Sources: World Bank, World Development Indicators (available at http://databank.worldbank.org); author's calculations.

be a significant source of volatility in years to come, and will continue to pose a challenge to Southeast Asia's macroeconomic policy makers.

The short-term vicissitudes of macroeconomic management notwith-standing, Southeast Asia's overall long-term economic prospects remain bright. The same forces that fueled growth in the past—sound macroeco-nomic management, open trading systems, favorable demographic trends, and relatively high savings rates—are likely to remain in place for the foresee-able future. Continued rapid and steady growth in India and China will help, and fiscal and financial recovery in advanced countries will provide a foun-dation for healthy global growth. Three megatrends will be at work to favor Southeast Asia's continued long-term growth: the seemingly unstoppable forces of markets and geography driving economic integration; the continued rapid growth of Southeast Asia's giant neighbors—China and India—which may slow from its previous highs but will still remain well above average global growth; and the implications of the demographic dividend for savings, investment, and economic growth.

The interplay between markets and geography will continue to play a cen-tral role in Southeast Asia's ongoing economic integration and transformation that will support further specialization and scale economies as well as help import and absorb new technologies, all of which will increase productivity growth and international competitiveness and continue to shrink the income gap with advanced economies. Already, the subregion is proving to be an indispensable source of energy, raw materials, and parts and components for China's rapidly growing manufacturing sector, and its production linkages with India are growing apace. In the next decade the forces of Asian inte-gration will likely accelerate, not weaken. Today, intra–East Asian trade as a share of GDP is approaching the level seen in the European Union. Soon, it may well exceed that level.

Geographical proximity, declining transport and communication costs, and a relatively free trade and investment environment—factors that helped create East Asian production networks in the first place and captured advantages of scale and specialization—will only intensify. Just as the liberalization of trade in goods was the engine of growth in East Asia over the past three decades, the liberalization of trade in services could further integrate the economies of the region and drive growth in the next three decades. The service sector accounts for a large part of the economies of Southeast Asia—but a very small share of its overall trade. And thanks to information and communications technologies, services are becoming increasingly tradable worldwide.

With development of the regulatory framework in Asia (including in China and India), trade in services could be set to grow rapidly if trade policies do not impose barriers that slow its potential expansion. Services trade has been included in revisions to the China-ASEAN and India-ASEAN FTAs, and is part of the proposed RCEP between ASEAN and its six FTA partners (Australia, China, India, Japan, Korea, and New Zealand). And while the AEC's end-2015 deadline to liberalize intra-ASEAN services trade is unlikely to be met, the combination of market forces and steady improvement in the regulatory frameworks for services in ASEAN member states will inexorably lead to greater liberalization in services trade.

Trade in goods and services within the region, and between the region and the rest of the world will be further supported by investment in transport and communications infrastructure that is now pouring into Southeast Asia—from the Asian Development Bank, World Bank, Japan, and China. Supplementing these efforts—perhaps even dwarfing them—China's initiatives to launch the New Development Bank (together with the other members of the BRICS) as well as the Asian Infrastructure Investment Bank (for which fifty-seven countries, twenty-one of which are Asian, have signed up as founding members) promise to channel some of China's large investable surpluses into long-term infrastructure financing for Asian infrastructure spending. In addition, China has announced the One Belt, One Road initiative that includes a Maritime Silk Road that potentially includes port development in several Southeast Asian countries.[18] Financial support from diverse Chinese sources (central and provincial governments, state banks, and state enterprises) could run into the trillions of dollars. These infrastructure investments will add to the forces of economic integration within Southeast Asia and between Southeast Asia and China. Japan has countered China's growing role in Southeast Asia by announcing a large infrastructure investment financing program of its own in the region. Finally, Myanmar's opening up has added new dimensions to these developments, raising possibilities of linking Southeast Asia with India across land-based infrastructure (and through the seaport of Sittwe) and linking Bangkok and its environs directly to the Bay of Bengal through the seaport of Dawei.

Of course, the two Southeast Asian maritime countries of Indonesia and the Philippines potentially benefit least from the growing infrastructure links on the Southeast Asian mainland. On the other hand, they could potentially leverage China's Maritime Silk Road initiative by accelerating investments in port infrastructure across their many islands and improving the efficiency of their interisland transport systems. This would not only lower interisland transport costs and improve international competitiveness of domestic industries, but also further integrate these large, sprawling archipelagic economies with the Asian mainland.

Much of Southeast Asia's integration with its Asian neighbors and further development of the Asian production network will depend on how Asia's two large economies—China and India—perform in the future.

Most observers project growth in China to slow to an average rate of near 7 percent a year for the next five to ten years, which is in line with the official target for the 12th five-year plan (7.5 percent a year). Recent policy announcements by the Chinese leadership give greater credence to the view that China's growth in the future, while slower than in the past, will become more sustainable. If China's growth were to slow more than expected, the impact on Southeast Asia would be felt through lower commodity prices and export volumes, fewer exports of manufactured components and final consumer goods, fewer Chinese tourists, and smaller levels of Chinese FDI in the region. True, a few observers have argued that China's growth rate could slow sharply to 3 to 4 percent—which, if it transpires, will have serious repercussions for Southeast Asia.[19] Such a "black swan" event—with low probability but high impact—is good reason for Southeast Asian policy makers to ensure their economies remain diversified in terms of markets and production networks. Much will depend on the future role of China's government in the economy and whether the government will be able to withdraw from direct involvement in production, distribution, and resource allocation, and instead focus on designing and implementing a regulatory framework that empowers the private sector and protects the environment, while building a fiscal system that provides equal opportunity and basic security for all.[20]

On the reasonable assumption that the Chinese authorities are able to guide the downward trajectory of GDP growth toward a sustainable rate of 5 to 6 percent a year, Southeast Asia stands to benefit through more channels than just trade. For example, as real wages continue to rise rapidly in China and its manufacturing moves up the value chain, labor-surplus Southeast Asian economies (Indonesia, Vietnam, Laos, Cambodia, and the Philippines) could potentially occupy the product space vacated by Chinese industries and become internationally competitive at lower rungs of the technology ladder. This migration of labor-intensive industries to Southeast Asia, albeit small, is already evident, and the trickle could rapidly turn into a flood. Multinational companies will be leading this trend as they continue to seek the best locations for the labor-intensive tasks in their production chains, but some, such as Japanese firms, may be seeking to diversify away from China in light of contentious bilateral relations between China and Japan.

Unlike China's, India's growth rate slowed dramatically in the past three years primarily on account of policy inertia. But the landslide election victory of the Bharatiya Janata Party and the elevation of its leader, Narendra

Modi, to the position of prime minister raised market expectations of decisive leadership to accelerate reforms and relieve these bottlenecks. Given India's fractious politics, such inflated expectations were inevitably punctured, but economic performance has nevertheless improved. Whether growth will accelerate further or not will depend on how effectively the Modi administration can ease transport and energy infrastructure bottlenecks, reduce labor market rigidities in the formal sector, lower barriers to foreign trade and investment, and expand the availability of skills.

Indeed, there are five good reasons to believe that India—and South Asia more broadly—could potentially become important trading partners with Southeast Asia, with the two regions becoming more interdependent and mutually supportive of growth in both. First is India's recognition that it must not only "look east" but also "act east." Over the past decade, India's trade with Southeast Asia has grown at near 20 percent a year (with China it has grown 40 percent a year). These rates of growth in trade could be higher still if India were to address its infrastructure, logistics, and regulatory constraints. Furthermore, an expected wave of liberalization in services trade, supported by revisions to the India-ASEAN Free Trade Agreement, will play to India's strengths and boost its exports further (services already account for 35 percent of India's total exports).

Second, Japanese and Southeast Asian investors consider India as a potential location for their export-oriented investments as a hedge against their perceived overdependence on China. A recent survey of Japanese investors places India as the most desirous investment location worldwide.[21] India offers a large domestic market, industrial depth, urban centers, and sophisticated financial services—comparable to what China offered in the 1990s. While India's progress in infrastructure and financial sector development has not been as rapid as China's, and its policy process may occasionally be baffling and frustrating, it is only a matter of time before it becomes an integral part of Asia's production networks and enjoys sustained rapid growth.

Third is Myanmar's pivot toward the outside world and away from autarky and dependence on China. This transition was given a further boost by Myanmar's recent national elections, which brought a landslide victory for Aung San Suu Kyi's opposition party, the National League for Democracy. Myanmar's economic and democratic transitions have created new opportunities for India and Southeast Asia directly and indirectly. A thriving and open Myanmar economy will add to India's trade and investment opportunities, especially for its poor and underdeveloped Northeast region. And a stable and growing Myanmar could also eventually open a land bridge between

India, Southeast Asia, and southern China, and put in place the last piece in the jigsaw for an integrated Indo-Pacific region.[22]

Fourth is the South Asian Free Trade Agreement signed in 2004, which is on track to create a South Asia Free Trade Zone by 2016 (including Afghanistan, Bangladesh, Bhutan, India, Maldives, Nepal, Pakistan, and Sri Lanka). Albeit still at low levels, intra–South Asian trade has grown at an average rate of 16 percent a year over the past decade—faster than growth in intra–Southeast Asian trade (12 percent a year). This is despite infrastructure weaknesses and lingering trade barriers. It is only a matter of time before markets and geography in South Asia overcome the suspicions and hostility that have plagued the region for more than half a century and build the trade and investment links that will drive South Asian growth in the future.

And fifth, there is a distinct possibility that India's recent growth acceleration can be enhanced further if the central government increases public investment in infrastructure and improves incentives for private investors, domestic and foreign. Furthermore, India's states have the constitutional authority and the critical mass to adopt many policies that can help spur growth, including those governing the availability of local infrastructure, water, and electricity. This independence of action in the states, coupled with decisive leadership and sound policies at the center, could provide the policy framework at all levels to accelerate growth significantly. As states compete for additional resources and new investments, and as better growth and welfare outcomes are rewarded in state and national elections, good practice policies should spread across most if not all states, providing new subnational sources of growth.

Southeast Asia's economic neighborhood, then, is likely to remain dynamic over the long term—in large part due to the future promise of China and India, its two neighboring giants. The proximity of Japan, Korea, Australia, and New Zealand will also contribute positively through trade, financial flows, and skills availability. Much of these forces will be driven by markets, geography, and the private sector. This makes it incumbent on Southeast Asian governments to ensure that stability, good governance, and the availability of public goods and services—at the national and regional levels—continue to support sustainable and inclusive growth. Yet this is where the biggest risks lie.

Consider how these issues are reflected in the medium-term outlook of key Southeast Asian economies.

Indonesia's growth is set to average near 5 to 6 percent over the medium term, but three structural reforms could help it grow faster. The first would be to lower barriers to entry and exit for private firms and reduce, if not eliminate, behind-the-border barriers to trade. The second would be to accelerate infrastructure investment, which currently forms an immediate binding constraint to growth. And the third is to alleviate a severe shortage in skilled workers by improving the quality of instruction in its schools, colleges, and universities.[23] Unfortunately, the pace of reforms slackened under President Yudhoyono's two 5-year terms and so little progress has been made on these fronts. The country chose a new president late in 2014—President Joko Widodo—but he too has found it difficult to build a consensus for reform in a politically fractious nation.[24] Moreover, President Widodo's statements on trade suggest that the rising trend in behind-the-border trade barriers and "resource nationalism" (restricting foreign investors in the natural resource sector) under President Yudhoyono could continue in his administration.

Malaysia's long-term growth projections remain at around 5 percent a year, but there is obvious upside potential. The government has launched an ambitious economic and government transformation program that focuses on twelve sectors (ranging from agriculture to tourism) and six cross-cutting reforms (from human capital development to inequality reduction). The program has had a positive effect on the private sector, and private investment picked up sharply in 2012 for the first time in years.[25] But rather than reforming a long-standing affirmative action program called the Bumiputera—or sons of the soil—policy, the government recently strengthened it. Unreformed, this policy, which distorts incentives, stifles innovation, and dampens growth, will continue to hold Malaysia back from achieving its full potential.

Thailand's economic projections show a growth deceleration driven by its deep political crisis that prompted a military coup in May 2014. The National Council for Peace and Order (NCPO), as Thailand's new military government is called, has made economic stabilization and the resumption of economic growth a top priority. It has taken steps to resume important infrastructure projects. The country needs additional roads and ports to lower logistics costs and water management systems to contain perennial flooding from Thailand's twenty-five river basins.[26] But sustaining reforms and economic growth rests crucially on a quick return to democratic norms and processes, including holding national elections and returning the country to a democratically elected civilian government. Unfortunately, the NCPO's decision to postpone elections to mid-2017 and other actions—including impeaching the previous prime minister, Yingluck Shinawatra, and banning her from politics for five years—have only exacerbated political tensions and increased investor uncertainty.

In the Philippines, the big imponderable is whether the recent acceleration in growth to 7 percent a year could continue into the medium term, and whether these economic gains can be translated into employment and poverty reduction (they haven't so far). Much will depend on whether the momentum of President Aquino's reforms can be maintained through his term (which ends in 2016) and after it.[27] The president has made important progress in combating corruption, improving public financial management, and bringing a tentative end to the Mindanao insurgency. But much more needs to be done, particularly in reforming land and labor markets, improving infrastructure, strengthening interisland connectivity, and raising the quality of governance. Part of this agenda has been addressed by President Aquino, but the brunt of it will need to be undertaken by his successor.

The remaining developing economies of East Asia—Cambodia, Lao PDR, Myanmar, and Vietnam—are confronted with the task of "breaking into" the production networks of East Asia. Apart from Myanmar, they have already made a remarkably successful start. For their level of per capita income, they are among the countries with the world's highest share of manufacturing relative to GDP. In Cambodia, value added in industry almost tripled over the past two decades (albeit from a low base), and so did the number of workers. And Vietnam is a favored destination for foreign investors seeking high returns from investments in labor-intensive production (10 percent of GDP in 2008).

Over the medium term, these countries undoubtedly will be helped by regional and global forces supportive of development—a rapidly growing neighborhood, a continued global trend toward specialization in tasks, and quickly rising labor costs in middle-income countries, including China. Thus far, however, Vietnam alone has been able to link to production networks—albeit only in a limited way. The challenges and opportunities confronting Cambodia and Lao PDR will be to upgrade physical and human capital and embrace regional integration. The development of regional and national infrastructure to improve connectivity and reduce transport costs across Southeast Asia is a critical step in this direction. This development will need to be complemented by "soft infrastructure"—namely, measures to facilitate trade, such as efficient transit arrangements, common border regulations, national single-window facilities for importers and exporters, and customs modernization.

Myanmar's dramatic political and economic "U-turn" after a half century of autarky makes it worthy of special attention. Although the country is a late starter, or perhaps because of it, its medium-term prospects are as bright as those of its low-income Southeast Asian neighbors. Its strategic location between China, India, and mainland Southeast Asia positions it well to benefit from intra-Asian trade and investment. Its rich soils and plentiful water give it the potential to become a major agricultural producer and Asia's largest rice exporter. Its large natural gas reserves promise bright energy prospects, and its generous mineral deposits could ensure a steady stream of foreign exchange earnings. But realizing Myanmar's huge potential will require resolving two fundamental and daunting challenges. The first is maintaining stability in a society fractured by deep ethnic and religious fault lines while rebuilding political and social institutions that were destroyed during a half century of military rule; and the second is overcoming the "resource curse" (when abundant natural resources and raw materials slow growth and employment creation) by developing agriculture, manufacturing, and tourism. Meeting both challenges will require visionary political and economic leadership that is capable of tackling vested interests, decentralizing political power, delivering public services, and opening the economy to genuine competition.[28]

Future Risks and Challenges

The previous section outlined the main reasons why Southeast Asia's economic future continues to look bright. But no region is devoid of challenges and risks—and the key risk facing Southeast Asia is the potential failure of public policy at the national and regional levels to provide the necessary policy and institutional framework supportive of sustainable and inclusive growth.

The Rise of China

For Southeast Asia, China's emergence in the next two decades as the world's largest economy poses arguably the biggest challenge. While this will bring enormous opportunities, it will also bring equally important risks. As China confronts economic, social, environmental, and international challenges, Southeast Asia will undoubtedly be buffeted by any instability that may emerge. China's transition to a more sustainable growth path is paved with uncertainty. Introducing economic reforms could prove difficult without parallel political reforms. Social and political pressures could erupt at any time and disrupt economic growth, perhaps for several decades until a new equilibrium is attained. As the fall of the Soviet Union and the more recent events related to the Arab Spring demonstrate, social and political forces, once unleashed, can undo seemingly impregnable political structures rapidly; building new political and economic systems and institutions in their place usually takes many years, if not decades.

Equally important, China's growing regional dominance is posing a security risk for Southeast Asian policy makers—a concern that has been highlighted by recent incidents in the East and South China Sea. The forty-year history of disputes in the region has seen a steady escalation in tension punctuated by occasional conflicts that have been quickly contained. Based on a vaguely defined "nine-dash line" (reduced from eleven dashes in 1953), China claims sovereignty over the Senkaku Islands in the East China Sea and the Paracel and Spratly Islands in the South China Sea. The competing claimants are Japan in the East China Sea and Brunei, Malaysia, the Philippines, and Vietnam, which have more modest, but equally important, claims in the South China Sea.

The territorial disputes in the East and South China Seas have been escalated by actions on both sides. China's rapidly growing military capabilities have given it an expanding capability to press its territorial claims against its smaller and weaker neighbors. Recent actions in contested waters—drilling for oil off Vietnam's coast, building structures on rocks and islets off the Philippine coast, issuing Chinese visas with maps that depict the nine-dash line (which go so far south as to include waters adjacent to Indonesia's gas-rich Natuna Islands)—have alarmed its Southeast Asian neighbors and triggered rapid growth in their military modernization and acquisition of new weapons systems in the region. The second has been the U.S. rebalancing strategy toward Asia, which, even though carefully crafted with economic, diplomatic, and strategic aims, has nevertheless been perceived by China as a move to contain its role as a regional power, thwart its expanding regional interests, and threaten its own security. The third has been the submission of a nearly four-thousand-page, ten-volume brief—called a "memorial"—by the Philippines to initiate arbitration proceedings against China in the Permanent Court of Arbitration under the United Nations Convention on the Law of the Sea. Vietnam has since submitted its own formal statement to the tribunal seeking due regard to its own rights and interests in the ongoing arbitration process, which is proceeding over the objections of China and without its participation. And finally, China's announcement of a new air defense zone in the East China Sea, which overlaps with similar ones established by South Korea and Japan, has raised tensions to an altogether new level. These actions have made the East and South China Seas and their adjacent territories, including Southeast Asia, a flashpoint in the new security dynamic posed by China's expanding regional interests and its growing military capabilities that can pursue and defend them.

Development of Regional Institutions

While regional tensions are rising on account of territorial disputes, markets and geography are driving further trade and financial integration within

Southeast Asia and between Southeast Asia and its giant neighbors. In dealing with the growing contradiction between these two trends, there is a high
risk that regional institutional structures will prove incapable of resolving
conflicts in their nascent stage before they jeopardize the rapid growth and
development of the region. The EAS, ADMM+, and ARF are useful building blocks for information exchange and cooperation on common security
issues, but they have neither the mandate nor the structures to mediate in
conflict situations. While there are a growing number of opportunities for the
key stakeholders—China, Southeast Asia, Japan, and the United States—to
resolve their differences through dialogue and confidence-building measures,
there is as yet no broad agreement on a way forward.

On the economic front as well, the regional institutional architecture faces
several challenges. For example, although the AEC is scheduled to herald free
trade in goods and services within the community by the end of 2015, the
ASEAN Secretariat lacks the institutional capability to verify implementation of the agreement or ensure convergence of trade regulations and procedures. Moreover, it is possible that Southeast Asian governments may abide
by the letter of the agreement by lowering at-the-border tariffs on goods and
services trade, but they may still abuse its spirit by using behind-the-border
protective measures to preserve the effective protection rate on key industries
or subsectors.

Effective regional institutions are also needed to cooperatively address
other regional cross-border challenges that include the risk of pandemics,
regional environmental crises, nontraditional security threats, natural disasters, freedom of navigation on the high seas, riparian rights over multicoun-
try river systems, and management over oceanic resources. While a start has
been made in addressing some of these issues in one or other of Southeast
Asia's regional institutions, the challenges seem to be growing more rapidly
than the ability of the institutions to deal with them. It is noteworthy that
following the devastating impact of Typhoon Haiyan in the Philippines, aid
poured in *not* from its immediate Southeast Asian neighbors, but from the
United States, Japan, and the United Kingdom. There clearly is a long way to
go before Southeast Asia's rhetoric of mutual help and cooperation is translated into reality.

The Middle-Income Trap

The middle-income countries in Southeast Asia—Indonesia, Malaysia,
the Philippines, and Thailand—face the medium-term challenge of raising
investment in physical and human capital, with the intention of moving up

the value chain. Following initial export successes (Malaysia and Thailand more than Indonesia and the Philippines), the pattern of production and exports in these countries has remained broadly unchanged for two decades. With the rise of China and India as favored investment locations for labor-intensive manufacturing, the middle-income countries of Southeast Asia have to reinvent themselves if they are to maintain rapid growth.

Some have suggested that Southeast Asia's middle-income economies could be caught in a "middle-income trap"—unable to remain competitive as high-volume, low-cost producers, but unable to move up the value chain and achieve rapid growth by breaking into fast-growing markets for knowl-edge- and innovation-based products and services.[29] Avoiding this trap is a challenge that many middle-income countries face. Only a handful of the 101 developing countries as of the 1950s have since made the leap to high-income status, many of them in Asia—Hong Kong, Japan, South Korea, Singapore, and Taiwan.

Moving up the value chain and competing with advanced economies re-quires many prerequisites—a highly educated and innovative workforce, a culture of excellence, entrepreneurial skills, access to finance and infrastruc-ture, and a competitive business environment. But acquiring these prerequi-sites will mean high levels of public and private investment in physical and human capital, institutions, and measures that encourage product and pro-cess innovation together with the adoption and adaptation of new technolo-gies. Yet investment in Southeast Asia's middle-income economies *declined* in the decade after the Asian financial crisis and currently falls well short of levels that existed in Japan, the Republic of Korea, and Singapore when they were at similar per capita income levels. The slowdown in investment does not stem from a lack of savings—indeed, for most of the past decade, domes-tic savings in all these countries exceeded domestic investment, resulting in external current account surpluses.

In fact, there is no single reason that explains why private and public in-vestment in Southeast Asia's middle-income countries has declined in the past decade. In Malaysia, rigidities in the labor market and entry barriers tend to discourage private investors; in Indonesia, public infrastructure and the reg-ulatory environment appear to be binding constraints; in Thailand, a deeply divided internal political system has raised risk and uncertainty; and in the Philippines, it has been a combination of corruption, inadequate interisland connectivity, and policy distortions affecting agricultural and labor markets.

Addressing these policy constraints is a priority for rapid growth to be sus-tained over the medium term—and there are good reasons to be optimistic on this score. In the past several decades, Southeast Asian governments have been showing themselves to be capable of rising to the economic challenges they confront. For example, the new economic model announced recently by Malaysia is representative of the reforms needed—empowerment of state and local authorities, development of cluster- and corridor-based economic activities (to capture economies of scale), attraction of local and foreign talent, removal of labor market restrictions, creation of incentives supporting innovation and risk taking, and a shifting of market orientation from the G-3 countries (the Euro Area, Japan, and the United States) to Asia and the Middle East. In Indonesia, urgent attention is being given to the core issue of infrastructure connectivity within and between its numerous islands to lower transport costs and crowd in private investment. In the Philippines, the Aquino administration is combating corruption, improving the quality of public financial management, and prioritizing infrastructure development. In Thailand, the new military government, the NCPO, has made economic stability a key priority and taken steps to restart an ambitious public investment program to address the economy's transport and energy infrastructure deficits. In all Southeast Asian middle-income countries, however, a key challenge remains largely unaddressed—improving access to secondary and tertiary education and raising its quality. One of the most common complaints of businesses in these economies is the lack of skilled labor, which is rapidly becoming a binding constraint to future sustained growth.[30]

Conclusions

Southeast Asia's ten economies continue to thrive in the shadow of their neighboring giants—China and India. Their openness to trade and investment has made the region among the most resilient and fastest growing in the world. This momentum is unlikely to fade. Straddling the Malacca Straits, Southeast Asia's strategic location is itself an asset that will continue to generate returns far into the future. Further economic integration within the region and with the rest of Asia, especially in services, has the potential to drive rapid growth for decades to come. Myanmar's recent political and economic reforms will add additional impetus to these forces. And unlike anywhere else in the developing world, a range of regional institutions, while far from perfect, provides constant opportunity for dialogue, cooperation, learning, and problem solving across a wide variety of common regional concerns.

Of course, nothing can be foreordained, and Southeast Asia faces its fair share of challenges in regard to its future. Not least among these is the rise of China itself and the risks it poses to Southeast Asia on two fronts: the first is the "black swan" possibility of a sudden growth deceleration or even economic collapse in China that could inflict severe repercussions for the neighboring Southeast Asian economies; and the second is the increased tension in the East and South China Sea as China's expanding interests in the region and its enhanced military capabilities to back them are together raising security concerns among its neighbors. Furthermore, the region's institutional architecture, while advanced, has yet to develop sufficiently to manage regional challenges that range from traditional and nontraditional security risks to further economic integration, disaster prevention and relief, and cross-border transmission of health pandemics. And finally, the middle-income Southeast Asian economies need to build a domestic policy and institutional framework supportive of adequate physical infrastructure, quality education, competitive products, and research and development.

These risks are well recognized among Southeast Asian policy makers and form an important part of their policy agenda. China promises to be by far their greatest economic opportunity as well as their greatest strategic risk. Southeast Asian leaders have been managing this risk with some success by leveraging their country's influence through regional and multilateral institutions and by forming strategic partnerships and alliances within and outside the region. Progress on domestic policy and institutional reforms has helped manage the other risks to rapid and sustainable growth, but there is little doubt that a lot more could be done in this regard. The best way to sustain economic progress will be to maintain a steady pace of structural reforms while at the same time ensuring macroeconomic stability in the face of periodic shocks. At the same time, Southeast Asia needs to build a security architecture that can defend its own territorial integrity while accommodating China's peaceful rise.

NOTES

The author wishes to thank Professor David Denoon and anonymous reviewers for their comments, and Yun Tang and Patrick Farrell, Junior Fellows at the Carnegie Endowment, for excellent research assistance.

1 "ASEAN as One Country? What Integration in Southeast Asia Will Look Like," *Economist*, http://aseaninsight.economist.com.

2 For a detailed explanation of Indonesia's meltdown, see World Bank, *Indonesia in Crisis* (Washington, DC: World Bank, 1998).

3 World Bank, *Emerging Stronger from the Crisis*, World Bank East Asia and Pacific Economic Update 2010, vol. 1 (Washington, DC: World Bank, 2010).

4 See box 1.9, p. 31 in IMF, *Asia and Pacific Regional Economic Outlook: Shifting Risks, New Foundations for Growth* (Washington, DC: IMF, April 2013).

5 IMF, *Asia-Pacific Regional Economic Outlook: Leading the Global Recovery; Rebalancing for the Medium Term* (Washington, DC: IMF, April 2010).

6   Vikram Nehru, "Indonesia: Survey of Recent Developments," *Bulletin of Indonesian Economic Studies* 49, no. 2 (2013): 139–66.

7   Hamid Alavi, Ralph Van Doorn, and Vikram Nehru, "Building a Neighborhood—One Policy at a Time: The Case for Deeper Economic Integration in East Asia," in *Engaging East Asian Integration: States, Markets and the Movement of People*, ed. Takashi Shiraishi and Jiro Okamoto (Singapore: ISEAS, 2012).

8   Werner Antweiler and Daniel Trefler, "Increasing Returns and All That: A View from Trade," *American Economic Review* 92, no. 1 (March 2002): 93–119.

9   Dani Rodrik, "Unconditional Convergence in Manufacturing," *Quarterly Journal of Economics* 128, no. 1 (2013): 165–204; Augustin S. Bénétrix, Kevin O'Rourke, and Jeffrey Williamson, "The Spread of Manufacturing to the Periphery, 1870–2007: Eight Stylized Facts" (NBER Research Working Paper 18221, 2012), www.nber.org; Margaret McMillan and Dani Rodrik, "Globalization, Structural Change and Productivity Growth" (NBER Working Paper no. 17143, 2011), www.nber.org.

10 See Ronald Lee and Andrew Mason, "What Is the Demographic Dividend," *Finance and Development* 43, no. 3 (2006), www.relooney.info; also see David Bloom, David Canning, and Jaypee Sevilla, *The Demographic Dividend: A New Perspective on the Economic Consequences of Population Change* (Santa Monica: RAND, 2003).

11 For the conceptual underpinnings of this argument, see Klaus Schmidt-Hebbel and Luis Serven, eds., *The Economics of Savings and Growth: Theory, Evidence, and Implications for Policy* (New York: Cambridge University Press, 1999).

12 However, an Asian Development Bank survey of firms in Singapore, Thailand, and the Philippines showed that 28 percent used preferential FTA tariffs. See Masahiro Kawai and Ganeshan Wignaraja, eds., *Asia's Free Trade Agreements: How Is Business Responding?* (Cheltenham: Asian Development Bank and ADB Institute with Edward Elgar, 2011), 34.

13 Alladin Rillo, Pitchaya Sirivunnabood, Ahmad Ahsan, and Jean-Christophe Maur, "ASEAN Integration Monitoring Report" (ASEAN Secretariat and World Bank Working Paper no. 83914, January 1, 2014), 3, http://documents.worldbank.org.

14 ASEAN and the World Bank, *ASEAN integration Monitoring Report: A Joint Report by the ASEAN Secretariat and the World Bank* (Washington, DC: World Bank, 2013), 105.

15 The twelve countries are Australia, Brunei, Canada, Chile, Japan, Malaysia, Mexico, New Zealand, Peru, Singapore, the United States, and Vietnam.

16 The six partners are Australia, China, India, Japan, Korea, and New Zealand.

17 The twenty-seven countries include the ten ASEAN member states (Brunei, Cambodia, Indonesia, Laos, Malaysia, Myanmar, Philippines, Singapore, Thailand, and Vietnam), the ten ASEAN dialogue partners (Australia, Canada, China, the EU, India, Japan, New Zealand, ROK, Russia, and the United States),

one ASEAN observer (PNG), as well as the DPRK, Mongolia, Pakistan, Timor-Leste, Bangladesh, and Sri Lanka.

18 Designed to increase connectivity and promote economic (including energy) security, President Xi's "one belt, one road" strategy announced in September 2013 includes a Silk Road Economic Belt, comprising road and rail connections between China and Europe through Central Asia, and the 21st Maritime Silk Road, which involves the developments of ports along a maritime route connecting the South China Sea, Strait of Malacca, India, the Middle East, and East Africa. President Xi's inspiration no doubt derives from China's fifteenth-century Ming period, when China established overland and maritime routes to Europe and South Asia, respectively, to facilitate trade.

19 Michael Pettis, *Avoiding the Fall: China's Economic Restructuring* (Washington, DC: Carnegie Endowment for International Peace, 2013).

20 See World Bank and Development Research Center of the State Council, *China 2030: Building a Modern, Harmonious, and Creative Society* (Washington, DC: World Bank, 2012).

21 See the 2014 JBIC Survey on overseas business operations by Japanese manufacturing companies, available at www.jbic.go.jp.

22 See Rory Medcalf, *The Indo-Pacific: What's in a Name?* (Washington, DC: Brookings Institution, October 25, 2013), www.brookings.edu.

23 See Vikram Nehru, Manufacturing in India and Indonesia: Performance and Policies," *Bulletin of Indonesian Economic Studies* 49, no. 1 (2013): 35–60.

24 See ibid.

25 Asian Development Bank, *Asian Development Outlook: Asia's Energy Challenge* (Manila: Asian Development Bank, 2013).

26 See Vikram Nehru, "Thai Floods a Wake-Up Call" (Washington, DC: Carnegie Endowment for International Peace, 2011), http://carnegieendowment.org.

27 The Philippines president is constitutionally prevented from serving longer than a single six-year term.

28 See Vikram Nehru, "Myanmar's Economic Policy Priorities" (Washington, DC: Carnegie Endowment for International Peace, November 15, 2012), http://carnegieendowment.org.

29 Indermit Gill and Homi Kharas, eds., *An East Asia Renaissance: Ideas for Economic Growth* (Washington, DC: World Bank, 2007).

30 For an account of the challenges that Indonesia faces in improving the quality of education, see Vikram Nehru, "Manufacturing in India and Indonesia: Performance and Policies," *Bulletin of Indonesian Economic Studies* 49, no. 1 (2013): 35–60.

2

ASEAN's External Policy

Caught between the United States and China

ANN MARIE MURPHY

Introduction

Southeast Asian states have long used the Association of Southeast Asian Nations (ASEAN) to promote their key interests in a peaceful and autonomous Southeast Asia. Recognizing that outside powers have interests in the region, ASEAN has created institutions such as the ASEAN Regional Forum (ARF), the ASEAN Plus Three (APT), and the East Asia Summit (EAS) to engage them in the hope of binding them to ASEAN norms and rules. Entry into the EAS, for example, requires applicants to sign the Treaty of Amity and Cooperation (TAC), which commits signatories to settlement of disputes by peaceful means and the "renunciation of the threat or use of force."[1] If ASEAN had a mechanism to ensure signatories to the TAC complied with its principles, the organization's goal of a peaceful Southeast Asia would be achieved.

ASEAN currently faces a series of challenges in promoting regional order and ensuring the region's autonomy from the hegemony of any great power. These challenges arise from domestic political changes within ASEAN countries, from disagreements among ASEAN members over visions of regional order, and from the changing balance of power in the Asia-Pacific. This chapter argues that these factors are increasingly undermining the factors that make ASEAN's external policy possible: a common set of interests and sufficient ASEAN cohesion to pursue these interests collectively vis-à-vis external states.

Today, Asia is in the midst of a major power transition. Scholars of small states agree that the safest environment for them is one of system equilibrium.[2] China's rise has upset that equilibrium, and as Beijing pursues its interests in ways that negatively impact some Southeast Asian countries, particularly those with claims to the South China Sea, tensions between China and these states have risen. ASEAN is divided over how to respond to China's rise and increasingly assertive maritime claims. ASEAN members also have divergent views over the U.S. Pivot to Asia, with some viewing Washington's strengthening of its offshore balancing role as a contribution to regional stability and others as an escalation of great power rivalry. As tensions between the United States and China increase, the efficacy of ASEAN attempts to maintain regional order through its traditional soft-power strategies of institutional binding and norm promotion is declining.[3] In the face of rising Sino-American competition, some in ASEAN fear being forced to choose between Beijing and Washington, a choice long considered ASEAN's nightmare scenario.

To illustrate ASEAN's current challenges, this chapter will proceed as follows. First, it will discuss Southeast Asian perceptions of the relationship between domestic politics, regional order, and great power intervention that led to ASEAN's creation. Second, it will review ASEAN's adoption of a collective external policy in the 1970s. Third, it will examine the internal factors that have undermined ASEAN cohesion and common interests, including ASEAN expansion, domestic political liberalization, and ASEAN's institutional weaknesses. Fourth, it will analyze the external conditions that influence ASEAN's ability to manage regional order, particularly ensuring great power participation within ASEAN-based regional architecture, and retaining ASEAN centrality within it. The chapter then will examine the disputes over the South China Sea to illustrate how that issue is threatening ASEAN unity and hence its ability to act collectively. This chapter argues that ASEAN's foreign policy is largely based on soft power, and its success is dependent upon an underlying balance of power in the region. It concludes that if the United States and China are unable to manage their power transition peacefully, it will be increasingly difficult for ASEAN to craft an effective external policy that maintains Southeast Asia's stability and autonomy.

Linking Domestic Politics, Regional Stability, and Autonomy from Great Power Hegemony

Southeast Asian leaders created ASEAN out of the recognition that if they could not prevent and resolve regional conflicts, then great powers would intervene to do so. ASEAN's creation was a direct outcome of the process of resolving *konfrontasi*, the low-intensity war initiated in 1963 by Indonesian President Sukarno (1945–65) against Malaysia and Singapore to divert Indonesian public opinion away from domestic problems.[4] Coming to the defense of Malaysia and Singapore, Britain and Australia ultimately stationed over forty thousand troops and a nuclear submarine in the area. This Western intervention combined with Sukarno's ties with China raised the prospect that if the conflict escalated, Southeast Asian states would lose control over their own destiny, as was then occurring in South Vietnam, Laos, and Cambodia.[5] The ending of *konfrontasi* by Sukarno's successor, Suharto (1965–98), and the creation of ASEAN were designed to avoid the fate of Indochina.

ASEAN's early leaders drew the following lessons from *konfrontasi*. First, high levels of domestic political contestation within Southeast Asia's ethnically, religiously, and ideologically diverse countries provided incentives for political leaders to pick fights with their neighbors. Second, once regional conflicts started, Southeast Asian states had an incentive to seek outside support. Given the intensity of Cold War competition, external assistance would likely be granted, but it would come with a price: retaliation by the opposing bloc through attempts to subvert domestic politics in Southeast Asia's fragile political systems and the loss of autonomy over regional events. These lessons led to the belief that to ensure regional stability, domestic political contestation must be suppressed. Regional stability was not just an end in itself, but also a means of ensuring that great powers have no incentive to intervene in Southeast Asian affairs.

These beliefs were enshrined in the Bangkok Declaration, through which Indonesia, Malaysia, Singapore, Thailand, and the Philippines created ASEAN in 1967. The preamble states, "the countries of South-East Asia share a primary responsibility for strengthening the economic and social stability of the region and ensuring their peaceful and progressive national development and that they are determined to ensure their stability and security from external interference in any form or manifestation."[6] Illustrating ASEAN states' belief that defense relationships should be maintained to enhance their own security and not imperil the security of their neighbors, the Bangkok Declaration also affirmed that "all foreign bases are temporary and remain only with the expressed concurrence of the countries concerned and are not intended to be used directly or indirectly to subvert the national independence and freedom of States in the area."[7]

These clauses from the Bangkok Declaration illustrate how domestic politics, regional relations, and autonomy from great powers were all interrelated in the minds of ASEAN's first generation of leaders. ASEAN states must exercise restraint in their relations with their neighbors, even if doing so might be costly domestically. In turn, they expect their ASEAN counterparts to manage their domestic affairs to prevent problems from spilling over into other countries. ASEAN's cardinal rules of noninterference in one another's affairs and respect for sovereignty of members countries are an outgrowth of these beliefs.

Factors Promoting ASEAN Cohesion and the Development of an ASEAN External Policy

ASEAN cohesion was promoted by a number of factors in its early years. First, all ASEAN countries were ruled by authoritarian leaders who consolidated their authority by suppressing leftist forces. Second, all ASEAN leaders viewed their domestic communist parties as the key threat to national stability. Fearing Chinese subversion through local communist parties, no ASEAN country had formal diplomatic ties with China in the organization's early years.[8] Third, believing that poverty provided fertile ground for communist appeals, all ASEAN leaders viewed economic development as a key national priority, adopted market-oriented policies, and sought economic aid from the West. Fourth, all ASEAN countries maintained security ties with the West. These factors produced a common vision of a stable, autonomous, Western-oriented Southeast Asian order.

To help promote this regional order, ASEAN enshrined a regional code of conduct in the TAC in 1976. The TAC codified ASEAN's bedrock principles of respect for sovereignty of member states, peaceful resolution of disputes, renunciation of the use of force, and effective cooperation. By making the TAC open to accession by all Southeast Asian states, ASEAN leaders hoped that its rules would provide the basis for rapprochement with the countries of Indochina following their communist victories. But it would take another two decades before the Indochinese countries joined ASEAN.[9]

An external ASEAN policy developed in the mid-1970s. Rajendran argues that ASEAN's shift to collective action was triggered by the need to grapple with the massive exodus of Indochinese boat people who washed up on ASEAN shores.[10] In that case, ASEAN lobbied for financial assistance from the countries of first asylum and a commitment from Western countries to offer permanent asylum, and it placed external pressure on Vietnam to stem the flow. ASEAN was fairly successful in achieving these objectives.

ASEAN policy toward Vietnam's December 1978 invasion of Cambodia brought ASEAN as an international actor to global attention. In this case, ASEAN had a collective agenda: to roll back the Vietnamese invasion, forge a Cambodian coalition out of its fractious political actors, and secure external assistance to implement the policy. Stating that ASEAN had a collective agenda does not mean that all members had identical interests. Indonesia and Malaysia disagreed with the policy of "bleeding Vietnam white" because they viewed China, not Vietnam, as the region's key external threat. But with Thailand's sovereignty at stake, leaders in Jakarta and Kuala Lumpur subordinated their national interests and prioritized Thailand's security and the interest of upholding ASEAN's bedrock principles of the pacific settlement of disputes. The Paris Peace Agreements that ultimately resolved the Cambodian situation were based largely on ASEAN's agenda.

In the Cambodian case, a number of factors made ASEAN's external policy possible and effective. First, the source of the conflict, Vietnam, was not an ASEAN member. Second, ASEAN remained a fairly cohesive body, despite its expansion to six members with the admission of Brunei in 1984. Therefore, its common perception of a regional order based on ASEAN norms, communist containment, and alignment with the West remained intact. Third, all major powers, including the United States, China, and Japan, supported ASEAN's position. Therefore, there was no reason for external powers to intervene in ASEAN's affairs to ensure an outcome congruent with their interests.

Internal Factors Undermining ASEAN Cohesion and Its External Policy

ASEAN Expansion

Sustaining ASEAN cohesion has become more difficult as membership has expanded to all ten Southeast Asian countries. In its first two decades, ASEAN states—despite their many ethnic, religious, economic, and political differences—were united by an anticommunist ideology, authoritarian regime, and Western political orientation. Today, ASEAN regimes range from a full-fledged democracy (Indonesia) to Islamic sultanate (Brunei) and two of the world's last remaining communist countries (Vietnam and Laos). The lack of a common ideological orientation creates divergent conceptions of regional order.

Furthermore, for almost three decades, ASEAN was mainly a maritime Southeast Asian institution; its center of gravity lay with Indonesia, Singapore, and Malaysia. Since ASEAN's expansion in the 1990s, its geographic orientation has changed. The entrance of Cambodia, Myanmar, Laos, and Vietnam (CMLV) has meant that ASEAN now has more members on mainland than maritime Southeast Asia. This geographic divide is reinforced economically.[11] The disparity between the older, richer ASEAN members and the newer, poorer ones is striking: 2010 per capita income for the original ASEAN six was US$3,211, versus US$819 for the CMLV countries.[12] The fact that ASEAN's poorest members are located on mainland Southeast Asia, next door to China's vibrant economy, means that their economic orientation is toward China, providing Beijing with an important source of influence.

Domestic Political Opening

Today, the political process is more open in virtually all ASEAN countries, making regional leaders much more dependent on public opinion. Public opinion can pressure leaders to adopt aggressive policies and raise the domestic political costs of restraint. During the 2005–9 Malaysian-Indonesian tensions over the oil-rich Ambalat block in the Celebes Sea, naval ships from the two countries were "bumping" into one another and the dispute threatened to escalate. Indonesian papers evoked Sukarno's *konfrontasi* with Malaysia and demanded that Indonesia *ganyang* or crush Malaysia. Indonesian leaders resisted these nationalistic appeals, ensuring that the bilateral dispute did not escalate with negative implications for regional stability and ASEAN cohesion. Indonesian leaders, however, paid a political price in public opinion. As Indonesia was ASEAN's largest country and de factor leader, its officials under the Yudhoyono administration were willing to incur domestic costs because they gained prestige from their purported ASEAN leadership, and placing broader regional interests ahead of narrow national interests is often a prerequisite for that leadership.

In contrast, Indonesia's new president, Joko Widodo (Jokowi), has stated that foreign policy must promote national interests, indicating a reduction in the importance Indonesia attaches to ASEAN. According to Rizal Sukma, a key foreign policy advisor to Jokowi, "We used to say ASEAN is *the* cornerstone of our foreign policy. Now we change it to *a* cornerstone of our foreign policy."[13] Indeed, Jokowi's promulgation of a maritime axis doctrine that envisions Indonesia as a global maritime power straddling the Pacific and Indian oceans clearly signals Indonesia's desire to expand its influence beyond Southeast Asia.[14] At the same time, the maritime axis strategy is focused on protecting Indonesian sovereignty, particularly its fishing stocks, from foreign exploitation. According to Indonesian authorities, over five thousand foreign ships operate illegally in Indonesian waters every day, resulting in approximately US$20 billion of lost revenue annually.[15] Since Indonesia lacks the naval capacity to patrol its vast waterways, Jokowi has instructed his security forces to sink foreign ships—after removing their crew—in order to deter future encroachments. To date, Indonesia has sunk illegal fishing vessels from Vietnam, Thailand, the Philippines, and Malaysia. The government has responded to foreign criticism by stressing that its actions are permissible under domestic law and the United Nations Convention on the Law of the Sea (UNCLOS), while Jokowi has emphasized that "this is a purely criminal issue and has nothing to do with neighborly relations."[16] Indonesia's neighbors clearly disagree. If Indonesia continues to take such public actions against its ASEAN partners, it will be difficult to envision anything other than a continued weakening of ASEAN cohesion.

Political leaders in other ASEAN countries have also often failed to exhibit restraint toward their ASEAN partners. Instead, political contestation can create incentives for politicians to provoke disputes with their neighbors as a means to strengthen their domestic political position. This was clearly the case in the Thai-Cambodian conflict over the Preah Vihear temple. At a time of intense political division in Thailand, some Thai leaders found it in their interests to accuse their political opponents of selling out Thai national interests in order to score political points at home. Coming at a time when Hun Sen was facing elections, the dispute also provided the Cambodian leader an issue that he could use to mobilize votes. Violence on both sides forced the evacuation of thousands along the border and left scores of soldiers and civilians on both sides dead and many more wounded.[17]

The temple dispute has had far-reaching implications for ASEAN's credibility, the basis of any ASEAN external policy. ASEAN often responds to criticism of its weakness by arguing that its greatest achievement is the fact that no ASEAN countries have fought one another. ASEAN attributes this achievement to the promulgation of its cardinal rules of noninterference in the affairs of others, respect for international sovereignty, and a commitment to the pacific settlement of disputes. In the Preah Vihear case, however, neither side adhered to these rules, despite attempts by Indonesian officials and others to mediate the conflict. This case illustrates the weakness of ASEAN as an organization—it lacks any mechanism to enforce compliance with its norms and sanction members when their actions threaten regional stability.

ASEAN'S Weak Institutional Structure

The disparity in size among ASEAN members, which include the world's fourth most populous country (Indonesia), two of its smallest (Brunei and Singapore), as well as a number of middle powers (Thailand, Vietnam, the Philippines, and Myanmar), illustrates that ASEAN is not an organization of equals. However, the organization's consensus decision-making rule means that each member has an equal vote. Stated differently, consensus voting gives each member a veto over ASEAN affairs. ASEAN's unwillingness to abandon consensus decision making even after its expansion can make reaching consensus difficult and ensures that the organization moves only at the pace of its slowest member. This has led to great frustration for some of ASEAN's original members, particularly Indonesia and Singapore, who do not like having ASEAN policy held hostage by the likes of Laos.

Moreover, ASEAN's institutional structure—a weak secretariat headed by a secretary general with no independent authority to speak or act on the organization's behalf—means that it is very difficult for ASEAN to respond to unfolding events quickly. Hopes by some members that the adoption of the ASEAN Charter, which gives the organization a legal basis, would strengthen the organization have been unrealized. Decision-making power remains fully vested with the national governments of ASEAN members, not the organization itself.

ASEAN Centrality and Great Power Participation in Regional Architecture

ASEAN's ability to bind great powers to ASEAN norms is dependent in part upon retaining ASEAN centrality in regional architecture and ensuring that countries like the United States and China participate in it. ASEAN centrality in regional organizations gives its members agenda-setting influence and helps prevent their domination by larger powers. Normally, international organizations are created and run by powerful states. In the Asia-Pacific, long-standing tensions between Asia's larger countries such as China and Japan created an opening for ASEAN to serve as the focal point for regional organization. Retaining ASEAN centrality will require balancing the interests of the larger powers, something possible if they value the status quo but not if they harbor revisionist ambitions.

ASEAN centrality will mean little if outside powers fail to participate in ASEAN-centered institutions. In managing its relations with the United States and China, ASEAN has traditionally faced a different set of challenges. China has long been an eager participant in ASEAN-based institutions and was the first outside power to sign the TAC. China's own ambitions for regional leadership, however, pose a threat to ASEAN centrality. In contrast, the United States has often been less than enthusiastic about ASEAN regionalism. The challenge facing ASEAN, therefore, is to ensure that the United States maintains a commitment to ASEAN-based institutions, while limiting China's influence in them.

To date, ASEAN has rebuffed Chinese attempts to usurp ASEAN's formal agenda-setting role. ASEAN members rejected China's proposal to host the second EAS because they feared China would use the organization as a vehicle for Chinese leadership. All EAS meetings are hosted by the ASEAN chairman. China has long pushed for regional institution building to take place on a "pan-Asian" basis that would exclude the United States, Australia, and New Zealand, thereby enhancing China's relative power in them. ASEAN members were divided on this issue: Myanmar, Cambodia, and Malaysia were vocal proponents of a pan-Asia framework, while Indonesia, Singapore, and Vietnam preferred a pan-Pacific basis that would dilute China's influence. Behind the scenes China objected to the expansion of the EAS to include the United States and Russia, but both became members in 2011.

The United States shares ASEAN's goal of promoting regional stability, but has not always been an enthusiastic supporter of ASEAN-centric institutions. Contending that ASEAN's consensus decision-making privileges process over substance, the U.S. secretary of state skipped a number of ASEAN meetings during the Bush administration. ASEAN members interpreted this absence as a sign that ASEAN might have to meet the China challenge without the United States as a counterweight. ASEAN members therefore welcomed the inauguration of President Obama, who expressed a desire to be the first Pacific president and whose administration increased its attention to Southeast Asia. Hillary Clinton became the first secretary of state to visit the ASEAN Secretariat, attended all ASEAN meetings, and called ASEAN "a fulcrum of the region's emerging regional architecture."[18] The United States signed the TAC in 2009 and joined the EAS in November 2011. Southeast Asian states are aware that the United States' newfound appreciation of ASEAN is driven largely by its concern with China. The Sino-American rivalry enhances ASEAN's regional status, but risks ASEAN becoming a forum for Sino-American competition, something its members want to avoid.

This fear of becoming a site of Sino-American rivalry led some Southeast Asian states to be wary of the security component of the U.S. Pivot to Asia, even as they welcomed greater U.S. participation in ASEAN-based organizations. Formally announced by President Obama in an October 2011 speech to the Australian Parliament, the U.S. Pivot was driven by the recognition that U.S. policy needed to focus more heavily on the strategically important and economically vibrant Asia-Pacific. In Australia, President Obama affirmed his intent to sustain U.S. regional leadership and announced plans to rotate twenty-five hundred marines through Australia's Darwin military base annually by 2017. This announcement, coming just days before Obama attended his first EAS Summit, led Indonesian Foreign Minister Marty Natalegawa to state that he feared the marine deployment would "provoke a reaction and counter-reaction precisely to create that viscous circle of tensions and mistrust."[19]

China responded as Natalegawa predicted, calling the U.S. Pivot a "conspiracy to hold down or actually disrupt China's rise."[20] As Kenneth Lieberthal has argued, the U.S. Pivot serves as an umbrella concept for a range of issues that China views as a threat: democracy promotion, pressure to revalue the renminbi, and the Trans-Pacific Partnership (TPP), which China views as a mechanism to prevent the internationalization of the renminbi.[21] In short, the United States and China have competing visions of what regional order in the Asia-Pacific should look like and who should lead it.

Policy makers in Washington and Beijing—as well as ASEAN capitals— are well aware that changes in the balance of power caused by rising powers have often triggered major wars. American and Chinese leaders have therefore called for a "New Type of Major Power Relationship" rather than the traditional zero-sum relationships that produce conflict. A scenario in which the United States and China manage their relationship without compromising the core interests of Southeast Asian states is ASEAN's desired outcome.

Power transitions themselves do not trigger conflict. Instead, revisionist behavior by the rising power typically does. China has taken a series of actions in the South China Sea that threaten the national interests of individual ASEAN members, particularly the Philippines and Vietnam. Viewing China's actions as unilateral attempts to revise the status quo, these nations have requested that ASEAN forge a united front to defend their interests, just as ASEAN united behind Thailand in the Cambodian case. Furthermore, as the world's leading naval power, the United States views many of China's actions as threats to its critical interest in freedom of navigation. For these reasons, this chapter now examines the South China Sea issue, and the challenges it creates for ASEAN in its pursuit of an external policy to ensure its key interests of regional stability and autonomy.

The South China Sea Dispute: A Major Challenge to ASEAN

Disputes in the South China Sea, with its strategic sea lanes of communication, rich fishing grounds, and significant oil and gas deposits, are not new. Overlapping territorial claims to the Paracel (China and Vietnam) and Spratly island chains (China, Taiwan, Malaysia, Brunei, the Philippines, and Vietnam) date back decades, as does competition to occupy and control them. The use of force by China to assert its claims is not new either: China forcibly took the Paracels from Vietnamese control in 1974.

What is new is China's 2009 submission to the United Nations Commission on the Limits of the Continental Shelf (UNCLCS), in which China claimed that it had "indisputable sovereignty over the islands in the South China Sea and their adjacent waters and enjoy sovereign rights and jurisdiction over the relevant waters as well as the seabed and subsoil thereof."[22] The submission was accompanied by a "nine-dash line" map that includes virtually the entire South China Sea. The Chinese claims are expansive, and its justification for them is ambiguous, relying mostly on its version of historical rights, not UN-CLOS. China's increasingly assertive maritime behavior—including harassment of the USS *Impeccable*, the detention of Japanese boats in the disputed Senkaku/Diaoyu islands, the 2012 military confrontation with the Philippines over Scarborough Shoal, the naval confrontation with the USS *Cowpens*, and its land reclamation projects—appear to indicate a policy of deterrence and denial through the South China Sea.[23] China's November 2013 declaration of an Air Defense Identification Zone (ADIZ) over the East China Sea has increased regional tensions and raised the prospect that China might declare an ADIZ over the South China Sea. To many in Southeast Asia and beyond, China's actions represent an attempt to revise the status quo unilaterally.

Vietnam and the Philippines have borne the brunt of Chinese assertiveness. In an effort to deter foreign oil companies from exploring for oil in waters disputed with Vietnam, China has threatened to punish oil companies that explore in disputed areas, even when those areas are well within Vietnam's two-hundred-mile Exclusive Economic Zone (EEZ). Chinese paramilitary boats have deliberately cut the sonar cables of Vietnamese survey ships. China has also imposed a unilateral fishing ban in disputed waters within Vietnam's EEZ. Imposed at the height of Vietnam's fishing season, the ban is purportedly to protect the fishing grounds from overfishing, but Vietnamese officials note that the fish are protected only from Vietnamese fisherman, while Chinese fisherman are permitted to exploit the catch. In 2014, China raised the stakes by placing a massive oil rig in disputed waters.

The Philippines, an archipelagic state with virtually no naval capacity, has long been a target of Chinese assertiveness. In 1994, the Chinese occupied Mischief Reef, located 130 miles off the cost of Palawan Island, well within the Philippines EEZ. Over official Philippine protests, the Chinese first fortified the reef with bamboo structures it claimed were shelters for Chinese fisherman and later built concrete bunkers that resemble military installations. The Philippines claims that China has a pattern of "creeping invasion," in which it plants buoys around islands and shoals, then lays down concrete markers on them, and later builds structures from which local authorities and fishermen can be kept out. The Philippine government claims this is currently playing out in Scarborough Shoal and will likely occur in the Second Thomas Shoal if China gains control of it. In 2014, Chinese ships unsuccessfully attempted to prevent the Philippines from resupplying the *Sierre Madre*, a naval ship deliberately run aground in Second Thomas Shoal to demonstrate Philippine control of the territory.

At the time, China's occupation of Mischief Reef, which occurred amid China's heated opposition to Vietnam's granting of oil exploration rights to

American oil company Crestone, led many ASEAN leaders to perceive China as a revisionist actor. Viewing China's actions as a test for the organization, ASEAN responded collectively by telling China, at the first ever ASEAN-China bilateral meeting held in April 1995 in Hangzhou, that ASEAN would not tolerate the use of force to resolve regional disputes.[24] Indonesia, as ASEAN's leading state and a nonclaimant, began a series of meetings between the disputants to explore resolution options and set parameters to avoid clashes at sea. Indonesia complemented its diplomatic response with a show of force, holding what was at that time the country's largest military exercise, involving over nineteen thousand soldiers, fifty warships, and forty aircraft in September 1996 around its Natuna Islands chain.[25]

As a result, Chinese leaders began to realize that its assertive policies were raising concerns in ASEAN. Furthermore, the strong U.S. response during the 1996 Taiwan Straits Crisis demonstrated the U.S. resolve to balance against China.[26] Chinese leaders feared that ASEAN states might join a balancing coalition against China, leading to its "encirclement." To forestall such an eventuality, China adopted a "win-win" strategy to convince its Southeast Asian neighbors that it was a benign great power.[27] China's adoption of its "peaceful rise" strategy is variously ascribed to the U.S. "hard power" response on Taiwan and ASEAN's strong stance of multilateral resolution through peaceful means.

In short, in the mid-1990s—before Myanmar, Cambodia, and Laos joined—ASEAN rallied behind the Philippines and Vietnam over their South China Sea disputes with China. ASEAN's soft-power diplomacy combined with the U.S. show of hard power convinced China to abandon its assertive policy and adopt a more conciliatory one. Today, Vietnam and the Philippines are pressing ASEAN for a similar show of support, while also seeking the assistance of the United States and others in the hope of inducing a similar shift in China's behavior.

The Philippines and Vietnam Seek ASEAN and Great Power Support, 2010–2012

At the 2010 ARF meeting, Vietnam used its position as ASEAN chair to confront China. China lobbied ASEAN not to raise the South China Sea issue, but twelve of the twenty-seven delegations did, including that of the United States.[28] Secretary Clinton used the occasion to state that the United States had a "national interest in freedom of navigation, open access to Asia's maritime commons, and respect for international law in the South China Sea." Clinton also stated that while the United States did not take sides on the sovereignty claim, it wanted to see the disputes resolved peacefully, through a collaborative process in accordance with UNCLOS, and offered to facilitate negotiations.[29] Clinton's statement supported the position of ASEAN members such as Vietnam, Indonesia, and the Philippines but challenged China's long-standing policy that the South China Sea disputes should be resolved bilaterally. Chinese Foreign Minister Yang Jiechi, blindsided by the coordination between the United States and ASEAN, responded furiously to the internationalization of the issue.

A key goal of Indonesia, as the 2011 ASEAN chair, was to produce guidelines to transform ASEAN's nonbinding 2002 Declaration on the Conduct of Parties in the South China Sea (DOC) into a legally binding code of conduct (COC). Indonesia has no territorial claims in the South China Sea, which Jakarta has traditionally believed positions it as an independent mediator. However, China's nine-dash line includes the oil-rich waters around Indonesia's Natuna Islands. Indonesia's decision to lodge a protest against China's 2009 UNCLCS submission, and its calls for resolution of the dispute according to UNCLOS, clearly support the positions of Vietnam and the Philippines but conflict with China's position.

In July 2011, ahead of the ARF meeting, ASEAN and China did agree on a set of guidelines for the implementation of the DOC as a prelude to the COC, but they studiously avoided the issue of sovereignty.[30] Hopes that the guidelines would include concrete proposals to reduce the potential for accidental naval clashes, such as advance notification of military exercises and rules of conduct for parties on the high seas, were dashed. Chinese officials called the guidelines a "milestone."[31] Secretary Clinton called them an "important first step" but also called for follow-up negotiations between ASEAN and China while reiterating that "the rest of the world needs to weigh in" because "all of us" have a stake in ensuring that the conflicts do not escalate.[32] The escalation of the South China Sea disputes since 2011 appears to indicate that China does not view the DOC as a restraint on its actions.

In its attempts to mediate the issue as the putative leader of ASEAN, Indonesia must seek to balance not only the diverse interests of its fellow ASEAN members, but also those of China and the United States. At risk is the prospect that if ASEAN cannot play a constructive role, then its members will seek support from outside powers, thereby raising the potential that local states will increasingly lose control. The Philippines has actively sought U.S. backing, and in November 2011 Secretary Clinton made a strong gesture of U.S. support for the Philippines by referring to the disputed waters as the "West Philippines Sea" during a speech from the deck of an American warship in Manila Bay.[33] China reacted strongly to the speech, illustrating that the challenge of maintaining ASEAN cohesion and balancing the interests of China and the United States are intricately intertwined.

Chinese analysts responded to Indonesia's attempts to forge a common ASEAN foreign policy by threatening to subvert ASEAN. In one editorial titled "On the South China Sea, an ASEAN United Front Won't Help Anyone, Especially Indonesia," the consequences of advocating anything other than China's current policy of "setting aside disputes and pursuing joint development" are enumerated.[34] First, China would weaken its support for ASEAN as an organization. Second, it would challenge ASEAN centrality in regional organizations because "China is becoming the focal point of regional integration." Third, China would pursue a subregional approach to economic integration, rather than an ASEAN-centered one. Chinese analysts argue that the Greater Mekong Subregion is geographically and economically more integrated than ASEAN. Given China's strong influence in tiny Laos and Cambodia, such a threat means that ASEAN's long-standing geographic divisions between mainland and island Southeast Asia could be reinforced geostrategically.

The challenges of preventing a geostrategic split in ASEAN and maintaining ASEAN unity when the ASEAN chairman is closely linked to China and China chooses to play hardball were illustrated in 2012. Cambodia failed to include the South China Sea dispute on its list of key agenda items for its chairmanship, contrasting with the 2011 and 2010 chairs. A visit by Chinese President Hu Jintao just ahead of the April 2012 ASEAN Summit triggered speculation that China was pressuring Cambodia to promote its interests. Cambodian Prime Minister Hun Sen denied such allegations, but Cambodia's proposal that China be included in the drafting of procedures to implement the DOC suggests otherwise. ASEAN's traditional position is that its members should agree on a policy draft first, then share it with outsiders. Any drafting role for China is starkly opposed by many ASEAN members and triggered what Philippine Foreign Secretary Albert del Rosario called a "big disagreement" at the summit.[35]

China's willingness to intervene in ASEAN affairs through Cambodia was clearly illustrated at the July 2012 ASEAN meetings in Phnom Penh. At issue was whether and how to mention conflicts in the South China Sea, particularly a tense 2012 military standoff between China and the Philippines over Scarborough Shoal, a chain of reefs approximately 140 miles off the coast of Luzon.[36] In April, Philippine naval forces found Chinese paramilitary ships in the shoal, protecting Chinese fisherman in the reef allegedly collecting coral and marine life in violation of international law. As the two sides faced off against one another, fears grew of an inadvertent clash. A deal was brokered for both sides to withdraw; the Philippines withdrew but the Chinese did not.[37] In the period since then, China has reinforced it presence around the shoal and laid an underground cable to keep Philippine fisherman out. The Philippines and its supporters argue that Chinese actions in the Scarborough Shoal constitute a concerted use of military force to seize territory, and revise the status quo in its favor.

Despite the desire of other ASEAN members to include a reference to the South China Sea, Cambodia—reportedly after conferring with Chinese officials—refused to do so and announced that ASEAN would not issue a joint statement for the first time in forty-five years, something Indonesian Foreign Minister Marty Natalegawa called "utterly irresponsible."[38] China's actions contravene ASEAN's norm of noninterference in the organization's affairs and illustrate that China is willing to violate ASEAN's bedrock principles. Recognizing China's threat to ASEAN cohesion and Indonesia's own regional leadership, Indonesian Foreign Minister Natalegawa embarked on a round of shuttle diplomacy to ASEAN capitals to secure agreement on six points that would be issued in place of the final statement. The six points included a desire to observe the Declaration on Conduct of Parties in the South China Sea and guidelines for its implementation; to work toward an early adoption of a Code of Conduct; to exercise self-restrain and avoid using force; and to uphold the peaceful settlement of disputes in keeping with universally recognized principles of international law, including UNCLOS.[39]

Natalegawa's diplomatic efforts papered over ASEAN's differences but did not resolve them. As Donald Weatherbee has observed, the real purpose of Natalegawa's work to gain a consensus was to demonstrate ASEAN solidarity, even if it did not advance ASEAN's agenda.[40] Indeed, the forging of an ASEAN agreement did not have the desired impact of inducing greater Chinese concern for ASEAN's position. Instead, on July 20, 2012, the same day that Natalegawa announced the agreement, China announced that its Central Military Commission had authorized the People's Liberation Army to form a Sansha Garrison Command over the Paracel and Spratly islands that would be on Hainan Island and that the new command's duties would include "defense mobilization" and activities to enforce China's maritime claims.[41]

ASEAN's lack of unity and Cambodia's willingness to privilege its relationship with China over its ASEAN partners continued at the November 2012 ASEAN Summit. Reflecting China's long-standing position that the South China Sea disputes should be resolved bilaterally between the claimants rather than internationalized, Cambodia attempted to insert a reference into the summit's joint communiqué that the leaders agreed not to internationalize the dispute. The clause was omitted from the communiqué due to objections by the Philippines, among others, but to many observers, Cambodia had clearly chosen sides.[42]

The South China Sea 2013–Present: A Philippine Move beyond
ASEAN, a Chinese Diplomatic Charm Offensive, and Greater
Maritime Assertiveness

*Leadership Change in ASEAN: Toward Greater Cohesion and Support
for ASEAN Claimants?*

Events in 2013 brought a number of changes to ASEAN that portended
an internal shift toward the coalition favoring a more assertive, collective
ASEAN response to China. First, veteran Vietnamese diplomat Le Luong
Minh became the new ASEAN secretary general. Second, Brunei assumed
the ASEAN chairmanship. The agenda-setting influence that comes from
these positions was now in the hands of representatives from maritime states
with South China Sea claims. Secretary Minh and Bruneian officials both
placed a priority on jumpstarting negotiations on the COC, and the sultan
of Brunei visited Philippine President Aquino ahead of the November 2012
ASEAN Summit to discuss the issue. Despite ASEAN splits in 2012, progress
had been made on the COC. Indonesia produced a "non-paper" on the COC
and presented it to ASEAN foreign ministers on the sidelines of the 2012 UN
General Assembly meeting. Brunei set an ambitious target date of October
2013 for the completion of the COC, so that it could be signed at the ASEAN-
China Summit.

Despite these favorable trends, on January 22, 2013, the Philippines made
a formal request to the UNCLOS Arbitral Tribunal to rule on the legality of
some of China's maritime claims. Recourse to UNCLOS procedures was included as one of two dispute mechanisms included in ASEAN's July 2012 draft
on proposed elements of a COC. However, the lack of Philippine consultation
with its ASEAN partners before approaching UNCLOS generated frustration
among some of them. The Philippine decision to take its claim to UNCLOS
can be viewed as recognition that ASEAN could not protect its interests.

China condemned the internationalization of the issue and refused to participate in the UNCLOS process. Since UNCLOS procedures do not require
China to appear before the Arbitral Tribunal, the case is moving forward
without Chinese representation. In October 2015, the tribunal concluded its
jurisdictional phase and agreed to rule on the legal entitlements of ten land
features in the merits phase of the case. The tribunal will not determine sovereignty to the disputed features, but will rule on whether the small reefs and
islands at issue generate maritime zones.[43] China's decision not to participate
in the legal process does not relieve it from being a party to the dispute, so
the Arbitral Tribunal's decision will be final and binding.[44] However, the UN-

CLOS dispute resolution system has no enforcement mechanism. As a result, should the tribunal hand down a ruling China perceives as harmful to its interests, it could refuse to comply with it, and it is unlikely that there would be any legal recourse. The impact of the tribunal's decision on regional politics is difficult to predict, and will depend in part on the ruling and in part on how China responds to it.

Manila's increasingly close cooperation with the United States could be interpreted to mean that the Philippines has "chosen sides" between the United States and China. Security ties between the United States and the Philippines weakened following the 1992 decision by the Philippine Senate not to renew the leases for the U.S. Subic Bay Naval and Clark Air bases.[45] Military ties revived following the September 11, 2001, terrorist attack, and since 2002, the United States has provided the Philippines US$132 million in military aid and surplus equipment including two cutters to enhance its maritime forces. In July 2013, the United States announced it would increase annual military assistance by two-thirds from US$30 million to US$50 million each year.[46] President Aquino has unveiled a US$1.82 billion military modernization program focused on naval capacity, designed to strengthen one of Asia's weakest militaries.[47] Most importantly, during President Obama's April 2014 visit to the Philippines, the two sides signed the Enhanced Defense Cooperation Agreement (EDCA), under which the two sides will strengthen defense cooperation and permit the rotational deployment of U.S. troops to Philippine bases and the forward deployment of supplies and equipment.[48] The two sides confirmed that the agreement would not permit the permanent basing of U.S. soldiers in the Philippines, which is prohibited under the Constitution. This contingency and the opposition to the EDCA by some segments of the Philippine public illustrate the outer limits on the defense relationship acceptable to Philippine public opinion, even at a time when control of its territory is under threat. What Philippine officials have repeatedly requested and will not be granted, however, is a public U.S. assertion that the 1951 Mutual Defense Treaty covers its disputed maritime territory. This stands in stark contrast to the Japanese case, where the United States has publicly declared that its treaty alliance with Japan extends to the disputed Senkaku/Diaoyu Islands.

The Philippines has also enhanced maritime security cooperation with Japan and in July 2013 the countries signed a strategic partnership. Japan has responded to China's assertive actions in the East China Sea by seeking support in Southeast Asia. President Aquino has offered both the United States and Japan, his country's only strategic partners, access to Subic Bay Naval Base, which faces the South China Sea. In a June 2013 visit to the Philippines, Japan's Defense Minister claimed that the two countries could cooperate "in defense of remote island chains."[49] If this were to occur, it would only raise tensions with China.

China responded to the Philippine decision to internationalize the South China Sea dispute by continuing to take punitive measures to isolate and punish Manila. During 2012, China banned Philippine banana imports and Chinese tourist visits to the Philippines. China's new Foreign Minister Wang pointedly omitted the Philippines from an early trip to the region.[50] More critically, when President Benigno Aquino announced that he would attend the Tenth China-ASEAN Expo in Nanjing, China requested that Aquino visit "at a more conducive time."[51] It was later revealed that China insisted that the Philippines drop its claim to the UNCLOS Arbitral Tribunal as a condition for the visit. In short, China has made an example of the Philippines to make the costs of contravening Chinese interests starkly clear to all ASEAN members.

China's Leadership Change: A Diplomatic Charm Offensive and Assertive Maritime Actions

China underwent a major leadership change in March 2013, which led to a new Chinese diplomatic charm offensive toward Southeast Asia, with the important exception of the Philippines. President Xi Jinping and Prime Minister Li Keqiang visited a number of ASEAN countries ahead of the 2013 APEC meeting in Bali and the EAS meeting in Brunei. Both leaders promised significant Chinese investment and trade. In Bali, Xi set a target of increasing Sino-ASEAN trade to US$1 trillion annually by 2020, up from US$400 billion in 2012.[52] Chinese leaders proposed an Asian Infrastructure Investment Bank, which would invest in ports, railways, roads, and other projects that would help further integrate China with Southeast Asian economies; the bank was formally launched in October 2014.[53] Wang Yi, the new foreign minister who is a veteran diplomat with extensive experience with ASEAN, is credited with overseeing this policy shift after what some viewed as China overplaying its hand toward ASEAN in Cambodia in 2012.[54]

Contrasting with China's diplomatic isolation of the Philippines, China and Vietnam exchanged high diplomatic visits recently. Foreign Minister Wang Yi visited Hanoi in August, and in a significant development, Chinese Premier Li Keqiang visited Hanoi in October, clearly signaling a desire to keep Sino-Vietnamese relations cordial.[55] While in Hanoi on August 5, 2013, Wang introduced a series of new points guiding China's approach to the COC: recognizing that a COC will take time and all countries should have reasonable expectations; consensus on negotiations; elimination of interference; and a step by step approach.[56] Some analysts viewed this support for a COC as a positive step, while others observed that China's approach held out little hope of significant progress anytime soon while sending a strong signal to ASEAN to keep nonclaimant countries such as the United States out of the picture.

The key issue, however, is whether anything substantive will come from the COC or if it is simply a mechanism to keep ASEAN engaged while China changes facts on the ground. Many of the issues on the COC agenda are already codified in the 2002 DOC, but ASEAN has no mechanism to ensure compliance with it. Indeed, in 2013 China took a number of actions designed to unilaterally revise the status quo. China's main focus was the Philippines, where in addition to its actions in the Scarborough Shoal, it also raised tensions over the disputed Thomas Shoal, located 106 miles off Palawan island. In 2013, President Aquino ordered the repair of the *Sierre Madre*, a Philippine ship deliberately run aground in Thomas Shoal in 1998 to demonstrate physical control. This triggered an angry response from China, which protested Philippine attempts to resupply the small contingent of marines on the *Sierre Madre* by sending Chinese vessels to the shoal, where they unsuccessfully attempted to block Philippine ships from approaching it. China claimed indisputable sovereignty over Thomas Shoal and called the presence of the Philippine marines illegal.[57]

China also engaged in a series of provocative actions toward areas disputed with other ASEAN countries. China sent tourists on forty-day fishing trips to the Paracel Islands, claimed also by Vietnam. From March 19 to April 3, 2013, China sent a flotilla of warships to conduct combat exercises as they circumnavigated the South China Sea. After storming the beach in Mischief Reef, the flotilla sailed to James Shoal, only eighty kilometers off the coast of Malaysia. There, the marines took an oath to "defend the South China Sea, maintain national sovereignty and strive toward the dream of a strong China."[58]

Malaysia has long taken a relaxed approach toward its overlapping claims with China. Prime Minister Najib is on record as stating that he favors joint development with China to prevent outside powers from interfering in the dispute. At the same time, Malaysia has been enhancing its naval ties with the United States. Malaysia's Naval Chief Abdul Aziz Jafar welcomed the June 2013 visit to Port Klang by the USS *Blue Ridge*, the first port call of a U.S. naval ship since 2008, by stating that the U.S. naval presence in Asia had a "positive impact."[59] Malaysian Defense Minister Hisammudin Hussein stated in August 2013 that Malaysia has sufficient trust in its relationship with China that so long as the Chinese had no intention to go to war, they could patrol the disputed waters every day. Nevertheless, following China's visit to James

Shoal, Malaysia announced that it was building a new naval base in Sarawak, one hundred kilometers from James Shoal, to protect its EEZ.[60]

Like the Philippines and Malaysia, Vietnam has strengthened ties with the United States. American restrictions on the sales of military equipment to Vietnam due to its human rights situation, however, limit the U.S. ability to strengthen Vietnam's military capacity. Vietnam, unlike the Philippines, has a range of security partners, and has recently strengthened its long-standing military ties with Russia. Vietnam has also awarded oil exploration contracts to a range of Western and Indian firms to give other countries an incentive to support Hanoi in its dispute with China.[61]

The U.S. Government Shutdown and Obama's Absence from EAS and APEC Undermine Pivot

The departure of staunch Pivot advocates Hillary Clinton and Kurt Campbell following Obama's January 2013 inauguration to a second presidential term and the appointment of John Kerry as secretary of state raised questions regarding the sustainability of the Pivot to Asia given Kerry's long-standing interest in the Middle East. Nevertheless, the new foreign team continued the policy of strengthening ties with ASEAN. At the Shangri-La Dialogue in Singapore in May, Defense Secretary Chuck Hagel invited all ASEAN defense ministers to meet in Hawaii as a group in 2014. In August, Hagel attended the ASEAN Defense Ministers Meeting Plus in Brunei in a trip that also included visits to Indonesia, Malaysia, and the Philippines. In July, Kerry attended the ARF, whose final communiqué dealt at length with the South China Sea, calling for the peaceful resolution of the disputes and the completion of the COC.[62]

After the ARF, the major opportunities for ASEAN to engage with outside powers were the EAS in Brunei and the APEC Summit in Bali, both scheduled for October to facilitate the travel schedules of world leaders. The hosting of these important events by two ASEAN members illustrates the centrality of ASEAN in regional architecture. Until 2013, Obama had supported the U.S. Pivot with his participation in the EAS and APEC summit meetings. But Obama cancelled his 2013 EAS and APEC participation, as well as bilateral visits to Malaysia and the Philippines, due to the government shutdown in Washington. Southeast Asian leaders expressed understanding, but were concerned with not only the president's absence, but also its cause. A Washington so polarized that it could not agree on a budget to keep the government functioning negatively impacts U.S. leadership and global economic stability. The shutdown also raised concerns about the administration's ability to complete the Pivot's economic component, the TPP: if the U.S. Congress could not agree on a budget, what confidence could foreign leaders have that it would grant the president authority to conclude the TPP negotiations? Singaporean PM Lee Hsien Loong publicly expressed the dismay of many when he stated, "Obviously, we prefer a U.S. government that is working to one that is not. And we prefer a U.S. president who is able to travel and fulfill his international duties to one who is preoccupied with national domestic preoccupations."

Chinese leaders emphasized China's economic dynamism. In Indonesia before the APEC summit, Xi Jinping became the first foreign leader to address the Indonesian Parliament, where he called for the creation of a Maritime Silk Road to strengthen economic ties between China and Southeast Asia. In this vision, the South China Sea becomes a source of connectivity, not a source of conflict, between China and Southeast Asia. At the APEC Summit, Xi highlighted China's economic vitality and warned that U.S. monetary politics were destabilizing and dangerous to developing countries. With China using economics in its competition for regional leadership, a senior Singapore Foreign Ministry official stated that the United States and Japan should step up their economic influence in Southeast Asia or risk ceding leadership to China.[63]

South China Sea issues were raised at the EAS in Brunei on October 10, but in contrast to previous years, Chinese officials reacted with measured language, arguing that the Philippines, Japan, and the United States were pushing too fast for a code of conduct. In Brunei, Li proposed a China-ASEAN treaty of good neighborliness, friendship, and cooperation. Some Chinese commentary characterized the proposal as a way to reduce regional concerns over China's rise, while others portrayed the treaty as a way to counter the U.S. Pivot. China directed harsh words not at ASEAN but at the United States, Japan, and Australia, who issued a declaration on the sidelines of the meeting opposing coercive, unilateral, and disruptive action in the South China Sea.

Representing the president at the EAS and the U.S.-ASEAN Summit, Secretary of State Kerry reiterated the U.S. commitment to a rule-based order in the region, something clearly incompatible with China's maritime actions. Weighing in on the South China Sea COC, Kerry stated, "[a] finalized code of conduct in which all abide by a common set of rules and standards is something that will benefit the entire Asia-Pacific community of nations."[64] At the EAS, Kerry also indirectly endorsed the Philippine submission to the Permanent Court of Arbitration on the Law of the Sea at the EAS by stating that all claimants have a "responsibility to clarify and align those claims with international law. . . . They can engage in arbitration and other means of negotiation."[65]

In short, contrasting with China's direct intervention in the 2012 ASEAN meetings, the 2013 EAS was marked by a more sophisticated diplomatic strategy stressing economic incentives for ASEAN members. Compared to the United States, China appeared to have an advantage coming out of the EAS and APEC Summits. Shortly thereafter, however, the swift and effective U.S. humanitarian response to Typhoon Haiyan in the Philippines reminded observers that the United States has unrivaled power projection capacity. And in the months after the EAS and APEC meetings, China's declaration of an ADIZ and a fishing ban in the South China Sea once again reinforced fears of China as a revisionist actor.

China Declares an ADIZ and a Fishing Ban in the South China Sea and Places a Rig in Disputed Waters

On November 23, 2013, China unilaterally declared an ADIZ in the East China Sea, without prior consultation with other countries, even South Korea and Japan, whose own ADIZs now overlap with the Chinese one. The fact the ADIZ covers the disputed Senkaku/Diaoyu Islands in the East China Sea has further raised tensions. The Chinese ADIZ requires aircraft passing through to notify China and register their flight plans. In contrast with ADIZs imposed by the United States that require notification only for flights intending to enter U.S. national airspace, China has demanded that aircraft passing through its new ADIZ file flight plans with China, and it has threatened to take action against aircraft who refuse to obey this rule. The United States has advised civilian airlines to comply with China's request, but Defense Secretary Chuck Hagel has stated that China's action "will not in any way change how the United States conducts military activities in the region." To underscore those words with action, on November 26, 2013, the United States sent two B-52 bombers through the ADIZ without any prior notification to China. The U.S. State Department claimed China's move constituted "an attempt to change the status quo in the East China Sea."[66]

The ADIZ has implications for ASEAN states because anything that raises Sino-U.S. or Sino-Japanese tensions makes ASEAN's attempts to retain its autonomy more difficult. Furthermore, China's ADIZ is perceived as another move in a pattern of unilateral attempts to change the status quo, and has raised fears that China might impose an ADIZ in the South China Sea. Chinese officials did not allay these fears when asked directly whether China intended to impose an ADIZ there. Instead, a Chinese Defense Department spokesperson, Yang Yujun, stated that "China will establish other Air Defense Identification Notification Zones at the right moment after necessary preparations are completed."[67]

Two days after its ADIZ announcement, China sent its aircraft carrier *Liaoning* on a training mission to the South China Sea. Long-standing fears that maritime competition in the absence of a code of conduct to prevent, manage, and resolve accidents could inadvertently cause accidents and escalate into unwanted conflicts were realized when one of the Chinese naval ships escorting the *Liaoning* crossed the bow of the USS *Cowpens*, which had been participating in relief efforts following Typhoon Haiyan.[68] According to the United States, the two ships narrowly avoided a crash due to the provocative action of the Chinese ships. In contrast, China's *Global Times* claimed that the USS *Cowpens* was tailing and harassing the *Liaoning*.[69]

Analysts have noted that the ASEAN reaction to the ADIZ has been fairly muted. As one analyst opined, given that the United States, Japan, South Korea, and Australia have taken a tough stance, the smaller states have an opportunity to free-ride on these attempts to influence China. The first meeting of ASEAN leaders following China's ADIZ announcement took place in Tokyo at the ASEAN-Japanese Summit. In a statement that never referred to the ADIZ directly but that Japanese analysts portrayed as a sign of support for Japan in its standoff with China, the leaders "agreed to enhance co-operation in ensuring freedom of overflight and civil aviation safety."[70]

Perceptions that China is unilaterally changing the status quo were reinforced once again by the announcement by China's Hainan province of new fishing regulations that as of January 1, 2014, all foreign vessels must seek permission before entering waters under Hainan's administrative control.[71] The new regulations cover not only China's two-hundred-mile EEZ around Hainan Island, but also contested and international waters that fall within China's nine-dash line, which one authority estimates covers 57 percent of the South China Sea.[72] In a familiar pattern, the Philippines and Vietnam opposed the ban vociferously.

In April 2014, President Obama visited the Philippines and Malaysia in an effort to demonstrate the U.S. commitment to Asia after the cancellation of his planned November trip and was received more warmly than he may have been in November as a result of the Chinese actions in the South China Sea, Typhoon Haiyan, and Malaysian Airlines Flight 370. In the Philippines, the EDCA was the main agreement and Obama described the U.S. commitment to its former colony as "ironclad."[73] The visit also provided an opportunity for President Aquino to thank President Obama for the massive U.S. response to Typhoon Haiyan, an operation that demonstrated the unique military response and projection capacities of the United States to the region. As Obama was the first American president to visit since Lyndon Johnson in 1966, his arrival in Malaysia in the wake of the deep freeze in Sino-Malaysian relations caused by the disappearance of Flight 370, carrying a large number of Chinese passengers, provided an opportunity to steer a new course in U.S. relations with Malaysia.[74] Bilateral ties have never been close, riven by differences over economic models, human rights, and democracy promotion. Obama's decision not to meet with opposition leader Anwar Ibrahim was welcomed by his Malaysian hosts, and the two sides signed agreements on halting the spread of nuclear weapons and continued negotiations on the Trans-Pacific Partnership. President Obama stated that the two sides were working "more closely together than ever before," and Malaysia's attitude toward the United States, long marked by deep suspicion, is moving toward a desire for greater cooperation.[75]

Conclusion

Forging an ASEAN external policy is becoming increasingly difficult as Sino-American competition heats up. Many years ago, Michael Leifer, a leading scholar of Southeast Asian Affairs, wrote that ASEAN's role in regional order building was predicated on a stable balance of power in the Asia-Pacific. Today, China's rise has upset the traditional balance of power. As a group of small and medium states, ASEAN lacks the hard power to restore the regional balance of power even if its members could agree that it was in their interests to do so. Instead, ASEAN's external policy is based on soft power: promoting regional norms and rules through institutions designed to bind larger states to them. ASEAN's external policy, therefore, is effective only when outside actors support the status quo, not when they want to change it in ways antithetical to the interests of key Southeast Asian states.

China's actions in the South China Sea have convinced some ASEAN members, particularly Vietnam and the Philippines, that China is a revisionist state that threatens their sovereignty. Officials in Hanoi and Manila have sought ASEAN backing against China, but it has not been forthcoming because nonclaimants do not want to pay the costs of opposing China when their national interests are not at stake. No one can predict the future. However, if current trends continue, ASEAN's two long-standing goals of regional stability and autonomy from great power influence may increasingly come into conflict, forcing ASEAN members to choose between them.[76]

NOTES
1 ASEAN Secretariat, "Treaty of Amity and Cooperation."
2 Rothstein, *Alliances and Small Powers*, 34.
3 On ASEAN strategies toward external actors, see Goh, "Institutions and the Great Power Bargain in East Asia."

4 See Weinstein, *Indonesia Abandons Confrontation.*

5 McMahon, *Limits of Empire.*

6 ASEAN Secretariat, "ASEAN Declaration."

7 Ibid.

8 Indonesia established relations with China in 1950 but suspended them in October 1967.

9 In 1987, the TAC was amended to open it to ascension to non–Southeast Asian countries.

10 Rajendran, *ASEAN's Foreign Relations.*

11 ASEAN Secretariat, "ASEAN Economic Community Chartbook 2010," 10.

12 Ibid., 10.

13 Parameswaran, "Is Indonesia Turning Away?"

14 Shekhar and Liow, "Indonesia as a Maritime Power."

15 Parameswaran, "Explaining Indonesia's 'Sink the Vessels' Policy under Jokowi."

16 "Indonesia Sinks Two Thai Boats."

17 Murphy, "Thai Foreign Policy in Crisis."

18 Clinton, "America's Engagement in the Asia–Pacific."

19 McDonell and Brown, "China, Indonesia Wary of US Troops in Darwin."

20 Lieberthal, "American Pivot to Asia."

21 Ibid.

22 Weatherbee, *Indonesia in ASEAN,* 70.

23 See Thayer, "The United States and Chinese Assertiveness."

24 Interview with ASEAN official present at the Hangzhou meeting, who also stated that it is difficult to imagine the blunt language that had been used then being used now.

25 Ian Storey, "Indonesia's China Policy," 161.

26 Christensen, "Fostering Stability or Creating a Monster?"

27 Glosny, "Heading toward a Win-Win Future?," 27.

28 Emmerson, "China's Frown Diplomacy."

29 Kate and Gaouette, "Clinton Signals U.S. Role."

30 Lohman, "U.S. Cannot Rely on ASEAN."

31 Junbo, "China Averts Collision in South China Sea."

32 McCartan, "Shallow Agreement on the South China Sea."

33 Whaley, "Clinton Reaffirms Military Ties."

34 Xunpeng Shi, "On the South China Sea."

35 "Cambodia Denies ASEAN Rift."

36 Emmerson, "Indonesia Saves ASEAN's Face."

37 Ely Ratner, "Learning the Lessons."

38 Strangio, "Cambodia as Divide and Rule Pawn."

39 Emmerson, "Indonesia Saves ASEAN's Face."

40 Weatherbee, *Indonesia in ASEAN.*

41 Emmerson, "Indonesia Saves ASEAN's Face."

42 Thayer, "New Commitment."

43 Kaskra, "Legal Analysis."

44 Lan Nguyen, "The South China Sea."

45 Some analysts contend that the Philippine Senate's decision encouraged China's taking of Mischief Reef.

46 Sheldon Simon, "US-Southeast Asia Relations."

47 Ibid.

48 Government of the Philippines, "Q&A on the Enhanced Defense Cooperation Agreement."

49 Simon, "US-Southeast Asia Relations."

50 Thayer, "South China Sea Developments in 2013," 4.

51 Thayer, "New Commitment."

52 Nguyen, "China's Charm Offensive."

53 Paal, "Contradictions in China's Foreign Policy."

54 Thayer, "New Commitment."

55 Thayer, "South China Sea Developments in 2013," 22.

56 Thayer, "New Commitment."

57 Ibid., 6.

58 Ibid., 16.

59 Simon, "US-Southeast Asia Relations."

60 Thayer, "South China Sea Developments in 2013," 23.

61 P. K. Ghosh, "Vietnam Ropes in Stakeholders."

62 ASEAN, "Chairman's Statement of the 20th ASEAN Regional Forum," July 2, 2013, www.asean.org.

63 Baker and Simon, "US-Southeast Asia Relations."

64 Ibid.

65 Ibid.

66 Kerry, "Statement on the East China Sea Air Defense Identification Zone."

67 Hui, "Muted ASEAN Response to China's ADIZ."

68 Campbell, "How China and America Can Keep a Pacific Peace."

69 Thayer, "USS Cowpens Incident."

70 Hasegawa, "Japan, ASEAN."

71 Thayer, "South China Sea: Hainan Province."

72 Ibid.

73 Guevarra and Rood, "Obama's Trip to the Philippines."

74 Landler, "In Malaysia, Obama Works."

75 Ibid.

76 One can argue that the Philippine decision to enter into the EDCA with the United States means it has already chosen security over autonomy.

BIBLIOGRAPHY

ASEAN. "Chairman's Statement of the 20th ASEAN Regional Forum." July 2, 2013. www.asean.org.

ASEAN Secretariat. "The ASEAN Declaration (Bangkok Declaration)." August 8, 1967. www.asean.org.

———. "ASEAN Economic Community Chartbook 2010." October 1, 2010. www.asean.org.

———. "Treaty of Amity and Cooperation in Southeast Asia Indonesia, 24 February 1976." February 24, 1976. www.asean.org.

Baker, Carl, and Sheldon Simon. "US-Southeast Asia Relations: Obama Passes." *Comparative Connections: A Triannual E-Journal on East Asian Bilateral Relations* (January 2014): 10.

"Cambodia Denies ASEAN Rift over Sea Disputes with China." *Jakarta Globe*, April 4, 2012. http://thejakartaglobe.beritasatu.com.

Campbell, Kurt. "How China and America Can Keep a Pacific Peace." *Financial Times*, January 2, 2014. http://blogs.ft.com.

Christensen, Thomas J. "Fostering Stability or Creating a Monster? The Rise of China and U.S. Policy toward East Asia." *International Security* 31, no. 1 (Summer 2006): 81–126.

Clinton, Hillary Rodham. "America's Engagement in the Asia-Pacific." Speech, Kahala Hotel, Honolulu, HI, October 28, 2010. http://m.state.gov.

Emmerson, Donald. "China's Frown Diplomacy." *Asia Times*, October 5, 2010.

———. "Indonesia Saves ASEAN's Face." *Asia Times Online*, July 24, 2012.

Ghosh, P. K. "Vietnam Ropes in Stakeholders to China Territorial Dispute." *East Asia Forum*, January 2, 2014. www.eastasiaforum.org.

Glosny, Michael A. "Heading toward a Win-Win Future? Recent Developments in China's Policy toward Southeast Asia." *Asian Security* 2, no. 1 (May 1, 2006): 24–57. doi:10.1080/14799850600575199.

Goh, Evelyn. "Institutions and the Great Power Bargain in East Asia: ASEAN's Limited 'Brokerage' Role." *International Relations of the Asia-Pacific* 11, no. 3 (September 1, 2011): 373–401. doi:10.1093/irap/lcr014.

Government of the Philippines. "Q&A on the Enhanced Defense Cooperation Agreement | Official Gazette of the Republic of the Philippines." *Official Gazette*, April 28, 2014. www.gov.ph.

Guevarra, Mark Lester A., and Steven Rood. "Obama's Trip to the Philippines: A Touchy Last Stop | In Asia." Asia Foundation, April 30, 2014. http://asiafoundation. org.

Hasegawa, Kyoko. "Japan, ASEAN Seek 'Freedom of Overflight' amid China Tensions." *Jakarta Globe*, December 14, 2013. http://thejakartaglobe.beritasatu.com.

Hui, Dylan Loh Ming. "Muted ASEAN Response to China's ADIZ." *New Straits Times*, December 30, 2013. www.nst.com.my.

"Indonesia Sinks Two Thai Boats." *Bangkok Post*, December 29, 2014. www.bangkokpost.com.

Junbo, Jain. "China Averts Collision in South China Sea." *Asia Times*, July 29, 2011. www.atimes.com.

Kaskra, James. "A Legal Analysis of the Philippine-China Arbitration Ruling." *Diplomat*, November 2, 2015. http://thediplomat.com.

Kate, Daniel Tan, and Nicole Gaouette. "Clinton Signals U.S. Role in China Territorial Dispute after ASEAN Talks." *Bloomberg*, July 23, 2010. www.bloomberg.com.

Kerry, John. "Statement on the East China Sea Air Defense Identification Zone." Press Release, U.S. Department of State, November 23, 2013. www.state.gov.

Landler, Mark. "In Malaysia, Obama Works to Mend Troubled Ties." *New York Times*, April 27, 2014. www.nytimes.com.

Lieberthal, Kenneth. "The American Pivot to Asia." *Foreign Policy*, December 21, 2011. http://foreignpolicy.com.

Lohman, Walter. "The U.S. Cannot Rely on ASEAN in the South China Sea." Heritage Foundation, August 5, 2011. www.heritage.org.

McCartan, Brian. "Shallow Agreement in the South China Sea." *Asia Times*, July 30, 2011. www.atimes.com.

McDonell, Stephen, and Helen Brown. "China, Indonesia Wary of US Troops in Darwin." *ABC News*, April 25, 2013. www.abc.net.au.

McMahon, Robert J. *The Limits of Empire: The United States and Southeast Asia since World War II*. New York: Columbia University Press, 1999.

Murphy, Ann Marie. "Thai Foreign Policy in Crisis." In *Bangkok May 2010: Perspectives on a Divided Thailand*, edited by Michael J. Montesano, Pavin Chachavalpongpun, and Aekapol Chongvilaivan, 351. Singapore: Institute of Southeast Asian Studies, 2012.

Nguyen, Lan. "The South China Sea: The Philippines versus China." *Diplomat*, July 27, 2015. http://thediplomat.com.

Nguyen, Phuong. "China's Charm Offensive Signals a New Strategic Era in Southeast Asia." Center for Strategic and International Studies, October 17, 2013. http://csis.org.

Paal, Douglas H. "Contradictions in China's Foreign Policy." Carnegie Endowment for International Peace, December 13, 2013. http://carnegieendowment.org.

Parameswaran, Prashanth. "Explaining Indonesia's 'Sink the Vessels' Policy under Jokowi." *Diplomat*, January 13, 2015. http://thediplomat.com.

———. "Is Indonesia Turning Away from ASEAN under Jokowi?" *Diplomat*, December 18, 2014. http://thediplomat.com.

Rajendran, M. *ASEAN's Foreign Relations: The Shift to Collective Action*. Kuala Lumpur: Arenabuku, 1985.

Ratner, Ely. "Learning the Lessons of Scarborough Reef." *National Interest*, November 21, 2013. http://nationalinterest.org.

Rothstein, Robert L. *Alliances and Small Powers*. New York: Columbia University Press, 1968.

Shekhar, Vibhanshu, and Joseph Chinyong Liow. "Indonesia as a Maritime Power: Jokowi's Vision, Strategies, and Obstacles Ahead." Brookings Institution, November 2014. www.brookings.edu.

Simon, Sheldon. "US-Southeast Asia Relations: Enhancing the Rebalance." *Comparative Connections: A Triannual E-Journal on East Asian Bilateral Relations* 16, no. 2 (September 2014): 12.

Storey, Ian James. "Indonesia's China Policy in the New Order and Beyond: Problems and Prospects." *Contemporary Southeast Asia* 22, no. 1 (April 1, 2000): 145–74.

Strangio, Sebastian. "Cambodia as Divide and Rule Pawn." *Asia Times Online*, July 18, 2012. www.atimes.com.

Thayer, Carlyle A. "New Commitment to a Code of Conduct in the South China Sea?" National Bureau of Asian Research, October 9, 2013, 5.

———. "South China Sea Developments in 2013: ASEAN Unity Restored, Sino-Philippine Tensions and ASEAN-China Consultations on a Code of Conduct." Paper, Fifth International Workshop on the South China Sea: Cooperation for Regional Security and Development, Hanoi, Vietnam, November 11–12, 2013. https://southeastasiansea.files.wordpress.com.

———. "South China Sea: Hainan Province All at Sea." Thayer Consultancy, January 10, 2014. www.iacspsea.com.

———. "The United States and Chinese Assertiveness in the South China Sea." *Security Challenges* 6, no. 2 (Winter 2010): 69–84.

———. "USS Cowpens Incident Reveals Strategic Mistrust between U.S. and China." *Diplomat*, December 17, 2013. http://thediplomat.com.

"U.S. Signals to China It Won't Keep Out of South Sea." *Bloomberg.com*, July 23, 2010. www.bloomberg.com.

Weatherbee, Donald E. *Indonesia in ASEAN: Vision and Reality*. Singapore: Institute of Southeast Asian Studies, 2013.

Weinstein, Franklin B. *Indonesia Abandons Confrontation: An Inquiry into the Functions of Indonesian Foreign Policy*. Sheffield: Equinox, 2009.

Whaley, Floyd. "Clinton Reaffirms Military Ties with the Philippines." *New York Times*, November 16, 2011. www.nytimes.com.

Xunpeng Shi. "On the South China Sea, an ASEAN United Front Won't Help Anyone, Especially Indonesia." *Jakarta Post*, June 13, 2012.

3

Nontraditional Security Threats in ASEAN and Beyond

AMY FREEDMAN

Introduction and Thoughts about Cooperation

While humanity has succeeded in creating mind-boggling technology, and life expectancy has skyrocketed over the past half century, we may again be faced with Malthusian-type problems of food insecurity, calamitous consequences from climate change, and the rapid spread of new and deadly diseases. There is a clear link between these three problems. Climate change is producing strains on living conditions and habitats (wetter/rainier conditions in some places, increased drought in other places, more extreme storms), agricultural conditions, and amounts of arable land. This impacts both food costs and supplies, and impacts the spread of conditions leading to increased incidence of disease. Furthermore, all three of these challenges demonstrate how what one country does within its borders impacts other countries. Therefore, states need to cooperate with each other, but they often find it difficult to do so because of sovereignty and self-interest.

Southeast Asia in particular is facing escalating challenges relating to climate change, food security, and the spread of infectious diseases. This chapter focuses on three specific elements of these problems: it looks at deforestation, rice security, and the spread of avian influenza and asks what efforts are under way in the region to address these problems, and what superpowers like China and the United States are doing (or not doing) to facilitate cooperation on these issues. Finally, the chapter assesses how cooperation, or lack of cooperation, on nontraditional security threats relates to the potential rivalry between the United States and China in Southeast Asia.

Scientists generally agree that without drastic reductions in carbon dioxide (or greenhouse gas, GHG) emissions, the earth's temperature could rise by as much as six degrees Celsius by the end of the century. Regions of the world will see increased drought in some places, increased rainfall in others, and increased storm activity. These changes could lead to potentially irreversible and catastrophic scenarios. Given Southeast Asia's similar geography and common ecological features, countries are destined for a shared future under current climate change projections. The Philippines, the Mekong River Delta in Vietnam, almost all regions of Cambodia and Laos, the greater Bangkok area, south and west Sumatra, and west and east Java are all threatened, but the most endangered is Jakarta; densely populated and Indonesia's capital, the megacity lies at the intersection of all but one of five climate-related hazards: droughts, floods, landslides, and sea-level rise.[1] Planning for and taking concrete steps to deal with the effects of climate change are difficult due to Southeast Asian countries' demographics (with densely populated urban areas and high levels of rural poverty), uneven levels of economic development (and the prioritization of short-term economic development over long-term contingency planning), high levels of corruption in most countries, and a lack of good governance.

Emerging infectious diseases (EID) pose international security threats the world over. EID have the potential to inflict harm upon humans, crops, and livestock. And they can do significant damage to countries' health infrastructures and overall economies, as the Ebola outbreak in West Africa clearly did to Sierra Leone and Liberia in 2014. Morgan Stanley's decision to relocate a hedge fund conference from Shanghai (May 2013) to New York later in the summer demonstrates fears about the Avian Flu (H7N9 is the most recent variation of bird flu; the more common strain is H5N1, and most of the data presented here relate to monitoring and combating H5N1) outbreak in China.[2] Other examples of this were seen with the SARS outbreak in Hong Kong and China in 2003, and the 2009 A/H1N1 impact on the Mexican economy in 2009, when it was estimated that almost one percent of that country's GDP was lost due to fears of the virus.[3] Developing countries, like most of those in Southeast Asia, are more likely to suffer from rapid and deadly disease transmission because of weak public health infrastructures, less technology, and less transparency and government accountability. Countries in the region vary greatly in their EID surveillance capabilities and treatment protocols.

The World Health Organization (WHO) defines food security as existing "when all people at all times have access to sufficient, safe, nutritious food to maintain a healthy and active life." Food security is built on three pillars: food availability (sufficient quantities of food, consistently available), food access (having sufficient resources to obtain appropriate food for a nutritious diet, affordability), and food use (appropriate use based on knowledge of basic nutrition and care, adequate water and sanitation).[4] We are looking ahead to a future of possible widespread food insecurity, particularly in the developing world.

Rice is a critical crop in Southeast Asia, and the discussion here over problems and possible cooperation over the rice trade demonstrates the larger questions and problems inherent to food security more generally. Thus, this work uses "food security" and "rice security" in interchangeable ways. Southeast Asia is a diverse region; it is home to some of the world's largest rice exporters, but also home to some of the largest importers and largest consumer populations in terms of rice consumption per capita. Southeast Asia continues to enjoy sustained economic growth (despite the European and American slowdown) and poverty reduction. Yet, over 15 percent of Asia's undernourished population lives in Southeast Asia. The region has abundant natural resources, and is rich agriculturally, but environmental stresses, changing demographics, lifestyles, and eating habits threaten many key ecosystems and thus pose a threat to future food production. Historically, food shortages have been a result of poor social, economic, and political policies, often combined with environmental problems of drought, floods, blight, and so on that can exacerbate unequal allocation of resources. Today, the most probable cause of food insecurity for millions of people around the world will be changing demographics coupled with the effects of climate change. The ability of societies and governments to effectively cooperate to deal with the effects of climate change will pose a significant challenge for states in the near term and longer into the future. Southeast Asia is faced with all of these challenges.

TABLE 3.1. Efforts at addressing nontraditional security threats

	Food security	Deforestation	Emerging infectious disease (EID)
National efforts	Yes	Yes	Yes
Regional efforts	Yes	No	No
Global efforts	No	Yes	Yes
Regional leadership	Weak (but better than on deforestation or EID)	Weak	Weak

There are some important actions being taken currently to address issues climate change and deforestation,[5] the spread of new and deadly diseases, and problems related to food security, but the most significant of these measures are being taken at the national level rather than through regional cooperative efforts, and adoption and implementation have been slow and uneven. This chapter looks at efforts in Southeast Asia to promote information sharing and policy coordination on deforestation, rice cultivation and trade, and protocols for EID. It also examines some individual national policies choices and challenges. Ongoing research shows that there have been some efforts to cooperate regionally on deforestation, food security, and EID, however, such measures are far from being firmly instituted and operational. I offer a theoretical lens with which to understand why efforts to cooperate on these problems have gotten under way, but why such efforts may not be enough to fully address potential crises.

Too often national policies on nontraditional security threats (undertaken by a number of countries in Southeast Asia at one point in time or another) exemplify "beggar thy neighbor" policies, where countries enact measures to protect their own producers, companies, and citizens. The larger effect of these policies can sometimes be a worsening of conditions across borders. While these actions are at times necessary and understandable, they illustrate a fundamental problem of international relations. What one country does impacts other countries. For example, when a food exporter decides to reduce or stop exporting a product, it can have dire consequences elsewhere for those who rely on importing that food commodity; or when one country builds a dam on a river or burns a forest, these actions impact other countries. Thus, states need to cooperate with each other, but often find it difficult to do so. Cooperation is hindered by a lack of leadership, imperfect information, a lack of regular mechanisms for designing agreements, and variation in the level of interest from states in cooperating on any given issue.

Hegemonic stability theory argues that great powers (a hegemon) help promote cooperation and stability in the international system by facilitating cooperation and collective action. A hegemon, Kindleberger and others argue, can encourage cooperation on common problems by demonstrating leadership and shouldering some or most of the cost involved in solving an international problem.[6] Such action could be taken unilaterally through the leadership of the great power, or more indirectly, through international organizations. International organizations (IOs) can provide the information and transparency needed in order for countries to come to an agreement and stick to it. These benefits can help countries feel less insecure, and so increase the likelihood that they will cooperate on economic issues and be less likely to resort to the kinds of beggar-thy-neighbor polices listed above. International cooperation can also be explained by the role of interest groups, or domestic politics more generally, within countries. When powerful groups favor protectionist policies, or uncooperative behavior, then it is more likely that cooperative efforts will fail. When interest groups stand to gain from international cooperation (on all kinds of issues such as trade policies, environmental agreements, research on new or EID), we are more likely to see policies implemented that lead to cooperation.[7]

This essay largely argues that weak cooperation on climate changes policies, on rice security, and on EID protocols in Southeast Asia can be best explained by a lack of leadership (from countries within Southeast Asia, and lack of leadership on the part of the United States or China), rather than simply saying that states don't see policies as in their interest. This essay shows that states do seem to see cooperation as in everyone's interest, and steps have been taken to try to create institutions and organizations to foster such cooperation. However, powerful domestic interest groups and lack of clear leadership in the region on issues relating to such nontraditional security issues seem to provide a comprehensive explanation of why we don't see robust cooperation.

If we want to see greater cooperation in Southeast Asia on nontraditional security threats, we need to ask who will take on leadership. In Asia, it isn't completely clear who the hegemon might be. China has the largest population and, according to World Bank figures,[8] the largest economy in the region. While China is playing more of a role in regional and international affairs, the Chinese are not yet in the position of wanting or trying to take on a leadership role. The United States, although geographically distant, has continued to exercise a significant role as a vital trade partner, and as a militarily presence in Asia. The U.S. "pivot" to Asia in 2009 aims to reorient significant elements of U.S. foreign policy toward Asia; this includes diplomatic attention, economic activity, people-to-people exchanges, and security interests. Despite this claimed set of objectives, economic woes, continued turmoil in the Middle East, and partisan politics in Washington have made operationalizing them problematic.[9] In addition, the United States is not a member of ASEAN or ASEAN Plus Three (APT) and has often been content to stay out of regional discussions about climate change, food security, and EID. The 2014 agreement between the United States and China on carbon emissions is an exception to this and will be discussed later in the chapter. To facilitate regional cooperation, institutions like ASEAN and APT have been tasked with addressing these problems. Indonesia has traditionally been viewed as the hegemon within Southeast Asia. However, since the fall of Suharto in 1998, Indonesia has preferred to lead by example, rather than taking on a more vigorous leadership style pushing for policies and changes, and has practiced quieter diplomacy and multilateralism. More on Indonesia's role in promoting cooperation in Southeast Asia will be discussed shortly.

Nontraditional Security Issues in Southeast Asia

Climate Change and Deforestation

The Intergovernmental Panel on Climate Change (IPCC), made up of hundreds of scientists from all over the world, issued a report in the fall of 2013 and the spring of 2014. Using the strongest language to date, the panel stated that it is extremely likely that human influence has been the dominant cause of the observed warming since the mid-twentieth century, and that climate changes pose risks for human and natural systems. The report offers assessments of impacts, adaptation, vulnerabilities, and possible mitigations of these changes. In discussing Asia specifically, the IPCC report found the following:

- warming trends and increasing temperature extremes have been observed across most of the Asia region over the past century
- water scarcity is expected to be a major challenge for most of the region due to increased demand and lack of good management
- the impact of climate change on food production and food security will vary by region, with most areas experiencing a decline in productivity
- coastal and marine systems are under increasing stress from climate and non-climate drivers
- stresses caused by rapid urbanization and industrialization will be compounded by climate change
- extreme climate events will have an increasing impact on human health, security, livelihoods, and poverty, with effects varying across Asia[10]

In advanced industrial countries, discussions about climate change generally lead to proposals to reduce carbon emissions from industrial sources. In Southeast Asia, deforestation is the largest contributing factor to the region's carbon dioxide emissions, and countries in the region are both some of the world's largest emitters and the most vulnerable to the effects of climate change. Between 1995 and 2005, 43.6 million hectares were deforested in the region, which released about 3.45 million tons of carbon into the atmosphere (according to the UN Food and Agriculture Organization).[11] In addition to contributing to climate change, deforestation is contributing to loss of biodiversity and posing problems for indigenous communities that rely on these ecosystems for their livelihoods. Indonesia, Cambodia, Laos, Burma, the Philippines, and Vietnam (in terms of old-growth forests) have all lost forest cover in the past forty years.[12] All countries in the region are vulnerable to the effects of climate change, whether from climate-induced migration, increasing water insecurity (and increased flooding in other places like Jakarta and Bangkok), new threats from invasive insects like the caterpillar explosion in Java and Madura in 2011,[13] or loss of cultivable land, which can lead to further food insecurity. It is these environmental problems that the region is attempting to tackle, both collectively and on a country-by-country basis.

TABLE 3.2. Annual forestation levels by country (1,000 hectares)

	1990	2000	2005	2010	2015	% loss/gain 1990–2015
Indonesia[a]	116,567	97,852	88,495	94,432	91,010	−22
Vietnam[b]	9,363	11,725	12,931	13,797	14,773	+58[d]
Cambodia[b]	12,946	11,541	10,447	10,094	9,457	−27
Thailand	14,005	17,011	16,100	16,249	16,399	+17
Laos[b]	17,314	17,532	16,142	15,751	18,761	−8
Malaysia[c]	22,376	21,591	20,456	20,456	22,195	−0.8
Philip-pines[b]	10,574	7,949	7,162	7,665	8,040	−24
Myanmar[a]	39,219	34,554	32,222	31,773	29,041	−26

a. FAO, "Global Forest Resources Assessment 2010, Main Report," FAO Forestry Paper 163 (FAO of the UN) (Rome, 2010).
b. FAO, "Global Resources Assessment, 2005. Country Reports for Vietnam, Cambodia, and the Philippines."
c. FAO, "Global Forest Resources Assessment, 2010, Country Report: Malaysia."
d. While Vietnam has seen levels of *overall* forest cover increase, this increase has come in new forest cover, not in primary forest cover, which has continued to be destroyed, particularly along the Mekong River.
Sources: FAO, "Global Forest Resources Assessment 2015" (Rome, 2015), www.fao.org; FAO, "Southeast Asia Subregional Report: Asia-Pacific Forestry Sector Outlook Study II" (Bangkok, 2011), www.fao.org.

Southeast Asian countries have (in theory) committed to sustainable forest management (SFM) to retain forest cover in the future. However, SFM is really an industrial strategy to keep trees standing until they are ready to be harvested. This allows industries to continue cutting tress during certain allowed periods. SFM as an ASEAN policy has failed to meaningfully reduce deforestation. Curtailing deforestation is the main goal of "Reducing Emissions from Deforestation and Forest Degradation," the strategy known as REDD. REDD aims to make conservation profitable by incentivizing users of the forest to practice sustainable forestry management, which will reduce carbon dioxide emissions.[14] At an international level, countries like Indonesia, Cambodia, and Vietnam would be paid for conserving forests and forgoing the economic gains that come from exploiting them. In 2008, the UNFCCC (United Nations Framework Convention on Climate Change) added three more strategic objectives to the original REDD goals of reducing emissions from deforestation and degradation: reducing emissions through conservation, sustainable forest practices, and enhancement of forest carbon stocks. The addition of these objectives has transformed REDD into REDD+.[15]

The Center for International Forestry Research (CIFOR), an independent research institution, contends that Indonesia is losing 1.1 million hectares of rainforest a year. Key drivers of deforestation in Indonesia are land use, weak spatial planning, tenure issues, ineffective forest management, poor governance, and weak law enforcement. Illegal logging, which is estimated to cost Indonesia $4 billion a year, is also a factor.[16]

Indonesia's forests are cleared not only for logging and the production of paper and pulp products, but also to convert land for agricultural, mining, and energy projects. Half of Indonesian GHG emissions are released not simply from the cutting down of trees, but from the clearing of peat land under the forest. Much of Indonesia's groundcover is peat, which can extend many meters underground. Peat lands emit huge quantities of emissions if drained for cultivation. Since 1999 it has been illegal in Indonesia to clear peat land over three meters deep. This law is often broken. Peat lands are critical to fighting global warming because their carbon density can be five to ten times higher than forests on mineral soil per unit of forest.[17] When fire is used to clear forests in areas rich in peat, they burn underground long after the forest is gone. The burning of peat land in Sumatra has been largely responsible for the "haze" that takes such a toll in Malaysia and Singapore.[18]

Fires in Indonesia were especially horrific in the second half of 2015. Tens of thousands of hectares of forest burned during the summer and fall of 2015. Estimates show that daily emissions from the fires surpassed average daily emissions from the entire U.S. economy, and five hundred thousand people were treated for acute respiratory tract infections and haze-related illnesses.[19] Citizens in Singapore and Malaysia were affected as well, leading to strong criticism of Indonesia by Singaporean and Malaysian leaders. President Joko Widodo (Jokowi) faced a great deal of domestic *and* international criticism for the 2015 peat fires. Indonesian environmental groups and ASEAN ministers called on Jokowi to invoke the strongest possible moratorium on burning of all peat lands and to revoke licenses held by companies that had not yet been used or planted. As of the end of 2015, the president's office said decrees of these sorts would be published shortly.[20] In late October 2015, ASEAN environment ministers met and issued a statement concerning the fires in Sumatra and Kalimantan: the ministers reviewed regional cooperation measures taken under the ASEAN Agreement on Transboundary Haze Pollution, expressed concern and sympathy for those affected by the haze, agreed to share information and cooperate to fight the fires, revised the Joint Emergency Response Agreement to operationalize the Alert Levels and Trigger Points and Actions, and noted that most member states had contributed to the ASEAN Transboundary Haze Pollution Control Fund. The ministers also expressed strong concerns over the impacts of climate change on fire regimes and vice versa—the contribution of vegetation fire emissions to climate change.[21] These remarks are consistent with earlier regional discussions and efforts to address environmental and climate-related issues. On the surface, there is a fair amount of consensus about the need to take action and work together. However, such niceties can get lost in the process of domestic policy making.

President Jokowi's efforts to address the fires are a perfect case in point. Even before this round of fires triggered such a horrific haze, Indonesia already had a moratorium on new licenses for primary forest and peat land development. This document was an informal presidential instruction to guide government ministries and local officials. In order to have legal force, a binding presidential decree (known as *perppu*) would need to be published to formally ban future development. Different industries (from agricultural groups to logging concerns) as well as local officials seeking to profit from land development have worked hard to prevent formal legal action. And, even if a ban is enacted, Indonesian laws have proved difficult to enforce at the local level because of both the decentralized nature of policy implementation and corruption.[22] Significant changes to the use of Indonesia's forests and peat lands would require much more than just presidential action.

ASEAN is attempting to build common approaches and understandings to deforestation and climate change: ASEAN first addressed REDD in a common position paper drafted in 2008. The five key points agreed upon were as follows:

1. The method for defining baseline or reference emission level should be left open to different approaches. Due to the erratic nature and scarcity of historical data on emissions in automated measuring systems (AMS), each country should be allowed to use an approach that best suits its national circumstances and capacity. Most importantly, the choice of method should be based on its effectiveness in reducing emissions from deforestation and forest degradation, including forest conservation and SFM practices.

2. Policy approaches should also be left open for a range of mitigation activities (reducing deforestation and forest degradation, SFM, conservation, enhancement of carbon stocks) depending on the capacity and the circumstances of the countries.

3. Positive incentives should be diversified and not by limited to market-based but also include fund-based approaches, depending on the readiness of the country.

4. Coverage or readiness activities under other related financial supports such as the Climate Investment Fund and the Forest Investment Program should be expanded (e.g., expanded to include improved forest management, conservation, and enhancement of carbon stock through SFM).

5. The need must be reiterated for Annex I countries to the UNFCCC to support capacity building, improvement of infrastructure, technology transfer, and exchange of knowledge and experiences for developing countries.[23]

There is nothing objectionable about these ideas; however, ASEAN is still in the planning stages of thinking about deforestation, and member states are not being asked to take action.

ASEAN's strategy to address climate change has been formulated in the ASEAN Socio-Cultural Community (ASCC), which is one of the three pillars of ASEAN. ASCC states that ASEAN will participate in global mechanisms to combat climate change and improve environmental sustainability. In paragraph D.10, ASCC specifically states actions that should be taken to mitigate and adapt to climate change. These steps relate to technology transfer, moving to a low-carbon economy, expanding research, developing baselines and common measurement tools, and reducing deforestation and degradation. Again, at recent ASEAN meetings, similar calls were made to address cross-border climate issues, and for technology transfer and international financial support.[24]

However, ASEAN has been largely ineffective in coping with the very real and present threats from climate change, such as floods, drought, infestations, and health crises and the way these problems directly impact local communities.[25] The ASEAN Economic Community also mentioned climate change, stating that ASEAN established the ASEAN Community in 2015, and that, as such, countries should also be working toward mitigating GHG emissions and investing in measures to mitigate climate change.[26]

REDD+ implementation is taking place in Southeast Asia, but more on a bilateral basis than through ASEAN or other regional organizations. Countries where communities are becoming involved in carbon trading for REDD+ include Thailand, the Philippines (they are not yet officially included in REDD programs, but the government wants to join and is preparing for REDD), Cambodia, Laos, Indonesia, and Vietnam. Most of the programs under way are funded by Western donor nations. For example, in Laos REDD program is being implemented in a test area supported by German and Japanese funds,[27] and in Indonesia, a letter of intent was signed between the governments of Indonesia and Norway, whereby Norway will pay Indonesia up to US$1 billion for documented reductions in GHG emissions.[28] It is too early to know if REDD+ will result in substantial changes in behavior in Indonesia and elsewhere in Southeast Asia. If it does work, it will largely be due to the financial help from individual countries like Norway, Germany, and others, rather than from key regional actors like China. China, as one of the sources of demand for timber, could be influential in helping to stop illegal logging (another cause of deforestation), but there is little evidence that it is interested in curtailing this demand.

Changes have been implemented in countries like Indonesia, Thailand, Vietnam, and the Philippines, but it will be years until we know if these changes have produced meaningful results. Indonesia created a cabinet-level body to oversee REDD in 2013, only to have newly elected President Jokowi fold that agency into the larger Forestry Ministry a year or so later.[29] The Philippines' national strategy for REDD+ calls for new laws and policies on government management of forest land, but this has only recently been initiated.[30] Thailand's military leaders, after seizing power in the coup of May 2014, called for an end to deforestation. The government went on to take back land from local village communities, from owners of resorts and rubber plantations, as well as from logging firms and even monasteries.[31] While the number of hectares of forest land appears to be increasing in Thailand and Vietnam, these gains are largely due to new forest growth, not to a complete halt in deforestation of primary forest cover, and these gains do not offset the continued loss of forest land in the region as a while.

In the United States (and to a lesser degree in Europe as well), one of the obstacles to greater policy action addressing causes and problems of climate change is climate skeptics. There are a small number of scientists and a larger number of industry-funded groups working in the United States and Europe to create public uncertainty and confusion over climate change. This has contributed to low levels of political support in the United States for stricter regulation of GHG emissions and policies like a carbon tax. In Asia, there is less scientific skepticism about the problem; instead obstacles to addressing climate change stem from several sources: First, there is a feeling that developing countries should not have to shoulder the burdens of addressing climate change when developed countries created most of the problems and enjoyed earlier and successful economic development from industrialization. Second, internal political opposition (and outright illegal activity) from industry groups, including mining companies, timber companies, and agricultural interests, as well as from small producers has made more vigorous political action difficult and sometimes risky for politicians. Finally, and related to the second factor, Western-owned firms (such as mining companies, oil, gas, and coal companies, etc.) also actively oppose further regulation of their activities in Southeast Asia.[32] Despite these obstacles, the United States and China in November 2014 agreed to a set of proposals to cut carbon emissions. The U.S. goal is to cut emissions between 26 and 28 percent by 2025 (using 2005 levels as a baseline). China set a target for its emissions to peak by 2030, and then has agreed to measures to cut emissions thereafter.[33] While there are no binding targets and no enforcement mechanisms, this agreement is still significant as a signal that China and the United States are now engaging seriously in climate discussions and that China is going to be a more willing partner in ongoing global negotiations. The U.S.-China agreement is viewed by some as a key factor leading to a historic agreement to combat climate change by 195 nations meeting in Paris in December 2015. The agreement's main aim is to keep the global temperature rise below two degrees Celsius and to strengthen nations' ability to deal with the effects of climate change. Countries agreed to take concrete measures to limit and roll back emissions and agreed to financial assistance flowing from wealthy to developing countries to help those most vulnerable.[34] While it is too soon to draw conclusions from this agreement, it could have significance down the road for how well the Asia-Pacific region addresses environmental problems like deforestation. China's new willingness to discuss curbing their own emissions and their cooperative behavior with the United States and the global community could have spillover effects in Southeast Asia.[35]

Emerging Infectious Diseases (EID)

The most written about and discussed EID in Southeast Asia is avian influenza (influenza A subtype H5N1). Outbreaks (particularly the one in 2003–4) in China, Vietnam, Cambodia, Thailand, and Indonesia have triggered concerns about a global health crisis that could start in the region. Sophal Ear has written about EID in Cambodia and Indonesia and has demonstrated how internal politics (within Indonesia and Cambodia) have stymied more effective efforts at establishing more comprehensive preventive measures and surveillance.[36] Some of the problems include low levels of training for laboratory personnel, political fears of loss of viral sovereignty, distrust of the U.S. or UN efforts at disease surveillance, and corruption and weak public health systems. In addition, low levels of political will from officials who fear electoral losses mean that efforts to cull bird flocks are halfhearted and underfunded in many countries in Southeast Asia.

The SARS outbreak in 2003 demonstrated the need for global cooperation on EID. SARS first appeared in Guangdong province in southern China in November 2002, then spread to twenty-eight countries, infecting 8,096 people and resulting in 774 deaths, according to WHO data.[37] China's reaction to the SARS epidemic in 2003 demonstrates exactly how countries should *not* deal with EID. Confronted with a growing health crisis and an unknown new disease, China chose to withhold information from the public and from the international community. The first case of the new disease occurred in the fall of 2003, and it wasn't until April 2004 that the Chinese government began cooperating with WHO and the global community and began to be somewhat more forthcoming regarding the extent of the outbreak.[38] They were extremely slow to allow

WHO officials or others (such as representatives from the U.S. Centers for Disease Control and Prevention, CDC) access to samples or accurate information. This led to widespread panic and rumors, and the lack of information may have contributed to the numbers of those who contracted the disease.

The regional question is this: how well, individually and collectively, can countries address outbreaks of infectious diseases? The answer (not surprisingly) is that there is wide regional disparity. Avian flu is one example of a regional epidemic where there are some commonalities and some differences in responses. H5N1 is largely spread through bird flocks and is carried and transmitted by both wild birds and livestock flocks. Humans contract the virus almost always from handling sick or infected birds. Effective protocols for preventing disease outbreaks in humans include quarantining new birds when introducing them to existing flocks and quarantining and culling infected birds, following proper rearing and handling practices and safety measures, and utilizing food handling and consumption techniques (including not consuming birds that die). Some countries in the region have been effective at instituting and applying such measures; Malaysia and China for example have seen rates of transmission fall since 2003, while Cambodia, Indonesia, and Vietnam are still struggling to fully address outbreaks of number human cases of H5N1.[39]

TABLE 3.3. Confirmed human cases of avian influenza (H5N1)

Year	Cambodia	China	Indonesia	Lao PDR	Malaysia	Thailand	Vietnam
2003	0	1	0	0	N/A	0	3
2004	0	0	0	0	N/A	17	29
2005	4	8	20	0	N/A	5	61
2006	2	13	55	0	N/A	3	0
2007	1	5	42	2	N/A	0	8
2008	1	4	24	0	N/A	0	6
2009	1	7	21	0	N/A	0	5
2010	1	2	9	0	N/A	0	7
2011	8	1	12	0	N/A	0	0
2012	3	2	9	0	N/A	0	4
2013	26	2	3	0	N/A	0	2
2014	9	2	2	0	N/A	0	2
2015	0	5	2	0	N/A	0	0

Source: Data from WHO, Regional Office for Southeast Asia, "Avian Influenza" (2016), www.searo.who.int; and WHO/GIP, "Cumulative Number of Confirmed Human Cases for Avian Influenza A(H5N1) Reported to WHO, 2003–2015," www.who.int, data as of December 15, 2015.

Reasons for the difficulty in either eradicating or reducing the incidence of H5N1 are multiple: First, in less well-off countries, it is prohibitively expensive to adequately pay farmers to cull sick flocks and to incentivize them to carry out accepted international protocols for cutting down on the transmission of the disease. Second, corruption and local-level political dynamics make it harder to successfully implement national programs in places where local officials may have significant power (China, Indonesia, and Cambodia). Bureaucratic disagreement, electoral politics where elected political leaders do not want to push unpopular policies like flock culling ahead of elections, and disagreements among bureaucracies over jurisdiction are widespread.[40]

Most international work on EID is conducted through the auspicious of WHO. The U.S. CDC in Atlanta works closely with WHO around the world in helping to identify and track global pandemics. ASEAN is also working to address EID. There are myriad existing ASEAN bodies (most under the ASCC pillar) already in operation to address the threat of pandemics, but ASEAN's difficulty in doing so lies with the wide capacity gaps in health systems among member states,[41] and perhaps the lack of willingness to create a regional fund to help poorer countries follow excepted protocols for culling diseased flocks. In July 2012, ASEAN's Expert Group on Communicable Diseases developed a plan to deal with EID. The plan has two focus areas: prevention and control of emerging infectious diseases and enhancing regional supportive environment. The first focus area, on prevention and control of EID, includes goals such as strengthening regional cooperative arrangements for integrated efforts at prevention, control, and preparedness for EID; developing regional support systems to narrow the gap among ASEAN member states in addressing EID; strengthening cooperation in tracking and health quarantine measures; strengthening surveillance measures for HIV, AIDS, malaria, TB, and so on; promoting collaboration in research and development on new medicines; and ensuring stockpiles of antiviral medications and supplies for all member states for rapid response and containment of potential pandemic influenza. The second focus area includes strengthening and maintaining regional support systems to narrow the gap in addressing EID; sharing of best practices in improving access to primary health care; strengthening regional clinical expertise through professional organizations; and sharing information to assist in response to EID as well as to other crises like climate change effects and food security problems.[42]

Despite sounding like a comprehensive ASEAN plan of action to deal with EID, the reality is much different. On many of these issues, funding is coming from WHO and wealthy donor nations like the United States. ASEAN seems to be making the most progress on the least controversial of these measures, such as establishing websites to share information on EID (maintained by

Indonesia). Countries have not always been forthcoming in sharing information, and compliance with best practices has been spotty at best. While the United States would seemingly like to be more involved, there is reluctance in the region allow more robust U.S. engagement. For different reasons, China is not taking a leadership role. The Chinese have not been able to deal with their own public health crises in a credible and transparent way, so it is hard to see how they could assume greater leadership on this issue.

Food Insecurity

The nations of Southeast Asia will need leadership and greater cooperation in the years to come if they are to address food needs in a changing global and regional context. There are many factors and trends emerging that threaten Asian and global food security. First, the number of people who are food *insecure* in Asia has been on the rise. While strong economic growth has bumped a number of states toward middle-income status, many of the world's undernourished live in Asia (India accounts for 43 percent of the undernourished, and China for 24 percent). Asia's population is projected to increase from 3.6 billion to 4.5 billion between 2010 and 2050. Most of that growth will occur in urban areas, as the urban population is set to surpass the rural population as early as 2028.[43] At the same time, there has been a global decline in investment in agriculture, from a 20 percent share of official development assistance for agriculture in 1979 to 5 percent in 2007.[44] There is also a paradox: economic growth and prosperity are unquestioningly a good thing; however, as societies become wealthier, they also eat differently, consuming more animal products. Thus, there is increased pressure on agriculture to produce for livestock instead of for human consumption. This can result in increased prices for grains, further hurting poorer citizens and areas and further straining food supplies.

Another complicating factor making food security difficult to tackle is that there is tremendous variation across borders in Southeast Asia, but also within countries as well. Not surprisingly, poorer countries in the region, such as Laos, Cambodia, Timor Leste, and Myanmar, have the highest levels of hunger. And, food crises are most acute as a result of humanitarian disasters. For example, after Cyclone Nargis hit southern Myanmar in 2008, close to a million people needed food assistance until the November 2008 harvest, while around three hundred thousand needed help until April 2009. "According to the Post-Nargis Joint Assessment (PONJA), 42% of all food stocks were destroyed and 55% of families only had stocks for one day or less."[45] Even within some of the wealthier countries in Southeast Asia, there are significant numbers of food-insecure people. Particularly vulnerable are poor, landless families (often this means the urban poor), female-headed families, and rural landless households.[46] Also the vulnerable are many ethnic minorities living throughout Southeast Asia. Some ethnic communities are being marginalized by changes in rural land use (for industrialization or biofuel production, to name just two), and these communities are among the poorest and most food-insecure in Southeast Asia. Tables 3.4 and 3.5 illustrate countries that import large amounts of grains and those that export these foodstuffs.

TABLE 3.4. Export data for maize, wheat, and rice

Export quantity (tons)		2002	2005	2008	2011	2014
Cambodia	Maize	3	22,788	311,572	5,890	300,000
	Rice—total (rice milled equivalent)	3,846	2,318	5,536	174,045	387,061
	Wheat	0	0	0	0	0
China	Maize	11,678,007	8,611,048	252,667	136,123	100,000
	Rice—total (rice milled equivalent)	2,064,467	666,729	963,069	501,073	300,000
	Wheat	687,629	260,356	125,950	39,808	1,000
Indonesia	Maize	16,306	54,009	107,001	12,717	20,000
	Rice—total (rice milled equivalent)	3,891	42,285	1,840	803	NA
	Wheat	35,916	13,269	39,500	30,000	33,000
Lao PDR	Maize	1,117	47,133	126,677	202,947	NA
Malaysia	Maize	16,266	4,241	248	3,405	10,000
	Rice—total (rice milled equivalent)	2,703	5,387	911	661	NA
	Wheat	1,036	869	1,194	7,703	150
Philippines	Maize	367	82	1,587	12	NA
	Rice—total (rice milled equivalent)	2	196	820	395	NA
	Wheat	0	0	0	0	25
Thailand	Maize	153,139	70,417	672,897	390,081	250
	Rice—total (rice milled equivalent)	7,328,418	7,508,581	10,186,678	10,671,194	9,200,000
	Wheat	11	29	2	11	200
Vietnam	Maize	4,774	2,515	12,334	762	500
	Rice—total (rice milled equivalent)	3,240,932	5,250,000	4,735,170	7,112,000	6,500,000
	Wheat	0	0	0	0	180

Source: Data retrieved from the United Nations Food and Agriculture Organization, http://faostat3.fao.org, and from indexMuni Commodity Export Data, www.indexmundi.com.

TABLE 3.5. Import data for maize, wheat, and rice

Import quantity (tons)		2002	2005	2008	2011	2014
Cambodia	Maize	165	1,525	3,012	1,380	NA
	Rice—total (rice milled equivalent)	68,741	40,209	27,600	12,128	54,839
	Wheat	15,681	24,512	8,795	15,744	NA
China	Maize	5,119,252	5,078,500	4,261,226	5,930,095	5,515,000
	Rice—total (rice milled equivalent)	695,350	932,962	729,948	1,059,294	4,500,000
	Wheat	1,766,618	4,801,480	1,015,719	2,612,288	1,926,000
Indonesia	Maize	1,154,063	185,597	286,541	3,207,657	3,381,000
	Rice—total (rice milled equivalent)	1,790,323	188,944	288,359	2,745,281	1,100,000
	Wheat	4,306,650	4,428,511	4,497,193	5,604,861	7,478,000
Lao PDR	Maize	13,335	938	1,517	856	3,381
	Rice—total (rice milled equivalent)	26,400	22,327	23,734	17,071	NA
	Wheat	0	30	0	0	NA
Malaysia	Maize	2,408,114	2,571,024	2,100,948	2,862,546	3,221,000
	Rice—total (rice milled equivalent)	496,102	583,654	1,106,743	1,031,033	1,100,000
	Wheat	2,097,769	2,220,049	1,004,010	1,142,454	NA
Philippines	Maize	278,246	70,972	22,966	66,193	NA
	Rice—total (rice milled equivalent)	1,196,159	1,821,641	2,432,001	706,471	1,850,000
	Wheat	3,099,749	2,049,843	1,703,463	2,766,569	5,099,000
Thailand	Maize	15,996	73,588	433,737	204,021	NA
	Rice—total (rice milled equivalent)	895	2,381	13,609	10,630	NA
	Wheat	877,170	1,148,363	694,909	1,426,210	348,9000
Vietnam	Maize	300,000	236,292	669,541	877,847	350,000
	Rice—total (rice milled equivalent)	40,000	340	683	2,409	2,296
	Wheat	702,000	1,121,000	701,889	2,421,217	1,850,000

Source: Data retrieved from the United Nations Food and Agriculture Organization, http://faostat3.fao.org.

NATIONAL CONCERNS AND ACTIONS ON FOOD SECURITY

Food security is a broad topic, so this chapter uses the example of the regional rice trade to understand the issue in Southeast Asia. Asian countries are some of the world's largest importers and exporters of rice, importing about 41 percent of rice traded on global markets: the Philippines accounts for about 3.6 percent of world rice imports, Bangladesh 3.4 percent, China 3.2 percent (but growing sharply), North Korea 2.4 percent, Japan 2.3 percent, Malaysia 1.8 percent, Indonesia 1.3 percent (but declining steadily), and Singapore 1.2 percent. On the export side, Asia farms produce more than 91 percent of the global rice harvest.[47] The largest rice exporters are Vietnam, Thailand, India, and Cambodia.

Malaysia, Singapore, and the Philippines are rice importers.[48] For Malaysia and the Philippines in particular, rice provision is a matter of national security. Both countries are instituting national policies to bolster national production.[49] In reaction to global price hikes in 2007–8, the government of Malaysia passed the Food Security Policy. Under this policy, RM506 billion was allocated for agricultural development, particularly rice cultivation and production. In the spring of 2011, the government extended this policy. Malaysia's National Agricultural Policy (NAP) for 2011 to 2020 will determine whether Malaysia will be able to achieve food security through self-sufficiency, or whether Malaysia will continue to be dependent on imports. The NAP involves both input and output subsidies in agriculture, guaranteeing a minimum price for paddy output, fertilizer paddy cultivation, and seed subsidies, and rice price supports. The coordinating agency for this is FAMA, the Federal Agricultural Marketing Authority (which is like Indonesia's coordinating agency, Bulog).[50] These policies may produce short-term self-sufficiency, but if the experiences of other countries are any guide, these policies are expensive to maintain and may not be environmentally sustainable.

Indonesia would like to reassume its leadership within Southeast Asia. However, when it comes to food security, particularly on the issue of rice cultivation and trade, Indonesia has not acted in a concerted way to change how trade and reserves are structured. This may in part stem from Indonesia's position of being mostly self-sufficient in rice production, neither importing huge quantities of rice nor economically reliant on exporting rice. Therefore, Indonesia may not see it as vital to its own interests to foster better cooperation.

Thailand, Vietnam, and Cambodia are rice exporters. In all three countries, the governments are seeking to protect both their own producers from price fluctuations and their own citizens from potential global shortages. Vietnam and Thailand are contemplating greater cooperation on creating a rice cartel under the umbrella of a regional federation for rice among ASEAN producing nations. The hope is that rice exporters will be able to command higher prices for their farmers if they work together as a group to set prices and control supply.[51] It is worth emphasizing here that the interests of rice importers and rice exporters are dramatically different. Creating a cartel-like organization would benefit suppliers over consumers because of their ability to control prices. Importing countries, like Malaysia, the Philippines, and others, would like to see as open, transparent, and competitive a market as possible for rice. Since the priorities and preferences are so divergent for importers and exporters, it is hard to envision a situation (short of repeated and intensifying crises) where greater coordination of rice trade policies will be possible.

Partly in response to the sharp increase in international food prices in 2007–8 leaders in Southeast Asia pledged to embrace food security as a matter of permanent and high priority. They adopted the Statement on Food Security in the ASEAN Region, which commits them, among others actions, to the implementation of the ASEAN Integrated Food Security Framework and the Strategic Plan of Action on Food Security in the ASEAN Region (2009–13). This is a five-year strategic plan to ensure long-term food security in the region through increased cooperation and mutual help.[52] The policies discussed in the next section demonstrate what is possible in terms of state cooperation on food security. While these measures do not overcome all of the problems related to self-interested decision making, they do help move countries toward a more cooperative situation.

COOPERATIVE EFFORTS ON RICE

The Senior Officials Meeting is the main ASEAN body that oversees cooperation in food and agriculture, with the guidance of the ASEAN Ministers on Agriculture and Forestry. Sectoral working groups, joint committees, boards, and experts groups have been established to implement the respective cooperation sectors of food, and the various subsectors of agriculture and forestry. The ASEAN Secretariat is charged with overall coordination of the programs. ASEAN has implemented numerous cooperative projects relating to food, agriculture, and forestry that cover a wide spectrum of activities ranging from exchange of information to crop production, postharvest handling, research and development, and trade promotion in the areas of crops, livestock, fisheries, and forestry.

In order to respond to globalization, ASEAN cooperation in food, agriculture, and forestry is now more focused on the enhancement of product competitiveness in international markets, while sustaining agricultural production, rather than on food security or climate change. Harmonization of quality and standards, assurance of food safety, and standardization of trade certification are among the priorities being addressed. These build upon the experience of some member states and attempt to meet international standards.

At ASEAN meetings in 2010, ministers welcomed and reaffirmed the ASEAN Plus Three (APT) Cooperation Strategy on Food, Agriculture, and Forestry, which provides a comprehensive framework to foster cooperation among the APT countries in the areas of strengthening food security, biomass energy development, SFM, climate change mitigation and adaptation, animal health and disease control, and cross-cutting issues (e.g., enhancement of capacity building and human resource development; strengthening of information and knowledge networking and exchange; enhancement of productivity, quality, and marketability of agriculture products; strengthening collaboration on research and development). The ministers agreed to formalize the APT Emergency Rice Reserve as a permanent scheme for meeting emergency requirements and achieving humanitarian purposes. The ministers urged all APT countries to sign the agreement and signal their support through early implementation. By 2010 members had created the ASEAN Food Security Information System to provide early warning systems and information on agricultural commodities; this was designed to provide information on food supplies before a crisis was full-blown. At the 2011 and 2012 ASEAN meetings, food security was again on the agenda. There was a renewed sense of importance and urgency at these meetings. Commodity prices were again climbing, and heavy rains in Thailand were threatening the rice harvests.

In addition, the events of the Arab Spring heightened government concerns over volatility of food prices because of the clear relationship between food security and political stability.[53] The protests throughout the Middle East and North Africa showed the world that the combination of high food prices, few opportunities for economic advancement, and authoritarian regimes that deny citizens meaningful participation and accountability and reward insiders with economic benefits is a recipe for feelings of deprivation and political unrest![54]

At the fall 2011 meeting, the APT members signed the emergency rice reserve agreement. Under the current plan, the thirteen signatory states will stock up to 787,000 tons of rice to be used in the event of sudden instability in rice supplies. This reflected nervousness among regional leaders over environmental conditions and the close connection between food supplies, costs, and domestic stability.[55]

One obstacle to greater cooperation is the nature of the rice market itself. Being relatively small (in comparison with other commodity markets), it is highly segmented and "imperfect," as economists would say. Most import and export deals on rice are made behind closed doors by governments with little transparency or accountability.[56] The basic problem is that the interests of food exporters and food importers are dramatically different, and they are able to influence their respective governments accordingly. It is hard to imagine large food exporters wanting to be constrained in how they control the distribution of such resources, and food importers will always want markets to be as open as possible. In Southeast Asia, Vietnam and Thailand are big exporters of rice, Philippines and Malaysia significant importers. Indonesia's position varies from year to year, some years importing significant supplies of rice, other years exporting.[57]

In theory, both importing and exporting countries would benefit from greater transparency and greater liberalization of the rice trade. There could be large payoffs from greater efficiency and better allocation of resources. There would be greater stability of prices and supplies, less of a tendency for actors to hoard stocks, and a reduction in the likelihood of price panics. So why don't countries liberalize trade in rice and increase their cooperative efforts? Peter Timmer views this cooperation challenge as a prisoner's dilemma. All countries would be better off if everyone cooperated. However, if a country defects (doesn't cooperate, implements import or export controls, etc.) while other countries cooperate, then the defecting country will come out ahead. This then generally produces the understandably rational decision of each individual country to forego cooperation in favor of beggar-thy-neighbor policies. Timmer explains that the way to resolve this dilemma is to agree on a formal mechanism for cooperation through ASEAN or a related organization with binding commitments (like those in the General Agreement on Tarrifs and Trade, which have governed other commodities). Alternatively, gradual learning by all actors can produce greater cooperative outcomes in prisoner's dilemmas. Through repeated rice price crises, countries may come to realize that cooperation is the best way forward. This of course is a painful way to achieve greater cooperation.[58] The rice trade could be impacted by the Trans-Pacific Partnership (TPP), currently awaiting ratification by 12 Pacific Rim countries, including the United States. The agreement includes provisions for freeing up trade in agriculture, including rice. Rough estimates are that the most significant impact of the agreement could be to bolster U.S. food exports to Asia, and countries such as Japan and Vietnam would end up importing larger quantities of food, including rice. If tariffs were eliminated for food commodities, the largest increases in intraregional trade would be for sugar, rice, animal fats and oils, and beef.[59] The USDA estimates that Japan, Malaysia, Vietnam, New Zealand, and Brunei will drop their tariffs and quotas on U.S. rice, bolstering U.S. exports to the region. Likewise, U.S. tariffs on rice will also be eliminated within fifteen years.[60]

Food security and public health problems of emerging diseases are also clearly linked to the larger challenges posed by climate change. Climate change will have profound effects on living conditions and human security, and will impact many diverse issues: water resources,[61] agriculture, forestry, the spread of diseases, migration patterns, energy systems, and arguably the larger economy itself. Stresses that arise from climate change can exacerbate and trigger new conflicts among groups within states and across national borders. The Center for Strategic and International Studies stated that climate change "could destabilize virtually every aspect of modern life."[62] The German Advisory Council anticipates that a global warming of between two and four degrees Celsius would lead to a drop in agricultural productivity worldwide and that this decrease will substantially increase desertification, soil salinity, and water security. One of the reasons that human security issues are often hard to tackle is that we live in a world still defined by states and national security interests. Addressing human security (which encompasses food security as well as economic, environmental, health, personal, community, and political security) requires a shift in focus from being concerned about state-centered approaches to focusing on people-centered approaches to security. This would require both a rethinking of notions of security, priorities, and actors, as well as vastly more cooperation across state boundaries. This is incredibly difficult, but not impossible.

Hegemonic stability theory would note that international organizations like the WTO and ASEAN often function best when there is strong leadership. So, one could imagine fostering greater cooperation on nontraditional security threats could come from a more active leadership by Indonesia (the largest player in ASEAN), China, or the United States. However, for reasons that will be discussed in the conclusion, leadership on nontraditional security issues is lacking, so free-riding behavior continues.

Conclusions

Indonesia, China, and the United States are all significant actors on economic and security matters in Southeast Asia, but for different reasons none of these states is currently playing a forceful enough role to foster greater regional cooperation on the issues examined here. Indonesia is the largest power in Southeast Asia and shows intermittent interest in acting like a regional great power. During Indonesia's time chairing ASEAN in 2011, officials pushed hard to strengthen the capacities and role of the ASEAN Intergovernmental Commission on Human Rights, pursued the goal of establishing a network of peacekeeping centers in ASEAN member states, and laid the groundwork for the Southeast Asia Nuclear Weapons Free Zone Treaty to be signed by the United States, United Kingdom, Russia, France, and China. These efforts reflect Indonesia's growing desire to be seen as a regional leader.[63] Indonesia's election of President Joko Widodo in the summer of 2014 may signal more of a return to an emphasis on domestic politics. Yet, it would behoove Indonesia to play a leadership role on issues of climate change, EID, and food security. Indonesia suffers the negative consequences from poor coordination on all of these issues and is vulnerable to the effects of all three problems. So, one would think that Indonesian leadership is likely on such issues. However, that has not been the case. As much as the government in Jakarta talks about wanting to deal with climate issues like deforestation and public health problems like avian flu, leaders have demonstrated considerable weaknesses in working on these problems within their own boarders, and have not played a significant role in promoting regional cooperation either. Likewise, one might expect to see Indonesia push for longer-term food security goals like policies to engage in better integration of the Asia rice market with more open trade policies and much greater transparency. But, this hasn't happened. The 2014 election of Jokowi provides further emphasis that domestic politics trumps international relations. Jokowi ran on a platform heavy on social and economic issues and has been outspoken about domestic politics taking priority over foreign affairs. There is little chance that Indonesia's leadership in the region will be enhanced by this position.

Domestic political factors are really at the crux of this discussion. Why are countries sometimes unable to cooperate on common problems even though it might be in their interest to do so? There are two broad sets of explanations: interest group politics and problems of state capacity and corruption. I will look briefly at each of these. Often the explanation for beggar-thy-neighbor policy choices is that domestic political forces or key interests work hard to promote policies that benefit their interests at the expense of the larger collective good. For example, logging companies, mining firms, or rice growers (or exporters) may be able to influence policies in ways that are helpful to their interests, even if they undermine efforts to combat climate change or address regional food supply issues. This happens in democratic and nondemocratic countries alike. Second, even when states do agree in principle to a set of policies, and even if they go so far as to sign an international agreement or pass laws (e.g., enacting prohibitions against clear-cutting forests), enforcement of such policies is often very difficult—either because monitoring agencies are weak and underfunded with little ability to offer carrots and sticks to get compliance or because national governments may not have the capacity to enforce policies at the local level. Corruption also plays a role, as local officials (or national ones as well) may be willing to turn a blind eye to policy violations in exchange for bribes or political support.[64] Many countries in Southeast Asia, such as Vietnam, Cambodia, Indonesia, the Philippines, and others, have high levels of corruption. This makes policy enforcement very difficult, regardless of if we are talking about measures to combat H5N1, where local officials may pocket money meant to be used to compensate farmers for culling infected flocks and thus infected birds are not properly dealt with, or where logging and mining companies use their political power, local patronage networks, and outright bribes to obtain a free pass to keep mining or leveling forests and destroying the peat layer (as happens in Indonesia). These domestic political dynamics occur throughout Southeast Asia and are a significant obstacle to countries like Indonesia and China being able to take on more of a leadership role in combating these nontraditional security threats.

How might we imagine countries overcoming these conditions that produce free-riding, uncooperative policy choices? As countries in the region continue to see strong economic growth rates and increasing levels of prosperity, this may get easier. As populations get richer, they will be better able to afford different diets and demand for rice may shrink. As demand drops, states may then have greater flexibility in how they view their control of and access to rice supplies, which may weaken the political power of rice growers throughout Southeast Asia. Likewise, continued economic development will make creating a social safety net easier as well. Citizens who have better access to public health networks, and more comprehensive social services will be less vulnerable to food insecurity, thus allowing for greater flexibility in policy making. Finally, interest groups like mining and logging firms are often kept in check by greater transparency in policy making and efforts to crack down on corruption. While these political elements are still lacking throughout Southeast Asia and China, things are changing. There is greater NGO activism from environmental groups all over the region. Local communities are more aware of and more willing to speak up against environmental problems that impact their lives. Over time, this may put pressure on policy makers to consider multiple perspectives, not just those of deep-pocketed corporations. This could make enacting and enforcing cooperative policies more likely.

In 2009, Indonesia and Malaysia initiated a series of bilateral discussions on cooperating on food security. The two countries stated their intention to jointly develop investment programs in agriculture. Indonesia has vast agricultural assets, and Malaysia is more technologically advanced. The goal would be that Malaysia would invest capital and technology into Indonesia's agricultural sector for mutual benefit. This would enhance regional cooperation and serve as a model for more multilateral efforts within ASEAN, and it would improve food security and help prevent food crises. As an example and a first step toward this larger goal, Indonesia and Malaysia agreed to cooperate on marketing of palm oil, this was viewed as a powerful indicator of what is possible by joining forces since together Malaysia and Indonesia control about 80 percent of the world's supply of palm oil.[65] But, like we see with the implementation of REDD+, states, including Indonesia, want to reap the benefits from partnering with advanced industrial countries, but either have difficulty (because of local autonomy issues and corruption, or because of the power of actors in the relevant industries) implementing better environmental policies or are unwilling to do so. Likewise, with food security, Indonesia, as neither a big exporter nor a big importer, could play a role in pushing for greater transparency and openness in the rice trade, but officials seem to have done little to this effect. Again, we see in Indonesia and elsewhere in the region (particularly Thailand) that domestic interest groups are able to impact national policies, and there is little political will to foster regional cooperation.

China, as the region's ascendant power, might be interested in greater leadership. However, on matters of food security, climate change, and the spread of diseases, China has a poor track record of addressing these issues at home, and thus it is hard to imagine leadership on these same issues within Southeast Asia. Chinese leaders are far more interested in preserving access to natural resources and sources of food that will contribute to China's continued industrialization (and CCP leaders assume that this will help them maintain power), than they are in conserving or preserving resources; and huge pollution problems and weakness with addressing public health problems at home make China unable to serve as a credible leader on issues of climate change or EID (this could change if China is successful at reigning in their emissions as per their agreement with the United States). China's behavior on water cooperation is telling. The Mekong River (called the Lancang in China), which begins in the Tibetan highlands and runs from China to Myanmar, Vietnam, Thailand, Laos, and Cambodia, has been a source of disagreement between China and its neighbors. China has built several enormous dams on the river and has been unwilling to share even the most basic information about their plans and actions for the river. This has had profound effects (with sudden, often unexplained, increases and decreases in the river's flow) for countries downstream and citizens who rely on the Mekong for fishing, agriculture, and transportation and communities' basic existence. The Mekong River Commission, an organization established in 1995 to facilitate cooperation over the shared resource, has had little success working with China. China is not a full member (if it was, it would be required to share information about activities on the river) but a "dialogue partner" and as such is required to provide only minimal information about their use of the river. The Southeast Asian countries impacted by China's use of the river have been relatively quiet in their protestations.[66] This reflects larger dynamics between China and countries in Southeast Asia. They would like China to be a constructive partner, not an adversary, and so seem to take pains not to antagonize China unless it is an issue of clear national sovereignty and security. And, for China's part, they seem disinclined to be more cooperative on sharing information and resources, let alone supplying public goods as hegemonic stability theory prescribes. There are reasons for possible optimism; the 2014 agreement with the United States on carbon emissions could prove to be a turning point on China's willingness to take the lead on environmental issues, but it is too early to tell. This agreement does seem to indicate that China may be willing to cooperate if prompted to do so by other great powers like the United States. Alone, Southeast Asian states may have fewer carrots and sticks to get China to act cooperatively. Likewise, without resolving the ongoing territorial disputes in the South China Sea, China will not be viewed as a neutral and credible broker on other common problems in Southeast Asia.

While the United States has signaled an interest and concern over food security issues and over EID, outside of ad hoc agreements and some aid contributions, the country has not tried to play a role in regional organizations like ASEAN to get specific long-lasting action on these problems. Likewise, the Obama administration has indicated a concern for climate change and related problems. However, the United States is preoccupied with its own internal political struggles and less willing and able to play the role of a strong leader on these issues in the region. Because the United States is not a member of ASEAN or APT, it is hard to see how the United States could play a more significant role within the context of these institutions (since that is where most of the cooperative measures are being built) in addressing these regional problems. The TPP is one possible mechanism for greater U.S. involvement in the region, along with the "pivot" to Asia promised by President Obama. However, there have been few tangible results from either of these developments. The United States is an important actor on the issues discussed here, from CDC involvement in EID to helping to fund some REDD+ activities and agreeing to allow Japan to use stockpiles of U.S. rice to end price spikes and panics over rice shortages in 2008. However, these actions should not be viewed as part of some larger shift in U.S. policy goals. The United States is still primarily focused on traditional security questions like the rise of Chinese power and instability in the Middle East. Nontraditional security issues, like those discussed here, remain secondary concerns. There seems to be little likelihood that either China or the United States will spearhead greater cooperative efforts within Southeast Asia to address these human security questions. The best chance for greater cooperation will have to come from Southeast Asian countries themselves. I think we will see increasing efforts to deal with the problems in moderate and incremental ways. Significant changes in how countries deal with these externalities may require additional crises and disasters (e.g., flooding, haze, EID outbreaks, food price spikes) for policy makers to overcome domestic interests and come up with shared strategies to deal with the issues presented in this chapter. Low levels of cooperation on these nontraditional security issues may also signal weak chances for cooperation on how Southeast Asia as a whole addresses more traditional security problems like maritime disputes with China. Countries in Southeast Asia have not shown robust cooperation in balancing against China in these disputes, and many Southeast Asian countries are quite reluctant to push back against Chinese actions (as seen in the example of China's selfish behavior on the Mekong). Countries in the region have continued their pragmatic policies of working with both the United States and China on economic and security matters, rather than choosing to balance against one or the other.

NOTES

1 Zelda Soriano, "Climate Change Demands That ASEAN's Future Is Cooperative," *Nation*, May 1, 2013, www.nationmultimedia.com.

2 Bei Hu and Natasha Kahn, "Morgan Stanley Said to Move Asia Hedge-Fund Event to US," *Bloomberg News*, May 28, 2013, www.bloombergnews.com.

3 Sophal Ear, "Emerging Infectious Disease Surveillance in Southeast Asia: Cambodia, Indonesia, and the US Naval Area Medical Research Unit 2," *Asian Security* 2, no. 2 (2012): 164.

4 World Health Organization (2012), www.who.int; Colin Butler, "Food Security in the Asia-Pacific: Climate Change, Phosphorus, Ozone and Other Environmental Challenges," *Asia Pacific Journal of Clinical Nutrition* 18, no. 4 (2009): 590–97.

5 The 2014 U.S.-China agreement on carbon emissions and the Conference of the Parties on Climate Change also based climate measures on voluntary national changes rather than international mandates. Susanne Goldenberg, "Lima Climate Change Talks Reach Global Warming Agreement," *Guardian*, December 14, 2014,

www.theguardian.com; and Josh Lederman "Surprise US-China Climate Deal Sets Aggressive Targets," *Christian Science Monitor*, November 12, 2014, www.csmonitor.com.

6 Charles Kindleberger, "An Explanation of the 1929 Depression," in *The World in Depression, 1929–39* (Berkeley: University of California Press, 1973), 291–308; Max W. Cordon, "American Decline and the End of Hegemony," *SAIS Review* 10, no. 2 (1990): 13–26; Michael H. Hunt, "American Decline and the Great Debate: A Historical Perspective," *SAIS Review* 10, no. 2 (1990): 27–40; and Helen Milner, "International Political Economy: Beyond Hegemonic Stability," *Foreign Policy*, no. 110 (1998).

7 One of the best examples of these dynamics can be seen in the change in U.S. policy toward the use of CFCs (chlorofluorocarbons) and the global environmental issue of ozone depletion. In the 1980s there were only a handful of large producers of CFC-based products. U.S. manufacturer DuPont was one of the largest such producers. Once DuPont developed a cheap substitute for CFCs for many applications, it actively lobbied the United States to regulate, and ultimately heavily restrict, CFC use domestically. This paved the way for U.S. leadership in negotiations leading up to the 1987 Montreal Protocol, which set targets for phasing out CFCs, halons, and other ozone-depleting substances and is widely held up as a model of international cooperation on an environmental problem. While U.S. leadership was not the only positive ingredient that led to the signing and success of this sort of international cooperation, there is no question that it was a necessary element of it. Domestic political dynamics, the significant role of interest groups in shaping American policies, contributed to strong U.S. leadership in the drafting, ratifying, and complying with the international agreement that would significantly reduce global use of ozone-destroying substances. This example shows that cooperation on issues of human security is possible as long as there are leadership and incentives for cooperation. Marvin Sooros, *The Endangered Atmosphere* (South Carolina: University of South Caroline Press, 1997), 160–61.

8 For information on world GDP rankings, see http://databank.worldbank.org.

9 Kurt Campbell and Brian Andrews, "Explaining the US 'Pivot' to Asia" (London: Chatham House, 2013), www.chathamhouse.org.

10 IPCC Working Group II AR5, "Asia," in *Climate Change 2014: Impacts, Adaptation, and Vulnerability* (Intergovernmental Panel on Climate Change, 2014).

11 Soriano, "Climate Change Demands."

12 John Vidal, "Greater Mekong Countries Lost One-Third of Forest Cover in 40 Years," *Guardian*, May 2, 2013, www.theguardian.com.

13 Bernadinus Steni, "Climate Change and ASEAN," *Jakarta Post*, May 10, 2011.

14 Center for International Forestry Research, "Simply REDD: CIFOR's Media Guide to Forests, Climate Change, and REDD," 5, http://blog.cifor.org.

15 Ibid., 5.

16 "SBY Vows to Protect Indonesia's Rainforests," *Jakarta Globe*, September 27, 2011.
17 Leony Aurora, "Indonesia Sets Aside 45% of Forest-Rich Kalimantan to Be World's Lungs," Center for International Forestry Research, http://blog.cifor.org.
18 Ann Marie Murphy, "Confronting the Challenge of Climate Change in Indonesia through REDD+: Technical Difficulties, Coordination Problems, and Politics" (paper, AAS, Toronto, March 15–18, 2012); Nadya Natahadibrata, "UNDP Report Shows Indonesia Is Struggling to Combat Deforestation," *Jakarta Post*, May 8, 2013.
19 Kate Lamb, "Indonesia's First Labelled a 'Crime Against Humanity' as 500,000 Suffer," *Guardian*, October 26, 2015, www.theguardian.com.
20 "Under-Fire Jokowi Prepares Biggest Shift Yet in Indonesian Haze," *Mongabay Haze Beat*, October 26, 2015, http://news.mongabay.com.
21 Global Fire Monitoring Center, "Land-Use Fires and Smoke Pollution in Indonesia," November 18, 2015, www.uni-freiburg.de.
22 "Under-Fire Jokowi Prepares Biggest Shift Yet in Indonesian Haze," *Mongabay Haze Beat*, October 26, 2015, http://news.mongabay.com.
23 ASEAN, "ASEAN Common Position Paper: On Reducing Emission from Deforestation and Forest Degradation (REDD) in Developing Countries" (2008), http://unfccc.int. See also Chris Lang, "Interview with Chris Lang, REDD-Monitor: Carbon Markets and REDD in Southeast Asia," *REDD-Monitor*, February 1, 2013, www.redd-monitor.org.
24 Soriano, "Climate Change Demands."
25 Steni, "Climate Change and ASEAN."
26 Ibid.
27 "REDD in Southeast Asia: A Political Economy Perspective" (summary of workshop, Bangkok, April 4, 2011), www.focusweb.org.
28 Murphy, "Confronting the Challenge of Climate Change."
29 Loren Bell, "Indonesia Dissolves Agency Charged with Forestry Reform," *Mongabay*, February 15, 2015, www.mongabay.com.
30 Department of Environment and Natural Resources: Forest Management Bureau, "The Philippines National REDD-plus Strategy," ed. Jacob Phelps (October 2010), http://www.unorcid.org.
31 "Thailand's Deforestation Solution," *World Policy Blog*, October 16, 2014, www.worldpolicy.org.
32 Gregore Lopez, "Mahathir's Regional Legacy," *East Asia Forum*, June 17, 2010, www.eastasiaforum.org.
33 Lederman, "Surprise US-China Climate Deal."
34 UNFCCC, "Historic Paris Agreement on Climate Change," December 12, 2015, http://newsroom.unfccc.int.
35 Asian countries (including the United States and Australia) involved in negotiating the Trans-Pacific Partnership (TPP) also have an opportunity to include environmental safeguards in this comprehensive trade agreement. However, in leaked drafts of the text of the TPP Environment Chapter in 2014, there are no enforcement mechanisms in the treaty and compliance will be left to industries

and states. Michael Kennedy, "How the TPP Could Make or Break Environmental Protection," *ABC Environment*, October 24, 2014, www.abc.net.au; Office of the U.S. Trade Representative, "Outlines of the Trans-Pacific Partnership Agreement, Fact Sheets," www.ustr.gov.

36 Ear, "Emerging Infectious Disease Surveillance"; and Sophal Ear, "Avian Influenza: The Political Economy of Disease Control in Cambodia," *Politics and Life Sciences* 30, no. 2 (2011): 2–19.

37 Elizabeth Wishnick, "Dilemmas of Securitization and Health Risk Management in the People's Republic of China: The Cases of SARS and Avian Influenza," *Health Policy and Planning* 25, no. 6 (2010): 454–66.

38 Amy Freedman, "SARS and Challenges to Regime Legitimacy in China," *Asian Affairs* (Summer 2005).

39 Ramona Gutierrez, Monica Naughton, Srey Viseth Horm, Sorn San, and Philippe Buchy, "A(H5N1) Virus Evolution in Southeast Asia," 1, no. 3 (2009): 335–61, www.mdpi.com.

40 Ear, "Avian Influenza"; Ear "Emerging Infectious Disease Surveillance"; and Wishnick, "Dilemmas of Securitization."

41 Gianna Gayle Amul, "ASEAN's Critical Infrastructure and Pandemic Preparedness," NTSblog (2013), www.ntsblog.sg.net.

42 ASEAN, "Information on EID," www.aseanplus3-eid.info.

43 RSIS Centre for Non-Traditional Security Studies, *International Conference on Asian Food Security 2011—Feeding Asia in the 21st Century: Building Urban-Rural Alliances* (Singapore, August 10–12, 2011), 7.

44 OECD, "Share of Official Development Assistance (ODA) for Agriculture (Percent)" (2009), https://stats.oecd.org.

45 UNDP, "Post-Nargis Joint Assessment Final Report" (July 10, 2008), www.mm.undp.org.

46 Le Danh Tyuen, "Food and Health Security in Southeast Asia," *Asia Pacific Journal of Clinical Nutrition* 18, no. 4 (2009): 493–97.

47 Daniel Workman, "Rice Import Dependent Countries Nigeria, Saudi Arabia and Philippines among Biggest Rice Buyers" (April 16, 2008). http://suite101.com. Also see International Rice Research Institute, "Data on Rice Importers and Exporters" (various years), www.irri.org.

48 David C. Dawe, ed., *Why Does the Philippines Import Rice* (International Rice Research Institute, 2006), http://irri.org.

49 Melody Aguiba, "Philippines to Play a Critical Role in Global Food Security with 2012 Golden Rice Launch," *Jakarta Globe*, March 19, 2011; Butler, "Food Security."

50 Hanim Adnan, "Food Security Policy May Be Extended," *Star* (Malaysia), April 10, 2011.

51 "Vietnam to Cooperate with Thailand on ASEAN Rice Cartel," *Angimex*, June 26, 2012, http://oryza.com.

52 AMAF (ASEAN Ministers on Agriculture and Forestry) Plus Three, "Joint Press Statement of the Tenth Meeting of the ASEAN Ministers on Agriculture and

Forestry and the Ministers of Agriculture of the People's Republic of China, Japan and the Republic of Korea" (10th AMAF Plus Three, Phnom Penh, October 24, 2010).

53 Yang Razali Kassim, "The 19th ASEAN Summit: Tackling Floods, Food and Stability—Analysis," *Eurasiareview*, November 17, 2011, http//www.eurasiareview.com.

54 Ted Gurr, *Why Men Rebel* (Princeton, NJ: Princeton University Press, 1970).

55 Yang Razali Kassim, "ASEAN's Role in Asian Food Security," *Business Times*, September 14, 2011, 21.

56 Peter Timmer, "Managing Price Volatility: Approaches at the Global, National and Household Levels" (Stanford University Symposium Series on Global Food Policy and Food Security in the 21st Century, May 26, 2011), 11.

57 "Indonesian Rice Production and Trade Policy," *Asiaone*, March 3, 2011, www.asiaone.com.sg; see also Edward B. Barbier, "Cash Crops, Food Crops, and Sustainability: The Case of Indonesia," *World Development* 17, no. 6 (1989): 879–95.

58 Timmer, "Managing Price Volatility," 14.

59 Mary E. Burfisher, John Dych, Birgit Meade, Lorraine Mitchell, John Wainio, Steven Zahniser, Shawn Arita, and Jayson Beckman, "Agriculture in the Trans-Pacific Partnership" (U.S. Department of Agriculture Economic Research Service, October 2014), www.ers.usda.gov.

60 USDA, "Trans-Pacific Partnership Benefits to US Agriculture" (October 20, 2015), www.fas.usda.gov.

61 While it is beyond the scope of this essay to comprehensively discuss water security, cooperation in Asia over water resources reflects similar dynamics to those on food security, climate change, and EID. China's track record of discussing water issues in the Mekong Delta is abysmal!

62 Jurgen Scheffron and Antonella Battaglini, "Climate and Conflicts," *Environmental Change* 11, suppl. 1 (2011): S27–S39, S31.

63 Lina Alexandra, "Indonesia Is Emerging," *Diplomat*, August 11, 2011, http://the-diplomat.com.

64 Some have even suggested that the forest fires in Sumatra and Kalimantan are linked to local elections held in December 2015. Incumbent local politicians needed money for reelection and thus might have been more likely to grant forest concessions for plantation projects to garner revenue. Leo Jegho, "Forest Fires Linked to Regional Elections?," *Global Indonesian Voices*, September 21, 2015, www.globalindonesianvoices.com.

65 Scheffron and Battaglini, "Climate and Conflicts," S31.

66 For information on the shared use of the Mekong, see Pilita Clark, "Troubled Waters: The Mekong River Crisis," *Financial Times*, July 18, 2014, www.ft.com; John Lee, "China's Water Grab," *Foreign Policy*, August 23, 2010, foreignpolicy.com; and Sophie Le Clue, "Water Treaties, a Question of Rights," *China Water Risk*, April 12, 2012, http://chinawaterrisk.org.

PART II

Southeast Asian Perspectives

4

Pragmatic Equidistance

How Indonesia Manages Its Great Power Relations

EVAN A. LAKSMANA

This chapter describes the rationale and nature of Indonesia's foreign policy vis-à-vis the United States and China. It places Indonesia's foreign policy pertaining to these two countries within the broader context of Jakarta's overall management of its great power relations. I argue that Indonesia's approach can be described as one of "pragmatic equidistance." As an approach to great power management, pragmatic equidistance captures the idea of fully engaging one great power in various forms of cooperation—from economic to defense matters—while simultaneously both maintaining strategic autonomy and keeping equal balance with other great powers. Put differently, it is about how a developing country with a rising regional and global profile like Indonesia can fully exploit the benefits of strategic partnerships with different great powers while maintaining autonomy and not being pegged as too close with one great power at the expense of another. I further argue that Indonesia's pragmatic equidistance with the United States and China is a function of (1) the historical legacies in bilateral relations, (2) the end of authoritarian rule in 1998 and the ensuing democratization process, and (3) the changing strategic environment in the broader Indo-Pacific. These conditions overlap and help explain the persistent ambiguity in the triangular Indonesia-U.S.-China relations.

The following sections expand these arguments. The first section describes two concepts—limited alignment and omni-enmeshment—as the underpinning theoretical framework for the pragmatic equidistance policy. It also places Indonesia's overall foreign policy strategy vis-à-vis the great powers within the broader pattern of how Southeast Asian countries engage the great powers. The second section describes the elementary foundation and domestic drivers of Indonesia's foreign policy. In particular, it highlights how the democratization process has overhauled Indonesia's foreign policy by expanding the complexity of foreign policy making, "democratizing" the Ministry of Foreign Affairs' foreign policy formulation process, and placing democratic values projection as of one of Indonesia's central foreign policy goals. The third section applies the insight from the previous sections to describe the complicated balancing act Jakarta has had to implement in its relationship with Washington and Beijing. The triangular relationship highlights how pragmatic equidistance works in practice. Finally, I draw some conclusions at the end and provide an initial assessment of how pragmatic equidistance can also help us make sense of, and even anticipate, Indonesia's foreign policy under the new Joko Widodo administration.

Limited Alignments, Omni-Enmeshment, and Pragmatic Equidistance

Indonesia's management of its great power relations is not unique. Indeed, the basic contours of how it manages its great power relations are consistent with the broader pattern of how developing countries, especially those in Southeast Asia, deal with regional major powers. As such, I propose that two interrelated concepts—limited alignment (Ciorciari 2010) and omni-enmeshment (Goh 2007/8)—provide us with a sound theoretical vantage point from which we can make sense of Indonesia's great power management strategy, which I call "pragmatic equidistance." Pragmatic equidistance describes a preferred balance between deeper engagement and strategic autonomy with several great powers simultaneously based more on pragmatic interests than normative concerns. The following elaboration of limited alignment and omni-enmeshment should clarify this proposition.

In the past decade, Indonesia's regional and global profile has been rising, partially due to its economic success story and its consolidating democracy. Indonesia is poised to be the next major economic power (already the tenth largest economy according to the World Bank in 2014), it has already been a historical leader in Southeast Asia, and it has tried to make distinctive contributions to G-20 deliberations while being among the most consistent contributors to UN peacekeeping operations (Laksmana 2011a; Reid 2012).[1] It has also begun its foray into global environmental and health policies, while maintaining its traditional leadership role in a wide range of security issues, such as the peaceful management of the South China Sea disputes, and an array of multilateral institutions, ranging from the Association of Southeast Asian Nations (ASEAN) to the Organization of Islamic Cooperation and the Asia-Pacific Economic Cooperation (APEC). How Jakarta deals with established great powers like China and the United States therefore cannot be decoupled from this context.

The story of Indonesia's rising profile however is also a story of domestic politics, which I will elaborate further in the next section. Suffice it to note for now that as Indonesia's economic, political, and military potentials are still in their early stages of development, its domestic politics often takes priority when it comes to foreign policy matters. But the nature of the regional environment has also shaped different foreign policy options and strategies available to policy makers. After all, developing countries are more likely to be concerned with their immediate neighbors than far-flung global interests. Taken as a whole, the primacy of domestic politics further explains why developing states, like Indonesia, are more likely to have limited alignment as their strategic outlook, while the regional environment explains why specific omni-enmeshment strategies were pursued.

We can see limited alignment when a state tilts toward one or more great powers to obtain some measure of security support but entails lower commitments and a less binding security relationship (Ciorciari 2010: 3–8). It typically includes arrangements for preferential arms sales, joint training exercises, and other forms of military aid without a general pledge of combat support. Developing states tend to pursue this strategy because they believe flexible security arrangements will provide the best ratio of risks to rewards—often seen through the lens of domestic politics—under conditions of strategic uncertainty (Ciorciari 2010: 8). This is because a tight alignment with established great powers can diminish the weaker partner's independence and alienate domestic actors (Ciorciari 2010: 9). In cases where the domestic political context is particularly problematic—when policy makers are polarized, for example—limited alignment can be a convenient default strategy between the more risky alternatives of tight alliance and strict nonalignment (Ciorciari 2010: 10).

While limited alignment draws our attention to the importance of domestic politics, it helps us understand only Indonesia's bilateral relationship with any given great power. Given the traditional centrality of Southeast Asia and ASEAN in Indonesia's foreign policy, we need a second concept to place the country's great power management within the broader regional and multilateral contexts. This is where omni-enmeshment comes in. Omni-enmeshment is the process of engaging a major power so as to draw it into deep involvement with a regional society and enveloping it in a web of sustained exchanges and relationships (Goh 2007/8: 121). As a pathway to regional order, omni-enmeshment functions through (1) *legitimate inclusion*, forging bilateral economic and political-military ties with the major powers and including them as partners in regional institutions to legitimize their regional security roles; (2) *institutionalized interaction*, enfolding the major powers within multiple bilateral agreements and multilateral frameworks to regulate and coordinate intraregional interaction; and (3) *cooperative security*, cooperating through ascription to norms and principles, and through informal dialogue and exchange to cultivate a climate of conflict avoidance and functional cooperation (Goh 2007/8: 130–31).

As a specific foreign policy strategy, omni-enmeshment can be pursued bilaterally and multilaterally. Bilaterally, we can see it in Indonesia's deliberate cultivation of multiple strategic relationships with major powers out of concern for diversifying security partners and cooperation over intraregional security concerns (Goh 2007/8: 126). We will discuss specific aspects of Indonesia's bilateral relations with the United States and China in the next section. Multilaterally, ASEAN and its "offspring" institutions such as the East Asia Summit and the ASEAN Regional Forum, are seen as channels for implementing enmeshment policies when member states have agreed that their incremental and informal processes were suitable to particular pursuits, such as the desire to boost regional leadership or to fulfill the imperative of strategic diversification (Goh 2007/8: 128–29). Historically, Indonesia has had such designs in mind when viewing ASEAN and its regional environment.

This is particularly the case when we consider that Indonesia's support for ASEAN and its associated institutions is also based on the notion that bringing the major powers into these organizations can tie them down by creating expectations and obligations (Goh 2007/8: 122–23). It does not hurt as well that ASEAN's greater effectiveness might boost Indonesia's competitive position in the global arena; Jakarta is a more significant actor and attractive partner in the eyes of extra-regional powers when leading a united ASEAN (Ruland 2013: 16). ASEAN has also been influential in allowing Indonesia to shape the broader regional dynamics beyond Southeast Asia. It is not surprising therefore that Indonesia's foreign policy elite have repeatedly stated that the promotion of multilateralism and cooperative security through ASEAN is a key priority (Novotny 2010: 19–20). After all, ASEAN has proven to be successful at reversing Indonesia's tarnished international image and brought back international investors in the 1970s (Haftel 2010). These positive expectations are not always borne out in reality, however. In cases where the key interests of the major powers are at stake, such as the case in the South China Sea, the immediate effects and utility of multilateral omni-enmeshment are not readily apparent. As such, despite recent criticisms that Indonesia does not seem to focus on ASEAN under its new president Joko Widodo (e.g., Poole 2015), the country's basic strategic lens with regards to ASEAN has not fundamentally changed.

Taken as a whole, limited alignment is a general outlook guiding developing and rising states like Indonesia in their engagement with established great powers as a function of domestic politics and highlights the value of maintaining strategic autonomy, while omni-enmeshment helps set the specific bilateral and multilateral foreign policies as a function of the regional environment. Together, these two concepts underpin Indonesia's pragmatic equidistance with both the United States and China. To specify this further, we shall now turn to the foundation and domestic drivers of contemporary Indonesian foreign policy.

Indonesia's Foreign Policy: Elementary Foundation and Democratic Consolidation

There is more continuity than change when it comes to the basic premise of Indonesia's foreign policy. For one thing, the ideational foundations of Indonesia's foreign policy are deeply nationalist and rooted in the vicissitudes of its history—including Dutch colonial rule, the Japanese occupation during World War II, and the subsequent armed struggle for independence as well as the exigencies of the Cold War (Ruland 2013: 7). All of these inculcated in Indonesian foreign policy elite a deep distrust toward a seemingly hostile external world and a profound sense of vulnerability (Weinstein 1976). As such, Indonesia's foreign policy has been traditionally shaped by the constant efforts to "eliminate various security threats" (broadly defined), and to maintain a sufficient strategic space for maneuvering and a favorable position vis-à-vis other states (Novotny 2010: 7). However, what those threats are precisely and how they affect specific foreign policy goals are seldom specified. Indeed, a survey of Indonesia's foreign policy elites reveals that there is substantial disagreement among the key decision and opinion makers about the conception of national interests and what these and the international context demand (Novotny 2010: 63).

This lack of consensus is a function of both the expansively normative conception of the "independent and active" foreign policy doctrine as well as the imperatives of domestic politics, especially presidential interests and styles. At its most basic, the independent and active doctrine—as defined by Vice President Mohammad Hatta in the late 1940s—is built upon four premises: (1) the conduct of foreign policy should be based on the state's *Pancasila* (five principles) ideology, (2) foreign policy should be aimed at safeguarding the national interest as defined in the Constitution, (3) the pursuit of national interest is best served through an independent policy, and (4) foreign policy should be conducted pragmatically, that is, it "should be resolved in the light of its own interests and should be executed in consonance with the situations and facts it has to face" (cited from Sukma 1995: 308). In short, given the Cold War context, Hatta argued that "Indonesia plays no favorites between the two opposed blocs and follows its own path through the various international problems. It terms this policy 'independent' and further characterizes it by describing it as 'independent and active.' By active I meant the effort to work energetically for the preservation of peace, through endeavors supported if possible by the majority of the members of the United Nations" (cited from Leiffer 1983: 29).

This doctrine has provided and will continue to provide the core foundation of Indonesia's foreign policy. Although it was initially formulated during the Cold War, its meaning has expanded and become synonymous with autonomy, which stands not only for foreign policy pragmatism but also for Indonesia's "self-styled role of a regional leader and major player in world politics" (Ruland 2013: 8). In short, the principle defines a foreign policy in pursuit of national interests as determined by the incumbent president, and the success or failure to promote or protect those interests is a function not of rhetorical appeal to the principle but of the mobilization and deployment of real capabilities (Weatherbee 2005: 155). Put differently, the foundational nature of Indonesia's independent and active doctrine is a "constant," but its implementation could be "recalibrated" by different presidents. Today, despite new foreign policy outlooks, such as President Joko Widodo's "global maritime axis," the essence of the independent and active doctrine remains.[2]

If the independent and active doctrine is the constant in Indonesia's foreign policy, then domestic politics has been the key variable for the past several decades (cf. Sukma 1995; Leiffer 1983; Novotny 2010). Most recently, the process of democratic transition and consolidation since 1998 has overhauled the operationalization and constrained the reinterpretation of the doctrine, as several studies have shown (Murphy 2012; Ruland 2013; Sukma 2011; Gindarsah 2012). I argue further that democratization has changed Indonesia's foreign policy system—"the input, process, and output"—through (1) the expansion in the number and different types of actors that can now shape foreign policy making, (2) the "institutional democratization" of the foreign ministry and how they formulate and execute their tasks, and (3) the growing centrality of democratic values projection.

Growing Complexity of Foreign Policy Making

Under the New Order regime, the president and his inner circle (many members of which came from the military) made most foreign policy decisions. And while the House of Representatives (DPR) had the power to ratify treaties, it acted for the most part as the president's rubber stamp (Anwar 2010: 128). The democratic transition in 1998, however, catapulted the DPR's role in foreign policy making through a series of constitutional amendments. The first amendment practically allows the DPR to approve or reject the president's ambassadorial candidates. This provision was meant to abolish the Suharto-era practice of using ambassadorial postings as sticks and carrots for aides or senior military figures (Anwar 2010: 128). The amendment also included a provision that gives the DPR the right to "approve" ambassadors being sent to Jakarta by other countries (Anwar 2010: 129). Law No. 24 of 2000 on International Agreements, which mandated an extensive consultation and coordination process between the executive, the legislature, and other relevant agencies, strengthened this amendment (Nabbs-Keller 2013: 65).

Beyond ambassadorial selections, the DPR has also been given more substantive oversight role in foreign policy making, including the ratification of international agreements signed by the government and over the budget of the Ministry of Foreign Affairs. For example, the parliament has been instrumental in persuading the government to elevate democracy and human rights as foreign policy norms, and after the ratification of the ASEAN Charter, it also ensured that the government pressed for substantive amendments (Ruland 2009). However, as the case of Indonesia's support for UNSC Resolution 1747 over Iranian nuclear program sanctions showed, the DPR's exercise of its foreign policy oversight often has to do less with their sound judgment of international affairs and more to do with domestic political squabbles and the parties' disenchantment over cabinet posts (Gindarsah 2012). Indeed, the DPR's review process and Indonesia's political culture, which favors coalition building between the president and the political parties, have increased the burden of the executive's responsibility in foreign policy making (Gindarsah 2012: 419–20).

In addition to the DPR's growing role, democratization has opened the door for various domestic public opinion makers as well as special interest groups to have further input in the country's foreign policy making. The effects of these non-state groups and the weight of public opinion vis-à-vis foreign policy making however are more indirect. As Indonesian political leaders tend to be more sensitive to a wider range of public opinion and aspirations during the democratic consolidation phase (Pepinsky 2010; Mietzner 2009), they are also more likely to be "image conscious." Indeed, President Yudhoyono's consideration over foreign policy issues has occasionally taken into account the views of civil society groups and the press for personal image-building reasons (Laksmana and Soesastro 2010). In other instances, however, civil society groups have occasionally tried to directly influence the direction of the country's foreign policy in areas such as climate change and the implementation of the "Responsibility to Protect" principle (Alexandra 2012; Nabadan 2010).

Institutional "Democratization" of Foreign Policy Making

The primacy of domestic politics, as defined by the president as well as the politicization and militarization of foreign policy making under Suharto, have contributed to the lack of the highest standards of "diplomatic professionalism" within the foreign ministry (Nabbs-Keller 2013). However, between 1999 and 2004, a series of laws and decrees placed Indonesia's foreign policy on a firmer institutional footing and augmented civilian authority and capacity, especially through the country's first national law on foreign relations (Law No. 37/1999) (Nabbs-Keller 2013: 65). The law redefined Indonesia's foreign relations as "all activities encompassing regional and international aspects conducted by the Government at the central and regional levels, or institutions, state agencies, business organizations, political organizations, community organizations, non-government organizations or Indonesian citizens." While this definition may seem too broad, it helped facilitate the institutional "democratization" of the foreign ministry and its activities.

Besides having to defer more closely to the wishes of the DPR, the foreign ministry began to involve other stakeholders to ensure a wider sense of ownership of the country's foreign policy. Indeed, former Foreign Minister Hasan Wirajuda made a conscious effort to democratize the foreign-policy-making process by actively consulting and engaging think tanks, academics, religious groups, the media, and civil society organizations. He also frequently commissioned papers from leading academics that would be openly discussed in workshops to provide policy inputs to the ministry and held regular closed briefings with opinion makers through informal forums such as the "foreign policy breakfast" (Anwar 2010: 131). According to one scholar, such a shift has increased the crucial role of the foreign ministry as an entrepreneur of new ideas and foreign policy practices (Nabbs-Keller 2013).

Projection of Democratic Values Abroad

In parallel with these developments, Indonesia has sought to project its democratic values across international borders—from the ASEAN Political Security Community (APSC) project to the Bali Democracy Forum and others.[3] While democratic projection initially entered Indonesia's foreign policy lexicon as a way to restore its battered post-transition image in the late 1990s (Murphy 2012: 90), it was not until under President Megawati Sukarnoputri that it was firmly established as one of the country's key pathways to burnish its soft power credentials. In addition, after several years of looking inward since 1998, the country's economic recovery helped to "improve the country's international image and also injected a new sense of self-confidence in the articulation and implementation of its foreign policy" (Anwar 2010: 127). All things considered, Indonesian leaders believe that their experience transitioning from an authoritarian rule to peacefully resolving conflicts, managing a terrorist threat, and overcoming an economic crisis gives them the credibility to address many of today's challenges (Murphy 2012: 85).[4]

The APSC project in particular was initially proposed as a way for ASEAN member states, individually and collectively, to promote their "people's participation, particularly through the conduct of general elections and human rights . . . [and] through the establishment of the ASEAN Commission on Human Rights" (cited from Sukma 2011: 114). Indeed, as highlighted by Wirajuda, "For Indonesia, the evolution of an ASEAN that is more alert to democratic principles and good governance is critical to ensure that there would not be a disconnect or divide between the transformation that has taken place in Indonesia and the regional milieu" (cited from Anwar 2010: 133).

Consequently, Indonesia now views its own regional neighborhood through the lens of democracy. We can see this, for example, in how Indonesia pressed for and supported ASEAN's regional efforts to gradually accelerate Myanmar's democratic transition and consolidation process in the past several years (Hlaing 2008; Dosch 2008; Ruland 2009) and, most recently, in its call to Thailand to end its May 2014 martial law and for the military to restore democracy (Ririhena 2014). Indeed, the foreign ministry has explicitly placed the expansion of Indonesia's global and regional identity as a democratic country as part of its long-term strategic plan through 2024 (Vermonte 2014: 208).

Normatively, the regional promotion of democratic and human rights norms—norms that are enjoying great international recognition—through ASEAN endows Indonesia with respectability and places its claims for regional leadership on a normative high ground (Ruland 2013: 14). Instrumentally, as discussed in the previous section, democratic value projection abroad can be seen as part of the foreign ministry's efforts to regain and strengthen civilian control over foreign policy decision making and to ameliorate widespread bureaucratic inefficiencies within the ministry. In addition, the projection of a democratic foreign policy also served important political functions in enhancing the government's legitimacy to both domestic and international constituencies (Nabbs-Keller 2013: 70).

The democratic value projection has also been associated with growing awareness of the broader society on foreign policy issues. This awareness however appears to be more closely aligned with a sense of self-entitlement. A 2012 survey suggests that around 80 percent of the public felt that the country has what it takes to become the next great power (Luftia 2012). But the poll also noted that any global role is measured more by Indonesia's state capacity—through its ability to provide a sufficient supply of food, clothing, and shelter (32 percent), for example—than global leadership.[5] Other polls also indicate a certain popular acknowledgment of Indonesia's special status. When asked in 2011 "about Indonesia's influence generally in the world compared to other countries," 20 percent of Indonesians put it among "the top 10 most influential countries" (Quayle 2013: 310). While the surveys might conflate the potential to become a great power, the necessary prerequisites to become one, and what it means to behave like one, they highlight the societal aspirations to a global profile. One scholar claimed that "all sectors of Indonesian society back the country's aspirations to take on a more active role in international affairs" (Sukma 2011: 117).[6]

Democratic value projection has not been without its challenges, however. Indonesia's democratic credentials have been constantly challenged by persistent problems of corruption, domestic political scandals, social violence, and terrorism as well as communal tensions, weak law enforcement, and growing religious intolerance (Sukma 2011: 118). In addition, the democratic gap in Southeast Asia, a region dominated by authoritarian and semiauthoritarian regimes, also makes Indonesia's democratic projection that much harder to fulfill. Indeed, Indonesia's neighbors have been less than enthusiastic about Jakarta's promotion of human rights and democratic values, especially given the long-standing history of "noninterference" in fellow ASEAN member states' domestic affairs (Anwar 2010: 134–35).

Taken as a whole, these contexts help us understand how Indonesia manages its pragmatic equidistance with the United States and China. For example, the DPR and business community have had more input over Indonesia's China policy, especially as it pertains to the ASEAN-China Free Trade Agreement. The professionalization of the foreign ministry has facilitated a more thoughtful, coherent, and consistent foreign policy strategy. Meanwhile, the projection of democratic values has partially facilitated efforts to fully normalize military-to-military relations with the United States and allowed Washington to further support Indonesia's growing regional and global leadership. We will explore these issues in the next section.

Squaring the Triangular Balance: Jakarta's Relations with Beijing and Washington

To be clear, Indonesia's great power management involves other countries than the United States and China, including Japan, Australia, Russia, and even India. For instance, Jakarta signed eighty-six bilateral defense and security agreements and partnerships with thirty-one countries between 1999 and 2014 (Laksmana 2014a: 37). Historically, however, Washington and Beijing have figured much more prominently in Indonesia's strategic thinking (Novotny 2010). This section thus focuses on Indonesia's efforts to balance its limited alignments with both countries, even as it still relies on various multilateral mechanisms (primarily through ASEAN) to sustain its pragmatic equidistance.

Indonesia has been considered "one of the clearest cases of limited alignments in modern Southeast Asia" (Ciorciari 2010: 136). For one thing, external threats have been relatively modest and internal security threats have historically been more prominent (Laksmana 2011b). For another, the possible rewards of a tight alliance with a great power have been unappealing because Indonesian officials rarely believe that the United States and other great powers possess the tools and credibility to deal with Indonesia's domestic security challenges (Ciorciari 2010: 136). Foreign policy makers also believe that great power alignments undermine policy independence and regime legitimacy and detract from Indonesia's regional ambitions. Indeed, the historically limited nature of its tilt toward one great power has allowed Jakarta to publicly characterize its foreign policy as essentially independent, preserve domestic and regional prestige, and claim a leadership role in ASEAN (Ciorciari 2010: 136). This is also one of the reasons why the independent and active doctrine noted above has withstood the rise and fall of different presidents for over sixty years.

Consequently, Indonesia's management of its great power relations may seem paradoxical and ambiguous. In the case of China, for example, Indonesia recognized its potential threat as a rising power and emphasized the need for a U.S. presence to counterbalance it. But on the other hand, Jakarta has also been expanding its bilateral relations with Beijing, from trade and investment to education and defense cooperation. At the end of the day, according to Sukma (2012: 42), "Jakarta cannot escape the imperative of having to conduct its foreign policy in the context of the complex relationship between the U.S. and China. Leaning to one side is not an option. Indonesia needs and wants both the U.S. and China as friends and partners, and would not want to see the superpowers become rivals, competing for influence in its neighborhood." After all, given Indonesia's concern to strengthen and capitalize on ASEAN as the primary regional institution, a Sino-U.S. rivalry could polarize ASEAN, which could turn the region once again into a "playing field" for the major powers (Sukma 2012).

This is a position that not just reflects geopolitical realities, but also has been influenced by the primacy of domestic politics in Indonesia's foreign policy, as we will discuss further below. For now, suffice it to note that the basis of Indonesia's pragmatic equidistance with both the United States and China has been to maintain its commitment to the independent and active doctrine that requires Indonesia to not take sides in any major power rivalry. Furthermore, its pragmatic equidistance also complements, if not better facilitates, Jakarta's proactive efforts to create what former Foreign Minister Marty Natalegawa calls a "dynamic equilibrium" in East Asia with ASEAN in the driver's seat of regional architecture building. However, this notion of "ASEAN centrality" is premised upon the willingness of the region's major powers—often contingent on Indonesia's perceived "neutrality" as the group's leader—to participate in the group's multilateral processes.

Taken as a whole therefore, Indonesia's pragmatic equidistance cannot be separated from the nature of its limited alignments with the United States and China and the omni-enmeshment of both countries through ASEAN as well as the imperatives of domestic politics. In practice, this further suggests that how Jakarta deals with Washington cannot be separated from how it deals with Beijing (Lanti 2008; Novotny 2010). We can see this, for example, in how Jakarta sought to strengthen the U.S. presence in the future East Asian community through the East Asia Summit, while simultaneously making the best out of the economic opportunities Beijing offered while embracing China within the ASEAN framework (Kosandi 2013: 198). This move was about maintaining Indonesia's strategic independence while attempting to balance the two powers. The following sections expand and build on these arguments.

Indonesia-U.S. Relations

Indonesia's pragmatic equidistance with the United States is rooted in the two country's close relations for over six decades, peppered with the ebbs and flows of temporary mutual interests and contradictory policies. At the elite level, one survey concludes that Indonesia's approach to its relations with the United States is ambiguous—Washington is seen to be both a source of potential threat as well as the main guarantor of regional stability (Novotny 2010). This ambiguity is also regularly borne out in several public opinion surveys. A Chicago Council on Global Affairs poll showed 64 percent of Indonesians lacked trust in the United States "to act responsibly" in the world, and a World Public Opinion poll found 63 percent agreed that "the US abuses its greater power to get Indonesia to do what it wants" (cited from Quayle 2013: 316). Polls conducted in the summer of 2008 showed that only 23 percent of Indonesians held either a favorable or very favorable opinion of the United States (cited from Pepinsky 2010: 4–5). But after Obama's election, according to the

Pew Research Global Attitudes Project, more than 60 percent of Indonesians had a favorable opinion of the United States (Wike 2010). This figure held until 2013.

These fluctuations notwithstanding, Indonesia's ongoing democratic consolidation process implies that foreign policy makers cannot fully ignore the weight of public opinion. Indeed, an increasingly open political system means that a wider range of actors can influence overall Indonesia-U.S. bilateral relations in ways antithetical to the interests of both (Murphy 2010: 375). That being said however, the United States has retained its primacy in the strategic calculus of the Indonesia's policy makers, though in somewhat ambivalent fashion.

On the one hand, Indonesian leaders have historically seen the United States as a highly useful economic partner and provider of military goods as well as the main guarantor of regional stability. Indeed, during the first few decades of Indonesia's independence, America's image among Indonesia's leaders was generally fairly positive (Ciorciari 2010).[7] In recent years, Indonesia has also tacitly supported and facilitated U.S. military predominance in the region to indirectly deter potential Chinese aggression or domination (Goh 2007/8: 135). It participates in the annual Cooperation Afloat Readiness and Training military exercises with the U.S. Navy and regularly hosts visiting U.S. vessels, and both currently hold approximately 140 joint exercises. Jakarta also seeks to increase its own domestic "internal balancing" by attracting U.S. military aid and training (fully restored in 2006), as well as trade and economic assistance (Goh 2007/8: 136–37). In 2010, the two countries signed a Defense Framework Agreement that covered a wide range of policy areas such as security dialogue, education and training, maritime security, and military equipment procurement (Murphy 2010: 376–77).

On the other hand, Indonesian policy makers have also been doubtful of Washington's capacity to solve Jakarta's domestic political and security problems, and many of them have even harbored suspicion of U.S. motives and credibility. If anything, the rocky history between the two countries during the Cold War,[8] various cultural sensitivities, and concerns over policy consistency have all contributed to those suspicions at different times (Ciorciari 2010: 140). More recently, various domestic political actors—from Islamic parties to civil society organizations—have also doubted American intentions over the extension of the global war on terror to Southeast Asia and Indonesia. Following the 2003 U.S. invasion of Iraq, for example, Colin Powell called Indonesian foreign minister Hassan Wirajuda to "persuade Indonesia to take sides"—to which he replied that Indonesia's condemnation of the invasion was "not just the government's position, but also that of the civil society and the people" (cited in Acharya 2015: 81). And yet, Presidents Megawati Sukarnoputri and Susilo Bambang Yudhoyono were often criticized for their support of various counterterrorism policies and for receiving U.S. and Western counterterrorism aid.

Jakarta also fully realizes that from Washington's viewpoint, distance and a lack of traditional ties imply that American interests in Indonesia are largely strategic. An archipelago of seventeen thousand islands stretching three thousand miles from east to west, Indonesia sits astride Southeast Asia's vital sea lanes of communications—the freedom of navigation through which is vital for U.S. strategic interests. According to one diplomat, Indonesia is also "the only country in the Asia Pacific which, I won't say it can stand up to China, but at least cannot be pressured into accommodating China. It has the mass, credibility to do this" (cited in Acharya 2015: 76). Washington therefore supports Indonesia's leadership and influence in broader regional institutions in which ASEAN plays an agenda-setting role. But because its interests are strategic, U.S. policy toward Indonesia has been driven by its overarching grand strategy (Murphy 2010: 364–65), and not by shared historical bond. Given these conditions, a policy of pragmatic equidistance makes perfect sense for many in Jakarta.

Indonesia-China Relations

Despite shared formative revolutionary experiences, Indonesia-China relations lacked warmth and substance from the outset, especially as powerful political elites in Indonesia (primarily the military and Islamic groups) were hostile toward communism and suspicious of Beijing's relationship with the country's small but economically powerful ethnic Chinese population (Storey 2011: 192; Goh 2007/8: 116n12). The peak of this acrimonious relationship took place in the latter half of the 1960s and early 1970s, when, following an alleged attempted coup by a group of military officers and the Beijing-backed Indonesian Communist Party, Indonesia broke off diplomatic relations with China.

By the mid-1980s, buoyed primarily by considerations over China's economic potential, Jakarta gradually moved to normalize its relations with Beijing (Storey 2011: 196). Yet, even after this initial step, Indonesia's engagement with China over the next few years was still tepid and tinged with suspicion, partially because of unresolved domestic political issues surrounding the state of Chinese Indonesians and partially because of the mounting unease within Indonesia's defense establishment over China's military modernization program and assertive behavior in the South China Sea (Storey 2011: 199).

Despite this historical strategic ambiguity, China began to further climb the ranks of Indonesia's strategic priorities during Sukarnoputri's presidency. Her government's emphasis on economic recovery became the focus of Sino-Indonesian relations between 2001 and 2004 (see details in Storey 2011: 203). It was also during her administration that China began to show a keen interest in Indonesia's energy sector, hoping to reduce its dependence on energy supply from the Middle East and hence the Straits of Malacca (Storey 2011: 203). In addition, Indonesia's increasingly resilient economy and huge market, as well as its strategic leadership role in ASEAN, were among the top reasons Beijing further engaged Jakarta to invest in a strategic partnership (Kosandi 2013: 193). This explains Beijing's "charm offensive," which included providing significant assistance during the 1997 economic crisis and the December 2004 tsunami. A year later, China announced that its investment in Indonesia could triple up to US$20 billion within five years; this is on top of the fact that China's aid by then was already double what the United States provided (Kurlantzick 2007: 88, 98). All of these helped alleviate some of Indonesia's earlier suspicions and concerns.

However, staying true to the impact of democratization, the implementation of the ASEAN-China Free Trade Agreement elicited domestic debates in Indonesia as the agreement had caused many small and medium-sized businesses in Indonesia to become less competitive and some even collapsed (Kosandi 2013: 186). While enjoying an increase in trade volumes with China, Indonesia had also suffered a bilateral trade deficit until very recently (Kosandi 2013: 186). Under these conditions, various domestic actors, including major businesses and corporations, have pressured the government and parliament to renegotiate terms with China—adding to the existing ambivalence in the bilateral relations.

The trade challenges notwithstanding, the strict visa control for visiting Chinese nationals has been lifted, and Chinese visitors can now obtain visas on arrival. Indonesia also granted concessions and permits to Chinese companies to be involved in Indonesia's strategic industries (Kosandi 2013). Indeed, after decades of U.S. dominance in Indonesia's oil industry, Jakarta has been diversifying its partners in the oil sector as officials begin to consider investment from other parts of Asia to be more attractive than from Western nations (Djalal 2011: 65–66). China's technological prowess has also attracted Indonesia's attention, with moves to develop closer science and technology cooperation between the two countries, including the formation of a joint committee to boost exchanges in aerospace surveying and satellite development, launch, and application (Anwar 2010: 137; "Chinese, Indonesian Presidents" 2013).

Taken as a whole, Indonesia has sought to develop closer ties with China by giving "strategic orientation" to the bilateral ties (Acharya 2015: 80). However, Indonesian officials have also said that Beijing's bilateral investment, trade, and military cooperation plans have been rife with promises but considerably lacking in delivery. For example, President Yudhoyono would like China to build power plants in Indonesia, but a protracted dispute over the price of a liquefied natural gas supply arrangement with Fujian province has somewhat marred relations (Djalal 2011: 67). And yet, in another testament to the pragmatic equidistance policy Indonesia has in place, Yudhoyono's China policy was more comprehensive as ties increased across a range of sectors: trade and investment remained the primary focus, but the political and security aspects of bilateral ties were also given much greater public attention (Storey 2011: 204).

In a move that highlights the complex Indonesia-U.S.-China triangular relationship, Indonesian officials and analysts suggested in 2005 that in light of America's arms embargo over the TNI (Indonesia Armed Forces) and the absence of fully normalized military-to-military relations between Jakarta and Washington, Indonesia might be forced to turn to the Chinese or the Russians as its major military supplier. In April 2005, Chinese President Hu Jintao signed a strategic partnership agreement with President Yudhoyono, committing initially to extend credit and loans for US$300 million worth of infrastructure projects and more than US$10 billion in private-sector investment. This agreement came a few weeks before a U.S.-Indonesia memorandum of understanding for a US$74 million aid package. But by late 2005 and early 2006 Washington had restored International Military Education and Training and Foreign Military Financing programs for Indonesia dsepite protesters who claimed that the TNI's human rights record had not changed (Goh 2007/8: 137).

Defense policy makers and military officers in Indonesia, however, remain concerned over China's position and claims in the South China Sea that effectively overlap with the exclusive economic zones (EEZs) of Indonesia's Natuna Islands. While this concern dates back to the mid-1990s, it has taken on a new life in recent years due to Beijing's growing assertiveness and the rising number of incidents involving the claimant states. This is why Western observers were quick to pick up on a statement by an Indonesian officer in March 2014 that the military is gearing up to strengthen the defenses of the Natunas due to China's claims as evidence of a shift in policy (Murphy 2014). This view is ultimately flawed (Laksmana 2014b; cf. Nabbs-Keller 2014). Officially, there's no maritime "dispute" between Indonesia and China. A few days following the officer's statement, Indonesian Foreign Minister

Marty Natalegawa clarified the matter: "We have to be absolutely clear about this. . . . Firstly, there is no territorial dispute between Indonesia and China, especially about the Natunas. In fact, we are cooperating with China in possibly bringing about foreign direct investment plans in the Natunas. Second, we are not a claimant state in the South China Sea. Third, on the nine-dash line, it is true that we do not accept that. This is why we have asked for a formal explanation from China regarding their claims' legal basis and background" (Prabowo 2014).

This policy is of course not new. Bottom line, Indonesia is concerned that the Natunas and its EEZs could be endangered by China's nine-dash line, but it will never officially admit a dispute with China because that would give credence to Beijing's claims. We can debate the merits of this position, but ultimately there's no significant policy shift on the matter. Furthermore, this policy allows Jakarta to maintain its nonclaimant status in the dispute and facilitate its leadership through ASEAN to push for an eventual Code of Conduct on the matter. After all, the concern over the Natuna Islands is only one of the strategic considerations in the broader bilateral relations with China (Acharya 2015: 80). More importantly, it also allows Indonesia to continue its strategic partnership with both the United States and China and reap the benefits of a pragmatic equidistance.

Conclusions and Implications

The preceding analysis suggests several key points. First, Indonesia's management of its great power relations, especially with the United States and China, is best captured by the notion of pragmatic equidistance. Historically, Jakarta has seen both the United States and China at various times as strategic partners and potential threats—whether politically, militarily, or economically. Second, the persistent ambiguity in the history of the triangular relations has been exacerbated by the growing complexity of Indonesia's domestic politics. While the primacy of domestic politics—and the highly valued strategic autonomy—has been a constant, Indonesia's foreign policy system has been gradually overhauled by the process of democratization. This makes any straightforward case for Jakarta to fully, unreservedly, and permanently lean on either Washington or Beijing in all policy areas to be without merit.

Finally, the nature of Indonesia's pragmatic equidistance with the United States and China should not be disentangled from the broader regional context and the role of ASEAN and its associated multilateral institutions. In other words, an understanding of why and how Indonesia engages with the United States and China should be placed within the broader context of how

Indonesia considers its regional environment and the primacy of ASEAN in its foreign policy thinking. This is not to say that such outlook is in Indonesia's best interest given the growing leadership gap in global governance issues and the growing view that as long as Jakarta is "caged" by ASEAN it will always "punch below its weight" (Sukma 2014: 163). But in any case, the overlap and entanglement between bilateral partnerships and multilateral institutions will likely continue, if not grow and expand, for the foreseeable future.

Taken as a whole, Indonesia's management of its great power relations is complex and driven by different domestic political considerations. This is of course not a novel insight; scholars of Indonesian foreign policy have underlined this feature over and over. What this chapter has demonstrated is how pragmatic equidistance gives a useful vantage point to better understand the complexity involved in and the manner through which Jakarta manages its great power relations. The concept can also help us better understand contemporary events like why and how Indonesia approaches the South China Sea in a particular way. As the concept was developed theoretically to explain the broader patterns of how developing states with rising profiles deal with established powers, it might be useful to consider the concept's applicability to other countries in the region and beyond.

This chapter's discussion of Indonesia's pragmatic equidistance policy also has broader implications pertaining to the new administration of President Joko Widodo (more popularly known as Jokowi). During the campaign, Jokowi ran a coherent foreign policy platform of turning Indonesia into a "global maritime axis."[9] The axis element entails an inward-looking and outward-looking duality—domestically, it focuses on the development of maritime infrastructure, interconnectivity, and resources, while zeroing in on maritime diplomacy and naval defense internationally (see Laksmana 2014a). After he was inaugurated in October 2014, the new president set out to implement this vision by establishing a Coordinating Ministry for Maritime Affairs, revamping the maritime and fisheries ministry, and supporting the creation of a unified coast guard along with the ongoing naval modernization process. He also sought to boost interisland connectivity and upgrade port infrastructure within the Indonesian archipelago, which encompasses thousands of islands and spans almost six million square kilometers (see details in Shekhar and Liow 2014).

As a foreign policy doctrine, the maritime axis concept represents both continuity and change in Jakarta's strategic thinking. On the one hand, as it remains focused on improving Indonesia's strategic autonomy and is driven by pragmatic concerns, the maritime axis still falls squarely within the "free and active" foreign policy premise. Viewed further under the pragmatic equidistance lens, Indonesia's maritime axis builds on the "dynamic equilibrium" concept proposed by Yudhoyono's Foreign Minister Marty Natalegawa, where no one power dominates the region but Jakarta is in good terms with all the major powers. After all, the maritime axis is the next step in the evolution of Indonesia's strategic thinking that began with Suharto's downfall in 1998 and, as we discussed above, was continually refined during the democratic consolidation process. In addition, as Jokowi himself is not considered a political "insider" with an independent, strong political base, nor is he the president of his own political party, we can expect domestic political considerations, including catering to shortsighted nationalist policies, to even further shape Indonesia's foreign policy.

On the other hand, an explicitly maritime outlook entails that some issues—such as conflict management in the South China Sea or the resolution of maritime borders—will be prioritized over others. Such a move is a departure from a generally bland internationalist outlook full with contradictions of the Yudhoyono presidency captured by his "one thousand friends zero enemies" slogan (see Alexandra and Basuki 2014). Furthermore, as the maritime axis concept is based on a sound understanding of Indonesia's geopolitical architecture—consisting of military, political, and economic dimensions at its core (Laksmana 2011b)—we can expect Indonesia's foreign policy to be more targeted on perhaps a smaller number of issues that may be considered less "globalist" in outlook compared to the Yudhoyono era.

Taken as a whole, while the maritime axis concept represents both continuity and change in Indonesia's foreign policy outlook, the notion of pragmatic equidistance can still help us make sense of Jakarta's thinking under a new presidency. Relationships with the established major powers—the United States, China, and Russia—will be maintained and developed further, while some policy areas with direct implications for Indonesia's ability to become a global maritime axis will be prioritized over others. When and how Jokowi can accomplish all he set out to do and to what extent remain to be seen.

NOTES

1 Critics argue however that Indonesia's economic growth has not yet given the state the resources to be a significantly more influential actor on the world stage, either diplomatically or militarily, and if Indonesia is to achieve great power status—a question that remains unclear—it will do so only in the longer term (McRae 2014: 3). This debate is why I prefer the term "rising profile" to "rising power" to describe Indonesia's global standing.

2 The previous Yudhoyono administration had used the phrase "navigating a turbulent ocean" as the latest extension of the doctrine to represent Indonesia's

foreign policy structured by current international challenges in a world of multipolarity where U.S. primacy is declining (Kosandi 2013: 197).

3 Indonesian foreign policy makers tend to draw a distinction between democracy "projection" and heavy-handed democracy "promotion," which may not take into account local conditions (Murphy 2012: 95).

4 Some even argue that there is an unmistakable "light on a hill" quality about Indonesia's self-identification on these matters, going back to previous historical periods (Quayle 2013: 319).

5 This perception is consistent with a cultural account of the foundations of Indonesia's strategic thought rooted in Javanese political ideas predating colonialism. Indeed, despite the spread of modern education and secularism, the belief in the ability of the state to provide public goods—peace, order, and prosperity—has remained an indication of the government's power and legitimacy (Nguitragool 2012: 738).

6 However, some anthropological accounts of Indonesian society's foreign policy views suggest that pan-Asiatic ideas of regional integration and regionalism remain mostly vague and do not feature strongly in everyday discourse, pertaining mainly to the elite's political and economic projects (Schlehe 2013).

7 Considering Indonesia's colonial background, some would consider it rather ironic that from the outset of its independence, Jakarta pragmatically opted to develop a strong relationship with the United States in particular and the West in general (Clark 2011: 292). Indeed, during the New Order period, the foreign ministry designated the United States, along with Japan, Australia, and the ASEAN states, with a "D1" code, indicating the "highest priority" in terms of strategic importance to Indonesia. See Nabbs-Keller (2013: 76n20).

8 Several events were salient during the Cold War: (1) Washington's blatant attempt to bring Indonesia into a quasi-formal alliance with the West—which brought down cabinets in Jakarta, (2) the United States' subversive intervention in the Outer Island rebellions directed against Jakarta in 1958, and (3) Washington's apparent neutrality but behind-the-scenes backing of the Dutch in their attempt to deny West Irian to Indonesia (Novotny 2010: 107).

9 "Global maritime axis" is a direct translation of the original concept dubbed *Poros Maritim Dunia*. Recently, analysts have begun to translate it as "maritime fulcrum." According to one cabinet insider, the preference for "fulcrum" instead of "axis" was proposed by Rizal Sukma, the executive director of the Centre for Strategic and International Studies in Jakarta and a foreign policy adviser to the president. The argument is that a fulcrum implies a more significant strategic advantage and a more proactive policy.

BIBLIOGRAPHY

Acharya, A. *Indonesia Matters: Asia's Emerging Democratic Power*. Singapore: World Scientific, 2015.

Alexandra, L. "Indonesia and the Responsibility to Protect." *Pacific Review* 25, no. 1 (2012): 51–74.

Alexandra, L., and T. Basuki. "Democracy, Human Rights, and Indonesia's Foreign Policy under Yudhoyono." *Indonesian Quarterly* 42, nos. 3–4 (2014): 183–200.

Anwar, D. F. "The Impact of Domestic and Asian Regional Changes on Indonesian Foreign Policy." In *Southeast Asian Affairs 2010*, edited by Daljit Singh, 126–42. Singapore: Institute of Southeast Asian Studies, 2010.

"Chinese, Indonesian Presidents Chart Course of Future Bilateral Cooperation." *Xinhua and Global Times*, October 4, 2013. www.globaltimes.cn.

Ciorciari, J. D. *The Limits of Alignment: Southeast Asia and the Great Powers since 1975*. Washington, DC: Georgetown University Press, 2010.

Clark, M. "Indonesia's Postcolonial Regional Imaginary: From a 'Neutralist' to an 'All-Directions' Foreign Policy." *Japanese Journal of Political Science* 12, no. 2 (2011): 287–304.

Djalal, D. "Indonesia: Domestic Transformation and the Implications for Maritime Energy Security in Southeast Asia." In *Maritime Energy Resources in Asia: Energy and Geopolitics*, NBR Special Report 35, edited by Clive Schofield, 61–84. Seattle, WA: National Bureau of Asian Research, 2011.

Dosch, J. "ASEAN's Reluctant Liberal Turn and the Thorny Road to Democracy Promotion." *Pacific Review* 21, no. 4 (2008): 527–45.

Gindarsah, I. "Democracy and Foreign Policy-Making in Indonesia: A Case Study of the Iranian Nuclear Issue, 2007–08." *Contemporary Southeast Asia* 34, no. 3 (2012): 416–37.

Goh, E. "Great Powers and Hierarchical Order in Southeast Asia: Analyzing Regional Security Strategies." *International Security* 32, no. 3 (2007–8): 113–57.

Haftel, Y. "Conflict, Regional Cooperation, and Foreign Capital: Indonesian Foreign Policy and the Formation of ASEAN." *Foreign Policy Analysis* 6, no. 2 (2010): 87–106.

Hlaing, K. Yin. "ASEAN's Pariah: Insecurity and Autocracy in Myanmar (Burma)." In *Hard Choices: Security, Democracy and Regionalism in Southeast Asia*, edited by Donald K. Emmerson, 151–89. Palo Alto: Walter H. Shorenstein Asia-Pacific Research Center, 2009.

Kosandi, M. "Shifting Paradigms and Dynamics of Indonesia-China Relations: Towards the Best Use of Theoretical Eclecticism." *Asian Politics and Policy* 5, no. 2 (2013): 183–210.

Kurlantzick, J. *Charm Offensive: How China's Soft Power Is Transforming the World*. New Haven: Yale University Press, 2007.

Laksmana, E. A. "The Enduring Strategic Trinity: Explaining Indonesia's Geopolitical Architecture." *Journal of the Indian Ocean Region* 7, no. 1 (2011a): 95–116.

——. "Indonesia's Rising Regional and Global Profile: Does Size Really Matter?" *Contemporary Southeast Asia* 33, no. 2 (2011b): 157–82.

——. "Indonesia's Strategic Thinking: Breaking Out of Its Shell?" In *CSCAP Regional Security Outlook 2015*, edited by Ron Huisken, 35–38. Canberra: Council for Security Cooperation in the Asia Pacific, 2014a.

——. "Why There Is No 'New Maritime Dispute' between Indonesia and China." *Strategist: Australian Strategic Policy Institute Blog*, April 4, 2014b. www.aspistrategist.org.au.

Laksmana, E. A., and H. Soesastro. "Indonesia." In *Does Fairness Matter?*, Global Economy and Development Working Paper no. 40, edited by Hakan Altinay, 23–25. Washington, DC: Brookings Institution, 2010.

Lanti, Irman, "Indonesia in Triangular Relations with China and the United States." In *China, the United States, and Southeast Asia: Contending Perspectives on Politics, Security, and Economics*, edited by Evelyn Goh and Sheldon W. Simon, 128–42. New York: Routledge, 2008.

Leiffer, M. *Indonesia's Foreign Policy*. London: George, Allen and Unwin, 1983.

Luftia, I. "Majority Believes Indonesia Can Be Next Superpower: Survey." *Jakarta Globe*, June 6, 2012.

McRae, D. *More Talk Than Walk: Indonesia as a Foreign Policy Actor*. Lowy Institute Analyses. Sydney: Lowy Institute for International Policy, 2014.

Mietzner, M. "Political Opinion Polling in Post-Authoritarian Indonesia: Catalyst or Obstacle to Democratic Consolidation?" *Bijdragen tot de Taal-, Land, en Volkenkunde* 165, no. 2 (2009): 95–126.

Murphy, A. M. "Democratization and Indonesian Foreign Policy: Implications for the United States." *Asia Policy* 13 (2012): 83–111.

———. "The End of Strategic Ambiguity: Indonesia Formally Announces Its Dispute with China in the South China Sea." *Pacific Forum PacNet Newsletter*, no. 26 (April 1, 2014).

———. "US Rapprochement with Indonesia: From Problem State to Partner." *Contemporary Southeast Asia* 32, no. 3 (2010): 362–87.

Nabadan, A. "Climate Change: Is Southeast Asia Up to the Challenge: Civil Society Engagement in the Current Negotiation on Climate Change." In *IDEAS Reports—Special Reports*, edited by Nicholas Kitchen, 63–65. London: London School of Economics and Political Science IDEAS, 2010.

Nabbs-Keller, G. "Is Indonesia Shifting Its South China Sea Policy?" *Interpreter: Lowy Institute for International Policy Blog*, April 16, 2014. www.lowyinterpreter.org.

———. "Reforming Indonesia's Foreign Ministry: Ideas, Organization and Leadership." *Contemporary Southeast Asia* 35, no. 1 (2013): 56–82.

Nguitragool, P. "God-King and Indonesia: Renegotiating the Boundaries between Western and Non-Western Perspectives on Foreign Policy." *Pacific Affairs* 85, no. 4 (2012): 723–43.

Novotny, D. *Torn between America and China: Elite Perceptions and Indonesian Foreign Policy*. Singapore: Institute of Southeast Asian Studies, 2010.

Pepinsky, T. B. *Politics, Public Opinion, and the U.S.-Indonesian Comprehensive Partnership*. NBR Special Report no. 25. Seattle, WA: National Bureau of Asian Research, 2010.

Pooler, A. "Is Jokowi Turning His Back on ASEAN?" *Diplomat*, September 7, 2015.

Prabowo, P. H. "Indonesia Pernah Sampaikan Keberatan Atas Peta Natuna." *Antara News*, March 19, 2014.

Quayle, L. "Power and Paradox: Indonesia and the 'English School' Concept of Great Powers." *International Relations of the Asia-Pacific* 13, no. 2 (2013): 301–30.

Reid, A., ed. *Indonesia Rising: The Repositioning of Asia's Third Giant*. Singapore: Institute of Southeast Asian Studies, 2012.

Ririhena, Y. "RI Calls for Restoration of Democracy in Thailand." *Jakarta Post*, May 24, 2014.

Ruland, J. "Constructing Regionalism Domestically: Local Actors and Foreign Policymaking in Newly Democratized Indonesia." *Foreign Policy Analysis* (2013). Advance online publication.

———. "Deepening ASEAN Cooperation through Democratization? The Indonesian Legislature and Foreign Policymaking." *International Relations of the Asia Pacific* 9, no. 3 (2009): 373–402.

Schlehe, J. "Concepts of Asia, the West and the Self in Contemporary Indonesia: An Anthropological Account." *South East Asia Research* 21, no. 3 (2013): 497–515.

Shekhar, V., and J. C. Liow. *Indonesia as a Maritime Power: Jokowi's Vision, Strategies, and Obstacles Ahead*. Washington, DC: Brookings Institution, 2014. www.brookings.edu.

Storey, I. I. *Southeast Asia and the Rise of China: The Search for Security*. London: Routledge, 2011.

Sukma, R. "The Evolution of Indonesia's Foreign Policy: An Indonesian View." *Asian Survey* 35, no. 3 (1995): 304–15.

———. "Indonesia dan Asia Timur: Reposisi Strategis sebagai Middle Power." In *Untuk Indonesia 2014–2019: Agenda Sosial-Politik dan Keamanan*, edited by Shafiah F. Muhibat, 157–68. Jakarta: Centre for Strategic and International Studies, 2014.

———. "Indonesia and the Emerging Sino-US Rivalry in Southeast Asia." In *The Geopolitics of Southeast Asia*, LSE IDEAS Special Report, 42–46. London: London School of Economics and Political Science, 2012.

———. "Indonesia Finds a New Voice." *Journal of Democracy* 22, no. 4 (2011): 110–23.

Vermonte, P. J. "Foreign Policy Begins at Home: Indonesia's Foreign Policy under SBY's Presidency." *Indonesian Quarterly* 42, nos. 3–4 (2014): 201–15.

Weatherbee, D. E. "Indonesian Foreign Policy: A Wounded Phoenix." In *Southeast Asian Affairs 2005*, edited by Chin Kin Wah and Daljit Singh, 150–70. Singapore: Institute of Southeast Asian Studies, 2005.

Weinstein, Franklin B. *Indonesia Foreign Policy and the Dilemma of Dependence: From Sukarno to Soeharto*. Ithaca, NY: Cornell University Press, 1976.

Wike, R. *Indonesia: The Obama Effect*. Washington, DC: Pew Research Global Attitude Project, 2010. www.pewglobal.org.

5

Economic and Strategic Trends in Southeast Asia

The View from Singapore

HENG YEE-KUANG

Introduction

An understanding of Singapore's perspectives on long-term economic and strategic trends in Southeast Asia will necessarily be conditioned and shaped by both its abiding sense of vulnerability and its leaders' fundamental assumptions about how international relations is conducted. The following sections outline the key components of this vulnerability to set the analytical framework, before moving to appraise how Singapore perceives strategic and economic developments in its neighborhood through this lens. Michael Leifer once described Singapore as an "exceptional state" in terms of not just its stellar economic achievements but also its "intensely innate sense of vulnerability."[1] It is therefore no exaggeration that "vulnerability and vigilance make up the adrenaline that drives Singapore's security perceptions and policies."[2] For founding Prime Minister Lee Kuan Yew, the island's vulnerability was not just an "obsession," but also the "inescapable, permanent condition of Singapore as an independent republic."[3] Singapore has been described as a mere "red dot" situated within "a swirling and turbulent sea of geopolitical and geo-economic forces."[4] This infamous term, coined by former Indonesian President Habibie, encapsulates Singapore's early postindependence sense of geostrategic vulnerability: "look at that map. All the green is Indonesia. And that red dot is Singapore." Singapore's strategic predicament is a function of its miniscule size—no natural resources, no water or foodstuffs, no hinterland—plus a multiethnic non-Muslim population surrounded by predominantly Malay-Muslim neighbors with whom it has had a tumultuous postcolonial history (a traumatic separation from Malaysia and military confrontation with Indonesia). This set of factors molded its leaders' strategic assumptions: "the Singapore Armed Forces' development has been driven by a pessimistic outlook of Singapore's PAP [People's Action Party] leadership."[5] The conventional wisdom that an independent urban Singapore was not viable "was exemplified, above all by the island's dependence on Malaysia's state of Johor for drinking water."[6] This "overwhelming reliance on outside sources for such basic needs highlights a major vulnerability—that is, due to some reason or other, those sources might be disrupted."[7]

Dealt with a grim geostrategic hand, the tiny island's first foreign minister, S. Rajaratnam, held out the vision of how Singapore could capitalize on its strategic weaknesses by becoming a global city: bereft of sizable populations or natural resources that other postcolonial states employed in import substitution industrialization strategies, Singapore would instead tap into the international system as a key node coordinating global flows of trade, money, materials, and goods and people. This explains the resources pumped into developing the relevant infrastructure for processing these global flows: Singapore's Changi Airport, global maritime port hub, and financial center. Not only would it overcome its lack of hinterland (the world has effectively become its hinterland), Singapore's hub status in maintaining the smooth functioning of the global economy would encourage external major powers to develop more of a stake in its survival. Being a global city for Singapore not only helps address its economic and developmental needs but also enhances its strategic position in the process. In this sense, economic and strategic developments in Southeast Asia are intertwined; both are seen to have bearing on the tiny city-state's continued prosperity and long-term survival as an independent sovereign country.

Combining this vulnerability with its leaders' beliefs in the nature of international relations, one gets a better sense of Singapore's foreign policy assumptions. Third-generation PM Lee Hsien Loong reiterated in 2011, "we will always be vulnerable, always a small country with an open economy, having to hold our own against larger countries, having to live by our hard work and our wits."[8] Its leaders believe that size matters in an anarchic international system. Singapore is a small state with a population of only five million in 2010 occupying almost the same land area as Chicago. Likening the arena of international relations to a "jungle with animals of different sizes," Foreign Minister K. Shanmugam rehashed this line of thought in 2011: "The smaller you are, the more likely you'll be eaten up. The bigger you are and the fiercer you are, more likely you will survive and the biggest and fiercest are usually the kings."[9] Based on such preconceived assumptions of how international relations is conducted and the central role that vulnerability plays in Singapore's foreign policy formulations, this chapter argues in the following sections that Singapore perceives long-term strategic and economic developments in Southeast Asia in dualistic terms of relentlessly forging new opportunities to enhance its prosperity and security, but at the same time continuously forecasting and averting potential threats to its national interests.

Strategic Issues

As a tiny city-state, Singapore has stressed self-reliance in developing a robust military capability to deter and inflict significant costs on a potential aggressor, if all else fails. From the relatively passive "poisonous shrimp policy," scholars argue this has evolved to the "porcupine strategy" predicated on more active deterrence and buildup capability to survive and outlast potential attackers.[10] However, much of Singapore's foreign and defense policy is designed first and foremost to minimize the chances of the country having to face a potentially larger aggressor alone on unfavorable grounds. Founding PM Lee Kuan Yew mused candidly that "as a small country, we are mindful that we need a balance . . . there should be as many powers with an interest in the region to maintain a balance and to make sure that no one power dominates the region."[11] The passing of Lee in March 2015 and the celebration of Singapore's fifty successful years of independence are likely to only reinforce this tried-and-tested belief in the need for a balance, mindful of Singapore's small size and vulnerability. Rajaratnam, advocate of the global city strategy, argued in a speech at the Asia Society in New York, "Like the sun the great powers will, by their very existence, radiate gravitational power. But if there are many suns, then the smaller planets can, by judicious balancing of pulls and counter-pulls, enjoy a greater freedom of movement."[12] There is no contradiction between this belief in a balance of power and Rajaratnam's global city strategy. As Leifer suggests, "in the interest of a distribution of power that will counter an innate vulnerability, Singapore's government has been quite eclectic about the mixture of means it is prepared to employ."[13] The overarching goal here was to encourage external powers to develop a stake in Singapore's continued survival, "by invoking wider international forces and interests in its support."[14] Singapore made itself increasingly relevant to the smooth functioning of the international economy, whether through its world-leading transshipment maritime port, financial center, or aviation hub at Changi Airport. Indeed, Rajaratnam's "Global City" strategy "was certainly a far more sophisticated exposition of the concept of the balance of power than that associated with eighteenth-century Europe."[15] Speaking in 2011, Deputy Prime Minister Wong Kan Seng presented the stakes in terms of survival, not just economic growth: "For Singapore, becoming a global city is not merely an aspiration. It is a prerequisite for our survival. Being open is the only viable option for us if we wish to be self-reliant and continue to prosper. Closing our doors would only turn us into an island of no consequence, unable to provide for our people. We will become irrelevant to the world. Being open allows us to connect and trade with the rest of the world, and in doing so attract investments and the best talent to Singapore."[16]

The need for Singapore to make itself relevant is crucial to understanding its views of strategic and economic trends: Nowhere is this more apparent than the much-touted U.S. "pivot" or rebalancing to Asia and the rise of China. Singapore has adhered to its tried-and-tested formula of being relevant and friendly with all the major powers in the region. To that end, Singapore's leaders have unabashedly stated their desire for a broader multipolar balance. Although Singapore in April 2013 hosted the first deployment of U.S. Navy littoral combat ships, Lee Kuan Yew has previously categorically stated that "our naval base is used by the Americans and next by the Japanese. And if the Chinese blue water fleet comes, we can also allow them to use the naval base."[17] Given Singapore's long-standing desire to be friendly to all major powers, this "open port" policy fits within that overall strategic paradigm. As Singapore has hosted South Korean, Japanese, Russian, and Indian warships in recent years, there is no practical reason why this policy would not be feasible, in light of the government's broader strategic desire to cultivate all major powers with interests in the region. Whether such an open policy is tenable if conflict appears imminent would likely depend on the circumstances surrounding any escalation and the extent to which Singapore's maritime lines of communication are threatened as a result. However, barring other nations' warships from its ports is not out of the question, as Singapore has recently blacklisted an Indonesian frigate named after two Indonesian marines who bombed a building in Singapore, killing several civilians in the 1960s. It is conceivable that if there is a clearly defined aggressor, then its warships may not call in Singapore, but the government will not make such judgment calls lightly. While the Chinese navy may well be uncomfortable being berthed next to U.S. or Japanese warships, such visits might also provide greater opportunities for military-to-military contacts that the People's Liberation Army Navy (PLAN) has belatedly demonstrated revived interest in. The PLAN conducted recent joint search-and-rescue drills in September 2013 with the U.S. Navy off Hawaii and accepted invitations to join the annual U.S.-led the Rim of the Pacific Exercises (RIMPAC) exercises in 2014. Many of these same navies berthing at Changi (such as the Indian, Japanese, Singaporean, and Korean maritime forces) will also be involved in RIMPAC. In an interview with the *Washington Post* in March 2013 about the rise of China, PM Lee restated Singapore's position that "everybody here would like to benefit from it. . . . At the same time we would like to remain friends with all our other friends, including the US, India, and the EU. We would like to have our cake and eat it and be friends with everybody. . . . We want the US to have constructive and stable relations with China. That makes it easier for us. Then we don't have to choose sides."[18] However, in response to the latest U.S.

moves to strategically "pivot" toward Asia and the deployment of Marines to Darwin, Australia, Singapore's Foreign Minister K. Shanmugam explained categorically Singapore's desire that ASEAN nations not get "caught between the competing interests" of major powers.[19] In February 2012, he warned against anti-China rhetoric in the U.S. election campaign: "We in Singapore understand that some of this is inevitable in an election year. But Americans should not underestimate the extent to which such rhetoric can spark reaction which can create a new and unintended reality for the region. . . . It's quite untenable—quite absurd—to speak in terms of containment of China." There is also a tendency, he added, in the media, to portray politics in "win-lose sporting terms" and the U.S. engagement in Asia "as a means to contain China." "Such rhetoric is a mistake on many levels." PM Lee Hsien Loong outlined Singapore's basic position on the U.S. pivot: "We are in favour of the US taking an active and constructive role in Asia. I'm not sure I would describe it as a pivot. First, it suggests this area has been neglected, which isn't quite so. Second, you really want a long-term implacable, inexorable presence, and I'm not sure if the pivot conveys that nuance." The United States could pivot back to the Mideast because it has so many global issues to address: "Asia is just one of them . . . it may not be on the front burner." The U.S. Seventh Fleet has a "stabilising influence on the security of the region, encouraging countries to exercise restraint with territorial disputes."[20]

The other strategic development for Singapore and its ASEAN partners is managing the dangers of steady escalation in the disputes over the South China Sea. Singapore has consistently made it a point to be neutral on its fellow ASEAN members' claims, and to use ASEAN as platform to manage the situation. Foreign Minister Shanmugam put it this way: "We don't want tension, instead, we want a Code of Conduct to progress the situation. We want a situation where parties resolve the disputes and differences in a way that is acceptable to all."[21]

Key ASEAN members such as Singapore are explicitly identifying themselves as "nonclaimant" states. As PM Lee Hsien Loong explained, "Singapore has taken a clear and consistent position on the South China Sea issue. We are not a claimant country, take no sides in any of the territorial disputes nor can we judge the merits of the various claims. However, Singapore does have certain critical interests at stake."[22] These are related to the city-state's status as a global city heavily dependent on free trade and the security of maritime sea lanes of communication as well as a small state with an interest in seeing disputes managed according to international law, rather than raw power. When tensions rose in 2015 over Chinese land reclamation activities, PM Lee stated that Singapore understood China wanted to assert its rights with its growing power after a long period of humiliation but also reminded Beijing to take a broader perspective because "the South China Sea issue will be seen as one marker of how a powerful China will assert its place in the world."[23] Government policy and public opinion appear concerned especially over Chinese activities because of its apparently large scale with before-and-after photos released to highlight the changes, although other claimants have undertaken similar smaller-scale activities. The fact that China, because of its size and power, could present a fait accompli in the South China Sea is not lost on small states like Singapore long concerned about how might makes right in international relations.

Singapore PM Lee Hsien Loong explained that "ASEAN centrality is key to the regional framework" for security cooperation. Once again, Singapore's size and vulnerability play a big role in how it perceives strategic trends in the region: "As a small Southeast Asian country, ASEAN is critical to Singapore. Singapore's security depends on a peaceful and stable Southeast Asia, which in turn depends on a cohesive ASEAN."[24] This idea of "centrality" however does not necessarily mean ASEAN will deal with the specific merits of delineation and settlement among claimant states. Instead, ASEAN's goal is a more minimalistic one: to set up a framework that would help facilitate claimant states negotiate a peaceful resolution of their competing claims. As Foreign Minister K. Shanmugam explained, "We have always been clear that ASEAN's role— ASEAN as a whole, 10 states' role—is in dealing with a framework and that's a principle that has been accepted because ASEAN came up with the Declaration of Conduct (DOC) and the implementation guidelines."[25] Recent incidents have put more stress on ASEAN. In May 2014, China deployed its largest oil rig into waters claimed by Vietnam, backed by a flotilla of vessels and fighter aircraft. When a Singapore national flag was mistakenly torched during subsequent anti-China protests at Singapore-run industrial parks in Vietnam, the Ministry of Foreign Affairs reacted sharply by condemning it as a "serious incident" and summoned the Vietnamese ambassador. Enjoying relatively good relations with China and other ASEAN claimant states, and with PM Lee labeling incidents in 2014 a "wake-up call," there is some renewed urgency in Singapore's attempts to encourage all parties to negotiate through an ASEAN framework to achieve a favorable outcome. This urgency, coupled with tensions over Chinese land reclamation activities in 2015, caused Foreign Minister Shanmugam to express frustration with the slow progress since the 2002 informal Declaration of Conduct: "We have got to move beyond philosophical discussions to actually say what is in the substance of the agreement."[26]

While China may have been probing ASEAN solidarity by placing its oil rig off Vietnam, the incident and ensuing anti-China riots in Vietnam may actually have enhanced ASEAN cohesion by highlighting dramatically their shared concerns.[27] ASEAN foreign ministers issued a joint statement calling for "restraint" (albeit without singling out China explicitly) and greater progress in negotiations on the Code of Conduct. The incident brought Hanoi and Manila closer together as fellow claimants. Vietnamese Prime Minister Nguyen Tan Dung visited Manila and issued a joint statement expressing concerns and calling on the world to condemn China's actions. This rare show of unity between the claimant states, according to analyst Carl Thayer, is an "admission that ASEAN is not going to go to the mat on this one." Indonesia has started voicing concerns over China's claims, which appear to overlap with Indonesian waters in the Natuna Sea. Singapore, as a small state, will doubtless be concerned at this display of strength by a major power against lesser ones, and the potential for domestic unrest highlighted in the anti-China riots. However, given its stated policy of neutrality and the hardening positions of all claimants, it is hard to see what more Singapore can do, besides expressing its concerns about regional stability more loudly. Perhaps Singapore can cooperate with other nonclaimants such as Thailand to provide venues for negotiations or propose joint development projects. But as long as Beijing continues to see the disputes on a bilateral basis, and other ASEAN countries like Philippines lose patience with the ASEAN route, Singapore's options appear rather limited.

The stakes are high, as PM Lee Hsien Loong highlighted: "The South China Sea is a major issue in the heart of ASEAN's own region. For ASEAN not to address it would severely damage its credibility. ASEAN must not take sides on the various claims, but it has to take and state a position which is neutral, forward-looking, and encourages the peaceful resolution of issues."[28] For ASEAN to somehow remain "neutral" when some members are claimant or "frontline" states engaged in tense maritime standoffs with China is becoming an increasingly difficult circle to square. Differences between claimant and nonclaimant members within ASEAN mean that ASEAN's long-standing method of slow methodical decision making based on consensus, consultation, and proceeding is under severe strain.

The Philippines' insistence (with Vietnamese support) on a reference to China's activities at Scarborough Shoal led to chair Cambodia's opting not to issue a statement at the ASEAN Foreign Ministers' Summit in June 2012 in Phnom Penh rather than accede to Manila's demands. Singaporean Foreign Minister Shanmugam considered the failure "a severe dent in ASEAN's credibility."[29] He pointed that "the lack of a Joint Communiqué reflects disunity within ASEAN. ASEAN unity and centrality are key to the vision of the ASEAN Community. An ASEAN that is not united and cannot agree on a Joint Communiqué will have difficulties in playing a central role in the region."[30] Singapore is concerned that ASEAN unity is possibly being undermined by differences over the South China Sea issue.

As Singapore is a nonclaimant state, its Ministry of Foreign Affairs (MFA) spokesman reacted pithily to Manila taking Beijing to UNCLOS in 2013: "What the Philippines has done is a national decision. Singapore first knew about this action from media reports."[31] There is little evidence here of any ASEAN consensus or prior consultation. Singapore has been at pains to rebut articles in the *Philippine Star* and *Manila Bulletin*, claiming that Singapore supported the Philippines' position in the South China Sea dispute. Singapore's MFA spokesman was caustic in the official response: "We have seen the reports in question. You all know how free the Filipino media is; they can even be very free with the facts. When PM Lee met President Aquino on 8 September 2012, he reiterated Singapore's consistent position, namely that we do not take sides on the merits or otherwise of the various specific disputes in the South China Sea. . . . Unlike the Filipino media reports you refer to, we deal with facts not fiction."[32]

As a small state, Singapore views ASEAN as a collective mechanism whereby it can try to ensure its interests are protected. However, ASEAN leaders continuously stressing ASEAN centrality in turn raises the stakes for the organization, particularly in light of divisions between its members. As PM Lee Hsien Loong noted, "Many countries are watching us closely. They will read how China deals with difficult bilateral problems with its neighbours as a sign of what China's rise means for the world. They will scrutinise ASEAN to see if it can deal with difficult issues effectively. ASEAN and China must not allow this isolated issue to affect their overall positive relationship."[33] Former Secretary-General Surin Pitsuwan summed up the challenge for ASEAN: "Knowing that the region is increasingly being interested and a lot of forces, a lot of players are converging on the region, therefore that principle of neutrality is extremely important. ASEAN must play a balancing act effectively."[34] Besides maintaining an increasingly fraught sense of unity among its members, ASEAN also has to engage a slew of great powers from China, the United States, and Japan on regional security issues. Singaporean leaders have continued to maintain that "only a united ASEAN can credibly play a central role in engaging major powers towards the common goal of promoting regional peace, stability and prosperity."[35] ASEAN's ability to present a united front and viable framework for conflict management over the South China Sea could determine whether regional security is driven by balance-of-power politics as ASEAN claimant states individually seek out powerful backers or regionalized consensual arrangements that help mitigate the vast power asymmetries between China and smaller states. In the hypothetical event of a conflict over the South China Sea issue, Singapore will likely maintain its long-stated stance that it is not a claimant party and not take sides. It will press for solutions to be negotiated through ASEAN diplomatically, preserving the global commons that all states enjoy: the freedom of maritime sea lanes of communications for trade. Here, it is likely to coordinate with other states such as Japan and the United States that share similar interests in maritime security. The espousal of a "global maritime axis" vision by Indonesian President Joko Widodo suggests that his administration will have a strong focus on maritime issues. Singapore has in general welcomed Jokowi's election and the smooth transition of power in its giant neighbor, and there could be opportunities for Singapore to cooperate more closely with Jakarta, particularly as both countries share concerns about freedom of maritime navigation. Singapore's PM Lee has also suggested that the city-state's sizeable maritime industry could assist in upgrading Indonesian maritime infrastructure.

Economic Trends

The previous section highlighted Singapore's position on strategic trends such as the American rebalancing and the dangers of escalating territorial disputes for Southeast Asia, but at the same time Singapore's leaders worry that "there is a de-sync between what is happening in the strategic arena and what is happening in the economic arena. While the US remains an important strategic partner for many ASEAN countries, China is overtaking the US in terms of trade and investment ties."[36] Once again, we see here how Singapore views strategic and economic developments as closely related. Southeast Asia is experiencing drives toward economic integration and free trade through various regional arrangements, a trend likely to only intensify. In 2012, real GDP of ASEAN economies grew by 5.7 percent, compared to sluggish growth rates in the developed world.[37] PM Lee points out that the Trans-Pacific Partnership, involving several ASEAN members such as Singapore, Malaysia, and Brunei, is "an important deal strategically for Asia-Pacific . . . [and] will make significant contributions to economic integration in APEC."[38] The U.S. State Department notes that "nearly 50 percent of world growth will be generated in the Asia-Pacific region, yielding almost one billion new middle class consumers."[39] For PM Lee, "[TPP] is not just a nucleus for promoting free trade in Asia-Pacific and for advancing America's interests, but also a signal that the US continues to believe in and to promote free trade around the world. . . . Promoting trade goes beyond securing markets and economic benefits.

It goes to enhancing your relevance and influence and it will complement and give substance to political and security relationships."[40] Once again, this demonstrates how Singapore views politics, economics, and security in tightly interlocking circles. While much has been said of the supposedly rival Chinese-promoted trade agreement, Regional Comprehensive Economic Partnership (RCEP), from Singapore's point of view both TPP and RCEP are not mutually exclusive as both will help to deepen regional economic integration. Singaporean Trade Minister Lim Hng Kiang stressed that both are envisioned as open and inclusive agreements, not meant to exclude any country.[41] Both are seen as "mutually-reinforcing parallel tracks for regional integration," according to a 2012 Ministry of Trade and Industry fact sheet.[42] This is consistent with Singapore's long-standing position as advocate of free trade and economic opportunities.

Singapore is located in a region that has many economic advantages to tap into. As Lee Hsien Loong observed in 2004, "Over the longer term, Southeast Asia remains a region of promise, with strong fundamentals. It is outward oriented, with a large and young population, strong emphasis on education, a positive work ethic, good infrastructure, and abundant natural resources."[43] Singapore Foreign Minister Shanmugam observed that "ASEAN's combined GDP of almost US$2 trillion is larger than India for example. ASEAN's GDP as a whole has increased four-fold since 1998. ASEAN was the world's 9th largest economy and 5th largest trading entity in 2011 after the EU, US, China and Germany."[44] Singapore is likely to tap onto these economic benefits of a growing ASEAN, but also by serving as a platform for external powers from Turkey to India seeking inroads into the Southeast Asian market. As Shanmugam noted, "We are a natural business centre for Turkish companies looking to expand in Southeast Asia." Singapore is seeking to position itself as not just a hub, but a "connector hub" to facilitate the entry of external players. Singapore has poured resources into developing higher value-added industries such as biotechnology, information technology, and pharmaceuticals. Through the government Agency for Science, Technology and Rsearch (A*Star) and state-of-the-art research facilities concentrated in Biopolis, for example, the country is consolidating its position as a regional hub attracting talents and major players from around the world in biomedical research. This is not forgetting Singapore's long-established economic links with the United States. Singapore is the United States' sixth largest Asian trading partner and largest among the ten ASEAN member states. Total goods and services trade between the United States and Singapore amounted to US$61.0 billion (S$76.7 billion) in 2011.

For many ASEAN countries however, the biggest trade partner is now China. Singapore is the largest recipient of Chinese foreign direct investment in ASEAN, accumulating US$10.9 billion worth of Chinese investment by end of 2011, nearly 50 percent of total Chinese investment in Southeast Asia.[45] ASEAN's trade with India is also booming, garnering about 10 percent of India's total foreign trade. Singaporean leaders, such as then-PM Goh Chok Tong, have recognized that "ASEAN must continue to enhance its external linkages"[46] with non-ASEAN powers. This need for ASEAN to strengthen its external linkages also explains why Singapore has embarked on a strategy to conclude FTAs with ASEAN's key partners. "Our FTAs are not exclusive agreements. They play a pathfinder role. Our FTA with the US, for instance, will help strengthen ASEAN's links with the world's largest economy. We hope that it will evolve into an ASEAN-wide FTA."[47] The country is ever alert to new opportunities that allow it to buttress its position. As part of its survival instincts and to overcome any potential vulnerability to disruption, Lee Hsien Loong has argued that "Singapore wants to strengthen its economic ties with many different centres of prosperity and growth, and not be overly dependent on one or two major trading partners."[48] This can be seen in how Singapore has played its cards with rising giants India and China.

From the establishment of the free trade area between ASEAN and China on January 1, 2010, until the end of 2012, ASEAN exports to China reached 195.8 billion. In March 2013, China signed an agreement with Singapore to double its existing currency swap facility for renminbi, allowing Singapore to position itself as a central player in the increasing use of the currency in Southeast Asia. President Xi Jinping's November 2015 visit to Singapore also brought with it agreements to double Singapore's renminbi quota, allowing fund managers in Singapore to offer more products denominated in Chinese currency. As a regional trading and financial center, Singapore is well placed to take advantage of both ASEAN's and China's growth. As for South Asia's rising giant, India-ASEAN bilateral trade was about US$58 billion in 2010–11, compared to the relatively miniscule US$2 billion two decades earlier and even the US$7 billion ten years ago. The Comprehensive Economic Cooperation Agreement was concluded with Singapore in 2006. Education Minister Heng Swee Keat (a key leader of the new-generation leadership team) has stated that Singapore fully expects to benefit because "ASEAN's geographical co-ordinates have helped it in functioning as an efficient intermediary for facilitating India and South Asia's interface with Northeast Asia and the Asia-Pacific. Southeast Asia, particularly Singapore, has played an enabling role in India's burgeoning trade with China and Australia. Much of the trade traffic between South Asia and the rest of the Asia-Pacific flows through the Straits of Malacca. . . . It is my hope that Singapore can play a catalytic role to further strengthen the linkages between the two regions."[49]

In light of China's and India's economic growth, PM Lee argued that Southeast Asia too faces challenges as well as opportunities: "We see Asia on the move, we understand that we, in Asean, have to band together to remain competitive and attractive to investors. Therefore, we are integrating our economies and we have a programme to establish an Asean Economic Community by 2015."[50] A similar point has been made by Lee Kuan Yew that "to remain at the centre of East Asia's economic and political evolution, ASEAN must integrate more closely and with urgency. Otherwise, it will be marginalized."[51] Singapore is faced with increasing initiatives within ASEAN to move toward greater openness in trade and services, a trend that will likely accelerate over the long term. Singapore's value of intra-ASEAN trade reached US$140.7 billion in 2009, with its ASEAN trade to total trade registering 27.3 percent. Connectivity is high on the region's agenda. The Master Plan on ASEAN Connectivity includes projects such as the Singapore-Kunming Railway, ASEAN Highway Network, and ASEAN Broadband Corridor. ASEAN has also launched an Infrastructure Fund that has been tapped by Indonesia to help upgrade and develop its ports to enhance connectivity with other ASEAN ports. The ASEAN logistics roadmap comprises key areas such as market access including behind-the-borders barriers, trade and customs facilitation, cross-border and multimodal transport, and public-private partnerships.

The Logistics Roadmap will greatly facilitate Singapore in assisting the development of fellow ASEAN countries as well as generate opportunities for Singaporean logistic firms. As ASEAN integrates, there will be questions that need to be addressed relating to supply chain integration, cross-border and multimodal transport, behind-the-border market barriers, trade and customs facilitation. Singapore's state investment arm, Temasek Holdings, has considerable investments in Thailand and joint ventures with Malaysia's Khazanah Nasional Berhad. Temasek is likely to seek long-term investments in this dynamic region, mainly driven by urbanization and demand from its growing middle-class population, and advanced health treatments and pharmaceutical products. Singapore's projects in the region have focused on real estate development, tourism, logistics, planning, and management, and include infrastructure projects and industrial parks. In terms of opportunities, Singaporean capital and firms have invested heavily in the Iskandar Corridor project in neighboring Malaysia as Kuala Lumpur seeks to develop its southern Johor state. This is likely to increase in the long term as lower land and labor costs in Johor are complementary to Singapore's capital skills and services expertise. Singapore's influential Economic Development Board sees the Iskandar project as mutually beneficial for Singapore to take advantage of cheaper labor and other costs in Malaysia, while not losing out on business opportunities altogether. Singapore has much at stake in the ASEAN economic community plans because there are new growth opportunities for a country that is increasingly concerned about rising wages and costs of doing business relative to its neighbors. Mutually complementary projects like Iskandar in Malaysia also provide a safety valve to capture overflow of businesses that might otherwise bypass Singapore's higher cost environment. A win-win situation develops for both states. Likewise, Singapore has invested heavily in the Riau Growth Triangle with Indonesia, to develop nearby islands not only for tourism but also for Singaporean businesses and factories to base their operations there on a lower cost basis. As part of moves toward regional economic integration, a common set of disclosure standards for companies wishing to issue shares or debt securities simultaneously in Singapore, Malaysia, and Thailand also came into force in April 2013, intended to forge closer links between these ASEAN members' capital markets. Other members like Indonesia and Philippines are not yet part of this agreement. Other ASEAN initiatives toward creating a common market include a cross-border equities trading platform, which allows brokers to jump between markets looking for the best opportunities. Singapore, with its financial hub status, is well poised to have first-mover advantage in the eventual opening up of ASEAN capital markets and financial flows.

In terms of potential challenges however, Singapore's relative advantage can erode as other ASEAN countries upgrade their infrastructure. As New Zealand's Ministry of Foreign Trade observed about Singapore, "increased regional competition, an aging population, and the need to upgrade and restructure its manufacturing sector are the three key challenges facing the Singapore economy. . . . Singapore's fiscal policy is designed to ensure that the economy continues to move up the value-added chain."[52] The need to constantly reassess and revamp its economic structure is not lost on the Singapore Economic Development Board (EDB), even as it attempts to grasp new opportunities in the ASEAN Connectivity Roadmap. This is reflected in the high-level Economic Review Committees that have been periodically established to fundamentally consider the state of the Singapore economy and future prospects. Singapore's airport and maritime hubs—which allow Singapore to achieve global city status and thus enhance its economic survival prospects—have been challenged in recent years. For instance, Bangkok and Kuala Lumpur have been positioning their air gateways as alternative hubs by building new terminals and runways and increasing capacity. Singapore's self-consciousness about its neighbors' challenges is reflected in PM Lee's August 2013 announcement that a new Terminal 5 will soon be built, in order to keep up with upgrades to regional airports.[53] Malaysia's Tanjong Pelepas Port Terminal in southern Johor state has also been credited with diverting some maritime traffic and shipping firms (in 2002 Evergreen Marine Corporation shifted its operations from Singapore to Tanjong Pelepas) that would otherwise have come through Singapore. Indonesia has also unveiled plans to develop several new ports, especially one on Batam Island, close to Singapore. These developments are on top of on-and-off rumblings that Thailand might cut through the Kra Isthmus, negating the need for maritime traffic to pass through Singapore waters. As other countries in the region move up the value chain as they develop their economies from manufacturing cheap textiles to electronics, Singapore has to continually adjust and upgrade its economy in order to keep finding its niche in an increasingly competitive economic climate. This explains why Singapore has heavily invested in its biomedical and pharmaceutical clusters in recent years. Singapore also sees the ability of ASEAN to achieve its long-term goals of integration and connectivity as a crucial test of the organization's future and collective political will. As PM Lee put it, "We must make sure that this project succeeds, both for its own merits and because it is the test of the credibility of ASEAN. The global business community is watching carefully to see if ASEAN can deliver on this key project."[54]

Besides confronting strategic dangers of being caught in between India, China, and the United States, dealing with these major global actors also carries with it potentially rich economic gains if the relationship and power transition are managed wisely and properly. It is this intricate and delicate relationship between strategy and economics that will characterize Southeast Asia for many years to come. Singapore has maneuvered itself into an position as a connector between its region and these major players. It has extensive economic ties, and in some cases free trade agreements, with these external economic actors and seeks to leverage these not just to build greater economic linkages on a bilateral basis, but also to transition these economic linkages into a regional footing as well. In the midst of attempts to manage the South China Sea disputes, ASEAN also has to somehow find sufficient political will and resources to push forward its long-stalled economic integration program with the ASEAN Economic Community launched on December 31, 2015. Once again, the characteristic Singaporean approach of perceiving both opportunities and threats is apparent. As its ASEAN neighbors ramp up their efforts to build region-wide connectivity and economic development, Singapore can reap significant economic gain not only from increasing levels of trade that better infrastructure and connectivity throughout the region bring about but also from finding more opportunities for investment in transport, logistics, and related sectors in developing ASEAN neighbors' infrastructure where Singapore firms have distinct advantages. At the same time, Singapore's planners have already started worrying about the long-term challenges that could possibly arise if the region's infrastructure and connectivity eroded Singapore's long-standing advantages in infrastructure, such as airports, roads, maritime ports, and financial expertise. The search is on once again for new niche areas where Singapore can find new opportunities.

Conclusion

Singapore's perceptions of international developments in its neighborhood, whether economic or strategic in nature, can be summed up by the following wry observation by founding PM Lee Kuan Yew in 2009: "Small countries have little influence on international trends. Singapore has always taken the world as it is. We analyse the world clinically, take advantage of opportunities that come our way or get out of harm's way."[55] Such foreign policy assumptions stem from Singapore's deep-seated and acutely felt sense of vulnerability as a small state and its leaders' assumptions about an international system that remains one of self-help and anarchy. Economic and security trends within the region are intertwined to the extent that they have the potential to impinge on Singapore's survival prospects. Singaporean leaders have always desired to have as many partners as possible, whether in economics or security, to minimize the chances of it being overdependent on one major power. To maximize opportunities and minimize threats, Singapore's leaders have honed the art of being relevant to the world: "We must make ourselves relevant so that other countries have an interest in our continued survival and prosperity as a sovereign and independent nation. Singapore cannot take its relevance for granted. Singapore has to continually reconstruct itself and keep its relevance to the world and to create political and economic space."[56] This constant desire to retain its "competitive edge" has led to a relentless desire to constantly innovate and restructure in ways that are relevant to the changing international system. Given its location in Southeast Asia, "a recurrent issue for Singapore is how to differentiate ourselves from our neighbours in order to compete and survive, and also get along with them. This is a perennial foreign policy challenge."[57] There is also a strategic element involved in such neighborly competition, as Lee Kuan Yew once argued: "we have not got neighbours who want to help us prosper."[58]

A triangular relationship is emerging between ASEAN, China, and the United States. Southeast Asia is experiencing potentially game-changing power shifts as Chinese military modernization challenges decades-old

American military dominance and Cold War alliance structures, coupled with destabilizing territorial disputes in the strategic sphere. Simultaneously, there are rich economic pickings from major powers like India and China and ASEAN's own focus on connectivity and growth. Singapore is inhabiting what will perhaps be the world's most exciting region in the years to come. The real challenge of China's rise for Singapore is how to peacefully enmesh a rising power into a regional security environment that has long been dominated by the United States, all within an ASEAN framework that has struggled for coherence and unity. The December 2015 deployment of an American Poseidon P-8 surveillance plane in Singapore can be read not as a significant shift in policy, but rather as a continuation and logical extension of long-standing attempts to facilitate U.S. military deployments in the region. The rotational deployments of U.S. Navy littoral combat ships and now the P-8 should be viewed in the same context. Indeed, Singapore has sought to play down the deployment, noting that the plane has also flown from other ASEAN countries such as Malaysia and the Philippines. China's relatively restrained response to the P-8 suggests that Singapore had informed Beijing in advance and that China appears to understand Singapore's long-standing dependence on Washington for security needs.[59] With strong commercial and economic ties to China, Singaporean leaders are highly sensitive to how China's growing economic clout is a two-edged sword: it confers opportunities but could also erode strategic pillars and security relationships in the region as major powers such as the United States and Japan are, rightly or wrongly, perceived to be fading. This is especially true when China has displaced the United States as the most important trade partner for erstwhile U.S. security allies like Japan and Australia. Singapore assumed the position of coordinator for ASEAN-China dialogue in August 2015. Above all, maintaining a peaceful and stable multipolar balance of power in this triangular relationship that enhances the survival and prosperity of small states remains the guiding lodestar of Singapore's foreign policy. When asked in July 2015 if he was feeling pressure from Beijing about being too "pro-U.S.," PM Lee sounded an optimistic note: "I think they understand the reason why we take the stand we do, and as a small country, we have to have our own independent stand, otherwise nobody will take us seriously, and in the case of strategic balance in the region, that we think that Americans make a constructive contribution and are an important player and still are."[60] Staying nimble enough to take advantage of opportunities while staying out of harm's way sounds straightforward enough, but operationalizing this in practice will challenge Singaporean leaders for years to come.

NOTES

1 Michael Leifer, *Singapore's Foreign Policy: Coping with Vulnerability* (London: Routledge, 2000), 9.

2 Mark Hong, "Singapore's Security Concerns Post-9/11," *RUSI Journal* 148, no. 1 (2003): 53.

3 Han Fook Kwang et al., *Lee Kuan Yew: Hard Truths to Keep Singapore Going* (Singapore: Straits Times Press, 2011), 9–10.

4 Kris Olds and Henry Yeung, "Pathways to Global City Formation," *Review of International Political Economy* 11, no. 3 (2004): 491.

5 Tim Huxley, *Defending the Lion City* (London: Allen & Unwin, 2001), 248.

6 Leifer, *Singapore's Foreign Policy*, 4.

7 Derek de Cunha, "Defence and Security: Evolving Threat Perceptions," in *Singapore in the New Millennium: Challenges Facing the City-State*, ed. Derek De Cunha (Singapore: ISEAS, 2002), 135.

8 Speech at People's Action Party Youth Wing 25th Anniversary Rally, April 17, 2011.

9 Cited in Tanya Fong, "Top Litigator, Now Top Diplomat," *Today*, May 21, 2011, www.todayonline.com.

10 See Ng Pak Shun, "From Poisonous Shrimp to Porcupine: An Analysis of Singapore's Defence Posture Change in the Early 1990s" (ANU Working Paper no. 397, Canberra, 2005), http://ips.cap.anu.edu.au.

11 Cited in Kwan Weng Kin, "Better to Have a Broader Balance of Power in Asia," *Straits Times*, May 21, 2010.

12 Cited in S. R. Nathan, speech at the Diplomatic Academy's Inaugural S. Rajaratnam Lecture, March 10, 2008, Singapore.

13 Leifer, *Singapore's Foreign Policy*, 26.

14 Ibid., 39.

15 Ibid., 36.

16 Keynote address by Mr. Wong Kan Seng, Coordinating Minister for National Security, Singapore Perspectives 2011 Conference, January 17, 2011, Singapore.

17 Cited in Kwan Weng Kin, "Better to Have a Broader Balance of Power in Asia."

18 Interview in *Washington Post*, March 17, 2013.

19 Cited in Anwar Faruqi, "Southeast Asia Caught between US and China," *Jakarta Globe*, November 17, 2011, www.thejakartaglobe.com.

20 Interview in *Washington Post*, March 17, 2013.

21 Cited in "Shanmugam, Kerry Reaffirm Bilateral Ties," *Asiaone*, May 16, 2014, http://news.asiaone.com.

22 Speech at Central Party School, China, www.pmo.gov.sg.

23 "China Wants Good Ties with Neighbours: PM Lee," *Channel News Asia*, July 23, 2015, www.channelnewsasia.com.

24 Speech at the Central Party School, China, September 6, 2012.

25 "Singapore Explains ASEAN's Role over South China Sea Dispute," *Channel News Asia*, September 15, 2012, www.channelnewsasia.com.

26 "Southeast Asian Nations Back Halt to Land Reclamation in South China Sea," *Today*, August 4, 2015, www.todayonline.com.

27 "China's 'Aggressiveness' Is Drawing ASEAN Together," *Deutsche Welle*, May 13, 2014, www.dw.de.

28 Speech at Central Party School, China, www.pmo.gov.sg.

29 Cited in "Severe Dent on ASEAN's Credibility," *Today*, July 14, 2012.

30 Singapore Minister of Foreign Affairs K. Shanmugam, Reply to Parliamentary Questions, August 13, 2012.

31 "MFA Spokesman's Comments in Response to Media Queries on the Philippines' Initiation of Arbitration Proceedings Against China under Article 287 and Annex VII of the 1982 United Nations Convention on the Law of the Sea (UNCLOS)," Singapore Ministry of Foreign Affairs, January 23, 2013, www.mfa.gov.sg.

32 "MFA Spokesman's Comments in Response to Media Queries on the South China Sea," Singapore Ministry of Foreign Affairs, September 10, 2012, www.mfa.gov.sg.

33 Speech at the Central Party School, China, www.pmo.gov.sg.

34 Cited in "ASEAN Seeks Early Talks with China on South China Sea Code," *Kyodo News*, November 19, 2012, http://english.kyodonews.jp.

35 Shanmugam, Reply to Parliamentary Questions.

36 Luncheon speech by Deputy Prime Minister and Minister for Defence Teo Chee Hean, Centre for Strategic and International Studies, Washington, DC, March 17, 2010.

37 ASEAN Secretariat, "ASEAN GDP Remains Robust" (October 21, 2013), www.asean.org.

38 PM Lee, interview in *Washington Post*, March 17, 2013.

39 U.S. State Department, "Factsheet on Trans-Pacific Partnership: Building on US Economic and Strategic Partnerships in the Asia-Pacific," September 5, 2013, www.state.gov.

40 Address to Chicago Council on Global Affairs, April 15, 2010.

41 "TPP and RCEP Are Meant to Deepen Economic Integration: Lim Hng Kiang," *Channel News Asia*, February 21, 2014, www.channelnewsasia.com.

42 Ministry of Trade and Industry, "What Is the Regional Comprehensive Economic Partnership?" (2012),www.fta.gov.sg.

43 Keynote address by Deputy PM Lee Hsien Loong at the Standard Chartered Bank's Singapore Conference, Mumbai, India, January 16, 2004.

44 Speech at the Annual Turkish Ambassadors' Conference, Ankara, Turkey, January 4, 2013.

45 Zhao Hong, "China's FDI into Southeast Asia," *ISEAS Perspectives*, January 31, 2013, 2.

46 Keynote address by PM Goh Chok Tong at the WEF East Asia Economic Summit, Kuala Lumpur, October 8, 2002.

47 Ibid.

48 Deputy PM Lee Hsien Loong keynote address.

49 Keynote address on "South and South-east Asia Engagements" by Education Minister Heng Swee Keat, Singapore, November 24, 2011.

50 Speech at Central Party School, China, September 6, 2012.

51 Lee Kuan Yew, speech at the US-ASEAN Business Council's 25th Anniversary Gala Dinner, Washington, DC, October 27, 2009.

52 New Zealand Ministry of Foreign Trade, "Singapore Economic Situation" (December 4, 2008), http://asean.fta.govt.nz.

53 Lee Hsien Loong, National Day Rally Speech, August 18, 2013.

54 Cited in "Members Urged to Press On with Integration," *Straits Times*, April 4, 2012.

55 Lee Kuan Yew, Minister Mentor, Speech at the US-ASEAN Business Council's 25th Anniversary Gala Dinner, Washington, DC, October 27, 2009.

56 Lee Kuan Yew, speech at the US-ASEAN Business Council's 25th Anniversary Gala Dinner, Washington, DC, October 27, 2009.

57 Ibid.

58 Han et al., *Lee Kuan Yew*, 25.

59 "China Gives Restrained Response to Singapore," *Straits Times*, December 9, 2015, www.straitstimes.com.

60 "China Wants Good Ties with Neighbours: PM Lee," *Channel News Asia*, July 23, 2015, www.channelnewsasia.com.

6

Tightrope Walking over the Sea of Trouble

Vietnam's Foreign Policy, Maritime Strategy, and Relations with China and the United States

TRAN TRUONG THUY

Vietnam's Foreign Policy Objectives

The priority of the Vietnam Communist Party (VCP) in foreign relations is protecting its national interests with three main objectives: development, security, and promoting the country's position in the international arena.

The goal of development was given highest priority after Doi Moi ("renovation") in 1986, and no signs of any reorientation of this objective have appeared. VCP considers economic development as the most important source to enhance not only national security but also regime legitimacy. It believes that economic underdevelopment will breed political instability and undermine its rule. On the contrary, economic development and improved living conditions will ward off other threats to the regime, especially that of "peaceful evolution" (codification of unintended democratization initiated by dissidents and/or sponsored by the West).[1]

The objectives of national security, safeguarding sovereignty, and territorial integrity are always foremost for any ruling party, particularly for VCP, which rose to and has maintained power by achieving these objectives. However, the party sees these goals of development and security (also internationally) not separately but in a dialectical way. Success in its economic development strategy will not only strengthen credibility and legitimacy of the regime, but also increase comprehensive national power, which, in turn, can help improve the country's capability in protecting national sovereignty and security and promoting the international prestige of the country. In 1998, the VCP Politburo adopted a resolution identifying the necessary conditions for protecting national security: "a strong economy, just-enough national defense capability, and expanded international relations."[2]

To achieve the development objective, Hanoi believes that a peaceful and favorable international environment is the necessary condition. Since 1988 VCP has stressed that "to preserve peace and to develop the economy are the most important strategic objectives and interests of the whole party and people in Vietnam."[3] One of the main objectives of foreign policy is to "create a favorable international environment and conducive conditions to serve the cause of national construction and defense."[4] That sort of priority partly explains why Vietnam has adopted a policy to settle all disputes, notably maritime and territorial disputes, with its neighbors exclusively by peaceful means, regardless of if these disputes are generally regarded as issues of protecting national sovereignty and security. This call is not simply rhetorical but is rooted in strategic calculations of maintaining a peaceful environment for economic development.

To achieve these objectives, Vietnam adopted the policy of "diversification and multi-directionalization of foreign relations" with "more friends, fewer enemies"[5] and sought to "become a friend to all countries in the world community."[6] By creating a favorable international environment and applying the policy of cordial relations with all countries, Hanoi's aim was to concentrate on economic development and take advantage of foreign resources, such as technology, markets, capital, and experience, to promote economic reforms. By diversifying and multi-directionalizing foreign relationships, Hanoi also sought an intertwining of interests of all major powers in the country and therefore avoid overdependence on any particular power, thus preserving independence of action. The best way to preserving its independence in peacetime and to maximize its strategic room to maneuver is not to ally with any country. Since the end of Cold War, Vietnam has adopted a policy of three noes: no foreign bases in Vietnam's territory, no military alliances, no alignment with any country against another countries.

To provide the policy rationale for cooperation with all countries, in mid-2003 the VCP Central Committee's eighth plenum provided important concepts: "partners of cooperation" (đối tác) and "objects of struggle" (đối tượng) in foreign relations. According to the eighth plenum's resolution, "with the objects of struggle, we can find areas for cooperation; with the partners, there exist interests that are contradictory and different from those of ours." In other words, international relations generally contain both elements. The Vietnamese leadership was of the conviction that their foreign relations with other countries (especially China and the United States) contained both areas of cooperation where their national interests converged and areas of struggle where their national interests conflicted.

In the implementation of this foreign policy, Vietnam sought to develop and expand relations with all countries, particularly neighboring countries, major powers, and traditional friends; join important regional and global intergovernmental organizations; expand trade relations; and attract foreign direct investment (FDI) and official development assistance. As a result, Vietnam

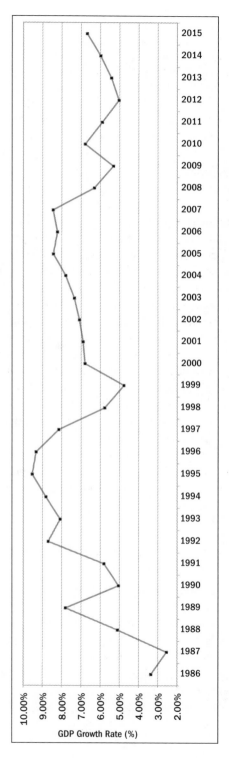

Figure 6.1. Vietnam's GDP growth rate from 1986 to 2015. Source: General Statistics Office of Vietnam, Ministry of Planning and Investment.

expanded overall relations with all neighboring countries in Southeast Asia, joined ASEAN, restored and developed relationships with all major powers, particularly China and the United States, and gained membership in various international organizations such as the World Trade Organization (WTO), Asia-Pacific Economic Cooperation (APEC), and Asia-Europe Meeting (ASEM). Before recent economic difficulties due to the global economic downturn, Vietnam was one of the fastest growing economies in Asia, with annual GDP growth around 7 to 8 percent.

With the success of its open-door policy, Vietnam has increasingly integrated into the world economy and gradually moved toward an export-led economy. One of the consequences of this process is that a peaceful and stable external environment has become more important than ever before. The top priority of foreign policy objectives, identified in the Eleventh and Twelfth National Party Congresses, in 2011 and 2016, respectively, remains "maintaining the peaceful environment and creating a favorable international environment conducive to national construction and defense, thus enhancing the position and prestige of the country in the international arena."[7]

Taking into account all the positive achievements of twenty-five years of reforms, the Eleventh VCP Congress stressed that Vietnam would continue the current foreign policy of multilateralization and diversification of international relations, proactively integrating with the rest of the world and being a friend, reliable partner, and responsible member of the international community.[8] The Twelfth VCP Congress reaffirmed "the foreign policy of independence, self-reliance, diversification and multidirectionalization of relations, proactive international integration; maintaining the peaceful and stable environment and creating a favorable international environment conducive to national construction and defense; promoting Vietnam's position and prestige in the region and in the world."[9]

Vietnam's Relations with China and the United States and the Role of ASEAN

For Vietnamese policy makers, the most challenging task in foreign policy has been maintaining sovereignty and political autonomy while keeping stable, peaceful, and beneficial relationships with its powerful neighbor, China. Although Vietnam has lived beside China for more than a thousand years, almost exclusively at peace, China's rise has created a renewed challenge for Vietnam. Hanoi wants to avoid repeating the history of falling within the sphere of Chinese influence. At the same time, Hanoi does not desire hostility with China. Memories of the brief and costly war in 1979, followed by more than a decade of hostile relations with China and international isolation, not least due to China's intentional policy of isolating Vietnam, are still vivid and offer valuable lessons for policy makers in Vietnam. Therefore, in its relations with China, Vietnam pursues a policy of both cooperation and struggle while maintaining a peaceful relationship.

Specifically, while cooperating with China on many issues where both countries have convergent interests—such as noninterference, democracy, economic cooperation, and instituting reforms while maintaining the Communist Party power monopoly—Vietnam has had to struggle with its northern neighbor on many issues. In addition to the territorial disputes in the South China Sea, which will be further analyzed in the next section, the Chinese construction of hydroelectric dams on the upper Mekong River,[10] competition for influence in Laos and Cambodia, increasing Vietnamese dependence on China as the principal supplier for its export-oriented economy, a widening trade deficit,[11] growing asymmetry of power—both hard power as well as the fear of being Finlandized—constitute the major concerns of Vietnamese policy makers. So while continuing to attach great importance to its relationship with China, Vietnam has great interest in deepening strategic relations with other major powers and ASEAN members. This move is also consistent with its overall policy of multi-directionalization and diversification of international relations in order to strengthen its independence and security.

In relation to this policy, Vietnam sees ASEAN as having increasing value in providing a platform to advance its interests despite the association's structural weaknesses associated with consensus principles and divergent interests and positions of other members on critical issues such as the South China Sea dispute. Hanoi understands ASEAN's role and its difficulties in the region. The resolution adopted at the Eleventh Party National Congress in 2011 acknowledges that "ASEAN will continue to speed up regional connectivity and build a community with a more important role in the region, however, many difficulties and challenges lie ahead for the bloc."[12] For Hanoi, enhancing Vietnam's role as a member within ASEAN not only consolidates the "sense of belonging to a community" and provides it with a huge market of more than six hundred million people and important sources of foreign investment, but also serves as a useful platform from which to conduct multilateral and bilateral diplomacy, thus boosting the country's international profile. Through various ASEAN internal mechanisms and related forums, Vietnam also expects to collectively engage China in multilateral discussions and negotiations to manage and settle the unresolved issues, particularly the maritime issues in the South China Sea, and to deal with ASEAN as a group, not with ASEAN individual members. The establishment of the ASEAN Community at the end of 2015 should strengthen solidarity among members.

The United States is considered to be one of the most important partners of Vietnam. The economic reforms during Doi Moi have integrated the country into the global economy and transformed Vietnam into an export-oriented economy. The United States became one of the leading sources of FDI in Vietnam, mainly from high-tech corporations, as well as Vietnam's largest export market. Two-way trade increased dramatically to reach almost US$45 billion in 2015 from US$1.5 billion in 2001, when both sides signed a bilateral trade agreement. It is worth noting that the trade surplus Vietnam enjoys in relation to the United States almost compensates for its trade deficit with China (almost US$30 billion in 2015).[13] Vietnam and the United States are participants in the Trans-Pacific Partnership (TPP), which is expected to diversify Vietnam's external economic relations with developed members in Asia-Pacific, helping Vietnam to depend less on China economically. TPP is also expected to boost two-way trade and investment from the United States, thus deepening not only bilateral and U.S.-led multilateral economic integration but also strategic congruence between Hanoi and Washington.[14] Strategically, both countries have shared interests in maintaining the current regional order, including China's peaceful rise and ASEAN's central role in the security architecture. On the South China Sea issues, Hanoi and Washington also have convergent interests, including peaceful settlement of disputes according to international law, particularly the UNCLOS 1982, freedom of navigation by sea and air, and unimpeded lawful commercial activities.

As a result of the gradual improvement of the nations' relationship, during President Truong Tan Sang's visit to the United States in July 2013, the countries announced the establishment of a comprehensive partnership, paving the way for more cooperation, ranging from political, security, diplomatic, and economic to science, technology, education, and environmental fields.[15]

However, the improvement to the U.S.-Vietnam relationship also has its limits. On the one hand, a significant segment of VCP is concerned that the United States maintains intentions to promote democratic changes and/or offer support to human-rights activists, who could undermine the VCP leadership. They worry that moving politically closer to the United States might endanger regime security through "peaceful evolution." However, more and more Vietnamese policy makers and experts believe that closer cooperation with the United States will reduce Washington's pressure related to human rights, democracy, and religious freedom. In fact, a number of visits to the

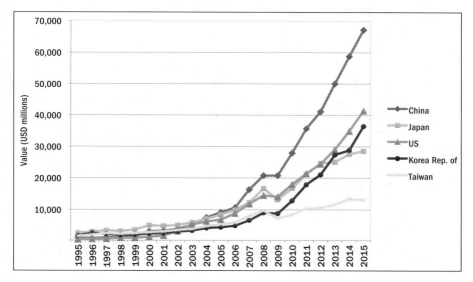

Figure 6.2. Import-export turnover of the five largest trading partners (1995–2015). Sources: WTO; General Statistics Office of Vietnam, Ministry of Planning and Investment.

United States in 2014–15 by Politburo members (Pham Quang Nghi, Head of the Party Committee of Hanoi City; Tran Dai Quang, Minister of Public Security; and Nguyen Sinh Hung, Chairman of the National Assembly) and especially the "historic" visit by VCP's General Secretary Nguyen Phu Trong in July 2015 indicated the growing consensus among VCP's leadership regarding the importance of Vietnam's relationship with the United States and, more critical, of the U.S. acknowledgment of VCP's rule in Vietnam, which helps strengthen the party's legitimacy and weaken the "hostile forces" pursuing "peaceful evolution."

On the other hand, while acknowledging that the United States is still the predominant superpower in the world, Vietnam analysts see the future as increasingly uncertain if China maintains its steady rise and the balance of power changes in favor of China. Officially, VCP forecasts that "the multipolar world is taking shape more clearly."[16] Therefore, Vietnam is also concerned over the perceived relative U.S. decline and the durability of U.S. commitments to a rebalancing strategy to Asia-Pacific, and, not without consequences, the possibility that the United States will cooperate with China and compromise on Vietnam's national interests. As mentioned previously, lessons from recent history seemingly prove to the Vietnamese that even treaty allies can abandon their commitments if their national interests are endangered, as clearly demonstrated in the case of the United States in relation to South Vietnam in 1974 when Beijing attacked Saigon's troops in the Paracel Islands. Consider also Moscow's stance toward Hanoi during the brief war between China and Vietnam in 1979 and military confrontation in 1988 in the Spratly Islands. Moreover, Hanoi views the relationships between the United States and China as containing elements of both "cooperation and struggle." While both are strategic competitors, Washington still needs to work with Beijing on issues of convergent interests: from the conflicts on the Korean Peninsula and in the Middle East to economic cooperation and climate change. Therefore, some fear that in certain circumstances Washington may trade Beijing's cooperation on issues of convergent interests in exchange for softening the U.S. position toward issues critical to China such as South China Sea sovereignty.

In the opposite scenario, Vietnam does not want to be forced to "take a side" and seeks to avoid being dragged into a deepening U.S.-China strategic rivalry, thus jeopardizing its independence and narrowing the room for strategic maneuvers. Within the limits of the three noes policy—no military alliances, no alignment with one country against another, no foreign military bases—Vietnam is careful not to allow developments in its relations with the United States to provoke China and inadvertently deteriorate their bilateral relationship.[17] In short, Vietnamese policy makers' thinking is heavily influenced by their traditional proverb—"distant water can't put out a nearby fire." Therefore, Vietnam will continue to develop a relationship with the United States to the extent that it will not undermine the regime's legitimacy or put Vietnam into a new confrontation with China. Hanoi's objective is to have the United States as balancer and, at the same time, not to antagonize China. Unless China pursues comprehensive aggression toward Vietnam, Hanoi will definitely not become Washington's ally. In this context, the dispute in the South China Sea and China's strategy toward Vietnam will determine Vietnam's balance between China and the United States.

A Test Case: The South China Sea Issues and Vietnam's Policy

The South China Sea Issues

The South China Sea issues continue to be the most important security challenge for Vietnam. In Hanoi's view, the South China Sea relates to almost all aspects of national security and development: protecting territorial integrity and national sovereignty; promoting maritime economic development;

maintaining a peaceful environment, especially peaceful relationships with China and other claimants; and safeguarding the regime's legitimacy and stability.[18] There are at least four issues that Vietnam has to tackle in the South China Sea disputes: (1) sovereignty over "land features" in the Spratlys; (2) sovereignty over "land features" in the Paracels; (3) sovereignty rights and jurisdiction within Vietnam's exclusive economic zone and continental shelf, including management and utilization of hydrocarbon and mineral resources and fisheries; and (4) China's arrest of Vietnamese fishermen and confiscation of their vessels in the Paracels.[19]

Although Vietnam has claims in the South China Sea that overlap with those of five other nations (China, Taiwan, Malaysia, Brunei, and the Philippines), ASEAN claimants have implicitly reached a common understanding in maintaining the status quo of occupation, settling disputes by peaceful means, and refraining from activities that can negatively affect the interests of other members.[20] Taiwan's activities have mainly concentrated on its occupied island Itu-Aba, the largest feature of the Spratlys, and therefore do not directly threaten Vietnam. China's excessive claims and growing assertiveness in the South China Sea, on the other hand, have stirred up nerves and made it harder for Vietnam to protect its legitimate interests.

China's renewed assertiveness in the South China Sea since 2007 has raised the occurrence of incidents in the overlapping area between the "U-shaped line," covering about 80 percent of the waters in the South China Sea, and Vietnam's exclusive economic zone and continental shelf. China has significantly increased its presence in the South China Sea with a comprehensive approach, expanding not only military but also paramilitary and civilian activities in the area, in order to achieve de facto control of the area.

Legally and administratively, China has initiated a number of steps to extend its claims to land features and maritime zones in the South China Sea. For example, in second half of 2012, the Chinese government issued new electronic passports depicting a map of the U-shaped line in the South China Sea. In November 2012 the Hainan provincial government announced new regulations allowing law enforcement officials to board, inspect, detain, expel, and confiscate foreign ships conducting "illegal" activities within "Chinese waters." On November 19, 2013, Hainan's authority issued new regulations on fishing in the South China Sea that require all foreign vessels to obtain advance approval from the "relevant and responsible department."[21] Foreign ships that do not comply will either be forced out of the area or subject to a fine of up to US$83,000.[22] Though Hainan officials and China's Ministry of Foreign Affairs spokesperson in both cases assured the international community that this rule applies only within twelve nautical miles of Hainan's coast and the Paracels,[23] the language of the regulation regarding Chinese "jurisdictional waters" and "Sansha city" is relatively ambiguous and can be exploited by Chinese law enforcement agencies to expand enforcement activities to all waters within the controversial U-shaped line. The area claimed by the Hainan government amounts to two million square kilometers, around 80 percent of the South China Sea.[24] ASEAN countries also worry that China, after establishing its Air Defense Identification Zone (ADIZ) encompassing the contested islands and maritime areas in the East China Sea, will announce a new ADIZ in the South China Sea, further escalating the disputes.[25] China's Defense Ministry spokesperson publicly said that it will "establish other air defense identification zones at an appropriate time after completing preparations."[26]

China's approach in the area has been "creeping expansion but non-confrontational dispute," with increasing presence and civilian and paramilitary forces in areas within the U-shaped line. Although the Chinese Navy has refrained from direct engagement with other claimants, it has sent deterrent messages by continuing to show force during standoffs and has conducted occasional military exercises. China's "Charm Offensive" is also arguably framed within its "divide-and-rule" strategy by offering economic incentives to ASEAN countries, especially to nonclaimants, and actively applying diplomatic pressure to prevent ASEAN from forming a common position on the South China Sea.

Resource exploitation (related to both hydrocarbons and seafood) in the South China Sea has become the most frequent source of tension between China and other claimants. China has accused other claimants of extracting "China's oil" and catching "China's fish," even while China has not obtained a single drop of oil from the Spratlys and Chinese fisherman are being captured and driven away.[27] Other claimants have been conducting resource development within the limits of their internationally recognized continental shelf, not the disputed Paracel and Spratly Islands. On the other hand, China has tried to prevent other claimants from the development of resources in overlapping areas between China's U-shaped line and others' exclusive economic zones (EEZs). This trend has become one of the main sources of tension in the South China Sea.

During the period of its unilaterally declared fishing ban between May and August (imposed annually since 1999), Chinese maritime security forces have repeatedly detained Vietnamese fishermen, confiscated fishing boats and charging fines for their release. This kind of incident has become more frequently in the Paracel Islands as Vietnamese fishermen continue catching fish in their "traditional fishing ground."

With regard to oil and gas exploitation, China has accused Vietnam of extracting "China's oil" and has tried to prevent Vietnam from developing resources in the overlapping areas between China's U-shaped line and Vietnam's continental shelf. Significantly, China's protests have incrementally escalated over time. From 2007 to 2010, China limited its protests to sending diplomatic notes directly to the Vietnamese government, issuing statements via its Ministry of Foreign Affairs, and verbally demanding that foreign oil and gas companies cease joint offshore exploration operations with Vietnam.[28] From 2011 to 2013, China escalated its protests by adopting the more aggressive tactics of using law enforcement vessels (from the Maritime Surveillance Agency) and/or fishing boats to harass vessels operating within Vietnam's EEZ and even cutting their seismic cables.[29]

On May 1, 2014, in a move widely considered as changing China's South China Sea approach to more "proactive assertive," for the first time the Chinese state oil company CNOOC stationed the huge oil rig HYSY981 (with construction costs approximately US$1 billion) for deep-sea drilling in the area just 120 nautical miles off the coast of Vietnam. The location is claimed by Vietnam as within its own EEZ and internationally is considered disputed. China also deployed more than one hundred ships, including law enforcement and military vessels, along with aircraft, to defend the rig. Tension intensified when Chinese vessels rammed, fired water cannons at, and chased away Vietnamese law enforcement vessels and fishing boats operating nearby.[30] This skirmish led to more than three months of diplomatic crisis and deteriorated the China-Vietnam bilateral relationship to its lowest level since normalization.

Other developments related to the oil rig crisis have ushered in a new dimension in the Vietnamese leadership's thinking regarding maritime issues and their implications for economic development. The oil rig incident not only inflamed anti-China sentiment among Vietnamese but also provoked large-scale anti-China riots in various Vietnamese cities. On May 13 and 14, unsanctioned anti-China protests in Vietnam escalated into riots, causing damage to a number of companies owed by foreign investors from mainland China and other Chinese-speaking territories and elsewhere (due to protesters' confusion over the companies' origins). The possibility of the sea-based skirmish between Chinese and Vietnamese vessels escalating into full-scale conflict deteriorated the business environment in Vietnam, which had been considered one of the safest and most stable in the region. The crisis also damaged Vietnamese tourism industry and the stock market. On May 8, 2014, Vietnam's benchmark stock index plunged 5.91 percent, its biggest drop since 2001.[31] A small-scale survey of 18 of Vietnam's 640 hotels showed that they

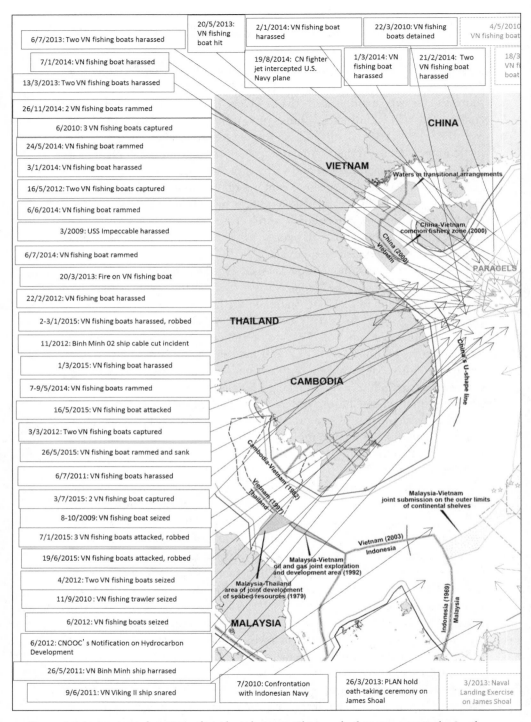

6/7/2013: Two VN fishing boats harassed

7/1/2014: VN fishing boat harassed

13/3/2013: Two VN fishing boats harassed

26/11/2014: 2 VN fishing boats rammed

6/2010: 3 VN fishing boats captured

24/5/2014: VN fishing boat rammed

3/1/2014: VN fishing boat harassed

16/5/2012: Two VN fishing boats captured

6/6/2014: VN fishing boat rammed

3/2009: USS Impeccable harassed

6/7/2014: VN fishing boat rammed

20/3/2013: Fire on VN fishing boat

22/2/2012: VN fishing boat harassed

2-3/1/2015: VN fishing boats harassed, robbed

11/2012: Binh Minh 02 ship cable cut incident

1/3/2015: VN fishing boat harassed

7-9/5/2014: VN fishing boats rammed

16/5/2015: VN fishing boat attacked

3/3/2012: Two VN fishing boats captured

26/5/2015: VN fishing boat rammed and sank

6/7/2011: VN fishing boats harassed

3/7/2015: 2 VN fishing boat captured

8-10/2009: VN fishing boat seized

7/1/2015: 3 VN fishing boats attacked, robbed

19/6/2015: VN fishing boats attacked, robbed

4/2012: Two VN fishing boats seized

11/9/2010 : VN fishing trawler seized

6/2012: VN fishing boats seized

6/2012: CNOOC's Notification on Hydrocarbon Development

26/5/2011: VN Binh Minh ship harrased

9/6/2011: VN Viking II ship snared

20/5/2013: VN fishing boat hit

2/1/2014: VN fishing boat harassed

22/3/2010: VN fishing boats detained

4/5/2010 VN fishing boat

19/8/2014: CN fighter jet intercepted U.S. Navy plane

1/3/2014: VN fishing boat harassed

21/2/2014: Two VN fishing boat harassed

18/3 VN f boat

7/2010: Confrontation with Indonesian Navy

26/3/2013: PLAN hold oath-taking ceremony on James Shoal

3/2013: Naval Landing Exercise on James Shoal

CHINA

VIETNAM

Waters in transitional arrangements

China-Vietnam, common fishery zone (2000)

China (2000)

Vietnam (2000)

PARACELS

THAILAND

CAMBODIA

China's U-shape line

Malaysia-Vietnam joint submission on the outer limits of continental shelves

Cambodia-Vietnam (1982)

Vietnam (1991)
Thailand (1997)

Vietnam (2003)
Indonesia

Malaysia-Vietnam oil and gas joint exploration and development area (1992)

Malaysia-Thailand area of joint development of seabed resources (1979)

Indonesia (1969)
Malaysia

MALAYSIA

Figure 6.3. Approximate locations of incidents between China and other countries in the South China Sea from 2009 to 2014. CN = China; MLS = Malaysia; PLP = Philippines; VN = Vietnam. Source: Compiled by the author based on press reports.

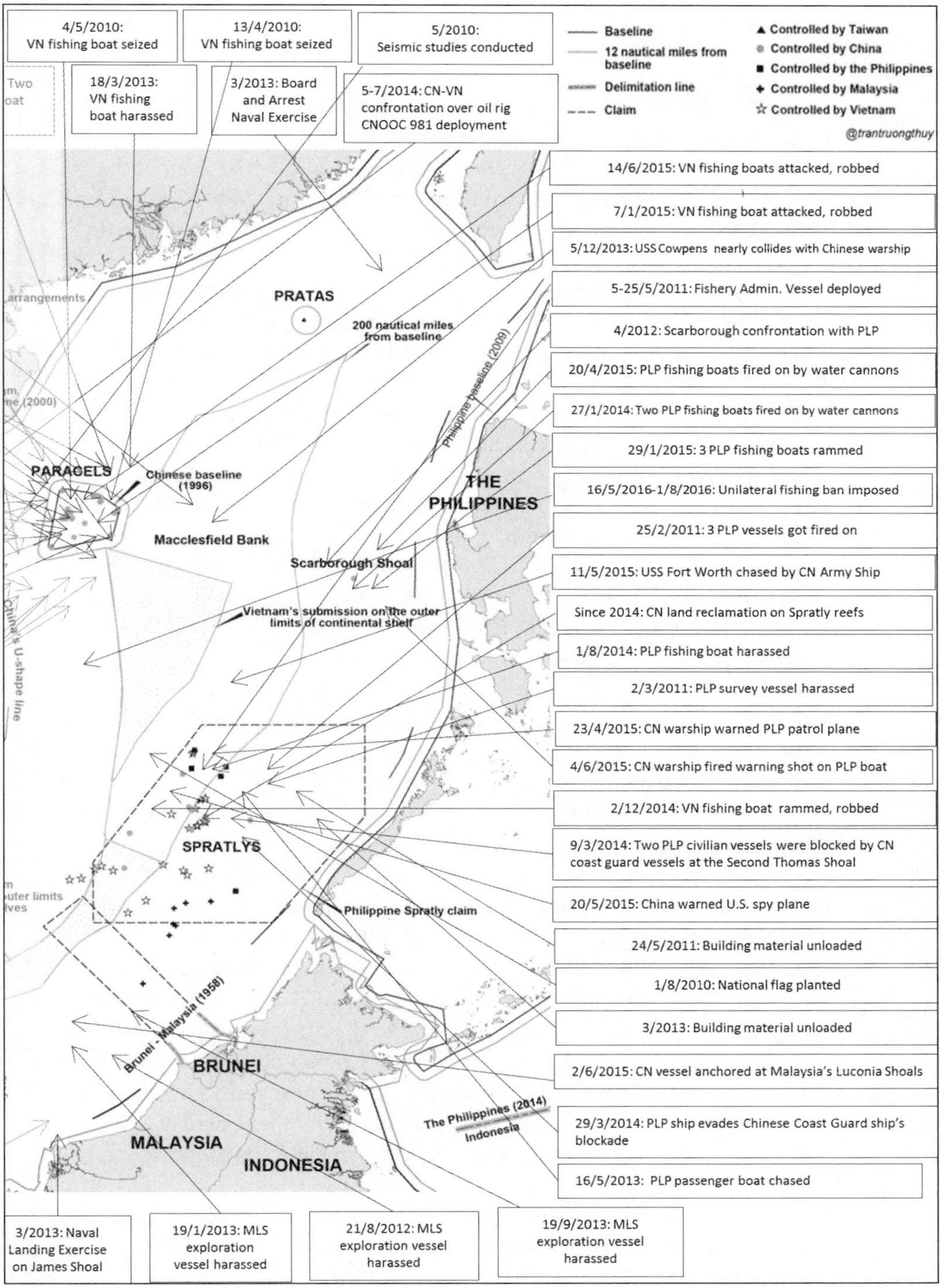
4/5/2010: VN fishing boat seized
13/4/2010: VN fishing boat seized
5/2010: Seismic studies conducted
Baseline
12 nautical miles from baseline
Delimitation line
Claim
Controlled by Taiwan
Controlled by China
Controlled by the Philippines
Controlled by Malaysia
Controlled by Vietnam
@trantruongthuy
18/3/2013: VN fishing boat harassed
3/2013: Board and Arrest Naval Exercise
5-7/2014: CN-VN confrontation over oil rig CNOOC 981 deployment
14/6/2015: VN fishing boats attacked, robbed
7/1/2015: VN fishing boat attacked, robbed
5/12/2013: USS Cowpens nearly collides with Chinese warship
5-25/5/2011: Fishery Admin. Vessel deployed
4/2012: Scarborough confrontation with PLP
20/4/2015: PLP fishing boats fired on by water cannons
27/1/2014: Two PLP fishing boats fired on by water cannons
29/1/2015: 3 PLP fishing boats rammed
16/5/2016-1/8/2016: Unilateral fishing ban imposed
25/2/2011: 3 PLP vessels got fired on
11/5/2015: USS Fort Worth chased by CN Army Ship
Since 2014: CN land reclamation on Spratly reefs
1/8/2014: PLP fishing boat harassed
2/3/2011: PLP survey vessel harassed
23/4/2015: CN warship warned PLP patrol plane
4/6/2015: CN warship fired warning shot on PLP boat
2/12/2014: VN fishing boat rammed, robbed
9/3/2014: Two PLP civilian vessels were blocked by CN coast guard vessels at the Second Thomas Shoal
20/5/2015: China warned U.S. spy plane
24/5/2011: Building material unloaded
1/8/2010: National flag planted
3/2013: Building material unloaded
2/6/2015: CN vessel anchored at Malaysia's Luconia Shoals
29/3/2014: PLP ship evades Chinese Coast Guard ship's blockade
16/5/2013: PLP passenger boat chased
PRATAS
200 nautical miles from baseline
Philippine baseline (2009)
PARACELS
Chinese baseline (1996)
Macclesfield Bank
THE PHILIPPINES
Scarborough Shoal
Vietnam's submission on the outer limits of continental shelf
China's U-shape line
SPRATLYS
Philippine Spratly claim
Brunei - Malaysia (1958)
BRUNEI
MALAYSIA
INDONESIA
The Philippines (2014)
Indonesia
3/2013: Naval Landing Exercise on James Shoal
19/1/2013: MLS exploration vessel harassed
21/8/2012: MLS exploration vessel harassed
19/9/2013: MLS exploration vessel harassed

lost over US$1.8 million—a total of 14,945 room-night cancellations—in July 2014.[32] According to one statistic, Chinese accounted for about a quarter of the nearly 4.3 million foreign visitors to Vietnam in the first six months of 2014. But in June 2014, arrivals from the Chinese mainland to Vietnam fell by about 30 percent and those from Hong Kong by 72 percent, compared to May 2014.[33]

Though the oil rig incident is worrisome, it was brief and the situation quickly normalized. Chinese development in the South China Sea since 2014 has altered the status quo permanently and has far-reaching strategic implications for the whole region.

Since the end of 2013, China has been conducting land reclamation operations on some occupied features in the Paracel Islands and on all seven occupied Spratly Islands. According to the U.S. Department of Defense, as of June 2015 China "had reclaimed more than 2,900 acres (= 11.7 km²) of land, 17 times more land in 20 months than the other claimants combined over the past 40 years, accounting for approximately 95 percent of all reclaimed land in the Spratly Islands."[34] China's work in the Spratlys has transformed submerged reefs and rocks into full-fledged islands with airstrips, harbors, and other military and civilian structures.

From the perspective of international law, it is clear that China's reclamation work constitutes a breach of international agreements, which require all parties to exercise restraint and not undertake unilateral actions that would permanently change the status quo regarding the disputed areas.[35] From a strategic competition aspect, the unprecedented land reclamation will tremendously impact major powers' competition and the dynamics of the claimants' in the South China Sea. On the one hand, Chinese fishing fleets, which already enjoy financial, technical, and administrative support from the central and local governments,[36] can utilize facilities on the enlarged islands to extend the duration and scope of their activities, which will likely stoke tensions with other claimants as they intrude into the EEZs of Vietnam, the Philippines, Malaysia, Brunei, and Indonesia. On the other hand, the enlarged islands with airstrips and harbors strengthen Chinese military capabilities and allow China to quickly deploy forces to the central and southern parts of the South China Sea in case of confrontation with other claimants. Those facilities also could enhance Chinese capabilities to block the supply routes of Vietnam and the Philippines to their controlled islands and rocks there. China's attempts to block Philippine supply routes to the Second Thomas Shoal in the first half of 2014 well illustrate this point.[37] China's expanded military presence there could also serve to enhance Chinese power projection. The web of Chinese military bases in the South China Sea, connecting Sanya (in

Hainan Island) in the north to Woody Island in the Paracels in the west to new unsinkable aircraft carriers on Fiery Cross, Johnson South, Cuateron, and Gaven reefs in the Spratlys in the center and the south to Mischief Reef and the possible base on Scarborough Shoal in the east,[38] will enhance Chinese capabilities to enforce an ADIZ above the South China Sea, if and when established, harass the U.S. military, hunt for American submarines, place Australia within Chinese strategic bombers' range for the first time,[39] and control or at least send a deterrent message of Chinese capability in blocking the critical energy supply routes from the Middle East to Japan, South Korea, and Taiwan.

Chinese land reclamation, construction, and deployment activities in the Spratlys and Paracels have attracted attention from the international community and are regarded by Vietnam as the most vivid and worrisome signs of China's increasing assertiveness in the South China Sea.

Vietnam's Policy

For Vietnam, in dealing with the South China Sea issues, the foreign policy principle of "maintaining peaceful environment" adopted since Doi Moi has also been reflected in the strategy of solving territorial and maritime disputes with other countries exclusively by peaceful means. Any confrontation with other countries relating to the disputed issues will inevitably be detrimental to the top foreign policy objective of maintaining a peaceful environment. The White Paper published in 2009 by the Ministry of Defense also reaffirms that "Vietnam's consistent policy is to solve both historical and newly emerging disputes over territorial sovereignty in land and at sea through peaceful means on the basis of international laws."[40] At the same time, Vietnam also applies the concept of "struggle and cooperation" as described above for dealing with China's South China Sea aggression with the objective to separate two aspects of the relationship so that the maritime issues will not negatively affect the overall Vietnam-China bilateral relationship.

Operationally, in response to China's increasing encroachments on its maritime interests in the South China Sea, Vietnam applies the policy of a weaker party in an asymmetric relationship to defend its national interests while seeking to preserve a peaceful relationship with China. This policy is a combination of engagement and (soft and hard) balancing toward China. It is relatively comprehensive and combines several features: First is *direct engagement*, including high-level exchanges, agency-to-agency interactions, and direct negotiations with China on maritime issues to defuse tensions and settle remaining bilateral issues. The second feature is *indirect engagement*, working with other members of ASEAN to engage China in the Declaration on the Conduct of Parties in the South China Sea (DOC) and code of conduct (COC) implementation. Third, *soft balancing* consists of raising the South China Sea issue in regional forums (particularly ASEAN-related forums), engaging the participation of other external powers in the South China Sea issues, and using international law, especially UNCLOS 1982, to defend its maritime claims. Finally, *hard balancing*, for deterrent purposes, includes improving military capacity, especially modernizing the navy, and strengthening law enforcement capability (the Coast Guard and Fishing Patrol Agency).

Regarding the *direct engagement* component of its policy, Vietnam emphasizes the exchange of high-level visits with China, and the South China Sea issue has become one of the main topics of discussion among leaders. The issue was a prominent topic during a meeting in Beijing on November 10, 2014, between presidents on the sidelines of the 22nd Summit of the APEC Forum.[41] In October 2013, during the visit of Chinese Premier Li Keqiang to Vietnam, both sides reached consensus on advancing maritime, onshore, and financial cooperation and establishing three working groups.[42] The two sides also "agreed to exercise tight control of maritime disputes and not to make any move that can further complicate or extend disputes" and set up a hotline between the two Agriculture Ministries (in addition to hotlines between General Secretaries of the Communist Parties, Defense Ministries, and Foreign Ministries) "to promptly and suitably deal with arising problems" in the South China Sea.[43] In addition to high-level exchanges, Vietnam and China also established (in 2006) the Steering Committee on Vietnam-China Bilateral Cooperation and a network of engagement with China through party-to-party and agency-to-agency cooperation. These include cooperative measures between military, fishery, criminal, and border patrol agencies directly and indirectly relating to the handling of maritime issues. Vietnam and China have also conducted direct negotiations on unresolved maritime issues. In October 2011, during the visit of VCP Secretary General Nguyen Phu Trong to Beijing, the nations signed the Agreement on the Basic Principles Guiding the Resolution of Maritime Issues, in which they pledged to address maritime issues incrementally and to hasten demarcation and cooperation in waters off the Tonkin Gulf and to foster cooperation in less sensitive fields including marine environmental protection, marine science research, search and rescue operations, and natural disaster mitigation and prevention.[44] The agreement also noted that the two sides should alternately hold biannual meetings between the heads of government-level border negotiation delegations and ad hoc meetings if necessary. The two sides also agreed to establish a direct hotline between the government-level delegations to help with timely resolutions of maritime issues.[45] Since the agreement was signed, Vietnam and China have conducted seven rounds of negotiations on delimitation and joint development in the waters outside the mouth of the Tonkin Gulf and have agreed to conduct a joint survey along the equidistant line between Hainan Island and Vietnam.[46] The two sides have also carried out six rounds of negotiations covering cooperation in less sensitive areas and have reached a draft agreement related to search and rescue cooperation at sea and agreements on two cooperative projects—joint research on the management of the marine and island environment in the Gulf of Tonkin and comparative research on sediment dating back to the Holocene epoch in the Red River and Yangtze deltas.[47]

Some Vietnamese analysts believe that by raising the South China Sea issues they can be elevated to a higher priority in China's foreign policy. Encouraging Chinese leaders to highlight these issues in bilateral and regional relations and better manage competition among various interest groups within China would reduce one of the main sources of tension in recent years. These engagements are also expected to promote mutual trust and cooperation and minimize misunderstandings among interest groups on both sides. On the other hand, cooperative mechanisms among agencies directly dealing with maritime issues can arguably help both sides prevent incidents from happening and/or deescalate tensions. However, it should be noted that the main competition between Vietnam and China in the South China Sea in recent years has been between law enforcement agencies protecting (and preventing the development of) resources (hydrocarbons and fish), but both sides have not yet established any cooperation between their Coast Guards. In May and June 2014, despite Vietnam's continuous efforts through high-level meetings, hotlines, and "more than fifty" diplomatic communications with China to resolve the oil rig crisis, the relatively long duration of the crisis indicated the limits to bilateral direct engagement in deescalating tensions. China withdrew the oil rig one month before it had planned, but arguably not as a result of bilateral Vietnam-China direct engagement.

Direct engagement proved to be more helpful in restoring the damaged relationship between the two countries once the crisis ceased. On August 26 and 27, 2014, Vietnam sent its special envoy, Politburo member Le Hong Anh, to China to meet with Chinese leaders. During Le Hong Anh's meeting with Chinese President Xi Jinping, both sides agreed to take measures to restore and develop their bilateral relations, which had been eroded by the oil rig deployment.[48] The visit was followed by a number of other important visits by other leaders and high-ranking officials from both sides to renormalize the China-Vietnam bilateral relationship and promote cooperation. During the visit of Vietnamese Defense Minister General Phung Quang Thanh to Beijing in mid-October, China and Vietnam signed a memorandum of understanding on establishing a direct communication line between their respective defense ministries, which could prove valuable in avoiding miscalculations and future tensions.[49] On October 16, Prime Minister Nguyen Tan Dung met with Premier Li Keqiang on the sidelines of the Asia-Europe Summit in Milan. News agencies reported that Vietnam and China agreed to "address and control" maritime disputes in the South China Sea. Prime Minister Dung was quoted as saying that "the two countries should properly address and control maritime differences and not complicate the situation further," "maintain high-level meetings to improve trust,"[50] and boost "cooperation in infrastructure, finance and maritime exploration."[51] Xinhua quoted Premier Li as expressing "thanks to the efforts from both sides," as "China-Vietnam relations have ridden out the recent rough patch and gradually recovered."[52] At the end of 2014, China sent Yu Zhengsheng, chairman of the National Committee of the Chinese People's Political Consultative Conference and the fourth ranking official in the Communist Party leadership, to Vietnam for a three-day visit. The main purpose of Yu's three-day stay in Hanoi, as the high-ranking Chinese official said, was "to consolidate political trust and beef up cooperation and exchanges between the two Parties and States."[53]

Vietnam's policy on its relationship with China is to separate aspects of the relationship so that the issues of struggle will not negatively affect the cooperation. For example, while demonstrating its determination in confronting China over the oil rig deployment, Hanoi maintained communications with their Chinese counterparts and successfully maintained commercial and investment cooperation, although tourism suffered. Soon after the oil rig crisis was over, Vietnam became one of the founding members of the Chinese-initiated Asian Infrastructure Investment Bank (AIIB).[54]

At the same time, keeping the issues of conflicting interests from negatively affecting cooperation has become a challenging task. Particularly, the issue of South China Sea dispute is a cancer that cannot be isolated, affecting the entire body. The more China becomes assertive in the South China Sea (or is regarded as assertive from Vietnam's perspective), the more anti-Chinese sentiment will increase among the Vietnamese both within the country and overseas. According to Pew Research surveys, 78 and 74 percent of Vietnamese people in 2014 and 2015, respectively, held an unfavorable view of China.[55] As Vietnam incrementally and increasingly becomes more democratic, VCP has to take into account public opinion and does not want to appear soft in protecting national sovereignty or appear too accommodating toward China. During the oil rig crisis in 2014, Prime Minister Nguyen Tan

Dung received nationwide praise when he declared that "we cannot trade our sacred independence and sovereignty for some elusive peace or any type of dependence."[56] Due to the maritime territorial dispute, the sharing of ideologies between Vietnam and China has become irrelevant in today's context.

Due to negative spillover effects from the maritime disputes, a number of Vietnam experts also perceive economic proposals from China with suspicion and seeing the strategic intentions behind the offers. Looking at China's grand initiative of One Belt, One Road (OBOR), for example, they see that China could advance its sovereignty propaganda with the creation of the Maritime Silk Road. OBOR could deepen the economic dependence of Vietnam and other ASEAN members on China, lowering these countries' position among ASEAN on the South China Sea issue.

Regarding *indirect engagement*, Vietnam tried to work with other ASEAN members to collectively engage China in multilateral discussions regarding the South China Sea within the framework of the ASEAN-China dialogue about DOC implementation and the new COC. This indirect engagement is currently considered to be one of the most important components of Vietnam's overall strategy toward the South China Sea issues.

Hanoi understands the internal and external dynamics of ASEAN. Due to divergent interests and external pressures, ASEAN countries have different viewpoints regarding the South China Sea issues. Even claimants in ASEAN, including Vietnam, the Philippines, Malaysia, and Brunei, sometimes do not share a common voice. Vietnam and the Philippines have had the most incidents with China and thus are the two most active players calling for ASEAN solidarity in handling the issues. Since the U.S. pronouncement of the Asian Pivot, the Philippines has become more confident and proactive, has frequently voiced concern about China's aggression in the South China Sea, and has proposed a number of new initiatives in ASEAN forums. Despite their status as claimants in the South China Sea disputes, Brunei and Malaysia to a lesser extent have not been directly intimidated by China at sea and often attach greater importance to their relations with China. Among nonclaimants, Singapore and Indonesia hold a neutral view. They do not support the claim of any party. Singapore's Ministry of Foreign Affairs spokesperson once commented that "Singapore is not a claimant state and takes no position on the merits or otherwise of the various claims in the South China Sea. But as a major trading nation, Singapore has a critical interest in anything affecting freedom of navigation in all international sea lanes, including those in the South China Sea."[57] Indonesia has a tradition of mediating, hosting many workshops on managing potential conflict in the South China Sea over the past twenty years and now is actively promoting ASEAN's common position on this issue. The country also is increasingly worried about China's intentions and behaviors in the South China Sea and also publicly protested China's U-shaped line as it encroaches upon the exclusive economic zone of the Natuna Islands.[58] Laos, Thailand, and Myanmar do not have direct interests in the South China Sea and so rarely express their positions. Having close political and economic ties with China, Cambodia to a certain extent supports China's preferences in bilateral negotiations.

While acknowledging that ASEAN countries have divergent interests in the South China Sea, Vietnam has made continuous efforts to work with member states to maintain at least minimum common positions on this issue. In fact, all ten ASEAN member states participated in negotiations and signed the Declaration of Conduct (DOC) in 2002 and all had also reached consensus to promote the negotiation of the COC with China in order to effectively manage the disputes and enhance peace and cooperation in the region.[59] While working toward the COC, Hanoi believes the DOC 2002 remains one of the most important documents (in addition to UNCLOS 1982) to regulate the behaviors of parties in the South China Sea, despite the fact that it is a political document and is not legally binding. Though some DOC provisions are ambiguous, the more clearly stated provisions, such as no use of force and no new inhabitation on unoccupied islands in the South China Sea, to a certain extent have helped prevent China from conducting adventurist activities. The process of DOC implementation and negotiation on COC arguably has facilitated China's discussion of the South China Sea issue within the ASEAN-China framework.

After the failure to release the joint communiqué at the forty-fifth ASEAN Foreign Ministers' Meeting (AMM45) in Phnom Penh in 2012, ASEAN realized the importance of maintaining consensus on the South China Sea issues so that it will not negatively affect its credibility and centrality in the evolving regional security architecture. ASEAN members now share common views and interests, which include, among others, protecting freedom of navigation and regional stability, respecting international law, and maintaining ASEAN's solidarity and centrality in the evolving regional security (and economic) architecture. In almost all important meetings within ASEAN and between ASEAN and its partners (AMM, ASEAN Summit, ASEAN Regional Forum, East Asia Summit [EAS]) under the chairmanship of Brunei, Myanmar, and Malaysia, in 2013, 2014, and 2015, respectively, the South China Sea issues were raised, discussed, and mentioned in concluding documents without any significant diplomatic rancor.[60] During the oil rig crisis, with some diplomatic pressure by Vietnam, ASEAN foreign ministers for the first time since 1992 consensually released a stand-alone statement to address the South

China Sea issues, in which they "expressed their serious concerns over the *on-going developments in the South China Sea*, which have increased tensions in the area" and "urged all parties concerned, in accordance with the universally recognised principles of international law, including the 1982 UN Convention on the Law of the Sea (UNCLOS), to exercise self-restraint and avoid actions which could undermine peace and stability in the area; and to resolve disputes by peaceful means without resorting to threat or use of force."[61] Although the ASEAN foreign ministers did not explicitly mention China or the oil rig incident to avoid negative reactions from Beijing, the phrase "on-going developments in the South China Sea" was carefully selected to indicate the oil rig incident.

At the same time, Vietnam understands the limits of indirect engagement with China through the ASEAN framework as it requires not only consensus within ASEAN but also, more importantly, political will from Beijing to accept some common understanding on the South China Sea issues. The three-level game of negotiation (internal within each country, within ASEAN, and between ASEAN and China) explains why the process of concluding any document is so protracted. For example, ASEAN took more than seven years to engage China to negotiate the DOC, which was signed in 2002,[62] and almost nine years to complete the symbolic guidelines for the implementation of the DOC, which was agreed in July 2011.[63] Similarly, the future of the ongoing negotiations on the COC remains uncertain, as ASEAN hopes to engage China in accepting a binding agreement that will, among others, regulate China's behaviors in the South China Sea. Nevertheless, for ASEAN, the process of engagement with China is as important as the results.

As discussed above, although direct engagement and indirect engagement through ASEAN provide useful channels for Vietnam in dealing with China on the South China Sea issues, they are insufficient to prevent China from advancing its claims there. Therefore, Vietnam has had to also rely on the soft and hard balancing elements of its strategy. Its soft balancing consists of bringing up the South China Sea issues in regional forums, particularly those related to ASEAN; engaging the participation of other major powers, especially the United States, in regard to the South China Sea; and using international law, especially the UNCLOS 1982, to defend its maritime claims and settle disputes peacefully.

As mentioned previously, Vietnam adopted a foreign policy of diversification and multi-directionalization of external relations, in which major powers play very important roles in strengthening its security and development. Some Vietnamese analysts believe that by creating a situation in which interests of major powers are intertwined in the country, coupled with the policy of "diversification and multi-directionalization" of external relations, other disputants, especially China, have to take into account the interests of these major powers as well. In these circumstances, the possibility of using military actions to solve the territorial disputes in the South China Sea can be minimized.[64] Moreover, Vietnamese policy makers also believe that by bringing up the South China Sea issues in regional forums and engaging the participation of other major powers, the issues will become major concerns in China's foreign relations, forcing China to contemplate its other interests in relations with major powers and thus soften its approach in South China Sea. On the other hand, once the South China Sea issue receives priority in China's foreign policy decision-making process, its approach will become much more coordinated and centralized. As a result, competition between and independent activities of interest groups—one of the main reasons for China's renewed assertiveness since 2007—were reduced.[65]

Another aspect, an important component of Doi Moi economic policy, has been attracting foreign direct investment into Vietnam, including in maritime and coastal areas. The Eighth National Party Congress of the VCP in June 1996 stated, "The maritime and coastal areas are strategically important in terms of economy, security and defense. These areas have advantages for economic development and serve as the gate for the country to connect with the world and main attraction for foreign investments."[66] As a result, oil and gas companies from almost all major powers (except China) have invested heavily in exploration and exploitation projects in Vietnam's exclusive economic zone, which have resulted in an established web of intertwining economic interests of major powers.

Among the major powers, the United States is playing the most important role. Policy makers in Vietnam understand that the United States is now the only country capable of constraining China's military expansions. Some analysts believe that although the United States conducts its activities according to its own interests, U.S. involvement has increased leverage for Vietnam in relations with China, making China soften its assertive approach and less willing to use force to solve the territorial disputes. In addition, U.S. policy has spillover effects on the positions of other countries, especially those that have close relationships with Washington, encouraging these stakeholders (such as Japan, Australia, India, and some European countries) to express concerns about developments in the South China Sea at many multilateral meetings (ARF, EAS, ASEAN Defense Ministers Meeting Plus [ADMM+], Asia-Europe Meeting, G-7, etc.). Consequently, the issue becomes even more internationalized and China has to take into account the relevant interests of these powers as well. This partly explains why Vietnam pays increasing attention to engaging and working with the United States in various regional and international forums. President Truong Tan Sang, during the visit to Washington in July 2013, "welcomed the United States' enhanced cooperation in the Asia-Pacific, which contributes to peace, stability, and prosperity of the region."[67] One particular aspect of the comprehensive partnership, announced during that visit, is that President Obama and President Truong Tan Sang "agreed to enhance cooperation at regional and international forums including APEC, ASEAN, EAS, ADMM+ to support peace, stability, cooperation, and development in the Asia-Pacific region."[68] The U.S.-Vietnam Joint Vision Statement, adopted during the historical visit to the United States by VCP's General Secretary Nguyen Phu Trong, stated, "Vietnam welcomes the United States' policy of enhanced cooperation with the Asia-Pacific region" and "the United States and Vietnam are also committed to strengthening cooperation on regional and global issues of mutual interest and concern."[69]

The United States, after a long engagement in the Middle East and Afghanistan in the war against terrorism, has "pivoted to Asia" to cope with a rising China.[70] The South China Sea has become one of the main focal points of the "Asian rebalancing" strategy adopted by the Obama administration. The shift in U.S. policy is relatively comprehensive. In terms of politics and diplomacy, the United States has engaged more deeply in the Asia-Pacific through an increasing number of visits by the president, secretaries of state and defense, and other high-ranking officials to the region. In the economic realm, after ratifying the free trade agreement with South Korea, the United States has concentrated on TPP, which has a strategic component of strengthening U.S. relations with other countries to counterbalance current China-centric multilateral economic mechanisms such as the China-ASEAN Free Trade Agreement and ASEAN+3. In military terms, despite cuts in defense spending, the budget for the U.S. Pacific Command (PACOM) will not be affected.[71] On the contrary, the United States will increase its presence in PACOM's areas of responsibility, including a new "rotating base" in Australia. The United States is also planning to move the majority of its naval forces to the Asia-Pacific region. In 2012 at the Eleventh Shangri-La Dialogue in Singapore, then U.S. Secretary of Defense Leon Panetta announced that 60 percent of U.S. warships would be based in the Pacific by 2020.[72] In recent years, the United States has also enhanced military and maritime cooperation with China's competitors in maritime domains, such as Japan and the Philippines. In April 2014 the United States strengthened access and readiness in the South China Sea by signing with the Philippines the Enhanced Defense Cooperation Agreement, which covers the full range of defense cooperation, including the deployment of U.S. "rotational troops" on Philippine territory and developing maritime security and domain awareness.[73] During 2015 and in the beginning of 2016, in a move to signal more direct engagement, the United States twice conducted freedom of navigation operations in the South China Sea to challenge "excessive maritime claims" of parties by sending Navy destroyers within twelve nautical miles of Subi Reef in the Spratly Islands and in the vicinity of Triton Island in the Paracel Islands on October 27, 2015, and January 30, 2016, respectively.[74]

High-ranking U.S. officials also referred to the South China Sea issue more often in their official speeches, especially within multilateral diplomatic meetings. For example, at the Seventeenth ASEAN Regional Forum in 2010, then U.S. Secretary of State Hillary Clinton declared for the first time U.S. "national interests" in the South China Sea, among which were freedom of navigation, peaceful settlement of disputes, and unimpeded commerce. The United States also indirectly rejected any argument of "historic waters" or "historic rights" of the U-shaped line when Hillary Clinton said, "consistent with customary international law, legitimate claims to maritime space in the South China Sea should be derived solely from legitimate claims to land features."[75] Speaking at a hearing before the U.S. Senate Committee on Foreign Relations, she said, "China's claims in the South China Sea exceed what is permitted by the UNCLOS."[76] In February 2014, Assistant Secretary of State Daniel Russel, while testifying before the U.S. Congress stated that, the United States "firmly opposes the use of intimidation, coercion or force to assert a territorial claim." He went on that "China's lack of clarity with regard to its South China Sea claims has created uncertainty, insecurity and instability in the region. . . . Any use of the 'nine-dash line' by China to claim maritime rights not based on claimed land features would be inconsistent with international law."[77] At the ARF meeting in Myanmar in August 2014, in a move indicating a new level of engagement from Washington on the South China Sea issue, Secretary of State John Kerry proposed the idea of "Freeze," asking claimants to voluntarily refrain from actions altering the status quo, including a moratorium on reclamation work on occupied features and militarization of the South China Sea. All of this was welcomed, quietly or bilaterally, by Vietnam and some other ASEAN members.

However, Vietnam also sees the current limits to U.S. involvement in the South China Sea issue. In addition to concerns about U.S. commitment and durability in the region due to global overreach, perceived power decline, and real military budget cuts, there are additional aspects. That the United States has not yet joined the 1982 UN Convention on the Law of the Sea reduces its legitimacy to criticize other countries, particularly China, for not respecting maritime law. The increasing presence and activities of U.S. naval forces in the South China Sea, for now, could not prevent China from (but may trigger) further expansion and militarization of its occupied islands. In response to U.S. freedom of navigation operations around Paracel, for example, China deployed HQ-09 surface-to-air missiles with a range of two hundred kilometers, signaling long-term Chinese plans to strengthen its military reach across the South China Sea.[78] On the other hand, the increasing presence of the U.S. naval forces has not had a significant impact on the competition for control of resources in the South China Sea, which is mainly among law enforcement vessels from claimant countries. The fact that in 2012 China successfully drove away the Philippines and established a permanent presence at Scarborough Shoal despite U.S. efforts to mitigate tensions showed the limits to U.S. involvement. In multilateral diplomacy, the effects of Clinton's remarks have diminished, since the United States has not expressed any significant new points in recent speeches at regional forums. If China continues using nonmilitary measures at sea and applying economic and diplomatic measures to influence ASEAN countries' policies, the United States cannot interfere with or influence the settlement of the South China Sea issues. The United States could add paramilitary and economic elements to its strategy, but the country has relatively neglected this option over the years.[79] Specifically, the United States may consider—in addition to helping other countries improve their maritime surveillance and law enforcement capabilities—deploying its Coast Guard directly in the South China Sea, possibly in the name of cooperation, to avoid provoking Beijing's negative reactions. The United States can help littoral states in improving their maritime domain awareness, individually or collectively, and sharing intelligence regarding the real picture on the sea. Regarding economic involvement, Washington should put more emphasis on the strategic aspect of TPP for reaching internal consensus to speed up the ratification process, which, once concluded, will strengthen U.S. economic engagement with the region—the permanent base for its rebalancing strategy.

Among other major powers, Japan is emerging as one of the most important partners to Vietnam, not just in terms of economic cooperation but also in the field of maritime cooperation and strategic concerns over China's long-term intention. Russia is the main arms provider for Vietnam and invests heavily in oil and gas exploration in the South China Sea. Both sides upgraded relations to the comprehensive strategic partnership level in 2013. However, Russia's main focus is on its immediate former republic neighbors—particularly Ukraine. Southeast Asia is a secondary priority for Moscow's foreign policy. Russia is also a "comprehensive strategic partner" and currently enjoys "the best relationship ever" with China,[80] and strongly needs Beijing's cooperation after suffering from Western sanctions due to its annexation of

Crimea. In addition, the Russian position that the South China Sea disputes should be resolved through bilateral negotiations and Moscow's mounting reactions to some serious incidents, particularly relating to China's oil rig deployment, did not meet the expectations of their Vietnamese counterparts. India is also involved in oil and gas exploration in the South China Sea, is improving its military cooperation with Vietnam, and also has territorial disputes with China, but it seems that India's "Act East" capacity has not yet met its "Look East" aspiration.

With other aspects of soft balancing, Vietnam has increasingly relied on international law, particularly the 1982 UNCLOS, to defend its maritime claims and settle the South China Sea disputes by peaceful means. So far, Vietnam has not resorted to third-party arbitration for the settlement of its territorial and maritime disputes with China. During the crisis ignited by the deployment of the Chinese oil rig, the Vietnamese government did consider various "defense options" against China, including legal actions.[81] Prime Minister Nguyen Tan Dung ordered relevant agencies to prepare documents for legal proceedings against China for "illegally placing a drilling rig in Vietnam's waters."[82]

Whether or not to undertake third-party arbitration, of course, would be a subject of careful consideration for the VCP's Politburo. Potential economic retaliation by China, a deterioration of bilateral relations, difficulties getting China's serious involvement in the UNCLOS dispute settlement mechanism, uncertainty toward international legal rulings, and lack of enforcement mechanisms in international arbitration all explain the reluctance of Vietnam to choose this path. However, if other soft balancing acts and hard balancing measures cannot help Vietnam deter China from impinging on Vietnam's national interests, Hanoi might seriously consider legal means as the last peaceful resort. In fact, Vietnam supports the Philippine move to bring their dispute with China to an arbitration established under Annex VII of the 1982 UNCLOS. On December 11, 2014, Vietnam submitted a statement to the Arbitration Panel, and its foreign ministry also rejected China's position paper, which was released days before laying out Beijing's legal objections to the arbitration.[83] Vietnam's statement to the Arbitration Panel made three main claims in opposition to China's stand. First, it recognized the court's jurisdiction over the case brought by the Philippines, directly contradicting China's position that the court had no such authority. Second, it asked the court to give "due regard" to its legal rights and interests in the Spratlys and the Paracels and in its exclusive economic zone and continental shelf when deciding on the merits of the case. Third and last, it rejected China's nine-dash line claim as being "without legal basis."[84] By recognizing the court's jurisdiction over the case and rejecting the nine-dotted line, Vietnam's statement arguably implicitly supported the Philippines in the case. Although the Arbitration Panel's decision will be legally binding only for parties directly involved, namely the Philippines and China, the case will affect Vietnam's legal standing and claims in the South China Sea, for better or for worse, regardless of outcome. If the Arbitration Panel rules against the nine-dotted line and/or declares that the land features in the Spratly Islands are rocks under UNCLOS 1982, meaning they cannot generate exclusive economic zones or continental shelves, it will undermine China's legal stand, minimize the area of dispute, and strengthen other claimants' legal bases for defending their sovereignty and jurisdiction within their maritime zones. The opposite scenario would be a nightmare for not only the Philippines but also other Southeast Asian claimants, notably Vietnam, since China would have free reign in advancing its claims in almost all bodies of water in the South China Sea.

Regarding hard balancing, although Vietnam considers diplomacy as "the first line of defense" and uses peaceful means to resolve the disputes, rising competition in the South China Sea has induced Hanoi to invest in improving its "deterrent" capacity, with more attention given to naval and air forces. Vietnam's success in economic renovations has provided additional resources for its expanding defense budget. However, as mentioned previously, Vietnam since Doi Moi has followed the guidance of a "strong economy, just-enough national defense capability, and expanded external relations" and therefore has to strike a good balance between security and development objectives within its government expenditure, which mirrors real growth in GDP. While the defense budget has been increasing in absolute terms, reaching US$3.397 billion in 2012, its rise is lower than that of economic growth, and its share of GDP remains between 2 and 2.5 percent—at the middle level in comparison with other countries around East Asia (see figures 6.4 and 6.5). Prime Minister Nguyen Tan Dung told the press that "we modernize our armed forces when the economic conditions allow, and that is normal." He also stressed that "Vietnam has a long coast and large maritime zone, which requires protection. Therefore, armed forces modernization is not a matter of contingency or arms race."[85]

After about a decade of inadequate investment, Vietnam is modernizing its deterrent capabilities through upgrading naval, air, and electronic warfare capabilities. For instance, in 2009, Vietnam signed contracts with Russia to buy six Project 636 Kilo-Class submarines with a value of up to US$1.8 billion. By January 2016 five submarines had been transferred to Vietnam by Russia, and the sixth is scheduled to be delivered during 2016.[86] The submarines represent almost an entire year's defense budget, demonstrating the seriousness with which Vietnamese leaders consider the security and sovereignty of their

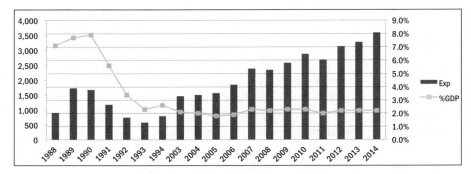

Figure 6.4. Vietnam's military expenditure and its share of GDP (1988–2014) (US$ millions). Note: Values are not available from 1995 to 2002. Source: SIPRI Military Expenditure Database.

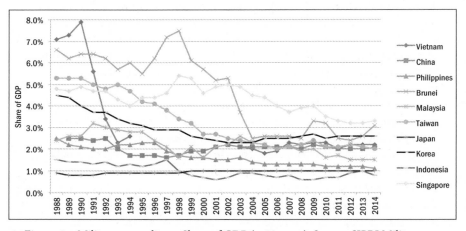

Figure 6.5. Military expenditure: Share of GDP (1988–2014). Source: SIPRI Military Expenditure Database.

maritime claims. Vietnam also ordered from Russia four Gepard-class light frigates, specially equipped for antisubmarine warfare, and in 2011 deployed the first two. In 2012 Vietnam also finalized a contract to purchase four Sigma-class corvettes from the Netherlands. To provide air cover for its naval fleet, Vietnam is acquiring at least twenty Russian-made Su-30MK2 multirole fighter aircraft, in addition to about a dozen relatively modern Su-27 and MiG aircraft.[87] In August 2013, Vietnam signed a contract with Russia for the purchase of an additional twelve Sukhoi Su-30MK2 multirole jet aircraft armed with antiship missiles in a deal valued at US$450 million.[88] To improve naval surveillance and patrols, Vietnam has procured six amphibious DHC-6 Twin Otter aircraft from Canada.[89] Vietnam's new military acquisitions will enhance its antiaccess/area-denial capabilities for protecting the country's sovereignty and interests in the South China Sea.

At the same time, Vietnam has also strengthened bilateral and multilateral defense cooperation with other powers to deal with national security challenges. The complex nature of security threats, not just in the South China Sea, has demanded Vietnam to "expand defense diplomacy and actively participate in defense and security cooperation in the regional and international community."[90] The 2009 Defense White Paper said, "defense cooperation is one of the most important factors to maintain peace and stability in the region and the world, and it is also an important factor to achieve Vietnam's defense goals."[91]

Vietnam's defense diplomacy actively contributes to "maintaining a peaceful and stable environment" and promoting regional cooperation. Alongside Vietnam's policy of tackling the challenges in the South China Sea by bringing up issues in international and regional forums to engage China and other countries to collectively find the solutions, Vietnam's defense sector also raises these issues in defense-related forums and participates in confidence-building processes, such as ADMM and ADMM+. Bilaterally, Vietnam "wishes to widen defense relations with all countries," and the range of prioritized activities includes "exchange of military delegations, information and sharing experience, cooperation in training and education, and solving humanitarian issues."[92] Significantly, Vietnam has established defense relations with sixty-five countries "spanning Asia-Pacific, Australia, Europe, North America, the Middle East, South America and Africa."[93] Concerning mil-to-mil relations with the United States, in September 2011, Vietnam and the United States signed a memorandum of understanding on defense cooperation, which sought to promote cooperation in five prioritized fields: the establishment of regular, high-level dialogues between the U.S. Department of Defense and Vietnam's Ministry of National Defense; maritime security; search and rescue; peacekeeping operations; and humanitarian assistance and disaster relief.[94] Amid rising tensions in the South China Sea, the two sides conducted noncombat naval exercises in the waters off Vietnam's coast. On July 15, 2011, after China's interference with a Vietnam oil-exploration ship in June, the United States and Vietnam launched a series of naval exchanges in the water off the coast of Da Nang as a sign of warming ties.[95] According to the assessment of Lieutenant Commander Clay Doss, a U.S. Navy public affairs official, "The quality and depth of the exchanges is increasing each year as our navies get to know each other better."[96] On April 8, 2014, the two navies launched six days of noncombat exercises in the South China Sea with the participation of two U.S. Navy ships and four hundred personnel. The exercises focused on search and rescue, shipboard damage control, and military medicine and classroom training on maritime security.[97] In October 2014, in a move indicating a closer level of bilateral cooperation, Washington announced that it would partially lift its long-standing policy of not selling lethal arms to Vietnam, with the main objective to enable transfers of "maritime security-related defense articles." According to the *Diplomat*, one of the first items that will likely be on Vietnam's wish list is Lockheed's P-3 Orion maritime surveillance aircraft.[98]

The other aspect of hard balancing is improvement of law enforcement capabilities. Vietnam considers that military confrontation is unlikely in the near future, and the main competition in the South China Sea is between law enforcement forces. In 2013, the Marine Police, established in 1998, was restructured, renamed the Coast Guard, and placed under the direct command of the minister of defense, instead of an agency within the Ministry of Defense. This restructuring aimed at avoiding blame for using military vessels for law enforcement purposes and expanding international cooperation with the Coast Guards of other countries. In 2013 Vietnam also established the Vietnam Fisheries Resources Surveillance (under the Vietnam Directorate of Fisheries) with a view to better protect the country's sovereign rights relating to fisheries within its exclusive economic zones.[99] Law enforcement vessels are prioritized to deploy in the contested area during confrontations to serve two purposes: demonstrating the country's sovereignty and jurisdiction and avoiding possible escalation or even military clash if using naval vessels. For example, from May to August 2014, during the skirmish around China's oil rig, Vietnam deployed more than thirty government ships from the Coast Guard and Fisheries Resources Surveillance to confront Chinese craft.[100]

Vietnam is also expanding international cooperation to improve its law enforcement capabilities with major countries that share concerns about China's maritime expansion. In 2013, Vietnam and Japan reached an agreement in which Tokyo will transfer patrol vessels to Vietnam to help strengthen maritime security capabilities.[101] On August 1, 2014, Japanese Foreign Minister Fumio Kishida announced during his visit to Hanoi that Japan would provide Vietnam with six used vessels to boost its Coast Guard and Fishery Surveillance forces.[102] During the visit to Vietnam in December 2013, U.S. Secretary of State John Kerry also announced a U.S. decision to provide up to US$18 million (with an additional US$32.5 million to help Southeast Asian nations) in assistance for Vietnamese maritime security, including five fast patrol boats for the Vietnamese Coast Guard.[103]

In mid-2015, the United States announced its Southeast Asia Maritime Security Initiative. This initiative is "helping Vietnam bolster its maritime Intelligence, Surveillance, and Reconnaissance (ISR) and command and control within Vietnam's maritime agencies; Lifting the ban on sales of maritime-related lethal capabilities to allow development of Vietnam's maritime capacity and encourage interoperability with other regional forces; and Expanding bilateral training and exercises, focusing on disaster relief and humanitarian issues."[104]

In April 2014, amid China's rising aggression in the South China Sea, the United States and Japan jointly declared their intention to assist ASEAN's littoral states "in building maritime domain awareness and other capacities for maritime safety and security so that they can better enforce law, combat illicit trafficking and weapons proliferation, and protect marine resources."[105]

Conclusion

As Vietnam becomes increasingly integrated into the world, Hanoi will continue the current foreign policy of diversification and multi-directionalization of international relations, proactively being a friend, a reliable partner, and a responsible member of the international community. One of the top priorities of Vietnam's foreign policy objectives remains "maintaining the peaceful environment and creating a favorable international environment conducive to national construction and defense." At the same time, Vietnam's leadership sees relations with other countries (especially with China and the United States) as containing elements of both cooperation in areas where national interests are convergent and struggle where Vietnam's national interests are adversely affected. The most challenging priority in Vietnam's foreign policy is maintaining its sovereignty and political autonomy while keeping stable, peaceful, and beneficial relationships with powerful neighboring China. While continuing to attach great importance to the relationship with China, Vietnam's prioritized policy is to deepen relations with ASEAN members and other major powers, especially the United States, to strengthen its independence and security and to promote economic development.

Walking a delicate balance between China and the United States, Vietnam will develop relationships with the United States to the extent that they will not undermine the regime's legitimacy and put Vietnam in jeopardy of a new confrontation with China. Unless China pursues a comprehensive aggressive policy toward Vietnam, Hanoi will definitely not become Washington's ally, though continuing to promote "comprehensive" cooperation with the United States. The dispute in the South China Sea, and particularly China's strategy toward Vietnam, will be a determining factor for Vietnam's policy in maintaining the balance between China and the United States.

Vietnam's policy of combining engagement and (soft and hard) balancing in dealing with China's assertive strategy in the South China Sea currently is considered as the most effective tool to defend national interests while simultaneously preserving a nonconfrontational and peaceful relationship with China, enhancing its role within ASEAN, and promoting cooperation with other major powers, particularly the United States. Whether this policy will remain relevant in the near future is an open question, because its effectiveness depends on several other external factors beyond Vietnam's control, including domestic politics within China, U.S.-China relations, and ASEAN development. From an internal dimension, Vietnam's strategic room to maneuver has not yet reached its limits, particularly with regard to two specific possibilities: using the international law channel and promoting cooperation with other stakeholders. If other soft and hard balancing acts cannot help Vietnam in deterring Chinese encroachment on its national interests, Hanoi might have to seriously consider legal means as the last peaceful resort and develop closer strategic relationships with the United States and other likeminded South China Sea stakeholders.

NOTES

1 Nguyen Vu Tung, "Vietnam's New Concept of Security in the Context of Doi Moi," in *Comprehensive Security in Asia: Views from Asia and the West on a Changing Security Environment*, ed. Kurt Radtke and Raymond Feddema (Leiden: Brill, 2000), 420.

2 Ibid., 420.

3 Text of the 13th Politburo Resolution, May 1988.

4 Political report presented by the Seventh VCP Central Committee to the Eighth National Party Congress held in Hanoi, June 28–July 1, 1996.

5 Text of the 13th Politburo Resolution, May 1988.

6 VCP, "Van kien dai hoi dai bieu toan quoc thoi ky doi moi" [Documents of national congresses in the era of Doi Moi], vol. 1 (Hanoi: National Political Publishing House, 2010), 403.

7 Press Conference on Foreign Policy and International Economic Integration, www.chinhphu.vn.

8 Political Report presented by the Tenth VCP Central Committee to the XIth National Party Congress, www.chinhphu.vn.

9 "Toàn văn dự thảo Báo cáo chính trị của Ban Chấp hành Trung ương Đảng khóa XI tại Đại hội đại biểu toàn quốc lần thứ XII của Đảng" [Full text of draft political report of VCP of 11th Central Committee to the 12th Party Congress], http://m.vietnamnet.vn.

10 Vietnam is greatly concerned about China's massive cascade of dams on the Upper Mekong in Yunnan province (and the dams proposed on the Lower Mekong Basin's mainstream in Laos, in Cambodia, and on the Thai-Lao border). First, dams in China and in the lower mainstream (with total reservoir storage capacity of about 40 billion m³) will trap a big portion of the Mekong's sediment that the river should naturally transport to the delta. The fertility of the delta, vital for rice cultivation, will suffer and productivity will decline. Second, most of the dams in China and all twelve dams in the mainstream of Lower Mekong basin are "run-of-river dams," but they are designed for daily regulation to meet changing power demands, mainly during the dry season. This poses a risk to downstream water levels, especially during the dry season, and gives way to salinity intrusion in the Mekong Delta. See Dao Trong Tu, "A Vietnamese Perspective on Proposed Mainstream Mekong Dams" (Stimson, December 8, 2011), www.stimson.org.

11 Since 2004, China has become Vietnam's largest trade partner with an annual two-way trade growth of over 20 percent in the past four years, amounting to more than US$50 billion in 2013. Vietnam's trade deficit with China is continuously rising and reached US$28.8 billion in 2014 and US$35 billion in 2015. Vietnam is exporting mostly raw materials, unfinished commodities, and low-value-added manufactured goods such as coal, crude oil, rubber, foodstuffs, seafood, and footwear, while imports from China include materials for manufacturing, machinery, equipment, and other high-value-added manufactured goods such as pharmaceuticals, computers, electronic products, and petroleum. Source: Vietnam Ministry of Industry and Trade, "Vietnam's Trade Deficit with China Likely to Reach $35bn in 2015: Ministry," *Tuoitrenews*, http://tuoitrenews.vn.

12 Resolution of the 11th Party National Congress, http://en.vietnamplus.vn.

13 U.S. Census Bureau, "Trade in Goods with Vietnam," www.census.gov. Vietnam's export-led growth model is relatively similar to the Chinese model, and its main export products face difficulty entering the Chinese market due to competitiveness. Conversely, Vietnam's economy complements that of the United States, and its main exports (including textiles and garments, seafood, farm and forest products, wooden furniture, and footwear) are low priced, high quality, and in high demand in the U.S. market.

14 American economist Samuel Rines estimated that "by 2025, Vietnam would stand to gain nearly $96 billion, or 28 percent of its GDP. This is largely due to exports increasing an estimated 37 percent." See Samuel Rines, "Trans-Pacific Partnership: Geopolitics, Not Growth," http://nationalinterest.org.

15 "Joint Statement by President Barack Obama of the United States of America and President Truong Tan Sang of the Socialist Republic of Vietnam," www.whitehouse.gov.

16 Resolution of the 11th Party National Congress, http://en.vietnamplus.vn.

17 Nguyen Tan Dung, "Building Strategic Trust for Peace, Cooperation and Prosperity in the Asia-Pacific Region" (Keynote address, Shangri-La Dialogue, 2013), www.iiss.org.

18 On February 2007, the VCP Central Committee introduced Resolution 09-NQ/TW on Vietnam's Maritime Strategy for 2020, which stressed that the South China Sea is of strategic geoeconomic and geopolitical importance to the cause of national development. The resolution set the target for 2020 that the maritime economy will account for between 53 and 55 percent of the GDP and between 55 and 60 percent of the total exports. Source: VCP, Propaganda Commission, "Documents to Study on the Resolution 09-NQ/TW on Vietnam's Maritime Strategy for 2020."

19 Tran Truong Thuy and Nguyen Minh Ngoc, "Vietnam's Security Challenges: Priorities, Policy Implications and Prospects for Regional Cooperation," in *Security Outlook of the Asia Pacific Countries and Its Implications for the Defense Sector*, ed. National Institute for Defense Studies (Tokyo: National Institute for Defense Studies, 2013), 96, www.nids.go.jp.

20 In addition to the Agreement with China on the Delimitation of the Tonkin Gulf and on Fishery Cooperation on December 25, 2000, Vietnam has signed the Agreement with Thailand on Maritime Delimitation on August 9, 1997, and the Agreement with Indonesia on the Delimitation of Continental Shelf on June 26, 2003. Vietnam is currently involved in negotiations over the delimitation of the Exclusive Economic Zone with Indonesia. In cooperation with neighboring countries, in 1992 Vietnam signed with Malaysia an MOU for cooperation in exploration and exploitation of petroleum in a defined area of the continental shelf in the Gulf of Thailand, which has been effectively implemented. The country and is currently engaged in negotiations with Thailand and Malaysia in cooperation over the Tripartite Overlapping Continental Shelf Claim Area. In early May 2009, Vietnam, in cooperation with Malaysia, submitted to the United Nations the Submission on the Limits of the Continental Shelf beyond 200 nm in the Southern Part of the South China Sea. See Ministry of Foreign Affairs, "Vietnam—A Responsible Party of UNCLOS Convention," http://english.vov.vn.

21 Taylor Fravel, "Hainan's New Fishing Rules: A Preliminary Analysis," *Diplomat*, January 20, 2014, http://thediplomat.com.

22 Carl Thayer, "China Escalates Fishing Disputes in the South China Sea," http://cogitasia.com.

23 "China Says 'Board and Search' Sea Rules Limited to Hainan Coast," http://in.reuters.com.

24 See text in Chinese at www.hq.xinhuanet.com.

25 "ADIZ Stirs Fears for South China Sea," *Asia Times*, December 6, 2013, www.atimes.com.

26 "China Exclusive: Defense Ministry Spokesman Responds to Air Defense Identification Zone Questions," *Xinhua*, November 23, 2013, http://news.xinhuanet.com.

27 Mingjiang Li, "Reconciling Assertiveness and Cooperation? China's Changing Approach to the South China Sea Dispute," *Security Challenges* 6, no. 2 (2010): 58.

28 Scot Marciel, "Maritime Issues and Sovereignty Disputes in East Asia," Testimony before the Subcommittee on East Asian and Pacific Affairs, Committee on Foreign Relations, U.S. Senate, July 15, 2009, http://foreign.senate.gov.

For a summary of leaked U.S. diplomatic cables released by WikiLeaks on China's protests against international oil firms signing exploration deals with Vietnam in the South China Sea, see Greg Torode, "Beijing Pressure Intense in South China Sea Row," *South China Morning Post*, September 23, 2011, http://topics.scmp.com.

29 There were at least three cable-cutting incidents between China and Vietnam: The first cable cutting incident, on May 26, 2011, took place in an area just about eighty miles off the south-central coast of Vietnam, within Vietnam's exclusive economic zone, when three Chinese patrol ships accosted and harassed the Vietnamese ship *Binh Minh 02*. See "Press Conference on Chinese Maritime Surveillance Vessel's Cutting Exploration Cable of PetroViet Nam Seismic Vessel," www.mofa.gov.vn.

The second incident occurred on June 9, 2011, when a Chinese fishing boat, with support from Chinese fishing patrol vessels, rammed the survey cables of the PetroVietnam ship *Viking II*, which was conducting a seismic survey in Block 136–03, an area within the two-hundred-nautical-mile exclusive economic zone of Vietnam. Foreign Ministry Spokesperson Nguyen Phuong Nga at the Press Conference, June 9, 2011, www.mofa.gov.vn.

Another incident happened on December 3, 2012, when two Chinese boats ran up behind and cut seismic survey cables of PetroVietnam's ship *Binh Minh 02* while this commercial ship was operating in the area outside the mouth of the Tonkin Gulf on Vietnam's side, about twenty miles from the median line between China's coast and Vietnam's coast. See "PetroVietnam Protests Chinese Ships' Breakage of Survey Cable," http://biengioilanhtho.gov.vn.

30 "Chinese Vessels Deliberately Ram Vietnam's Ships in Vietnamese Waters: Officials," *Tuoitrenews*, http://tuoitrenews.vn.

31 "Chứng khoán giảm cực mạnh vì biển Đông," http://vnmoney.nld.com.vn.

32 "Struggling Businesses Urge Vietnam to Expand Visa Waiver to Lure Back Tourists," *Thanh Nien News*, June 12, 2014, www.thanhniennews.com.

33 "China Tensions Choke Off Tourism to Vietnam," *New York Times*, July 22, 2014, www.nytimes.com.

34 U.S. Department of Defense, "The Asia-Pacific Maritime Security Strategy: Achieving U.S. National Security Objectives in a Changing Environment," 16, www.defense.gov.

35 Robert Beckman, "Large Scale Reclamation Projects in the South China Sea: China and International Law," http://cil.nus.edu.sg.

36 "Satellites and Seafood: China Keeps Fishing Fleet Connected in Disputed Waters," Reuters, July 27, 2014, www.reuters.com.

37 "Second Thomas Shoal Tensions Intensify," *Diplomat*, March 13, 2014, http://thediplomat.com.

38 Yoji Koda, "Recent Trends in the South China Sea and U.S. Policy: Perspectives on U.S. Policy toward the South China Sea," CSIS, July 11, 2014, http://csis.org.

39 "Construction of an Airfield on the Disputed Spratly Islands Puts Australia in Reach of China's Strategic Bombers: Reports," November 25, 2014, www.news.com.au.

40 Defence White Paper 2009, 19, http://admm.org.vn.

41 "Vietnam, China to Boost Ties, Settle Disagreements Satisfactorily." *Tuoitrenews*, November 11, 2014, http://tuoitrenews.vn.

42 "Chinese Premier Li Keqiang Visits Vietnam," *VietNamNet*, October 14, 2013, http://english.vietnamnet.vn; "Premier Li Keqiang Holds Talks with Prime Minister Nguyen Tan Dung of Vietnam," www.fmprc.gov.cn.

43 "Chinese Premier Li Keqiang Visits Vietnam."

44 "Vietnam-China Agree on Basic Principles to Resolve Maritime Issues," *Nhan Dan*, June 20, 2013, http://en.nhandan.org.vn.

45 Ibid.

46 "Seventh Talk Round on Sea Area Off Gulf of Tonkin Held," *VietnamPlus*, http://en.vietnamplus.vn.

47 One project is on joint research on the management of the marine and island environment in the Gulf of Tonkin, and the other is on conducting comparative research on sediment dating back to the Holocene epoch in the Red River Delta and the Yangtze River Delta. See "Vietnam, China Discuss Sea Borders," *VietNamNet*, http://english.vietnamnet.vn.

48 "Vietnam, China Agree to Restore Ties after Oil Rig Rift," *Tuoitrenews*, August 28, 2014, http://tuoitrenews.vn.

49 Carl Thayer, "China-Vietnam Defense Hotline Agreed: What Next?," *Diplomat*, October 20, 2014, http://thediplomat.com.

50 "Vietnam, China Pledge to Address and Control Maritime Differences," *Thanh Nien News*, October 16, 2014, www.thanhniennews.com.

51 "China, Vietnam Pledge to 'Address and Control' Maritime Disputes," Reuters, October 17, 2014, www.reuters.com.

52 Ibid.

53 "VN, China Need to Treasure Bilateral Ties," *VGP News*, December 26, 2014, http://news.chinhphu.vn.

54 "Vietnam Joins AIIB to Seek New Funding Source," *Saigon Times*, June 30, 2015, http://english.thesaigontimes.vn.

55 Pew Research Center, "Opinion of China" (2016), www.pewglobal.org.

56 Tuong Lai, "Vietnam's Overdue Alliance with America," *New York Times*, July 11, 2014, www.nytimes.com.

57 Singapore MFA Spokesperson's Comments on Visit of Chinese Maritime Surveillance Vessel Haixun 31 to Singapore, www.mfa.gov.sg.

58 Indonesia sent a diplomatic note to the UN secretary-general on July 8, 2010, saying the map lacks international legal basis and was tantamount to upsetting

the UNCLOS 1982. Note available at www.un.org. See also Ann Marie Murphy, "Jakarta Rejects China's 'Nine-Dash Line,'" *Asia Times*, April 3, 2014, www. atimes.com.

59 In July 2012, ASEAN foreign ministers reached consensus and adopted the "proposed elements" of the COC and tasked the ASEAN senior officials with meeting with the senior official from China to negotiate the code. Michael Lipin, "Cambodia Says ASEAN Ministers Agree to 'Key Elements' of Sea Code," *Voice of America*, July 9, 2012, www.voanews.com.

60 See related documents on the ASEAN website at www.asean.org.

61 ASEAN, "ASEAN Foreign Ministers' Statement on the Current Developments in the South China Sea," www.asean.org, emphasis added.

62 ASEAN, "Declaration on the Conduct of Parties in the South China Sea," www. asean.org.

63 ASEAN, "Guidelines for the Implementation of the DOC," www.asean.org.

64 Author interview with Vietnam Ministry of Foreign Affairs senior officials, Hanoi, July 2012.

65 In March 2013, China announced plans to restructure the country's top oceanic administration by bringing China's maritime law enforcement forces, currently scattered in different ministries, under the unified management of one single administration, to "enhance maritime law enforcement and better protect and use its oceanic resources." See "China to Restructure Oceanic Administration, Enhance Maritime Law Enforcement," *Xinhuanet*, October 10, 2013, http://news. xinhuanet.com.

66 Dang Cong san Viet Nam, *Van kien Dai hoi Dai bieu Toan quoc lan thu VIII* [VCP, documents of the Eighth National Party Congress] (Hanoi: National Political Publisher, 1996), 211.

67 "Joint Statement by President Barack Obama of the United States of America and President Truong Tan Sang."

68 Ibid.

69 Full text of the Joint Vision Statement, http://iipdigital.usembassy.gov.

70 Hillary Clinton, "America's Pacific Century," *Foreign Policy*, October 11, 2011, www.foreignpolicy.com.

71 Author's interview with U.S. PACOM senior officials, Honolulu, HI, June 2013.

72 Leon Panetta, "The US Rebalance towards the Asia-Pacific" (Washington, DC: International Institute for Strategic Studies, June 2, 2012), www.iiss.org.

73 Government of the Philippines, "Q&A on the Enhanced Defense Cooperation Agreement," www.gov.ph.

74 "Return of the FONOP: US Navy Destroyer Asserts Freedom of Navigation in Paracel Islands," *Diplomat*, January 31, 2016, http://thediplomat.com/2016/01/ return-of-the-fonop-us-navy-destroyer-asserts-freedom-of-navigation-in-paracel-islands/

75 Ibid.

76 "China's Sea Claims Excessive, Says US," *Manila Bulletin*, www.mb.com.ph.

77 "Maritime Disputes in East Asia," Testimony by Daniel R. Russel, Assistant Secretary, Bureau of East Asian and Pacific Affairs, before the House Committee on Foreign Affairs Subcommittee on Asia and the Pacific, Washington, DC, February 5, 2014, www.state.gov.

78 "Paracels Build-Up a Pointer to China's Broader South China Sea Ambitions," Reuters, February 21, 2016, http://mobile.reuters.com.

79 Tran Truong Thuy, "The South China Sea: Interests, Policies, and Dynamics of Recent Developments" (paper, Managing Tensions in the South China Sea, Washington DC, June 5–6, 2013), https://csis.org.

80 Author's interview with senior researchers at the Diplomatic Academy of Russia, Moscow, January 2014.

81 "Exclusive: Vietnam PM Says Considering Legal Action Against China over Disputed Waters," Reuters, May 21, 2014, www.reuters.com.

82 "Vietnam's PM Calls for Preparation of Lawsuit Against China," *Thanh Nien News*, July 2, 2014, www.thanhniennews.com.

83 "Vietnam Dismisses China's Position Paper on East Sea Claims," *Thanh Nien News*, December 12, 2014, www.thanhniennews.com.

84 "Beijing Rejects Hanoi's Legal Challenge on Spratly, Paracel Islands Disputes," *South China Morning Post*, December 12, 2014, www.scmp.com.

85 Quoted in Nguyen Vu Tung, "Vietnam's Security Challenges: Ha Noi's New Approach to National Security and Implications to Defense and Foreign Policies," in *Asia Pacific Countries' Security Outlook and Its Implications for the Defense Sector*, edited by National Institute for Defense Studies (Tokyo: National Institute for Defense Studies, 2010), 121, www.nids.go.jp.

86 However, it will take time for the Vietnamese Navy to build a full-fledged submarine capability, as it requires not only the submarines themselves, but also a concerted effort in investing in infrastructure, maritime aerial surveillance, proficient crews, submarine rescue capabilities, and international cooperation with regional navies. See Koh Swee Lean Collin, "Vietnam's New Kilo-Class Submarines: Game-Changer in Regional Naval Balance?," (Singapore: Rajaratnam School of International Studies, 2012), www.rsis.edu.sg.

87 "Vietnam Builds Naval Muscle," *Asia Times*, March 29, 2012, www.atimes.com.

88 Carl Thayer, "With Russia's Help, Vietnam Adopts A2/AD Strategy," *Diplomat*, October 8, 2013, http://thediplomat.com.

89 For information on Vietnam's Major Defence Acquisitions since 1995, see Le Hong Hiep, "Vietnam's Hedging Strategy Against China since Normalization," *Contemporary Southeast Asia* 35, no. 3 (2013): 354–55.

90 *Vietnam Defence White Paper*, 24.

91 Ibid., 24.

92 Ibid., 24.

93 Carlyle A. Thayer, "Vietnam People's Army: Development and Modernization" (Research monograph, April 30, 2009), 26.

94 Lewis M. Stern, "Adding Strategic Depth to U.S.-Vietnamese Defense Relations," *Stratfor*, May 17, 2012, www.stratfor.com.

95 "U.S., Vietnam in Exercises amid Tensions with China," *Wall Street Journal*, July 16, 2011, http://online.wsj.com.

96 "U.S.-Vietnam Naval Exercises Begin amid Sea Tensions," *Bloomberg*, April 8, 2014, www.bloomberg.com.

97 Ibid.

98 Ankit Panda, "United States Lifts Vietnam Arms Embargo (with a Catch)," *Diplomat*, October 3, 2014, http://thediplomat.com.

99 "Ra mắt lực lượng Kiểm ngư Việt Nam" [Launching Vietnam fisheries resources surveillance force, government's website], http://baodientu.chinhphu.vn.

100 "Chinese Vessels Deliberately Ram Vietnam's Ships in Vietnamese Waters: Officials," *Tuoitrenews*, May 7, 2014, http://tuoitrenews.vn.

101 "Japan Coast Guard Vessels and Equipment in High Demand in S.E. Asia, Africa," *Asahi Shimbun*, September 30, 2013, http://ajw.asahi.com.

102 "Japan to Supply Six Ships to Vietnam, Intended for Patrolling: Sources," *Japan Times*, August 1, 2014, www.japantimes.co.jp.

103 "US Boosts Maritime Security Aid to Vietnam," AP, December 13, 2013, http://news.yahoo.com.

104 White House, "Fact Sheet: U.S. Building Maritime Capacity in Southeast Asia," www.whitehouse.gov.

105 White House, "U.S.-Japan Joint Statement: The United States and Japan: Shaping the Future of the Asia-Pacific and Beyond," www.whitehouse.gov.

7

Not between Scylla and Charybdis

Malaysia's Relations with China and the United States

ZAKARIA AHMAD

The visit of U.S. President Barack Obama to Kuala Lumpur at the end of April 2014—the second such visit by a U.S. leader after President Lyndon Johnson in 1966 (a gap of forty-eight years)—signified to many Malaysians that Malaysia was an actor of no small measure in Southeast Asia, the Asia-Pacific, and indeed the world. U.S. watcher and strategist Elina Noor declared the Obama visit (an earlier, scheduled visit in 2013 had been canceled because of a U.S. budget crisis) as the "best opportunity to lay an enduring framework for the future development of the U.S.-Malaysia relationship."[1] That opportunity nonetheless would have to be balanced against U.S. resolve from the first U.S. "Pacific President" and its recent policy of "rebalancing" or "pivot to Asia," all of which may be seen as a response to rapidly evolving geostrategic and politico-economic circumstances and a changing balance of power scenario, including a more assertive China as a rising power and a declining United States.

In contrast to Obama's delayed visit, China's President Xi Jinping was able to visit as planned, and did so ahead of the 2013 APEC meeting in Bali. That visit to Malaysia resulted in an agreement between Kuala Lumpur and Beijing to elevate bilateral ties to a "comprehensive strategic partnership"— again succinctly noted by Elina Noor as a focus "to deepen already expanding trade and increase nascent cooperation in defence and security matters."[2] Beijing's overtures in Malaysia and Southeast Asia, in general, however, are not so salutary and benign as outwardly indicated; in the past several years, Beijing has increasingly flexed its naval presence in Southeast Asian waters and elsewhere, and in some sense displays a two-faced policy even as it offers its hand of friendship. Beijing's steadfast policy of its sovereign right to the Spratlys has led to clashes with Vietnam and the Philippines. With Malaysia, there have been no such clashes, but Chinese Coast Guard vessels are regularly stationed off James Shoal, and Chinese Navy ships have come close to territorial waters.[3]

The juxtaposition of these two high-level visits by the leaders of the United States and China to Malaysia puts into relief the large issue of the roles of Big Powers in their interactions with smaller countries such as Malaysia. From a military viewpoint, the United States is seemingly benign, whereas China has indicated its presence with muscle, especially in the South China Sea. Yet, both Big Powers are important and have good diplomatic and economic linkages with Malaysia, and the result of the two aforementioned visits have been underscored by agreements that suggest "strategic" partnerships and mutual desires to deepen ties. It is more than apparent that Malaysia faces an extraordinary challenge in its foreign policy dealings with both the United States and China in the second decade of the new millennium. Malaysia itself, after more than five decades of independence, is an actor of increasing stature and significance in international affairs and certainly an important actor in world trade. How, then, should it deal with these two Big Powers—should or can it tread a careful path between the two, as between Scylla and Charybdis, or will it be trampled (as the Asian saying goes) by the two elephants, whether they fight or make love? Or even pretend as though neither elephant is in the room.

The reference to Scylla and Charybdis may be seen as an overdrawn analogy, or even a false construct. But one may be reminded of an earlier period of Southeast Asia's modern history, in the period of the 1950s through the 1990s, when Cambodia's efforts not to be engulfed between the United States and China failed.[4] The tragic outcome resulted precisely from Cambodia's inability to steer clear of Scylla and Charybdis. Perhaps an important element to consider is any nation's strength and ability to maintain its independence and integrity in a context of Big Power contestation. The issue of Big Power contestation or that of Big Power intervention and interference is not novel to Malaysia or the rest of Southeast Asia, and has been an existential scenario since World War II. Malaysia's desideratum has been and is to prevent such intrusions even as it remains open to external influences. In the prevailing context of more than apparent Sino-U.S. rivalry, Malaysia is eschewing taking sides. But in attempting to maintain a relationship with both, but not at the expense of the other, it is treading a journey through perilous waters while avoiding dangerous rocks. Indeed, at the outset, it can be stated that Malaysia is attempting not to be between Scylla and Charybdis as it develops its relationships with both the United States and China.

The primary scenario that unfolds is that Sino-U.S. rivalry is a reality that affects Southeast Asia, and indeed all of Asia. Such a rivalry is not just about military or strategic empowerment and displacement but is a complex web of political, economic, technological, and social relationships and developments occurring at different levels and intertwined with varying rates of progress in the nations of Pacific Asia. Competition and cooperation coexist, and complexities abound within and across nations. Such has been the situation of the Trans-Pacific Partnership Agreement (TPPA) talks among the United States and countries like Malaysia in which debates swirl not only about competitive advantages in trade of goods and services, but a whole gamut of issues that encompass environmental protection, the development of small and medium-sized enterprises, fair trade, and the intrinsic needs and priorities of developing countries against those of developed economies. Although both houses of the Malaysian Parliament assented to Malaysia's entry into the TPPA in early 2016, there are still voices of dissent within Malaysia as well as concerns that doing so will complicate relations with the Chinese.

It is against such scenarios that this chapter attempts to address Malaysia's forays into the external environment—amid a changing balance of power in Pacific Asia and the challenges of change in political economy and technological transformation. More specifically, the remainder of this chapter reviews Malaysia as a Southeast Asian/ASEAN actor and its relations with the United States and China in the second decade of the twenty-first century. The chapter addresses Malaysia's foreign policy priorities and its dealings and views of China and the United States, and it includes a brief discussion of the issue of the South China Sea in terms of Malaysia's interests vis-à-vis China and the United States.

Malaysia's own stature as a "Middle Power"[5] in Southeast Asia and ASEAN is an important consideration in its relations with the United States, China, and other power actors. That sense of entitlement was underscored by its role as chairman of ASEAN in 2015 and its nonpermanent membership in the UN Security Council. As 2015 ASEAN chair, Malaysia enjoyed its position of having established as fact the ASEAN Economic Community, the ASEAN Political Security Community, and the ASEAN Socio-Cultural Community.

Malaysia's Priorities

Malaysia aspires to be a "Westphalian" nation of stature, pulling its weight and exercising its rights and prerogatives in the ever-evolving regional and global landscape. Noted foreign policy analyst J. Saravanamuttu argues that "despite being one of the smaller states in Southeast Asia, Malaysia has been able to punch above its weight in foreign policy and particularly vis-à-vis the major powers in the region," and "has been at the forefront of policy innovation in the face of the region's ever changing geopolitics."[6]

Such boldness in foreign policy has been and is being pursued even as it continues on a path of state- and nation-building against the realities of a divided, multiethnic and multireligious society; even as it professes to be a "moderate, Muslim-majority" country, it grapples with the challenge and desideratum of the call to be an Islamic state, inter alia, with the possible replacement of English-derived civil law by *Sharia* law.[7] Although it has achieved middle-income status, Malaysia has also fallen into the "middle-income trap," and Prime Minister Najib is attempting to elevate the country's economic modernization through the Economic Transformation Programme and the Government Transformation Programme. Politically, Najib's ruling Barisan Nasional coalition is also under siege and attempting to reestablish its previous dominance in the political process,[8] to obtain the two-thirds parliamentary majority it had enjoyed before the 2008 general election.

In 2014–15, controversies plagued Malaysia's domestic political context as allegations of corruption of Prime Minister Najib arose when it was revealed that he had received political donations from a Middle Eastern source. Such innuendoes of impropriety were concomitant with other events such as public demonstrations and tumult in the upper echelons of the ruling party such as the removal of stalwarts Deputy Prime Minister Muhyiddin Yassin and UMNO Vice-President Shafie Apdal. Such denouements led one observer to note that such domestic upheavals tarnished Malaysia's standing even as it chaired ASEAN in 2015 and held a nonpermanent seat in the UN Security Council.[9]

As Malaysia is an ASEAN state located somewhat in between continental and maritime Southeast Asia, its relations with the United States and a "rising" China at the outset may be described as not wanting to be drawn in a bilateral tussle of influence in the ever-important Asia-Pacific. In terms of foreign policy goals, Malaysia has welcomed China's rapid economic growth (since Deng Xiaoping) as an opportunity, and no longer sees Beijing in adversarial terms or as a threat as was the case during the Cold War. Malaysia's changing perception of the "China threat" may be traced to the 1950s through the 1970s, at which time the communist insurgency not only was waged by local ethnic Chinese but also was supported by and drew its ideological inspiration from China under Mao Zedong. Developments and modernization in post-Mao China, concomitant with Sino-U.S. rapprochement, from the 1970s to the present have presented Malaysia's leaders with the view that China is no longer a political or security threat and conversely presents more of an opportunity for commerce and bilateral trade.[10] It needs to be noted that Malaysia was the first ASEAN country to establish diplomatic relations with China, in 1974, and Sino-Malaysia links, in their fifth decade, continue to deepen and grow from "strength to strength,"[11] especially in the economic realm. Currently, Malaysia is ASEAN's largest trading partner with China, and China is Malaysia's largest trading partner.

On the other hand, while Washington has often been lambasted in rhetorical terms (especially during the Mahathir years), American investment and trade have always been welcomed, and U.S.-Malaysia military and security cooperation has been sustained, if not deepened, on a mutually rewarding basis. U.S. warships (presumably including submarines) make frequent port visits to Malaysia, and small U.S. troop detachments conduct periodic training exercises there. Nonetheless, there is as much ambiguity as a sense of continuity in terms of Malaysia's strategic perspectives and foreign policy stances, even as Malaysia pushes ahead to achieve economic modernity and competitiveness as a trading and industrializing nation.

Not unlike many other developing states, Malaysia's foreign policy and engagement with its neighbors, far and wide, are a function of both the external environment as well as the domestic imperatives of elite stances and ongoing political denouements. Malaysia's foreign policy has traversed several periods of emphasis, responding in large part to the changing external environment, but after more than five decades of independence the country has also exhibited a self-assured confidence in forging initiatives as a maturing nation-state. Rather than being a closed society and isolationist state and shutting itself off from external influences, Malaysia has remained a relatively "open" society receptive to outside ideas, and has continuously pursued an independent, pragmatic, and forward-looking foreign policy. In large part, Malaysia's quest for economic development and its policies of export-driven growth have resulted in it being one of the top forty largest trading nations in the world. It is a significant trading partner of the United States and China and looks to *both* Washington and Beijing for foreign direct investment, as well as other incentives.

In terms of politics and security, Malaysia has pursued a policy of non-involvement in Big Power politics and has veered more to being part of the "nonaligned" world. In doing so, it has pushed for guarantees of noninterference in its affairs from all external Big Powers, as when it presented its idea of the Zone of Peace, Freedom and Neutrality (ZOPFAN), a concept coinciding with the period of the Second and Third Indo-China Wars. ZOPFAN was a notion of neutralism, but not necessarily neutrality. The roots of this notion are traceable to the early beginnings of Malay(si)a's foreign policy journey. Thus, under the nation's first prime minister, Tunku Abdul Rahman, it pursued a policy of being a "committed neutral"—not involved in Big Power politics or the East-West ideological divide, but yet staunchly anticommunist and committed to "Western" ideals of freedom and democracy. While it has

moved away from being "pro-Western," it is the view here that it has not necessarily become "anti-Western."

A persistent theme in its foreign policy of noninvolvement with Big Powers was labeled "equidistance," or keeping at arm's length the influence of Big
Powers, and more involvement in the Non-Aligned Movement. It is apparent that this stance still prevails; although the nomenclature of "equidistance"
seems to have been cast aside with the end of the Cold War, occasional reference to it indicates a lack of clarity and direction or ambiguity as to its intent
as a plank of policy.

Even as it has pursued the notion of noninvolvement in Big Power politics,
Malaysia has nonetheless continued to engage the Big Powers and other actors. It has sustained its links with Britain, Australia, and New Zealand, all of
which may be seen as part of the "Western" alliance. Not only have these three
Commonwealth countries been very involved in Malaysia's fight against communist insurgency, but they also played a robust role in the defense of Malaysia during the period of Indonesian Confrontation (or Konfrontasi, 1963–66),
and therefore may be seen as important to Malaysia's strategic interests. It is
instructive that as a result of the experience Malaysia continues to be committed to the quasi-alliance Five Power Defense Arrangements, initiated in 1967,
that groups it with Britain, Australia, New Zealand, and Singapore.[12] More
importantly, that Malaysia continues to have such linkages is indicative of the
fact that, in the final analysis, its interests and survival may reside in being
part of "Western" security parameters.

Although foreign policy remains largely an elite activity and is not a matter
of active parliamentary debate, there is some relevance of domestic parameters in Malaysia's external affairs. Thus, in deference to Islamic credentials, it
has no diplomatic relations with Israel and has allowed Palestinian diplomatic
recognition (even as it subscribes to a "two-state solution" for the disputed
territory). Within the domestic context, however, there are developments that
suggest more inward-looking concerns, thus leading to an observation of Malaysia "looking outward and moving inward."[13] This theme may indicate a
schizophrenic tendency, but its essence underlies the domestic emphases of a
polity tied to the reality of being an open economy subject to the vicissitudes
of international change and yet attempting to shield itself from all the mani-
festations and challenges of globalization and its concomitant challenges.
Thus, to be competitive means not only a dynamic response to external factors of production but also the need to adjust to domestic considerations that
offer resistance as well as adoption; one consequence is an influx of foreign
labor into the Malaysian economy and society (and polity), with both negative and positive repercussions. The approach toward foreign labor is often

xenophobic in character, but the large numbers of immigrants demonstrate both an official and a societal recognition of their need in the industrial, manufacturing, service, and even domestic sectors of the economy.

While not an arcane subject restricted only to an elite few, the scope, direction, and objects of foreign policy have been reviewed periodically both within and without the foreign policy establishment. In 2014–15, the quasi-official think tank, the Institute of Strategic and International Studies (ISIS Malaysia), prepared a foreign policy blueprint for the future, a report dealing with the changing balance of power in Asia and the world and the many other facets of rapid change in economics, trade, and technology.[14] At the time of writing, it is not clear as to the status of the study after submission to the prime minister's office. Be that as it may, foreign policy desiderata, goals, and implementation are a function of the domestic political milieu of policy making and direction; there is little political debate on foreign policy issues in Malaysia within the political spectrum, and as such, discussion as may take place is concentrated with the agency or agencies of foreign policy (principally the Ministries of Foreign Affairs, International Trade, Home Affairs, and Defence) and a select group of elite thinkers, practitioners, and analysts.[15] Foreign policy is an elite endeavor, and decisions on national stances in both domestic and external contexts are more often than not a prime ministerial prerogative. Sometimes, even the Foreign Ministry is oblivious of actions enacted by the prime minister on foreign policy issues.[16]

If prime ministerial prerogative is a key locus of policy, and not merely an idiosyncratic factor, it may well be that structure and national interest(s) in Malaysian foreign policy are overshadowed by subjective inclinations. It is patently clear that foreign policy is guided by all of Malaysia's successive prime ministers. With reference to the issue of the United States and China and Malaysia's "equidistance" policy, it can be observed "that the Najib government has sought to *concurrently* enhance Malaysia's relations with America and China, building stronger bilateral relationships with both powers without departing from its non-alignment stance, with effects serving to reinforce its fallback position."[17] According to C. C. Kuik, in August 2014, in responding to a question raised at a student conference about "who Malaysia should choose" between the two major powers, Najib replied that Malaysian foreign policy "is based on principle" and that the country "did not really need to choose between United States and China" because of "the strength of both countries."[18]

Malaysia, ASEAN, and Beyond

Even as there are constraints and domestic political conditionalities in Malaysian foreign policy, Kuala Lumpur's approach has been enduring in its notion of being a Southeast Asian state, or by extension an ASEAN state, leading to the posture that its external relationships will be based on ASEAN as a "cornerstone of its foreign policy."[19] That said, it is also apparent that it is not hostage to a presumably "ASEAN position," and that it retains flexibility and pragmatism even as it exhorts a commitment to ASEAN solidarity.

That ASEAN is accorded a central parameter in Malaysian foreign policy is a recognition of the country having been a founding member of the regional organization and a belief that Malaysia is a stalwart ingredient of its workability and substance. It also rests on the notion that Malaysia's geopolitical location in Southeast Asia is a fundamental given. Perhaps, if ASEAN did not exist, Malaysia would have to invent it. For a substantial period in the history of foreign policy making, certain cohorts and personalities, especially Ghazali Shafie (a top Wisma Putra official who later also was minister of foreign affairs)[20] were instrumental in embedding the notion that Malaysia's fate, fortunes, and future rested on it being an integral part of Southeast Asia/ASEAN and conversely as well that ASEAN as a regional entity draws strength from Malaysia as a core member.[21]

What is less clear, however, is if Malaysia will be subject to an ASEAN position that is inimical to Malaysia's interests. This begs the issue of the so-called consensual decision-making process (or the "ASEAN Way") itself, usually arrived at the ASEAN Ministerial Meetings (and duly endorsed by ASEAN leaders or at the level of the ASEAN Summits). Thus far, there does not appear to be any unified stand concerning the United States and China that would signify a unanimity of views and approaches among the ASEAN member states. This may well be, however, in Malaysia's interest. Paradoxically as it may seem, Malaysia's subscribing to ASEAN unity does not bind it not to forge its own stance in its relationship with other countries, including Big Powers. As much as there is ambiguity, Malaysia's ability to forge policy views independent of ASEAN exemplifies a high degree of pragmatism and a subtlety in regional leadership.

As Malaysia is a core member of ASEAN, it can be observed that Kuala Lumpur/Putrajaya has been, under successive prime ministers, an instrumental leader of regionalism and in initiatives promoting ASEAN/Southeast Asian centrality and resilience. It is in this sense that one may recognize the attributes of a "middle power" approach on Malaysia's part. Such an approach is perhaps more aspirational and linked to Malaysia's ASEAN position under

Prime Minister Najib. At a keynote address at the Eighth Heads of Malaysian Missions Conference in 2014, he stated, "As a Middle Power that means playing a greater part in Asia and helping Asia play a greater part in the world." Also in reference to ASEAN, he declared, "We sink or swim with our region. If we don't have an influential voice here, we won't have an influential voice anywhere."[22] He opined "that Malaysia must embrace its position as one of the region's middle powers in its path towards becoming a developed nation by 2020."[23]

In addressing foreign policy making and implementation, it is germane to ask if developments regarding the United States and China, and Sino-U.S. relations, are salient areas of enquiry. Without doubt there is interest in Malaysia-U.S. and Malaysia-China relations and events and awareness of global and regional events that have an impact on Malaysia's own travails as an actor in the international system. In a situation in which foreign policy may be characterized by the nature of prime ministerial leadership, in style and substance, even if idiosyncratic, Kuala Lumpur's stances and relations with external actors have also varied according to evolving international circumstances and domestic political developments. Thus, during the early years of the Cold War, and China's earlier revolutionary forays in Southeast Asia, Malaysia saw Beijing as threatening but nonetheless did not see it fit to be part of the U.S.-sponsored Southeast Asia Treaty Organization (SEATO). Following the U.S.-China rapprochement, however, Malaysia recognized the PRC in 1974—an event of both regional and domestic significance—and today engages with gusto the former "enemy to the north," in economic linkages, trade and development, and the advancement of an Asian regional identity.[24] As the Asian region has grown economically, its political stature has also increased, and there have been greater interactions among Asian nations. In this regard, Malaysia not only has been active in ASEAN but also has been at the forefront in pursuing intra-Asian linkages, and has been a strong proponent of the ASEAN Plus Three—that is, plus China, Japan, and South Korea—framework. However, it is not clear yet if region-wide initiatives and ideas proposed by China's leaders, such as the Maritime Silk Road and One Belt, One Road, have been readily accepted by Kuala Lumpur.[25] Although Malaysia has signed on to be part of the China's Asian Infrastructure Investment Bank, the indication for its action seems to be more opportunistic than prompted by geostrategic considerations.

As has been argued, informed policy in Malaysia is limited to a small coterie of political policy makers, academics, and public bureaucrats in the Ministries of Defence, Home Affairs, and Foreign Affairs. Emphasis on trade and export-led strategies since the 1970s has meant a greater involvement of the Ministry of International Trade and Industry. Civil society participation and interest re-volves around specific trade issues and challenges, but for the most part this concerns essentially the enhancement of business linkages. There have been bilateral initiatives to enhance linkages extending to education, sports, youth exchange, and even military cooperation. But generally these do not form a substantive addition to existing trade and political ties, in both Malaysia-U.S. and Malaysia-China relations. Form and substance in Malaysia's respective, bilateral relations with the United States and China constitute a major future chal-lenge if Kuala Lumpur were not only to engage, but also manage its relations with Big Powers, and more generally its conduct of foreign policy. It is evident that expert knowledge in foreign area studies is lacking in spite of the rapid expansion of tertiary educational centers, and therefore policy advice from ex-perts is not readily available—a shortcoming that is evident now. Expert knowl-edge as it exists today may be more impressionistic in nature and shaped by superficial observations. Arguably, Malaysia's perceptions toward the two Big Powers seem to shed a positive take on China but a negative one on the United States. This may suggest that the U.S. role in the past and elsewhere is seen as part of U.S. unilateralism, if not "big power bullying," whereas China has not been seen to interfere or intervene in other parts of the world. On the other hand, it can be noted that the American impact on the political imagination—especially in the visual media—is also larger than knowledge or awareness of China and its society, and this shapes perceptions of Malaysians beyond the policy-making coterie.[26]

Perceptions of the United States

U.S.-Malaysia relations during the Cold War developed due to convergence arising out of a common concern of resisting or countering communism.[27] The United States was therefore viewed as a legitimate actor, with political, economic, and strategic stakes in Malaysia and Southeast Asia. The United States has also been a source of new ideas in knowledge and technology and, in the period of the 1970s and 1980s, the Malaysian student population in the United States was among the largest of all national foreign student cohorts. At the same time, the United States has been an important contributor of invest-ment, especially in the electronic industry. In economic terms, the United States has been a robust source of FDI, and Malaysia has risen over time to be one of the United States' largest trading partners. The U.S. military and security services also enjoy good cooperative arrangements with Malaysian defense and security organizations—an activity set to increase within the ambit of "cooperative security."

Since September 11, 2001, with the advent of the Global War on Terror (GWOT), Malaysia has been cooperative with the United States in information sharing and, in its own way, has pursued the active elements of putative terrorist organizations (such as Jemaah Islamiyah). However, Malaysia also believes that the best way of dealing with post-9/11 terrorism is to delve into the root causes and does not subscribe to the notion that the U.S. invasion of Iraq in 2003 was proper or vital in the GWOT. On the other hand, Malaysia is engaged with the West in countering Islamic State (IS) militants and clearly shares the conception of this threat. The Malaysian police have been very active in keeping a close track of IS supporters and have conducted many arrests. In early 2016, Malaysia organized an international conference on "Deradicalizing and Countering Violent Extremism."

The ethno-religious factor is also salient here. Malay identification with Islam—"all Malays are Muslim"—is a factor of domestic political import. A perception exists of the United States as "anti-Islam" since September 11; the U.S. invasion of Afghanistan and Iraq and its unstinting support of Israel in spite of Washington's efforts to broker peace in the Middle East are viewed as part of this "anti-Islam" image. But Malaysia-U.S. ties on the whole are good, if not excellent, at least on a government-to-government basis, even if the rhetoric suggested otherwise during Prime Minister Tun Dr Mahathir's years in office. Under Najib, the U.S.-Malaysia relationship can be described only as cordial, smooth, and positive, and is likely to be sustained for a considerable time.

Nevertheless, there is a perception of uneasiness that while the United States may be an important element of stability and offers insurance against unwanted military aggression, it has a proclivity to interfere in the domestic politics of Asia and, indeed, its very actions in Vietnam, Iraq, and Afghanistan demonstrated a policy of ill-advised intervention. Over the past two decades, numerous speeches have been delivered by Malaysian politicians regarding unwarranted U.S. interference in the whole world, and, in this regard, the United States is viewed as less than "benign."

There is, therefore, an ambiguity in perceptions of the United States. In strategic terms, its presence and military wherewithal suggest a countervailing capacity to deal with forces inimical to regional peace, but on the other hand there is an anxiety over its true intentions, over whether it is acting in its own interest of remaining dominant and powerful in the region, to the detriment of the member states. Such ambiguity is reflected in Malaysia's reactions and views regarding an earlier U.S. suggestion for a role in enhancing the security of the international waterways, such as the Straits of Malacca, against increasing acts of piracy and the possibility of terrorist strikes against targets in the littoral states. Malaysia's position has been that such a U.S. role (for example, providing warships for maritime patrols) would be against Kuala Lumpur's sovereign rights. However, it welcomes assistance and aid from external powers to enhance maritime surveillance and security. Malaysia, indeed, has benefitted from U.S. aid in the form of radar surveillance equipment, as utilized in the Borneo (Sabah/Sarawak) theater to prevent incursions by insurgent and terrorist elements like Abu Sayyaf and the like, and is very keen on acquiring U.S. aerial surveillance ("eyes in the sky") technology, especially in dealing with nontraditional threats.

As already alluded to above, Malaysian foreign policy is often a function of prime ministerial prerogatives and perceptions. During the Mahathir years, the United States was often portrayed publicly in negative terms, but in official relations was dealt with pragmatically. After Mahathir, the Malaysia-U.S. relationship endured vicissitudes and was at best a "bumpy" one. In the words of one observer, during the tenure Prime Minister Abdullah Badawi (preceding Najib),

> By the time Najib Razak came into office, the US-Malaysia relationship had lost the optimism it had when Abdullah assumed office. While the bilateral relationship became more engaged and the security relationship remained strong, the economic and political disconnect described above, shaped by both sides, had undermined strengthening ties. In many ways, relations had worsened economically, given the loss of US investment in Malaysia tied to the economic crisis and failure of the FTA. The decline of US support in other parts of the Muslim world was replicated in Malaysia. The fact is that from the start, Malaysia was more important strategically for the Bush administration than the other way round. There were many opportunities to change this path. For numerous reasons, from failure of delivery on promises and limited diplomatic communication to different world views, a strong bilateral relationship was not meant to be. The US became less relevant for Abdullah, as Malaysia became less central in US policy toward Southeast Asia. US attention moved to Indonesia and Vietnam. The storms—the ASEAN meeting in particular—could not be repaired by the smiles, as a situation of better civility emerged without a clear commitment to more robust bilateral connection.[28]

Perceptions of China

China's emergence as a power of considerable magnitude has not yet translated into a fear that Beijing will exercise hegemony in the region in the long run. In the present policy environment in Malaysia, the view is that China's rise is to be embraced, not only as the new boy on the block, but to be welcomed into the club of the "dragons" (or "tigers") of the Asia-Pacific. In other words, China's spectacular rise is legitimate as it relentlessly and vigorously pursues its policy of economic modernization. It may be speculated that China's emergence may be positive as a "countervailing" force vis-à-vis the United States, but a primary consideration is that it is an opportunity, not a threat.

That China is viewed in positive terms is indicative of a reversal of policy, when heretofore China not only had been a threat, but in fact had been a source of a revolutionary movement committed to the overthrow of the legitimate government in Malaysia. From the 1940s until the Communist Party of Malaya's (CPM) surrender in 1989, fear of Maoist China and its support of the CPM was the uppermost external security concern of Kuala Lumpur, even if the communist insurgency was essentially an internal security challenge. This Chinese-based insurrection that challenged the legitimacy of the sovereign Malay-based polity from the onset remains ingrained in the memories of Malaysia's decision makers. Once the CPM underwent its demise though, Beijing began to be viewed in very positive terms. This change of stance toward Beijing is not just pragmatism, but is grounded in the belief that China's role in the region and the world is benign and that it fosters no ill-will toward Malaysia.

Significantly, China and Malaysia have overlapping claims in the Spratly archipelago, but such a contentious matter seems to have been relegated to the back burner under the logic of the ASEAN Declaration on the Conduct of Parties (DOC) between China and ASEAN (including Malaysia). While a Code of Conduct (COC) is now being prepared for the South China Sea between ASEAN and China, issues persist with regard to legality, territoriality, sovereignty, and ultimately ownership of the Spratlys. The major challenge is whether resolution of the issues will be peaceful or otherwise. The notion does not prevail that China is likely to overrun Malaysia and Southeast Asia as it emerges as a strong power, but there is still a lingering suspicion it may wish to enact a Middle Kingdom suzerainty and force subservience on Southeast Asians states. That Southeast Asia is seen as part of Chinese territory in Beijing maps only contributes to such a lingering suspicion. Such views are indicative of Malaysia's strategic ambiguity, in that it seems to pretend the issue will fade away.

As already indicated, the Chinese have begun to flex their military capability in the disputed Spratlys, as evidenced by their presence at Beting Serupai and James Shoal. Malaysia's position is one of calm concern, seeking a more amicable resolution.[29] In the next decade, China will likely not just demonstrate its presence but assert more rigorously its right to and presence in the area; under such circumstances, both Malaysia and China would have to ponder all associated ramifications. It can therefore be asked if Sino-Malaysia relations, good as they currently are, can contain untoward developments.

For the most part, Malaysia's good relations with China have been spurred by growing trade ties. According to one observer, already as early as 2002, "Malaysia for the first time overtook Singapore as China's largest trading partner in the Association of Southeast Asian Nations (ASEAN) grouping."[30] According to another report, by 2013, "China was Malaysia's largest trading partner for the fifth consecutive year, with a two-way trade that year valued at US$62 billion. Deep energy ties exist between the two since Malaysia is the third-largest supplier of liquefied natural gas to China."[31] As has been noted, Malaysia is now ASEAN's largest trading partner with China. It has also been observed that Malaysia's trade with China is more complementary than competitive in nature and that China seems sensitive to concerns about its possible currency revaluation and the impact on countries like Malaysia.

The author of an early observation remarked that "no matter what twists and turns Malaysia-China relations may take, it can be observed that Malaysia has, and will in the foreseeable future regard China as its greatest threat in one form or another."[32] In the short term at least, it is not inconceivable that the "China threat" looms large among some of Malaysia's decision makers, especially those dealing with security issues. Such security issues pertain to not only the question of China's claims in the South China Sea and its actions with various claimants, including the use of force, but also the larger strategic question of the prospect of not only Big Power competition and the rise of China and India, but also the repercussions of a Pax Sinica that may replace a Pax Americana in Pacific Asia. The contrary view is that China is a "benign" power enveloped in its relentless pursuit of economic modernization.

Although an earlier (in the Cold War days) view had held that the domestic Chinese community may be a potential fifth column for Beijing, and indeed trade conducted by local ethnic Chinese with China had to be channeled by a government agency previously, business and other linkages between China and Malaysian Chinese presently have no barriers or curbs. Even increasing Chinese investment (from China) that is now more than apparent is not seen in negative terms. However, a speech by the Chinese ambassador in September 2015 "warning those who used violence to disrupt public order in the country" was interpreted as "tantamount to interfering in Malaysia's domestic affairs."[33] The speech was delivered in the light of certain disturbances that had racial connotations in Kuala Lumpur's Chinatown. That it drew flak is suggestive that Sino-Malaysia relations may be affected by domestic factors.

Malaysian China scholar Cheng-Chwee Kuik argues that Malaysia's policy toward China is essentially one of "hedging,"[34] that Malaysia retains traditional military ties with Western powers to "guard against uncertainty surrounding the rise of a big power."[35] Kuik elaborates that over time Malaysia has pursued elements of economic pragmatism, engagement, and "limited bandwagoning"—"which are driven by a desire to maximise economic and foreign policy returns from a close and cordial relationship with the rising China, implemented in conjunction with a counteracting position that was aimed at hedging against the risks of strategic uncertainty surrounding the rise of a Big Power in close proximity."[36]

Viewed on the larger plane of the Asia-Pacific, Malaysia's engagement with China seems predicated on a partnership that can foster regional collaboration and cohesion, especially in the ASEAN Plus Three framework. In addition, Malaysia is keen to develop economic and educational linkages. But therein lies the rub of Malaysia's overtures with China: basically they are competitors in many endeavors, including the attraction of foreign direct investment (FDI). Yet, China's own political strength as it advances economically has not perceptually signaled the prospect of Chinese political domination in regional collaboration. On the contrary, Chinese investment, trade, and collaboration in other areas suggest a salutary Chinese stance toward Malaysia.

China's adherence to international norms in both policy and behavior is of course welcomed, but a profound understanding of China's political, economic, and strategic developments is a matter not yet seriously being pursued. The belief exists that China will not enact policies harmful to Malaysia and that it will be benign. Thus, it is not clear if enough attention is being given to policies that can deal with the devaluation of the yuan or the impact of hostilities as a result of a Chinese military solution for Taiwan. In most instances, developments in China are seen as "internal matters" not subject to outside interference. Indeed, Malaysia sees U.S. comments and actions on China as Washington's interference in another country's affairs.

It is not apparent if Malaysia is actively engaged in deliberations with other ASEAN states as to the possibility of a joint approach in policy toward China. But neither is there a sense of rivalry with other ASEAN states to ensure that Malaysia enjoys an advantage over others in its dealings with Beijing. Kuala Lumpur does subscribe to an ASEAN-wide approach to dealing with China, but how this is translated into action remains less clear. At the 2014 ASEAN Summit, there was a joint statement on the need for more restraint in China's actions relating to maritime disputes, but at the 2012 Phnom Penh summit, a joint statement was less forthcoming; as reported by Nguyen Huu Tuc, "The failure of the ASEAN foreign ministers in their Cambodia meeting in 2012 caused by differences over the South China Sea disputes is still vivid."[37]

Malaysia's relations with China have seen an intensification that augurs well; indeed, in spite of Malaysia's negative image in China because of the disappearance (with a majority of Chinese passengers) of Malaysia Airlines Flight 370 in March 2014, and only limited pieces of airliner debris recovered despite massive international recovery efforts, both countries look to an improvement and strengthening of relations. Such a view has been expressed by leaders on both sides, especially on the occasion of Najib's 2014 visit to China to celebrate forty years since the establishment of Sino-Malaysian ties.

Concluding Remarks

It is more than apparent that Malaysia is a significant actor in Southeast Asia and the larger Asia-Pacific, its stature buttressed by having achieved middle-income status, and that it pushes its weight as an important international actor, perhaps even as a Middle Power, through contributions to UN peacekeeping and in regional peace efforts in the southern Philippines. In terms of the changing balance of power in the Asia-Pacific, it is clear that it steers away from being embroiled in Big Power politics and does not wish to be drawn into having to decide in favor of the United States or China as the rivalry between these two latter powers intensifies. Yet, based on the preceding discussion, it is apparent that even as there has been continuity in policy and its premises, there is as well ambiguity, and perhaps even vacillation, among the lead architects of Malaysia's foreign policy.

In any event, Malaysia continues to engage both the United States and China, even to the extent that there is a "strategic" connotation to relationships with both. But whether Kuala Lumpur will be a willing partner to any Chinese or U.S. overture at the expense of the other is clearly a position to be eschewed, or at least only tacitly acknowledged as existential. Thus, it is not patently clear if the recent U.S. "rebalancing to Asia" is welcome or not as it may only exacerbate tensions in situations in the South China Sea.

In the larger context of U.S.-China relations, it is unclear how Malaysia is perceived in the United States, as to whether it can be an important third party. A nongovernmental view in Washington is that Malaysia could play a "gateway" role for U.S. businesses and other interests, but as of yet this remains an opportunity to be pursued. The United States has hoped that Malaysia might play a larger role in antiterrorism efforts, such as engaging the U.S. Navy in the Straits of Malacca, but clearly Malaysia is not keen on extra-regional physical involvement in that strategic waterway. Nonetheless, Malaysia has been a willing participant in many of the cooperative security exercises conducted by U.S. forces in the Pacific.

This situation may be envied by the Chinese, who for their part have begun to pursue more bilateral military cooperation activities such as exchanges of officers in military training institutes, table-top exercises, and in 2015 a joint Malaysia-China five-day exercise, Managing Non-Traditional Threats and Humanitarian and Disaster Relief, code-named Peace and Friendship 2015.[38] While ostensibly there seems to have been an incremental element in China-Malaysia military cooperation, there is also caution and perhaps even disquiet if not unease, especially with regard to China's increasing presence in the South China Sea. Such caution, in part, is illustrated by Malaysia sending only a low-level delegation to the September 2015 military parade in Beijing celebrating the seventieth anniversary of the end of World War II. In the context of the larger bilateral relationship, "China's audacity" in the South China Sea has caught Malaysia authorities "off balance," not expected given Kuala Lumpur's perceived special relationship with Beijing.[39] Elina Nor opines that "the Malaysian government might be better off tempering its own expectations of a mutually recognized or reciprocal special relationship with China. If both sides were really placing stock in such a relationship, then it should be reflected across the board, including in the South China Sea. This does not mean that Malaysia should or will begin choosing sides between China and others in any conceivable future. But it means that in the face of rising Chinese assertiveness and a rapidly changing South China Sea landscape, Malaysia will no longer be as averse to recalibrating its policy as needed to protect, preserve, and advance its national interest."[40]

In Malaysian conceptions of the future, there is no notion of the United States being a strategic partner to "balance," counter, or neutralize China's "big power" mentality and actions, should Beijing choose to actualize them. But the view exists that U.S.-China relations will be stable and conducive to Asia-Pacific security, fostering peaceful conditions for regional countries to thrive and prosper. The problem might be that the United States will be uneasy about not only the emergence of China, but more of its ability to surpass the United States. In other words, the United States may not be able to retain its "top dog" position in Pacific Asia that it has held since the end of World War II. In this context, the United States may actually pursue what George W. Bush has described as "strategic competition" with China.

Concern over China and Asia more generally, however, may be overshadowed by other U.S. concerns. Since 9/11, the United States has devoted more attention to the GWOT and certainly has been preoccupied with its invasion and occupation of Iraq and its actions in Afghanistan. The issue may be not so much if the United States will intervene in Asia, but whether it intervenes for its own interests, parochial or otherwise, and then retreats into neo-isolationism. Indeed, it may even be that Southeast Asia does not rank as the "problem area" it was in the 1960s. But the current U.S. "rebalancing" posture has now rendered Southeast Asia greater relevance in U.S. policy predispositions, at least outwardly.

Under Prime Minister Najib, the view from Kuala Lumpur is not hopeful but seemingly desirous of a more substantive relationship in which sinews can develop bilaterally. Efforts have already been undertaken to strengthen U.S.-Malaysian ties, in part based on a binational think tank's recommendations.[41] In this regard, Barack Obama's visit to Malaysia at the end of April 2014, brief as it was, generated hopes and aspirations that a more robust and vibrant relationship will blossom. Obama's visit to Malaysia at the end of 2015 to attend the U.S.-ASEAN and East Asia Summits reaffirmed Washington's strategic commitment to Asia and indeed may have garnered creditability to Najib's beleaguered prime ministership and as such underscores the depth of a U.S.-Malaysia relationship.

A good relationship with both the United States and China is important to Malaysia's long-term interests. It is therefore significant that Malaysia does not want to choose between Scylla and Charybdis, but as noted by Najib himself, "Malaysia is caught between two mega world powers, . . . and the future is about how this country and others in the region manage that relationship between the US and China."[42] Malaysia's posture, in this regard, is not about hedging but rather about amicable relations with the United States and China.[43]

The hope in Kuala Lumpur is that conflict will not erupt between the claimants in the South China Sea dispute and that untoward maritime incidents will not occur between the United States and China; indeed the hope is that there will be safety of navigation and no interdiction of goods and services in Asia-Pacific and world trade. In this respect, it is to be expected that Malaysia will push in its diplomacy with ASEAN to achieve the COC for the South China Sea.

Similarly, while the United States and China are welcome as Asia-Pacific actors, Kuala Lumpur's hope is for not only a deepening of relationships with these two Big Powers, but also a stable, peaceful, and harmonious Sino-U.S. relationship in the region and in relation to Malaysia. That said, it can be expected that Malaysia will increase its efforts at engaging China and the United States in ever-widening fields of cooperation.

NOTES

1 Elina Noor, "President Obama in Malaysia: The Substance of Symbolism," *Asia Pacific Bulletin*, no. 261 (May 8, 2014).

2 Elina Noor, "Of Symbols and Substance," *New Straits Times*, October 8, 2013, reprinted in Pacific Forum CSIS PacNet, no. 76 (October 9, 2013).

3 Royal Malaysian Navy sources inform that two Chinese Coast Guard vessels are constantly stationed off James Shoal, off the Sarawak coast. They disappeared during Xi Jinping's visit to Malaysia in 2013, but reappeared after he left. James Shoal, also known as Beting Serupai, is about eighty kilometers from the Sarawak coast. Chinese Navy ships first appeared there in March 2013. A year later, China conducted a military exercise in the area, deploying marines and hovercraft. See Tang Siew Mun, "The Beting Serupai Incident," *PacNet Newsletter*, April 22, 2013, and Nguyen Huu Tuc, "Malaysia and the South China Sea: Will KL Abandon Its Hedging Policy?," *RSIS Commentary*, no. 003/2015 (January 5, 2015).

4 See R. M. Smith, "Cambodia: Between Scylla and Charybdis," *Asian Survey* 8, no. 1 (January 1968).

5 For a discussion on this theme, see Kim R. Nossal and R. Stuhbs, "Mahathir's Malaysia: An Emerging Middle Power?" in *Niche Diplomacy: Middle Powers after the Cold War*, ed. F. Cooper (London: Macmillan, 1971). See also notes 22 and 23.

6 J. Saravanamuttu, "Malaysia in the New Geopolitics of Southeast Asia" (London School of Economic IDEAS report, November 2012), www.google.com.

7 Malaysia's present Federal Constitution is based on a secular nation of governance. Calls for the imposition of Syaria and Hudud have become more strident in recent years, just as there have been issues of conversions and even the use of Allah in church literature. For one version of the issue between religion and government policy in Malaysia, see *International Religious Freedom Report* (2013), www.state.gov. Provisions for Hudud implementation were introduced and passed in the Kelantan State Assembly in March 2015.

8 See Yang Razali Kassim, "Malaysia's Political Outlook 2014: Key Challenges Facing Najib," *RSIS Commentary*, no. 236/2013 (December 26, 2013) ; Ooi Kee Beng, "Let's See Some Nation-First Leadership on the Road to 2020," *Edge*, December 30, 2013; Khadijah Md Khalid and Zakaria Haji Ahmad, "Coalition Politics in Malaysia," in *Coalition Politics and Democratic Consolidation in Asia*, ed. E. Sridharan (New Delhi: Oxford University Press, 2012); "Malaysia's Political Challenges," *IISS Strategic Comments* 21 (November 2015): 32.

9 See Rashaad Ali, "From ASEAN Chair to UN Security Council: Malaysia Foreign Policy in 2015," *RSIS Commentary*, no. 274/2015 (December 18, 2015).

10 See the discussion in Kuik Cheng-Chwee, "Malaysia's China Policy under Abdullah," in *Awakening—The Abdullah Badawi Years in Malaysia*, ed. Bridget Welsh and James U. H. Chia (Petaling Jaya: Strategic Information and Research Development Centre, 2013), 590–608.

11 This phrase was used by Prime Minister Najib in his keynote address at the Shangri-La Dialogue in 2011: "Malaysia . . . is equally determined to ensure that our bilateral relationship remains unaffected and in fact, continues to grow from strength to strength." Cited in Tuc, "Malaysia and the South China Sea," 3.

12 See Zakaria Ahmad, "A Quasi-Pact of Enduring Value: A Malaysian Perspective of the FPDA," in *Five Power Defence Arrangements at Forty*, ed. Ian Storey, Ralf Emmers, and Daljit Singh (Singapore: ISEAS, 2011), 98–104.

13 See Zakaria Ahmad, "Malaysia Foreign Policy and Domestic Politics: Looking Outwards and Moving Inward?," in *Regional Dynamics—Security, Political and Economic Issues in the Asia-Pacific Region*, ed. R. Scalapino et al. (Jakarta: CSIS, 1990).

14 Malaysian Foreign Policy Study Group, "Malaysia's Foreign Policy Towards and Beyond 2020 Vision, Goals and Recommendations" (Kuala Lumpur: ISIS, 2013). This is a confidential report that was prepared on the basis of many meetings and discussions with a host of luminaries, thought leaders, and intellectuals.

15 For an insightful analysis, see Johan Saravanamuthu, *Malaysia's Foreign Policy, the First Fifty Years* (Singapore: Institute of Southeast Asian Studies, 2000), 22–47.

16 Karminder Singh Dhillon, *Malaysian Foreign Policy in the Mahathir Era, 1981–2003* (Singapore: NUS Press, 2009), 57–59.

17 Cheng-Chwee Kuik, "Malaysia's Relations with Major and Middle Powers" (Asia Centre, French Ministry of Defense, 2014/2015).

18 Ibid.

19 For a critique, see Muthiah Alagappa, "Is ASEAN the Cornerstone of Malaysia's Foreign Policy?," *Edge*, November 19, 2012.

20 Wisma Putra is the name accorded to the Ministry of Foreign Affairs. For an analysis of the ministry's evolution, see Zakaria Haji Ahmad, "Malaysia, Change and Adaption in Foreign Policy: Malaysia's Foreign Ministry," in *Foreign Ministries: Change and Adaption*, ed. Brian Hocking (London: Macmillan, 1999), 117–32.

21 This notion was never explicit, but Kuala Lumpur in the 1970s through the 1980s did understand the Indonesian argument of "national resilience" leading to "regional resilience" and vice versa.

22 "Prime Minister Najib: Malaysia Must Embrace Middle Power Position in ASEAN," *New Straits Times*, February 24, 2014. See also note 5.

23 Ibid.

24 Zakaria Haji Ahmad, "Malaysia," in *Betwixt and Between—Southeast Asian Strategic Relations with the US and China*, ed. Evelyn Goh (Singapore: Institute of Defence and Strategic Studies, Nanyang Technological University, 2005), 52.

25 For a thoughtful analysis, see Cheng-Chwee Kuik, "China's Maritime Silk Road (MSR) Initiative and ASEAN's Trilemma: A Preliminary Analysis" (unpublished paper).

26 Zakaria, "Malaysia," 52–53.

27 The bulk of the discussion in this section is drawn from an earlier study. Ibid.

28 Bridget Welsh, "Smiles and Storms—Abdullah Badawi's Navigation of US Waters," in *Awakening—The Abdullah Badawi Years in Malaysia*, ed. Bridget Welsh and James U. H. Chin (Petaling Jaya: Strategic Information and Research Development Centre, 2013), 586.

29 For an insightful analysis, see Tang Siew Mun, "What Is at Stake in the South China Sea Dispute?," in *Diplomatic Voice*, vol. 3 (Kuala Lumpur: Institute of Diplomacy and foreign Relation, 2012).

30 Shee Poon Kim, "The Political Economy of Malaysia's China Policy: Economic Cooperation, Political and Strategic Ambivalence" (International University of Japan Research Institute Working Paper 2004–6, Asia Pacific Series, 2004), 2.

31 Tuc, "Malaysia and the South China Sea," 2.

32 See J. N. Mak, "The Chinese Navy and the South China Sea: A Malaysian Assessment," *Pacific Review* 4, no. 2 (June 1991): 150.

33 "Wisma Putra Summons Chinese Ambassador over Petaling Street Remarks," *Malaysian Insider*, September 25, 2015.

34 Cheng-Chwee Kuik, "Malaysia's China Policy under Abdullah," in Welsh and Chin, *Awakening*, 591.

35 Ibid.

36 Ibid., 595.

37 Tuc, "Malaysia and the South China Sea," 3.

38 Sumathy Permal, "China and Malaysia's First-Ever Joint Military Is an Important Strategic Move," *STAR*, September 28, 2015.

39 Elina Noor, "Malaysia: Recalibrating Its South China Sea Policy?" (Asia Maritime Transparency Initiative, January 8, 2016).

40 Ibid.

41 Ernst Bower, Murray Hiebert, and Gregory Poling, "From Strength to Empowerment: The Next Generation of US-Malaysia Relations" (CSIS Southeast Asia Program and ISIS Malaysia, May 17, 2012).

42 "The Mark of Friendship," *New Straits Times*, April 26, 2014.

43 The view was expressed by Cheng Chwee Kuik, "Malaysia's Balancing Act," *New York Times*, December 6, 2015. See also note 34.

8

The Mainland minus One

Power Dynamics in Thailand, Laos, Cambodia, and Myanmar

CATHARIN DALPINO

The ancient cultural threads that linked Thailand, Laos, Cambodia, and Myanmar—the so-called "Indianized" states in Southeast Asia—have long since frayed. Theravada Buddhism, with Hindu architectural overtones and Brahmin monarchies, set the four countries apart from Chinese-influenced Vietnam to the east and the maritime Southeast Asian nations with Malay and Muslim notes to the south.

If this quartet ever formed a coherent group of polities—a questionable proposition—precolonial wars on mainland Southeast Asia quickly divided them. The kingdoms of Lan Xang (Laos), Khmer (Cambodia), Siam (Thailand), and Burma (Myanmar) each conquered their neighbors before receding. In the nineteenth century, European colonization put Cambodia and Laos in the French colonial empire, added Myanmar to British India, and left Thailand the rare country that was never colonized. The Cold War imposed a new structure on the subregion, with Thailand a treaty ally of the United States, Cambodia and Laos would-be neutral states that would fall into the Eastern Bloc at the end of the Vietnam War, and, by the mid-1960s, Myanmar in self-isolation.

Shifts beginning in the 1990s signaled yet another new regional order, which is still in formation. The end of the Cold War, the Cambodian peace agreement and the subsequent enlargement of ASEAN, the rise of China and India, a modest renewal of U.S. interest in Southeast Asia, and Myanmar's reform process have forged new relations with old adversaries but also created new (or renewed) tensions. This essay examines the transformation of the foreign relations of Thailand, Laos, Cambodia, and Myanmar in this new regional environment, with a focus on the following:

- *New economic and geostrategic realities*: New power dynamics in the Asia-Pacific region and the global environment boost the geostrategic importance of some countries, such as Myanmar; at the same time, the demise of the Cold War paradigm has diminished interest in other countries. However, tensions between China and Southeast Asian claimants to the Spratly Islands in the South China Sea suggest that a new geostrategic competition may be in play.

- *Connectivity*: The construction of new transportation corridors (north-south and east-west) on mainland Southeast Asia will increase the flow of people and goods within the subregion and open new trade routes with China and India. However beneficial these new routes may be to the countries through which they pass, they are likely to be even more beneficial to the region's larger economies, particularly China. At this stage, however, the new connectivity is also a catalyst for local opposition, particularly in Myanmar. The costs of constructing new ports and roads—and the "special economic zones" that often accompany them—to local populations and the environment have forced governments and their funders back to the drawing board in some cases.
- *Regional leadership*: Under ASEAN's system of rotational chairmanship, even the smallest member countries have regional leadership roles thrust upon them once a decade. Myanmar chaired ASEAN for the first time in 2014, and in 2016 Laos is chair for the second time. However, Cambodia's leadership of ASEAN in 2012 was a cautionary tale of the vulnerability of smaller, weaker states in the face of pressure from an external power.
- *Economic factors*: China's determination to mount a new "charm offensive" with Southeast Asia and its ambitions to install a China-led regional economic framework, evidenced by the Asian Infrastructure Investment Bank, present ASEAN with more pronounced choices between Washington and Beijing. The United States and Japan have answered with the Trans-Pacific Partnership (TPP); with the exception of Vietnam, however, the countries of mainland Southeast Asia are not candidates for early accession. In addition, China's recent economic slowdown exerts a greater gravitational pull toward the United States and Japan for Southeast Asian economies.
- *Domestic dynamics*: Although the Northern Tier of Southeast Asia represents a broad spectrum of political systems, governments of every stripe are under increasing domestic pressure, which affects foreign policy. Thailand, Myanmar, and Cambodia are engaged in long-term struggles to balance political stability with demand for more open politics. Thailand's decade-long political crisis has distracted the government from external relations at times. Moreover, the May 22, 2014, military coup has triggered low-level sanctions from the United States, the European Union, and Australia, and raised questions about the near-term course of the U.S.-Thailand security alliance. Political reform in Myanmar has thus far enabled Naypy-

idaw to strengthen relations with the United States, the European Union, and Japan, but that dynamic could falter if the reform process stalls.

In this regard, much will depend upon the performance of the newly elected government in Myanmar, and the military's willingness to let it govern. As the 2018 elections approach, Cambodia's political problems present China with an advantage, since Beijing is less inclined to factor human rights or democratization concerns into its foreign policy and economic assistance than are the West or Japan.[1]

- *China, the United States, and other new triangles*: Cold War patron-client patterns are fading and new arrangements are emerging. Some of these place China and the United States into competition, however inadvertent. Others in time may exacerbate rivalries between China and India. Japan's renewed interest in Southeast Asia under the leadership of Prime Minister Shinzo Abe appears to pit Tokyo against Beijing in Myanmar at present, and its more forward-leaning military posture helps strengthen the maritime security capabilities of Vietnam and the Philippines, but at the cost of further irritating China. Russia is raising its profile in Southeast Asia and reinvigorating its partnership with Vietnam in particular.

Thailand: Equilibrium Gone Awry?

With the end of the Vietnam War, Thailand began a gradual return to the principle of equilibrium in foreign policy that had helped to preserve its sovereignty against the Western colonial push in the nineteenth century. After the fall of Saigon in 1975, fear of Vietnamese incursions westward prompted the Thai government to open a diplomatic window to China. In the late 1970s and into the 1980s, Bangkok and Washington reconfigured the U.S.-Thailand alliance. During this time, trade with China (facilitated by the Sino-Thai community) helped to spark double-digit growth rates in Thailand and the emergence of a new commercial class that pressed for greater political liberalization.

As a result of these shifts, Thailand today is the only treaty ally of the United States on mainland Southeast Asia, but a country that arguably has the closest and most comfortable relationship with China of any Southeast Asian state. American security analysts are often confounded by the seeming contradiction. Thais appear to be more comfortable with this balancing act, which is rooted in an implicit division of labor: the enduring alliance with the United States enables Thailand to maintain close economic ties with China, while the Thailand-China trade relationship helps to insulate Thailand from downturns in the U.S. economy, such as the 2008 financial crisis.

However, this dynamic is changing, if only to a modest degree. The 2014 coup in Thailand and the direct form of military rule has been imposed have set Bangkok and Washington further adrift. U.S. policy makers do not believe that Thailand will overinvest in its relations with China, but the U.S.-Thailand alliance is no longer the leading edge of U.S. security relations in Southeast Asia.

To be sure, the drift in the U.S.-Thailand alliance is due more to the lack of a common threat—and so a rationale for continued cooperation—than either the 2014 coup or China's overtures to Thailand for a stronger security relationship. However, these more recent factors prevent the two countries from serious dialogue on the direction of the alliance. In the meantime, a decision by Bangkok to withhold permission for U.S. planes and ships to use Thai military facilities for refueling and repair and to deny flyover rights for U.S. planes (as former Prime Minister Thaksin attempted to do at the beginning of the U.S. intervention in Iraq) would require Washington to reexamine its assumptions about access routes in Southeast Asia.

Thailand's Regional Vision

In the late 1980s, with a booming economy and the prospects of Indochina's opening to the international market, Thai Prime Minister Chatchai Choonhavan revived the national dream of the "golden peninsula," in which Thailand would function as the economic hub of Southeast Asia. The thread of this theme continued into the administration of Thaksin Shinawatra, who expanded Thailand's commercial presence in the three neighboring countries and inaugurated economic assistance programs for them. But much of this Thai regional momentum has dissipated in the past decade because of internal political instability; among other casualties of Thaksin's "good neighbor" policy, the 2006 military coup against Thaksin ended the subregional assistance program.

More important, since 2006 the country has been largely inward-looking, consumed with political ruptures and public uprisings that spilled over into Thailand's regional relations. Bangkok's eighteen-month tenure as ASEAN chair in 2008–9 was marred by disrupted meetings and an increasing loss of confidence in Thailand's leadership on the part of the other ASEAN member states. After Yellow Shirt demonstrators seized the Bangkok International Airport for four days in November 2008, the ASEAN Summit was relocated to Jakarta. During this time, tensions between Thailand and Cambodia over the Preah Vihear temple on the border flared, further compromising Bangkok's ability to lead the regional group.[2] This dismal state of Thailand's regional leadership was underscored when Red Shirt protestors disrupted an

ASEAN meeting in Pattaya in April 2009, forcing diplomats to be evacuated from the hotel roof by helicopter. The six-week Red Shirt siege of Ratchap-rasong, the commercial district of Bangkok, in 2010 was a more direct hit on the Thai economy by protestors.

The three-year tenure of Prime Minister Yingluck Shinawatra, Thaksin's younger sister, appeared to offer some stability, but that image dissipated rapidly in 2014, when Thailand's polarized politics ultimately resulted in a military coup. The ASEAN chair will rotate to Bangkok again in 2019, but it is not assured that Thai domestic politics will have stabilized sufficiently by that time to enable Thailand to be a strong regional leader, particularly if the country is in the midst of a tumultuous transition to monarchy at that time.

Can Thailand Sustain a Regional Role?

But whatever the state of its internal politics, Thailand's importance to main-land Southeast Asia will be maintained by the new web of transportation links, road and rail, that will run east to west (funded by international development banks) and north to south (funded by China and partner states) regardless of its internal political dynamic. The 873-kilometer China-to-Thailand seg-ment is critical to China's Trans-Asian Railway and an early notch in Beijing's broader One Belt, One Road regional initiative.[3] However, the negotiation of the project signals some inherent difficulties in China's ambitions to domi-nate regional infrastructure: although ground was broken on the China-Thai line in January 2016, the precise financial arrangements were not finalized at that time.

The major powers are not the only architects of regional infrastructure. A growing investor in mainland Southeast Asia, Bangkok is planning to fund such joint infrastructure projects as the Dawei port in Myanmar, which will enable Thai exports to avoid shipment through the Straits of Malacca. After years of hesitation, in mid-2015 Japan agreed to provide some funding for the Dawei project.[4]

But political instability in Thailand could also impact ASEAN's attempts to forge an agreement with China on a Code of Conduct in the South China Sea, albeit indirectly. Thailand is a reluctant actor in the issue of territorial disputes between China and some Southeast Asian countries (Vietnam, the Philippines, Malaysia, and Brunei) in the South China Sea. Until recently, Bangkok had maintained that it had no interest in this issue, but growing ASEAN concerns about China's maritime ambitions—including claims of sovereignty over the "nine-dash line"—have forced Thailand, albeit reluc-tantly, to adopt this as a policy concern.

Thailand, the United States, and China

Although Japan has been Thailand's largest trading partner in recent years, China is likely to replace Japan in the next few years.[5] The United States is Thailand's third largest trading partner. China and Thailand have been in a free trade arrangement since 2003 by virtue of the ASEAN-China Free Trade Agreement, while negotiations for a U.S.-Thailand FTA broke down in 2006 in the midst of Thailand's growing political instability. As well, Thailand has episodically negotiated a free trade agreement with the European Union, but the EU suspended talks in the wake of the 2014 coup.

As yet, Thailand has not made a formal decision to seek entry into the TPP, although Washington encouraged Bangkok (as well as Manila and Jakarta) to do so after the current group of TPP countries finished negotiations and leaders are ready to consider a new slate of entrants. The Thai technocratic sector is expressing increasing interest in the TPP, perhaps because it can safely assume that concrete possibilities for new entrants are still several years away. Beijing views the TPP as an attempt by the United States to undermine China's role in the regional economy, although Chinese officials are reportedly considering accession to the TPP in view of Japan's entry and South Korea's newly expressed interest.[6]

Although Thai government officials often profess to see no conflict in maintaining close relations with both Washington and Beijing, prior to the coup Thai military officers were more likely to express fears of a rising China in the region.[7] Thailand has often found it easier to balance relations between the two powers in the economic realm than in security affairs. Objectively, the U.S.-Thailand alliance far overshadows the emerging Thailand-China security relationship. The two countries are the foundation of the annual Cobra Gold exercises, the largest multilateral military exercises in the world, and continue to expand their security relationship; in 2012, for example, Thailand signed the Proliferation Security Initiative. Abridged Cobra Gold exercises were held in both 2015 and 2016, despite U.S. security sanctions on Thailand because of the 2014 coup.

The Thai coup will likely present China with a short-term advantage in its security relations with Thailand. The Foreign Assistance Act (FAA) requires that the United States suspend economic assistance to a country whose elected government has been overthrown by forcible means. As a result, Washington has suspended roughly half of US$10 million in economic assistance to Thailand (the other half being tied up in regional projects that are managed with Bangkok and may therefore be exempt from the FAA provision); Thai participation in the International Military Education and Training

(IMET) program has also been suspended. As well, low-key trilateral training on humanitarian assistance with U.S., Thai, and Burmese forces was halted after the coup.[8] However, since the original suspension of some programs after the coup, both sides have taken steps to retain as much of the relationship as U.S. law and political dynamics will allow. This is particularly true of U.S.-Thailand cooperation that involves regional activities. For example, U.S. assistance to the International Legal Education Academy based in Bangkok was suspended in May 2014, but quietly resumed the following August.[9]

U.S. defense officials note that China increasingly objects to the presence of a U.S. security ally on mainland Southeast Asia and attempts to undermine that by expanding its military-to-military relations with Thailand. This includes joint exercises, weapon sales, and military training. At the same time, Thailand's present security cooperation with China is modest in comparison to that with the United States, and fears that U.S. negativity about the coup will drive Bangkok "into the China camp" are likely exaggerated.[10]

However, the current political situation leaves Beijing free to expand its security ties to Thailand and greatly constrains Washington from doing the same. This dilemma comes at an ill-timed interval, as the United States looks for opportunities to strengthen security relations with Southeast Asia in pursuit of the "pivot" to Asia.

Laos: A New Finlandization?

With its usual incremental pace, Laos has moved slowly in the past two decades to broaden its regional relations and to strengthen its relations with the United States. Although Washington and Vientiane never severed relations completely after the communist takeover in 1975, for the first decade following the end of the Vietnam War Laos's only bilateral relationship of any significance was with Vietnam. This configuration moved to a triangular dynamic in the late 1980s when Laos normalized relations with Thailand. With a larger and more developed economy, expertise in market economics, commonality between the Lao and Thai languages that made education in Thailand accessible to Lao students, and similar schools of Buddhism, Thailand rapidly became an appealing external partner for Laos, if Laotians sometimes chafed under the pi-nong ("big brother–little brother") dynamic. By the early 1990s, Vietnam remained Laos's closest political relationship but Thailand had become its most important economic partner.

Although Laos had also commenced normalization with China in the late 1980s, Beijing's "charm offensive" did not really bear fruit until the 2000s. Geography (in particular Laos's mountainous terrain) and colonial history had prevented Laos and China from developing deep historical ties. Even today, Laos's sparse population (six million) and low income levels make it an unlikely manufacturing destination and unattractive market for China. However, its natural resources, agricultural land, and position in the north-south transportation corridor have drawn Chinese officials to this southern neighbor. This new quadrilateral dynamic makes both Vietnam and Thailand nervous, although China has thus far confined most of its efforts to the northern half of the country, leaving the south to Thai and Vietnamese influence. Nor is the growing Chinese presence in Laos viewed without reservation in the Lao population. Large "plantation" deals, which import tens of thousands of Chinese workers, have lately been the subject of domestic discontent and some Lao-style push-back.

Even surrounded by its more powerful neighbors, Laos is exerting its own regional, sometimes controversial, influence. Determined to secure a national budget that is not dependent upon external donor funds, Laos aspires to be the "battery of Southeast Asia," by exporting hydropower, primarily to Thailand, through dams on the Mekong River. Although China is the ultimate upriver Mekong country, and Laos is therefore subject to the impact of Chinese mainstream dams, to Vietnam and Cambodia Laos is decidedly upriver and able to inflict damage on its southern neighbors.

The latest project, the Xayaburi dam, was initially on hold to enable the Mekong River Commission to assess its likely environmental impact, but ground was broken in November 2012. The dam will exert a long-term ecological effect on Vietnam, but it delivered an immediate political shock: Hanoi's inability to dissuade Vientiane from the Xayaburi project was an indication that Vietnam was losing its influence on Laos faster than Vietnamese officials had realized.[11] China's role in the Laos's "battery" initiative has been to offer financial guarantees when international development banks or other parties raise concerns about environmental impacts, as it did with the Nam Theung II dam. In this dynamic, China, Laos, and Thailand are pitted against Vietnam and Cambodia.

Despite some discernible anti-Chinese sentiment in the Laotian population, to many Lao businesspeople and officials China represents an ally in the country's new drive for economic independence from Western donors. However, China will see an increase in competition for Vientiane's attention in the coming years from regional powers, if only to solidify relations with ASEAN as a whole. Japanese Prime Minister Shinzo Abe's trip to Vientiane in late 2013 was groundbreaking.[12] President Obama's participation in the 2016 East Asia Summit made him the first American president ever to visit Laos.

Mekong Rivalries

Apart from competing bilateral relations, Laos stands at the nexus of competition between the United States and China over influence on the development of the Mekong River. China's six dams on the Mekong and, as noted above, its support for the construction of dams in Laos have an impact not only on geopolitical dynamics but also on the ecology of mainland Southeast Asia. The ultimate impact of these dams will be on Cambodia and Vietnam, the two downriver countries, in terms of unseasonal floods, droughts, and dwindling fisheries.

The United States does not take a strident position on the new Mekong dams, but supports the World Bank, Asian Development Bank, and other international organizations in urging that environmental and demographic concerns be taken into account in decisions on construction. Partly in this vein, in 2009 the Obama administration established the Lower Mekong Initiative (LMI) and its companion organization, the Friends of the Lower Mekong, which brings the Mekong countries together with the United States, Japan, the European Union, and Australia. China is not a member of either organization. Apart from attempting to influence development of the Mekong River region, Washington also uses the LMI as a diplomatic tool in its relations with Vietnam, Cambodia, Laos, Thailand, and Myanmar.[13]

To counter Washington's influence in the LMI, in March 2015 China indicated that it would establish its own Lower Mekong Initiative.[14] Although the parameters of such a group are still under discussion with the downriver countries, there is broad speculation that it may follow the lines of the new China-led Asian Infrastructure Investment Bank, through which China provides capital to fund projects (in this case dams) with guidelines on the environment and other areas that are less stringent than those imposed by the West and international financial institutions. Laos would be a major beneficiary of a new Chinese Lower Mekong Initiative.

Cambodia: Inevitable Client State?

On the surface, to many Western analysts Cambodia is a small state that has been all but consumed by its powerful neighbor China. China's pervasive economic and diplomatic influence in Cambodia becomes apparent when Phnom Penh accedes to Beijing's demands on specific issues. The return of Uighur asylum seekers to China in 2009, immediately followed by an increase in Chinese investment, and the Cambodian government's resistance to putting South China Sea issues on the ASEAN agenda in 2012 are recent examples.

However, many Cambodians maintain that, as with other vulnerable Northern Tier countries in Southeast Asia, Phnom Penh is pursuing an intricate, if imperfect, balancing act. Closer relations with China are a hedge against dependence on Western-led international financial institutions, on which Cambodia has been dependent for roughly half its annual budget since the UN peace process in the early 1990s. Stronger ties with China also balance an assertive Vietnam, although Cambodia's long-serving prime minister, Hun Sen, was an official in the government installed in Phnom Penh by Hanoi after the 1978 Vietnamese invasion of Cambodia. And, as with both Laos and Myanmar, domestic resentment of China is apparent, particularly when the government makes economic concessions to Chinese firms. Some Cambodians argue that the domestic factor, which includes resentment toward Beijing for its prior support of the Khmer Rouge, acts as a brake on Chinese encroachment.

This school of thought also holds that U.S.-Cambodian relations have had a similar flowering in the past two decades but that Americans seldom realize it because of a strong U.S. focus on human rights in Cambodia that publicly overshadows other aspects of the relationship. The United States is the largest market for Cambodian garments—receiving approximately 70 percent of Cambodian garment exports—and favorable labor standards make Cambodia an attractive, if small, target for U.S. investors. The bilateral security relationship has also expanded, in quiet increments, and included joint exercises in 2012 for the first time (which displeased Cambodia's neighbor Thailand).[15]

But although Cambodia's relations with the United States have arguably expanded as significantly as its relations with China, Cambodia's political dynamic gives Beijing an edge. Washington's continued concern with human rights abuses and electoral irregularities constrain relations. Beijing, on the other hand, emphasizes its unconditional approach to aid and trade with Cambodia. Nor are Chinese leaders above specific moves to counter or trump U.S. influence. In November 2012, just before President Obama arrived in Phnom Penh for the East Asia Summit meeting, the serving U.S. president ever to visit Cambodia, Chinese Prime Minister Wen Jiabao upped Beijing's ante with Phnom Penh with a US$100 million loan to establish Cambodia's largest cement plant.[16]

Although several ASEAN countries—particularly those with claims in the South China Sea—share the perception that Cambodia is increasingly in China's orbit, Phnom Penh's actions in the region might be explained as small state behavior, particularly in a country with few realistic ambitions for regional leadership. The issues on which Cambodia appears to have yielded to China (Uighurs, South China Sea) are not perceived as vital interests in the Cambodian policy apparatus. Thus, Phnom Penh's could more easily acquiescence to Chinese demands that the South China Sea be kept off the agenda of ASEAN meetings when Cambodia was the 2012 chair. Cambodia has signed but not ratified the United Nations Convention on the Law of the Sea, but has no substantial claims in the South China Sea that would motivate it to side with those ASEAN countries (Vietnam, the Philippines, Malaysia) that do.

Instead, Cambodia's concerns appear to be on its borders. Despite the Cambodian People's Party's fraternal history with the Vietnamese Communist Party, anti-Vietnamese sentiment is evident in the Cambodian public and often sparks internal instability: the formal demarcation of the Cambodia-Vietnam border in 2012 resulted in strong demonstrations. So too relations with Thailand are continually in flux, over issues ranging from border disputes to Prime Minister Hun Sen's close relationship to exiled Thai Prime Minister Thaksin. In contrast to Laos, with its political ties to Vietnam and its cultural ties to Thailand, Cambodia can look to neither of its more powerful neighbors as an ally. As a result, Phnom Penh is likely to remain focused in its foreign policy on the regional level rather than on larger geostrategic shifts.

However, as a small and vulnerable state, Cambodia is more inclined toward global multilateral intervention when that suits its interests. Cambodia placed more emphasis on the use of the International Court of Justice to settle its dispute with Thailand over the Preah Vihear temple than did Bangkok. More recently, Cambodia was the first ASEAN state to publicly support Malaysia's call for an ASEAN peacekeeping force, although the scope and mandate of that body are yet to be discussed among the member states.[17] Cambodia's comfort level with multilateral intervention goes against China's preference for settling disputes bilaterally where possible and could complicate the China-Cambodia relationship.

Myanmar: Emerging Balancer?

Following the 2010 national elections, Myanmar has initiated political and economic reform movements and accelerated its emergence from half a century of self-isolation. This has sparked an international surge into Myanmar, with Asian powers—particularly Japan—moving more quickly than the West. However, the reform era is not a total blank slate. Domestically, the role of former regime officials—"cronies"—continues to affect the pace of progress. As well, Myanmar's prereform relations continue to figure prominently in its foreign policy. By far the most significant of these are Myanmar-China relations.

China's Changing Role and Image

As in most Southeast Asian states, officials in Myanmar espouse a policy paradigm of a multiplicity of foreign relations and an attempt to balance them all equally. In particular, they deny any element of U.S.-China rivalry or conflict in the country's foreign policy. However, adjustment in Myanmar-China relations is inevitable in the new policy environment. China finds its former status as the country's most important external partner challenged on several fronts by several countries. Although Chinese officials initially appeared to believe that the warming of U.S.-Myanmar relations under the Obama administration was an attempt to diminish Chinese influence there, they seem more focused at present on Japan's meteoric reengagement with Myanmar in the past few years.[18]

However, the larger problem in Myanmar-China relations is Beijing's increasingly unfavorable image with the Myanmar public. There are several sources of rising public suspicion of China:

1. *Large Chinese infrastructure projects*, many of which were contracted before the reform movement began. The "poster child" of public discontent in this regard is the Mytisone dam, which President Thein Sein has suspended for the time being. However, Chinese officials are lobbying top political figures—Thein Sein, Shwe Mann, and Aung Sang Suu Kyi—to allow work on the dam to resume when it is politically possible to do so.

   Another recent example was the 2012 protests against a copper mine in Latpaduoung, in northern Myanmar, jointly built with the Chinese Wanbao Mining company. The government's crackdown on the protestors, many of whom were monks, drew additional controversy.[19] A parliamentary investigatory commission, led by National League for Democracy chair Aung Sang Suu Kyi, found fault with the government response but recommended that work on the mine continue, sparking new public outrage and accusations that the government had chosen relations with China over the welfare of its people. In fact, Suu Kyi specifically cited the need to maintain positive relations with China when the commission's findings were publicly released.[20]

2. *The perception that China does not comply with agreements.* In several instances, Myanmar partners in Chinese business ventures have had the experience of signing an agreement with a Chinese firm, only to have that firm push for more concessions after signing. This is a fairly common Chinese negotiation tactic across the region, and Southeast Asians are beginning to realize that the conclusion of an agreement is only the beginning of negotiations. While this can have benefits for both sides in some circumstances,

new international investors in Myanmar are more inclined toward a more open and contractual approach.

3. *The perception that China is supporting border minority groups against the central government.* China has a considerable stake in Kachin province, not only because of the energy pipelines but also because of the number of ethnic Chinese in Kachin (and the number of ethnic Kachin across the border in China). However, China also has a close relationship with the Wa, which uses Chinese currency. The closeness of this relationship with the Wa has given rise to the suggestion that the Wa region is more a part of the Chinese province of Yunnan than of Myanmar. This is a complicated situation, because many ethnic groups had fought against the People's Liberation Army during the Cold War. However, this perception creates suspicion among central Burmans that China is pursuing a divide-and-conquer strategy with the ethnic minorities.

This problem between neighbors was exacerbated in early 2015 with the eruption of conflict in the Kokang Special Region in the northern part of Myanmar's Shan State, on the Myanmar-China border. The conflict sent tens of thousands of Myanmar nationals of Chinese ethnicity across the border into Yunnan province. Naypyidaw has charged Yunnan officials with giving sanctuary to Peng Jiashen, the eighty-five-year-old leader of the Kokang rebel group, the Myanmar National Democratic Alliance Army. For their part, Chinese officials are worried that a conflict on the Myanmar side of the border will stir discontent within its own nationals on the China side, and they are critical of the Myanmar armed forces for not putting down the Kokang rebellion more forcefully.[21] To date, the MNDAA remains outside the ethnic peace negotiations with the government. However, China's greatest concern is the Kachin state. Chinese officials have fostered dialogue between the Myanmar central government and the Kachin Independence Organization but prefer to be the sole external actor in this regard—attempts by Naypyidaw to include U.S., British, and UN observers in the dialogue process met with initial resistance from Beijing.[22] Washington and London have not since pressed for a formal role in the peace process. The Thein Sein government was able to craft a national cease-fire, in which half of the armed ethnic groups participated, but it will be up to the new government to draw the remaining ethnic groups into the peace process and complete difficult political negotiations before any concrete agreement is reached.

4. *China's availability as an easy scapegoat.* China's prominence in Myanmar also makes it vulnerable to myriad conspiracy theories, including those surrounding violence against Muslims in Rakhine state, where the Chinese pipelines also transverse. Persistent rumors that China has sparked inci-

dents of violence to draw attention away from its increasingly unpopular infrastructure projects seem to be counterintuitive, since increased instability in Rakhine would threaten the security of the pipelines. Beijing has called for calm in Rakhine but has avoided comments that would make China appear to side with either Muslims or Buddhists. However, protests against the pipeline are mounting in Rakhine over conditions for the local population,[23] which help fuel charges of Chinese meddling in communal disputes. The recent outbreak of anti-Muslim violence in Mandalay, which represents a significant leap in this trend, undermines arguments that communal tensions are orchestrated by China.

However, focusing exclusively on anecdotes of emerging public resistance to China's role in Myanmar would create an inaccurate sense of relations between the two countries. A considerable spectrum of Myanmar officials and nongovernmental actors regard China as Myanmar's most important bilateral tie, and caution that the relationship is "special."[24] There are several reasons for China's continued centrality in Myanmar's foreign policy, the reform movement notwithstanding. Geography is undeniable, and the shared border between China and Myanmar gives Beijing (and Kunming) a direct interest in Myanmar's internal stability. In addition, many Myanmar officials feel some loyalty to China for supporting the country during two decades of international sanctions. (Myanmar's relations with Moscow also strengthened during the sanctions period, but those have a lower profile than Myanmar-China relations.)

At the same time, leaders across the spectrum appear to be seeking greater balance in its foreign relations. Given its potential position on mainland Southeast Asia, that new policy paradigm may give Myanmar a new role as a regional balancer. In the near term, however, Naypyidaw is finding that rebalancing can be a difficult proposition. For example, although the government is pressed to respond to new relations with several powers, it worries that some of these relations are not moving along as quickly as others. Many Myanmar interlocutors are also worried that relations with India—which they had hoped would be a counterweight against China—have not developed as expected. Indian companies are not as prominent in infrastructure projects, primarily because the decision-making process is too cumbersome. Myanmar officials find India's slow start particularly alarming because of new pathways being forged between the Pacific and the Indian Oceans through various ASEAN interconnectivity projects, as well as more private infrastructure projects. Without a more robust Indian presence in Myanmar, China may be able to exploit these new connections to their advantage. However,

India's "Look East" policy remains limited in Southeast Asia as a whole, in part because of resistance within the Indian bureaucracy to sudden shifts.

But despite China's continued prominence in Myanmar's foreign affairs and Washington's increasing interest, Naypyidaw is not likely to find itself in a triangular relationship with Washington and Beijing. Although U.S. relations with Myanmar have expanded dramatically since the onset of the reform process following the 2010 elections, the United States has not yet established a strong footprint in the country. Many sanctions have been suspended by presidential executive order but not formally removed from U.S. law; in addition, many U.S. companies are reluctant to enter the Myanmar market in the absence of a strong regulatory framework. A fuller U.S. embrace will likely be delayed until Myanmar satisfies concerns—in both the U.S. Congress and the executive branch—about continued military influence and control in the political process and ethnic issues, particularly violence against Muslims.

Myanmar's Integration into Southeast Asia

Myanmar's debut as ASEAN chair in 2014 was both a watershed and a test in Naypyidaw's new regional and international role. To be sure, ASEAN chairmanship is a drain on the host country's foreign policy apparatus, although many of the thousand-plus ASEAN meetings in any given year are held in other member countries. The most important meetings are the high-profile ones: the two ASEAN Summits held each year; the ASEAN Regional Forum; the ASEAN Defense Ministers Meeting (ADMM, and the ADMM-Plus, which includes eight external partners); and, most prominently, the East Asia Summit.

Apart from the constant round of meetings, Naypyidaw was challenged by the need to move ASEAN's institutional development forward in several directions, including moving the group toward completion of the ASEAN Economic Community (AEC) in 2015 and addressing significant issues with external partners, such as tensions with China in the South China Sea. In reality, some tasks—such as harmonizing the economies in preparation for the AEC—are left to high-ranking technocrats rather than political leaders, but leaders are required to maintain the political will to move these arrangements forward.

Myanmar received basically positive marks from its fellow ASEAN states and the international community for its chairmanship in 2014. With help from the ASEAN Secretariat, other ASEAN governments, and some external partners, including the United States, Naypyidaw was able to manage the large number of meetings in ASEAN's growing basket of issues.

However, Naypyidaw's chairmanship sparked internal debate over pressures on ASEAN states and the likely impact of major ASEAN initiatives on the domestic population. The AEC will be a mixed blessing for Myanmar. Essentially a free trade agreement for goods and, to a lesser extent, services, it will lower barriers to trade within ASEAN. Although this will no doubt stimulate intraregional trade, it could also exacerbate inequities between ASEAN's wealthier and poorer members. Moreover, the mechanics of the AEC require that members revise and harmonize certain structures, such as customs regulations. This adds an additional burden to Myanmar at a time of large-scale revision of its economic and administrative framework. Another worry for Myanmar officials is the free movement of professional labor within ASEAN under the AEC. Although this will make greater skilled labor available to strengthen Myanmar's own economic development, it could also inhibit the growth of these sections within Myanmar itself. The four "new" ASEAN members—those that entered in the 1990s—were given a longer lead time in which to reform their regulatory frameworks to conform to AEC standards, but the deadline will probably slip further for these poorer ASEAN states.

Myanmar is also under some pressure to move forward sensitive areas of cooperation within ASEAN, such as human rights. Since it entered ASEAN in 1997, Myanmar has customarily caucused with the other new members— Vietnam, Laos, and Cambodia—to encourage an incremental (and slow) pace toward an ASEAN human rights framework, in keeping with the long-standing institutional principle of noninterference in the internal affairs of member states. In contrast, ASEAN's democracies—Indonesia, the Philippines, and (in its democratic periods) Thailand—have tended to take a more vigorous (and slightly more interventionist) approach toward regional human rights, driven in part by their domestic populations' demands for a policy shift.[25] Naypyidaw's approach to the issue area is all the more complicated by Myanmar's own internal rights problems. ASEAN has encouraged its member states to form national human rights commissions, with the eventual aim of linking these bodies together into one regional organization. To date, all ASEAN members have formed commissions of some sort, except for Vietnam, Laos, and Cambodia. Although Myanmar has had a national human rights commission since 2012, decreed by President Thein Sein, it is under the Ministry of Home Affairs and is criticized by human rights groups for its lack of independence.

ASEAN's gradual move toward a security community also presents challenges and opportunities for Myanmar. While the United States is identified with Cobra Gold, China is more closely associated with the establishment of the ADMM. At present, the U.S. Congress is holding firm to sanctions on the Tatmadaw, while the Obama administration supports the inclusion of Myanmar officers in the IMET program.[26] The ADMM process could offer an entry point for stronger U.S.-Myanmar security relations, since it offers regional rather than bilateral cooperation. However, the ADMM meets with its external partners only every three years, which does not suggest fast-paced institutional development, and any direct benefit from U.S.-Myanmar security relations through the ADMM will take years to be realized.

Conclusion

Generalizations about this group of four Mainland Southeast Asian countries are inadvisable, if not impossible. The exception to this may be the fact that none of the four countries is a claimant in the South China Sea, and all four generally would prefer to avoid becoming embroiled in the disputes surrounding that area. Cambodia's apparent deference to China on this issue when Phnom Penh chaired ASEAN in 2012 was a much-criticized example of this reality. However, with Laos serving as the ASEAN chair in 2016 and Thailand in 2019, this will be a recurrent dynamic in internal ASEAN affairs.

Comparisons among the four countries may be more useful. Two states, Myanmar and Laos, share borders with China and have specific issues with that country as a result. Of the two, the situation on the Myanmar-China border is more significant and potentially more destabilizing because of continued tensions between the Myanmar central government and the Kachin state. However, shared borders also facilitate the flow of natural resources from these two countries into China, and Myanmar and Laos will be special trade targets as a result. Three of the four states—Myanmar, Laos, and Thailand—are embroiled, with one another and with China and Vietnam, in various issues related to energy competition. As competition increases and major energy consumers seek multiple sources and transportation routes, these mainland Southeast Asian countries will become even more critical.

Three (Myanmar, Laos, and Cambodia) are among the region's smallest and least developed economies. Their immediate destiny is determined by their place in the supply chain, with external trade dominated by natural resources and light manufacturing. By virtue of their exclusion from APEC, these three countries are ineligible for such high-end trade agreements as the Trans-Pacific Partnership. For the time being, they will be challenged enough to meet the regulatory requirements in the "lower end" free trade agreements in the region, including the ASEAN Free Trade Agreement and the Regional Comprehensive Economic Partnership. On the brighter side, lower wages will make these three countries—especially Myanmar and Cambodia—attractive to foreign investors. However, because of the size of its population, its natural resource base, and its educated elite, Myanmar's prospects for economic development and regional prominence are obviously brighter than those of Laos and Cambodia.

As a sometime-democracy and as a newly liberalizing system, Thailand and Myanmar, respectively, have stronger connections between domestic political dynamics and foreign policy. However, Thailand is far less vulnerable to external pressure than are its three neighbors; for Bangkok, the challenge will be in stabilizing internal politics so as to pursue a more coherent and effective foreign policy. External interference in internal political affairs is no more welcome in Myanmar, Laos, and Cambodia than in Thailand, but Thailand's economy and its position as a regional hub (as well as its history of unbroken independence) are better fortifications against external pressure.

Moreover, Thailand's position in the emerging connectivity grid of mainland Southeast Asia, as well as its larger and more developed economy, will ensure its place as the regional power within this subregion of four countries regardless of its current political situation. The "golden peninsula" moment for Thailand on mainland Southeast Asia may have passed, but Myanmar's increasing openness to the region and the international community will strengthen Thailand's role as a regional hub in the near term. Relations between Thailand and Cambodia have seldom been smooth, and Bangkok will continue to view Phnom Penh as an irritant on its border. Thailand has greater leverage in Laos and will seek to maintain its influence there as competition from China intensifies.

A longer-term issue for Myanmar will be the political and social consequences of greater regional connectivity. Special economic zones and related transportation projects will further open the country to regional influence, but they will also create new domestic pressures that will in turn affect Myanmar's relations with its major economic partners.

Over the next decade, the political and economic fortunes of mainland Southeast Asia's three largest countries—Thailand, Vietnam, and Myanmar—will largely determine dynamics in the subregion. Of these three, Myanmar's development will be the most influenced by its relationship with China, because of its lower economic levels. However, Myanmar's opening to the West—particularly the United States—is indicative of its intention to diminish China's considerable influence. By contrast, the two smaller countries, Cambodia and Laos, have few if any prospects of genuine regional leadership (their rotational chairmanships of ASEAN notwithstanding) and will be more vulnerable to the persuasions and intimidations of external powers.

Completion of the TPP will give Vietnam the greatest access to the U.S. and Japanese markets of any mainland Southeast Asian country and less economic dependence upon China as a result. However, strong party-to-party relations with China, combined with continued tensions over the South China Sea, ensure that the love-hate nature of Vietnam's relations with China will continue, which in turn will ensure Hanoi's continued vigilance toward China's presence and influence in Laos and Cambodia. By comparison, Thailand and Myanmar are less entangled with China historically and therefore more free to form stronger relations with other regional powers.

As well, mainland Southeast Asia's relations with China (and the United States) will depend in part on the trajectories of other regional actors—Japan, Russia, India, and Australia—in developing relations with Southeast Asia. The current triangle of greatest concern—Southeast Asia–China–United States—could in time be replaced by other dynamics (e.g., Southeast Asia–China–Japan or Southeast Asia–China–India). However, with its greater proximity to China in comparison to maritime Southeast Asia, these dynamics will likely be felt first on mainland Southeast Asia.

NOTES

1   For a discussion of this, see Ciorciori, "China and Cambodia."

2   These tensions have abated to some extent with the decision on Preah Vihear handed down by the International Court of Justice in November 2013. The ICJ reaffirmed Cambodian sovereignty over the temple itself but ceded only a tiny portion of the surrounding territory to Phnom Penh, effectively forcing the two governments to jointly administer the temple area. The decision can be found at www.icj-cij.org.

3   Li Renliang, "Dancing with the Dragon.".

4   Matsui, "Japan Tries to Check China."

5   Ton Han Shih, "China Trading on Top Thai Trade Spot."

6   Keck, "China May Join US-Led Trans-Pacific Trade Talks."

7   Author's interviews with senior officers of the Royal Thai Army, Bangkok, January 2012.

8   Author's interview with U.S. Department of Defense official, Washington, DC, July 30, 2014.

9   Author's interview with U.S. State Department official, Washington, DC, February 27, 2015.

10 Author's interview of U.S. Department of Defense official, Washington, DC, July 30, 2014.

11 Author's interview with Vietnamese Ministry of Foreign Affairs official, Washington, DC, April 4, 2014.

12 "Japan Reinforcing ASEAN Ties."

13 Myanmar draws only 6 percent of its water supply from the Mekong, but was incorporated into the Lower Mekong Initiative to strengthen its relations with the United States and the other states in mainland Southeast Asia.

14 "Mekong Competition May See China/US Diplomatic Crisis."

15 See, for example, Cheang, "US-Cambodian Relations."

16 Szep, "Obama Visit to Cambodia."

17 Moss, "Malaysia Proposes Joint ASEAN Peacekeeping Force."

18 Author's interviews with Myanmar Ministry of Foreign Affairs officials in Naypyidaw, October 2013.

19 Lintner, "Burma."

20 "Aung Sang Suu Kyi Support for Copper Mine."

21 "Myanmar and China."

22 "Presidential Visit to Push US-Myanmar Economic Ties."

23 "Hundreds Protest Pipeline in Burma's Rakhine State."

24 Author's interviews with Myanmar officials in Naypyidaw and Yangon, October 2013.

25 For example, the movement in 2004 to deny Myanmar its rotation as the ASEAN chair was largely driven by nongovernmental organizations and opposition politicians in ASEAN's more democratic member countries.

26 See the testimony of Judith Cefkin, U.S. State Department senior advisor for Burma, and Vikram Singh, deputy assistant secretary of defense for Southeast Asia, at the "Oversight Hearing of U.S. Policy toward Burma" before the House Committee on Foreign Affairs, Subcommittee on Asia and the Pacific, December 4, 2013, http://foreignaffairs.house.gov.

BIBLIOGRAPHY

"ASEAN Leaders Eye Stronger Integration Beyond 2015." *Xinhua*, October 10, 2013. www.globaltimes.cn.

"Aung Sang Suu Kyi Support for Copper Mine Outrages Burmese Activists." *Guardian*, March 12, 2013. www.guardian.co.uk.

Cheang, Vannarith. "US-Cambodian Relations: Human Rights Is One Variable." Pac-Net no. 80. *Pacific Forum*, November 30, 2012. http://csis.org.

Chongkittavorn, Kavi. "China Renews Its Efforts to Re-engage ASEAN." *Nation*, September 16, 2013. www.nationmultimedia.com.

Ciorciori, John. "China and Cambodia: Patron and Client?" IPC Working Paper Series no. 121. Ann Arbor: Gerald R. Ford School of Public Policy, University of Michigan, June 14, 2013. http://ipc.umich.edu.

Dalpino, Catharin. "An Old Alliance for the New Century: Reinvigorating the US-Thailand Alliance." NBR Special Report no. 40. Seattle: National Bureau of Asian Research, June 2012.

Galluci, Daniel. "China and Thailand Vie for Influence with Thai Rail Projects." *Financial Times*, March 3, 2015. http://blogs.ft.com.

"Hundreds Protest Pipeline in Burma's Rakhine State." *Radio Free Asia*, April 18, 2013. www.rfa.org.

"Japan Reinforcing ASEAN Ties as Check to China." *Nation*, November 22, 2013. www.nationmultimedia.com.

Keck, Zachary. "China May Join US-Led Trans-Pacific Trade Talks." *Diplomat*, May 31, 2013. http://thediplomat.com.

Li Renliang. "Dancing with the Dragon: The Trans-Pacific Railway and Its Impact on Thailand." *Perspective, Institute of Southeast Asian Studies*, no. 9, March 4, 2016. www.iseas.edu.sg.

Lintner, Bertil. "Burma: Brewing Trouble for China." *Yale Global*, November 2, 2012. http://yaleglobal.yale.edu.

Mahtani, Shibani, and Myo Myo. "Myanmar Signs Draft Peace Deal with Armed Ethnic Groups." *Wall Street Journal*, March 31, 2015. www.wsj.com.

Matsui, Motokazu. "Japan Tries to Check China with Dawei Development Project." *Nikkei Asian Review*, July 7, 2015. http://asia.nikkei.com.

"Mekong Competition May See China/US Diplomatic Crisis." *Oxford Analytica Daily Briefs*, March 26, 2015. www.oxan.com.

Moss, Trefor. "Malaysia Proposes Joint ASEAN Peacekeeping Force." *Wall Street Journal*, March 18, 2015. www.wsj.com.

"Myanmar and China: The Han That Rock the Cradle." *Economist*, March 14, 2015. www.economist.com.

"Presidential Visit to Push US-Myanmar Economic Ties." *Oxford Analytica Daily Briefs*, May 20, 2103. www.oxan.com.

Szep, Jason. "Obama Visit to Cambodia Overshadowed by Row over South China Sea." *Christian Science Monitor*, November 19, 2012. http://m.csmonitor.com.

"Testimonies of Judith Cefkin, US State Department Senior Advisor for Burma, and Vikram Singh, Deputy Assistant Secretary of Defense for Southeast Asia, at the 'Oversight Hearing of U.S. Policy toward Burma' before the House Committee on Foreign Affairs, Subcommittee on Asia and the Pacific." December 4, 2013. http://foreignaffairs.house.gov.

Ton Han Shih. "China Trading on Top Thai Trade Spot." *South China Morning Post*, February 27, 2013. http://m.scmp.com.

PART III

The Outside Powers

9

Japan's Relationship with Southeast Asia

The Perpetual Potential Partner

EDWARD J. LINCOLN

Trade

Given the relatively rapid growth of nations in Southeast Asia, the region should have become both a more important destination for Japanese exports and origin for imports. This is certainly the experience Japan (and much of the rest of the world) has had with China. While Southeast Asia has not grown as rapidly as China, economic growth has been well above the global average. Furthermore, since 1985 (when the Japanese yen strengthened sharply against the U.S. dollar and other currencies) Japanese firms have been relocating production to lower-wage countries, and Southeast Asia would be a natural destination for them. That relocation process should enhance the trade relationship, with sophisticated components flowing from Japan to Southeast Asia and finished products flowing from there back to Japan.

Figure 9.1, however, shows that ASEAN has not become a significantly more important destination for Japan's exports. Except for an unusual dip between 1982 and 1986 (when a weak yen led to an explosion of Japanese exports to the United States), ASEAN has been the destination for roughly 15 percent of Japan's exports. Exports rose from the unusually low level of 5 percent in 1986 to 17 percent in 1995, but subsequently fluctuated in a narrow 12 to 15 percent range.

Since the mid-1980s, some Japanese manufacturing production has shifted through foreign direct investment to lower-wage countries. This shift should have caused a corresponding shift in trade patterns, with, for example, a shift from exports of finished goods from Japan to the United States, to exports to the new production bases in Asia and rising exports from those locations to the United States. However, this effect shows up only for Japan's trade with China (including Hong Kong) and the United States. The share of Japan's exports destined to the United States has fallen dramatically (from 39 percent in 1985 to only 20 percent in 2015) and those to China have risen equally dramatically (from 8 percent in 1986 to 23 percent in 2015). While some Japanese production

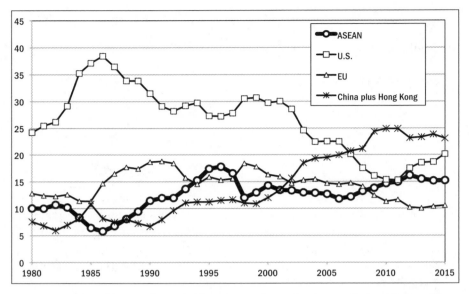

Figure 9.1. Japan's exports by region (percentage share of exports to the world). Source: Ministry of Finance, Government of Japan, "Trade Statistics of Japan," www.customs. go.jp/toukei/suii/html/time_e.htm.

in China is for the local market, much of it is exported to traditional Japanese export destinations such as the United States, as well as back to Japan.

Figure 9.2 presents data on the origin of Japan's imports. The story is similar to that for exports, with ASEAN countries representing a relatively constant 15 percent share of all of Japan's imports. A small decline occurred in the 1980s from 15 percent to 12 percent (mainly due to the fall in the price of oil and gas, which are significant Japanese imports from Indonesia), but the share soon returned to the plateau of 15 percent. As with exports, the pattern with ASEAN contrasts sharply to that with China. Due primarily to the relocation of final assembly production to China, its share in Japan's imports exploded from only 3 percent in 1980 to 25 percent by 2015. The rise in imports from China has been so strong that the share of imports from both the United States and Europe has fallen.

These trade trends present something of a puzzle. Why doesn't the pattern of trade with ASEAN more closely resemble that with China? For example, while global GDP growth averaged 2.7 percent in the period from 2000 to 2014, the ASEAN countries averaged 5.3 percent, lower than that of China but still well above the global average.[1] On investment, wages in a number of

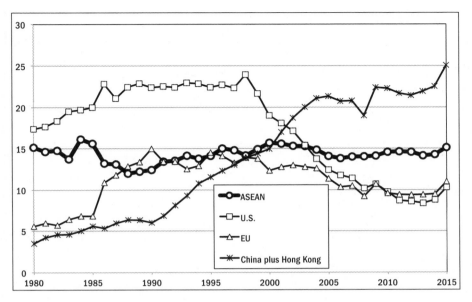

Figure 9.2. Japan's imports by region (percentage of total imports from the world). Source: Ministry of Finance, Government of Japan, "Trade Statistics of Japan," www. customs.go.jp/toukei/suii/html/time_e.htm.

ASEAN members have been as low or lower as those of China. These countries also share (as does China) a longitudinal proximity to Japan; being close in terms of time zones generally enhances investment flows due to greater ease in communication (just as American firms locate production in Mexico due to both geographical proximity and similar time zones). The probable answer to this puzzle, explored in the following section of this chapter, is that while Japanese manufacturing firms have relocated production to ASEAN, much of the output has not been exported back to Japan. Instead, the output is sold locally, shipped to Japanese-owned factories elsewhere in ASEAN, or sent to China. This conclusion is at least crudely supported by ASEAN trade data, with the share of ASEAN exports to Japan falling from 1990 to 2014 (from 16 percent to 9 percent of ASEAN global exports), while the share to China rose, as did intra-ASEAN exports.[2]

Investment

Part of the trade puzzle might be answered by Japanese foreign direct investment patterns, shown in table 9.1. That is, perhaps Japanese firms have chosen to invest heavily in China (enhancing the trade ties), but not in ASEAN countries. However, as indicated in table 9.1, this is not the case. The data prior to 2005 are not entirely consistent with the numbers since then due to a change in data collection procedures, but the relative shares should be roughly comparable.

TABLE 9.1. Japan's foreign direct investment by destination (percentage of total annual flow)

Calendar year	ASEAN	United States	European Union	China
2000	0.7	44.8	34.8	3.0
2001	10.4	18.3	46.5	5.6
2002	13.3	23.2	30.5	8.2
2003	1.5	37.2	27.9	13.8
2004	9.0	24.4	23.7	18.9
2005	11.0	27.0	17.1	14.4
2006	13.8	18.5	35.7	12.3
2007	10.6	21.4	27.3	8.4
2008	4.9	33.7	17.7	5.1
2009	9.4	14.3	22.8	9.3
2010	15.6	16.1	14.5	12.7
2011	17.0	12.6	31.2	11.0
2012	8.8	26.1	23.7	11.0
2013	17.6	32.4	23.0	6.7
2014	17.1	35.2	20.5	5.6
2015	15.1	33.2	25.9	6.7
2000–2015	12.2	27.1	24.9	8.6

Source: Ministry of Finance, "Balance of Payments (Historical Data)," www.mof.go.jp.

The data in table 9.1 reveal sharp fluctuations in the destination of investment from year to year. Nonetheless, summing up the amounts for the fifteen-year period from 2000 through 2015, two significant points emerge. First, the notion of investment flowing on the basis of seeking lower wages is only a partial explanation for Japan's investment behavior. Half of all Japanese foreign direct investment in this time period went to the United States and the European Union, not to developing countries. Second, ASEAN has received somewhat more investment from Japan than has China. For the entire time period, ASEAN countries received 12.2 percent of cumulative flows while China received a somewhat lower 8.6 percent.

These data would seem to present a further puzzle concerning Japan and Southeast Asia. If the region has absorbed as much investment from Japan as has China, why are the trade patterns so different? The answer may lie in the nature of Japanese investment in ASEAN and China. When Japanese firms began a major effort to seek lower-cost bases of production, they moved factories into a number of countries around the region, and it is possible that pattern of trade generated by those in ASEAN countries has been different from those in China. If, for example, ASEAN countries received factories producing component parts while China received more factories involved in final assembly, then plants in China would be more likely to ship output to the United States, Europe, and even Japan than those in ASEAN. With Japanese firms invested in a number of ASEAN countries, components (that used to come from Japan) are produced locally and then shipped to other ASEAN countries for incorporation in the next stage of production. Japanese statistical data on foreign direct investment flows show a broad distribution of investments across six of the ten ASEAN member countries, shown in table 9.2.

TABLE 9.2. Japan's foreign direct investment flow to individual ASEAN countries (¥ billions)

Calendar year	Singapore	Thailand	Indonesia	Malaysia	Philippines	Vietnam	Other ASEAN
2005	63	36	134	59	47	17	202
2006	44	231	86	346	43	54	5
2007	263	306	121	38	124	56	9
2008	112	209	74	62	74	113	8
2009	271	152	46	58	77	53	2
2010	332	198	41	91	43	64	3
2011	352	558	288	115	81	150	7
2012	128	46	304	105	58	205	12
2013	355	1,013	382	123	120	318	22
2014	812	551	471	107	52	142	193
2015	792	433	430	342	169	168	-213
Total flow 2005–2015	3,524	3,733	2,376	1,445	889	1,339	249

Source: Ministry of Finance, "Outward/Inward Direct Investment (Historical Data)," www.mof.go.jp.

Investment by Japanese firms is spread broadly among the five original ASEAN members plus Vietnam, and although the amounts vary there is significant investment in each of them (in contrast to the very small amounts in the other four ASEAN countries). This spread is due in part to local conditions (investment in the financial sector in Singapore; investment in oil and gas in Indonesia) but also results in part from the distribution of manufacturing facilities across the region depending on availability of raw materials, the level of wages, and other conditions. Put in dollar terms, the total flow ranges from roughly US$8 billion to Philippines to US$30 billion to Singapore and Thailand. This spread increases trade within ASEAN as components move from one factory to another. Thus, Japanese foreign direct investment in ASEAN creates trade, but not necessarily more trade between ASEAN and Japan, as discussed in the previous section on trade.

A further significant aspect of these investment data is the continued strength of investment in China. The series of confrontations over the past decade concerning the "history question" (denial or downplaying of responsibility for the war and associated atrocities in the public statements of Japanese politicians) and the Senkaku Islands have led to a questioning in Japan of the advisability of expanding trade and investment ties with China. These provocations began to escalate when then Prime Minister Junichiro Koizumi made a series of annual trips to the infamous Yasukuni Shrine in the early 2000s (where the spirits of soldiers are enshrined, including those of the Class-A war criminals executed by the Allies after the war). More recently, in the fall of 2012 (after the Japanese government purchased the Senkaku Islands from a private Japanese owner) sales of Japanese goods, including automobiles manufactured in China, fell temporarily as Chinese consumers boycotted them.[3] Prime Minister Shinzo Abe (who came into office at the beginning of 2013 following an election victory of the Liberal Democratic Party and who is discussed later in this chapter) visited the Yasukuni Shrine in December 2013 (the first prime minister to do so since Prime Minister Koizumi almost a decade earlier), provoking official protests from China and Korea. However, even though he was known as a staunch nationalist, the formal response by the Chinese government to his visit was quite muted compared to that during the 2012 tensions and there were no public protests. However, as table 9.1 shows, the share of investment flowing to China fell somewhat after 2012. In 2015 the share was 6.7 percent, down from 11 percent in 2012 (while the share going to ASEAN in 2015 was 15.1 percent). If the drop was motivated by Japanese business fears of deteriorating relations with China under Prime Minister Abe, then the gradual improvement in relations since 2013 could cause the level of foreign direct investment to rebound. Economic factors may be in play to prevent a rebound, though, with rising wages and slowing economic growth in China making it a less attractive location for Japanese investment.

Looked at a different way, the question might be this: why is the share of Japanese investment in China not much higher than in ASEAN? The turmoil of the Asian Financial Crisis of 1997 caused many foreign firms to relocate investments away from countries hit by the crisis (especially Thailand and Indonesia), and especially relocate to China. For several years foreign direct investment inflows in ASEAN fell from pre-crisis levels while inflows to China increased. Consider also that China is much larger in terms of GDP and population than all of ASEAN, which ought to lead to relatively more inward investment, especially to the extent that investments exist to serve the local market. China also has a reputation for better physical infrastructure (roads, harbors, railways, electrical supply, water supply, sewage, etc.) to support foreign investments. Given these differences that favor investment in China, the fact that ASEAN has continued to attract as much investment from Japan as does China might be an indication of the extent to which Japanese firms want to hedge their risks by avoiding a high reliance on investments in any single country. China presents problems related to the possibility of a major rupture in bilateral relations with Japan (though this remains unlikely), periodic anti-Japanese outbursts (by consumers and occasionally by rock-throwing crowds), intellectual property theft, and rapidly rising wages. ASEAN countries, in turn, have had problems with political stability (Indonesia in the wake of the Asian Financial Crisis, or Thailand since the coup in 2006) and inadequate physical infrastructure. In such an environment, it behooves firms to spread the risk of investment by locating it in a number of different countries. Furthermore, as wages continue to rise rapidly in China, a number of ASEAN countries will look increasingly attractive to Japanese firms that are seeking inexpensive labor.

Although ASEAN countries have received somewhat more investment from Japan than has China, it is also important to put Japanese investment into an ASEAN perspective. That is, to what extent do ASEAN countries as a whole receive direct investment from Japan relative to investments from other countries or regions? Table 9.3 shows the cumulative flow of foreign direct investment into ASEAN countries for the period from 2006 through 2013.

TABLE 9.3. Foreign direct investment flow into ASEAN (cumulative
2006–13, percentage of total)

European Union	22
ASEAN	16
Japan	14
United States	9
China	5
Other	35

Source: ASEAN Secretariat, *ASEAN Statistical Yearbook* (2014), 110.

Although Japanese firms invested more in ASEAN countries during this time period (14 percent of total foreign direct investment inflows) than did American firms (9 percent), the margin is not huge. Of greater significance, both intra-ASEAN investments (16 percent) and those by European firms (22 percent) are larger than those of Japanese firms. These numbers are somewhat at odds with the impression one gets from presentations at Japanese academic conferences. One would think that Japanese firms invented the concept of overseas production networks and that, therefore, Japanese firms are dominant investors in ASEAN. In reality, American and European firms are as adept at this evolution of multinational corporate behavior as their Japanese competitors (and more flexible than the Japanese in terms of buying outside their own network of subsidiaries). In sum, Japan is certainly an important source of direct investments into ASEAN, but hardly a dominant one, lagging behind investments from the European Union.

Foreign Aid

Historically, Southeast Asia was a major recipient of Japanese foreign aid, absorbing over 50 percent of bilateral aid in the 1970s and 1980s. However, over time Japan diversified its foreign aid (to areas such as Africa). As recently as 2000, 40 percent of Japan's bilateral aid was still directed to countries in Southeast Asia, but by 2010–11 the share was down to 10 percent and in 2013–14 sank to a tiny 1.3 percent (according to OECD data, which are different from what the Japanese government data in table 9.4 show).[4] In addition, the total amount of Japan's foreign aid has been flat for almost two decades. In 1995–96, Japan disbursed US$12.0 billion in net foreign aid, and in 2014 the amount was US$9.3 billion (with relatively little fluctuation in the intervening years other than that due to exchange rate movements).[5] Much of bilateral foreign aid has been extended in the form of subsidized loans rather than grants. With most Southeast Asian nations receiving less from Japan in new aid other than relatively small grants, the region as a whole is actually returning money to Japan on a net basis, as indicated in table 9.4. The only countries in the region receiving net new loans are Cambodia, Laos, and Vietnam, with the bulk of the new loans going to Vietnam. For some, the repayment of loans is substantial (Indonesia, Philippines, and Thailand). Japan continues to extend new official development assistance (ODA) loans to the region, but not as much as is being repaid on existing loans. In 2013, ASEAN as a whole received US$5.3 billion in new loans from Japan, while making repayments of US$6.7 billion.[6] Therefore, Prime Minister Abe's pledge in 2014 of US$20 billion in new ODA loans to ASEAN over the next five years (i.e., US$4.0 billion per year) does not represent much of a change, as discussed later in this chapter.

TABLE 9.4. Japan's net bilateral official development assistance to Southeast Asia 2012 (US$ millions)

Country/region	Grants	Loans	Total
Southeast Asia	3,939.0	−1,438.8	2,499.2
Brunei	0.1	0.0	0.1
Cambodia	120.5	21.0	141.5
Indonesia	97.2	−918.1	−820.9
Laos	78.4	−2.5	76.0
Malaysia	23.9	−29.1	−160.5
Myanmar	3,287.1	−758.8	2,528.3
Philippines	122.9	−524.4	−401.5
Singapore	0.3	0.0	0.3
Thailand	72.0	−265.0	−193.1
Timor-Leste	20.5	1.7	22.2
Vietnam	129.3	1,177.6	1,306.9
World	9,840.9	−1,317.1	8,523.6

Source: Ministry of Foreign Affairs of Japan, *Japan's Official Development Assistance White Paper 2013*, 179, 183.

With a thaw in relations with Myanmar in 2013, Japanese foreign aid to that country jumped, at least temporarily. Prime Minister Shinzo Abe visited Myanmar in June of that year and promised to both cancel existing debt owed to Japan (US$1.8 billion) and extend new foreign aid loans of US$500 million. The debt cancellation appears as part of the very large grant for 2014 of US$3.3 billion shown in table 9.4. The new interest of the Japanese government in helping Myanmar, though, appears to come from the old-fashioned stance of providing infrastructure in locations where Japanese firms are eager to invest (in this case, a new industrial park and port facilities in Thilawa near Yangon).[7]

While new flows of foreign aid are no longer a substantial link between Japan and Southeast Asia (with the exception of Vietnam and now possibly Myanmar), Japan did respond with some additional aid during the Asian Financial Crisis of 1997–98. Dubbed the "New Miyazawa Initiative" after then-Finance Minister Kiichi Miyazawa (and called "New" because there was an earlier Miyazawa Plan for Mexico during its 1984 financial crisis), this plan was announced in October 1998 and was supposed to amount to US$30 billion—US$15 billion in short-term financial support and an additional US$15 billion in medium- and long-term financing. However, according to Japanese data, not all the loans were disbursed. The Ministry of Finance indicates that US$21 billion was actually used, although that sum includes swap lines of credit for Malaysia and Korea of US$7.5 billion that may not have been used. The swap credits were to be used for direct intervention in foreign exchange markets by the Korean and Malaysian governments to defend their currencies, but since those currencies had stabilized by the time the money was made available, it is unlikely that the swap arrangements were activated. If so, then the actual net supply of new loans could have been as low as US$13.5 billion. The bulk of this aid was directed at infrastructure projects and trade finance, both areas of direct impact for Japanese firms (by obtaining construction contracts and exporting construction equipment, as well as Japanese exporters in general). Furthermore, the Japanese government indicated that the loans were made in line with IMF policies toward the involved countries, that is, Japan gave approval to the conditionality attached to IMF loans at that time (though these had been considerably scaled back or altered after the heavy criticism of the initial conditionality attached to the IMF loans in the fall of 1997).[8]

Regional Economic Leadership?

Even though the economic relationships between ASEAN and Japan are not of unusual or outstanding strength, the robustness of the trade and investment ties certainly suggest that the Japanese government could see Southeast Asia as having strategic importance because it is a market for Japanese products, source of imports (and especially oil and gas from Indonesia), and location for Japanese investment. Japan, therefore, has a strong national interest in the political and economic well-being of Southeast Asia as well as an interest in pursuing policies favorable to Japanese firms.

Involvement with Southeast Asia has long roots. For example, Southeast Asia was a key issue in the outbreak of the Pacific War in 1941. Japan desperately needed access to oil, rubber, tin, and other raw materials from Southeast Asia in order to pursue its war in China, especially when the U.S. government embargoed the export of oil to Japan in the summer of 1941. The need to protect its Pacific flank while invading Southeast Asia then led to the disastrous decision to attack the U.S. Pacific naval base in Pearl Harbor. The occupation of most of the region by the Japanese from 1941 to 1945 was quite mixed. The period of time was too short to generate the kind of long-lasting animosities that have continued to hinder good relations between Japan and Korea (annexed by Japan in 1911), and insufficiently brutal to generate feelings similar to the long-term enmity of the Chinese. And the arming and training of local military units created some goodwill because these forces in some countries aided the postwar independence efforts against European colonial powers. Some residual anger remained until the early 1970s, when Japan's prime minister had to cancel a trip to the region due to anti-Japanese demonstrations. Nonetheless, relations since the 1970s have been quite favorable, enhanced by the jobs provided by Japanese firms investing in the region since the mid-1980s.

Japanese policy toward the region, while friendly, was characterized at least until the 1990s by a gratuitous condescension embodied in the concept of the "flying geese." This Japanese view of the region originated with Professor Akamatsu of Hitotsubashi University in the 1930s. The concept was that Japan was the (permanent) lead economy in Asia, with the rest of the region developing in Japan's wake, like the v-shaped flying formation of a flock of geese.[9] As the lead goose, and implicit leader of the region, the Japanese prime minister used to routinely visit several ASEAN countries each year in the late 1970s and 1980s just prior to attending the G-7 summit meetings, in order to claim to be speaking on behalf of East Asia.

During the 1990s, Japan enhanced its implicit leadership role with Southeast Asia during the 1997 Asian Financial Crisis. First, the Japanese government (or, more accurately, one high official in the Ministry of Finance—Eisuke Sakakibara) advocated creation of an Asian Monetary Fund. While never fleshed out, the concept was to create a purely regional IMF-like organization that would not have the U.S. or European governments as members. Angry with the United States and IMF over the initial response to the Asian Financial Crisis (indifference and no assistance on the part of the U.S. government and onerous, somewhat misguided conditionality attached to loans from the IMF), ASEAN governments appreciated Japan's attempt to propose a radical response to undermine or distance itself from the U.S. and IMF approaches.

Even though the proposal was quickly dropped, with Sakakibara losing influence on Japanese international economic policy, the symbolic gesture helped create a favorable view of Japan in the region.

Second, when that proposal failed due to strong objections from the United States and China, the Japanese government announced the unilateral New Miyazawa Plan discussed in the previous section. This package of assistance came late (an entire year after the Asian Financial Crisis hit, at which point the crisis countries were already recovering), was much smaller in amount than advertised, focused on lending that would benefit Japanese firms as much or more so than the Southeast Asian countries, and endorsed IMF (by then revised) conditionality. One could argue, therefore, that this package showed far less independence and had far less impact than the Japanese government wanted the region and the world to believe. Nonetheless, the package was appreciated as an independent gesture by the Japanese government that stood in some contrast to the continued criticism directed at the U.S. government and the IMF.

At the same time Japan became a member of the new ASEAN+3 (ASEAN plus Japan, China, and Korea) grouping, although this was not a Japanese initiative. Originating as a proposal by then-Malaysian Prime Minister Mahathir in the late 1980s for an East Asian Economic Caucus, ASEAN+3 came into existence in 1995 as a ministerial-level meeting and added a meeting of leaders in 1997. Japan did not officially support Prime Minister Mahathir's original EAEC concept due to strong opposition from the U.S. government, even though the concept of a regional organization without a U.S. presence was quite popular among both Japanese government officials and academics as a way of demonstrating independence from U.S. foreign policy. But by 1995, the U.S. government was no longer objecting, so the Japanese government felt comfortable joining ASEAN+3.

Initially the Japanese government viewed this new organization as a venue in which it could exercise leadership within the region without interference by the United States. What the government discovered quite quickly, however, was that China was an activist participant in these meetings, with proposals often at odds with Japanese preferences. In fact, concern over China's leadership role led the Japanese government to advocate creation of a broader East Asia Summit that would include (in addition to the ASEAN+3 participants) India, Australia, and New Zealand. The first meeting of this group occurred in 2005, tacked on to the end of the annual ASEAN+3 meeting. This successful initiative by the Japanese government was specifically intended to get at the table another large country (India) that might be able to help counter the role of China. The United States and Russia eventually became members of the East Asia Summit in 2011, adding additional large-nation participants to counter China, but also negating the original intent of a regional group without U.S. participation. ASEAN+3 remains more structured than the East Asia Summit, with sub-cabinet-level committees similar to the structure of APEC, but the Japanese government clearly prefers the East Asia Summit format for high-level regional discussions. In addition, Japan has continued a bilateral approach to the region, characterized by both visits by prime ministers to the region and negotiation of bilateral free trade agreements (a role that Prime Minister Abe expanded, as discussed later in this chapter).

The one major accomplishment of ASEAN+3 was the creation of the Chiang Mai Initiative (CMI) in 2001. The concept behind the CMI was identical to that behind the Asian Monetary Fund proposed by Japan in 1997. Swap agreements enable the central bank of one country to lend dollars to the central bank of a country attempting to defend its currency in foreign exchange markets. The original 2001 agreement was to expand existing bilateral swap arrangements between the potential lenders (Japan, Korea, and China) and various ASEAN member countries. In 2010 a common pool of funds was established, set initially at US$120 billion and expanded in 2012 to US$240 billion. In this pool both Japan and China/Hong Kong each provide 40 percent of the funds, and the rest of the members 20 percent.

The CMI would appear to be a major success, amounting to virtual fulfillment of Japan's 1997 Asian Monetary Fund proposal. However, there are three reasons to regard the CMI as a much more modest accomplishment. First, the CMI is not an organization like the IMF; it has no office and no staff, at least not yet. This means that there is no CMI capability of evaluating loan requests from member governments. More generally it lacks the IMF's role of monitoring member economies and making recommendations to them on a regular basis about economic policy, something that is a major part of the IMF's annual functions. The Asian Development Bank, covering all of Asia and with American and European participation, has offered to provide monitoring and loan evaluation on behalf of the CMI, but this is a weak solution. Therefore, the CMI still falls short of what Eisuke Sakakibara envisioned in 1997.

Second, the Japanese government insisted on a clause that limited activation of any loans to only 10 percent of the total available amount prior to approval from the IMF (though this limit was first raised to 20 percent, and in 2012 it was raised again to 30 percent). The 1997 Japanese proposal appeared to be an effort to escape from the tyranny of the IMF and its onerous conditionality by creating a similar regional organization that would not bother borrowers with such conditions. But when the time came to craft a true regional agreement, the Japanese government was sufficiently fearful of "throwing good money after bad" and of offending the U.S. government that it wanted to tie most of the funds to IMF endorsement. Even though the portion of funds promised to a borrower that can be activated without sanction by the IMF has been expanded to 30 percent, the majority still requires explicit approval from the IMF.

Third, while the CMI became an example of regional cooperation, it has never been used. During the 2008 global recession, the Korean government asked the Japanese government to lend it money under its bilateral CMI agreement, but the Japanese government refused, telling Korea to go to the IMF. In another example, the Indonesia rupiah (floating since 1997) declined sharply in 2013 as domestic economic indicators worsened. The Indonesian government undertook a variety of measures in response (such as raising interest rates), but requesting loans through the CMI to defend its currency was not one of them. Therefore, the CMI so far has been just a symbolic gesture.

The Japanese AMF proposal and the eventual evolution of the CMI occurred against a backdrop of broader informal discussion of eventually moving toward a common currency in East and Southeast Asia. This was an idea pushed mainly by the Japanese, and was common topic at international conferences sponsored by the Japanese in the late 1990s and early 2000s, as well as the subject of a number of articles and books.[10] However, interest in this topic appears to have waned, especially since the onset of economic crisis in Europe in 2008 and the difficulty keeping the euro together in face of the debt problems of Greece, Spain, and Ireland. With greater economic disparity in size, affluence, growth rates, and inflation in East Asia compared to Europe, the notion of currency unification or even yen dominance as the currency of choice in regional trade and investment was never viable, and academics and pundits in Japan appear to have dropped the topic.

On the trade front, Japan has engaged in the same expansion of bilateral and regional free trade agreements as many other nations around the world. Many of those agreements (but not all) involve Southeast Asian partners. By 2015, Japan had bilateral agreements with Indonesia, Malaysia, the Philippines, Singapore, Thailand, and Vietnam, as well as with ASEAN as a whole.[11] The proliferation of agreements between Japan and ASEAN countries might appear to be a sign of Japanese leadership in the region. But that image is at least partly incorrect for two important reasons.

First, the initiative for these agreements did not always originate with Japan. The first agreement was with Singapore (negotiated in 2000–2001 and signed in 2002) and the initiative was by the Singapore government, not Japan (which at that time was not committed to a strategy of negotiating bilateral trade agreements). Only after this agreement was completed did the Japanese government begin to propose free trade negotiations on its own. Second, the agreement with ASEAN as a whole was prompted by the start of negotiations between ASEAN and China, so that it was a reactive decision by Japan. The Japanese government was concerned by both the potential economic loss if ASEAN economic ties with China were to strengthen at the expense of ties with Japan, and the loss of reputation as an informal leader in the region. Thus, while this negotiation was a Japanese proposal to ASEAN, the request came a year after negotiations between ASEAN and China were already under way. A repeat of this pattern occurred in 2012–13 when Japan joined the Trans-Pacific Partnership (TPP) negotiations, involving a total of eleven countries including the United States and a number of Southeast Asian countries, only after those negotiations had already been ongoing for a couple years. TPP is an American-driven negotiation, not Japanese.

Second, Japan's bilateral and subregional agreements are not very robust. To be sure, like all free trade agreements, they zero out many tariffs. However, exceptions (especially on agricultural products entering Japan) are numerous and the agreements are weak on non-tariff barriers and on services. Indeed, after embracing the concept of bilateral and regional trade agreements in the wake of the Singapore negotiation, the government recognized that such agreements provided a better opportunity to avoid concessions on agricultural import barriers than was the case in WTO negotiations.[12]

Japan's bilateral and subregional agreements stand in sharp contrast to the TPP negotiations, in which the U.S. government was pressing quite aggressively for a very robust and extensive lowering or removal of non-tariff barriers (including agriculture) and restraints on trade in services. One reason for the hesitation of the Japanese government in joining the TPP negotiations was concern that the U.S. government (as well as other participants) would push Japan aggressively for more robust commitments on eliminating tariffs and other market barriers. Thus, the slow and somewhat reluctant decision of the Japanese government to join TPP made Japan look like a follower rather than a leader on regional trade arrangements. Furthermore, as of early 2015, Japan continued to be a major obstacle in reaching an agreement on TPP. If Japan really wanted to play a strong leadership role in the region, it could show its commitment by taking a more proactive role in the TPP negotiations. Instead it resisted pressures from the United States and other governments on agriculture and other aspects of the negotiations. Agreement on TPP finally occurred in the fall of 2015, but reflecting the vehemence of Japanese opposition, that agreement included relatively modest reductions in Japan's agricultural import barriers (to be phased in over a long time period).

In 2013 a new regional free trade negotiation began that included Japan and excluded the United States—the Regional Comprehensive Economic Partnership (RCEP). This negotiation involves all the ASEAN countries plus China, India, Japan, South Korea, Australia, and New Zealand. An East Asian trade agreement of some sort had been a topic of discussion in Japan since the 1980s (from the time of Malaysian Prime Minister Mahathir's East Asian Economic Caucus proposal). Nonetheless, Japan does not appear to have been the major player in the starting of the RCEP (with ASEAN and China pushing for it in the ASEAN+3 meeting of 2011), although the inclusion of India, Australia, and New Zealand was favored by the Japanese government. China, not a member of TPP, saw a diplomatic advantage to creating a regional negotiation excluding the United States, but the government preferred restricting non-ASEAN participants to Japan, Korea, and itself. ASEAN continued to prefer settings that at least symbolically put it in a central position (with all ASEAN members participating in RCEP while only Brunei, Malaysia, Singapore, and Vietnam were in TPP). Furthermore, ASEAN brokered acceptance of the larger participant list desired by Japan, and insisted on allowing other countries (such as the United States) to join in the future.[13]

Constraints on Japanese Regional Leadership

Japan and Southeast Asia share a common concern about the rise of China. Both Japan and various Southeast Asian countries have territorial disputes with China that have served as focal points for the broader concerns about shifting economic power—the Spratly Islands for Southeast Asia and the Senkaku/Diaoyu Islands for Japan. And as noted earlier, the series of provocations by China around the Senkaku Islands in the past several years has led Japanese firms and the government to question their relationship with China, even though this has not (yet) affected trade and investment patterns. As Japan has the largest economy and the most affluent one in non-China East Asia, it would be natural for the nation to play a leadership role in crafting the region's response to the economic and strategic rise of China. However, this was not the case until Shinzo Abe became prime minister in 2013. Three factors explain why Japan has played a modest, peripheral role in Southeast Asia relative to what its economic and strategic interests would imply: primacy of the United States, the Constitution, and the dominance of more local relations.

Since the creation of the U.S.-Japan Security Treaty of 1952, Japan's foreign policy has been strongly oriented toward the United States. Keeping the U.S. government sufficiently satisfied with Japan's behavior on a wide variety of fronts to ensure the continued existence of the security treaty has been the key goal of Japanese foreign policy since that time. At various times over the past thirty years, both American and Japanese analysts have predicted that this era was coming to an end, but it has not. For example, Japan sent a small contingent of noncombat soldiers to Iraq (2004–6) not because the government saw participation in Iraq as critical to Japan's broad foreign policy goals but because Prime Minister Koizumi wanted to keep the Bush administration satisfied (a decision motivated by remembrance of the difficult relations with the United States during the Gulf War, when Japan initially expressed no concern over Iraq's invasion of Kuwait but eventually provided US$13 billion to the United States to help finance the war after heavy U.S. pressure to do "something"). This deployment also furthered a conservative political agenda of bending the rules concerning the allowable international use of Japan's military.

When the Democratic Party of Japan (DPJ) gained control of the government following the elections of 2009, incoming Prime Minister Yukio Hatoyama appeared to shift foreign policy somewhat away from the United States toward stronger relations with China. However, the public's dismay at his very clumsy handling of the issue of relocating an American military facility in Okinawa (in the town of Futenma) was a major factor in his short tenure as prime minister. Prime Minister Hatoyama wanted to reopen an agreement concerning relocation of the military base, and made vague promises to voters in Okinawa about reducing the American military presence. He also managed to send rather different signals to U.S. and Okinawan audiences. In so doing, Prime Minister Hatoyama managed to confuse, bewilder, and annoy the U.S. government. Media coverage of these antics caused his approval ratings to plummet, and his tenure as prime minister ended after less than nine months. Hatoyama's DPJ successors reverted to a U.S.-centered foreign policy.

Japan's strong orientation toward the United States means that the government is generally reluctant to undertake policy initiatives without at least tacit U.S. approval. The 1997 Asian Monetary Fund proposal, for example, foundered immediately because of strong opposition from the U.S. government. Japan appeared to strike a more independent posture with its role in supporting creation of the CMI, but as described earlier, the government pressed for a 10 percent limit on use of swap funds pending IMF approval partly out of fear of a negative U.S. reaction. In the spring of 2013 Japan finally decided to join the TPP regional trade negotiations, but that decision was often cast in domestic debate as a response to U.S. government pressure to join (even though the alleged pressure was nonexistent). Therefore, the primacy of the

U.S.-Japan relationship in Japan's foreign policy limits what the government is willing to do in terms of independent policy initiatives toward Southeast Asia.

Second, Japan continues to be constrained by Article 9 of its Constitution, which prohibits the use of military force. Article 9 has been reinterpreted by Japan's Supreme Court over the years as permitting self-defense, and Japan spends a sizable one percent of its GDP (roughly US$50 billion per year) on its Self-Defense Force. Changing interpretations over time have allowed a somewhat wider scope of international involvement, including participation in a few UN peacekeeping missions, a refueling operation for NATO forces in the Indian Ocean supporting the Afghanistan war, noncombat deployment to Iraq, and participation of some Japanese naval vessels in international antipiracy patrols off Somalia. Nonetheless, the ability or willingness of the Japanese government to push the boundaries has been limited. In Southeast Asia, the government has participated to a limited extent in international antipiracy activities in the vicinity of the Malacca Straits, but this engagement has been restricted to some training missions and financial support to governments in the region.[14]

In 2015, the government took a new step in altering the interpretation of the Constitution by passing security legislation that would permit collective defense (i.e., coming to the assistance of an ally militarily even if the territory of Japan were not under direct attack). This step was touted in the press as the biggest change in Japan's defense policies in decades. However, as discussed later in this chapter, the change is actually quite modest and probably does not open the way for Japan to play a larger military role in Southeast Asia.

Third, to the extent that Japan is absorbed with regional issues in Asia, that focus is closer to home: Korea (both North and South) and China. Arguably, North Korean belligerence (including launching a ballistic missile over Japan in 1998 and the more recent nuclear tests) was the major factor in Japan launching its own spy satellite and upgrading the Self-Defense Agency to a cabinet-level Ministry of Defense. With both China and South Korea, Japan has a combination of territorial disputes over islands and lingering issues regarding Japan's military aggression (the annexation of Korea in 1911, the takeover of Manchuria in 1932, and the war with China 1937–45) and associated atrocities such as the forced recruitment of prostitutes for the military during the war (the so-called "comfort women" issue). These disputes dominate Asian foreign policy news, debate, and government policy in Japan, not Southeast Asia. This situation is unlikely to change in the near future.

The focus on China, however, provides the obvious opportunity for rhetorical declarations of solidarity. Prime Minister Taro Aso (serving for a year in 2008–9) spoke of an "arc of freedom and prosperity," with the aim of supporting young democracies on the rim of the Asian continent. This was an obvious effort to align Japan with other countries on China's borders, not that all of them can be described as democracies or even as having a good record on human rights. However, neither Prime Minister Aso nor his three successors through 2012 were very active in turning this rhetorical flourish into policy. Only beginning in 2013 did Prime Minister Abe pursue a more active policy, considered in the next section of this chapter.

These three constraints have limited Japan's implicit leadership role in the region in the past, but one can argue that a stronger role was not necessary for the Japanese government to achieve its regional foreign policy goals. In fact, Japan appears to have achieved its modest goals quite successfully. Since Japanese firms began actively investing abroad in the mid-1980s, Japan has had a strong interest in peace, stability, creation of physical infrastructure in support of inward foreign direct investment, reasonably robust rule of law on commercial issues related to foreign firms, and generally favorable treatment of Japanese firms by host governments. The government had a particular interest in pursuing these foreign policy goals in Southeast Asia as a hedge against China, as discussed in the earlier section on direct investment. To achieve these goals, it was not necessary to push strongly for an Asian Monetary Fund or to press regional partners in free trade negotiations for complete market liberalization. For the Asian Monetary Fund, the fact that Japan was willing to (temporarily) annoy the U.S. government was sufficient to enhance regional attitudes toward Japan. Other policies, such as the New Miyazawa Plan or the symbolic CMI, were also sufficient to build good will in Southeast Asia toward Japan. And, in the 1980s and 1990s, bilateral aid flows that helped build infrastructure helpful to incoming Japanese firms was appreciated by governments eager to attract more foreign direct investment. As a result, whatever lingering bad feelings remained from the Second World War were erased, replaced by a new image of Japan as a friendly regional power. Therefore, playing a modest regional role that was less than one might expect for a large, affluent economic power was sufficient for the accomplishment of Japan's national interests in the region.

A Changing Agenda under Abe?

In December 2012 the Liberal Democratic Party (LDP—the conservative party that held the majority for virtually all of the period from 1955 to 2009) won an election for the Lower House of the Diet, bringing it back into power after a two-and-a-half-year absence. With this victory Shinzo Abe became prime minister. He had served a year in this post in 2006–7, stepping down for alleged physical ailments, though mainly for inept leadership. The second time around, Prime Minister Abe proved to be better organized and longer lasting (a longevity helped when the LDP won control of the Upper Houses of the Diet (along with a coalition partner, the Komeito Party) in the summer of 2013. He reaffirmed this grip on power by calling a snap election for the Lower House in December 2014 in which his party (and the Komeito) retained its majority. Prime Minister Abe had long been known as a very conservative nationalist—favoring revisionist views of the Second World War and revision of Article 9 of the Constitution. As prime minister, he has pursued several policies that alter Japan's relationship with Southeast Asia.

First, under Abe, policy toward China has hardened. For the Chinese government, he was a known right-wing politician, which also contributed to worsened relations. Prime Minister Abe, in turn, clearly saw China as the principal threat to Japan. His visit to Yasukuni Shrine mentioned earlier was a snub to China, whose government had thought he had promised not to do so when he had been prime minister in 2006–7. Eventually the relationship thawed somewhat—with Abe meeting with Xi Jinping on several occasions in 2014–15 on the sidelines of larger multilateral meetings (as well as some lower level meetings between officials of the two governments). Nonetheless, the largely negative attitude of both Abe and his government toward China remained.

Prime Minister Abe's approach toward Southeast Asia must be seen in the context of his antagonism toward China. That is, under his leadership, Japan is not improving relations with ASEAN because doing so is economically beneficial to Japan or because friendly relations with neighbors make intuitive sense. Instead, Abe has been quite explicit about containing China. Whereas the U.S. government has generally gone out of its way to officially deny any containment policy toward China, Japan is now doing the opposite. To reinforce the new emphasis on Southeast Asia, Abe made a point of visiting all ten ASEAN countries in 2013 while pointedly not visiting either China or Korea and became the first prime minister ever to visit all ASEAN members. The Japanese media interpreted this pattern of visits as demonstrating Abe's China containment policy.[15] This interest is containing China has also driven visits and consultations with both India and Australia.

Abe furthered this policy in 2014 by delivering the keynote address at the annual Asian Security Summit (often referred to as the Shangri-La Dialogue), a broad group of government officials (that includes representatives from China) hosted by the Institute of International Security Studies in Singapore. In this speech he announced an intent to play a larger role in supporting Southeast Asian countries in their territorial disputes with China. As he put it, "Japan will offer its utmost support for the efforts of the countries of ASEAN as they work to ensure the security of the seas and skies and thoroughly maintain freedom of navigation and freedom of overflight."[16] This more hawkish stance came under the umbrella of Japan's first-ever National Security Strategy published at the end of 2013 that called for a "more proactive contribution to peace" around the world. Following up on Prime Minister Abe's speech, Japan's Defense Minister Akinori Eto met with his counterparts in the first-ever Japan-ASEAN cabinet-level defense meeting in November 2014.[17] While both Prime Minister Abe and Defense Minister Eto are always clear to couch their remarks in general terms of promoting peace and security, including antiterrorism and antipiracy, it is entirely clear that the main intent is to join with other nations in opposing China's aggressive moves on territorial disputes. No previous prime minister had been so clear or active in pursuing such a strong tilt.

Second, pursuant to the intention to be more "proactive" on security issues, Prime Minister Abe pursued an active agenda of bending the interpretation of Article 9 of the Constitution (which prohibits use of military force). Revision of the Constitution itself remains a goal, but is not likely to occur. The December 2014 election reduced the probability of revision since the LDP lost three seats while its more pacifist coalition partner, the Komeito Party, gained four seats. Reinterpretation, however, was a different matter. In the spring of 2014 the government softened a longtime ban on exports of military equipment (a ban imposed decades ago through a Cabinet resolution, not through legislation). In August 2014, Foreign Minister Fumio Kishida promised during a visit to Hanoi to provide six used naval surveillance vessels to Vietnam.[18] And Defense Minister Eto raised the possibility of further military exports to ASEAN in his November meeting. Also in 2014, Japan reached an agreement to provide Australia with advanced (non-nuclear) submarine propulsion technology (and outside the region individual defense technology deals were discussed with the United States, Britain, and France).[19]

Even without changing the Constitution, Prime Minister Abe pressed successfully in 2015 to enact new legislation permitting collective defense. While the symbolic change in defense policy was significant, the changes were actually rather modest. In order for the Japanese military to join in collective action, three rather restrictive conditions must be met. First, attack by a foreign power must threaten the "life, liberty and pursuit of happiness" of the Japanese public, even if the attack is not on Japanese territory. Second, military action will be authorized only when all other options have been exhausted. Third, the response must be limited to the minimum necessary. The language of the new law is sufficiently vague that a variety of situations could conceivably be declared as meeting the criteria in the future, but it would be difficult for the government to make the case that joining the United States in something like the 2002 invasion of Iraq met the three requirements of the law. Furthermore, the law speaks of coming to the assistance of an "ally." Technically, Japan has only one ally—the United States. While Japan has friendly relations and an enhanced defense dialogue with ASEAN and Australia, it does not have formal defense treaties. Therefore, if the United States were to become involved in military action related to territorial disputes in the South China Sea, for example, Japanese forces could conceivably participate. Without American involvement, though, any effort of the government to join military action in the South China Sea would be highly controversial at home.

Third, Prime Minister Abe has attempted to mute opposition at home to his bolder nationalistic stance by emphasizing domestic policy. The Japanese economy has underperformed and suffered from deflation, on average, for almost a quarter century. Abe proposed a coordinated policy (quantitative easing to expand the money supply, temporary fiscal stimulus, and broad structural change and deregulation) to end deflation and restore growth, quickly dubbed Abenomics. The LDP won the election of December 2012 in large part on the basis of Abe's proposals. The enthusiasm for Abenomics meant that the public was willing to accept his more nationalistic foreign policy—especially controversial measures such as easing the ban on military exports and the new law allowing collective self-defense—as an undesired but unavoidable cost of fixing the economy.

The aggressive agenda established by Prime Minister Abe gives the appearance that Japan has entered a decisively different era in relations with Southeast Asia (as well as with India and Australia). However, the extent and durability of this new approach should not be overestimated for several important reasons.

Abe's ability to pursue his hawkish foreign policy depends on success of his economic policies. If the public loses faith in his ability to accomplish the goals of Abenomics, then its tolerance of his controversial reinterpretation of the Constitution would diminish. The announced goal was to end deflation and raise inflation to 2 percent, while restoring real GDP growth to an annual level of 2 percent. Compared to the bungling of economic policy by the DPJ when it was in power (2009–12) or even LDP policies prior to 2009, Abenomics appeared to be well conceived. Implementation got off to a quick start (with a sizable supplementary budget in January 2013, and a strong dose of quantitative easing from April 2013). However, by 2015 its success and even the commitment of the prime minister to pursuing its success were in doubt. The goals of 2 percent inflation and 2 percent GDP growth remained elusive.

After the brief burst of fiscal stimulus, concerns over the size of the government deficit led to a decision to implement a planned 3-percentage-point increase in the national consumption tax (an American-style sales tax on most consumer goods and services). That increase, on April 1, 2014, from 5 percent to 8 percent threw the economy into a temporary recession for the next two quarters. Despite a second round of quantitative easing at the end of October 2014 (when the Bank of Japan determined that the first round was not working to end deflation or restore growth), prices were falling once the impact of the consumption tax increases was removed from the data. And progress on deregulation and structural reform of the economy was weak and diffused among too many minor issues. Joining the TPP negotiations in 2013 had been touted by Abe as an important part of the structural reform "arrow" of Abenomics—with the elimination of trade barriers forcing Japanese farmers and businesses to face global competition at home. However, as noted earlier, the concessions made by the Japanese government in the 2015 TPP agreement in areas such as agriculture were rather weak.

Should Abenomics continue to fall short of the announced targets for inflation and growth in 2015 and beyond, public tolerance of his aggressive defense and foreign policies will wane. To be sure, the public has had its own antagonistic feelings toward both Korea and China, fueled by the territorial disputes with both, as well as fear of North Korea fueled by repeated nuclear tests. But public opinion is not in favor of constitutional revision or radical reinterpretation of Article 9. Public opposition to the new defense legislation in 2015 was quite strong. For the first time in decades people took to the streets for sizable demonstrations, and the popularity of the prime minister quickly dipped below 40 percent when the new law passed. In response, Abe quickly assured the public that he would drop his emphasis on defense policy and return to a focus on economic performance. His approval ratings returned to the 50 percent level by the end of the year, but the message from the public was quite clear: Abe got his new defense law, but he had better not try to actually use it. What the public wants is not an activist defense agenda but an improved economy. Even with renewed focus on economics by the prime minister, though, Abenomics remains unlikely to achieve its twin goals of 2 percent real GDP growth and 2 percent consumer price inflation.

If the concept of collective self-defense were to result in actual Japanese participation in military action, the most likely candidate to pass muster with domestic public opinion would be action related to North Korea (in a case where U.S. forces become involved on the Korean Peninsula, but Japan has not been hit directly by North Korean weapons). Absent constitutional change, therefore, Japan's cooperative actions with Southeast Asian nations are most likely to remain confined to rhetorical flourishes about solidarity buttressed by occasional antipiracy patrols or training sessions offered in Japan.

To be sure, the new arms export policy is moving forward. But even there domestic politics will inhibit major changes. Giving half a dozen small, obsolete coast guard vessels to Vietnam hardly makes Japan a major supplier of military equipment to ASEAN. Equally important, the fragmented, high-cost Japanese defense industry is not likely to be cost competitive in providing very many weapons systems to Southeast Asia or anywhere else.

Prime Minister Abe's approach to Southeast Asia is also largely one-dimensional, focused mainly on security policy. In contrast, the economic aspects of policy engagement with Southeast Asia under Abe have been relatively weak. In 2014 Abe announced both a US$100 million contribution to the Japan-ASEAN integration fund (a fund established under Prime Minister Taro Aso in 2007, to which Japan had committed US$70 million to further intra-ASEAN efforts on regional issues such as antiterrorism and avian flu). The purpose of the new donation was not specified by the Japanese government, but is likely to be at least partially used for security efforts rather than to further ASEAN economic integration. In addition, Abe announced that Japan would provide US$20 billion in new ODA loans over a five-year period. However, as noted earlier in this chapter, ASEAN countries are paying back previous loans at the rate of close to US$4 billion per year. Therefore, new loans of US$20 billion over five years imply only that the total level of ODA loans to the region will stop shrinking. This is hardly a bold new initiative.

TPP provides yet another demonstration of relatively weak economic engagement. As discussed earlier, Japanese negotiators strongly resisted concessions in agriculture and a number of other areas of the negotiations. Some of these areas, and especially agriculture, are of importance to Southeast Asian participants in TPP. Japan's ability to minimize concessions in these areas in the TPP agreement—a pattern that ASEAN countries have seen before in their separate free-trade negotiations with Japan—sends a negative signal about Japan's willingness to embrace Southeast Asia economically.

Overall, the economic side of engagement of ASEAN represents no change from the past. Modest amounts of new foreign aid and the positive but very incomplete nature of Japanese offers in TPP may be enough to keep ASEAN countries welcoming Japanese firms without creating any tight economic community. And as long as Japanese firms are able to invest in Southeast Asia as a hedge against possible problems (as well as sharply rising wages) in China, they will be content. This continuation of past patterns on the economic side, though, stands in stark contrast to Prime Minister Abe's security approach to Southeast Asia.

Diplomatically, Abe must also contend with the continued centrality of the security relationship with the United States. His visit to Yasukuni Shrine in 2013 was publicly deplored by the U.S. government—an unusual and deliberate rebuke. In general, the Obama administration was privately unhappy with Abe's belligerence toward China and Korea while publicly defending Japan in the face of Chinese provocations at sea and in the air around the Senkaku Islands. The Abe government even managed to pursue its agenda of altering historical memory by attempting to get a local town in New Jersey to dismantle a memorial to the comfort women, get the Virginia state government to reverse a decision to refer in school textbooks to the body of water between Japan and Korea as both the Japan Sea and the East Sea, and get the wording of references to the comfort women in a McGraw-Hill high school history textbook changed. This latter intrusion included public statements of outrage by the prime minister in the Diet in January 2015 that American textbooks would include such references (i.e., that the textbook used the phrase "forcibly recruited"), and he directed Foreign Ministry officials to meet with McGraw-Hill (to no avail).[20] This kind of aggressive pursuit of a history-bending agenda in the United States was an embarrassment to the Obama government, with its hopes to work with Abe to conclude TPP and encourage successful implementation of Abenomics.

Of course, on some issues, the U.S. government stands firmly behind its ally Japan. In April 2014, President Obama officially declared that the United States would defend militarily Japan's administration of the Senkaku Islands (without saying that the islands necessarily belong to Japan). But this affirmation of support for Japan on the territorial issue presumably came with some private understanding that Prime Abe would back off of provocations of China that might make the situation in the vicinity of the Senkaku Islands tenser. In general, though, the unease of the U.S. government over Abe implies a limit to how much of an expanded mission in Southeast Asia the U.S. government will welcome.

Conclusion

Japan has a substantial economic engagement with Southeast Asia, although it has not expanded as much as the rapid economic growth in the region might suggest. That engagement and particularly Japanese firms' investments in the region create a natural national interest in peace, stability, and growth in the region. Furthermore, the rapid rise of China implies a common interest between Japan and Southeast Asia to manage the peaceful integration of China into the region and to jointly oppose Chinese aggressive posturing on island territorial disputes. Nonetheless, Japan continued to play a rather modest role in the region until the advent of the Abe administration in 2013. Claims of emerging Japanese regional leadership have been around for a three decades, but relatively little has happened, and even the Abe-led tilt toward the region remains constrained. American dominance in Japan's foreign policy, the pacifist Constitution, and the primacy of Japan's disputes with China and Korea plus security concerns about North Korea remain firmly in place as factors that limit the government's ability to play more of a leadership role in Southeast Asia. Despite Abe's new activism, Japan largely remains the perpetual potential partner for the region. Were Prime Minister Abe to adopt a less nationalistic and negative stance toward China (and with Korea), it would do a lot to improve Japan's standing in the region as a partner for Southeast Asia. But such a change by the fundamentally conservative, nationalistic Shinzo Abe is unlikely. The big question, therefore, is whether he has put in motion a process of stronger engagement that his successors can build on without his heavy nationalism, or whether his approach will simply fade once he leaves office.

NOTES

1 ASEAN Secretariat, *ASEAN Statistical Yearbook*, 2013, 36–37; 2010, 34–35; and 2004, 36. Also see ASEAN Secretariat, "Selected Key Indicators," plus World Bank, *World Development Indicators*.

2 ASEAN Secretariat, "External Trade Statistics"; and International Monetary Fund, *Direction of Trade Statistics*.

3 "Poll: Two-Thirds of Chinese Boycotted Japanese Goods."

4 Organization for Economic Cooperation and Development (OECD), *Statistics on Resource Flows to Developing Countries*, Table 28.

5 Ibid., Table 4.

6 Ministry of Foreign Affairs of Japan, *Japan's Official Development Assistance White Paper 2014*, 189.

7 "Japan and Southeast Asia," 44.

8 For details on the New Miyazawa Initiative, see Lincoln, *East Asian Economic Regionalism*, 216–20.

9 Terutomo Ozawa, "Classical Origins of Akamatsu's 'Flying-Geese' Theory."

10 See, for example, Kwan, *Yen Bloc*. Kwan saw currency unification happening mainly in an informal manner, as the yen would become the common currency for trade and investment in Asia.

11 Ministry of Foreign Affairs of Japan, "Free Trade Agreement."

12 On the somewhat odd notion that a bilateral "free trade" negotiation offers an opportunity to maintain politically sensitive trade barriers, see Frost, *Asia's New*

Regionalism, 157. She notes that East Asian governments, and not just Japan, see this as an advantage to these negotiations.

13 Hiebert and Hanlon, "ASEAN and Partners Launch Regional Comprehensive Economic Partnership."
14 Vavro, "Piracy, Terrorism and the Balance of Power in the Malacca Strait."
15 "With Visits to All 10 ASEAN Nations."
16 Ministry of Foreign Affairs of Japan, "Peace and Prosperity in Asia."
17 "Japan, ASEAN Defence Officials Hold Talks in Myanmar."
18 Panda, "Vietnam to Acquire Japanese Maritime Surveillance Ships."
19 Pfanner, "Japan Inc. Now Exporting Weapons."
20 Fackler, "U.S. Textbook Skews History."

BIBLIOGRAPHY

ASEAN Secretariat. *ASEAN Statistical Yearbook, 2013.*
———. "External Trade Statistics; Table 19 ASEAN Trade by Selected Partner Country/ Region." January 29, 2015. www.asean.org.
———. "Selected Key Indicators." www.asean.org.
Fackler, Martin. "U.S. Textbook Skews History, Prime Minister of Japan Says." *New York Times*, January 29, 2015.
Frost, Ellen. *Asia's New Regionalism*. Boulder, CO: Lynne Rienner, 2008.
Hiebert, Murray, and Liam Hanlon. "ASEAN and Partners Launch Regional Comprehensive Economic Partnership." Center for Strategic and International Studies, September 30, 2013. http://csis.org.
International Monetary Fund. *Direction of Trade Statistics.* www.imf.org.
"Japan, ASEAN Defence Officials Hold Talks in Myanmar." *BBC Monitor in Asia Pacific*, November 20, 2014.
"Japan and Southeast Asia: Hand in Hand." *Economist*, June 1, 2013, 44.
Kwan, C. H. *Yen Bloc: Toward Economic Integration in Asia.* Washington, DC: Brookings Institution, 2001.
Lincoln, Edward J. *East Asian Economic Regionalism.* Washington, DC: Brookings Institution, 2004.
Ministry of Foreign Affairs of Japan. "Free Trade Agreement (FTA) and Economic Partnership Agreements (EPA)." May 20, 2013. www.mofa.go.jp.
———. "Peace and Prosperity in Asia, Forevermore; Japan for the Rule of Law; Asia for the Rule of Law; and the Rule of Law for All of Us." In *Japan's Official Development Assistance White Paper 2013.* www.mofa.go.jp.
Organization for Economic Cooperation and Development. *Statistics on Resource Flows to Developing Countries.* September 27, 2013. www.oecd.org.
Ozawa, Terutomo. "The Classical Origins of Akamatsu's 'Flying-Geese' Theory: A Note on a Missing Link to David Hume." Working Paper Series no. 320. New York: Center for Japanese Economy and Business, Columbia University, April 2013.
Panda, Ankit. "Vietnam to Acquire Japanese Maritime Surveillance Ships." *Diplomat*, August 2, 2014. http://thediplomat.com.

Pfanner, Eric. "Japan Inc. Now Exporting Weapons." *Wall Street Journal*, July 20, 2014. www.wsj.com.

"Poll: Two-Thirds of Chinese Boycotted Japanese Goods over Senkakus Dispute." *Japan Times*, January 6, 2014.

Vavro, Caroline. "Piracy, Terrorism and the Balance of Power in the Malacca Strait." *Canadian Naval Review* 4, no. 1 (2008): 15.

"With Visits to All 10 ASEAN Nations, Abe's China Containment Strategy Complete." *Asahi Shimbun*, November 18, 2013. http://ajw.asahi.com.

World Bank. *World Development Indicators*. http://data.worldbank.org.

10

India and Southeast Asia

From Looking to Acting East Policy

G. V. C. NAIDU AND GULSHAN SACHDEVA

If the global center of gravity is inexorably shifting to the East, Southeast Asia is at the heart of it and hence developments here will have significant implications not merely for East Asia but beyond the region too. Today's Southeast Asia is characterized by unprecedented economic vibrancy with virtually the entire region performing exceptionally well (reforms in Myanmar are expected to bear fruit sooner rather than later) and the region has never been more peaceful and stable than in the past several decades. The only hitch is China continuing to up the ante with its assertive actions in the South China Sea and an elusive code of conduct (COC). Yet, concerns remain on how long the current calm will last as the region is on the cusp of profound changes. Whereas these shifts are wide-ranging and fundamental, the Asian great powers are becoming significant players in regional economic and security architecture. It needs to be noted that there are also many other factors that could undermine regional security. The challenge for Southeast Asia, therefore, is in ensuring ASEAN's principal role in maintaining regional stability, continued economic prosperity, and orderly integration. Not least is the management of great power engagement. The idea is that regional autonomy is not threatened and the great powers remain engaged without unbridled domination by any one power. It is not an easy task since doubts have arisen about ASEAN's cohesion and ability to put up a united front in the backdrop of steadily intensifying contest for supremacy among the great powers in the face of a power vacuum in Southeast Asia and tricky unsettled boundary disputes.

Ever since New Delhi launched the much celebrated Look East Policy in the early 1990s, it has been one relentless diplomatic endeavor to strengthen its relationship with East Asia in general and with Southeast Asia in particular. This policy has gained so much traction that it is one of the most successful initiatives ever undertaken in the recent past. It has over the years evolved into a multifaceted approach encompassing political, diplomatic, economic, and strategic aspects. Thanks to deepening and expanding relations, from being a marginal player when the Cold War ended, New Delhi has gradually emerged as a key factor in the evolving regional security architecture. Now that India has earned a niche for itself, a qualitative shift in India's strategy toward Southeast Asia can be expected as it unveils a new phase in what Prime Minister Modi calls the "Act East Policy." Conscious that reticence and tentativeness that marked its policy so far are untenable in the rapidly changing context and given its rising economic and strategic stakes, India is likely to step up its involvement in regional affairs, which may manifest in a lot more proactive initiatives from exploiting the soft power potential to forging greater cooperation across a wide spectrum of areas, including defense and security. Elevation of relations with ASEAN to strategic partnership, setting up of a separate diplomatic mission to ASEAN, forging strong defense and security links at the bilateral level, active participation in regional multilateralism, a nuanced approach in dealing with China, and a willingness to work closely with the United States and others are indicators that India is accelerating its engagement qualitatively. In this backdrop, besides providing a brief background, this essay sets out to examine the various contours of India's policy toward Southeast Asia including the China factor, the U.S. dimension, and India's role in emerging regional security.

Backdrop

To understand India's interests and stakes in Southeast Asia in perspective, it is imperative to keep in view the remarkable transformation the entire East Asia is witnessing. Its rise is represented not merely by China and India but by the entire region, an unprecedented development in global history. The East Asian economy covers a vast region spread from India to Australia and from Korea to Indonesia. It has a combined GDP of around US$38 trillion (in PPP terms according to IMF), composing over 37 percent of global GDP, and by 2013 was already larger than the United States and EU combined; it is by any measure the most dynamic in the world. Besides being home to nearly half of the global population, the world's fastest and largest growing markets are in this region.[1] Both globalization and regionalization processes are taking place remarkably rapidly even as the countries in the region vigorously pursue greater regional economic cooperation and integration. At around 57 percent in 2015, the intra-Asian trade is greater than trade in North America and is not far behind the EU; it is growing faster than its trade with rest of the world. Similarly, many East Asian investments are bound within the region as opportunities expand in what is called "networked FDI," which is

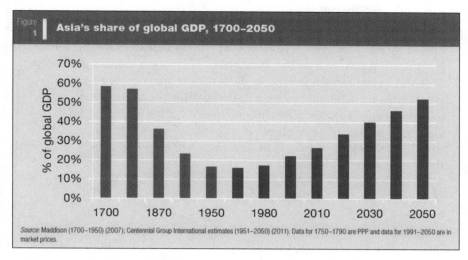

Figure 10.1. Asia's share of global GDP, 1700–2050. Source: *Asia 2050: Realizing the Asian Century* (Manila: Asian Development Bank, 2011), 15.

contributing to greater regional economic cooperation integration. And, if the Regional Comprehensive Economic Partnership (RCEP) proposal that is being discussed materializes by 2016 as envisaged along with ASEAN Economic Community idea and innumerable bilateral free trade agreements, the region will integrate itself much more strongly, aided by a robust regional value chain. This region already holds more than half the world's foreign exchange reserves and accounts for nearly a quarter of global financial assets. It has logged double the average of the world's growth rates, and indications suggest the buoyant outlook will continue for the foreseeable future.[2] Indeed, most credible studies have forecast that Asia's share of global output will increase from 27.7 percent in 2010 to 52.3 percent by 2050.[3] According to the U.S. National Intelligence Council's *Global Trends 2030*, "The diffusion of power among countries and from countries to informal networks will have a dramatic impact by 2030, largely reversing the historic rise of the West since 1750 and restoring Asia's weight in the global economy and world politics. In a tectonic shift, by 2030, Asia will have surpassed North America and Europe combined in terms of global power, based upon GDP, population size, military spending, and technological investment."[4] Similar trends are also forecast by the Asian Development Bank.[5]

While there are strong reasons for optimism on Asia's future, one cannot discount potential impediments that could upset the above projections.

Large economies such as China and India could falter on the way of rapid growth or can get caught in the "middle-income trap," which can seriously affect the rest of the region, as is seen at present in the case of China, which is trying to grapple with a slowing economy. Attempts to transit the economy from export and FDI dependence to domestic consumption and services have not exactly been smooth, as seen in the volatility in China's stock market in early January 2016 and problems associated with devaluation and depreciation of the yuan. The ripple effect could be felt across virtually the entire world. Nonetheless, there is optimism since Beijing is expected to weather these challenges as it has in the past.

Probably more alarming is the regional security that is witnessing tectonic changes. The Asian great powers are redefining their roles and increasingly becoming more assertive. East Asia is also home to the largest number of land and maritime boundary disputes, and vestiges of the past linger on. While the post–Cold War unipolarity is giving way to East Asian multipolarity, it is not without problems. The dichotomy between high economic performance and continued concerns about security is a reflection of the huge complexity the region is afflicted with, and hence we are still stuck with a post–Cold War kind of framework. Since the existing security multilateralism has failed to live up to expectations, there is an urgent need to construct a new security paradigm. While China's economy is crucial, the rest of the region, in particular Southeast Asia and India, is faring well, which can offset China's slowdown. Moreover, greater regional cooperation and integration will contribute to additional growth and trade opportunities in the region.

In this scenario of East Asia, Southeast Asia occupies a unique place, located as such at the center of the region and also at the crossroads of the Pacific and Indian oceans, and hence it has a key role to play in the evolving regional equation. Although relatively far more peaceful and prosperous now than almost ever before, Southeast Asia is not devoid of potential dangers, including in the nontraditional security domain. In the backdrop of the region, for the first time in over two centuries not having a military presence by extra-regional powers, probably the foremost security issue that is under focus relates to the rise of new power centers, especially China, not so much due to its economic rise but because of its actions that suggest that it wants to be the region's preeminent power. A near simultaneous rise of Asian great powers coupled with continued American dominant position has resulted in a situation in Southeast Asia wherein never before have the interests of these powers intersected as sharply as they do at the present. It is evident in their new strategies: The United States has announced vociferously its "rebalancing" strategy toward Asia in which Southeast Asia is the centerpiece; Japan under Prime Minister Shinzo Abe has made Southeast Asia a top priority as part of its "reengagement" policy and is not hesitant to fully utilize tensions over the South China Sea to enhance its security role (the new security laws that the Diet approved in September 2015 would greatly facilitate this); China, which has always considered Southeast Asia its backyard, is trying to consolidate immense diplomatic and economic gains it has made in the past two decades by launching the "diamond decade"; and India is upping the ante with its own "pivot" to the region by further upgrading relations through the Act East Policy. Perhaps never in the past have so many powers vied with each other with such vigor and passion to make themselves consequential players in Southeast Asia. Equally important, ASEAN is bracing to be at the helm of regional affairs by deftly pushing its own agenda by its community-building exercises and by spearheading regional multilateralism.

The great power interest is an opportunity as well as a challenge for Southeast Asia. If the involvement is managed skillfully, the region can gain enormously politically and economically, or it can end up becoming an arena for their competition and rivalry. Notwithstanding the fact that there is no unanimity of opinion, most take a positive view on the growing great power involvement with the belief that instead of one dominant power, several will countervail each other and hence provide greater stability and thus more leeway to smaller and medium powers. While ASEAN is a successful subregional multilateral organization, it remains to be seen whether it has what it takes to face the looming challenges now that Southeast Asia's future in many ways is linked to developments in the rest of East Asia. The foremost challenge is to find an amicable solution to the tricky issue of the South China Sea dispute. The contest over sovereignty involving China and a few ASEAN members (though to varying degrees) has created a division of views within the association as to whether it should risk its credibility as well as relations with China by taking a hard-line position because some of its members are party to the dispute. On the other hand, if ASEAN fails to express solidarity with some of its own member states, it risks losing the enormous faith members have reposed in it. Consequently, ASEAN has to play the delicate role of an honest broker in resolving the issue while simultaneously not giving the impression that it is undermining the unity and solidarity among members that it has so assiduously built over the decades. The enormous delay in concluding a COC agreement in the South China Sea has already cast serious doubt on ASEAN's ability to manage serious security issues. Probably for this reason, the United States unilaterally undertook the so-called freedom of navigation operation in October and November 2015 in the wake of Beijing's relentless island-building practices.

The second daunting task before ASEAN is to balance the interests of great powers at a time when their competition in Southeast Asia is intensifying. Beijing is concerned about some recent American moves such as "rebalancing" and the Trans-Pacific Partnership (TPP), for it believes that they are basically aimed at containing China. China is also worried about India's strong forays into East Asia through the Look East Policy and growing strategic and defense cooperation with the United States and Japan, and Tokyo's moves to beef up its defense capabilities as tensions mount over the Senkaku/Diaoyu Islands in the East China Sea. On the other hand, these three powers are anxious that a rapidly rising China is becoming too aggressive in grabbing the strategic space at the cost of their interests. What is apparent is that with its accretion of vast economic and military power, China strongly feels that the old order has to surrender to a newer one reflecting current realities of its dominant status; in other words, a China-led hierarchical Asian order, which is something others think is inimical to their interests. Thus, a clash of interests and divergent perceptions is at the root of current friction between China and others. Consequently, as noted, ASEAN has to brace for growing assertive stances of not just China but other great powers too, although less muted since they are not involved in territorial disputes. For instance, the American "rebalancing" strategy, further strengthening its military presence in Asia along with building new "strategic partnerships" with certain countries, besides consolidating alliance partnership, is an assertion of its predominance. Perhaps the country that is witnessing remarkable shifts is Japan, striving hard to become a "normal" nation, which is reflected in a series of bold decisions in its security policies. Of course, theses changes are not a recent phenomenon, but the momentum has picked up pace under Shinzo Abe. The revisions began with Tokyo joining the U.S. ballistic missile defense program in 2003 under Junichiro Koizumi, after resisting Washington's pressure for over a decade, followed by a series of other significant decisions such as replacing the Japan Defense Agency with the Ministry of Defense, contributing troops (for noncombat activities) to the U.S. war efforts in Iraq and Afghanistan, and so on. However, Prime Minister Abe is determinedly charting a new course for Japan, including exporting arms, signing joint defense R&D agreements with friendly countries, forging new security partnerships with countries that share security concerns, strengthening the Self-Defense Force, and proposing new legislation to exercise the right of "collective self-defense." Equally noteworthy are India's efforts to carve a niche for itself in the Indo-Pacific region. Besides being the preeminent maritime power, possessing the largest navy among the Indian Ocean littorals, and asserting its status as a rising power with rapidly expanding interests, the Indian Navy is acquiring capabilities that would enable it to project power far beyond its immediate vicinity (more on this below).

The Southeast Asian problem is, first, that there is no uniformity of opinion on the question of great power involvement in regional affairs and, second, that China is becoming too pushy for the comfort of several ASEAN states. Nonetheless, most agree that the last thing ASEAN wants is to get caught in the crossfire of a great power rivalry, as exemplified by the Chinese and U.S. standoff over the South China Sea. As a result, ASEAN is compelled to undertake the delicate task of involving great powers to the extent that they counterbalance each other and at the same its own autonomy of action is not imperiled. That is how ASEAN, while forging strong links with Beijing, has convinced Washington to loudly pronounce its "rebalancing" strategy as a signal to China and also involving India and Japan robustly.

The third set of issues that confront ASEAN are domestic issues with spillover effects on neighbors (ethnic minorities and religious extremism), interstate problems and historical suspicions (minor but highly emotive unsettled border/territorial problems and others such as Preah Vihear temple), regional economic integration (problems associated with the creation of the ASEAN Economic Community), uneven development, environmental issues, and so on. Numerous security issues in the nontraditional domain such as religious extremism, piracy, security of sea lines of communication, natural disasters, and others are also often quite daunting. This background needs to be kept in view in order to understand India's policy toward Southeast Asia and the latter's responses.

India and Southeast Asia

For India, Southeast Asia is critical for both strategic and economic reasons. Apart from geographic proximity, sharing land and/or maritime boundary with three Southeast Asian countries, India's links with the region are probably the oldest compared with other great powers, and its immense cultural, linguistic, and religious influences are unparalleled. However, a long hiatus due to colonialism that badly disrupted the ancient linkages and later a combination of several factors—such as the entire region coming under the grips of the Cold War and India's own security and domestic problems—severely constrained India's role, notwithstanding a brief period of New Delhi's activism in the aftermath of its independence in support of freedom struggles and in promoting Asian identity and solidarity.[6] Thus, the end of the Cold War and acute domestic economic compulsions led to a kind of rediscovery of Southeast Asia in the early 1990s. However, by then New Delhi had become politically marginal, economically inconsequential, and irrelevant to regional security. Thus, in a way India had to start from scratch by keeping in view a sense of purposefulness and a set of realistic objectives, which marked the launch of the Look East Policy in 1991. It must, however, be mentioned that it was not a well thought out or a clearly laid policy initiative except that New Delhi sought to align more closely with the world's fastest growing region toward its east.[7]

Attempts at renewed engagement with Southeast Asia in the early 1990s had elements of both economic exigencies and geopolitical imperatives. The reforms that were introduced, resulting in the opening up of the economy, grew from fears of getting left out in the wake of the creation of mega trading blocs in Europe, North America, and East Asia and left New Delhi with little choice but to somehow hitch its economic wagon to East Asia. Not least a consideration was China's steadily rising profile in Southeast Asia—especially its close links with Myanmar (with which India shares its second longest border)—which injected a sense of urgency to begin fresh political initiatives.

It may be kept in mind that virtually no one, including the United States, Japan, and most Southeast Asian countries, saw much value in involving India in regional affairs. Although early on New Delhi talked mostly of the larger Asia-Pacific, ASEAN became the cynosure of its policy because by then ASEAN was beginning to shed its reticence and play a larger role in the management of regional affairs and also because it became the primary driver of a plethora of regional multilateral frameworks that were coming into being after the Cold War's end. This is the backdrop in which India began its odyssey toward the East, which two and a half decades later has evolved into a robust, multifaceted, and successful policy encompassing political, strategic, and economic dimensions.

Since it was a relatively new entrant, New Delhi had to undertake a sustained diplomatic effort to hard-sell itself politically, that it would be a useful partner for Southeast Asia, which in turn warranted developing substantial institutional linkages with ASEAN. Thus, India became a Sectoral Dialogue Partner in 1992, a full Dialogue Partner in 1995, and a Summit Partner in 2002, which cleared the way for India to join other regional multilateral mechanisms such as the ASEAN Regional Forum (ARF), East Asia Summit (EAS), the ASEAN Defense Ministers Meeting Plus (ADMM-Plus), and the RCEP.[8] Singapore, Indonesia, Myanmar, and Vietnam were targeted for strengthening of bilateral relations. For some inexplicable reasons, the one country with which India had somewhat frosty relations at times was Malaysia, when Mahathir was at the helm, but there has been a remarkable turnaround since his exit. Of note is the dramatic shift one can see in India-Myanmar relations, especially in the past decade or so.

Not least are ASEAN's own compulsions that played a significant part in making India's Look East Policy a major success, if seen in the background of certain key developments during 1992–93. The Soviet and later especially the American military withdrawal from the Philippines transformed Southeast Asia from a predictable, stable Cold War bipolarity into a region of post–Cold War uncertainty and power vacuum. This alone would not have been a major worry, but for other developments that followed, which were mostly to do with China's generally assertive stances over its claims in the South China Sea in particular and exhibiting greater ambitions to be the predominant power in the region. The Standing Committee of the National People's Congress of China in February 1992 adopted the Law on the Territorial Waters and Their Contiguous Areas (Territorial Sea Law), asserting China's sovereignty over the Spratly and Paracel Islands and published a map indicating that the entire South China Sea from Hainan up to Indonesia's Natuna Islands represents its territorial waters. Soon a series of low-level military spats ensued between China and Vietnam and China and the Philippines, with Beijing not hesitant to use force to realize its claims, which set off alarm bells across Southeast Asia. In these circumstances, while the United States was in no mood to reestablish its military presence in Southeast Asia, ASEAN started to weigh other options as it was forced to come to terms with new realities in the changed circumstances wherein its security role had come to a sudden sharp focus.[9] Thus, India, a large country with formidable military power, came to the table as a potential counterweight to China. This is evident if one looks at the debate on the creation of a regional security multilateral framework, the ARF, in which not only India hardly figured but its attempts to join it were politely rebuffed. By 1995, however, a perceptible change in ASEAN's attitude was apparent when India was made a full Dialogue Partner and invited to join ARF. Undoubtedly, Singapore played a pivotal role in support of India's active involvement. Still, for most ASEAN countries, India was an unknown quantity, trying to reestablish links after more than three decades without properly laying out its objectives. Thus, most countries were basically betting on its future potential.

It is useful to mention two key developments, one of which set India–Southeast Asia relations back, but the other, ironically, actually increased India's stature as a consequential military power. When it appeared the Look East Policy was picking up steam after successfully overcoming the initial hitches, it suffered a major blow with the 1997–98 financial crisis that afflicted several Southeast Asian countries. Whereas the crisis catapulted China's critical role (leading to the creation of ASEAN Plus Three in 1998) in regional economic issues, India hardly mattered. Since India had been less consequential to Southeast Asia economically, only after the recovery were these countries ready to engage New Delhi once again. By then China had a big advantage over India. On the other hand, the July 1998 ARF meeting in Manila was an important occasion when for the first time India came into ASEAN's security reckoning. In response to India's May 1998 nuclear tests, a group of countries led by Australia, Japan, the Philippines, and China sought to corner and condemn India;[10] however this movement was thwarted as some ASEAN countries—prominently Indonesia, Singapore, and Vietnam—that came out strongly in defense of India. Then Indonesian Foreign Minister Ali Alatas, while regretting the tests, dubbed India as a "non-aligned nuclear power" and strongly castigated the "double standards and hypocrisy" and lacking sincerity on nuclear disarmament by the nuclear-five countries.[11] It was a clear indication that these countries were looking at India, which had broken China's monopoly over nuclear weapons in Asia, as a potential contributor to regional security. Thus, beside forging institutional links with ASEAN, nothing substantial occurred in the 1990s, but things began to change dramatically starting in the early 2000s.

Look East Policy since 2000

A decade after the launch of the Look East Policy, India's economic reforms began to pay rich dividends as it became the second fastest growing economy. By the early 2000s, riding high growth rates and burgeoning defense capabilities, India was ready to unleash the second phase of the policy. Unlike in the early 1990s, this time around the political environment was far more favorable to India—India-U.S. relations were back on track, Japan was beginning to cozy up to India, and wariness about a powerful China in Southeast Asia was palpable. The tentativeness that marked the first phase had been replaced by more tangible steps that also reflected an India that had become far more confident, both economically and militarily. This had an enormous impact on the way New Delhi sought a role for itself commensurate with its size and growing stature.

As its economy began to log impressive growth rates (averaging 7.55 percent between 2001 and 2011), India not only could afford to fund generously to augment its military capabilities but could even visualize a larger security role in the Indo-Pacific region. This is starkly visible by looking at the attention the Navy in particular received. After enduring what was called the dark decade of the 1990s in the wake of defense budget cuts, which badly affected capital spending and led to a severe curtailing of modernization and expansion plans, the Navy from the 2000s onward has embarked on an ambitious modernization program.

It is noteworthy that the current modernization plans of the Indian Navy are qualitatively different from the previous ones. Despite two fleet carriers (including the recently procured one from Russia), a lone attack submarine on lease from Russia, some conventional submarines, and other principal combatant ships, the Indian Navy could not be considered truly blue-water capable as it was virtually incapable of embarking on any out-of-area operations given its very limited sealift and power projection capabilities. That began to change in the mid-2000s with the addition of more oceangoing ships: between April 2007 and March 2012 (Eleventh Plan Period), close to two hundred acceptances of necessity—the initial process of obtaining approval—with a total value of nearly US$50 billion were obtained; a total of 161 contracts worth US$16.7 billion were finalized.[12] Corresponding to the growing profile of the Navy, military funding also witnessed a steady rise: from 12.7 percent in 1990–91 to about 19 percent by 2012–13 of the total defense budget, excluding the Coast Guard.[13] Despite inordinate delays and cost overruns, the Indian Navy is aiming to build three carriers by the end of this decade, so that operationally at least two carriers will be available at any given time. In August 2013 India also launched a forty-thousand-ton indigenous aircraft carrier and missile-capable nuclear submarine called *Arihant*. Attempts are also in the works to augment the sealift and surveillance and reconnaissance capabilities considerably.

In order to brace for the protection of rapidly expanding economic and strategic interests, India has been quietly reordering its defense strategy. It is more pronounced in the case of its maritime strategy. With continental threats becoming less severe and the Indian Ocean environment more favorable, there has been a greater appreciation of the unique role the Navy can perform in advancing diplomatic and strategic interests and to deal with a variety of maritime security challenges. As the Indian Navy strives to graduate from being a brown-water to a blue-water navy, a new strategy has also been unveiled. For instance, the 2007 paper *Freedom to Use the Seas: India's Maritime Military Doctrine Strategy* "clearly delineates the regions of primary and secondary interest in the Indian Ocean and beyond."[14] The former include the "Arabian Sea and the Bay of Bengal, which largely encompass our EEZ, island territories and their littoral reaches; the choke points leading to and from the Indian Ocean—principally the Strait of Malacca, the Strait of Hormuz, the Strait of Bab-el-Mandeb and the Cape of Good Hope; the Island countries, the Persian Gulf, which is the source of the majority of our oil supplies; and the principal international sea lines crossing the IOR." And the secondary areas are "the Southern Indian Ocean Region; the Red Sea; the South China Sea, the East Pacific Region."[15]

There is little wonder that the Indian Navy is attracting huge attention at a time when the maritime security environment in the Indo-Pacific is undergoing profound shifts with especially India and China emerging as major maritime powers on one hand, and rapidly growing geostrategic and geoeconomic salience of the Indian Ocean on the other. Equally striking is the strengthening of naval force on India's eastern flank facing Southeast Asia. Many Southeast Asian countries have begun to forge strong links in particular with the Indian Navy in view of its strengths as well as its potential stabilizing role in the region.

Since the Indian Navy is gearing up to emerge as a force that can embark on operations in far-flung regions, in addition to equipping itself with sufficient capabilities, increasingly the emphasis is on creating a sophisticated communication network: what is called the shift from "platform-centric to network-centric operation."[16] With a view to keep the dispersed formations linked, the Indian Space Research Organization has launched a dedicated naval communication satellite, called *Rukmini* GSAT-7, in late August 2013.[17] The Navy announced that the satellite "seamlessly networked" around sixty warships and seventy-five aircraft during a massive month-long theater-level readiness and operational exercise (Tropex) in the Bay of Bengal that ended in late February 2014.[18] This also underscores the fact that India's robust and fast-growing space capabilities will serve military purposes as well.

It is important to keep the above discussion in view in order to understand India's likely role in the rapidly changing maritime security environment in the region. No question that focus is increasingly shifting to the maritime domain not merely because of the emergence of maritime boundary disputes as major security concerns but also because of the rise of Asian great powers as great maritime forces. Besides numerous maritime nontraditional security challenges, the region is bereft of either institutional mechanisms or robust confidence-building measures or tangible dialogues. Furthermore, there is very little maritime cooperation in the region. In this background, the Indian Navy is expected to play a significant role in the Southeast Asian region and thus is at the forefront in forging defense links.

India's Defense Diplomacy in Southeast Asia

As the Look East Policy began to gather momentum, a number of important developments took place. One dimension that has come into bold relief pertains to the alacrity with which New Delhi has been quietly pursuing strategic and defense cooperation by forging strong bonds at the multilateral and bilateral levels with the countries of Southeast Asia. Indeed, these appear to be more robust than economic or political aspects of India's Look East Policy, taking into account the scale and degree of the agreements and interactions. No doubt that they have remained low-profile but are reflective of growing Southeast Asian concerns about regional security and India's potential contribution. From an Indian perspective, they would entail enhancing its overall strategic heft and making itself part of the regional security equation. At the multilateral level, apart from being a member of the regional security mechanism, the ARF, the Regional Cooperation Agreement on Combating Piracy and Armed Robbery, and ADMM-Plus, the Indian Navy undertook a unique initiative in 1995 to host biennial naval gatherings called the Milan, at Port Blair in the Andaman and Nicobar Islands. Purported to be a confidence-building measure comprising littoral countries of the Bay of Bengal, it has been steadily expanding with the participation of most countries of Southeast Asia and the island states of the Indian Ocean. It is emerging as a key platform to address myriad maritime security issues in the region in the unconventional domain. From being a small gathering of just five navies (Indonesia, Malaysia, Singapore, Thailand, and Sri Lanka) at its launch, it had grown to sixteen participants by 2014.[19] The event is spread over five days and involves an assortment of activities, with the intent to promote interoperability, build confidence, and discover ways to deal with a variety of nontraditional security challenges in the region such as maritime terrorism, piracy, humanitarian assistance, search and rescue operations, and protection of the sea lanes near the Malacca Strait, through which over 30 percent of global trade passes.

The idea of forging defense links began in 1990 as an attempt to assuage Southeast Asian concerns about the Indian naval expansion in the mid- and late 1980s, which had generated apprehensions about the intent of major modernization. The Navy thus took the initiative to reinvigorate contacts with counterparts in Indonesia initially and Malaysia, Singapore, and Thailand a little later. It resulted in holding simple bilateral passage exercises to begin with, which were gradually expanded. The other significant development was the 1993 agreement under which India trained Malaysian air force personnel to operate Russian MiG-29 aircraft that it had acquired and to provide spare parts because of turmoil in Russia. However, starting from the early 2000s the defense and security cooperation began to gather unprecedented momentum to include a wide array of activities such as strategic dialogues, bilateral and multilateral exercises, training programs, high-level visits, technology cooperation agreements, and some instances of arms transfers as well. Concerns about China's military might and India's deft diplomacy helped New Delhi to position itself as a potential security contributor to the region.[20] A measure of the success of defense diplomacy can be gauged from the fact that a section on "Defence Relations with Foreign Countries" has been appearing in the Annual Reports of the Ministry of Defence since 2003–4. Since most of the above activities are done under its auspices, the Navy created a separate Directorate of Foreign Cooperation at its headquarters in 2004.

India's most expansive defense cooperation is with Singapore in terms of both degree and intensity. What began as simple naval maneuvers have now become advanced air, surface, and subsurface exercises, which since 2005 have been upgraded to SIMBEX (Singapore Indian Maritime Bilateral Exercise). According to an Indian naval officer, these have "graduated from purely training oriented ASW (anti-submarine warfare) exercises to complex exercises, involving multiple facets of operations at sea."[21] These exercises take place not only in India's territorial waters but also in the South China Sea. India even stationed four of its Dornier maritime reconnaissance aircraft in Singapore to undertake surveillance sorties in the South China Sea to "carry out coordinated patrols in the waters and will operate in coordination with the Indian Navy ships in the region."[22] The air exercises that began in 2003, called SINDEX, involving major frontline aircraft such as MiG-29s, Su-30s, Jaguars from India, and F-16s from Singapore, are held in both countries. The level of India-Singapore defense cooperation can be gauged by the fact that Indian pilots for the first time flew F-16 fighters in air combat exercises held at Paya Lebar Airbase in 2006.[23] Under the 2005 memorandum of understanding, the armies of the two countries have also conducted joint exercises involving mainly armor and artillery units.[24] Singapore has also been involved in multilateral maneuvers by participating in the India-French Garuda Air Advanced Exercises starting from 2010 involving Indian Su-30 fighters backed by Il-76 heavy-lift and Il-78 midair refuelers, French Rafaels and Mirages, and Singaporean F-16 aircraft.[25] Singapore also trains all three wings of its military in India. Singapore has also used India's Chandipur facility to test out its guns and missiles and was the first country to train in India to operate submarines.[26] It entered into a long-term agreement in 2007 to use the Kalaikunda Air Force Station for training purposes (the agreement also allows Singapore to place its personnel and equipment in the country over the long term), and under another agreement in 2008 its army has been given greater access to Indian facilities.[27]

The 2001 defense cooperation agreement between India and Indonesia has given impetus to otherwise limited bilateral exchanges to move into substantive areas of cooperation that include joint efforts to ensure peace in the region and prevent illegal activities such as smuggling, piracy, robbery, drug trafficking, and transnational crimes. The biannual India-Indonesia Coordinated Patrols (Ind-Indo CORPAT) in the Six Degree Channel of the Andaman Sea by the Indonesian and Indian Navies since September 2002 are significant because this channel is the main conduit for international shipping that passes through the Malacca Strait.[28] A similar arrangement has also been agreed upon under a 2005 comprehensive memorandum of understanding signed in 2005 between Thailand and India to conduct biannual coordinated exercises close to their maritime boundary near the Malacca Strait.[29]

As part of the 2000 fifteen-point defense cooperation agreement, India and Vietnam have been expanding their military-to-military interaction and a variety of other activities.[30] Hanoi has already taken Indian assistance in "submarine training, conversion training for its pilots to fly Sukhoi-30, modernization of a strategic port and transfer of medium-sized warships."[31] In a first deal of its kind, India has offered a US$100 million credit line to Vietnam to purchase four patrol boats.[32] In one of those rare instances, the Myanmar Navy has been participating in Milan naval gatherings since 2003. Apart from imparting counterinsurgency training and helping in hydrographic surveys, India has also started training the Myanmar Air Force.[33] In April 2007, a leading Indian daily claimed, "After equipping [Myanmar] with 105 mm artillery guns, T-55 tanks and Islander aircraft, New Delhi plans to help set up a naval aviation wing and to provide training to their personnel."[34]

Furthermore, as part of proactive defense diplomacy to leverage its military might, New Delhi has also created a variety of defense/security dialogues with most countries of the region and has signed the largest number of strategic partnership agreements with the countries of Southeast Asia—Indonesia, Vietnam, Malaysia, Thailand, and Myanmar.

Economic Dimension

The collapse of the Doha Development Round of WTO negotiations pushed many countries including India to look for alternatives to multilateral negotiations to improve their trade positions. This has been happening within the broader context of India making a successful transition from an excessively inward-oriented economy to a more globally integrated economy. As a result of new policies, India has become one of the fastest growing economies of the world. Despite some serious challenges like global slowdown, energy security, poverty, infrastructure limitations, regional disparities, and internal security issues, there are strong indications that rapid growth will continue. Apart from expansion, the Indian economy has also been diversified significantly in the past decade. Traditionally, the economy was dependent on markets in Europe and the United States. In the past two decades, there has been a rapid integration of the Indian economy within Asia, which has been reinforced by India's Look East Policy that was initiated in the early 1990s. This is clearly evident from rapidly increasing India-China trade as well as India-ASEAN trade. The Twelfth Five-Year Plan (2012–17) targets faster, more inclusive, and more sustainable growth. The focus is on creating human, physical, and institutional capabilities to achieve targeted 8.2 percent growth in the next five years. Although rapid growth in the first decade of the twenty-first century raised expectations, domestic and global circumstances have been less favorable in recent years. Still, the overall aim is to bring 9 percent growth back by the end of Twelfth Plan.[35] As a result of these changes, India is adapting itself simultaneously to the economic globalization and to the emerging balance of power. Changes in India's internal and external economic policies also coincided with the end of the Cold War.

Within this broader framework, India has put its proposed regional trade agreements on a fast track since 2005. In the past, India had adopted a cautious approach to regionalism, and was engaged in only a few bilateral/regional initiatives, mainly through preferential trade agreements or through open regionalism. In recent years, it has started concluding comprehensive economic cooperation agreements (CECAs) with many countries. The CECAs cover free trade agreements (with limited negative lists of items not covered under the pact) in goods, services, investments, and other identified areas of economic cooperation. Some important signed agreements include the South Asian Free Trade Area (SAFTA) and agreements with ASEAN, Japan, Singapore, Afghanistan, Bhutan, Sri Lanka, Nepal, South Korea, Mercosur, and others. Serious negotiations are on with the EU, the Gulf Cooperation Council, the India-Brazil-South Africa Dialogue Forum, Australia, Malaysia, and more.

According to the Asian Development Bank Asia Regional Integration Centre database, at different stages India was involved in at least thirty-four free trade agreements by 2013, out of which thirteen agreements were already signed, including four framework agreements, and several FTAs were under negotiation. Similarly, negotiations are ongoing in another ten agreements, and seven new FTAs have been proposed. As seen in table 10.1, most of India's engagements are within Asia. Within Asia, one significant aspect of this phase of economic growth is India's increasing economic cooperation with Southeast Asia through regional, subregional, and bilateral engagements (eight initiatives).

TABLE 10.1. India's engagement with regional integration through bilateral/multilateral initiatives

Name of the agreement	Status
ASEAN-India Comprehensive Economic Cooperation Agreement	Signed and in effect
Asia-Pacific Trade Agreement*	Signed and in effect
Bay of Bengal Initiative for Multi-Sectoral Technical and Economic Cooperation** (BIMSTEC) Free Trade Area	Framework FTA signed
Comprehensive Economic Partnership for East Asia (CEPEA/ASEAN+6)	Proposed/under consultation and study
India-Afghanistan Preferential Trading Agreement	Signed and in effect
India-Australia Free Trade Agreement	Negotiations launched
India-Bhutan Trade Agreement	Signed and in effect
India-Canada Economic Partnership Agreement	Negotiations launched
India-Chile Preferential Trading Agreement	Signed and in effect
India-Colombia Preferential Trading Arrangement	Proposed/under consultation and study
India-Egypt Preferential Trade Agreement	Negotiations launched
India-Eurasian Economic Union of Armenia, Belarus, Kazakhstan and Russia FTA	Proposed/under consultation and study
India-European Free Trade Association Free Trade Agreement	Negotiations launched
India-European Union Broad Based Trade and Investment Agreement	Negotiations launched
India-Gulf Cooperation Council Free Trade Area	Framework agreement signed
India-Indonesia Comprehensive Economic Cooperation Arrangement	Negotiations launched
India-Israel Preferential Trade Agreement	Negotiations launched
India-Korea Comprehensive Economic Partnership Agreement	Signed and in effect
India-Mauritius Comprehensive Economic Cooperation and Partnership Agreement	Negotiations launched
India-Mercosur Preferential Trade Agreement	Signed and in effect
India-Singapore Comprehensive Economic Cooperation Agreement	Signed and in effect
India-Southern African Customs Union Preferential Trade Agreement	Negotiations launched
India-Sri Lanka Free Trade Agreement	Signed and in effect
India-Thailand Free Trade Area	Framework agreement signed
India-Turkey Free Trade Area	Proposed/under consultation and study
India-Uruguay Preferential Trading Arrangement	Proposed/under consultation and study
India-Venezuela Preferential Trading Arrangement	Proposed/under consultation and study
Indo-Nepal Treaty of Trade	Signed and in effect
Japan-India Comprehensive Economic Partnership Agreement	Signed and in effect
Malaysia-India Comprehensive Economic Cooperation Agreement	Signed and in effect
New Zealand-India Free Trade Agreement	Negotiations launched
Regional Comprehensive Economic Partnership	Negotiations launched
South Asian Free Trade Area	Signed and in effect

*Earlier Bangkok Agreement.
**Membership includes Bangladesh, Bhutan, India, Myanmar, Nepal, Sri Lanka, and Thailand.
Source: Asian Development Bank Regional Integration Centre Database.

After years of difficult negotiations, India finally signed a free trade agreement with ASEAN in 2009, which became operational in 2011. The fully functional India-ASEAN FTA will eliminate tariffs in a phased manner on 80 percent of the traded goods by 2016. Import tariffs on 10 percent of goods on the sensitive list will not be eliminated, while the tariffs on the remaining 10 percent of items will be brought down to 5 percent by 2019 in a phased manner. Another regional cooperative initiative has been the Bay of Bengal Initiative for Multi-Sectoral Technical and Economic Cooperation (BIMSTEC), which groups together Bangladesh, Bhutan, India, Myanmar, Nepal, Sri Lanka, and Thailand. Launched in 1997, this seven-country forum is aiming to achieve its own free trade area soon. The Mekong-Ganga Cooperation initiative is another subregional program that was launched in 2000 by India and the five countries from the Mekong region, namely, Cambodia, Lao PDR, Myanmar, Thailand, and Vietnam, to build cooperation in the region defined by two great rivers. Apart from regional arrangements, India also concluded bilateral trade agreements with Thailand (2003), Singapore (2005), and Malaysia (2011). In 2014, the India-ASEAN FTA in services and investments was also signed.

In 2011–12, India's goods trade with ASEAN was about US$80 billion, surpassing the trade target of US$70 billion by 2012. With the operationalization of FTA in goods in 2011, it grew by 41 percent in 2011–12. Indian officials are now hoping that it will increase to US$200 billion by 2022. Compared to China-ASEAN trade, it may look small, but one has to realize that it has grown from a meager US$2.3 billion in 1990–91.

TABLE 10.2. India's trade with ASEAN 2000–2001 to 2015–16 (US$ billions)

Year	Exports to ASEAN	Imports from ASEAN	Trade turnover
2000–2001	2.91	4.15	7.06
2001–2	3.46	4.39	7.85
2002–3	4.62	5.15	9.77
2003–4	5.82	7.43	13.25
2004–5	8.43	9.11	17.54
2005–6	10.41	10.89	21.30
2006–7	12.61	18.11	30.72
2007–8	16.41	22.68	39.09
2008–9	19.14	26.20	45.34
2009–10	18.11	25.80	43.91
2010–11	25.63	30.61	56.24
2011–12	36.74	42.16	78.90
2012–13	33.01	42.87	75.87
2013–14	33.13	41.28	74.41
2014–15	31.81	44.71	76.52
2015–16 (Apr–Sep)	11.79	20.96	32.75

Source: Export Import Databank, Ministry of Commerce, Government of India.

Within ASEAN, India's major trading partners are Singapore, Indonesia, Malaysia, Thailand, and Vietnam. Among these, Singapore is the largest destination for Indian goods (45 percent of total exports to ASEAN in 2011–12), followed by Indonesia, Malaysia, Vietnam, and Thailand. Similarly, Indonesia has emerged as the largest source of imports for India (34 percent of India's total imports from ASEAN), followed by Malaysia, Singapore, and Thailand.

TABLE 10.3. India's bilateral trade with ASEAN countries (US$ millions)

Country	2007–8	2008–9	2009–10	2010–11	2011–12	2012–13	2013–14	2014–15
Brunei	238	415	454	257	1,501	855	796	882
Cambodia	56	50	51	75	107	124	154	160
Indonesia	6,985	9,266	11,720	15,619	21,444	20,211	19,599	19,048
Laos	4	10	37	13	104	168	89	153
Malaysia	8,588	10,605	8,012	10,395	13,454	14,395	13,428	16,934
Myanmar	994	1,151	1,498	1,338	1,927	1,957	2,183	2,005
Philippines	825	999	1,062	1,311	1,434	1,691	1,811	1,819
Singapore	15,502	16,010	14,047	16,965	25,246	21,106	19,273	16,934
Thailand	4,111	4,462	4,672	6,546	8,245	9.086	9,043	9,331
Vietnam	1,784	2,147	2,361	3,716	5,442	6,282	8,036	9,262
Total ASEAN	39,087	45,115	43,914	56,235	78,904	75,875	74,412	76,528
India's total trade	414,786	488,992	467,124	620,905	795,284	791,137	764,605	758,371

Source: Export Import Databank, Ministry of Commerce, Government of India.

As shown by Ayako Obashi (2011), ASEAN has become a relatively more important trading partner for India, in compassion to India's importance to the ASEAN's trade.[36] In manufactured goods as well as in machinery, the percentage of ASEAN as an export destination almost doubled in the first decade of the twenty-first century.

TABLE 10.4. The proportions of India/ASEAN as ASEAN's/India's export destination and import origin (percentages)

For ASEAN	India as export destination			India as import origin		
	1990	2000	2009	1990	2000	2009
All commodities	1.3	1.6	3.3	0.9	1.0	2.1
Manufactured goods	1.1	1.3	2.7	0.9	0.8	1.7
Machinery	0.9	1.0	2.4	0.3	0.3	0.9
For India	ASEAN as export destination			ASEAN as import origin		
	1990	2000	2009	1990	2000	2009
All commodities	5.4	6.5	10.6	6.3	11.0	9.1
Manufactured goods	5.3	5.9	9.2	5.7	9.9	7.5
Machinery	12.7	11.6	19.2	6.4	17.1	9.9

Source: Obashi (2011: 61).

Two-way investments have also grown to more than US$60 billion in the past fifteen years. In fact, Singapore has emerged as a top investor in India in the past fifteen years, ahead of the United States, the United Kingdom, Japan, and Germany (table 10.5). Between 2004 and 2010, Indian investments in ASEAN grew to about US$22 billion.[37]

TABLE 10.5. FDI inflows into India (US$ millions, April 2000–September 2015)

Country	FDI inflow	Country	FDI inflow
Mauritius	91,222	Cyprus	8,328
Singapore	38,882	France	4,767
United Kingdom	22,563	UAE	3,307
Japan	19,167	Malaysia	760
United States	72,315	Indonesia	623
Netherlands	15,769	Thailand	212
Germany	8,337	Philippines	129
		Total	265,265

Source: Department of Industrial Policy and Promotion, Government of India, *FDI Factsheet* (September 2015).

In addition to the FTA in services with ASEAN, India is also negotiating similar agreements with members of the group. India has already implemented CECAs with Singapore and Malaysia and is negotiating with Indonesia and Thailand. The operationalization of the India-ASEAN FTA in goods and the signing of an FTA in services and investment would also clear the way for discussions on the RCEP that ASEAN plans to negotiate with its six key economic partners—Australia, China, India, Japan, South Korea, and New Zealand.

It is clear that compared to China's, India's economic exposure to ASEAN is still limited. One of the major reasons for this is physical connectivity with the region. Although FTAs in trade, services, and investments are central to India's strategy, India has realized that infrastructure challenges could hamper growth in linkages. Emerging nodes of India-ASEAN connectivity—Myanmar and Northeast India—are both weak in infrastructure.[38] At the same time, this is also an area that has a difficult topography and is home to many insurgencies. In the past fifteen years, however, the Indian government has given a special emphasis to economic and infrastructural developments in the Northeast, with many positive results.[39] The new opening in Myanmar will definitely help to build the connectivity further. Therefore, economic development strategies within Myanmar as well as the Indian Northeast could

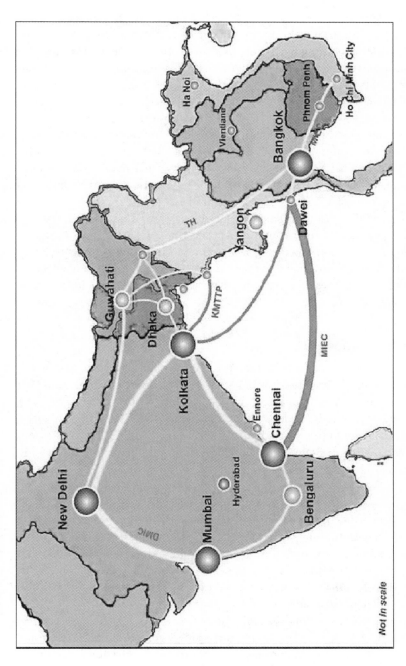

Figure 10.2. Framework to enhance India-ASEAN connectivity. Source: Prober De, "ASEAN India Connectivity: An Indian Perspective," in *Asean-India Connectivity: The Comprehensive Asia Development Plan, Phase II*, ERIA Research Project Report no. 7, ed. Fukunari Kimura and So Umezaki (Jakarta: ERIA, 2011), 138.

have a significant impact on India-ASEAN connectivity in the coming years. To enhance India-ASEAN connectivity, currently two main routes that would need further upgrading have been identified: the sea route and west link of the Mekong-India Economic Corridor (MIEC), and the land route, with various possible paths, along the trilateral highway between India, Myanmar, and Thailand. The MIEC would enhance connectivity between Ho Chi Minh City, Phnom Penh, Bangkok, and Dawei by road, and further to Chennai in India by sea; and the trilateral highway would improve connectivity between Northeast India and ASEAN. These roads would be further connected to Indian Golden Quadrangle project connecting major metropolitan areas as well as the Delhi-Mumbai Industrial Corridor. These plans are part of phase 2 of the Comprehensive ASEAN Development Plan.

So, a major thrust of India's policy in the past two decades has been economic, which has led to further political and strategic closeness with ASEAN nations. At the conclusion of negotiations on services and investments, Prime Minister Manmohan Singh said that India-ASEAN relations were at an "exciting stage" and expressed confidence that these agreements would transform bilateral relations.[40]

The China Factor

The discourse on India and Southeast Asia is incomplete without reference to China. Almost as large and aspiring to emerge as strong as China, India has nearly equivalent military might, although it lags far behind economically. One way or another China has figured in India's policy since the late 1970s, when it came out openly in support of Vietnam when the latter sent troops to dislodge the pro-Beijing Pol Pot regime in Cambodia. By the early 1990s, China had a head start as it was already well poised to be the major economic actor in the region when it began reforms to its economy. Although India has made considerable progress since then, it still lags far behind China, particularly in economic interactions with Southeast Asia. Since 2008, China has been the largest trading partner for ASEAN, with bilateral trade in excess of US$400 billion, compared to India's US$76 billion in 2013. China is also far better connected with and far more deeply embedded in the regional value chain than is India. However, several countries have taken note of India's potential to emerge as an economic giant in the longer run.

To be sure, India-China bilateral relations are witnessing an unprecedented transformation. They are becoming increasingly complex, multifaceted, and mature and are no longer confined to the border dispute, China's support of Pakistan, or the Dalai Lama issue, as had been the case from the 1962 war to the early 2000s. They now compete for resources, investments, and markets, and also for political influence. The contest for greater strategic space between the two is most visible in Southeast Asia, concomitant with their growing interests and expanding stakes. Historically Southeast Asia had been heavily influenced by India and China, and after remaining on the margins for more than two centuries during the colonial interlude, the countries are meeting once again in Southeast Asia. In a remarkable shift of events, they are now significant players in the emerging regional economic and security order. With China's rise as the predominant power in Southeast Asia and India's emergence as a great power, it is obvious that their interests will intersect, which has generated considerable unease between the powers.

Nevertheless, one must exercise caution in drawing hasty inferences merely because there have been occasions in the recent past that may have sent signals implying these two Asian giants were headed toward an irreconcilable rivalry. Yet, questions arise as to whether this region will emerge as the theater for India and China to play out their competition/rivalry and what the implications will be for the rest of the region, or if they will find ways to peacefully coexist by joining hands in the management of regional security.[41] There is no question that they continue to harbor suspicions: the Chinese are anxious about India's rising role in East Asia, in particular its participation in what China considers a U.S.-led containment strategy, along with Japan, and its involvement in the South China Sea, even if ostensibly in search of energy resources. It should be noted that the Indian public-sector oil company ONGC Videsh Ltd. (OVL) has been involved in South China Sea oil exploration since 1988, when it acquired a block on the southeast of Vung Tau with an area of 955 square kilometers and began commercial production in January 2003. Subsequently, in 2006 OVL also secured a license for blocks 127 and 128.[42] Beijing's response has become far shriller in recent times than it was earlier. For instance, *People's Daily* suggested that there is strong political motivation behind the exploration projects and that "China must take practical and firm actions to make these projects fall through."[43] It must have rattled China when the Indian naval chief inadvertently stated during a press conference that the Indian Navy was ready to defend Indian interests in the South China Sea.[44] So far India has stood pat, repeating its refrain that it is within its rights to undertake exploration activities in the territorial waters of Vietnam and that any dispute should be settled peacefully without affecting freedom of navigation or access to maritime commons in the South China Sea. Interestingly, New Delhi has started airing this viewpoint only recently, which resembles the stand taken by Washington. After withdrawing from blocks 127 and 128, as they are commercially unviable, India has given in to

Vietnamese pressure by committing to resume exploration activity in block 128 while relinquishing 127.[45]

The way India managed to rebuild its relationship with Myanmar starting from the mid-1990s and thus to an extent blunting Chinese influence is a good example of the subtle but noticeable contest for influence. Similarly, India has always been wary of close links between Beijing and Islamabad and is skeptical of every Chinese move in India's immediate neighborhood, its long-term ambitions in the Indian Ocean, and its attempts to keep India away from East Asian affairs. Beijing's discomfort at the bonhomie with Japan and the United States in the region is obvious. While their interactions have historically been peaceful and marked by vibrant exchanges for more than two millennia, that may not be the case now. Yet, Beijing is becoming less hostile to India and has on more than one occasion stated that India has vital stakes in East Asia and that the region is large enough to accommodate more than one power. Hence, India and China are most unlikely to allow the competitive elements to degenerate into an open political and/or military showdown. A number of institutional mechanisms have been created, such as the 2005 Strategic Partnership and the 2014 Maritime Dialogue, on the eve of President Xi Jinping's 2014 visit. This helped manage relations as the stakes mount in the Indo-Pacific region. India and China also started a Strategic Economic Dialogue in 2011 to underscore how vital their economic relations are.[46] Despite occasional incidents along their border, there has not been a single exchange of fire in more than forty-five years, and the nations have evolved tangible confidence-building measures to ensure tranquility along the border. Both certainly will face the challenge of keeping their relationship on an even keel through a set of self-imposed limits. Consequently, elements of both competition and cooperation are seen in bilateral relations, and attempts to keep them under control will continue to characterize India-China relations in Southeast Asia.[47]

Within ASEAN there is no uniformity of views on China and India, but there is a broad understanding that the rise of these two powers in close vicinity and their rising stakes in the region will have implications. ASEAN's strategy has been to enmesh China and India in regional affairs in such a way that they will contribute to regional stability and development.[48] It is true that at present China is far more attractive economically than India, but most countries are also concerned about its aggressive attitude and unrelenting stance on maritime disputes. Logically Southeast Asia is the region into which China is most likely to project its power as it emerges as a major maritime state with its goal of control up to the first island chain in the Pacific. On the other hand, India is relatively better placed not only because it has a limited number of pending territorial disputes, unlike China (or other great powers for that matter). India's geostrategic location, dominating the East Indian Ocean, gives it a uniquely advantageous position. These factors offer New Delhi considerable political leeway, which it seems to be exploiting to build strong defense and strategic links.[49] Thus, from ASEAN's perspective India serves three purposes: a countervailing force against China, an option vis-à-vis China, and a solution to a variety of nontraditional security challenges.

India, the United States, and Southeast Asia

The other significant dimension that will have enormous bearing on Southeast Asia is India's strategic partnership with the United States. Driven by a convergence of interests and shared concerns, for the first time India and the United States have begun to cooperate closely in managing regional security. Many factors such as the relative decline of the United States, the rise of China and India, and a fluid political environment in Asia are warranting a major review of American strategy. Instead of exclusive dependence on bilateral alliances and forward deployment, Washington is increasingly trying to incorporate potential strategic partners and to make use of regional multilateralism in addressing complex economic and security issues in the region. Thus, the emphasis is shifting from "allies" only to "allies and friends/ partners," wherein India figures prominently (along with a few other Southeast Asian countries) in the new "rebalance" strategy.

While it is true that both India and the United States share a similar objective of ensuring that a rapidly rising China will not resort to force in settling the disputes that might seriously undermine regional stability or take actions that will adversely affect their vital interests, their agenda in fact goes beyond China such as tackling several nontraditional security issues, in particular in the maritime domain and in building a stable East Asian balance of power. These led them to start working together on counterterrorism in 2002, and their navies joined hands in providing relief to the victims after the deadly 2004 tsunami in Indonesia. This was the beginning of forging interoperability between their navies. The second objective is to work closely to build a stable multipolar regional architecture. One of the initiatives is high-level consultations on East Asian security and increased interactions between the armed forces as part of building the strategic partnership. The upshot was two massive multilateral naval exercises in the Pacific (the first time the Indian Navy went to the Pacific to participate in a large exercise) and in the Bay of Bengal in 2007, which India hosted (involving carriers, attack submarines, advanced destroyers, etc.).

India-U.S. cooperation has acquired enormous significance ever since the East Asia Summit became a location for high-level discussions. It figured for the first time in the post-summit Joint Statement between Singh and Obama in November 2010: "The United States welcomes, in particular, India's leadership in expanding prosperity and security across the region. The two leaders agreed to deepen existing regular strategic consultations on developments in East Asia."[50] Then Secretary of State Hillary Clinton maintained that "in all of these areas, India's leadership will help to shape positively the future of the Asia Pacific. That's why the United States supports India's Look East policy, and we encourage India not just to look east, but to engage East and act East as well."[51] Defense Secretary Panetta contended that "defense cooperation with India is a linchpin in this [rebalancing] strategy."[52] This was once again reiterated by a senior official of the National Security Council, who claimed that "in so many ways, as the U.S. implements our re-balance, we see India as a fundamental provider of security and economic growth across the region."[53] Almost every major statement or assessment that has emanated from Washington has made references to India's key role in the Indian Ocean and East Asia.[54]

When Secretary of State Hillary Clinton declared during the 2010 ARF meeting in Hanoi that the United States was "back in Asia," leading subsequently to the announcement of the pivot or "rebalancing" strategy, New Delhi was one of the first to enthusiastically welcome it on the understanding that a robust and enduring American presence in East Asia would be a better guarantor of stability at a time when the region was staring at an uncertain future with disputes in both the East and South China Seas rising. As Secretary Clinton claimed, one of the issues in the U.S.-India Strategic Dialogue "is India's growing engagement and integration into East Asia, because we believe that India is a key player in this region."[55] In addition, two more bilateral institutional mechanisms have been launched specifically aimed at East Asia: the India-U.S. Dialogue on Asia-Pacific and the U.S.-India-Japan Trilateral.[56]

Obama's two visits to India while in office and the fact that he was the first ever president to be the chief guest at the Republic Day celebrations carry enormous symbolism. That considerable time was spent discussing China is also a clear indication that they will cooperate more closely in the Indo-Pacific region on a range of issues. Still, it is difficult to sidestep some amount of ambivalence that dogs India's policy to throw its lot behind the United States. Indian reticence results from its desire not to do something that might give rise to unnecessary concerns in China and to not get caught in the U.S.-China crossfire. The conflicting signals that New Delhi has sent in the recent past on its involvement in the South China Sea are a reflection of this.[57] However, both of these seem to be misplaced since rebalancing is not a containment strategy because, as Washington is well aware, it is evidently counterproductive. The U.S. stakes in China are immense, so Washington is seeking to engage China more productively. Rebalance is meant more to regain lost political ground and inject a sense of confidence in its allies and partners, besides greater engagement of China. Perhaps India should see its role as a stakeholder in terms of not merely managing regional security but also actively working toward crafting a new regional security order. Apparently, New Delhi, while recognizing the benefits of close strategic links with Washington, wants to keep some amount of strategic autonomy open. Yet, as far as Southeast Asia is concerned, it appears India and the United States share many common interests and concerns. Both do not want China's shadow looming over the region and want ASEAN and ASEAN-led multilateralism to play a key role in managing regional affairs.

The Indian foreign minister stated that India-U.S. cooperation through bilateral and trilateral talks will aim at creating a "peaceful and stable Asia, Pacific and the Indian Ocean region, and the evolution of an open, balanced and inclusive architecture in the region. We will continue to work together, and with other countries, toward this goal through various mechanisms, such as our bilateral dialogue, the regional forums and our trilateral dialogue with Japan."[58] Furthermore, the emergence of the Indo-Pacific as the new strategic template underscoring growing interdependence and interface of the Indian and Pacific oceans will add greater strategic heft to the India--U.S. partnership. This comes across quite clearly in the Joint U.S.-India Joint Strategic Vision for the Asia-Pacific and Indian Ocean Region, issued during President Obama's visit on January 25, 2015. Specific reference was made to the South China Sea: "Regional prosperity depends on security. We affirm the importance of safeguarding maritime security and ensuring freedom of navigation and over flight throughout the region, especially in the South China Sea."[59] References were also made to strengthening regional dialogues, deepening regional integration, and exploring multilateral opportunities for engagement.

After resisting for a long time on the assumption that it would foreclose its strategic autonomy and options, India has become far more comfortable with the idea of regional balance of power and with a role for itself and even with working closely with others. A former foreign secretary underscored that "India and the US could contribute to a better balance of power in the Asian region at a time when a major process of realignment was taking place on the continent with the emergence of China as a global economic power house and New Delhi poised to be a major player as well."[60] An unprecedented transformation in India-Japan relations since the signing of the Joint Declaration on Security Cooperation in 2008 has brought India, the United

States, and Japan much closer. Their trilateral dialogue and trilateral maritime exercises have come about due to Japan's initiative.

India and Southeast Asian Security

The ambivalence that characterized the 1990s from both sides largely was over by the early 2000s with respect to India's role in Southeast Asia. India's keenness to increase its security profile was matched by ASEAN's enthusiasm to involve it in regional affairs.[61] As the Indian Navy acquires blue-water capabilities,[62] its strong presence in the crucial Bay of Bengal in the close vicinity to several Southeast Asian countries has acquired considerable salience, especially at a time when much of the focus is on maritime security. The kind of capabilities that India is seeking to acquire are obviously aimed at its Navy emerging as an expeditionary force, a fact acknowledged in the Twelfth Defence Plan by making clear that the objective is to "build adequate standoff capability for sea lift and expeditionary operations to achieve desired power projection force levels, influence events ashore and undertake military operations other than war."[63]

India's rise and willingness to play a larger security role have coincided with continued uncertainty in Southeast Asia, which is still coming to terms with an economic and security environment that is rapidly shifting. A detailed discussion on regional order is beyond the purview of this study, but two aspects warrant attention. First, by the early 2000s, Northeast Asia and Southeast Asia had become very close, and hence the latter's security had to be analyzed in the context of East Asia rather than in isolation. Second, notwithstanding a few claims to the contrary, there is hardly a regional order that could be construed as viable and enduring. Numerous multilateral forums—ARF, EAS, and ADMM-Plus—have been created but have not proved to be dependable for dealing with complex security problems. ASEAN's own unity and cohesion came under question after its foreign ministers for the first time in its history failed to issue a joint communiqué in 2012. The current security environment in East Asia is marked first by the fact that the region is in the throes of transition from U.S. to Chinese hegemony. Second, the region is beset with security dilemmas, which are reflected in the military buildup across the region, which has not yet become a typical arms race. Finally, the limitations to cooperative security have become clear. In these circumstances there is no option but to build a robust regional balance of power with multilateralism playing a supplementary role at the most. New Delhi's ASEAN-centric policy and its evolving relations with great powers reflect this broad approach.

A corollary to the above is this question: does India have a well-defined strategy? There is no way to know if there is one because New Delhi officially never articulates its strategy on any security issue, not least toward Southeast Asia. The problem is that India publishes few official documents or White Papers on security issues; only the Navy has issued a few papers on doctrine and strategy in the recent past.[64] Although there is no clarity on what role India seeks to play, given that it has articulated its growing interests well, it certainly seems to be preparing to play a bigger role. Conscious of the fact that India's economic interactions with East Asia are growing faster than any other region (it has signed the largest number of bilateral and multilateral free trade agreements compared to any other region) and its enthusiastic participation in attempts to create a pan–East Asian region-wide free trade zone, India is poised to substantially increase its role in the region. Prime Minister Modi's announcement of the Act East Policy is a harbinger of India's enhanced engagement with the region. There is always the question of how many resources, diplomatic and otherwise, New Delhi is willing to devote to Southeast Asia. If India were to make good its intent to shift its policy from "Look East" to "Act East," it will require a lot more attention and further consolidation of defense and economic ties. A major constraint to deepening relations with Southeast Asian countries is poor connectivity by road, rail, and air, which has also been largely responsible for its low participation in the regional value chain, which is playing a pivotal role in bringing the region closer. The lack of substantial economic links with Southeast Asia is the weakest attribute of India's Look East Policy.

On the other hand, if the Indian Navy is acquiring blue-water capabilities, the focus is unmistakably toward its east.[65] It has also gained considerable respectability because of its role as a net security provider in the Indian Ocean region and its ability to respond quickly to nontraditional security challenges such as December 2004 tsunami or the May 2008 Nargis super cyclone that devastated Myanmar or counterpiracy operations in the Gulf of Aden from late 2008 onward. Given its capabilities and reach, the Indian Navy will play a critical role in facing up to the challenges the nontraditional security challenges pose in the Indo-Pacific.

While India's keenness to engage Southeast Asia matters, how the region is responding to Indian overtures is equally significant. The region's initial reaction when India launched the Look East Policy in 1991 was one of indifference, but that began to change dramatically as the events unfolded soon after, especially the American military withdrawal and China's assertive claims over the Paracels and the Spratlys in the South China Sea. It then became apparent that India's involvement would contribute to regional security. The Indian economic reforms were also seen as offering economic opportunities. Singapore has had been the most proactive among the ASEAN countries in engaging New Delhi not only bilaterally but also with the association. Singapore was very disappointed with excruciatingly slow reforms, minimal progress in building infrastructure, and a bureaucracy that refused to give up old habits. Thus, whereas the progress on the economic front remained tardy, on the security front one can see remarkable progress. Of course, not all ASEAN countries shared a uniform opinion on India. But for the concerns about post–Cold War power vacuum and an uncertain security environment, India's Look East Policy would not have been as successful. This was evident during the deliberations over ARF before its launch when India was totally ignored but was invited to be a part of it in 1994. There is no question that today there is much broader support for India's involvement in ASEAN compared to the early 1990s, especially from Indonesia and Malaysia and more recently the Philippines.

Act East Policy

Prime Minister Narendra Modi's Act East Policy is under intense scrutiny. Since no official enunciation of the contours of the policy has been made, it has led to considerable speculation. However, the policy's overall thrust appears to be on strengthening economic relations with East Asia since it is generally recognized that India's economic future lies in that region. Moreover, Modi secured a huge mandate in the 2014 general elections due to the development goals that he advocated, so he has to meet people's high expectations. As noted, East Asia remains the brightest spot in the world in terms of economic performance, but India, despite more than two decades of effort, remains a marginal power. Its share in regional trade is small, and its participation in the rapidly growing regional production chain is limited, so India is not able to reap the benefits. While regional cooperation and integration are expanding apace, India is lagging. The attempts to strike free trade agreements and active participation in the RCEP are part of the new strategy. The fact that Modi has undertaken more visits to East Asia than to any other region (up to early 2016) is an indication of how important this region is. His actions highlight three points: augment connectivity (land, rail, air, and sea), exploit the vast soft power potential that India possesses, and engage the Indian diaspora especially in Southeast Asia to figure prominently in the new thrust toward East Asia. The second dimension of Modi's proactive Act East Policy is to focus on strengthening bilateral relations with select countries. The third aspect is a far more purposive engagement of great powers. While strengthening the trilateral talks with the United States and Japan, Modi is trying to recast the relationship with China not by simply looking at the narrow prism of the security or border issue but with the intent to make links more expansive and broad-based with a lot of emphasis on economic ties. Thus, the Act East initiatives under Modi will have considerable implications for India's policy toward Southeast Asia.

Conclusion

Southeast Asia will remain in the spotlight for two reasons: first, due to its geostrategic location connecting the East Indian Ocean and the West Pacific regions, which have emerged as the new global center of gravity, and, second, because of the role of ASEAN as the glue that brings major stakeholders together through a variety of regional multilateral forums to manage regional affairs. How effectively ASEAN can accomplish this onerous task is something to be seen given its limitations and drawbacks amid growing competition among great powers for regional supremacy.

After remaining on the sidelines for a long time, India's destiny lies in East Asia and the nation must anchor its future here. The Look East Policy has become a major success story for India, over the years becoming multifaceted and comprehensive, encompassing political, economic, and defense/strategic aspects. While two distinct phases of this policy are discernible, it appears poised to move to the next stage, which is likely to be far more robust and broad-based by bringing in newer elements such as soft power and strengthening economic links. Contrary to the past when New Delhi had a limited role and even more limited influence, today without a doubt India has become a significant player in regional affairs. Considerable reticence and ambivalence that characterized the initial interactions are being replaced by more assertive actions and articulation of stakes. If economic exigencies and political compulsions forced New Delhi to look east, no less important was the rise of China and its steadily increasing role. Fortunately for India, many Southeast Asian countries saw India as a likely counterweight to China, besides its potential to emerge as an option for economic interactions.

With nearly 30 percent of India's external trade being with ASEAN, a large number of comprehensive economic partnership agreements, and its active participation in the RCEP, New Delhi cannot afford to be indifferent to the phenomenal shifts East Asia is witnessing. With the expansion of economic and strategic interests, New Delhi is also enlarging the security perimeter from the limited South Asian neighborhood to an "extended neighborhood" that now includes all of East Asia, of which Southeast Asia constitutes the core region.

Among the three distinct dimensions of the Look East Policy, that is, robust institutional linkages with ASEAN, strong defense and security cooperation arrangements with most countries, and economic relations, the last is the weakest. India's economic relations with Southeast Asia are nowhere near comparable to those of the other great powers. Thus, in the Act East Policy that the Modi government has announced, the emphasis is likely to be on increasing connectivity and qualitatively improving economic links.

Invariably the China factor comes up quite prominently in any discussion on India's Look East Policy. The United States has been exhorting New Delhi for a more active role, and Japan is seeking to deepen its strategic partnership with India primarily with an eye on East Asian security. Indications suggest that India's competition with China will grow, but it will exercise caution in joining an anti-China bandwagon unless compelled to do. Obviously India cannot match China economically, but the Southeast Asians are conscious that India can contribute significantly to regional security, not merely as a counterweight to China but even in crafting a stable balance of power, to tackle myriad nontraditional security challenges, and to aid in regional prosperity as its economy progresses. Consequently, the expectations from India as a net security provider have also increased considerably, which is reflected in the huge progress in defense and strategic cooperation. Against the above backdrop, the U.S. "rebalancing strategy" and Japan's redoubling of efforts to deepen its engagement are welcome signs from an Indian perspective, for they are likely to help in creating a multipolar East Asian order in which India too will have a substantial role.

In the quest to find a rightful place in Southeast Asian affairs, India is mostly likely to intensify its interaction and involvement in the coming years. New Delhi has been successful in forging close links with ASEAN and other regional organizations, and now the emphasis is likely to shift to qualitatively upgrade bilateral relations with select countries, which is already visible in the cases of Indonesia, Vietnam, Singapore, and Myanmar. Strong India–Southeast Asia relations are mutually beneficial, but it is a different matter to what extent New Delhi will be forthcoming in stating its strategy and in taking tangible, proactive initiatives afresh.

NOTES

1 According to Kissinger, one of the three revolutions the world is witnessing is the "shift in the centre of gravity of international affairs from Atlantic to Pacific and Indian Oceans." Kissinger, "Three Revolutions."

2 Kohli, Sharma, and Sood, *Asia 2050*.

3 *Australia in the Asian Century*.

4 National Intelligence Council, *Global Trends 2030*, 16.

5 *Asia 2050: Realizing the Asian Century*.

6 The March 1947 Asian Relations Conference, January 1949 Conference on Indonesia, April 1955 Afro-Asian Relations Conference, etc.

7 Except Prime Minister Narasimha Rao's Singapore Lecture titled *India and the Asia-Pacific: Forging a New Relationship*, there were hardly any official documents, statements, or pronouncements on what the contours and objectives of the Look East Policy were. In fact, the Ministry of External Affairs began to use the phrase "Look East Policy" in its annual reports only beginning in 1995.

8 India and ASEAN have since entered into several other agreements on functional cooperation in such areas as counterterrorism, education, human resource development, science and technology, health and pharmaceuticals, space science, agriculture, new and renewable energy, information and communication technology, telecommunications, transport and infrastructure, and tourism and culture.

9 This explains why ASEAN, which was initially unenthusiastic in its support of the Japanese idea of a regional security platform to replicate the European example, came around as a major benefactor of the ASEAN Regional Forum (ARF) in 1993.

10 The Clinton administration even went so far as to suggest a partnership with China to compel India to reverse its ongoing nuclear decisions, leading to strong reactions from New Delhi.

11 "ASEAN Rebukes India, Pakistan for Nuclear Tests."

12 Verma, "Indian Navy's Recent Milestones."

13 The naval share of the defense budget does not include the Coast Guard, whose funding is provided by the Ministry of Finance. Data are computed from "Defence Services Estimates" (various years), Ministry of Defence, Government of India.

14 For details, see Naidu, "India and the Indian Ocean," 252.

15 *Freedom to Use the Seas*, 59. Also see Mukherjee, "Admiral A.K. Chatterjee Memorial Lecture."

16 Bhatt, "Navy Building High-Speed Data Network."

17 Madhumati, "Navy's First Satellite GSAT-7 Now in Space."

18 Pandit, "Navy Validates Massive Exercise."

19 The countries represented in the February 2014 session were Australia, Bangladesh, Cambodia, Indonesia, Kenya, Malaysia, Maldives, Mauritius, Myanmar, New Zealand, Philippines, Singapore, Sri Lanka, Tanzania, and Thailand.

20 Two incidents brought Indian naval capabilities into focus: the swift and dramatic rescue of Japanese freighter *Alondra Rainbow* from pirates in 1999 and the United States seeking Indian assistance to escort logistics ships in the Bay of Bengal for its counterterrorism war in Afghanistan after the 9/11 attacks.

21 "Navy Gears Up for Singapore Drill."

22 "Indian Navy Deploys Four Dornier Aircraft in Singapore."

23 "IAF Pilots Flying High in Singapore."

24 *Hindu*, January 18, 2005.

25 "Op Garuda."

26 *Times of India*, May 13, 1992.

27 Singapore was the only Southeast Asian country to participate in the first-ever mammoth five-nation joint exercises that India hosted in September 2007, called Malabar-07. The other participants were the United States, Japan, and Australia.

28 "Joint Patrolling of Andaman Sea."

29 Embassy of India in Bangkok, "List of Agreements," www.indianembassy.in.th.

30 *Hindu*, March 29, 2000.

31 Dikshit, "Vietnam's Plea."

32 Dikshit, "India Offers Vietnam Credit."

33 "India to Firm Up Military Ties with Myanmar."

34 *Hindustan Times*, April 19, 2007.

35 See Planning Commission, *Twelfth Five Year Plan (2012–2017)*.

36 Obashi, "Development and Current Status of Machinery Trade."

37 Hoang, "Foreign Direct Investment," 66.

38 For details, see *ASEAN-India Connectivity Report: India Country Study*.

39 Sachdeva, "Preparing the Northeast Economy."

40 *Hindu*, December 12, 2012.

41 Hong, "India and China."

42 Das, "India in the South China Sea."

43 "India-Vietnam Oil Exploration Deal Must Be Stopped."

44 Unnithan, "Indian Navy Prepared to Defend Its Interest."

45 Dikshit, "India Within Its Rights."

46 China is India's largest trading partner; their bilateral trade in 2012 was as large as India's trade with ten ASEAN countries.

47 See Naidu, "India, China and East Asia."

48 See Thayer, "Rise of China and India."

49 India has signed defense cooperation agreements with all the countries of Southeast Asia except Brunei.

50 "Joint Statement of Prime Minister Dr. Manmohan Singh and President Barack Obama."

51 U.S. State Department, "Remarks by Secretary of State Hillary Rodham Clinton."

52 Panetta, "Partners in the 21st Century."

53 "India a Fundamental Provider."

54 For instance, the 2010 *Quadrennial Defense Review* stated, "As its military capabilities grow, India will contribute to Asia as a net provider of security in the Indian Ocean and beyond."

55 Clinton, "America's Engagement in the Asia-Pacific."

56 A Quadrilateral, an informal consultative mechanism suggested by then PM Shinzo Abe comprising the United States, Japan, India, and Australia, with its origins in the December 2004 joint tsunami relief operation, was created in 2007

but failed to take off partly because of intense diplomatic pressure by China and partly because of the Labour Party coming to power, which abruptly withdrew, openly expressing its serious reservations. The withdrawal also halted high-profile naval exercises, two rounds of which were held in 2007. The Trilateral was revived as more of a formal mechanism consisting of senior officials in 2011. The naval exercises that had been limited to India and the United States have been extended to include Japan since early 2014. New Delhi appears to be reluctant to expand the Trilateral to Quadrilateral given its earlier experience.

57 The Indian Naval Chief announced, "Not that we expect to be in those waters very frequently, but when the requirement is there for situations where the country's interests are involved, for example ONGC Videsh, we will be required to go there and we are prepared for that." "Indian Navy Prepared to Defend." On the other hand, the Indian Foreign Minister made it clear that "there are fundamental issues there (South China Sea) that do not require India's intervention . . . (and the disputes) need to be resolved between the countries concerned." "India Sails into Troubled South China Sea."

58 "Joint Press Interaction of Indian External Affairs Minister and U.S. Secretary of State."

59 White House, "U.S.-India Joint Strategic Vision."

60 Baruah, "India, US Can Contribute to Better Balance of Power."

61 See, for instance, Yong and Mun, "Evolution of India–ASEAN Relations"; Brewster, "India's Defence Strategy."

62 According to former Admiral Nirmal Verma, by 2027 the Indian Navy will sport a brand-new look, with some 150 principal combat ships and another 500-odd aircraft. Nearly 50 new warships and submarines, which are on order, are likely to be launched in the next few years. *SP's Naval Forces Roundup.*

63 Pubby, "12th Defence Plan."

64 These are "Indian Maritime Doctrine" (2004) and a revised version in 2009, and the 2007 "Freedom to Use the Seas: India's Maritime Military Strategy."

65 See Vasudeva, "High-Tech Naval Base."

BIBLIOGRAPHY

ASEAN-India Connectivity Report: India Country Study. New Delhi: RIS, 2012.

"ASEAN Rebukes India, Pakistan for Nuclear Tests." *United News of India,* July 25, 1998. www.rediff.com.

Asia 2050: Realizing the Asian Century. Manila: Asian Development Bank, 2011.

Australia in the Asian Century. Canberra: Government of Australia, October 2012.

Ayoob, Mohammed. *India and Southeast Asia: Indian Perceptions and Policies.* London: Routledge, 1990.

Baruah, Amit. "India, US Can Contribute to Better Balance of Power in the Asian Region: Shyam Saran." *Hindu,* November 29, 2005. www.thehindu.com.

Bhatt, Arunkumar. "Navy Building High-Speed Data Network." *Hindu,* December 6, 2004. www.hindu.com.

Brewster, David. "India's Defence Strategy and India-ASEAN Relationship." *India Review* 12, no. 3 (2013): 151–64.

Clinton, Hillary Rodham. "America's Engagement in the Asia-Pacific." Speech, Kahala Hotel, Honolulu, HI, October 28, 2010. http://m.state.gov.

Das, Rup Narayan. "India in the South China Sea: Commercial Motives, Strategic Implications," *China Brief* 13, no. 20 (October 10, 2013): 14–17.

Dikshit, Sandeep. "India Offers Vietnam Credit for Military Ware." *Hindu*, July 28, 2013. www.thehindu.com.

———. "India Within Its Rights to Explore for Oil in South China Sea: Vietnam." *Hindu*, July 11, 2013. www.thehindu.com.

———. "Vietnam's Plea Puts South Block in a Predicament." *Hindu*, November 9, 2011. www.thehindu.com.

Freedom to Use the Seas: India's Maritime Military Doctrine. New Delhi: Ministry of Defence, 2009.

Hoang, Nguyen Huy. "Foreign Direct Investment and ASEAN-India Joint Ventures in Third Countries." In *ASEAN-India Strategic Partnership Perspectives from the ASEAN-India Network of Think-Tanks*, 64–69. New Delhi: Research and Information System for Developing Countries, 2013.

Hong, Zhao. "India and China: Rivals or Partners in Southeast Asia?" *Contemporary Southeast Asia* 29, no. 1 (2007): 121–42.

"IAF Pilots Flying High in Singapore." *Times of India*, December 13, 2006.

"India a Fundamental Provider of Security Growth in Asia-Pacific: White House." *Press Trust of India*, February 5, 2015. www.thehindu.com.

Indian Maritime Doctrine 2004. New Delhi: Ministry of Defence, 2004.

Indian Maritime Doctrine 2009. New Delhi: Ministry of Defence, 2009.

"Indian Navy Deploys Four Dornier Aircraft in Singapore." *Sify News*, June 14, 2010. http://sify.com.

"Indian Navy Prepared to Defend Its Interest in South China Sea Says Admiral D.K. Joshi." *Mail Today*, December 3, 2012. http://indiatoday.intoday.in.

"India Sails into Troubled South China Sea." *IPS*, February 4, 2013. www.ipsnews.net.

"India to Firm Up Military Ties with Myanmar." *Hindu*, June 24, 2007. www.thehindu.com.

"India-Vietnam Oil Exploration Deal Must Be Stopped." *People's Daily*, October 14, 2011. http://english.peopledaily.com.cn.

"Joint Patrolling of Andaman Sea." *Hindu*, September 11, 2006. www.thehindu.com.

"Joint Press Interaction of Indian External Affairs Minister and U.S. Secretary of State." July 19, 2011. http://mea.gov.in.

"Joint Statement of Prime Minister Dr. Manmohan Singh and President Barack Obama," November 8, 2010. http://meaindia.nic.in.

Kissinger, Henry A. "The Three Revolutions." *Washington Post*, April 27, 2008.

Kohli, Harinder S., Ashok Sharma, and Anil Sood, eds. *Asia 2050: Realizing the Asian Dream*. Manila: Asian Development Bank-Sage, 2011.

Madhumati, D. S. "Navy's First Satellite GSAT-7 Now in Space." *Hindu*, August 30, 2013. www.thehindu.com.

Mukherjee, Pranab. "Admiral A.K. Chatterjee Memorial Lecture." Kolkata, June 30, 2007. http://mea.gov.in.

Naidu, G. V. C. "India, China and East Asia." In *India and China in the Emerging Dynamics of East Asia*, ed. G. V. C. Naidu, Mumin Chen, and Raviprasad Narayan, 9–25. New Delhi: Springer, 2015.

———. "India and the Indian Ocean." In *India-ASEAN Defence Relations*, edited by Ajaya Kumar Das, 236–59. Singapore: Rajaratnam School of International Studies, 2013.

National Intelligence Council. *Global Trends 2030: Alternative Worlds*. Washington, DC: National Intelligence Council, December 2012.

"Navy Gears Up for Singapore Drill." *Telegraph*, April 3, 2010. www.telegraphindia.com.

Obashi, Ayako. "Development and Current Status of Machinery Trade between ASEAN and India." In *ASEAN-India Connectivity: The Comprehensive Asia Development Plan, Phase II*, ERIA Research Project Report no. 7, edited by Fukunari Kimura and So Umezaki, 57–94. Jakarta: ERIA, 2011.

"Op Garuda: IAF Tests Skills Against French, Singaporean Air Power." *Times of India*, June 15, 2010. http://timesofindia.indiatimes.com.

Pandit, Rajat. "Navy Validates Massive Exercise under Country's First Military Satellite's Gaze." *Times of India*, March 1, 2014. http://timesofindia.indiatimes.com.

Panetta, Leon E. "Partners in the 21st Century." Address, U.S. Defense Secretary to the Institute for Defence Studies and Analyses, New Delhi, June 6, 2012.

Planning Commission. *Twelfth Five Year Plan (2012–2017): Volume 1*. New Delhi: Planning Commission, Government of India, 2012.

Pubby, Manu. "12th Defence Plan Focus on Navy's 'Expeditionary' Ops." *Indian Express*, May 4, 2012. www.indianexpress.com.

Quadrennial Defense Review. Washington, DC: U.S. Department of Defense, February 2010.

Rao, Narasimha. *India and the Asia-Pacific: Forging a New Relationship*. Singapore Lecture. Singapore: Institute of Southeast Asian Studies, 1994.

Sachdeva, Gulshan. "Preparing the Northeast Economy for the ASEAN Linkage." In *India-ASEAN Economic Integration*, edited by R. Lianzela, S. Ratna, and Vanlal Chhawna, 147–62. New Delhi: Macmillan, 2012.

SP's Naval Forces Roundup 7, no. 1 (February–March 2012).

Thayer, Carlyle. "Rise of China and India: Challenging or Reinforcing Southeast Asia's Autonomy." In *Strategic Asia 2011–12: Asia Responds to Its Rising Powers China and India*, edited by Ashley Tellis, Travis Tanner, and Jessica Keough, 313–46. Seattle: National Bureau of Research, 2011.

Unnithan, Sandeep. "Indian Navy Prepared to Defend Its Interest in South China Sea, Says Admiral D.K. Joshi." *Mail Today* (New Delhi), December 3, 2012. http://india-today.intoday.in.

U.S. State Department. "Remarks by Secretary of State Hillary Rodham Clinton, India and the United States: A Vision for the 21st Century" (Chennai, July 20, 2011). www.state.gov.

Vasudeva, P. K. "High-Tech Naval Base to Counter Chinese Expanding Navy." *Indian Defence Review,* April 3, 2013.

Verma, Nirmal. "Indian Navy's Recent Milestones." Statement at farewell press conference, August 7, 2012. www.indiastrategic.in.

White House. "U.S.-India Joint Strategic Vision for the Asia-Pacific and Indian Ocean Region." January 25, 2015. www.whitehouse.gov.

Yong, Tan Tai, and See Chak Mun. "The Evolution of India–ASEAN Relations." *India Review* 8, no. 1 (January–March 2009): 20–42.

11

China's Economic Approach to ASEAN

CHEN SHAOFENG

Introduction

The rise of China has become a historical event capturing the attention of academia and politicians across the world. Thanks to China's rise, "the traditional underpinnings of international relations in Asia are undergoing profound change."[1] As China's neighbors, the Southeast Asian countries are in a position to benefit from the dragon's rise. The growing economic ties between China and ASEAN have reinforced this trend.

The signing of the Framework Agreement on Comprehensive Economic Cooperation (FACEC) between China and ASEAN in November 2002 marked a watershed in bilateral economic relations. This agreement set up the goal of establishing the China-ASEAN Free Trade Agreement (CAFTA). Prior to the full implementation of CAFTA, both sides signed the Trade in Goods Agreement, Trade in Service Agreement, and Investment Agreement under FACEC in November 2004, January 2007, and August 2009, respectively.

The idea of forming a CAFTA was first proposed by former Chinese Premier Zhu Rongji at the ASEAN Plus Three Summit in November 2000. One year later, at the ASEAN-China Summit in November 2001, Premier Zhu formally proposed building a CAFTA within ten years. To that end, China took on its own initiative to offer market openness in some key sectors to ASEAN countries five years before they reciprocated, and agreed to provide preferential treatment to Cambodia, Laos, and Myanmar.

China towers over each individual ASEAN member, and all of them combined. Among the combined CAFTA countries, ASEAN together constitutes only 29 percent of the population, 32 percent of the GDP, and 46 percent of the trade volume. Moreover, according to scholars' estimates, ASEAN could also gain more than China in the early 2000s. It is important to ask, what motivated China to build an FTA with its Southeast Asian neighbors?

Beginning on January 1, 2010, CAFTA came into effect between China and ASEAN-6 (Brunei Darussalam, Indonesia, Malaysia, the Philippines, Singapore, and Thailand). These agreements have greatly facilitated bilateral economic exchanges. Since 2009, China has replaced the United States as the largest trading partner of ASEAN. Foreign direct investment (FDI) flows and the number of tourists between China and ASEAN have also skyrocketed in the past years. Against the backdrop of a global financial crisis and the United States' proactive pivot to Asia (part of the strategy is to push forward the Trans-Pacific Partnership [TPP] in the economic sphere), will CAFTA maintain its momentum? What challenges is CAFTA confronting?

I would argue that China concluded CAFTA primarily out of political considerations, notwithstanding a modest economic benefit from the deal, but the final result is mainly driven by market forces, represented by regional production networks in East Asia, with China at the hub. Looking toward the future, bilateral economic relations will be further enhanced with more trade- and investment-facilitating measures enacted. Despite that, some challenges remain. Prominent among them is the mismatch between economic ties and strategic mistrust. How to cope with such a discrepancy remains a daunting challenge for China.

China's Motivations

China was primarily out of political options to deepen regional integration, and for that reason Beijing was willing to make economic concessions in the process of concluding and implementing CAFTA. This policy intends to ameliorate China's neighboring environment through deepening economic ties and cultural diplomacy. By integrating itself into regional development, China has become a key economic partner and development assistance provider in Southeast Asia.

China has great stakes in boosting regionalization in East Asia. For a long time, Beijing dealt with its foreign relations with neighboring countries predominantly through bilateral channels, rather than from a "region" perspective.[2] In other words, it rarely put bilateral relationships into its regional strategy and had no such a strategy either. Implementation of the North American Free Trade Agreement (NAFTA) in 1994 and the European Union prompted China to be more committed to regional cooperation. In Beijing's view, big powers tried to enhance their future competitiveness in the world by engaging in regional integration in each of their regions. Without being left behind in this wave, China understandably prioritized East Asia for its regional integration efforts.

East Asia matters for China not only because it is the anchor for the country's economic development, but also because it is the major source of security threats to Beijing.[3] Economically, while bordering on China's economic powerhouse, East Asia, including its expansive seas, houses the major routes through which China transacts trades goods and natural resources with the outside world. Strategically, China may face security threats in its surroundings, but the most vital one may come from the Pacific. Hence, East Asia is most relevant to the dragon's survival and development.

China had expected to push forward East Asian integration based on 10+3 cooperation, or ASEAN Plus Three, but it had to relinquish this goal due to the challenges ahead. In Beijing's view, 10+6 would involve countries not belonging to East Asia. Compared with 10+1 or an FTA among China, Japan, and South Korea, deepening 10+3 cooperation could generate more economic benefits and even contribute to defusing tensions in East Asia. Nonetheless, Japan and ASEAN, two key members of 10+3, had different preferences for the platform for regional integration. Both expected that the United States could have a larger presence in this process so as to counterbalance a rising China. Japan was also concerned that China would take the lead in the integration process.[4] Moreover, the United States was quite wary of an East Asian block excluding its involvement. In view of the bleak prospect of 10+3, China had to turn to another regional arrangement. There were two options for China: building an FTA with Japan and South Korea, its Northeast Asian neighbors, or forming an FTA with Southeast Asian countries.

Choosing ASEAN rather than its Northeast Asian neighbors as partners indicates that China kick-started its first FTA at the cost of greater economic gains. When deciding its regional integration arrangement (RIA) partners, China chose Southeast Asian countries, rather than Japan and South Korea, although an FTA with the latter would be more economically beneficial to China. According to Maurice Schiff and L. Alan Winters, when defining a country's ideal partners for RIA, the country should embrace the comparative advantage principle as it directly determines the size of the economic welfare brought about by regional integration, as well as the convergence or divergence of the RIA members' incomes.[5] Apparently Japan and South Korea were more economically complementary with China than most of its Southeast Asian neighbors. In contrast, at a similar development stage, China and ASEAN countries in general had a similar industrial structure with a predominance of labor-intensive industry. As shown in table 11.1, the industrial structure similarity between China and ASEAN was nearly 100 percent, indicating that they were competing not only for export markets, but also for foreign investments. Hence, the economic welfare brought about by regional integration with Japan and South Korea would be much larger than integration with ASEAN, including greater trade creation, more investment, faster economic growth, and so on. Despite this, Beijing pressed on with ASEAN rather than its Northeast Asian neighbors.

TABLE 11.1. Industrial structure similarity between China and ASEAN (1996–2004, percentages)

Indonesia	Brunei	Thailand	Vietnam	Malaysia	Philippines	Cambodia	Singapore	Laos	Myanmar	ASEAN
0.98	0.98	0.97	0.97	0.94	0.92	0.89	0.81	0.74	0.73	0.99

Source: Yinghong Su, "Woguo yu Dongmeng guojia de chanye fengong yu xiezuo" [Industrial division and cooperation between China ASEAN states], *Tequ Jingji* [Special zone economy], no. 11 (2007).

As a matter of fact, before signing the agreement, Chinese analysts expected the agreement to favor the ASEAN states, and many Chinese scholars expressed reservations about such a proposal. For instance, it was estimated that CAFTA would boost ASEAN's GDP by 0.9 percent and China's by 0.3 percent.[6] Chinese scholars also underscored the difficulty in building CAFTA not only because of the vast economic differences among the member states, but also because of the absence of what they call a "nucleus," like the Germany-France axis in the EU or the central role of the United States in NAFTA. China cannot and should not play the leading role in view of its low level of GDP and the possible "China threat" thesis.[7]

Why did the Chinese government proceed with an ASEAN FTA despite the aforementioned factors? I argue that political considerations were foremost. One of the considerations was to alleviate the strategic pressure China was facing at that time.[8] The rise of China has proceeded in tandem with the "China threat" thesis in some countries. In order to create a peaceful and stable environment, in the late 1990s China worked out a New Security Concept, trying to appease other countries that China's rise will not pose a threat to them. The concept articulates that countries in the post–Cold War period can enhance their mutual security through diplomatic and economic interactions, and that countries should relinquish the Cold War mentality of competing and antagonistic blocks. At the core of this concept are mutual trust, mutual benefit, quality, and coordination. CAFTA could be used as a battlefield for the application of the New Security Concept. By building such an FTA block, the Chinese government anticipated that ceding more economic interests to its Southeast Asian neighbors would help stabilize its political relationship with ASEAN countries and even win over their hearts. Joshua Kurlantzick called the Chinese modus operandi a "charm offensive."[9]

The second consideration was to diffuse ASEAN's worries about its entry into the WTO.[10] In the mid-1990s, many ASEAN countries held misgivings about China's economic rise, and China's embrace of the WTO further entertained their apprehension, as illustrated by two prevalent views in East Asia. One view contended that the rise of the Chinese economy would form a "black hole," which would "engulf" other homogeneous Asian economies including South Korea and Southeast Asian countries.[11] In particular, they worried that China's expanding foreign trade resulting from its entry would be at the cost of ASEAN economies thanks to their similar industrial structures. The other view was of the belief that both China and the ASEAN countries were competing for FDI. Such advantages as low costs, fewer trade barriers, and vast market potentials brought about by China's entry into the WTO would further take substantial FDI from ASEAN markets.[12] Even Singapore, the most developed economy in Southeast Asia, was alarmed. Lee Hsien Loong, then the Deputy Prime Minister of Singapore, declared, "Southeast Asian countries are under intense competitive pressure, as their former activities, especially labor-intensive manufacturing, migrate to China. One indicator of this massive shift is the fact that Southeast Asia used to attract twice as much foreign direct investment as Northeast Asia, but the ratio is [now] reversed."[13]

In order to alleviate their misgivings, China offered to build an FTA block with Southeast Asia despite the lack of a solid economic foundation for an FTA between them. CAFTA could weave new bonds gluing China and ASEAN countries more tightly, and the deepening economic integration through FTA could convince Southeast Asian countries that the rise of China would provide more opportunities for them, therefore reinforcing mutual trust and smashing the "China threat." Hence, after China joined the WTO in 2001, it soon started the FTA negotiation process with ASEAN. To materialize its goal of pursuing good neighborly relations, friendship, and cooperation with ASEAN countries, China took a series of moves in the following years, including signing the Declaration on the Conduct of Parties in the South China Sea, becoming the first ASEAN dialogue partner to join the Treaty of Amity and Cooperation, and establishing the Strategic Partnership for Peace and Prosperity with ASEAN.

Another way to comprehend China's motives is through the lobbying efforts by some provinces, mainly Guangxi, Yunnan, Chongqing, and Sichuan. Since the Chinese economy is export-oriented, its exports mainly originate from the coastal provinces. With higher logistic costs, the interior regions are unable to emulate their coastal counterparts in exporting goods to China's major trade partners like the EU, the United States, and Japan. They thus turned their attention to the neighboring ASEAN countries. It is manifest that CAFTA will not only bring down tariffs, but also greatly diminish logistics costs, thus boosting their exports. It is the same logic that drove Guangxi and

Yunnan to lobby the central government for creating a pilot area for cross-border trade settlements in RMB.[14]

Moreover, building an FTA with ASEAN, as mentioned previously, was also a result of China's learning efforts and response to challenges posed by competitive regionalisms in the world economy, particularly competition from the EU and NAFTA. An FTA with ASEAN would deepen the latter's economic dependence on China and change the power structure and mode of cooperation in East Asia, thus furnishing China with preemptive leverage in regional integration. Therefore, China was keen to play a leading role in East Asian regional cooperation.[15]

China's political motivations have been reflected in its unilateral concessions in the process of creating CAFTA. Its concessions can be found in the two-track system and an "early harvest" program. The two-track system allowed new ASEAN members (Cambodia, Laos, Myanmar, and Vietnam [CLMV]) five more years to join the FTA. CAFTA also incorporated a special and differential treatment, wherein China accorded the three non-WTO ASEAN members (Vietnam, Laos, and Cambodia) most-favored-nation status. In fact, given the complexity and differences among ASEAN member states, China also accepted a multitiered phasing in of the mercantile agreement and different treatment for "sensitive" and "highly sensitive" products and "general exceptions."[16] Moreover, China unilaterally granted CLMV with the "early harvest" program, which covers tariff cuts on six hundred agricultural products, including live animals, meat, fish, dairy produce, other animal products, live trees, vegetables, fruits, and nuts. In 2004, the year the "early harvest" began, China's trade deficits with ASEAN soon reached US$20.08 billion.[17]

CAFTA: Trade and Investment Performance

CAFTA was designed primarily out of political considerations, but as it has gone into effect, its performance and effectiveness will decisively be tested by market forces. Indeed, after years of implementation, FACEC has greatly enhanced the economic ties between China and ASEAN. After CAFTA was implemented on January 1, 2010, bilateral economic relations gained new momentum. Since then, import duties on more than seven thousand products classified by China and the ASEAN-6 (Brunei, Indonesia, Malaysia, the Philippines, Singapore, and Thailand) that were in the Normal Track have been removed, and the remaining 150 tariff lines (NT2) were eliminated by 2012. For CLMV, they are allowed to fully implement the ASEAN-China Free Trade Agreement (ACFTA) on January 1, 2015, with flexibility on 250 tariff lines under NT2 to be eliminated in 2018. China's offer of an "early harvest program" in 2004 favored CLMV and has greatly promoted trade in agriculture and marine products. According to the Agreement on Trade in Services between China and ASEAN signed in January 2007, the first package of commitments and the second package of commitments were implemented beginning in July 2007 and January 2012, respectively.

In terms of goods, trade between China and ASEAN saw a ninefold jump from US$39.5 billion in 2000 to US$480.4 billion in 2014,[18] with an annual growth rate of over 20 percent. The two sides tried to reach the bilateral trade target of US$500 billion by 2015 and came close, reaching $472 billion in 2015. As shown in figure 11.1, the proportion of bilateral trade in China's foreign trade keeps rising, growing from 1.08 percent in 2000 to 11.16 percent in 2014. During the same period, the ratio of exports to ASEAN to China's total exports rose from 6.96 percent to 11.61 percent, while the ratio of imports from ASEAN to China's total imports showed only a small increase, from 9.85 percent to 10.63 percent.[19] Since 2009 China has become ASEAN's largest trading partner, while ASEAN has replaced Japan to become China's third largest one. During the period of 2000 to 2011, China registered a trade deficit with ASEAN, and the deficit reached US$22.8 billion in 2011. In 2012, for the first time China gained a trade surplus of US$8.45 billion in its trade with ASEAN, and this trade surplus further rose to US$45 billion and US$64 billion in 2013 and 2014, respectively. But ASEAN member states have shown different performances in their trade with China. Malaysia, Singapore, and Thailand (in that order) were China's three largest trading partners in terms of total foreign trade in goods in 2013 (in 2014 they were Malaysia, Vietnam, and Singapore), but in terms of growth rate of foreign trade with China in 2013, Laos, Myanmar, and Vietnam were the top three. In 2011 Vietnam, Singapore, Myanmar, Cambodia, and Brunei (in that order) saw trade deficits with China, whereas the rest had trade surpluses, with Malaysia, Thailand, the Philippines, and Indonesia being the four largest. In 2013, except for Malaysia and Thailand, the other ASEAN member states had trade deficits with China, with Vietnam, Singapore, and Indonesia being the top three. China's three largest export markets in Southeast Asia in 2012 included Singapore, Malaysia, and Indonesia (in 2013 they were Vietnam, Malaysia, and Singapore), whereas the top three import markets were Malaysia, Thailand, and Indonesia (Malaysia, Thailand, and Indonesia).

In terms of investment, in August 2008 both sides signed the China-ASEAN Investment Agreement, which began to be implemented on January 1, 2010. This agreement aims to promote investment flows and to establish a free, convenient, transparent, and competitive investment regime in China

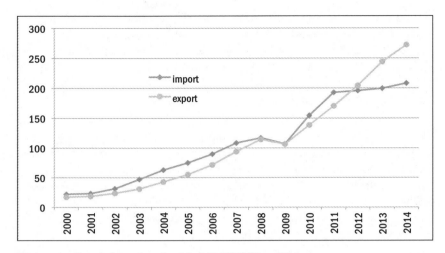

Figure 11.1. China's foreign trade with ASEAN (billion US$).

and ASEAN. Apparently, the institutionalized China-ASEAN integration process not only has fueled bilateral trade, but also led to the jump in China's FDI to ASEAN. FDI flows between them keep expanding. By the first half of 2012, accumulated two-way FDI between China and ASEAN came close to US$93 billion.[20] As shown in figure 11.2, China's actual use of FDI from ASEAN countries rose from US$2.8 to 8.35 billion from 2000 to 2013. Among ASEAN countries, Singapore remains the primary investor in China. In 2013, Singapore, Thailand, and Malaysia had the three largest FDI outflows to China, and Singapore alone accounted for 86.6 percent of ASEAN's FDI outflows to China. Striking are the annual fluctuations of ASEAN outward FDI into China. For instance, Brunei used to be very active in venturing in the Chinese market. FDI from Brunei was merely US$100,000 in 2001, but since then Brunei has boosted its investments, and this figure peaked at US$348 million in 2009, when many countries were severely hit by the global financial crisis. Then investments from Brunei plummeted to US$133.2 million in 2013. Similarly, FDI contributed from Indonesia shrank very rapidly. From 2000 to 2011, its investment in China diminished from US$146.9 to 46 million, and then rebounded to US$126 million in 2013.

In terms of FDI inflows to ASEAN from China, ASEAN has become an important FDI destination for China's overseas investment. It is also China's important foreign project-contracting market and labor services export market. According to ASEAN statistics, in 2013 FDI flows from China to ASEAN remained much lower than those to the EU and Japan, but they have grown

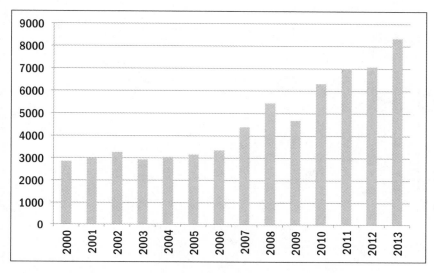

Figure 11.2. Actual utilized FDI inflows to China from ASEAN-10 (million US$).
Sources: 2000–2013 data: National Statistical Bureau of China; 2014 data: www.cafta.
org.cn/show.php?contentid=74049.

very fast and for the first time overtook flows to the United States. As indicated in table 11.2, this figure increased significantly from US$1.85 billion in 2009 to US$8.6 billion in 2013. With US$21.88 billion, China's FDI accounted for 6.55 percent in total FDI inflows to ASEAN from 2011 to 2013, while the EU and Japan had shares as high as 22.4 percent and 16.9 percent, respectively, indicating there remains a large gap for China to close.

In the financial sector, bilateral financial cooperation has made strides in recent years. Having been launched on March 24, 2010, ASEAN+3 has expanded the size of the Chiang Mai Initiative Multilateralization (CMIM) agreement to US$240 billion from the original US$120 billion. As a multilateral currency swap arrangement among ASEAN+3, the CMIM aims to address balance-of-payments and short-term liquidity difficulties in the region and to supplement the existing international financial arrangements. China has so far signed four local currency swap agreements with ASEAN counterparts that total 1.4 trillion yuan (US$228 billion), while yuan-denominated cross-border settlements between China and ASEAN reached 1.12 trillion yuan (US$183.1 billion) by June 2013.[21] Thus far Malaysia, Thailand, Indonesia, the Philippines, and Cambodia have brought Chinese yuan into their foreign currency reserve systems as a way to improve the local financial structure and reduce financial risk. Singapore has become one of the impor-

TABLE 11.2. Top ten sources of foreign direct investment inflows in ASEAN

Country/region	Value (in US$ million)					Share to total inflows (percentage)				
	2009	2010	2011	2012	2013	2011–13	2011	2012	2013	2011–13
European Union	8,063.1	17,012.1	29,693.3	18,084.9	26,979.6	74,757.8	30.4	15.8	22.0	22.4
Japan	3,789.9	10,756.4	9,709.0	23,777.1	22,904.4	56,390.5	10.0	20.8	18.7	16.9
ASEAN	6,300.2	14,322.7	15,228.4	20,657.6	21,321.5	57,207.6	15.6	18.1	17.4	17.1
China	1,852.6	2,784.6	7,857.7	5,376.8	8,643.5	21,878.0	8.1	4.7	7.1	6.5
Hong Kong	5,667.4	344.0	4,273.8	5,029.9	4,517.3	13,821.0	4.4	4.4	3.7	4.1
United States	5,704.3	12,771.6	9,129.8	11,079.5	3,757.5	23,966.9	9.4	9.7	3.1	7.2
Republic of Korea	1,794.0	3,764.2	1,742.1	1,708.4	3,516.2	6,966.7	1.8	1.5	2.9	2.1
Australia	NA	NA	1,530.2	1,831.0	2,002.3	5,363.5	1.6	1.6	1.6	1.6
Taiwan, Province of China	1,130.5	1,088.8	2,317.0	2,242.3	1,321.7	5,880.9	2.4	2.0	1.1	1.8
India	NA	NA	(2,230.5)	2,233.4	1,317.5	1,320.4	(2.3)	2.0	1.1	0.4
Total top ten sources			79,250.8	92,021.0	96,281.6	267,553.4	81.3	80.5	78.7	80.1
Others	11,191.8	23,678.8	18,287.3	22,263.1	26,095.0	66,645.3	18.7	19.5	21.3	19.9
Total FDI inflow to ASEAN	46,896.7	98,872.8	97,538.1	114,284.0	122,376.5	334,198.7	100	100	100	100

Source: ASEAN Secretariat, "Foreign Direct Investment Statistics," www.asean.org. (Data here have been updated.)

tant offshore RMB centers. Since October 2013, China and Singapore have introduced direct trading between their currencies. The Bank of China and the Industrial and Commercial Bank of China are allowed to conduct yuan-clearing services in Singapore. Since October 2013, China has extended the Renminbi Qualified Foreign Institutional Investor (RQFII) program to Singapore, with an aggregate quota of 50 billion yuan (US$8.2 billion). The RQFII program allows qualified Singapore-based institutional investors to channel offshore RMB from Singapore into China's securities markets, and the RQFII license holders to use the RQFII quota to issue RMB investment products to investors in Singapore.[22] Chinese companies are also able to be listed on the Singaporean stock market.

In the area of infrastructure construction, China and ASEAN have worked out a Strategic Plan for China-ASEAN Transport Cooperation, aiming to pave the way for local poverty reduction, explore more substantive cooperation, and accelerate regional integration in East Asia. The sides proposed two corridors, rail and road, from Nanning to Singapore. Currently both sides have made some progress in China-ASEAN connectivity, covering projects like the Kunming-Bangkok Highway, the Trans-Asian Railway, and more flight linkages. They have also begun to carry out maritime connectivity cooperation. However, Vietnam is hesitant about the two corridors as it is concerned that far more goods will be coming down the corridors from China than going up from Vietnam, and much of Vietnam's exports would continue to be raw materials and resources. Nonetheless, as the performance of the free trade zone will be affected by infrastructure, it is expected that China may accelerate infrastructure projects covering not only roads, rails, water transportation, and airlines, but also telecommunications and energy. In order to buttress the development of more than fifty infrastructure projects in ASEAN countries, in 2009 China set up a US$10 billion China-ASEAN Fund on Investment Cooperation and a US$15 billion credit, including US$1.7 billion in preferential loans, which was subsequently increased to US$6.7 billion. To support the implementation of the Master Plan on ASEAN Connectivity formulated at the Seventeenth ASEAN Summit in October 2010, China proposed to provide an additional US$10 billion credit including US$4 billion in preferential loans and US$6 billion in commercial loans.[23]

To provide financial support to enterprises in China and ASEAN so as to promote their economic cooperation in this region, both sides have set up a China-ASEAN Fund on Investment Cooperation with an amount of US$10 billion. The fund requires that the total amount for each investment project range between US$50 million and US$150 million and that it mainly be used for infrastructure construction, including transportation projects, power plants and power distribution, renewable energy, utilities, telecommunications, pipelines and storage, and social infrastructure. During Chinese President Xi Jinping's state visit to Indonesia, he proposed to establish an Asian Infrastructure Investment Bank (AIIB) to promote interconnectivity and economic integration in the region.[24] The proposed bank was to be open to other Asian countries and seek to cooperate with other sources of funds like the Asian Development Bank (ADB), rather than fighting with them.[25] According to estimates from the ADB, Asia would need "about $8 trillion in national infrastructure and $290 billion in regional infrastructure between 2010 and 2020 to sustain its growth trajectory,"[26] but ASEAN could raise only a few hundred million dollars for the Master Plan for ASEAN Connectivity by end of 2012.[27] Given such a tremendous gap, ASEAN countries in general welcomed such a proposal. Both Indonesia and Brunei welcomed China's proposal, which would prioritize ASEAN projects.[28] On October 24, 2014, twenty-one Asian nations signed an agreement to establish the AIIB. Indonesia was absent from the inauguration ceremony, but it later signed a memorandum of understanding to join.[29] With US$50 billion in capital at the start, the AIIB can hardly meet what is needed but provides a helpful boost. Moreover, unlike both ADB and the World Bank, whose loans cover a wide range of issues such as environmental protection and gender equality, the AIIB focuses solely on infrastructure.

The BRICS Development Bank, proposed to be established at the BRICS Summit in Durban, South Africa, on March 27, 2013, could be an additional and supplemental financing source for infrastructure construction in Southeast Asia in the long run. The proposed bank aims to finance long-term infrastructure projects first and foremost within the member states, and then expand to other low-income countries. Apparently its setup reflects the dissatisfaction of emerging economies with the World Bank and International Monetary Fund, dominated by developed countries, as well as their will to build a more just world order. Thus far, beyond a consensus of US$50 billion in start-up capital that will be distributed equally among the five member states, many key issues remain to be decided, such as the payment of the capital and the structure, location, and management of the bank. Due to a lack of detailed information, it is hard to judge its impact, but the BRICS Bank may become a serious competitor for the World Bank if it can achieve the two goals: (1) respond to developing countries' needs as opposed to the priorities of the lending institution and (2) lend to key areas where the private sector is indifferent, such as small and medium-sized enterprises, infrastructure, and agriculture.[30] The latest report revealed that the BRICS Development Bank (later referred to as the New Development Bank) was to start lending in 2016, and the bank will be open to any other country as well.[31] Expansion of membership is planned in 2017 and 2018.

China and ASEAN also decided to boost their cooperation in other areas. At the 2013 China-ASEAN Expo, the two parties signed three economic agreements covering ports, technology transfer, and an entrepreneur association. In November 2011, they also set up a China-ASEAN Maritime Cooperation Fund, for which China provided 3 billion yuan (US$490 million). The fund aims to enhance bilateral maritime connectivity and cooperation in light of the guidelines on conduct in the South China Sea.[32] Overall, with the implementation of CAFTA, bilateral economic interdependence has been greatly enhanced.

Challenges and Future Prospects

Looking forward, it is projected that economic ties between China and ASEAN will be further boosted with more trade and investment facilitating measures and intraregional connectivity being in place. Against the backdrop that markets in the developed world have more uncertainty thanks to the economic recession and trade frictions, ASEAN is more important for Chinese exports while ASEAN's rise would hardly be possible without an economically fast-growing China. To a great measure, the Chinese market has become a safety valve for its Southeast Asian countries. For instance, according to China's Ministry of Commerce, Sino-ASEAN trade totaled US$443.61 billion in 2013, an increase of 10.9 percent. In contrast, Sino-U.S. trade and Sino-EU trade rose 7.5 percent and 2.1 percent, respectively, during the same period.[33] Two-way FDI also has risen sharply in recent years. By the end of 2014, China's outbound FDI in ASEAN nations totaled more than US$40 billion, and FDI outflows from ASEAN into China exceeded US$90 billion. By contrast, in 2011 these two figures were merely US$7 billion and US$6.03 billion, respectively.[34]

Moreover, Southeast Asian countries will gain more in the medium to long run based on the following three reasons. First, thanks to big power tussles in Southeast Asian, particularly between China and Japan, ASEAN has become a "seller's market" where every big power endeavors to woo the member states. Second, and related to the first point, in his first state visit to Southeast Asia, Chinese President Xi Jinping vowed "to ensure that China and ASEAN are good neighbors, friends and partners, and jointly build a more closely-knit China-ASEAN community of common destiny."[35] During his keynote speech at the tenth anniversary of the China-ASEAN strategic partnership and the Tenth China-ASEAN Expo held in Nanning from September 3 to 6,

2013, Chinese Premier Li Keqiang described the past ten years as a "golden decade" for China-ASEAN cooperation, and declared that China is devoted to creating a "diamond decade" in the future. In order to promote bilateral economic ties, he proposed to build an "upgraded-version" of CAFTA and expand cooperation of "a greater scope and higher quality." Under the new version of CAFTA, bilateral trade is projected to hit US$1 trillion by 2020 from US$400 billion in 2012, and two-way investment is planned to grow to US$150 billion by 2020. To that end, he suggested the two sides should expand free trade agreements to cover more goods, further lower taxes, reduce nontax barriers, launch a new round of talks over services, and create a more convenient platform for bilateral trade and investment. Politically, in order to embrace a "diamond decade" to come, China will continue prioritizing ASEAN member countries in its peripheral diplomacy, strengthening its strategic partnership with ASEAN and cooperating with ASEAN to build peace in the region, including in the South China Sea. Financially, China offered to implement bilateral and regional local currency swap agreements to bolster financial and economic stability in the region. It will also expand best practices in cross-border yuan settlements, creating more commercial opportunities for financial institutions on both sides. Moreover, China will offer more assistance in developing infrastructure in this region.[36]

On the other hand, primarily due to appreciation of the yuan and increases in labor costs in China, ASEAN countries are in a more competitive position in attracting foreign investments and industrial migration. First, rising wages in China have been pushing Chinese enterprises, except for than foreign invested enterprises, to transfer their factories to Southeast Asia. Second, values of the Chinese yuan have a notable effect on China's outward FDI into Southeast Asian states. Early studies show that depreciation of the host currency relative to the home country would encourage more FDI inflows, and vice versa.[37] Indeed, studies by some Chinese scholars have indicated that appreciation of the Chinese yuan would boost China's FDI in general,[38] an argument that holds in the case of Chinese outward FDI to ASEAN.[39] Of course, other than the exchange rate, there are other major factors affecting Chinese companies' FDI to ASEAN, such as market size, resource endowment, political risks, bilateral trade, unemployment, and so forth.[40] Third, as an Investment Agreement has been incorporated into CAFTA, CAFTA has also facilitated China's FDI to ASEAN. More specifically, the primary motives of Chinese firms investing in Southeast Asian countries encompass the market, resource and technology seeking, as well as trade barrier aversion.[41] Singapore, Myanmar, Thailand, and Cambodia were major recipients of Chinese FDI in 2010.[42] In the meantime, it should be noted that the scale of

China's outbound FDI to ASEAN remains small. With a stock investment of US$30 billion by June 30, 2013, it merely accounted for 5.1 percent in China's total outward FDI.[43] Fourth, the expansion of regional production networks in East Asia with China at the hub means that Southeast Asia can gain more benefits from the rise of China. China's participation in production networks has deepened production fragmentation in East Asia, and production networks centered on China have contributed significantly to the growth in East Asia.[44] Moreover, the pressure from the U.S.-led West to rebalance the world economy has forced China to make efforts to diversify its export market. To that end, CAFTA plays a more important role for China.

Doubts may arise regarding whether the trend is more in favor of ASEAN when it comes to the changed trade surplus position of China vis-à-vis ASEAN. The Chinese trade surplus with ASEAN started to emerge later in 2012. Before that, China for a long time had trade deficits, which on average accounted for 15 percent of bilateral trade and in 2003 and 2004 even hit 21 percent and 19 percent, respectively. ASEAN's imports from China have grown in recent years largely because of trade diversion, namely, China has replaced Japan to be its top importing source. Moreover, China's trade surplus with ASEAN accounted for only 2 percent in bilateral annual trade, which is still within the range of trade balance.[45]

However, challenges remain ahead. Despite growing economic ties and an irreversible interdependence, distrust and uneasiness toward a rising China have mounted rather than decreased. Countries in Southeast Asia have endeavored to hedge against China by actively involving big powers into this region. I summarize the challenges into four categories.

The first challenge pertains to the South China Sea dispute. The dispute, if not appropriately handled, may not only hold back Southeast Asian countries from furthering economic ties with China, but may damage the peaceful relations in the region. The tension between China and some Southeast Asian states over conflicting claims in the South China Sea has loomed large in recent years. The "Declaration on the Conduct of Parties in the South China Sea," signed in 2002, was a watershed event in regional confidence building, but there has been little further progress. With the rise of China, some claimant countries like the Philippines and Vietnam have become anxious as they feel the resolution to the maritime dispute is China's responsibility. Hence, they are keen to internationalize the dispute. While referring to their tussles with China as a dispute between China and ASEAN, they also tried to incorporate South China Sea into the scope of ASEAN defense cooperation.[46] In particular, they took advantage of Washington's rebalancing strategy, trying to involve the U.S. military presence in the region.

On the Chinese side, Beijing has strongly rebutted such an assertion that the maritime dispute is between China and the ASEAN and has underscored that this dispute "should not, and will not undermine the overall relationship."[47] But Beijing is very nervous about the U.S. pivot to Asia and has tended to regard it as a hedging strategy against China. In its 2013 Defense White Paper, the Chinese government observed, "The Asia-Pacific region has become an increasingly significant stage for world economic development and strategic interaction between major powers. The US is adjusting its Asia-Pacific security strategy, and the regional landscape is undergoing profound changes." In response to this changing political and strategic context, China needs to review and redefine its regional strategy by enhancing and nurturing regional dialogue and consultation mechanisms and institutions.

ASEAN maintains a long-standing neutral position in this dispute, but the pending tensions over the South China Sea are set to put ASEAN in a tricky position and even tear it apart. A recent example occurred in the meeting of ASEAN foreign ministers during Cambodia's time in the ASEAN chair. For the first time in ASEAN's history, the foreign ministers were unable to agree on a joint statement due to discord over the South China Sea issue. As a matter of fact, ASEAN is more proactive in playing a central role in pushing for settlement of the dispute. In recent years, the South China Sea dispute has been entangled with and stolen the spotlight from almost every meeting sponsored by ASEAN.[48] ASEAN needs to play the balancing act, serving as a fulcrum to balance all power plays in the region, but doing so is very challenging.[49] At critical junctures, it is likely that escalating tensions over the South China Sea may become a flash point that will split ASEAN. The dispute over the South China Sea is bound to have some adverse impact on China-ASEAN economic ties. On one hand, the likelihood that this tension may escalate into interstate confrontation may scare off investors. On the other hand, some ASEAN member states may feel hesitant and even reluctant to be more economically integrated with China.

Second, China is in a more disadvantageous position in the contest of weaving regional free trade networks. When China took the initiative to enter into an FTA with its ASEAN partners, it figured it would be able to take the lead in pushing forward regional integration in East Asia and that CAFTA could be drawn upon to buttress its rise in the global economic competition. However, after years of development, Beijing gradually found itself being left behind on both fronts. On the first front, due to tussles between China and Japan, neither of them can succumb to the other in the integration of this region. ASEAN has gradually undertaken this role. While signing an FTA with China, ASEAN countries are active in engaging with other big powers and building FTAs with them as well. As such, ASEAN has become the hub of regional integration in East Asia. On the second front, China is surrounded by an array of bilateral and regional FTA blocks. Besides the multilateral trade arrangement like WTO, which is now stagnant, East Asia has witnessed a growing number of signed and implemented FTAs in the region, from three in 2000 to more than sixty in 2012.[50] These trading blocks are not necessarily competing with each other, but different countries in this region, especially big powers, are inclined to sign different arrangements whose contents, agendas, and member states vary greatly. The major ones include ASEAN, ASEAN+1, ASEAN+3, Regional Comprehensive Economic Partnership (RCEP, or ASEAN+6), TPP, Asia-Pacific Economic Cooperation (APEC), and CJK (China, Japan, and South Korea) Trilateral FTA. Furthermore, they spark concerns about an Asian "noodle bowl" of agreements, adding more operation costs for firms, especially small and medium-sized enterprises in this region. With all these agreements in play, China has no way to push forward its own preferred agenda.

Among these various economic arrangements, TPP, which was confirmed in October 2015 and is expected to "set the rules for the 21st century for trade,"[51] may bring about strong percussions for China. In China, there are debates regarding its attitudes toward TPP. Proponents tend to regard TPP as an opportunity for China's long-term development.[52] In their eyes, TPP is being promoted as a "gold-standard FTA" covering a variety of sensitive areas such as environmental criteria, labor rights, government procurement, and state-owned enterprise (SOE) reform. It is expected to develop a level playing field for businesses in the Asia-Pacific by focusing on liberalizing cross-border trade and investment, and strengthening regulatory reforms. Joining TPP may be detrimental to China in the short term, but as verified by China's entry into WTO (at that time many people also saw it as potentially disruptive), economic sectors like automobiles and steel, which used to be considered uncompetitive and vulnerable, in fact developed so successfully that they have leapt to the front ranks of the world economy. Another reason the proponents offered is that China will benefit from TPP's trade liberation rules. They argued that China has become a victim of trade protectionism in the form of antidumping, particularly after the eruption of the global financial crisis, and TPP will push forward free trade that is in the interest of China. In the meantime, proponents also underscore the backlash effect brought about by TPP's high standards. Namely, the advent of TPP would prompt China to speed up its industrial upgrading and restructuring, reduce its reliance on the foreign market, and build an economy whose growth is mainly driven by domestic demands. Finally, they perceived TPP as an opportunity to push forward regional integration in the Asia-Pacific.

The opponents, in contrast, perceive TPP as a conspiracy by the United States to contain China and its attempt to regain a prevailing influence over East Asia. According to them, TPP would create a pronounced trade diversion effect on China, dealing a severe blow to China's exports. But TPP is not merely an economic pact; it contains important security objectives.[53] Politically, TPP is part and parcel of America's Asia pivot strategy, which reinforces its linkage with Asian countries, divides East Asia, and dwarfs the China-ASEAN economic linkage so as to further marginalize China in the Asia-Pacific region. Hence, China cannot limit itself by joining TPP.[54]

Meanwhile, to reduce the adverse effects brought about by TPP, Beijing has prepared its own agendas. First, its top priority rests with an effective multilateral trade regime. Hence, Beijing is still hopeful that the WTO will be reinvigorated. Second, China is at pains to revive APEC's role as a platform for economic integration of multiple free trade zones in the Asia-Pacific so as to facilitate the creation of a Free Trade Area of the Asia-Pacific (FTAAP).[55] Initially proposed back in 2006, the building of FTAAP has been mentioned at every APEC Summit since, but it was during the APEC Summit 2014 in Beijing that China made moves to initiate its formation by launching a two-year study into its feasibility. However, in the view that APEC for long has been reduced to mere talking sessions without being able to work out any effective rules and regulations for trade liberalization, facilitation, and integration, Beijing has to resort to other alternative schemes. Third, besides proactively pursuing more bilateral FTAs with other countries, China is also making efforts to build FTAs with Japan and South Korea. Because of escalating territorial disputes and issues of history among the three, success on this front seems unlikely in the short run. Fourth, China is ready to join hands with and render full support to ASEAN to advance the goal of forging RCEP,[56] an ASEAN-led (specifically Indonesia) trade agreement comprising ASEAN and its six FTA partners—China, India, Japan, South Korea, Australia, and New Zealand. It includes 3.4 billion people, has a combined GDP (in PPP) of about US$33 trillion, and accounts for about 28 percent of world trade. Hence, the RCEP will be much larger than TPP, NAFTA, and the EU (see table 11.3). Negotiations began in early 2013, but have failed to meet the expected deadline of the end of 2015, and now are even expected to miss the deadline of December 2016. Although China is very interested in the

RCEP, it is aware that its success is not up to China or ASEAN alone. Understandably, RCEP's completion presents mounting challenges. Above all, it is composed of sixteen countries at different stages of development, making it extremely difficult to reconcile their different preferences toward trade and investment liberation. Moreover, unlike TPP in which the United States has played a leadership role, there is no such counterpart for RCEP, which means it would be much more difficult to achieve compromise. Also, with an aim to remove the spaghetti bowl effect resulting from a variety of bilateral FTAs, RCEP will be based on the five "10+1" FTAs, but the problem is determining which version to use as the benchmark. As Sanchita Basu Das summarized, the problems that RCEP faces are "managing different relational dynamics among its sixteen members; historical conflicts and unsettled territorial disputes between China, Japan and Korea; significant development gaps among RCEP members that may prevent countries from pursuing aggressive trade liberalization policies; lack of commonality across ASEAN+1 FTAs and varying domestic policies; the lack of domestic support; and concurrent regional integration agendas which could put pressure on a country's scarce resources of personnel and budget."[57]

The attitude of the Chinese government has undergone some changes, from the initial "observe the situation cool-headedly" to "intensive study and weigh the advantages and disadvantages."[58] When the United States decided to join TPP in a high-profile move, Beijing tended to consider it as a move to undermine China's economic links with ASEAN. The very strict standards were believed to "target" China so that it had no chance of joining. But eventually China came to realize that TPP per se is undergoing some dynamic changes since its overambitious goals came up against reality.[59] As the Xi Jinping administration endorsed the concept of building a new type of relationship with the United States that will defy the so-called zero-sum theory, Beijing deemed it important to keep confident in face of TPP. On May 30, 2013, a spokesman for the Ministry of Commerce said in a statement that "we will analyze the advantages, disadvantages and the possibility of joining TPP, based on careful research and according to principles of equality and mutual benefit."[60] Nevertheless, China is encountering some barriers to its access: (1) TPP sets restrictions on the existence of SOEs; (2) TPP has high requirements on labor rights protection; and (3) TPP will have too much of an impact on China's finance and agriculture. Looking forward, it is very likely that China will join TPP as Beijing is fully aware that further liberalization of the international economic system is not only an irreversible trend but also in the interests of China.

TABLE 11.3. Comparing the regional initiatives

	GDP (nominal, US$ trillions)		GDP (PPP, US$ trillions)	Population (billions)		Total merchandise trade (US$ trillions)
	2011	2015ᵃ	2011	2011	2015ᵃ	2011
RCEP	19.9 (28)	26.2 (32)	26.1 (39)	3.4 (48)	3.5 (48)	10.1 (28)
TPP	20.7 (29)	24.4 (30)	20.8 (26)	0.66 (9.49)	0.68 (9.4)	7.8 (21)
ASEAN	2.1 (3.1)	3.1 (3.8)	3.4 (4.2)	0.60 (8.7)	0.64 (8.8)	2.4 (6.5)
APT	16.5 (23)	21.8 (26)	20.7 (26)	2.1 (31)	2.2 (30)	8.8 (24)
CJK	14.3 (20)	18.7 (23)	17.3 (22)	1.5 (22)	1.5 (21)	6.4 (17)
APEC	38.8 (56)	48.5 (59)	43.9 (56)	2.7 (40)	2.8 (39)	17.6 (48)
NAFTA	17.9 (26)	21.1 (25)	18.1 (23)	0.46 (6.6)	0.47 (6.5)	5.4 (15)
EU	17.6 (25)	17.5 (21)	15.8 (20)	0.50 (7.2)	0.50 (7.0)	12.3 (33)

Note: Values in parentheses are the percentage of the world value. APEC = Asia-Pacific Economic Cooperation; APT = ASEAN Plus Three; CJK = China-Japan-Korea Trilateral FTA; EU = European Union; NAFTA = North American FTA; RCEP = Regional Comprehensive Economic Partnership; TPP = Trans-Pacific Partnership.
a. Implies IMF forecast.
Sources: IMF, World Economic Outlook database (October 2012); World Trade Organization database; author's calculations.

Yet TPP will have great impacts on ASEAN as well. On one hand, it may marginalize the central role of ASEAN in weaving regional cooperation networks, particularly dealing a blow to the progress in forging the RCEP. Furthermore, it may divide ASEAN since currently only Brunei, Singapore, Malaysia, and Vietnam have joined TPP and many of them are at different stages of economic development. On the other hand, as a high standard FTA, TPP is set to dwarf CAFTA in the short term as it would generate some trade diversion effects and shift investment.

Third, challenges arise due to growing concerns over losing competition with China. Some ASEAN countries have developed a growing sense of fear after the realization of CAFTA. First, largely because of the South Sea territorial dispute, ASEAN member states have growing misgivings about deepening their economic reliance on China. Take the Philippines as an example. Due to the intensified maritime dispute, the Philippines is much more cautious to jump onto the Chinese economic bandwagon. As a result, China's investment commitments in this country remain relatively small. In 2011, Chinese FDI in the Philippines was US$294 million, accounting for only 4.5 percent of China's total FDI in ASEAN. By the end of 2011, China's cumulative investment in the Philippines was only US$494.3 million, just 2.2 percent of its total investment in ASEAN. Second, as mentioned previously, ASEAN member states are in different positions in their trade with China, and even within a country different sectors are faring differently. In competition with their counterparts in the CAFTA block, it is comprehensible that some states with trade deficits and those sectors suffering from market openness may lodge complaints against the implementation of CAFTA. Take Indonesia as an example. Its textiles, electronics, iron, and steel used to enjoy high tariff protection. With the advent of CAFTA, they were hit hard by the reduction of tariffs and the flood of low-cost Chinese-made goods. Opposition from these sectors has been translated into the Indonesian government's request for renegotiating 228 tariff categories in eight sectors so as to leave more time for local industries to cope with the blitz of foreign imports.[61] Last but not the least important, ASEAN is also afraid that it could lose its competitiveness in both labor-intensive manufacturing and high-tech sectors when dealing with China. It was reported that during Obama's visit to Asia, almost every ASEAN leader expected the United States to enlarge the American presence in the region so as to strike a balance and avoid their being China's backyard.[62]

Finally, and more broadly, that the present trade patterns are unsustainable may defy Sino-ASEAN economic relations as well. At present, the dominant trading pattern correlates with regional production networks in East Asia. Acting as an assembly country for firms seeking low labor costs, China has become their magnet for new investments. As the hub of the production networks, in many sectors firms investing in China primarily import from its neighbors parts, components, and intermediary goods, such as machinery, minerals and fuels, plastics, fats and oils, rubber, and organic chemicals. China then assembles, processes, or reprocesses these goods and exports the products mainly to the American and European markets. This is often called "triangular trade," and almost half of China's exports are related to this trade. As a result, "China's exports to the EU and the US have skyrocketed and have displaced Japan's and newly industrialized economies' exports at accelerated pace."[63] Hence, the traditional way of calculating aggregate trade in light of the principle of country of origin is quite problematic, resulting in highly exaggerated trade imbalances between China and the United States or European Union. Prema-chandra Athukorala's study confirmed that trade in parts and components and final assembly within production networks has normally achieved faster growth than total world trade in manufacturing, and East Asia in particular outperforms other regions in the world in this regard.[64] Such a trade pattern can work well as long as the economies of developed countries are in good shape and the United States is willing to continue its consumption on debt. However, the "trilateral trade" is very vulnerable to economic downturn in developed countries. As verified by the global financial crisis, East Asian countries were dealt a heavy blow when exports to the United States shrank dramatically. Furthermore, China's position as the hub largely depends on its comparative advantage of specialization in labor-intensive products, which have produced very low value-added. Nonetheless, China's rise of labor costs and its struggle for upgrading industrial structures have posed challenges to the triangular trade pattern. Hence, Asian countries need to adjust their economic growth mode and trade patterns as well. One way is to enlarge China's domestic consumption. Although the Chinese government is making efforts toward that end, doing so takes time, and it remains unclear to what extent China can restructure its economy.

Conclusion

This essay has analyzed China's motives to build an FTA with ASEAN, the progress of CAFTA, and its future prospects. China was mainly out of political considerations to forge economic ties with ASEAN. Despite larger potential economic gains from an FTA with Japan and South Korea, Beijing opted for an FTA with ASEAN first. Beijing's decision was primarily driven by the purpose of diluting fears of its Southeast Asian neighbors arising from China's rise and accession to the WTO, the lobbying battle by local governments, and its fears of losing competitiveness in the new wave of regionalization across the globe. Despite similar economic development stages and industrial structures between the two sides, China had to make economic concessions to initiate the agreement and win the hearts of ASEAN states. Despite the political motivations in launching CAFTA, the performance of CAFTA will be determined by market forces. Indeed, it has made tremendous progress in the sense that both economies are more interdependent and bilateral cooperation has achieved a broader scope and deeper depth. In order to foster a closer China-ASEAN community of common destiny, China and ASEAN in November 2015 nailed down a protocol on upgrading their FTA, which is conducive to meet the target of scaling up two-way trade to US$1 trillion by 2020.[65] Hence, Sino-ASEAN trade is bound to hit a new peak with the removal of more trade barriers and more sectors being covered by free trade. Two-way investments will skyrocket with the completion of interconnectivity and implementation of more investment facilitation measures. The two sides will also deepen their cooperation in finance, high technology, and many other areas.

China hopes that deepening bilateral economic ties will lubricate overall relations and that political relations with its Southeast Asian neighbors will be firmly anchored. Nonetheless, economic interdependence seems unable to buy political trust. As a matter of fact, its Southeast Asian neighbors still have strong misgivings about a rising China strategically. I thus foresee two trends: On the one hand bilateral economic ties will be further enhanced, likely in favor of the ASEAN side. On the other hand, distrust and misgivings about China are mounting among Southeast Asian countries largely due to the unresolved territorial disputes. Such a gap between close economic ties and strategic mistrust will tend to grow. How to cope with such a discrepancy remains a daunting challenge for China.

NOTES

1 David Shambaugh, "China Engages Asia: Reshaping the Regional Order," *International Security* 29, no. 3 (2004–5): 64–99.

2 Angang Hu and Honghua Men, *Zhongguo: Dongya Yitihua Xin Zhanlue* [China's new strategy for East Asia integration] (Hangzhou: Zhejiang Renmin Chubanshe, 2005), Introduction.

3 Zhidong Ren, "Dongya shi Zhongguo Diyuan Zhanlue de Zhongxin" [East Asia is China's geostrategic center of gravity], *Huangqiushibao* [Global times], August 7, 2013.

4 Chong Wu, "Zhongguo yu Dongya '10+3' Jizhi" [China and "10+3" mechanism in East Asia], *Jingji Luntan* [Economic forum], no. 14 (2001): 32–37.

5 Maurice Schiff and L. Alan Winters, *Regional Integration and Development* (Washington, DC: World Bank and Oxford University Press, 2003).

6 Amitav Acharya, "China and Southeast Asia: Some Lessons for Africa?," in *Crouching Tiger, Hidden Dragon? Africa and China*, ed. Kweku Ampiah and Sanushu Naidu (Scottsville: University of KwaZulu-Natal Press, 2008), 322; Marwaan Macan-Markar, "ASEAN-China FTA: Boon for Whom?," *Asian Times*, October 22, 2002, www.atimes.com.

7 Cao Yunhua, "Zhongguo yu Dongmeng Guanxi: Xianzhuang he Qianjing" [Sino-ASEAN relations: The status quo and prospect], *Dongnanya Yanjiu* [Southeast Asian studies], no. 1 (2002): 55–63.

8 Mei Kuang and Zhou Zhou, "Zhongguo-Dongmeng Ziyou Maoyiqu Chuangjian yu Fazhan de Zhengzhi Jingji Fenxi" [Political economy analysis of the establishment and development of the CAFTA], *Dangdai Yatai* [Contemporary Asia Pacific], no. 3 (2008): 50–60.

9 Joshua Kurlantzick, *Charm Offensive: How China's Soft Power Is Transforming the World* (New Haven: Yale University Press, 2007).

10 Lijun Sheng, "China-ASEAN Free Trade Area—Origins, Developments and Strategic Motivations" (Institute of Southeast Asian Studies Working Paper, International Politics & Security Issues Series no. 1, 2003); Kevin G. Cai, "The ASEAN-China Free Trade Agreement and East Asian Regional grouping," *Contemporary Southeast Asia* 25, no. 3 (2003): 387–404.

11 Anshan Long, *Zhongguo-Dongmeng Ziyou Maoyiqu Jianshe: Lilun, Shijian, Qianjing* [Construction of the CAFTA: Theory, practice and prospect] (Shanghai: Shanghai Shehui Kexue Chubanshe, 2008), 211.

12 David Rosenberg, "China-ASEAN Relations: Economic and Legal Dimensions," *China Journal* 61 (2009): 246–48.

13 John Ravenhill, "Is China an Economic Threat to Southeast Asia," *Asian Survey* 46, no. 5 (2006): 653.

14 "The China-ASEAN Free Trade Agreement: Who's Happy, Who's Not?," Knowledge@Wharton, May 12, 2010, www.knowledgeatwharton.com.cn.

15 See, for example, Shambaugh, "China Engages Asia"; Peter J. Buckley et al., "China's Inward Foreign Direct Investment Success: Southeast Asia in the Shadow of the Dragon," *Multinational Business Review* 13, no. 1 (2005): 3–31; Juliana W. Chen, "Achieving Supreme Excellence: How China Is Using Agreement with ASEAN to Overcome Obstacles to Its Leadership in Asian Regional Economic Integration," *Chicago Journal of International Law*, no. 7 (January 1, 2007): 655–74; Kurlantzick, *Charm Offensive*, 271–76.

16 Walter Lohman, "More Charm Than Harm: Lessons from China's Economic Offensive in Southeast Asia" (Heritage Lectures no. 1149 on China and Southeast Asia, Heritage Foundation, February 24, 2010).

17 National Statistical Bureau of China, *China Statistical Yearbook 2005*.

18 Trade data from 2000 to 2013 come from National Statistical Bureau of China, while trade data for 2014 can be found in China-ASEAN Free Trade Area, www.cafta.org.cn.

19 Calculated by the author based on data from the National Bureau of Statistics of China. Data for 2014 are from the General Administration of Customs of the PRC.

20 "Zhongguo-Dongmeng Maoyi e nian zengzhanglv tongji fenxi," Zhongguo Hangye Yanjiu wang, August 12, 2012, www.chinairn.com.

21 Based on Zhou Xiaoyan, "The 'Diamond' Decade," *Beijing Review*, no. 38 (September 19, 2013).

22 "China to Extend RQFII Program to Singapore," *Xinhua*, October 22, 2013.

23 ASEAN Secretariat, "ASEAN-CHINA Dialogue Relations," www.asean.org.

24 "China Proposes an Asian Infrastructure Investment Bank," *Xinhua*, October 3, 2013, www.chinadaily.com.

25 Banyan, "An Asian Infrastructure Bank: Only Connect," *Economist*, October 4, 2013.

26 Philip C. Erquiaga, "For a Better Road to Development, Asia Must Attract Private Partners," *Jakarta Globe*, May 3, 2012, www.adb.org.

27 Prashanth Parameswaran, "Beijing Unveils New Strategy for ASEAN–China Relations," *China Brief* 13, no. 21 (2013).

28 Ibid.

29 The founding members now number twenty-two: Bangladesh, Brunei, Cambodia, China, India, Indonesia, Kazakhstan, Kuwait, Laos, Malaysia, Mongolia, Myanmar, Nepal, Oman, Pakistan, the Philippines, Qatar, Singapore, Sri Lanka, Thailand, Uzbekistan, and Vietnam.

30 Caroline Bracht, "Will the Brics Bank Deliver a More Just World Order?," *Guardian Professional*, May 8, 2013, www.theguardian.com.

31 Alonso Soto, "Exclusive—Brics Emerging Nations Close to Launching Bank; to Start Lending in 2016," Reuters, May 30, 2014.

32 "China to Boost Maritime Cooperation with ASEAN Countries," *Xinhua*, December 16, 2011.

33 Comprehensive Department, Ministry of Commerce, "2013 nian Zhongguo duiwai maoyi fazhan qingkuang" [China's development of foreign trade in 2013], May 4, 2014, http://zhs.mofcom.gov.cn.

34 For figures for 2014, see Suya Zhou, "Shangwubu: Jiezhi qunian Zhongguo he Dongmeng shuangxiang touzi chao 1300 yi meiyuan," *Renminwang*, July 29, 2015, http://finance.people.com.cn; for figures for 2011, see Qingfen Ding and Wei He, "'Diamond Decade' Ahead for China, ASEAN," *China Daily*, September 4, 2013, http://usa.chinadaily.com.cn.

35 "China Vows to Build Community of Common Destiny with ASEAN," *Xinhua*, October 3, 2013, http://news.xinhuanet.com.

36 Based on Zhou Xiaoyan, "'Diamond' Decade."

37 D. O. Cushman, "Real Exchange Rate Risk, Expectations, and the Level of Direct Investment," *Review of Economics and Statistics* 67, no. 2 (1985): 297–308; K. A. Froot and J. C. Stein, "Exchange Rates and Foreign Direct Investment: An Imperfect Capital Markets Approach," *Quarterly Journal of Economics* 106, no. 4 (1991): 1191–1217; S. W. Kohlhagen, "Exchange Rates Changes, Profitability, and Direct Foreign Investment," *Southern Economic Journal* 44, no. 1 (1977): 43–52.

38 See, for example, Fengli Wang, "Renminbi huilv dui woguo duiwai zhijie touzi de yingxiang—Jiyu ECM moxing de jianyan" [Impact of exchange rate of RMB on China's foreign direct investments—Based on the test of ECM model], *Jingji Wenti Tansuo* [Inquiry into economic issues], no. 3 (2008); Bin Hu and Chunli Tu, "Renminbi huilv yu Zhongguo duiwai zhijie touzi—Jiyu kuaguo mianban shuju de shizheng fenxi" [Exchange rate of RMB and China's foreign direct investments—Based on the empirical study of some cross-state panel data], *Dangdai Jingji Yanjiu* [Contemporary economic research], no. 11 (2012); Kun Guo, "Renminbi Shengzhi dui Zhongguo duiwai zhijie touzi de yingxiang yanjiu" [Study on the impact of RMB appreciation on China's outward foreign direct investment] (Doctoral diss., Northeast Normal University, December 2013).

39 Huichao Qiao and Wenbin Sha, "Zhongguo dui Dongmeng zhijie touzi jueding yinsu de shizheng yanjiu—Jiyu Dongmeng shiguo de Panel Data jianyan" [An

empirical research of FDI determinants from China to ASEAN—Based on panel data test of ASEAN], *Guangxi Caijing Xueyuan Xuebao* [Journal of Guangxi University of finance and economics] 25, no. 3 (2012); Yan Zhang and Li Wang, "Zhongguo dui Dongmeng guojia zhijie touzi de jueding yinsu yanjiu" [Study on the FDI determinants from China to ASEAN], *Inquiry into Economic Issues*, no. 7 (2013); Lei Zheng, "A Study on Outward Foreign Direct Investment from China to ASEAN" (Doctoral diss., Dongbei University of Finance and Economics, December 2011).

40 Lei Zheng, "Study on Outward Foreign Direct Investment."

41 Ibid.

42 Ministry of Commerce, "Zhongguo Duiwai Touzi Hezuo Fazhan Baogao" [Report on development of China's outward investment and economic cooperation] (2011–12), 10.

43 Ministry of Commerce, "Zhongguo yu Dongmeng shuangbian maoyi e 2015nian jiang tupou 5000 yi meiyuan" [China-ASEAN bilateral trade will surpass 500 billion dollars by 2015] (July 24, 2013).

44 Mona Haddad, "Trade Integration in East Asia: The Role of China and Production Networks" (World Bank Policy Research Working Paper 4160, March 2007).

45 Based on Fashan Chen, "Zhongguo dui Dongmeng maoyi shuncha yuanzi maoyi zhuanyi" [China's trade surplus with ASEAN originated from trade diversion], *Caixin*, July 23, 2013.

46 Guojun Zhao, "Lun Nanhai wenti 'Dongmeng hua' de fazhan—Dongmeng zhengce yanbian yu Zhongguo yingdui" [On the development of "ASEAN-ization" of the South China Sea issue—ASEAN's policy evolution and China's counter-measures], *Guoji Zhanwang* [World outlook], no. 2 (2013).

47 Speech by China's Defense Minister Chang Wanquan during the ASEAN Defense Ministers' Meeting-Plus convened in Brunei; see Zhang Yunbi and Li Xiaokun, "'Don't Flaunt ASEAN Banner' on the S. China Sea Issue," *China Daily*, August 30, 2013.

48 Guojun Zhao, "Lun Nanhai wenti."

49 Guy De Launey, "Has Chinese Power Driven ASEAN Nations Apart?," *BBC News*, July 19, 2012, www.bbc.co.uk.

50 Masahiro Kawai and Ganeshan Wignaraja, "Dealing with the 'Noodle Bowl' of Asia's Free Trade Agreements" (Asian Development Bank Institute, April 24, 2012), www.asiapathways-adbi.org.

51 Jessica Glenza, "TPP Deal: US and 11 Other Countries Reach Landmark Pacific Trade Pact," *Guardian*, October 5, 2015.

52 Such views can be seen in Lei Wei and Hanlin Zhang, "Meiguo Zhudao kua Taipingyang guanxi xiexi tanpang de yitu ji Zhongguo duice" [The intent of the United States in dominating the TPP negotiation and China's countermea-sures], *Guoji Maoyi* [International trade], no. 9 (2010); Tianlong Wang, "Zhongguo ke shishi canyu TPP tanpang" [China can consider joining TPP

negotiations at appropriate time], *Zhongguo Jingji Daokan* [China economy and trade guide], no.1 (2012); Li He, "TPP yu Zhongguo de jingji yitihua fa Dongxiang he duice" [TPP and the direction of China's economic integration law and countermeasures], *Zhengfa Luntan* [Politics and law forum], no. 3 (2011).

53 C. Fred Bergsten and Jeffrey J. Schott, "Submission to the USTR in Support of a Trans-Pacific Partnership Agreement" (Peterson Institute for International Economics, January 25, 2010).

54 Such views can be seen in Bin Sheng, "Meiguo shijiao xia de Yatai quyu yitihua xin zhanlue yu Zhongguo de duice xuance" [New strategy of regional integration in the Asian-Pacific from the U.S. perspective and China's policy choice], *Nankai Xuebao* [Nankai University Journal philosophy and social science version], no. 4 (2010); Minghui Shen, "Dongya hezuo zhong de Meiguo yinsu—yi 'Fan Taipingyang huoban guanxi xieyi' weili" [The American factor in East Asian cooperation—a case on TPP], *Taipingyang Xuebao* [Pacific journal], no. 6 (2010); Zhongwei Liu and Jiawen Shen, "Kua Taipingyang huoban guanxi xieyi: Yanjiu qianyan yu jiagou—Zhongguo de shijiao" [TPP: Current research and framework—China's perspective], *Contemporary Asia-Pacific Studies*, no. 1 (2012); Xiangyang Liu, "Kua Taipingyang jingji zhanlue huoban guanxi xieding yu Meiguo de Yatai quyu hezuo xin zhanlue" [TPP and America's new strategy on regional cooperation in Asian Pacific], *Guoji Maoyi* [International trade], no. 6 (2010).

55 "China Calls on APEC to Promote FTA Integration," *Xinhua*, September 30, 2013, www.chinadaily.com.cn.

56 ASEAN Briefing, "The China-ASEAN 'Diamond Decade,'" September 9, 2013, www.aseanbriefing.com.

57 Cited in Sanchita Basu Das, "Challenges in Negotiating the Regional Comprehensive Economic Partnership Agreement," *ISEAS (Institute of Southeast Asian Studies) Perspective*, no. 47 (August 12, 2013).

58 Jing Song, "Guanfang Taidu weibian: Zhongguo Jiaru TPP de Li yu Bi," *21 Shiji Jingji Baodao* [21st century economic herald], June 5, 2013.

59 There are two layers of meanings. First, many sensitive sectors with very high requirements are incorporated into TPP, which may stall the negotiation process; second, Washington's initial intent of "encircling" China is set to fail given that China's economic influence in East Asia is primarily a result of market forces, specifically the regional production networks in East Asia, whereas the decline of U.S. influence in this region has mainly been brought on by Washington itself.

60 "China to Study Possibility of Joining TPP: MOC," *Xinhua*, May 30, 2013, http://news.xinhuanet.com.

61 Qi Chen, Zhou Zhou, and Tang Tang, "Dongmeng dui Zhong-Dongmeng Zimaoqu de gulv" [ASEAN's misgivings about the CAFTA], *Guoji Zhengzhi Kexue* [Quarterly journal of international politics], no. 4 (2010): 59–68.

62 "China-ASEAN Free Trade Agreement: Who's Happy, Who's Not?"

63 Guillaume Gaulier, Françoise Lemoine, and Deniz Ünal-Kesenci, "China's Integration in East Asia: Production Sharing, FDI & High-Tech Trade" (CEPII Working Paper no. 2005–09, June 2005).

64 Prema-chandra Athukorala, "Production Networks and Trade Patterns in East Asia: Regionalization or Globalization?" (ADB Working Paper no. 56, August 2010).

65 "China, ASEAN Seals Deal to Upgrade Bilateral FTA," *Xinhua*, November 23, 2015, http://news.xinhuanet.com.

12

China and the United States in Southeast Asia

CHU SHULONG

The Role of Southeast Asia to China

China is a big country, and big countries are important to China. In Northeast Asia there are big countries such as Japan and Russia, whose far eastern region forms a large part of Asia and borders China. But in Southeast Asia, there is not really a big country. Indonesia might be a big nation in terms of geography and population, but in national power it has not become a big country in Asia or the world.

Southeast Asia is important to China not because there is big power there, but because there are many Asian nations there. This gives the subregion importance to China's economy, diplomacy, and society/culture, and some security significance.

China's Trade and Economic Interests in Southeast Asia

Southeast Asia is increasingly significant to the Chinese economy. China has focused on economic development and modernization for more than three decades since 1978, when Deng Xiaoping launched "reform and opening" in China. Economic development and modernization have been national priorities for China since. And Chinese economic development has followed the East Asian "export-led growth" model, with exports as the major driving force for the country's economic takeoff. China has intended to change the model since the Asian Financial Crisis in 1997 and especially since the International Financial Crisis in 2008, but so far has not been quite successful. That is, export and foreign trade are still very significant to China's economic growth and interests. And even as China is trying to shift its growth model from export- and investment-driven to domestic consumption in the future, foreign trade will always be an important part of any modern economy, especially a large economy such as China's.

Southeast Asia is one of the largest areas of China's foreign trade and economic relations. In 2012, the ten countries of the Association of Southeast Asian Nations (ASEAN) together formed the third largest trade partner of China, next only to the EU and the United States. The trade value was US$400.93 billion: Chinese exports totaled US$204.27 billion, and imports from ASEAN amounted to US$195.82 billion. Southeast Asia is not only one of the largest trade partners of China, but also a quickly growing trade partner, with an annual trade growth rate around 20 percent; in the past five years, China's trade with Europe has increased slowly, but that with Japan has actually decreased.[1] In 2014, the total trade value of trade between China and Southeast Asia was US$480.3 billion, there was an increase of 8.3 percent over 2013, and it accounted for 11.16 percent of total China's foreign trade. Thus, Southeast Asia is the third largest trade partner of China, the fourth largest foreign market, and the second largest source of imports.[2]

According to Chinese Minister of Commerce Gao Hucheng, exports to developing countries accounted for almost 60 percent of total Chinese exports in the first half of 2013, while exports to developed markets, including the United States, Europe, and Japan, accounted for only 40 percent.[3] Clearly, exports to the developing world, including Southeast Asia, have become significant to China's economy.

In addition to trade, Southeast Asia is also a major source of foreign investment in China and a destination for China's foreign investment. By the end of 2012, China had invested about US$30 billion in the region. Southeast Asia accounts for 5.1 percent of the Chinese international investment and represents the fourth largest destination for China's foreign investment. By the end of June 2013, the cumulative ASEAN investment in China was US$80 billion, accounting for 6.6 percent of total Chinese FDI, the third largest source of China's foreign investment.[4] And at the end of September 2014, two-way investment between China and Southeast Asia had reached US$132.1 billion; Southeast Asian investment in China was US$90 billion.[5]

Diplomatic Significance

Southeast Asia is one of the most important areas for Chinese foreign relations. The significance lies not just in concrete interests, but also in symbolic importance. Southeast Asia determines the image and the nature of China's diplomacy. Because almost all countries in the region are small or midsize nations and more nations are here than anywhere else in Asia, relations with Southeast Asia determine the nature of China's overall foreign relations. With productive relations in the region, China can show the whole of Asia and the world that Chinese foreign relations are sound and positive. China's relations with ASEAN hence have become a test case for whether China can maintain good relations with smaller and weaker neighbors. In other words, relations with Southeast Asia determine whether China's rising is peaceful or not.

This point is clearer when we think about China's relations with Northeast Asia. Unlike Southeast Asia, where all nations are small in size and/or stature, there are big nations and powers in Northeast Asia, such as Japan and Russia. If China fails to maintain good relations with Japan or Russia, it could be the fault of the Japanese or Russians because they are roughly equal to China in power. But when China has poor relations in Southeast Asia, observers are bound to conclude that it must be the fault of the Chinese, the stronger power. When issues arise between China and the Southeast Asian nations, many criticize China for "bullying small countries," an interpretation not propagated when China and Japan have problems.

If China desires to have good foreign relations and to rise peacefully, it has to maintain positive relations with most if not all countries in Southeast Asia. Good relations with these countries might not be as significant to China economically, militarily, politically, and strategically as relations with Japan and Russia, but they might determine the image and nature of China's foreign relations across Asia and throughout the world.

Security Interests

China shares many borders in Southeast Asia: land borders with Myanmar, Laos, and Vietnam and national or international sea borders with other six countries of the region.

In its past China has had territory disputes with Vietnam, and two countries fought a war regarding their border in 1979. The South China Sea remains one of the three major territorial disputes China has today in Asia, next to Diaoyu Islands with Japan and disputed territory with India. In South China Sea China has disputes with Vietnam, the Philippines, Brunei, and Malaysia.

In terms of national security, the South China Sea disputes themselves do not pose a major security problem or threat to China because the parties to the disputes are unlikely to declare war, and even if there were armed conflict, it would not cause large problems for China. The bigger security interests here lie in China's relationship with the United States. The Americans may become involved in the disputes because of the U.S. alliance with the Philippines, U.S. positions on the issue, and American interests in sea lanes. Therefore, the South China Sea disputes involve not just China and Southeast Asian claimants, but also the United States.

Even considering all security threats in Southeast Asia, the region is unlikely to pose a major national security problem for China today or in the future. China's primary security challenge is the Taiwan independent movement, which could cause full-scale war across the Taiwan Straits and could even draw U.S. involvement. The second major Chinese security challenge is in Xinjiang, where a separatist movement, combined with terrorist and extremist groups, threatens Chinese national unity and people's lives. The third major security challenge that China faces is in the East and South China Seas, where territorial disputes with other Asian nations could engender some degree of conflict.

Tensions between China and Southeast Asian countries have grown in recent years. The Philippines has filed a complaint with the UNCLOS Tribunal on its disputes with China, and Vietnam reacted aggressively toward China's oil rig in the South China Sea in May 2014. Vietnam might also file a lawsuit China relating to the territorial disputes.

Social and Cultural Ties

Southeast Asia is a special region to China and the Chinese. Many ethnic Chinese live in the region, including 25 million of the 30 million overseas Chinese.[6] There are thus close social and cultural ties between China and these Southeast Asian nations. Close to one-third of Malaysians are ethnic Chinese, and in Thailand, the Philippines, Indonesia, and Cambodia, ethnic Chinese account for 10 to 20 percent of the total population. Singapore is basically a Chinese nation.

Socially and culturally speaking, China is closer with Southeast Asia than any other world region, even as this sometimes causes problems in China's relations with these countries.

The overseas Chinese factor has been important to China's foreign relations with Southeast Asia. Overseas Chinese have been a trouble issue in China's relations with a number of countries in the region. It was a very serious and disputed issue in the 1960s when Indonesia cracked down on ethnic Chinese living there, damaging diplomatic relations between China and Indonesia for a long time. The relations between the two countries were not "normalized" until the 1980s. For a long time, the Indonesian government was suspicious that China would utilize its overseas Chinese population to influence, maybe even control, Indochina's politics and economy. From the Chinese perspective, the Chinese government had to intervene when the media depicted the rude treatment of Chinese in Indonesia. Such a dispute arose again in the late 1990s, when a large number of ethnic Chinese were attacked and killed in Indonesia.

The overseas Chinese also was a major factor in the Sino-Vietnamese War in 1979, when the Vietnamese government expelled two hundred thousand ethnic Chinese from Vietnam. Bilateral relations between the two communist states became hostile. The Chinese government and its leader, Deng Xiaoping, could not accept this mistreatment of the Chinese. China launched the war to "teach" the Vietnamese "a lesson" that they should not bully other nations and people, including ethnic Chinese, in Indochina.

Overseas Chinese has also been a dedicated problem between China and Myanmar, including the fighting between Myanmar government and local Chinese military and authority in the border area between China and Myanmar. The Chinese government tries to mediate the dispute between the local and central forces in Myanmar in recent years.

The overseas Chinese population is a less controversial problem between China and Malaysia, the Philippines, Cambodia, and Thailand. But all of these governments understand this is a sensitive issue both externally and internally and handle it with caution.

The Chinese also believe that overseas Chinese can be a positive issue between China and Southeast Asia because it ties the two sides together. It provides for cordial relations as many in Southeast Asian countries, including some royal families and leaders, have Chinese blood. It has become a very positive force in economic and social relations between China and the subregion. In fact, most investment from Southeast Asia to China and a large portion of the trade between the subregion and China is performed by overseas Chinese. And most of the thousands of Southeast Asian students enrolled in Chinese universities each year are ethnic Chinese.[7] These economic, social, and cultural ties are always positive in the bilateral relations between China and the Southeast Asian countries. The Chinese government understands this and utilizes this fact in its relations with the region.

China So Far Has Not Had a Clear "Regional Strategy" in Asia

China has not yet outlined a clear regional strategy in Asia, including Southeast Asia, not delineating a goal of what Asia should become. Other countries such as Malaysia, Australia, the United States, Russia, Japan, and South Korea have all proposed some regional structures or frameworks in Asia, such as the Asia Community or the Pacific Community, but China has never proposed a vision. None of the Asian multilateral frameworks, such as APEC (the Asia-Pacific Economic Cooperation), ASEAN Plus Three, ARF (ASEAN Regional Forum), and the East Asia Summit, have been initiated by the Chinese. The

Chinese just react and follow others' initiatives. The Asian Infrastructure Investment Bank (AIIB) is a recent exception.

A major power's global or international strategy presents a vision of the world and a strategy to achieve it, to turn the world in a certain direction. The Soviet Union had a vision to shape the world toward a "communist" or "socialist" future, while the West, including the United States, Western Europe, Canada, Australia, and New Zealand, has always had a vision of a "free" or "democratic" world. During the 1960s and the first half of the 1970s, China under Chairman Mao Zedong had a vision of a "Red World" and supported revolutions in Asia, Africa, and Latin America. That was the only time when modern China had a clear and long-term vision of and strategy to remake the world.

During most of the post–Cold War era, China did not present a clear vision of the world. But in September 2005, Chinese President Hu Jintao proposed a "harmonious world" as a long-term goal for the world. He had proposed a "harmonious society" for China after ascending to power in 2002. The Chinese government did repeat the proposal for a few years,[8] but appeared to stop around the time of the Eighteenth Party Congress of the Chinese Communist Party. Therefore, except for a short time, the Chinese did not present a clear vision of the world.

Today, China's leadership and government still do not propagate a grand vision for global development. China's current foreign strategy is to maintain good relations with each nation, to have a peaceful world that is good for Chinese development and modernization. It also desires to increase China's role and influence in the world.

Although China lacks a specific vision, Beijing does have a commercial interest in the world. China seeks to export its products across the globe and seeks raw materials everywhere. China today is a global power with a global reach and interests, economic and commercial.

The fundamental reason why China does not present a clear world vision is not its leadership and government, but traditional Chinese philosophy, culture, and values. Chinese culture, philosophy, and tradition are basically "inward looking" and "internal oriented." Chinese culture and philosophy were founded by Confucians around 700 BC and have been based on the concept of *junzi* (gentleman). Confucians told generation after generation of Chinese to become a *junzi* but never to spread Chinese culture, to spread God's message, or to save the world. Chinese culture has always been nonreligious and inward-looking, emphasizing what is within rather than the outside world.

This fundamental part of the Chinese culture is based the country's size. With its size, agricultural resources, and immense population, China prospered during the thousands years of *xiao nong jingji* (small agriculture economy), which served China well until 1978, when it began policies of modernization, industrialization, and openness to the outside world.

Since "reform and opening up" in the late 1970s, great changes have taken place in China, including its foreign relations with the outside world. However, as Samuel Huntington pointed out, culture changes slowly.[9] Today, China is vastly different from thirty years ago, but its culture, philosophy, and social values have changed very little. It remains an inward-looking culture, emphasizing the internal development of China. To the international community, the Chinese leadership has always been occupied with internal affairs, not foreign affairs.

As China continues its ascent, its economy has integrated with the global economy, but China remains an "inward-looking" nation in regard to politics, security, and strategy. Not only Chinese leadership and government focus on internal issues; its people and society do too. China's diplomats do not want to be posted abroad, senior businesspeople do not stay long overseas, and most elite university students do not go abroad for further studies or their career, a different situation from ten to fifteen years ago. "Foreign affairs" in the Chinese media concentrates on "Chinese affairs" because if the reports are not "related to China," nobody will consume them.

China lacks an Asian strategy, and it has not openly stated its goals in the Middle East, Africa, or Latin America. Yet China has a clear strategy for dealing with the United States and Russia.

China's Asian Policy

China emphasizes the "Asian Policy." And since 2002, China's Asian policy has been *mulin, anlin, fulin* ("neighborhood, reassuring neighbors, and enriching neighbors").[10]

The policy is sincere and true, at least from the intentions and goals, even though whether China can be successful in implementing the policy is another issue. China seeks good relations with all of its neighbors, except maybe Japan, because the Chinese have no ill will toward others. And China does not want to see competition between itself and any of its other neighbors, including India. The Chinese are confident that they do not need competition, because China has played a major role in Asia for thousands of years.

The Chinese understand that China is larger than all its neighbors and is becoming stronger, so it is quite natural for the neighbors to worry about China now and in the future. China does not desire its neighbors to be fearful, so it reassures its neighbors that it will not be a threat. The problem is the balance between protecting basic national territorial interests and having good relations with others.

China is also aware that there is economic competition between the rising China and the other economies in the region, whose development levels are similar to China's. All are lower-level to midlevel economies, and all target developed countries for exports, foreign investment, and technological transfers. China is at an advantage among them because of its size, population, market, and economy, which enable the country to export more to the developed markets and absorb more foreign investment and technological transfers. China certainly would not give up its advantages, but the Chinese do like to consider sharing their opportunities with other Asian countries.

There are also some nontraditional security frictions between China and other Asian countries that might become more serious and troublesome in the future. The frictions are related to water, the environment, air pollution, crime, illegal immigration, and others.

China's Asian policy has been carried out in the following three areas.

Neighborhood Diplomacy

China seeks positive relations with all of its neighbors by strengthening economic, political/diplomatic, social, and cultural ties with them. This includes encouraging tourist, student, academic, and journalist exchanges between China and the Southeast Asian nations.

In the political and diplomatic arena, China tries to maintain good relations through intensive official contacts with the neighboring countries. Under the ASEAN Plus Three, ASEAN Plus One, ARF, and East Asia Summit frameworks, the Chinese government and military have many regular meetings and contacts with their Southeast Asian counterparts each year, related to such topics as foreign affairs, finance, trade, investment, the environment, law enforcement, culture and sports, and many others.

In addition to these frequent engagements, China has had regular and intensive high-level and official contacts with the leaderships and governments of almost all Southeast Asian nations, including heads of state and government visits, agreements, statements, and communiqués. Each year, many of these events take place between China and Southeast Asian countries. This at least makes the relationships between them amicable.

A good neighborhood relationship is a general goal of China's Asian policy. Certainly nobody in the world will pursue any goal without principles and conditions. While China wants to have good neighborhood relations, it does have some differences and disputes with a number of neighbors. China, like all other nations, would not suffer any cost just to maintain good relations. This common sense is true of every nation in the world, and is equally true to China.

Economic Cooperation

In the past decade, China has actively promoted the trade, investment, and financial cooperation with Southeast Asian nations for China's own interests and to "enrich the neighbors." China proposed the free trade agreement (FTA) with ASEAN in 2001, and the two sides have come to agreements on the "early harvest," trade, and service. The China-ASEAN FTA formally started in 2011, and trade has grown by more than 20 percent, some years by 40 percent. China and ASEAN have become major trade partners.[11]

China has also encouraged its companies to invest in Southeast Asia, after decades as a major destination of Southeast Asian capital, in energy, infrastructure, manufacturing, and service. Chinese tourists have become numerous in the region. In 2012, 2.7 million Chinese tourists visited Thailand alone.[12]

Security Exchange and Constraint

The Chinese military has established and engaged in military exchange relations with almost all of the Southeast Asian nations, and there are some annual security consultation dialogue mechanisms between China and several ASEAN countries. Joint military exercises, including in antiterrorism and other nontraditional security areas, have been conducted between China and some Southeast Asian countries.

The ASEAN Defense Ministers Meeting (ADMM) is a new phenomenon, and so far China has had no problems with the meetings. Although they might talk about the South China Sea issues, China opposes any multilateral discussion on the disputes that China sees as bilateral in nature. But China does not worry that all ASEAN countries, including their defense ministers, will take a common position against Beijing, because the country has relatively good relations with most of the ASEAN countries.

China has not used People's Liberation Army naval forces in the South China Sea disputes since 1995. Instead, it has used Maritime Agency ships, which are equivalent to the coast guard vessels of other states. When the Philippines sent its largest naval vessel to Huangyan Island (Scarborough Shoal) and tried to catch Chinese fishing boats and control the island in May 2012, China sent its Maritime Agency ships to block the Philippine military forces.

As some people in Asia and the United States have argued, even though China did not use military force, its coastal protection ships are powerful and aggressive. But China claims there is an important difference between using or threatening to using military force and using civilian law enforcement ships. Thus, the Chinese government asserts there has been a certain degree of self-restraint from China toward its disputes with other countries in Asia.

At the same time China worked hard to negotiate with Vietnam and reached the land territory agreement and maritime agreement on the Gulf of Tonkin (Beibu) in the early 2000s, resolving another longtime major territory dispute between China and its neighbor. In fact during the more than thirty years of China's rise, the general trend of China on the territorial disputes has been resolving them through talks, negotiations, and other peaceful means. China negotiated and resolved a dispute with the Soviet Union and later Russia regarding their five-thousand-kilometer border. This might be the longest disputed border in the world and the two countries had fought serious battles over it in the past. It has become a peaceful border between two of the world's big countries. China has also resolved border issues with all Central Asian and most South Asian states. The history of rising China over more than thirty years has been a history of China trying to resolve territorial disputes through peaceful means, not military force.

Here one can compare China's history to that of another major country in Asia, Japan, which has had territorial disputes with all of its neighbors—Russia, China, and the Koreas—and which has not resolved any of the disputes after more than thirty years. China, on the other hand, has resolved a number of major territorial disputes with its neighbors through talks and negotiations. And Japanese territorial disputes have become more serious and troublesome in recent years.

China's Position and Actions over the South China Sea Disputes

The territory disputes in the South China Sea have been the most serious problem between China and Southeast Asian countries and have become more controversial in recent years.

The Chinese position and policy on the South China Sea, *Zhuquan guiwuo, gezhi zhengyi, gongtong kaifa* ("Sovereignty belongs to China, put the disputes aside, and engage joint exploitation of the resources there"), were formulated by Deng Xiaoping in the early 1980s.[13] Chinese President Xi Jinping restated that principles at a Politburo meeting on July 31, 2013.[14]

But this official Chinese policy has not been successful. Countries that dispute this claim do not recognize Chinese sovereignty. Vietnam and the

Philippines have actively stated their differences with China; and the Philippines took its claims all the way to the International Tribunal for the Law of the Sea (ITLOS).

For a long time, China did seek to maintain peace and stability and the status quo in the South China Sea. In the early 2000s, China proposed the principles of code of conduct in the South China Sea. China and ASEAN agreed to the Declaration on the Principles of Code of Conduct over the South China Sea disputes in 2002.

The central part of the agreement is that nobody should take any unilateral action to change the status quo of the disputes, so that peace and stability can be maintained. In fact, all parties to the disputes have basically followed this agreement. No power has taken any unilateral action to change the status quo of de facto control since the agreement was signed in 2002, even though there have always been some disputes, including incidents related to fishing, research, energy exploitation, and other activities.

The long-term position of the Chinese government on the disputes in the South China Sea is that China has "indisputable sovereignty in the South China Sea," even while China clearly recognizes that there are disagreements. This means that the territory, including the territorial waters, in the South China Sea belong to China in terms of sovereignty, while China recognizes that other countries have different positions and claims over those territories, including the associated territorial waters. China has proposed bilateral talks on these disputes:

Like those of other Asian countries, the Chinese claims are based on "history." The Chinese believe that their territory rights were formed thousands of years ago, not by modern law. The specific evidence is always based in ancient times, that Chinese governments claimed the territory, including the territorial waters; Chinese fishermen traveled there to go fishing. the central Chinese governments placed those areas under local administrative control; Chinese and other countries' maps clearly depicted those areas as Chinese territories.

The Chinese claims are much more solid in the twentieth century. The Chinese government and military gained exclusive control over the South China Sea. In 1945 at the end of the Second World War, Japan withdrew from the South China Sea and China took control and sent troops to Taiping Island. At the same time no other countries exercised any control in the South China Sea. And before 1974, the Philippine government did not claim sovereignty over the sea; all of its maps depict the area as Chinese territory. The Northern Vietnamese government indicated the whole of the South China Sea, including the northern and southern parts, as Chinese, in its official statements and documents.

The South China Sea disputes have become more serious and trouble-some in recent years. And to the Chinese understanding, this has much to do with the American "return to Asia" or "rebalancing strategy" in recent years, especially Secretary Hillary Clinton's speech in Hanoi in July 2010, which highlighted the disputes among the countries and called for a "multilateral" approach to end them.[15]

To the Chinese, the U.S. government intends to utilize the tension over the territory disputes between China and other Southeast Asian countries to contain or encircle China's rising and "rebalance" the region, maintaining strengthening the American role and influence in the region.

Most Chinese see the American gesture, especially the secretary of state's speech in Hanoi, as unnecessary and unreasonable. Because the Chinese believe that the South China Sea situation, including the territorial disputes, had been basically stable, peaceful, and quiet since 2002, when China and ASEAN reached the agreement on the Principles of Code of Conduct on the South China Sea. The agreement was proposed by the Chinese in the early 2000s, and the central part of the agreement is that no concerned parties should undertake unilateral action to change the status quo of the South China Sea, so that peace, security, and stability can be maintained.

In almost ten years following the agreement, its principles had basically been followed by countries in the region. No country undertook military action to change the situation, even though the disputes were maintained and some incidents occurred. In fact, there had been general peace and stability among the countries over the territorial disputes in the South China Sea between 2002 and 2010. Therefore, the Chinese could not understand why the American government, especially through Secretary Clinton's speech, brought up the relatively quiet issue in July 2010. Americans claim that a number of countries went to Washington to tell Americans about the wrongdoing of China in the South China Sea and demanded that the Americans stop the Chinese aggression.

That might be true. But who are those "countries"? Yes, they might be the Philippines and Vietnam. And more important is what they were saying about the Chinese "aggressive actions." They might include the cutting of seismic cables and harassing of fishing vessels and boats of other countries. Those incidents may have occurred, but they are nothing new. Those incidents have taken place among all parties at all times in the decades of the disputes. We have to understand that the South China Sea has been a disputed area among a few countries for a long time, and many minor incidents and conflicts have taken place every year. There was nothing unusual. The important thing is that no fighting, no war, no military confrontations, and no new taking of territory had occurred for ten years. The situation was basically okay. It would be unrealistic for anyone, including Americans, to expect that nothing at all would happen in the disputed South China Sea.

Therefore, the Chinese have sufficient reasons to be suspicious that the American high position toward the relatively quiet situation in the South China Sea is not because Americans thought the situation was serious but because they wanted to "return to Asia," to "rebalance" the rising China in Asia. For their pivot strategy, the Americans needed a "reason," and highlighting and aggrandizing the situation in the South China Sea was a good enough "reason" to justify their "returning" and "rebalancing."

In other words, there were not big troubles in the South China Sea for long time after 2002, but the Americans invented trouble there to "return to Asia" and "rebalance" the Chinese rising role and influence in Asia. It is quite a pity for American policy makers. Ten years ago when another Democratic administration was in power in Washington, the American Asian strategy was stated as "three pillars": economic interests, security, and democracy.[16] That America was confident and equally active in Asia. But ten years later, after the Iraq War and International Financial Crisis, Americans were not as confident as before; they see China continuing to rise and taking the American place as the largest trading partner in the region, and they believe that America's role and influence have been seriously threatened by the rising Chinese power and influence in Asia. And Americans believe they must do something to stop and change the trend.

That is fine. Every country wants to see its role and influence rising. Nobody likes to see its role and influence declining anywhere in the world. Here the problem is not the will of competition but the way. Ten years ago, Americans used three means—economy, security, and democracy—to compete with others, to reach American goals in the region. Ten years later, the new Democratic administration finds it can now use only security issues to advance American interests in the Asia-Pacific region. After losing the position of largest trade partner, Americans can do little to change the trends of competition of economic influence between the United States and China in the region. And after the Iraq War, especially abusing the human rights of their prisoners, and setting "secrete jails," seriously damaging America as the leader of freedom and democracy in the world, the Americans find they can no longer advance their interests and goals through advocating "democracy and human rights" in Asia and in the world, because nobody trusts and respects Americans as much as before the Iraq War.

Then American leaders find that their only strength and advantage is military and security. The best way that America can change the unfavorable trend in Asia is in the security arena, where America remains the most powerful and influential. This is the only strength and advantage that America can use in the region. Here the basic problem is that security issues are always negative and troublesome; they are not like economic and "democratic" issues that are always positive to everybody, except for a few nondemocratic regimes. Emphasizing security issues as a strategy means emphasizing problems, troubles, and disputes. Indeed, the American "return to Asia" and "rebalance" strategy emphasizes problems, troubles, and disputes in Asia, to utilize them to maintain the American role and influence, to maintain the American alliance system, to persuade Asians that they still need Americans. Therefore, it is a pity that a sole superpower can depend on only troubles to maintain its regional role. That is negative and destructive to the region. In fact, since the American "pivot" to Asia, more trouble has been taking place in the region, and tensions among Asians are growing, not diminishing, including between American allies in the region, Japan and South Korea.

To the Chinese, other countries in the region, especially American security alliances such as Japan and the Philippines, see the American strategic pivot and would utilize the movement to advance their own interests and agenda, and thus take some action in the territory disputes in the East and South China Seas, leading Japan to "nationalize" the disputed Diaoyu Islands, denying that it is a disputed issue, and the Philippines to send its largest naval ship to Huangyan Island and try to take over the disputed island in May 2012.

In addition to Huangyan Island, China and the Philippines have increasing tension over another territory: Renai Reef/the Second Thomas Shoal. It is a disputed territory between the two countries. The Philippines had trouble with a ship and left it on the reef in 1999. The Philippine government said it would repair the ship and remove it, according to the Chinese government. And the Philippines has not left the island since 1999. Chinese ships nearby have tried to stop the shipment of materials, but not the food and water meant for Philippine military personnel aboard the ship.

China has stated clearly it would not take part in nor accept any outcome of the Philippines' arbitration at ITLOS, because the Chinese government believes that the UN Convention at Sea in 1982 is about the exclusive economic zone (EEZ), not about the sovereignty of nations at sea or land, and the nine-dash line is a sovereign issue, not an EEZ matter, so the ITLOS does not have the authority to make any decisions over those sovereignty/territorial disputes, including the nine-dash line and Huangyan Island. China's government made a clear statement that it does not recognize that the convention has authority on sovereign issues.[17]

Another country that China has serious territory disputes in the South China Sea is Vietnam. Vietnam claims sovereignty over both Nansha and Xisha Islands. The Chinese government rejects the Vietnamese positions and states that all territories and waters within the nine-dash line belong to China.

The Sino-Vietnamese disputes over the South China Sea became very serious in the summer of 2014, when China launched an oil rig to drill 17 nautical miles away from its controlled Zhongjian Island and about 150 nautical miles from Vietnam's coast. The Chinese believe this is reasonable. First, China believes that all territories and waters within the nine-dash line are Chinese. Second, even considering Vietnamese claims to the Xisha Islands, this drilling was not near a place that Vietnam controls. Third, this was a commercial operation that countries, including Vietnam, have done for decades in the South China Sea.

The Vietnamese reactions by the government and citizens included riots against the Chinese and other Asian investments in Vietnam and the killing of three Chinese workers and wounding of about a hundred of them. The Chinese government stood firm against the Vietnamese reaction and warned the Chinese tourists about traveling to Vietnam. The political, economic, and social relations between the two countries suffered in the following months.

The Chinese withdrew the oil rig in the middle of July, after two months of operation. The stated reasons for the withdraw were that the company did not find oil or gas there and that a strong typhoon was imminent. Many Chinese doubt these are the true reasons for the withdraw, believing that the Chinese government yielded to Vietnamese and American pressure.

No matter the real reason for the Chinese withdrawal, it contributed to the improvement of relations between China and Vietnam and other countries, including the United States. The oil rig event may make the Chinese government more cautious in the future in the South China Sea, understanding that even a commercial action a Chinese claim can have a big impact on China's relations with other countries interested in the area.

But the general and basic position of China on the South China Sea has not changed. China remains tough over the disputed territory. Facing the American aggressive strategic movement of "rebalancing" China in Asia, and some countries' hard-line actions over the disputes in East and South China Seas, encouraged by the American "pivot" and "rebalancing" strategy, the Chinese government and people believe that they have no alternative but to stand up to the aggressive movements by Americans and their allies in the region. This is the situation we have today: more negative actions, words between China and other nations in the region, especially between China and Japan and China and the Philippines, over the disputed areas.

The "new" Chinese action in the South China Sea might be construction on the reefs that China controls in the sea, including airfields and seaports. China believes this is their national right to do in their sovereign territories, and China says Vietnam, the Philippines, and others have done the same over the years in the disputed territories in the sea. It looks as though China will continue to finish the current projects, which will enhance Chinese strength in the South China Sea.

But there are still some positive trends. After years of hesitation, the Chinese government has agreed to have China-ASEAN meetings to discuss the Code of Conduct in the South China Sea, and a meeting was held in Suzhou, China, on September 14 and 15, 2013. A "joint working group" was authorized to have specific consultations on the code of conduct. Chinese Vice Foreign Minister Liu Zhenmin spoke at the meeting and emphasized that the meetings between China and ASEAN should focus on improving cooperation in the South China Sea, not resolving those territorial disputes.[18]

China and the United States in Southeast Asia

When reviewing U.S.-China relations in the post–Cold War era, we can see that the major controversial areas between China and the United States in the 1990s were China's human rights, most favored nation trading status, the 1996 Taiwan crisis, and the embassy bombing in 1999. Then in the twenty-first century, China and the United States were heavily troubled by the Taiwan independence movement when Chen Shui-bian and the Democratic People's Progress Party were in power in Taiwan between 2001 and 2008.

And in recent years, China and the United States have seemed to focus on regional security and economic issues in East Asia and the Western Pacific. Southeast Asia, including the South China Sea, is certainly a major part of this regional conflict and competition between the United States and China.

The official position of the United States has been that it does not take a position over sovereignty in territory disputes in the East and South China Seas. The United States cares only about the freedom of sea lanes, and the peaceful means to deal with disputes among nations. Its position sounds neutral, but in fact the United States is not and cannot be neutral toward the disputes, because it is an ally of a number of concerned parties in the territorial disputes in Asia. For every time the Chinese did something over the disputes, the United States always made statements to criticize or attack the Chinese, including the Senate passing a nonbinding resolution condemning China's action in the East and South China Seas in late July 2014. Meanwhile the United States kept silent when Japan, Vietnam, and the Philippines took actions over the disputes, including some clearly aggressive and provocative words and actions.

In early 2014, the U.S. government took a position over the sovereignty issue in the South China Sea and challenged the Chinese sovereign position there. Assistant Secretary of State Daniel Russel and other U.S. government officials stated in early 2014 that the United States does not find a basis in international law for China's claim based on the "nine-dash line."[19]

The Chinese Foreign Ministry spokesman criticized the American position for "taking [a] position on the sovereignty disputes," which stands against the long-stated American position, and restated that China's sovereignty rights over the South China Sea are "historical and solid."[20]

Most Chinese support their government's position. They believe that territory in Asia, and in the world, was determined by historical developments, most not by law or treaties and agreements. In fact boundaries were formed long before the establishment of international laws, which are basically modern phenomena. And there has been a fundamental legal principle that any law cannot and should not apply to something that predates the law. If new laws apply to the historical development before the law, then everything in the world should be reset again, including the territory of the United States.

However, over the years, including in the past year when China and the Philippines intensified their dispute over Huangyan Island in May 2012, the United States, as the security ally of the Philippines, tried hard not to take a position.

Certainly as a major ally, the Philippines expects and demands that the United States show its support of the Philippine side over the dispute. But in years of the dispute over Huangyan Island, the American government did not highlight the issue and did not show its support to the Philippines. The American long-term position is that its security agreement/treaty does not cover the territory that was not controlled by the partners in the alliance when the agreement or treaty was signed.

The State Department spokesman and other American government officials clearly criticized the Chinese over the South China Sea dispute, such as in reaction to China's established "Sansha Administration" in 2012, but most of time Americans keep a lower profile. During the frequent visits and meetings at all the levels, including the summit meeting between Presidents Obama and Xi at the Annenberg Estate in California in early June 2013, American leaders and officials did talk with their Chinese counterparts about the South China Sea issue, but the general tone was hoping that China and other parties would exercise constraint, not increase tensions. In other words, the general American approach was lowering, not increasing, tensions. This is constructive for maintaining peace and stability in the region.

But the situation and American position have changed dramatically since the first half of 2014. The president, the secretaries of state and defense, the national security advisor, and many high-level officials of the United States came out to attack China for its actions in South China Sea, including the oil rig as "proactive," and even "invasion."[21] To the Chinese, Americans seem to have gone crazy in opposing China on every dispute China has with Asian countries. China does not fear this American hard-liner approach. It seems that the United States and China are engaging in a new confrontation over the regional security issues in Asia, and China would be even stronger to defend its security and sovereignty interests as it did over six decades, even if that means war with the United States, such as in Korea and Vietnam in the Cold War era.

For more than twenty years, Vietnam has been exploiting oil and gas resources in the disputed areas with China in the South China Sea, yet the United States never said anything about unilateral actions taken in disputed areas by the Vietnamese. But when China launched the oil rig, all high-level U.S. officials immediately came out to criticize China. National Security Advisor Susan Rice even attacked China's drilling in the South China Sea as a "provocative and aggressive action."[22] Rice and other American officials should know that the drilling takes place 150 nautical miles from the coast of Vietnam, so it is at best in the disputed area of the EEZ between Vietnam and China, according to the UN Convention on the Law of Sea 1982, rather than the territory of any country, and if this is "provocative and aggressive" action, then the American officials should know that the U.S. warplanes and ships go into China's EEZ almost every day, also "provocative and aggressive" actions.

It is quite clear that with regard to territorial disputes in the East and South China Seas, the United States does not care about either the facts or the historical background, or who is right and who is wrong; it looks at these disputes only as China versus other countries. It would oppose anything China says or does over those disputed issues, and it would support any other countries that confront China. This is a reflection of the "pivot" or "rebalancing" strategy aimed to counter the rise of China in Asia and protect the U.S. role and influence in the region.

Such a biased confrontational approach would not help the United States in reaching its goal to deter or balance, if not contain, China. Since it is so clear that this approach is targeting China, China should and will choose to ignore it. While China does not want to, it equally does not fear the confrontation that the United States has initiated. China certainly had the capability to cope with U.S. confrontation decades ago in Korea and Vietnam, and has the capacity to protect its legitimate rights in the Western Pacific today.

One "bilateral" difference or dispute between the United States and China in the South China Sea is about the freedom navigation. High-level officials, including the secretary of state and the secretary of defense, have frequently stated that freedom of navigation in the South China Sea is a key interest of the United States. The Chinese government says all the time too that China respects the right of freedom of navigation at sea. It states that this is also a key Chinese interest because China is a big trade and transportation power. The Chinese government argues that there has been no problem of freedom of navigation in the South China Sea, and in the future China would not deny that right to the United States or other countries.[23]

But the United States seems not to be convinced by the Chinese confirmation, because Americans worry about the Chinese position claiming all the islands and reefs in the sea, and the "nine-dash line" that claims that around 80 percent of the water of the South China Sea is Chinese territory. American logic is that since China claims those waters are the Chinese, China can and might deny passage at any point in the future and freedom of navigation would be lost.

Like the Taiwan issue, the United States and China do have serious differences on the South China Sea disputes and others in the region. But one should not conclude that the two countries are at conflict in Asia. Now the two countries have a dialogue mechanism about "regional issues" of Asia, and China and the United States also have common ground on many regional issues such as Korea. The experiences over Taiwan, the most controversial problem between the countries, demonstrate that the two big powers can manage their differences, even if they cannot resolve them. Therefore, through intensive dialogue and consultation and mutual influence, China and the United States might control and narrow their differences in Southeast Asia and across Asia, and develop a "new type of major powers' relations" now and in the future.

Over the years, the Americans and Chinese have seemed to reach consensus on a "new type of major power relations" between them, even though they may use different words or terms. President Obama, Secretary Clinton, and Secretary Kerry all have stated that the U.S.-China relationship is not a zero-sum game, it is not a U.S.-Soviet type of relationship.[24] The two countries have tried to avoid a confrontational or conflictual relationship. The intensive dialogues, such as summit meetings and the Strategic and Economic Dialogue each year, indicate the intention of the two countries to have a cooperative not confrontational relationship.

And the testing ground for the new type of relationship is Asia, especially in the East and South China Seas. Here Americans and Chinese do have differences, and there is a danger of military and security confrontation. But over the years, the United States and China have worked hard to discuss the disputed issues. They may not be able to resolve their differences, but they can keep engagement over the disputed territories and manage their differences.

The Strategic and Economic Dialogue between the two countries in Washington in July 2013 produced some good news: the two sides agreed to discuss a mechanism to give advanced notice to each other for major military actions in the region of Asia-Pacific.[25] This would be another major measure of confidence building, which can reduce the dangers of misunderstanding and incidents.

In fact, the United States and China, and other countries in Asia, need more codes of conduct and confidence building to manage their differences and disputes. China and the United States should go along this constructive direction in dealing with the disputed issues between them, and among China and other countries in Southeast Asia. The foreign ministers' meeting between China and ASEAN in July 2013 reached an agreement to engage in dialogue on a real code of conduct for the South China Sea.[26] This is certainly good news for the region and for managing the disputes between China and Southeast Asian countries in the region.

More than twenty naval leaders, including those of the American, Japanese, and Philippine fleets, on the sidelines of the Western Pacific Naval Symposium in Qingdao, China, in April 2014, reached the Code for Unplanned Encounters at Sea, a navy-to-navy template designed to reduce misunderstandings and avoid maritime accidents.[27]

Besides managing the differences or disputes between China and the United States, and between China and other Southeast Asian countries, China has to manage its rising issues. First is the rising of Chinese military power and activities in the Asia-Pacific region. China is rising and thus has the right to modernize its military and to engage in military activities in the seas in Asia-Pacific, as the United States and other countries have done for decades. But China should fully understand that other Asian countries have the right to worry about the increasing Chinese military power and activities near them. So China should engage in more dialogues, explanations, consultations, transparency, confidence-building measures, and code of conduct with all other Asian countries and the United States in the region. This is necessary to reduce and avoid misunderstandings, incidents, and tension over many security issues in the region.

The second issue is managing the territorial disputes between China and other nations in Asia. Territorial disputes are very important and emotional issues to all the nations, and they are often difficult to resolve. Every country, including China, should understand the sensitivity and complexity of the issues, and should not seek quick solutions of these difficult and complicated issues. Maintaining the status quo and keeping the balance is the best approach before the final solution. Then, every country should not seek a superiority toward the disputed issues. It should be fine enough for countries to can maintain the status quo and balanced situation of the territorial disputes. Everyone should take some self-restraint toward bilateral disputes. The Chinese government should resist the will of its general public for taking advantage of the territorial disputes, and even to finally resolve the disputes favoring China alone.

Southeast Asia is not the only place where the United States and China interact; there is certainly a bigger area where the two countries have important interests, and the two countries' relations in Southeast Asia are in fact determined by those bigger areas and issues.

One of the bigger issues for the United States and China is their strategic goal in the whole of Asia. Here the two powers have common interests and differences, if not conflicts. American Asian strategy has been clear—maintaining its leadership role and alliance system in the region. And the regional goal of China, as a rising power, has not been given. President Xi Jinping offered a slogan in May at a pan-Asian meeting in Shanghai of "Asia for the Asians." To the Chinese, this is a long-term vision, and there is nothing wrong with it. It is no difference from saying Europe is for Europeans or Africa is for Africans. Xi's words show the Chinese anger over Americans' harsh words in the first half of 2014. Attacking China over the East and South China Seas issues is not a strategy or policy, and nothing follows it. It is just a general slogan and thinking.

The United States and China may have differences on some real Chinese proposals. One is RCEP and TPP. It looks like RCEP is more general and TPP more specific and serious in promoting economic relations in Asia-Pacific. The Southeast Asian countries may benefit from both processes. While RCEP will not cost Southeast Asian nations too much, TPP will force Vietnam, the Philippines, and other countries in the subregion to reform their economic, political, and social practices. TPP is much more serious and demands major changes to countries' internal policies.

While the United States has been pushing for TPP in Asia, China has been busy in promoting the New Silk Road, Maritime Silk Road, and Asian Infrastructure Investment Bank (AIIB). Those are big proposals that require massive effort. Therefore, the Asians and the world will witness that Chinese leaders and government will be working hard now and into the future to implement those plans. They will take lots of Chinese time, money, and other resources to push them to fruition. These Chinese proposals do not mean that China wants to replace the existing international institutions such as the World Bank, IMF, and ADB. China will continue to try to play a bigger role in these institutions. But the fact will be that China will not have equal resources to offer the existing international institutions. China will have to spend more on its own proposals.

On the still bigger issue of regional architecture in Asia, China in the past preferred ASEAN+3 as the "main channel" for regional cooperation in Asia. And Americans, Australians, and even the Japanese were not happy with it and worried that China might dominate the process. Then they made EAS (East Asia Summit) to counter the ASEAN+3. With this dual situation, China can no longer expect the ASEAN+3 to be the "main channel." Then what is and will be the "main channel"? The Chinese government has not given a clear idea. China still has not given a clear indication on regional architecture in Asia-Pacific. It has given clear ideas on some smaller and specific things such as One Belt, One Road and AIIB, but not on a bigger framework for the whole region, because, as argued by this essay, China for thousands years has been a power without global and regional strategies. This is not likely to change now and in the future, even as China is "rising."

China has always had a vision and strategy for bilateral relations with Asian countries and subregions. In the security arena, China's major concerns are the United States and Japan, and the strategy to deal with the concerns is to have a relatively good political and economic relationship with them, and strengthen Chinese military capacity. China so far has not had a regional security strategy, as it has not had a comprehensive regional strategy. China's security strategy amounts to monitoring the American threat in the Pacific, largely the Western Pacific, opposing American interference in Taiwan, the Diaoyu Islands, and the South China Sea disputes, and pushing American spy planes and ships away from Chinese territory.

Conclusion

China will keep rising, even at a somewhat slower pace compared with the annual growth rate of 9.9 percent in the past thirty years. The rise of China does include its military strength and activities in the Western Pacific, including in the South China Sea.

China seems unlikely to change its long-term policy of having good relations with the Southeast Asian countries, at least most of them, if not all. China would continue to develop its economic, diplomatic, and social/cultural relations with the Southeast Asia countries. But at the bottom line, Southeast Asia is not a strategic region to China, as the Northeast Asia has been. Southeast Asia has much economic, diplomatic, and symbolic importance to China. Thus, China will continue to strengthen its economic, social, and cultural relations and ties with the subregion. At the same time China does not have a big strategic goal in Southeast Asia, just because the subregion is not of strategic importance to China. It has big influence over Chinese foreign economic and diplomatic relations, but the subregion does not determine China's security and economic future, even though the United States is deeply involved in the region. The bigger picture for China is Japan, Northeast Asia, Russia, India, Europe, and the United States; those determine China's great power relations and diplomacy, economic modernization, and strategic environment, now and in the future. Compared with those major powers and areas, Southeast Asia is always a relatively smaller and less powerful area to China. Therefore, China will continue to have better economic, social, and diplomatic ties with Southeast Asia, but not seeking a great role for China in the subregion. And China does not see the subregion as of great strategic importance to China, now or in the future.

China and the United States now are becoming more confrontational in the South China Sea. This seems to be the new area of Sino-U.S. tensions now and into the future, but the growing confrontation is not likely to change the trends and direction of China-U.S. relations, because the relationship has become more solid, complicated, and comprehensive, it is not likely to be determined by one area of the relationship and issues.

NOTES

1 Cheng Hui, "China and ASEAN," 3.
2 *China's Foreign Trade*, February 2015, 8.
3 Minister Gao Hucheng interviewed by China Central Television (CCTV), evening news, August 1, 2013; Li Jiarao, "Nation 'Confident' on Trade," 13.
4 Cheng Hui, "China and ASEAN," 3; and Zhong Sheng, "Taking the New Opportunities," 5.
5 Cheng Cheng, "Accumulative Bilateral Investment between China and ASEAN Reached $123.1 Billion in 2014" (November 7, 2014), www.asean168.com.
6 Chao Shaochong, "New Chinese Immigrants," 31.
7 Zhong Sheng, "Taking the New Opportunities," 5.
8 Hu Jintao, "Building Long-Term Peace," 1.
9 Huntington, *Clash of Civilizations*, 242.

10   Jiang Zhemin, "Report to the 16th Congress," 4.
11   Zhong Sheng, "Taking the New Opportunities," 5.
12   Zhou Wa, "Wang Aims above Regional Rows," 11.
13   Deng Xiaoping, "Speech at the 3rd Meeting of the Advisory Commission," 87.
14   Xi Jinping, "Speech at the 8th Study Meeting," 1.
15   U.S. Department of State, "Hillary Rodham Clinton Remarks."
16   "Roth 7/22 Remarks," 19; and Liu Liandi, *Major Documents on China-U.S. Relations*, 381.
17   Zheng Sheng, "China's Sovereignty," 3; Lu Yang, "Tribunal Arbitration," 5.
18   Zhang Yunbi, "China, ASEAN to Ignore 'Distractions,'" 11.
19   Dyer, "U.S. Toughens Line on China Sea Clash."
20   Xiao Qiang and Yu Wen, "China and U.S. Diplomatic 'Oral Confrontation,'" 3; and Chen Weihua, "US Must Cease Biased Remarks," 8.
21   White House, "Remarks of President Barack Obama."; Li Xiaokun et al., "US 'Must Respect History,'" 1.
22   "National Security Adviser Susan Rice."
23   U.S. Department of State, "Hillary Rodham Clinton Remarks"; Wang Qian and Zhang Yunbei, "Xi Vows to Protect Maritime Interests," 2; and Wu Jiao, "China Calls for Regional Peace," 1.
24   "Secretary Clinton's Interview," 42; Zhu Zhe, "Redefining Relations," 1.
25   Wen Xian et al., "The 5th Economic and Strategic Dialogue Completed," 3.
26   Li Xiaokun, "Foreign Minister Makes ASEAN Debut as Tensions Flare," 12.
27   Zhao Shengnan, "Pact to Reduce Sea Conflicts," 1; Zhao Shengnan, "Worries over Beijing's Maritime Ambitions 'Unnecessary,'" 11.

BIBLIOGRAPHY

Chao Shaochong. "The New Chinese Immigrants and Chinese Society in the U.S." *Shijie Minzhu* [World nationalities], no. 6 (2005): 31.
Chen Weihua. "US Must Cease Biased Remarks on China, Warns Top Diplomat." *China Daily*, February 22, 2014, 8.
Cheng Hui. "China and ASEAN: Bilateral Trade Expected to be $500 Billion by 2015." *Renmin Ribao* [People's daily]. July 24, 2013.
Clinton, Hillary. "America's Pacific Century." *Foreign Affairs*, October 2011.
Deng Xiaoping. "Speech at the 3rd Meeting of the Advisory Commission of the CPC Central Committee." In *Selected Works of Deng Xiaoping*, vol. 3. Beijing: Ren Min, 1993.
Documents Editing Committee of the Communist Party Central Committee of China. *Selected Works of Deng Xiaoping*. Beijing: People's Publishing House, 1993.
Dyer, Geoff. "U.S. Toughens Line on China Sea Clash." *Fortuna's Corner*, February 9, 2014. www.fortunascorner.com.
Hu Jintao. "Building Long-Term Peace, Mutual Prosperous, and Harmonious World." *Renmin Ribao*, September 16, 2005.

———. "Report to the 17th Congress of the Communist Party of China." *Renmin Ribao*, October 25, 2007, 1–4.

———. "Report to the 18th Congress of the Communist Party of China." *Renmin Ribao*, November 18, 2012, 1–4.

Huntington, Samuel P. *The Clash of Civilizations and the Remaking of World Order.* Beijing: Xinhua Publishing House, 2002.

Information Office of the State Council of China. "The Diversified Employment of China's Armed Forces." Defense White Paper. *China Daily*, April 16, 2013, 8–11.

Jiang Zhemin. "Report to the 16th Congress of the Communist Party of China." *Renmin Ribao*, November 18, 2002, 1–4.

"Kerry Offers View of U.S. Role in More Interconnected World." *Washington File*, January 24, 2013, 1–2.

Li Guoqiang. "Prospecting and Developing South China Sea Oil and Gas Resources." *China International Studies* 49 (November/December 2014): 126–43.

Li Jiarao. "Nation 'Confident' on Trade." *China Daily*, August 2, 2013.

Li Keqiang. "Creating the New Future Asian Development Together: Speech at the Baoao Asian Forum." *Renmin Ribao*, April 11, 2014, 2.

———. "Time for Harvest and Sowing for Future: Speech at Tenth China-ASEAN Expo and the China-ASEAN Business and Investment Summit." *China Daily*, September 5, 2013, 9.

Li Xiaokun. "Foreign Minister Makes ASEAN Debut as Tensions Flare." *China Daily*, July 1, 2013, 12.

Li Xiaokun et al. "US 'Must Respect History.'" *China Daily*, February 15–16, 2014, 1.

Liu Liandi. *Major Documents on China-U.S. Relations.* Beijing: Shisi Publishing House, 1998.

Liu Zhenmin. "Laying the Foundation of Peace and Stability for an Asian Community of Shared Destiny." *China International Studies* 49 (November/December 2014): 17–26.

Lu Yang. "Tribunal Arbitration on S. China Sea Neither Fair Not Just." *China Daily*, December 19, 2015, 5.

"National Security Adviser Susan Rice on This Yesterday at the Women's Foreign Policy Group." *Nelson Report*, May 15, 2014.

National Intelligence Council of the U.S. *Global Trends 2030.* December 10, 2012.

"Roth 7/22 Remarks to Senate Foreign Relations Committee." *USIS Bulletin*, July 23, 1997, 19.

"Secretary Clinton's Interview at Global Town Hall." *Washington File*, January 29, 2013, 42.

U.S.-China Joint Statement. *Washington File*, January 20, 2011.

U.S. Department of State. "Hillary Rodham Clinton Remarks at the ASEAN-U.S. Ministerial Meeting Hanoi, Vietnam, July 22, 2010." www.state.gov.

Wang Qian and Zhang Yunbei. "Xi Vows to Protect Maritime Interests." *China Daily*, August 1, 2013, 2.

Wen Xian et al. "The 5th Economic and Strategic Dialogue Completed." *Renmin Ribao*, July 11, 2013, 3.

White House. "Remarks of President Barack Obama Graduation Ceremony West Point." www.whitehouse.gov.

Wu Jiao. "China Calls for Regional Peace." *China Daily*, April 14, 2013, 1.

Xi Jinping. "Speech at the 8th Study Meeting of the Politburo." *Renmin Ribnao*, August 1, 2013, 1.

———. "Speech at the Foreign Affairs Meeting of the CPC Central Committee." *Renmin Ribao*, November 30, 2014, 1.

———. "Working Together toward a Better Future for Asia and the World: Speech at the Boao Forum for Asia Annual Conference 2013." *China Daily*, April 9, 2013, 8.

Xiao Qiang and Yu Wen. "China and U.S. Diplomatic 'Oral Confrontation.'" *Global Times*, February 10, 2014, 3.

Yang Jiechi. "Go Along the Road of Peaceful Development." *China Daily*, December 14, 2012, 6.

———. "Innovations in Diplomatic Theory, Practice." *China Daily*, August 17, 2013, 5.

Zhang Yunbi. "China, ASEAN to Ignore 'Distractions.'" *China Daily*, September 16, 2013, 11.

Zhao Shengnan. "Pact to Reduce Sea Conflicts." *China Daily*, April 23, 2014, 1.

———. "Worries over Beijing's Maritime Ambitions 'Unnecessary.'" *China Daily*, April 14, 2014, 11.

Zheng Sheng. "China's Sovereignty over South China Sea Territory Is Not Deniable." *Renmin Ribao*, December 15, 2015, 3.

Zhong Sheng. "Taking the New Opportunities of China-ASEAN Relations." *Renmin Ribao*, May 7, 2013.

Zhou Wa. "Wang Aims above Regional Rows." *China Daily*, August 5, 2013.

Zhu Zhe. "Redefining Relations." *China Daily*, June 9, 2013, 1.

Zoellick, Robert. "The Great Powers' Relationship Hinges on the Pacific." *Financial Times*, June 5, 2013, 9.

13

U.S. Security Strategy and Southeast Asia

MARVIN C. OTT

The Historical Setting

With the exception of the Philippines, America's strategic interest in and engagement with Southeast Asia begins with World War II. Prior to that "Monsoon Asia" was remote and exotic—a place of fabled kingdoms, jungle headhunters, and tropical seas. By the end of the nineteenth century European powers had established colonial rule over the entire region except Thailand. Then, as the twentieth century dawned, the Spanish colonial holdings in the Philippines suddenly and unexpectedly became available to the United States as an outcome of the Spanish-American War and Admiral Dewey's destruction of the decrepit Spanish fleet in Manila Bay.

This presented a quandary. Post–Civil War America was emerging as a major industrial power, and many, like President McKinley's high-voltage vice president, Theodore Roosevelt, thought economic capacity must perforce translate into military strength. Alfred Mahan was providing the intellectual scaffolding to justify a modern navy with global reach. But America's traditional self-image and moral vocation were overtly anticolonial; "American empire" did not sound right or sit well with much of the citizenry or the Congress. The president prayed on the matter and announced that American moral standards and rightful international stature could be reconciled if the United States took over administration of the Philippines with the avowed purpose of preparing the archipelago for independence. And so it happened. The Tydings-McDuffie Act committed the United States to a thirty-year timetable that would see the Philippines become independent in 1947.

By the early 1930s it seemed likely that America's Philippine adventure would go down as a colorful sidebar in the historical narrative. There was little to suggest it might portend a serious strategic engagement with Southeast Asia. The Philippines is geographically distant from the rest of Southeast Asia, and the United States had little interest in fostering ties with British, French, and Dutch holdings in the region. The greater implications of America's colonial enterprise seemed to be none.

That all changed with World War II. Japan's war aims gave a high priority to capturing and exploiting the resources and geographical position of Southeast Asia. U.S. forces in the Philippines were attacked as part of the same military operation that targeted Pearl Harbor. Inevitably, Southeast Asia became a major theater in the global military contest. In fact, the term "Southeast Asia" was coined when Britain's Lord Mountbatten was given command of Allied ground forces operating in the territory between India and China. For Americans, the war for the future of East Asia, including Southeast Asia, was to be largely fought as a naval and air campaign in the vast maritime stretches from Australia to Hawaii to the home islands of Japan. As it happened, the U.S. commander of these forces, General Douglas MacArthur, had been stationed in the Philippines at the outbreak of the war.

With the defeat and occupation of Japan, the United States found itself with extensive territorial holdings in the South Pacific, an army-led occupation administration of Japan, and no plans to retain a large military presence elsewhere in Asia, much less Southeast Asia. The Philippines received its independence in 1947 on the schedule laid out by Tydings-McDuffie.

Again, events conspired to profoundly alter U.S. strategic expectations. The advent of the Cold War and the North Korean attack across the Thirty-Eighth Parallel in Korea created an utterly new security environment. President Truman surprised allies and adversaries alike by committing U.S. forces to the defense of South Korea. Suddenly the Philippines became important as a location for U.S. air, naval, and other military support facilities. In 1951 the U.S.-Philippines Mutual Defense Treaty codified a large U.S. military footprint in the Philippines centered on the massive naval base at Subic Bay but comprising at its height over eighty facilities of one kind or another.

Most Americans understandably think of the Cold War as "cold"— involving a military standoff in Europe and a frightening strategic stability based on offsetting intercontinental ballistic missiles and the doctrine of mutual assured destruction. It is easy to forget that in Southeast Asia the Cold War was hot. A postwar Comintern decision set in motion active communist insurgencies and revolutionary movements throughout the region intent on overthrowing (first) returning colonial regimes and (later) indigenous postcolonial governments. As part of its global containment strategy the United States became an active protagonist in the contest for the political future of Southeast Asia. This was particularly evident in the Philippines, where the United States provided advice, technical and logistical support, and intelligence assistance to the Philippine government and armed forces in its long-running struggle with communist insurgents—first, the Hukbalahap and then the New People's Army. Indochina became the other principal Southeast Asian arena for U.S. forces, culminating in the decade-long Vietnam War. That grinding conflict cost fifty-eight thousand American lives—sacrificed to the proposition that a noncommunist Southeast Asia was a vital U.S. national interest.

Given the magnitude of the costs and effort, it was startling to watch how rapidly and thoroughly the United States unwound its strategic position in Southeast Asia following the 1973 Paris Peace Accords and the final withdrawal of all U.S. forces and diplomatic personnel from Saigon in 1975. It became clear very quickly that key components of the U.S. security establishment including the Pentagon and the CIA wanted nothing more to do with Southeast Asia. Both organizations rapidly divested themselves of expertise on the region and on counterinsurgency more generally. The entire experience in Vietnam had been ugly and painful, and America was going to shift its focus to more congenial areas—Europe (NATO), the Middle East, and the "Revolution in Military Affairs" (the application of advanced technology to military systems, including in space).

The final shoe dropped in 1991 when the United States and the Philippines agreed (acrimoniously) to end the lease that authorized the U.S. military bases in the Philippines. Southeast Asia effectively fell off Washington's security map; it became instead a place of high interest to U.S. corporations and banks as the region enjoyed explosive economic growth. Any lingering U.S. security attention faded with the withdrawal of the Vietnamese army from Cambodia in 1989 and the subsequent diplomatic settlement that stabilized an independent Cambodia.

The Post–Vietnam War Era

In geopolitical terms, Southeast Asia in the post–Vietnam War period enjoyed remarkable regional stability. Over the three-plus decades following the war (1975–ca. 2009) the region was largely free of either cross-border conflicts or major domestic revolutions.[1]

The sources of this strategic quiescence were multiple and interesting.

First, the entire region shared a consensus that the overriding task facing governments was economic development and societal modernization. The results have been striking; regional growth rates have transformed a largely rural, poor, and premodern region into the great economic success story of the postcolonial Third World. The shared commitment to modernization powerfully supported cross-border synergies and positive-sum relationships across the region.

Second, Japan played a major economic role as investor, trader, and banker to the region—but Tokyo never translated its economic prowess into an active strategic role.

Third, the overthrow of the Sukarno regime in 1965 removed a radical, destabilizing force in the region and brought an end to Indonesia's "Konfrontasi" aimed at the destruction of Malaysia. The successor Suharto government in Jakarta joined with Kuala Lumpur in helping create ASEAN.

Fourth, beginning with the formation of ASEAN in 1967, Southeast Asia produced a noteworthy edifice of regional institutions fostering economic, diplomatic, cultural, political, technical, and even security linkages among the ASEAN states and between them and the wider Asia-Pacific. Along the way ASEAN became what the late political scientist Karl Deutsch termed a "security community"—a collectivity of states that have effectively foresworn warfare as a means of dispute settlement among them.

Fifth, a potentially potent destabilizing factor, China, became instead a constructive partner. China joined the development consensus relatively late (following the death of Mao) but join it did, becoming an integral, dynamic part of the overall regional growth formula. Beijing's support for communist revolutions in Southeast Asia in the 1950s, 1960s, and even 1970s had not been forgotten. But under paramount leader Deng Xiaoping that policy was abandoned wholesale. In its place Beijing mounted a very skilled diplomatic/public affairs campaign to convey an image to Southeast Asia of a good neighbor that shared the aspirations of the region. The rhetoric was given tangible effect by a series of free trade agreements and other arrangements between China and Southeast Asia bolstered by massive infrastructure projects (roadways, railways, IT networks, energy grids, riverine transport systems, and airline connections) linking China with Southeast Asia.

Finally, the United States played a key role in this bucolic circumstance. Despite strategic indifference from Washington, the U.S. Pacific Command continued to maintain a substantial naval and air presence in the region that included regular patrols through the South China Sea and Straits of Malacca into the Indian Ocean. The net effect was to retain the U.S. position as the strongest military power in the region—one with no territorial ambitions and primary interests in regional peace, prosperity, and stability. U.S. interests were coincident with those of the ASEAN governments, and America, in effect, became the village cop who threatened no one and reassured everyone. In the language of political science, the region was spared a security dilemma spiral and the arms races that would accompany it.

For the U.S. armed forces in and around Southeast Asia, the post–Vietnam War period was one this writer has characterized previously as "policy without strategy." Pacific Command was active throughout the region: naval patrols, air deployments, port visits, joint exercises and training with local militaries, VIP exchanges, military sales, and natural disaster responses. The list was a long one, and it kept thousands of sailors and airmen occupied. Moreover, the formal defense obligations that attended U.S. treaties with Thailand, the Philippines, New Zealand (until 1984), and Australia remained operative. It all had strategic implications, but it was not animated or guided by an overall strategy.[2] This, in turn, reflected a lack of attention to the region at the highest levels of U.S. policy making—the Office of the Secretary of Defense, the National Security Council, the Seventh Floor of the State Department, and the White House. The ways that secretaries of state have chosen to allocate their time and travel is illustrative. In the Clinton administration Secretary Christopher chose to devote his energies heavily to the Middle East and the Israeli-Palestinian dispute. His successor, Madeleine Albright, was consumed by the postcommunist transformation of Central Europe. George W. Bush's secretary, Condoleezza Rice, received annual entreaties to attend ASEAN ministerial conclaves but was a reliable no-show.

Institutional arrangements within the Department of Defense exacerbated the problem. Security cooperation was (and is) run out of PACOM's J4 (Logistics) not the more logical J5 (Policy and Plans). This is the last major U.S. Command organized in this fashion. This in turn may contribute to what one military officer familiar with the system describes as "a great leap from the Office of the Secretary of Defense to PACOM policy wonks and then out to country teams. This sometimes leads to policy breakdowns since State and Defense are organized very differently."[3]

The dearth of strategy can also be illustrated by how specific issues and countries were handled. In 1988 oppressive military rule in Burma produced a popular uprising led by the iconic Aung San Suu Kyi. To placate the populace the military allowed elections that it tried to rig and then annulled—while imprisoning the leaders of the prodemocracy movement. Washington reacted with condemnation and increasingly severe sanctions. The policy was characterized and implemented as a morality play—standing up for good and punishing evil. The policy had serious strategic consequences by providing an opening for Chinese influence and presence, but that never became a consideration in U.S. policy. In the case of Vietnam, Washington began a slow process of postwar reconciliation with Hanoi in the early 1990s. For years the issues in play were essentially political and moral—the search for the remains of American servicemen who had died in combat and the mitigation of the environmental and health effects of the use of Agent Orange. Again, there were strategic implications involving China that went *largely* unnoted.

The 9/11 attacks in New York and Washington galvanized the Bush administration into a strategic response—the Global War on Terror (GWOT). The overall merits of that construct are outside the purview of this essay. The GWOT did impact Southeast Asia, a region the president characterized as the "second front" in that campaign. U.S. forces in small numbers were deployed into the southern Philippines to assist the Philippine army in their operations against a nominally jihadist group (Abu Sayyaf) that was mainly a criminal gang in the business of kidnapping for ransom. September 11 revivified defense (and intelligence) contacts with several Southeast Asian states, notably Indonesia, and the president visited the region. But it was not long before regional governments began to complain that the U.S. focus was limited to counterterrorism, to the exclusion of virtually everything else. Counterterrorism was too narrow a pedestal on which to build a strategic relationship.

On December 26, 2004, a massive tsunami hit northern Sumatra, causing damage of apocalyptic dimensions. In the days and weeks that followed the U.S. Seventh Fleet provided critical search and rescue capabilities along with disaster relief that could be provided by no one else. For security strategists there were important strategic consequences, but the event was treated and portrayed purely in terms of disaster mitigation. In the eyes of many, the most important mission of America's vast naval power in the Pacific wasn't military at all; it was humanitarian.

There were limited exceptions to this picture of a strategy-free zone. When it became clear that U.S.-Philippine negotiations over a renewal of the bases agreement were in trouble, Prime Minister Lee Kuan Yew of Singapore made it clear that his small country was prepared to do whatever it could to provide the United States with facilities that would offset those being lost in the Philippines. The Singaporeans were thinking strategically. They were deeply concerned that with the Cold War over and the Philippine bases gone, the U.S. military would simply turn its back on Southeast Asia, leaving the region to its own devices. That was profoundly unsettling because Singapore officials saw a rising China as a future dominant power in the region. Chinese power, unconstrained and unbalanced by a U.S. presence, was not a comfortable prospect. Lee Kuan Yew, incidentally, had long argued that the Vietnam War had an important strategic benefit for Southeast Asia in that it "bought ten years" for Southeast Asian nations to strengthen their capacity ("resilience") to resist communism. It was an argument that almost never appeared in America's long, angry internal debate over that conflict. In the event, Singapore built specialized facilities, notably including a pier for aircraft carriers, designed to service U.S. naval vessels during their Southeast Asian deployments.

Admiral Charles Larson, the Commander of U.S. Pacific Forces (1991–94), responded to the loss of bases in the Philippines with a strategic concept he labeled "places not bases." It envisioned U.S. forces present in Southeast Asia with a smaller, more diversified footprint. It was designed to preserve U.S. combat capabilities while placing a lighter political burden on host governments in the region. It was a creative, thoughtful construct, but there was little evidence it ever generated serious attention or interest at the top levels in Washington.

In 1990 Congress actually tried to compel the Pentagon and State Department to think strategically about Southeast Asia by requiring a report (with State Department input) titled the East Asia Strategy Review (EASR). That study, and a follow-up in 1992 titled "A Strategic Framework for the Asian Pacific Region," emphasized unimpeded freedom of navigation through the major sea lanes of communication (SLOCs) as a critical U.S. security interest. The most consequential implications of that assertion—that it apparently contradicted a Chinese claim that those same sea lanes were inside Chinese sovereign jurisdiction—went unnoted. A subsequent iteration of the EASR released in 1995 inexplicably omitted all references to the SLOCs. That omission was actually inadvertent—the product of too many editors exchanging too many drafts. Tellingly, almost no one in official Washington even noticed, and the oversight was never publicly corrected. This, in itself, said volumes about the lack of strategic awareness regarding the region. With Chinese naval power growing and the contemporaneous Chinese seizure of Mischief Reef (within the Philippines EEZ) it never occurred to responsible officials that the United States, by dropping the language of the 1990 version, was sending a signal to Beijing that the United States was less likely to stand in the way of China's ambitions in the South China Sea. In 1992 China enacted the Law of Territorial Waters and Contiguous Land Claims, asserting its jurisdiction over the South China Sea, and in 1999 Beijing closed off the Paracels Archipelago for eight weeks to all fishermen. In 2009 the closure was extended to ten weeks. None of this generated any discernible reaction from the U.S. government. It was no accident that some years later U.S. officials visiting China encountered an insistent message that America's days in Asia were numbered and U.S. power was on its way out of the region.

The Contemporary Strategic Context

By the midpoint of the first decade of this century, Southeast Asia had settled into a distinctive geopolitical pattern. Economic development and modernization remained the priority enterprise of government and nongovernment elites. China was an increasingly prominent partner in that enterprise as economic connectivity between Southeast Asia and southern China grew at a breakneck pace. At the same time, China was investing a significant proportion of its growing wealth into building a modern military—with particular emphasis on naval and air maritime forces. Published Chinese statistics showed annual increments in military spending at a stunning 16 to 17 percent.

There was something else. From the outset, the People's Republic adopted and reissued maps first drawn by the Nationalist regime showing almost the entire South China Sea encompassed by a "nine-dash line." The Nationalist government characterized that line as an international boundary demarcating the rightful territorial extent of China—a position the government, now on Taiwan, still affirms. The PRC did nothing to disavow, modify, or clarify that claim. In 1995–96 the Philippines discovered that China had constructed a military outpost on Mischief Reef, a South China Sea atoll near Palawan in an area claimed by the Philippines. A démarche from ASEAN expressing concern and requesting clarification signaled to Beijing the need to put its South China Sea claims on the diplomatic back burner. Rather than inflame ASEAN opinion, and lacking the military capacity to enforce an expansive claim, China opted to soft pedal the issue. Deng Xiaoping often reminded his countrymen of a traditional Chinese aphorism that roughly translates as "bide your time and conceal your capabilities until you are ready to act." For Beijing, clarity was a danger and ambiguity an asset when it came to the South China Sea.

In the years following (until ca. 2010), a dense conceptual fog enveloped the Chinese position. The result was uncertainty and disagreement in the small community of outside analysts who tried to follow the issue. The prevailing view was that China was claiming something less than full *sovereignty*, largely because Beijing refrained from using that word. The nine-dash line presumably denoted something other than a legal international boundary, but just what remained murky. And there were ample grounds for confusion— consider the following.

- At various times, Beijing has cited as a basis for its claim different and mutually inconsistent rationales, including historic presence, the archipelagic principle, the EEZ principle, and the continental shelf principle.
- China rebuts Japanese claims in the East China Sea by noting that the outcroppings of land cited by Tokyo are not habitable, as required under international law. However, China has cited the same kind of land features to justify its claims to the South China Sea.

- Legislation adopted by China in 1992 that put the dashed line into law refers to "historic waters," a category that has no standing under international law.
- A 1958 governmental "Declaration on China's Territorial Sea" refers to the South China Sea as "high seas"—a characterization that contradicts the notion of a territorial sea.
- China has drawn archipelagic baselines around the Paracel Islands, which it claims (and occupies), but not around the Spratly Islands, which it also claims.
- China has ratified the UN Convention on the Law of the Sea but with reservations that render ratification almost meaningless.
- By declaring a "coastal economic exclusion zone," China has given the concept of an EEZ an interpretation unrecognized in international law.
- In an effort to rebut a joint Malaysian-Vietnamese submission to the United Nations, China submitted a map with its nine-dash line boundary but gave no explanation or justification. Indonesia responded with a formal request to the UN that Beijing clarify its claim. China has remained silent.
- The nine-dash line has never been precisely demarcated, and large sections of it, for example the waters near Indonesia's Natuna Islands, remain entirely opaque.

The fog began to dissipate when the nine-dash line was considered from the perspective that it might be exactly what many Chinese official statements seemed to indicate—a demarcation of China's maritime boundary. Consider the following.

- The line that appears on all Chinese produced maps actually has eleven, not nine, dashes and encompasses Taiwan as well as the South China Sea. There is no doubt whatsoever that China views Taiwan as sovereign territory.
- In 1974, China deployed naval forces to seize the Paracels from Vietnam. That archipelago has not been characterized by China as in any way separate and distinct from the rest of the South China Sea.
- The People's Liberation Army (PLA) has built an impressive military outpost on Mischief Reef, located 120 nautical miles from the Philippines and over 600 nautical miles from China.
- China's 1992 Territorial Law affirms the dotted line and mandates its armed forces to defend China's maritime territory.
- China's rapid buildup in military capabilities has focused on naval and air power projection beyond China's shores.

- The Chinese navy has stopped Vietnamese fishing boats operating well within Vietnam's EEZ, while Beijing has warned international oil companies away from Vietnamese offshore leaseholds.
- While China agreed to sign a "Declaration on the Conduct of Parties in the South China Sea," it has refused to make the agreement legally binding or to refrain from building new structures.
- At a public symposium hosted by the U.S. Pacific Command in 1994, two PLA senior colonels answered "no" when asked if America's Seventh Fleet has a right to traverse the South China Sea without China's permission.
- In a recent display of technological prowess, a Chinese submersible descended to the deepest portion of the South China Sea, where the crew was instructed to plant a Chinese flag on the ocean bottom.
- The proposition that the nine-dash line is intended to demarcate a sovereign boundary is powerfully buttressed by the fact that Beijing has never authoritatively disavowed that interpretation over more than six decades and in the presence of repeated appeals from the region to "clarify" the line.

Nevertheless, from the mid-1990s, China invested considerable effort and skill presenting itself to Southeast leaders and general publics as a benign presence that posed no threat to its smaller southern neighbors. An American official visitor to Southeast Asia during the late 1990s and early 2000s who asked about China received a consistent and insistent response; China says it has good intentions, and its actions support that contention. During this period, China's behavior toward Southeast Asia had been, on the whole, exemplary. If official Washington had been inclined to portray China's intentions toward Southeast Asia as having a darker side, there would have been little receptivity throughout most of the region—including in Kuala Lumpur, Manila, Phnom Penh, Vientiane, Jakarta, Rangoon, and Bangkok. It hardly mattered because official Washington at this time shared the prevailing Southeast Asian view. The cautious dissenters in the region would have been found in Singapore and Hanoi. The Singaporean leadership has strategic thinking in its blood, and they understood the remorseless geopolitical logic of a rising great power and aspirant superpower to their north. Vietnam has its own lengthy history of carving out independent space in the face of China's imperial ambition. The price of Vietnamese independence from China has often been paid in blood. As recently as 1979 China launched thirty army divisions in an attack on Vietnam designed to teach Hanoi "a lesson."

That same American official visitor to Southeast Asia in 2009–10 would have begun to detect a new tone of uneasiness with regard to China. China's value as an economic partner was undiminished, but its military buildup was now on such a scale that Southeast Asian officials were beginning to wonder. China faced no credible military threats; why was it building so formidable a capability—particularly one that seemed to be designed almost exclusively to project power offshore? Those concerns were reinforced by a growing number of incidents involving "arrests" of non-Chinese (primarily Vietnamese) fishing boats and Chinese pressure on international oil companies not to sign exploration leases on tracts in the South China Sea with Southeast Asian governments.

These concerns remained largely sotto voce until July 2010 when the ASEAN Regional Forum (ARF) held its annual Foreign Ministerial meeting. The ARF is a twenty-six-nation grouping for the purpose of discussing security issues facing Asia. Like many other Asian groupings, it is convened and hosted by the ASEAN states. For several years Vietnam had attempted to get the South China Sea and its growing problems with Chinese actions on the ARF agenda. But each of the ASEAN host governments had in turn refused, knowing that to accept Vietnam's request would anger China. But in 2010 Vietnam was the host and chair and was determined to use that position to raise the South China Sea issue. Hanoi sought U.S. support, and when the meetings convened Secretary Clinton was there—the first time a U.S. secretary of state had attended. Secretary Clinton noted the competing territorial and maritime claims in the South China Sea and made two principal points: (1) a territorial dispute involving multiple claimants should be settled without resort to force through a multilateral negotiation and (2) the major sea lanes that bisect the South China Sea, like SLOCs elsewhere in the world, are not subject to the ownership or authority of any state but are part of a "global commons." In the context of international diplomatic practice, both points were pretty much axioms.

Then things got interesting. Eight of the ten ASEAN foreign ministers spoke in support of Secretary Clinton's statement—tangible evidence of growing disquiet regarding China's actions in the maritime domain. The reaction of China's foreign minister to all this was incendiary; he became angry, emotional, and demanding. At one point he completely lost his composure. At another he turned to the foreign minister from Singapore (an ethnic Chinese) and said, "There are small countries and there are big countries, and don't you forget it!" For the Southeast Asian ministers it was a revelatory moment concerning the seriousness of China's strategic ambitions and the implications for

Southeast Asia. If there was any doubt as to what it all meant, a few days later in a public setting the official spokesmen for the Chinese Defense Ministry asserted China's "indisputable sovereignty" over the South China Sea. The fog had lifted; "bide your time" had ceased to be Beijing's operative principle.

The Maritime Challenge to U.S. Security Strategy

U.S. National Interests

American national interests regarding Southeast Asia are consistent with those that have animated U.S. policy elsewhere in the world. Fundamentally, the United States wants Southeast Asia's autonomy and self-determination to be preserved. The basic strategic rationale for American involvement in World Wars I and II was to prevent Europe and East Asia from being subordinated to the imperial ambitions of Germany and Japan. A similar strategic concern animated U.S. resistance to Soviet ambitions during the Cold War. Regarding Southeast Asia, America is a status quo power; it views the current configuration of independent states and regional institutions as well as the international status of the South China Sea as fully consonant with U.S. interests. Those interests include economic, diplomatic/political, and security access to the region. U.S. companies are free to trade and invest subject to local laws and international agreements. The American armed forces can establish collaborative relationships with receptive governments in the region. A related U.S. interest is the universal acceptance of the major sea lanes through the region (notably the Malacca Strait and the South China Sea) as international waterways open to global commerce and innocent passage of military forces as a matter of right. Integral to this paradigm is an acceptance of the legal provisions and norms of the UN Convention on the Law of the Sea (UNCLOS) regarding the definition and extent of territorial seas and exclusive economic zones. All of this, from an American standpoint, will preserve the region as accessible and autonomous—a full participant in global commerce and politics and secure from external threat and intimidation.

The SLOCs bear special mention. With regard to ongoing territorial disputes in the South China Sea, U.S. officials have repeatedly stated that America has no claims of its own nor a position on the merits of the claims and counterclaims of others. The U.S. national interest in the South China Sea has two elements: (1) disputes should be resolved or managed peacefully without coercion or intimidation and (2) the sea lanes themselves must be preserved as an "international commons" not subject to the ownership or sovereign jurisdiction of any state. Of the two, it is a fair surmise that the latter is much

more important. China, at Scarborough Shoal, has already successfully de-
fied the U.S. stricture against coercion. The status of the SLOCs, however,
is another matter. There can be little doubt that freedom of navigation as a
matter of international right is a principle that the United States will defend
militarily.

As for China, the U.S. strategic interest lies in establishing a cooperative
partnership with a country that Washington is fully prepared to recognize
as a regional great power and prospective superpower. From an American
standpoint, the two countries have no inherent conflict of vital interests. East
Asia is big enough and dynamic enough to accommodate the interests and
ambitions of both Washington and Beijing. Moreover, the two countries are
hugely interdependent economically—and as China's economy grows so does
its interest in fostering international stability and globalization. This is all
very different from the security landscape that confronted the architects of a
strategy to contain the Soviet Union in the 1950s. For most of the past three
decades the prevailing assumptions animating U.S. policy have embraced this
vision of a cooperative U.S.-China relationship. U.S. security agencies including the Pentagon and the CIA have invested considerable sustained effort to
implement this goal. The language surrounding the recent California summit between Presidents Obama and Xi regarding a "new type of great power
relationship" reflected—from an American standpoint—an affirmation that
a genuine partnership is not only possible but necessary. Only the skeptics
noted that Xi and Obama seemed to have very different ideas what "the new
type" of relationship should look like. And despite the determined optimism
of official Washington, there has very recently—within the past two or three
years—been a dawning realization that U.S.-China relations are to some significant degree hostage to China's relationship with regions to its south.

The Pivot and Air-Sea Battle

The strategic "pivot" or "rebalance" is a response to two overriding considerations: (1) U.S. economic and commercial interests that are increasingly
weighted toward Asia—most notably East and Southeast Asia—and (2)
increasingly overt claims to Chinese sovereignty over nearly all of the South
China Sea. The escalating rhetoric supporting the South China Sea claim has
been matched by a rapid buildup of Chinese naval and maritime coast guard/
police forces, which in turn have been used to assert Chinese control over
fishing grounds, offshore oil exploration areas, and actual land features. In
short, China's vocabulary and actions have taken on an increasingly hegemonic, even aggressive, character.

If the United States is not prepared to accept that its strategic preeminence in East Asia will be displaced by China, the pivot will have to have an overtly military dimension. That will in turn signal to China and to the U.S. allies and other security partners in the region that the United States is not prepared to accede to a new Sino-centric security order in Southeast Asia and its maritime littoral. In broad brush such a military strategy will seek to signal reassurance to allies and friends, defend the sea lands and high seas as a global commons, and dissuade China from pursuing a path of crude territorial expansion. All this is a central component of the Obama administration's declared "rebalance" toward East Asia, particularly Southeast Asia.

The rebalance or "pivot" received its first articulation in an article in *Foreign Policy* magazine (October 2011) by Secretary of State Hillary Clinton. In addition to Clinton, a prime architect of the new policy was Assistant Secretary Kurt Campbell. The rebalance was (and is) envisioned as a multidimensional initiative with diplomatic outreach, a far-reaching trade agreement (Trans-Pacific Partnership), and a shift of military resources and attention toward the Asia-Pacific as American military commitments in Iraq and Afghanistan wound down. In the two and a half years since it was articulated, the most tangible outcomes of the rebalance have been military—including an agreement with Australia for the deployment of U.S. Marines to Darwin, an agreement with Manila for the regular rotation of U.S. forces to Philippines facilities, and an agreement with Singapore for the berthing of three or four latest-generation "littoral combat ships." Finally, both Secretary of Defense Panetta and Secretary of Defense Hagel have reiterated that cuts in the overall defense budget will not affect deployments and commitments in Asia.

In 2000 the U.S. Defense Department began long-range planning for an upgrade in U.S. military activity in East Asia. That planning effort became public in the 2010 Quadrennial Defense Review in the form of a new overarching concept designated "Air-Sea Battle" (ASB). In 2011 DOD created the Air-Sea Battle Office (ASBO) with a small elite staff of seventeen planners unaligned with any one military service or unified combatant command. ASBO was tasked with developing the ASB concept without any authority to initiate new forces, weapons, or command structures. ASBO's public mandate does not mention China—or any specific geographic region. But there is no doubt that the office was created with China in mind and is tasked to develop the military methodology that can defeat Chinese "anti-access/area denial" (A2/AD) capabilities—capabilities that are intended to prevent U.S. military forces in the Pacific from entering the maritime region inside the first island chain and to constrain the movement and communications of any forces that do penetrate that area. China's rapidly growing A2/AD capabilities include long-range antiship cruise and ballistic missiles particularly designed to attack U.S. carrier battle groups, improved air defense missiles, nuclear submarines, stealth fighter aircraft, high-capacity marine mines, new radars, impressive cyber warfare capabilities, and the recent deployment of China's first aircraft carrier—with another under construction. All this poses a major, and very real, challenge to the U.S. Pacific Command. The challenge facing ASBO planners is how to operate effectively in what is euphemistically identified as "degraded or denied environments."

If it is to be successful, ASB must not only be capable of defeating an increasingly capable A2/AD effort by China but also do so without triggering a major U.S.-China war. This is a tall order—analogous to the Cold War containment strategy that ultimately defeated the Soviet Union without a shot fired. China's strategic ambition and reach are clearly fueled by an intense and broadly embraced nationalism that takes as axiomatic that the territories inside the first island chain are to be China's security monopoly by historic right—just as the South China Sea is Chinese sovereign territory. If this perception of China's intentions is correct, the only hope for deterring increased hegemonic behavior will be a powerful, visible deterrent. Deterrence was the strategic mainstay throughout the Cold War and will be required to once again do the strategic heavy lifting in the early twenty-first century in East and Southeast Asia. Richard Andres of the National War College in Washington summarized the challenge: "How we shape our forces and doctrine has the potential to dramatically influence the chances that we will get into a hot war with China. If we are too weak, we invite China to call our bluff. If our force posture requires us to attack targets the Chinese see as vital to regime survival (and it is hard to know what they will consider vital), we are inviting escalation to—hopefully—limited and localized nuclear war. If we base our strategy on too few technologies and too few bases, we invite a Chinese preemptive action. This is not rocket science—it's much more complicated than that."[4]

The initial thinking and planning around ASB has focused, for obvious reasons, on the Navy, Marines, and Air Force. Whereas America's recent (and ongoing) wars in the Near East have been overwhelmingly land and counterinsurgency campaigns that relied primarily on Army and special operations forces, the Asia/Pacific is a largely maritime domain involving huge distances. As Admiral Locklear, commander of U.S. Pacific forces, likes to note, "You can take all the land masses in the world and push them together and put them in the Pacific Ocean and you still will have room for a couple of more continents." The end of American combat responsibilities in Iraq and the pending withdrawal of most (if not all) of U.S. forces from Afghanistan has released manpower, equipment, and some money for redirection to East Asia. Money is in especially short supply given the overall pressures on the federal budget generally and the defense budget specifically. Nevertheless, the "rebalance" of U.S. forces has begun with a near-term target of putting 60 percent of total U.S. naval assets into the Pacific theater. As previously noted, a small contingent of Marines has begun what will be a regular rotation into northern Australia, and the latest U.S. Navy warships designed for shallow-water operations are being based in Singapore while discussions involving a more substantial U.S. military presence in the Philippines are well advanced.

These events highlight an important element of the ASB concept—it is very much focused on near-term capabilities. ASBO "can only really focus on existing weapons and organizations . . . [with] . . . little time to explore potentially revolutionary new technologies not already embedded in the Pentagon's seven-year plan, the Program Objective Memorandum (POM)." In sum, the ASBO is tasked with maximizing the effectiveness of existing service structures, weapons systems, and communications systems. It is all about synergies, improved coordination, and enhanced communication across services and platforms. It is also about dispersal, movement, speed, and the capacity to operate autonomously even while blinded by an adversary's disruption of radar, satellite links, and other communications.

Not surprisingly, the Army has viewed the shift of strategic priorities away from land to sea and air with ill-disguised alarm. With the exception of Korea, the Asia/Pacific theater is not an obvious natural habitat for the Army—particularly if one assumes that future presidents will take to heart the advice of former Secretary of Defense Robert Gates: "Any future defense secretary who advises the President to again send a big American land army into Asia . . . should have his head examined." The Army doesn't necessarily see things that way. For the first time since 1974 the Army has assigned a four-star general to PACOM as commander of the U.S. Army Pacific. The new incumbent, General Vincent Brooks, has launched a campaign to raise the Army's profile and presence in the region—a concept designated "Pacific Pathways." "We intend to put into motion a pathway of activity (for the Army) into multiple countries for extended periods of time, linking a series of events and exercises on a variety of topics," he said. General Brooks's vision includes tactical missile defense, multipurpose units including amphibious brigades, and manned and unmanned air units (some operating off of Navy ships). These units will engage resident Asian armies in joint exercises and training and will assist with natural disaster mitigation.[5] Predictably, the U.S. Marines Corps already in the area of responsibility (AOR) sees much of this as an effort to replicate capabilities already extant.

The Alliance System

The foundation of U.S. security strategy in Southeast Asia since World War II has been a "hub and spoke" system of formal bilateral alliances with initially four—then three—countries in the region: Thailand, the Philippines, Australia, and New Zealand. Initially, these relationships were embedded in two multilateral alliances: SEATO and ANZUS. A similar system in Northeast Asia included Japan and the Republic of Korea. These arrangements were part of Secretary of State John Foster Dulles's "pactomania" approach to a global containment of the Soviet empire. SEATO never functioned as an Asian counterpart to NATO and died a quiet death in the 1970s. In 1984 New Zealand was effectively read out of ANZUS when a new Labor government adopted an unbending antinuclear posture that precluded nuclear-powered and armed vessels of the U.S. Navy from entering New Zealand ports. ANZUS became, for Washington, another bilateral security alliance in the region.

During the Cold War these alliances became the primary vehicle for U.S. and allied governments to prosecute counterinsurgency campaigns against communist guerrilla forces. American assistance helped the Philippine government beat back the Hukbalahap threat in the 1950s, and military and economic assistance buttressed Thailand's government in its long-running struggle with communist insurgents centered in the northeast part of the country. Both Manila and Bangkok allowed the Pentagon to establish major facilities (Utapao and Udorn airfields in Thailand and Subic Bay and Clark Field in the Philippines) that were critical to America's largest counterinsurgency war—in Indochina.

With the termination of the Vietnam War in 1975, the strategic landscape changed dramatically. The Nixon administration's "Guam Doctrine" signaled a sharp diminution of the U.S. military presence in Southeast Asia. Congress and the Pentagon were happy to turn what the Nixon White House viewed as a gradual, almost stealthy, exit from the region into a stampede. Not surprisingly, this helped fuel a major change in attitudes toward U.S. alliances in Bangkok, Manila, Canberra, and Wellington. The Thai government was deeply angered and hurt by what it saw as an American decision to cut and run, leaving Thailand naked and exposed to a triumphant Vietnam. Bangkok's worst fears were soon reinforced when the Vietnamese army occupied Cambodia and moved forces to the Thai border. In extremis, Thailand turned to the erstwhile supporter of the Thai communist insurgents—China. Thailand's timing was fortuitous. Mao had died and the new paramount leader, Deng Xiaoping, was not interested in supporting Maoist insurgencies and, in fact, saw Vietnam's occupation of Cambodia as a threat to China. The result was negotiations that ushered in a new era of Thai-Chinese strategic collaboration that brought the Thai communist insurgency to an end and facilitated Chinese logistical support to Khmer Rouge guerrillas fighting the Vietnamese army in Cambodia.

In the Philippines, the U.S. military presence had become deeply tainted in the eyes of many of the Philippine elite by its perceived association with the Marcos dictatorship. Despite American assistance in Marcos's overthrow and the subsequent warm relations with Cory Aquino's government, Washington remained the favorite target of a new nationalism centered in the Philippine Senate. The result was a decision to allow the lease that provided the legal and monetary basis for U.S. military facilities to lapse. In 1992 U.S. forces completed their withdrawal from Subic Bay—and an era came to an end.

Down Under the Whitlam Labor government won election in 1972 with a pledge to withdraw all Australian forces from Vietnam. Subsequently, the Keating government (also Labor) in the 1990s sought to redefine Australia's strategic priorities, at least rhetorically, in terms of Asia-first. Meanwhile New Zealand had slipped out of the ANZUS fold in the 1980s. It all suggested a strategic uncertainty and flux—and when the North Star in the form of the Soviet threat disappeared that sense was magnified.

No surprise, the value and relevance of the U.S. alliance system was, at the very least, thrown into doubt. The story of Southeast Asia in the post–Vietnam War period, particularly in the 1990s (after the withdrawal of the Vietnamese army from Cambodia), was one centered on economic growth and societal modernization. It was a heady time captured in the title of a major World Bank study, *The Asian Miracle* (1993). There was much talk about the "Pacific century" and the ascendance of "Asian values"—displacing the flawed and tired values of the West. These tendencies were powerfully reinforced by the dramatic growth in China's economy validating Deng's reform agenda. All this had profound strategic implications—but none so directly as the loss of U.S. military bases and joint facilities in Southeast Asia—particularly Clark and Subic. The effect was to remove the southern anchor of U.S. military power in Asia and shift the specific gravity of U.S. Asia strategy decisively northward to Japan and the Republic of Korea.

In many respects it is remarkable that the entire "hub and spoke" setup didn't just dissolve. There are several plausible reasons: (1) the alliances were sunk costs—the facilities, relationships, and programs they engendered were created at considerable expense and effort over time and were not something to be lightly tossed aside; (2) the Pacific Command (PACOM) was deeply invested in the alliance system and kept it going, often with little high-level attention from Washington; (3) the military-to-military relationships tended to have a dynamic unto themselves and were highly valued by the officer corps in all the countries involved; and (4) a steady drumbeat of natural disasters and humanitarian crises in PACOM's AOR tended to reinforce the utility of a highly capable military presence in situ—even without a major traditional security threat.

There were also factors in the region that supported a continuation of the traditional U.S. security role. Prime Minister Lee Kuan Yew in Singapore not only spoke out about the critical importance of a continued U.S. security presence in Southeast Asia; he offered facilities in Singapore to compensate to the extent possible for the loss of Clark and Subic. These included a carrier pier constructed for the express use of the U.S. Navy. The election of John Howard in Australia brought into office a prime minister dedicated to revivifying the Australian-U.S. alliance. The 9/11 terror attacks produced a flurry of attention from the Bush administration toward Southeast Asia (particularly the Philippines) as the "Second Front" in the GWOT. The discovery in the mid-1990s that China had established a military outpost on Mischief Reef, well within the Philippines EEZ, set off tremors in ASEAN and produced a joint démarche to Beijing. Finally, the epic Boxing Day (2004) tsunami that devastated western Sumatra graphically demonstrated the unique value of the U.S. Seventh Fleet for search, rescue, and medical and logistical support in a crisis. Nevertheless, the alliance system as a whole remained at a low ebb in terms of public visibility and strategic priority until late in the first decade of this century.

The system remains in place today, but the regional context is far different and far more complex than even a few years ago. Consider the changes.

- When ASEAN was established in 1967 its architects repeatedly characterized the new organization as what it was not—it was not a military alliance, nor did it have an overt security agenda. Yet today, ASEAN is at the center of a web of defense/security forums including the ASEAN Regional Forum (ARF), the ASEAN Defense Ministerial Meeting (ADMM) and ADMM-Plus, and the East Asia Summit (EAS), which has addressed security issues in recent years. Where this is headed is uncertain; Beijing remains resolutely opposed to these trends, arguing that security issues should be addressed in bilateral discussion only. Washington argues to the contrary, and so far the U.S. view seems to be prevailing. In any case, the mil-to-mil interaction within ASEAN has, with rare exceptions, been in the form of discussions rather than operations.
- China's economic ties to Southeast Asia have grown dramatically—as have economic relationships within ASEAN. China has become the top

trading partner with nearly all the ASEAN countries as well as Australia. Trade statistics are only part of the story. In the case of Australia, foreign investment ties with the United States far exceed those with China, and the disparity is growing. Infrastructure projects (railways, riverine transport, road networks, power grids, IT networks) link Southeast Asian economies to south-central China. All this poses a question of whether economic ties also shape security relationships or whether the two can be delinked—and whether intra-ASEAN economic ties can engender a collaborative security agenda.

- The U.S. pivot/rebalance, if seriously implemented over time, will substantially upgrade American military capabilities in the region and effectively reverse some of the effects of three decades of relative inattention and diversion of hard military assets to other geographic regions. Doubts about whether the president was truly serious regarding the rebalance became prominent with the departure of Secretary Clinton and the evident preoccupation of her successor, Secretary Kerry, with the Middle East. However, the fact that the president made two trips to Asia (one in 2014 and one in 2016) and the fact that former Secretary of Defense Hagel has made repeated trips suggest that the administration's commitment is real.

- As China's territorial ambitions in the South China Sea have come into focus, U.S. alliances have been provided a hard rationale that would have been almost unimaginable to the region even five years ago. Suddenly, old-fashioned concepts like deterrence and power balance have come back into fashion.

- Partly as a result, U.S. security "partnerships"—outside the formal alliance system—have developed significantly. Singapore has long been the most intensive and substantive of these—amounting to something close to a de facto alliance. U.S. military ties with Indonesia have evolved from minimal and arm's length in the 1980s and 1990s to close and collaborative today, with a growing sense of shared security interests. The most dramatic trajectory in improved ties involves Vietnam. From a protracted, bloody war in the 1960s and 1970s and commencing with initial military-to-military contacts in the mid-1990s, relations have developed to the point where an American Secretary of Defense could stand side by side with senior Vietnamese military officers on the deck of a U.S. Navy ship in Cam Ranh Bay and extol the prospects for increased U.S.-Vietnamese strategic cooperation. Although less dramatic and visible, security cooperation with Malaysia has always been good but is now growing. Within the Pentagon, Malaysia is routinely identified as a country with upside potential in this regard. For all these countries, South China Sea developments loom large. Burma/Myanmar is a different and interesting case. Long a pariah, subject to a full suite of U.S. sanctions due to a military coup and subsequent human rights abuses, Burma has undergone a startling democratic transformation. U.S.-Burmese relations have been largely normalized as a result. This process has yet to extend to military ties, but if present trends continue, that day is not far off.

- The traditional alliance system is also in some flux. This is most notable in the Philippines where China's military reach into maritime space claimed by the Philippines, plus the advent of the Aquino administration have transformed thinking in Manila. Suddenly, the Mutual Security Treaty with the United States is no longer a controversial artifact of the Cold War; it is vital to the defense of the Philippines. There is no prospect for a full reconstitution of U.S. bases at Subic and Clark; the Philippines constitution now forbids it. But military-to-military cooperation is on a rapid upward trajectory to include military equipment (sales and donations); joint exercises, training, and education; and a formal agreement for longer and more frequent rotation of U.S. military units to the Philippines. In the case of Australia, an already intimate defense relationship has gotten even closer with Marines in Darwin and a new Conservative government in Canberra. Meanwhile, Wellington and Washington have taken steps to ease their defense estrangement short of fully restoring the ANZUS status quo ante. Thailand is the most notable exception to this overall pattern of deepening U.S. security ties. Bangkok has developed close relations with Beijing and is largely unaffected by South China Sea developments. Thailand is far more comfortable with China's growing power than is true throughout most of Southeast Asia (Cambodia and Laos being the other notable exceptions). Bangkok has also been in a state of near policy paralysis due to a protracted political standoff between urban ("yellow shirt") and rural ("red shirt") elites. Thailand continues to efficiently and effectively host the annual Cobra Gold multilateral military exercise and support other alliance activities—but the U.S.-Thailand alliance is not a growth industry; it is basically in maintenance mode.

- Finally, the advent of the Abe administration with the prime minister's clear desire to assert a Japanese strategic role (in coordination with the United States) in Southeast Asia has added new complexities and opportunities from outside the immediate region. Tokyo, most notably, is supplying the Philippines and Vietnam with Coast Guard cutters—even as the prime minister faces political resistance at home to his proposals to amend Article 9 of the Japanese Constitution.

In sum, the United States is a key and integral part of a de facto security system/architecture in the region. To be effective, the U.S. role obviously requires much more than a series of agreements and understandings; it requires an ambitious range of operational activities: military sales and transfers, logistical assistance, training and education, strategic dialogues, natural disaster response, and a high tempo of regular bilateral and multilateral military exercises—as PACOM deploys its assets around the region. All these activities are calibrated to match the needs, preferences, and capabilities of counterpart armed forces. For optimal effectiveness these support programs need to proceed in coordination with other allied assistance. This is not always the case. For example, Japan is providing eighteen Coast Guard cutters to the Philippines. But they can't communicate with the Coastal Watch System being provided by the United States.

Strategic Imperatives

The United States, in Southeast Asia and the maritime domain that encompasses it, is an avowedly status quo power. The established configuration of independent states integrated into the global economy and accessible to U.S. commercial and security interests and sea lanes that function as a global commons is optimal from an American perspective. Unlike in Europe, peace and stability are not underwritten by formal security architecture analogous to NATO and the EU. Historically, the relative tranquility of the maritime regions has been maintained by several factors.

First, the fishermen who had traditionally worked these waters—whether Vietnamese, Chinese, Filipino, or Malay—had always viewed them as a commons. So the indigenous maritime inhabitants of the South China Sea worked and interacted peacefully.

Second, none of the governments claiming territory in the South China Sea had the logistical or military capability to effectively enforce its claim. So these expansive territorial ambitions remained just that—ambitions but not more. Moreover, none of the claimants had the technological capabilities to mount their own deep-water petroleum exploration and drilling operations. Thus the sometimes fevered speculation concerning massive reserves under the South China Sea remained speculation.

Third, the establishment of ASEAN in 1967 and its subsequent expansion (notably the inclusion of Vietnam in 1995) created an interesting and significant incentive to avoid conflict among the members—whether over the South China Sea or anything else. ASEAN, though often derided as a mere "talk shop," was created during the Vietnam War with one overriding goal in mind: prevent conflict within the region that would weaken it in the face of external pressures and would jeopardize the all-important march toward economic development and modernity. Peace and development would produce, in the favorite phrase of the time, "resilience." ASEAN became what Deutsch called a "security community"—a grouping of states committed to resolving or deferring their disputes without resorting to violent conflict. In an innovative elaboration of this idea, ASEAN initiated an increasingly elaborate "dialogue" process with non-ASEAN states designed to mute external threats and exploit opportunities for collaboration. It has produced the remarkable and unexpected outcome of placing Southeast Asia (and ASEAN specifically) at the center of much of Asia's diplomacy. It has also put a firm damper on the possibility that the overlapping South China Sea claims of Malaysia and the Philippines, for example, could spark a military clash.

Fourth, because China lacked the military capacity to enforce its sovereign claim, it was tactically and strategically prudent for it to adopt a low (nonprovocative) posture in the South China Sea. A key element in this strategy was to foster uncertainty, even confusion, on the part of outside observers as to the actual meaning of the "nine-dash line." Contradictory rationales, actions, and initiatives surrounded the Chinese claim in a dense fog of ambiguity that Chinese strategists were in no hurry to dispel.

Fifth, the U.S. Navy, as the strongest military force in the theater, acted as a potent constraint on conflict in the South China Sea. PACOM's Seventh Fleet traversed the region on a regular basis in defense of U.S. interests, but those interests did not include the competing territorial claims. As former Secretary of State James Baker might have put it, "the U.S. had no dog in that fight." The American interest, articulated most clearly in the East Asia Strategy Review (1995) produced jointly by the Department of Defense and the Department of State, was limited to maintaining the sea lanes through the South China Sea as international and open to all countries and urging the respective claimants to seek a peaceful resolution of the disputes. The United States was cast in the role of the neighborhood gendarme—a neutral peacekeeper—because that was what the U.S. interest required.

The combination of a U.S. defense presence with growing ASEAN-based diplomatic processes produced what Victor Cha has aptly described as a "complex patchwork" security framework in which the two largely separate phenomena complemented and reinforced one another in largely unnoticed ways.[6] One result was a remarkably placid South China Sea.

Three of these five factors have eroded or disappeared—leaving regional maritime peace and security resting on two factors that generate more questions than certainties: (1) Can the web of multinational forums centered on

ASEAN and the growing density of economic ties between Southeast Asia and China act as a serious constraint on Chinese hegemonic ambitions? Can they effectively obviate Beijing's determination to handle all strategic issues bilaterally and raise the costs of a latter-day lebensraum campaign in the South China Sea? Will an increasingly integrated Southeast Asia make a divide-and-rule strategy increasingly infeasible? (2) Can the United States deploy and maintain (with the cooperation and support of regional allies and partners) sufficient hard power to deter further Chinese territorial acquisitions by intimidation, stealth, or force using Chinese military and quasi-military assets? By definition, deterrence is successful only if a hot war is avoided.

An effective U.S. counter to Chinese ambitions will require a strategy of considerable sophistication.

First, it should explore in depth how the region's complexity can be harnessed for U.S. interests. As a theoretical proposition, systemic complexity with multiple diverse actors is, other things being equal, a source of stability. In Southeast Asia the most effective brake on Chinese ambitions will be the presence of multiple actors all defending their own interests. For a Chinese strategist, a binary face-off between the United States and China in the South China Sea is far more promising than one that also involves several ASEAN countries and non–Southeast Asian regional actors. The more numerous the players and the more complex and dense the interactions, the less China will be able to determine outcomes. A central task of U.S. strategy will be to cultivate and utilize that complexity by, for example, facilitating the presence of Indian and Japanese security forces and security assistance programs in the region.

Second, the SLOCs must be unambiguously asserted as a vital or "core" U.S. interest—one shared by every major maritime country as well as the Southeast Asian littoral states. The U.S. insistence that the SLOCs are a "global commons" should be clearly embraced by that broader array of interested parties. Perhaps most important, there must be no doubt that this is an interest that the United States *will* defend militarily.

Third, a U.S. strategy should identify itself closely with UNCLOS.[7] This too is an important constraint on Chinese actions—particularly since Beijing is a signatory to the convention. The recent initiative by the Philippines to enlist the UNCLOS adjudication process to pass judgment on the legal validity of Chinese claims is both interesting and important in this regard.

Fourth, ASEAN and the "ASEAN-Plus" mechanisms provide an additional and important element of complexity and constraint in the regional strategic context. China has blown hot and cold on whether Southeast Asia's multilateral processes are an asset or an obstacle for Chinese strategy. For the United

States they are an unambiguous asset. A strategy must address ways these institutions can become sotto voce partners of U.S. strategy.

Fifth, U.S. military assets under PACOM are obviously a critical component of any U.S. strategy—particularly given the rapid buildup and deployment of Chinese naval and maritime enforcement capabilities. At the end of the day, the only real constraint on a Chinese decision to seize additional territory in the South China Sea is the U.S. Navy and Air Force. That is what ASB is all about. But these forces have a far larger role than that. In the nearly four decades since the conclusion of the Vietnam War the U.S. PACOM has never engaged in actual military hostilities. The crucial questions concern how U.S. forces can be utilized to provide presence, reassurance, and assistance to buttress American influence and leverage. This is not new. PACOM has been doing it for decades and doing it well. But in a more superheated regional security environment these "nonkinetic" activities will become more important and demanding.

Sixth, a successful strategy will have to be built on a close understanding with regional governments. This will require substantive strategic exchanges at many levels with ASEAN counterparts (defense, foreign ministry, intelligence, and think tanks) and with other Asian governments (Australia, India, etc.). The Pentagon has already initiated several "strategic dialogues" in the region (Vietnam, Malaysia, etc.). It is a worthy beginning, but will require substantial elaboration and development. A critical objective of such exchanges will be a shared (or mutually understood) view of China and its strategic intentions. This would include an agreement regarding where Chinese interests and ambitions should be accommodated (e.g., Chinese naval ship visits and patrols, joint development with Chinese enterprises of seabed resources) and where they cannot (e.g., SLOCs as global commons, the seizure by force of disputed maritime land features). Finally, and critically, there should be detailed shared planning regarding possible confrontations and contingencies in the South China Sea with an eye to avoiding inadvertent military conflict.

Seventh, U.S. political and military leaders must continue a long-standing effort with their Chinese counterparts to improve mutual understanding regarding defense issues. The holy grail of this endeavor would be a strategic accommodation regarding Southeast Asia's maritime domain on terms acceptable both to Washington and to major Southeast Asian capitals.

The drumbeat of daily headlines may still suggest otherwise, but the central strategic challenge facing the United States now and for the foreseeable future is in the maritime regions of East Asia. The pivot/rebalance in U.S. strategy reflects that understanding in the White House and Pentagon. The tests that confront U.S. security strategists will be on the same order of difficulty and importance as those faced by the architects of Cold War containment. The mission, now as then, will be to craft a strategy that preserves a rules-based, non-hegemonic future for the region—and to do so without a war. No one should underestimate the difficulty or the magnitude of that undertaking.

The President's Trip

In late April 2014 President Obama took his fifth official trip to Asia—this one to Japan, South Korea, Malaysia, and the Philippines. Set in the context of the rebalance, three of the four countries visited were treaty allies. The leitmotif of the trip was strategic reassurance—that America's security presence will remain robust and effective even as China seeks to establish a new Sino-centric order in the region. In terms of reassurance, the greatest potential payoff came in the presidential visits to Malaysia and the Philippines, particularly the former. Shortly after China's Xi Jinping assumed office, he made it clear that Chinese strategy would focus on winning the support of key Southeast Asian states, notably Malaysia. It was no accident that in October 2013 (while President Obama was confined to Washington by the government shutdown), President Xi made a state visit to Kuala Lumpur, where he gave an address to the Malaysian Parliament and announced a series of dramatic trade and investment initiatives. Malaysia's Prime Minister Najib Razak was a gracious host, but he is no fool. He knows that China's ambitions for regional dominance will eventually come at the expense of Malaysian sovereignty and independence. America, by contrast, seeks a future for Southeast Asia that is entirely congruent with Malaysia's national interests. But would the prime minister dare to bet Malaysia's future and risk China's anger and retribution on the conviction that the United States will be there to protect Malaysia now, tomorrow, and for the foreseeable future? That is a weighty question and one likely to keep Prime Minister Najib awake at night. For President Obama the task was to persuade him that he can rest easier—and then deliver on that promise.

The Philippines, more so than any other country in Southeast Asia, has, under President Aquino, opted for closer ties to the United States at the cost of growing Chinese irritation and anger. This is the direct product of China's seizure of maritime territory very close to the Philippines and very far from China, coupled with the six-decade-old security alliance with the United States. Aquino, like Najib, needed reassurance that American power will be real, credible, and adequate to cope with China. There have already been a series of physical confrontations between Chinese and Philippines vessels. If things turn violent in the future, as they well may, Manila will expect its ally to come to its rescue. Such contingencies were presumably on the minds of both presidents when they met. They will certainly be on the agenda for both governments in the months ahead.

Current Considerations

Any analysis of a dynamic strategic environment like Southeast Asia is potentially perishable. That consideration argues for a final update taking into account developments at the end of 2014 and the outset of 2015. That said, it is striking the degree of strategic continuity the region exhibits.

- The "pivot/rebalance" remains an odd admixture of substance, promise, and skepticism. On the substantive side, the Department of Defense continues to plan, build, deploy, and augment U.S. military assets in the region. One representative example is the ongoing PACOM sea and air buildup on the island of Guam. In terms of promise, the White House has announced a busy schedule of visits by Asian leaders to Washington over the next year. At the same time, anyone who follows the news is aware how renewed tensions and conflict in the Middle East and Ukraine have captured the attention of senior policy makers including the president and the Joint Chiefs. Conceptually a key component of the pivot is economic; the proposed Trans-Pacific Partnership will bolster U.S. commercial and financial ties to a region increasingly influenced by multifaceted economic links to China. But despite prolonged diplomatic negotiations, the ultimate membership and viability of the TPP remain very much in question.
- The strategic uncertainty surrounding the pivot is ironic given the fact that the reception to it in Southeast Asia has been broadly positive—even enthusiastic. There is nothing surprising in this; countries like Vietnam, Indonesia, Malaysia, and Singapore are at increasingly close quarters with China's growing power and ambition. The only plausible strategic counterweight they can turn to is the United States. The widely shared wish in the region is that American power will be present, effective, and sufficient to discourage overt Chinese attempts to subordinate the region—without provoking actual military hostilities and without compelling Southeast Asian governments to "choose sides" between the United States and China.
- An additional irony is Washington-based. For years the U.S. political system has been riven and semi-paralyzed by partisan political battles. Often it seems that political disagreements have become reflexive; whatever one

party is for, the other is automatically against. In that context it is noteworthy that U.S. policy and presence in Asia have been immune to political infighting. The pivot enjoys broad, virtually unquestioned, support across the political spectrum. Thus the electoral earthquake of 2014 that left Republicans with solid majorities in both the House and Senate will, from all indications, have no impact on U.S. strategy in the Pacific. The one possible exception—another irony—is that the administration's TPP effort enjoys stronger support among Republicans than Democrats.

- The other side of the strategic equation in the region is, of course, China. Beijing's strategic objective concerning Southeast Asia is increasingly clear—a region led and dominated by China. In the Chinese mind, this is a natural, historically validated ambition that sees China's ultimate role as a benign, beneficial, but unquestioned overlord. The pursuit of that objective remains unrelenting and multifaceted. Its military dimension is most evident in the South China Sea. If any reminder of China's determination was needed, it came in the first weeks of 2015 when Chinese sources revealed that a second aircraft carrier, slated for deployment in 2020, was under construction. Equally consequential, and with equal determination, Beijing has continued to build an increasingly robust network of economic ties between China and the region. These include an Asian Infrastructure Investment Bank (AIIB) with a proposed capitalization of US$100 billion (most of it from China) that will serve as a rival and alternative to the Asian Development Bank dominated by the United States and Japan. China has also heavily promoted a proposed free trade arrangement, the Regional Comprehensive Economic Partnership to include the ASEAN ten and six other Asian trading nations. Multiple rounds of negotiations on RCEP have been undertaken, but have been inconclusive, as the countries involved are waiting to see if TPP will be ratified. All this takes place against the backdrop of rapidly growing trade ties and infrastructure links (land, riverine, maritime, air, information technology, and power grids) between China and Southeast Asia. If fully developed, China's economic ties to Southeast Asia may become so substantial that the U.S. presence will be marginalized to the point of strategic irrelevance. The implications for plans concerning the TPP and related economic arrangements are obvious.

All this assumes China's continued growth trajectory. A modest, and predicted, slackening of the rate of growth suggested by recent statistics will not alter the prevailing picture. A major economic and/or political crisis in China could create a new strategic context—one that is beyond the scope of this essay.

Addendum

The South China Sea—and Southeast Asia more broadly—remained a very dynamic strategic arena through 2015 and early 2016. Chinese initiatives and the reactions they engendered continued to shape the region. Key developments in the South China Sea included an acceleration of China's "island building," two U.S. Naval "freedom of navigation operations" (FONOPS), further steps in the Philippines legal filing before the International Tribunal for the Law of the Sea (ITLOS), and shifting patterns of Chinese influence in peninsular/mainland Southeast Asia.

Chinese construction activity includes seven artificial islands built with sea floor sediment dredged onto coral reefs. The "islands" are platforms where China is constructing port facilities, military structures, and three airstrips—including one that can receive any aircraft in the Chinese inventory. Along with China's rapid buildup of maritime military capabilities, these facilities will greatly enhance China's ability to project power throughout the South China Sea. Beijing asserts "indisputable sovereignty" within the nine-dash line that encompasses over 80 percent of that maritime domain. It should be noted that power projection in this case is more geopolitical than military. In an actual armed conflict the new Chinese facilities would be highly vulnerable to attack—including long-range artillery from Palawan Island in the Philippines. For the marine environment including the coral reefs and atolls, China's activities have been catastrophically destructive.

The two most notable responses to China's activities have come from the United States and the Philippines. Washington announced on two separate occasions that it had sent a Naval destroyer within twelve nautical miles of a Chinese "island" (one in the Spratlys and the other in the Paracels) to implement Secretary of Defense Carter's assertion that "the U.S. will fly, sail, and operate wherever international law allows." The FONOPS produced heated Chinese protests and demands that they not be repeated. The Philippines, which has already lost Mischief Reef, Scarborough Shoal, and traditional fishing grounds to Chinese encroachment, mounted a novel legal challenge to China's expansive maritime claims. After reviewing Manila's submissions, ITLOS agreed to assert jurisdiction and consider the Philippines case. China has already declared it will not recognize or accept an ITLOS judgment, but Beijing is clearly concerned over the effect of an ITLOS validation of Manila's position. In another legal arena the Philippines Supreme Court affirmed the constitutionality of the U.S.-Philippines Enhanced Defense Cooperation Agreement that will inter alia facilitate a more substantial U.S. military presence in the Philippines.

China's drive for increased strategic weight elsewhere in Southeast Asia produced mixed results. In Myanmar/Burma, the startling political transition from autocracy to democracy reached a milestone with the electoral victory of Aung San Suu Kyi's National League for Democracy. One consequential side effect of this transformation has been a sharp diminution of Beijing's leverage reflecting widespread resentment of China's heavy-handed influence under the prior junta regime. But next door in Thailand a reversal of this process seemed under way as General Prayut's military regime reacted to U.S. criticism of the coup he led by turning toward China, which has been far more accepting of developments in Bangkok. Meanwhile, Vietnam continued to seek closer strategic ties with the United States while carefully gauging Chinese reaction. Two VIP visits served as a barometer of this process. Communist Party General Secretary Nguyen Phu Trong visited Washington, and his schedule included a meeting in the Oval Office—the first time a Vietnamese party secretary had met with the president of the United States. The occasion was marked by obvious public cordiality. Not long thereafter, President Xi of China visited Hanoi and spoke before the Vietnamese parliament. That visit was marked by an equally obvious tension.

NOTES

1 The single major exception was the continuation of the Indochina Wars after 1975, including the Vietnamese invasion and occupation of Cambodia (1978–89), the anti-Vietnamese insurgency in Cambodia staged from Thailand, and the Chinese attack across the Vietnam border (1979).

2 There are institutional echoes of this divorce between policy and strategy to the present time. Security Cooperation under PACOM is run by J-4 (logistics), not J-5 (policy and plans). Nor is it always clear that coordination and communication among the policy staffs in the Office of the Secretary of Defense, PACOM, and the in-country teams—and between State and Defense—are what they should be.

3 Interview with an Army Major (Foreign Area Officer) with experience at PACOM and at OSD/Policy in the Pentagon.

4 Caitlin Lee, "Planning Beyond the Pivot," *Jane's Defence Weekly* (IHS Jane's), October 31, 2012, 26–32.

5 USARPAC, the U.S. Army headquarters at the Pacific Command, has labeled this new initiative "Pacific Pathways."

6 Victor Cha, "Complex Patchworks: U.S. Alliances as Part of Asia's Regional Architecture," Asia Policy 11 (Seattle, WA: National Bureau of Asian Research, January 2011).

7 The Obama Administration has repeatedly tried, and failed, to persuade the Senate to approve U.S. accession to UNCLOS. Senate rules allow a small minority to block an initiative that is overwhelmingly in the strategic national interest.

14

U.S. Policy Options in the South China Sea

MICHAEL MCDEVITT

Introduction

The aim of this chapter is to discuss U.S. policy in the South China Sea (SCS) as well as speculate about additional policy options the United States might pursue in dealing with the complex problem of finding a peaceful solution to China's uncompromising efforts to reclaim sovereignty over all the land features in the SCS. While Washington has been very publicly involved in urging restraint since 2010, the Obama administration's pursuit of this objective took a decided turn for the worse in 2015. For much of the year, the SCS was either at the top, or nearly so, of Sino-U.S. trouble spots. This happened because in 2014 China quietly began dredging operations aimed at turning the three rocks and four low-tide elevations (a land feature submerged at high tide) it has occupied in the Spratly Islands for over twenty years into quite large (relative to other Spratly features) man-made islands.[1] This action came to a head in 2015 because China's island building included infrastructure such as airfields, harbors, and buildings that provide Beijing with the means to literally change overnight the balance of military power in the southern half of the SCS in its favor.[2] This greatly exacerbates extant disputes between China and four ASEAN members over the maritime features in the South Sea—the islands, rocks, shoals, and cays claimed in whole or in part by China, Taiwan, Vietnam, the Philippines, Malaysia, and Brunei, and put pressure on Washington to respond, even though the United States has no claims at stake and is essentially indifferent to how the sovereignty claims are eventually solved so long as it is through a process that is lawful, is peaceful, and does not involve coercion.

The issue of Chinese behavior in the SCS is also related to China's so called nine-dash line (NDL) that encloses most of the SCS and appears on all of China's maps of the area. Is the line simply a cartographical annotation indicating China's claim to all the land features within it, or since it cuts through the exclusive economic zones (EEZs) of all of the SCS coastal states, is it also an attempt to claim a significant portion of the resources that, under the Law of the Sea, legitimately belong to the coastal states? Beijing has long refused to officially clarify what this line signifies, but acts as though it is infringing on coastal state EEZs by claiming both land and water within the line. The United States has already made clear that it thinks the line has no legal basis under the Law of the Sea.[3] So has the Philippines. Manila took legal action permitted to UNCLOS signatories and legally challenged China at the Permanent Court of Arbitration (PCA) in The Hague in January 2013.[4] The NDL as well as Chinese appropriation of low-tide elevations on the Philippine continental shelf are at the center of its request for an arbitral finding.

China has opted not to participate in the arbitration, and said it would not be bound by any finding. It did however argue, using a position paper, that the PCA should dismiss the Philippine case on the grounds that it does not have jurisdiction because the Philippine arguments are really about sovereignty, and UNCLOS does not address sovereignty issues.[5] This legal strategy failed. The PCA found it did have jurisdiction.[6] The PCA then focused on the merits of the Philippine request for arbitration and decided in favor of the Philippines on all but one item in its July 12, 2016, ruling.[7]

The United States strongly supports the use of arbitration as a mechanism to resolve the overlapping claims in the SCS. This is not surprising, since U.S. policy is based on the notion that "following the rules" is the key to stability in East Asia. This policy approach is repeatedly reflected in public declaratory U.S. policy. As Secretary of State John Kerry said during his December 2013 visit to Vietnam, "Claimants have a responsibility to clarify their claims and to align their claims with international law and to pursue those claims within international peaceful institutions. Those countries can engage in arbitration and other means of negotiating disputes peacefully."[8] This policy approach was stated even more forcefully in congressional testimony by Assistant Secretary of State for East Asian and Pacific Affairs Daniel Russel in February 2014: "International law makes clear the legal basis on which states can legitimately assert their rights in the maritime domain or exploit marine resources. . . . We do take a strong position that maritime claims must accord with customary international law. This means that all maritime claims must be derived from land features and otherwise comport with the international law of the sea."[9]

Finally, it is important to highlight the fact that when it comes to the competing claims of sovereignty, the United States takes no position on the relative merits of the sovereignty claims in the SCS. This policy approach dates to 1995 in response to China's occupation of Mischief Reef, a low-tide elevation in the Spratly Island chain that rests on the Philippine continental shelf.[10] Beyond the SCS, not taking position on Asian maritime island disputes has antecedents that date back to at least 1971 when the Okinawa Reversion Treaty was being deliberated in the U.S. Senate, and sovereignty over the Senkaku/Diaoyu Islands was an issue.[11] In this regard it is useful to note that Washington has accepted without protest the activities of various claimants since 1946 to occupy features in the SCS they have claimed as their own.

Background

China and Taiwan (the Republic of China) claim all of the land features in the SCS. Vietnam claims the Spratly and Paracel chains, which include most, but not all, of the features. The Philippines claims a large portion of the features in the Spratly chain, as well as Scarborough Shoal in the central portion of the SCS. Malaysia claims a small number of land features in the Spratly Islands, and Brunei claims one. With the exception of Brunei, the other five claimants occupy some of the islands or features with military or paramilitary forces. China also apparently makes claims based on assertions of "historic rights" that are delimited by a vague dashed line with no precise coordinates on maps. Known as the "U-shaped" or "nine-dash" line, it encompasses virtually the entire SCS. This line is the cause of significant anxiety, because Beijing has so far refused to define what it thinks this line means legally. As already mentioned, this line overlaps the legitimate EEZs and the continental shelves of the other SCS coastal states.[12]

A main reason why the ASEAN claimants care who "owns" the many largely uninhabitable above-water land features is that sovereignty carries with it certain rights to the resources of the surrounding waters. Fishing rights are important to all the SCS littoral states, as is the prospect of significant quantities of gas and oil beneath the seabed. No one knows for sure the extent of hydrocarbon resources because the entire SCS has yet to be surveyed, but informed judgments from Washington's International Energy Administration hold that most of the hydrocarbon resources are on the continental shelves of the Philippines, Vietnam, Malaysia, Brunei, and Indonesia.[13]

A small number of the land features have strategic value for China because they have, or soon will have, runways long enough to accommodate tactical jet aircraft. The Spratlys are located well east of heavily traveled shipping lanes, but are within easy tactical aircraft range. China has an obvious strategic interest in ensuring that its sea lanes are not interdicted by forces operating from the Spratly Islands, and the de facto military facilities being built on its man-made islands on all of the Spratly Islands it currently occupies represent one way to prevent that.[14] Beyond this, nationalism focused on not giving up "any of our sovereign territory," especially in China, plays an important role in shaping and limiting the governmental options of the claimants. As Xi

Jinping reportedly said in a speech in Singapore in November 2015, "Islands in the South China Sea have been China's territory since ancient times, and the Chinese government must take responsibility to safeguard its territorial sovereignty and legitimate interests."[15]

Publicly Stated U.S. Policy

Because of China's SCS island building, U.S. policy has evolved and taken a harder edge. A new policy formulation specifically focused on land reclamation activities was included in a presentation made by Secretary of Defense Ashton Carter at the annual Singapore-hosted Shangri-La Dialogue on May 30, 2015. He said, "There should be no mistake: the United States will fly, sail and operate wherever international law allows. . . . America, alongside its allies and partners . . . will not be deterred from exercising these rights. . . . After all, turning an underwater rock into an airfield simply does not afford the rights of sovereignty or permit restrictions on international air or maritime transit."[16] Carter was referring to a central interest of the United States: high seas freedoms, and what is permitted by international law on the high seas. He was making clear that newly created SCS islands will not constrain legal U.S. maritime activity on, under, and above the high seas. This was a clear expression of traditional U.S. policy, but it was also a bit of preemptive diplomacy since as of this writing in January 2016, China has yet to officially claim any maritime entitlements associated with its artificial islands.

In a speech at George Washington University on the eve of President Xi Jinping's September 2015 state visit to Washington, National Security Advisor Susan Rice both provided an excellent overview of administration policy in East Asia and made clear that the mantra "the United States of America will sail, fly, and operate anywhere that international law permits" was an unambiguous statement of U.S. policy.[17] President Obama also made this point publicly during his press conference with President Xi.[18]

For context, a review of the many authoritative public statements of U.S. SCS policy is helpful. There are a number of examples from both Secretary Kerry and former Secretary of State Clinton that could be cited. Consider a typical statement from Secretary Kerry:

> As a Pacific nation, and the resident power, the United States has a national interest in the maintenance of peace and stability, respect for international law, unimpeded lawful commerce, and freedom of navigation in the South China Sea. As we have said many times before, while we do not take a position on a

competing territorial claim over land features, we have a strong interest in the manner in which the disputes of the South China Sea are addressed and in the conduct of the parties. We very much hope to see progress soon on a substantive code of conduct in order to help ensure stability in this vital region.[19]

A very important official statement from the U.S. government regarding the SCS was made on February 5, 2014, by Assistant Secretary Russel. Because of its specificity and candor, it is worth including several verbatim sections, because Russel's testimony remains the most comprehensive public statement available.

On the U.S. desire for a Sino-ASEAN Code of Conduct to prevent escalation:

> In the South China Sea, we continue to support efforts by ASEAN and China to develop an effective Code of Conduct. Agreement on a Code of Conduct is long overdue and the negotiating process should be accelerated. This is something that China and ASEAN committed to back in 2002 when they adopted their Declaration on the Conduct of Parties in the South China Sea. An effective Code of Conduct would promote a rules based framework for managing and regulating the behaviour of relevant countries in the South China Sea. A key part of that framework, which we and many others believe should be adopted quickly, is inclusion of mechanisms such as hotlines and emergency procedure for preventing incidents in sensitive areas and managing them when they do occur in ways that prevent disputes from escalating.[20]

On the importance of customary international law (the UN Convention on the Law of the Sea, UNCLOS, has become customary international law), Russel had this to say:

> International law makes clear the legal basis on which states can legitimately assert their rights in the maritime domain or exploit maritime resources. . . . We take a strong position that maritime claims must be derived from land features and otherwise comport with the international law of the sea. So while we are not siding with one claimant against another, we certainly believe that claims in the South China Sea that are not derived from land features are fundamentally flawed.[21]

Russel was the first U.S. government official to convey a position on China's NDL. He said,

> There is a growing concern [that] . . . China is [attempting] to assert control over the area contained in the so called "nine dash line," despite the objections of its neighbors and despite the lack of any explanation or apparent basis under international law regarding the scope of the claim itself. China's lack of clarity with regard to its South China Sea claims has created uncertainty, insecurity and instability in the region. It limits the prospect for achieving a mutually agreeable resolution or equitable joint development arrangements among the claimants. I want to emphasize the point that under international law, maritime claims in the South China Sea must be derived from land features. *Any use of the "nine-dash line" by China to claim maritime rights not based on land features would be inconsistent with international law.*[22]

The importance of the Russel testimony is that it reflects an evolution of U.S. policy from general exhortations asking for all parties to abide by international law to becoming more specific in its public views regarding maritime claims that are not in accordance with the UNCLOS. This more explicitly "legalist" approach is certainly warranted, and has been encouraged by both the Philippines and Vietnam. China tends to be dismissive of U.S. policy statements that harp on following UNCLOS since the U.S. Senate has not ratified the UNCLOS treaty,[23] and as a result some question Washington's credibility when it criticizes others for not abiding by the treaty.[24]

This is nonsense; not only did Washington play a large role in crafting the treaty, it has abided by its provisions since 1982, when President Reagan so directed.[25] In addition, while it is unfortunate that Washington has not ratified UNCLOS, that does not mean that America's many excellent maritime legal specialists are incapable of reaching judgments regarding what claims are, or are not, in compliance with UNCLOS. The fact that the United States has not ratified the treaty, and given the partisan divide on Capitol Hill is unlikely to do so in the foreseeable future, should not deter the U.S. government from speaking out regarding noncompliance by claimants involved in SCS disputes. As Russel put it, "all claimants—not only China—should clarify their claims in terms of international law, including the law of the sea."[26] This is why the U.S. policy includes support for the Philippine decision to institute arbitral proceedings against China under Annex VII of the 1982 UNCLOS.[27]

In December 2014, Vietnam surprised the international community by revealing that it had officially expressed an interest in the outcome of the Philippine arbitration case. Vietnam scholar Carl Thayer writes,

> By expressing its interest in the case Vietnam is not joining the Philippines in taking legal action against China. But Vietnam's statement of interest will

be noted by the arbitrators of the China-Philippines case. This will have the effect of raising—however slightly—the importance of this case. In other words although the case is a bilateral matter, the judgment of the arbitrators must take into account the interests of other parties likely to be affected by the outcome. It may be likely that by filing a statement of interest that the Arbitral Tribunal could invite Vietnam to make a presentation of its rights and interests. In other words, Vietnam can make its legal case "through the back door."[28]

Finally, it is also important to note that U.S. policy involves more that words; it also involves closer security cooperation with treaty allies such as the Philippines and strategic partners like Singapore to improve U.S. military access to facilities proximate to the SCS. Of equal significance, U.S. policy also includes helping SCS littoral states, especially the Philippines and Vietnam, improve their capacity to police their own territorial waters and EEZs by providing excess naval hardware to the Philippines and fast patrol boats to Vietnam and the Philippines. The provision of capacity building assistance was announced by Secretary Kerry in Hanoi in December of 2013.

> No region can be secure in the absence of effective law enforcement in territorial waters. And because of that, today I am also pleased to announce $32.5 million in new U.S. assistance for maritime law enforcement in Southeast Asian states. This assistance will include, among other things, training and new fast-patrol vessels for coast guards. Building on existing efforts like the Gulf of Thailand initiative, this assistance will foster greater regional cooperation on maritime issues and ultimately provide the ability of Southeast Asian nations . . . to police and monitor their waters more effectively.
>
> In particular, peace and stability in the South China Sea is a top priority for us and for countries in the region. We are very concerned by and strongly opposed to coercive and aggressive tactics to advance territorial claims. Claimants have a responsibility to clarify their claims and to align their claims with international law and to pursue those claims within international peaceful institutions. Those countries can engage in arbitration and other means of negotiating disputes peacefully. We support ASEAN's efforts with China to move quickly to conclude a code of conduct.[29]

Following his stop in Vietnam, Secretary Kerry went on the Philippines, where he was very explicit in his comments that linked Philippine security, the SCS, and U.S. security assistance together:

The United States is committed to working with the Philippines to address its most pressing security challenges. That's why we are negotiating a strong and enduring framework agreement [which has subsequently been concluded] that would enhance defence cooperation under our alliance, including through an increased rotational presence of U.S. forces in Philippines. And that's why we have committed $40 million for a new initiative to improve the Philippines's maritime security and maritime domain awareness.

Second, we support internationally recognized dispute resolution mechanisms such as those that are provided in the Law of the Sea Convention. The United States strongly opposes the use of intimidation, coercion, or aggression to advance territorial claims. And I assured the foreign secretary that the United States remains firmly committed to the security of the Philippines and the region.[30]

Once the magnitude of Chinese island building became clear, U.S. policy responded by calling for a freeze on this activity because it was considered destabilizing. Assistant Secretary Russel took advantage of an ASEAN senior officials meeting in the summer of 2014 to make "suggestions" regarding how ASEAN might respond to China's reclamation activities:

The other suggestion that I made . . . is based on the 2002 Declaration of Conduct that was agreed upon between the ASEAN countries and China. . . . Would they be willing to make a pledge as simple as not to occupy any of the land features in the South China Sea that are currently unoccupied? That is the sort of thing that is very consistent with, if not actually implicit in, the Declaration of Conduct. And the point that I tried to make is that while they work at making progress on a long-term binding code of conduct, the pace of incidents and the level of tension in the South China Sea is going up, and going up quickly.

As the press has reported, there are signs of large-scale reclamation projects in the South China Sea and the construction of military facilities, and so on. And my suggestion was that if the claimants themselves engaged in a voluntary process [of freezing activity], they would have an opportunity to lower the temperature, improve the prospects for the code of conduct negotiation, and minimize the risk of other dangerous incident.[31]

A year later, Washington decided to double down on its willingness to help improve the maritime security capacity of SCS littoral states, and in May 2015 Secretary Carter used the Shangri-La venue in Singapore to announce a US$425 million Southeast Asia Maritime Security Initiative, originated by Senator John McCain, chair of the Senate Armed Services Committee.

Focused on Indonesia, Malaysia, the Philippines, Thailand and Vietnam, this program is designed to provide equipment, training, supplies, and small-scale construction.[32]

Importantly, in addition to the capacity-building aspect of U.S. policy, there is a low key but very visible hard power element to U.S. policy in South East Asia. Starting in August 2013, the U.S. Seventh Fleet stepped up its military capacity in the SCS by instituting a full-time U.S. Navy warship presence, along with periodic aircraft reconnaissance missions, somewhere in the SCS. On average there are two U.S. Navy warships patrolling that body of water daily. (Unofficially, this compares with five to six People's Liberation Army [PLA] Navy warships plus some number of Chinese Coast Guard vessels operating in the SCS.)[33]

In sum, U.S. policy consists of the following elements.

- No use of force or coercion by any of the claimants to resolve sovereignty disputes or change the status quo of disputed SCS features.
- Freedom of navigation, which includes unimpeded lawful navigation for commercial, private, and military vessels and aircraft. Coastal states must respect the UNCLOS language that all "high seas freedoms," including peaceful military operations, are applicable in the EEZs of coastal states. The United States will sail or fly wherever international law permits.
- All maritime entitlements to any of the waters of the SCS must be based on international law and must be derived from land features in the SCS. China's NDL does not meet these criteria. In short, only land (islands and rocks) generates maritime zones, not vice versa.
- The United States takes no position on the relative merits of competing sovereignty claims. It does not choose sides; nor does it favor one country's claim over another's.
- An effective Code of Conduct that would promote a rules-based framework for managing and regulating the behavior of relevant countries in the SCS is essential. A key part of such a document would be mechanisms such as hotlines and emergency procedures for preventing incidents in sensitive areas and managing them when they do occur in ways that prevent disputes from escalating.
- China as well as other parties that occupy Spratly Island features should "freeze" potentially destabilizing improvements to those features. China's island reclamation activities are especially unhelpful in this regard.
- The United States supports internationally recognized dispute resolution mechanisms, including those provided for in the UNCLOS treaty.

- Washington will respond positively to small SCS littoral countries that are U.S. allies, officially designated "strategic partners" or "comprehensive partners," who want to improve their ability to patrol and monitor their own territorial waters and EEZs.[34]
- The U.S. government wants to improve access for the U.S. military in areas proximate to the SCS, especially in the Philippines, where an Enhanced Defense Cooperation Agreement with the Philippine government has been concluded.[35]

What U.S. Strategic Interests Are Involved?

Freedom of Navigation and U.S. Military Activities in China's EEZ

When U.S. government officials speak about "freedom of navigation" in the SCS they are combining two distinctly different aspects of freedom of navigation. The first has to do with unimpeded lawful trade and commerce. During testimony before the Senate in 2012, then Secretary of State Hilary Clinton made the point that freedom of navigation in the SCS was a "vital interest."[36]

The data tend to support this claim. More than half of the world's annual merchant fleet tonnage passes through the Indonesian Straits of Malacca, Sunda, and Lombok that link the Indian Ocean with the SCS, with the majority of that maritime traffic continuing on to the SCS. According the U.S. Energy Information Administration, almost a third of global crude oil and over half of global LNG trade passes through the SCS, making it one of the most important trade routes in the world. The United Nations Conference on Trade and Development Review of Maritime Transport 2011 estimated 8.4 billion tons of total world maritime trade in 2010 transited the SCS—this volume equates to more than half of the world's annual merchant fleet tonnage.[37]

It is important to point out that the SCS is not the only route for ships to reach East Asia from the Indian Ocean and vice versa, it just happens to be the most efficient; it is a shorter route, and making it cheaper to transport goods via the SCS. But if a crisis did occur that made it unsafe for commercial traffic to transit the SCS, other less efficient routes are available.[38]

When the United States speaks to China regarding "freedom of navigation," it is not speaking about any Chinese hindrances to legitimate maritime trade; China rightly points out that it has no interest in obstructing maritime commerce, and has never done so.[39] Beijing has to some degree appeared perplexed at why Washington keeps raising the issue of "freedom of navigation." In truth it appears that each side is talking past the another. The real issue for Washington has to do with Chinese objections to U.S. surveillance activities in its EEZ. There is a decided difference of opinion regarding what military activities are permitted in the EEZ of China. Washington argues that UNCLOS permits nations to exercise "high seas freedoms" in the EEZs of coastal states. These freedoms include the right to conduct peaceful military activities, including, inter alia, surveillance and military surveys. China disagrees. It claims that these are "hostile" activities. This disagreement regarding surveillance has already caused two serious incidents: the 2001 midair collision between a U.S. Navy surveillance aircraft (EP-3) and an intercepting Chinese navy fighter and the 2009 harassment by Chinese fisherman and paramilitary ships of USNS *Impeccable*, which was conducting undersea surveillance.[40]

The United States believes that nothing in UNCLOS or state practice changes the right of any nation's military forces to conduct military activities in EEZs without first notifying the coastal state and gaining its consent. China disagrees; it claims that any nation that undertakes reconnaissance activities in China's EEZ without having notified China and gaining its permission is in violation of Chinese domestic law and international law.

The U.S. view is most succinctly spelled out by a retired U.S. Navy maritime lawyer, Captain Raul (Pete) Pedrozo, who formerly taught at the U.S. Naval War College:

> China's views on coastal State authority in the exclusive economic zone (EEZ) are not supported by State practice, the negotiating history of the United Nations Convention on the Law of the Sea (UNCLOS), or a plain reading of Part V of the Convention. All nations may legitimately engage in military activities in foreign EEZs without prior notice to, or consent of, the coastal State concerned. Efforts were made during the negotiations of UNCLOS to broaden coastal State rights and jurisdiction in the EEZ to include security interests. However, the Conference rejected these efforts and the final text of the Convention (Article 58) ultimately preserved high seas freedoms of navigation and overflight and other internationally lawful uses of the seas related to those freedoms, to include military activities, in the EEZ.[41]

Peter Dutton, also a retired U.S. Navy international lawyer, elaborated in a separate article on how and why the decisions leading to the current language of Article 58 were reached:

> The creation of the exclusive economic zone in 1982 by UNCLOS . . . was a carefully balanced compromise between the interests of the coastal states in managing and protecting ocean resources and those of maritime user states in ensuring high seas freedoms of navigation and over flight, including for mili-

tary purposes. Thus in the EEZ the coastal state was granted sovereign rights to resources and jurisdiction to make laws related to those resources, while high seas freedoms of navigation were specifically preserved for all states, to ensure the participation of maritime powers in the convention.[42]

Despite the clear negotiation record, China is attempting to undo this carefully balanced compromise between coastal states and user states. China's desire to limit military activity in its EEZ is likely to be an ongoing source of direct Sino-U.S. friction.[43] On a positive note, during the Obama and Xi summits in November 2014 and September 2015, memoranda of understanding on procedures associated with surface ship and aviation encounters between the United States and China were signed; the hope is that while China has not changed its objections to U.S. surveillance activity, it will make encounters between military and paramilitary forces, including those occasioned by these activities, safer by reducing the possibility of a future incident.[44]

Rule-Based Stability in East Asia

U.S. policy toward the SCS and Southeast Asia is intertwined with the Obama administration's overall East Asian policy—the "rebalance to Asia." Starting in the earliest days of President Obama's first term, there was a focus on Southeast Asia. This was evidenced by Secretary Clinton's visit to the ASEAN secretariat in February 2009, and Washington's accession to ASEAN's Treaty of Amity and Cooperation in 2009, which then made it possible for the United States to become a member of the annual heads of state meeting called the East Asia Summit (EAS).[45]

The real turning point of more direct U.S. involvement in the SCS happened at the July 2010 meeting ASEAN Regional Forum (ARF) in Hanoi when Secretary Clinton indicated that Washington was willing to facilitate multilateral discussions on the disputed territories of the SCS. Because of Chinese behavior, she took a much more assertive position, saying the United States is opposed to any use of coercion or threats of force to resolve conflicting claims. Clinton justified her statement of concern by stating, "The United States, like every nation, has a national interest in freedom of navigation, open access to Asia's maritime commons and respect for international law in the South China Sea."[46]

This policy step directly involved the United States in the SCS in a strategic rather than tactical fashion. Not surprisingly, China was furious over Clinton's comments, not least because previously it had succeeded in keeping the sovereignty issue off the agenda of ARF and other Asian multinational meetings. Chinese officials denounced Clinton's efforts to "internationalize" the issue; both the Chinese foreign and defense ministries criticized her for intervening in the SCS dispute.[47]

By inserting itself more directly into SCS sovereignty issues, Washington was responding to a perceived demand signal from Vietnam and the Philippines, which were worried about Chinese assertiveness in the SCS.[48] Washington was also more attuned to aggressive Chinese behavior following the USNS *Impeccable* incident in the spring of 2009.[49] The Clinton statement at the Hanoi ARF reminded the participants, including China, that the United States intended to remain a serious strategic player in East Asia and *that peace and stability in the SCS was a U.S. interest.*

It also foreshadowed by a year the rollout of the Obama administration's strategic approach to Asia; initially dubbed the pivot, subsequently known as the rebalance, this strategy includes an integrated mix of diplomatic, economic, budgetary, and security-related initiatives.[50] Specific military posture changes are focused on Southeast Asia and intended to increase U.S. presence through rotational deployment, more frequent port visits, and improved military-to-military engagements and training exercises with the Philippines, Vietnam, and Singapore.[51] Whether the administration wished it or not, the renewed emphasis on Southeast Asia, a deeper policy involvement in the SCS, and initiation of a long-term Asia-focused strategy (the rebalance) transformed public consciousness of the SCS (as well as the Senkaku dispute between China and Japan) into litmus tests of the effectiveness of the Obama approach to Asia.[52]

Reassuring the Region That the "Rebalance" Is Still an Administration Goal

Because of defense budget reductions, political dysfunction in Washington, and perceived weakness in how the White House has responded to the Syrian civil war and Russia's aggression in seizing Crimea, regional skepticism regarding how committed the administration is to the rebalance strategy and to its security guarantees to Asian friends and allies is a problem the administration faces. Fueling this skepticism is the fact that neither the new National Security Advisor nor the Secretary of Defense was considered an "Asia hand." One of the key aspects of the current policy approach is to emphatically reassure the region that the administration remains committed to the rebalance strategy in general, and to Southeast Asia in particular. During his visit to Brunei in July 2013 for the ASEAN ministerial meeting Secretary of State John Kerry spoke directly to the Obama second-term commitment to the rebalance strategy:

I know that some people have wondered whether in the second term of the Obama Administration, and with a new Secretary of State, are we going to continue on the path that we have been on? And the answer, I say to all of you directly, is yes. Not just yes, but we hope to increase the effort. So we are committed to ensuring a peaceful, stable, and prosperous Southeast Asia, and that's why we're working together on a whole range of both traditional and non-traditional security issues from wildlife trafficking to human trafficking—trafficking in persons—to non-proliferation, humanitarian assistance, and disaster relief, and so much more.

In November 2013 Ambassador Susan Rice, the current National Security Advisor, delivered an address laying out the administration's continued commitment to the rebalance. She stressed the multidimensional nature of the rebalance—it is not just about security—and provided more specificity on what the administration hopes to achieve during its final three years in office. "Rebalancing toward the Asia Pacific remains a cornerstone of the Obama Administration's foreign policy. No matter how many hotspots emerge elsewhere, we will continue to deepen our enduring commitment to this critical region. Our friends in Asia deserve and will continue to get our highest level attention."[53] After specifically highlighting that the administration is showing commitment to the region by dispatching a number of high-level delegations to the region, which is viewed in East Asia as an important indication of administration interest, Rice went on to say,

> I'd like to take this opportunity to outline what we aim to achieve in the Asia Pacific over the next three years. Ultimately, America's purpose is to establish a more stable security environment in Asia, an open and transparent economic environment, and a liberal political environment that respects the universal rights and freedoms of all. . . . In the near term, President Obama will continue to lay the critical foundations for lasting progress in four key areas—enhancing security, expanding prosperity, fostering democratic values, and advancing human dignity.[54]

While she did not specifically address the maritime disputes in East Asia, including the SCS, she did address the importance the rebalance places on strengthening allied relationships as well military posture aspects of the rebalance strategy:

> We are making the Asia Pacific more secure with American alliances—and an American force posture—that are being modernized to meet the challenges of

our time. By 2020, 60 percent of our fleet will be based in the Pacific, and our Pacific Command will gain more of our most cutting-edge capabilities.

We are updating and diversifying our security relationships in the region to address emerging challenges as effectively as we deter conventional threats. We are urging our allies and partners to take greater responsibility for defending our common interests and values. . . . To diversify the network of security relationships in the region, we are strengthening trilateral cooperation with our allies and our security partners and encouraging them to cooperate more closely among themselves.[55]

Defense Treaty Obligations to the Philippines

Another U.S. interest is the reality that one of the major disputants in the overlapping sovereignty claims to the Spratly Islands and Scarborough Shoal is the government of the Philippines. While Philippine claims in the Spratly Islands overlap with those of Vietnam, China, and Taiwan, Manila's most worrisome issues are with China, which takes serious issue with all of Manila's claims. In April 2012, the SCS was the site of a confrontation between the Philippines and China over an uninhabitable feature known as Scarborough Shoal. This dispute has quieted, but with the result that China is now in effective control of the feature.[56]

It is not that the mutual defense treaty with the Philippines obligates Washington to take sides over the sovereignty question of Scarborough Shoal; it does not. In fact U.S. policy has repeatedly pointed out that Americans take no position on sovereignty claims, which includes those made by the Philippines on portions of the Spratly group *after* the Mutual Defense Treaty with the Philippines was signed on August 30, 1951.

This probably means the United States would not become militarily involved if the Chinese seized an island the Philippines claimed, as they have essentially done in the case of Scarborough Shoal. But if in the process of doing that China were to attack a Philippine naval or coast guard vessel, shoot down a Philippine military aircraft, or kill or wound members of the Philippine armed forces, treaty language related to attacks on "[the Philippines'] armed forces, public vessels or aircraft in the Pacific" suggests that the treaty would apply.[57]

The treaty requires that either party will, in the event of an attack, "act to meet the common dangers in accordance with its constitutional processes."[58] The U.S. decision regarding its response in accordance with the terms of the treaty would immediately be under the regional microscope. America's friends and allies, along with China, would watch Washington's response very closely and reach their own conclusions regarding how effective the rebalance strategy was in maintaining a stable and peaceful East Asian region. The premise rationalizing forward U.S. military presence is that it deters conflict; for deterrence to be effective, however, the United States must be perceived as having both the ability and the political will to act.

Although credibility is an essential part of Washington's attempt to reassure friends and allies that the United States is a force for stability in the face of Chinese power, Washington does not want to get into a conflict with China over inconsequential rocks and shoals in the SCS claimed by the Philippines, particularly since Philippine claims to sovereignty over portions of the Spratly Islands are legally very suspect.[59]

Concluding Thoughts on U.S. Policy and Options

Starting in the summer of 2010 the Obama administration clearly signaled, through a combination of diplomacy and enhanced military engagement with SCS littoral states, that the United States does consider *creating rule-based stability in the SCS an important U.S. national interest.* Since that time the United States has become increasingly involved in the day-to-day security dynamic between China and the SCS littoral states. China's island building activities have resulted in greater U.S. involvement "on the ground" as it were. These unilateral changes to the status quo in the Spratly Islands have triggered changes in declaratory policy; then as a tangible demonstration of the U.S. policy of "sailing wherever international law permits," they led to the direct involvement of the U.S. Navy. On October 27, 2015, Washington directed a U.S. Navy destroyer to sail within twelve nautical miles of one of China's reclaimed islands (Subi Reef). This was intended as a tangible demonstration that the United States would not recognize any maritime entitlements associated with Beijing's island building. Since Beijing has yet to make any claims to entitlements, the legal reasoning behind this demonstration is convoluted, triggering an exchange of correspondence between an unhappy U.S. Senator John McCain, seeking an explanation of why the operation was characterized as "innocent passage," and Secretary of Defense Ashton Carter. A passage from the Department of Defense response explaining the reasoning behind the involvement of USS *Lassen* follows:

> With respect to Subi Reef, the claimants have not clarified whether they believe a territorial sea surrounds it, but one thing is clear: under the law of the sea, China's land reclamation cannot create a legal entitlement to a territorial sea,

and does not change our legal ability to navigate near it in this manner. We [the Obama administration] believe that Subi Reef, before China turned it into an artificial island, was a low-tide elevation and that it therefore cannot generate its own entitlement to a territorial sea. However, if it is located within 12 nautical miles of another geographic feature that is entitled to a territorial sea—as might be the case with Sandy Cay—then the low-water line on Subi Reef could be used as the baseline for measuring Sandy Cay's territorial sea. In other words, in those circumstances, Subi Reef could be surrounded by a 12-nautical mile-territorial sea despite being submerged at high tide in its natural state. Given the factual uncertainty, we conducted the FONOP in a manner that is lawful under all possible scenarios to preserve U.S. options should the factual ambiguities be resolved, disputes settled, and clarity on maritime claims reached.[60]

While Senator McCain was not happy, the intended message was clearly received by Beijing. The Chinese too were not happy, but in this case that was the point of the operation—it was the operational equivalent of diplomatic protest. In response, Beijing eventually used carefully chosen language that avoided making Washington's case that China was making an unlawful maritime claim associated with the newly created islands. In short, Beijing did not argue that the United States had violated Chinese sovereignty,[61] but did indicate the United States had "harmed" China's security. This is not the last we will hear about SCS freedom of navigation operations, since the U.S. Department of Defense apparently remains committed to periodic freedom of navigation operations in 2016—activity that could result in a direct military confrontation between Washington and Beijing.[62]

The unsettled situation in the SCS also brings attention to the future role of the United States in the region. Having more directly involved itself starting at the ARF in Hanoi, the Obama administration has over the years increased the amount of "skin it has in the game." This is very unfortunate, since short of the actual use of force it appears there is little Washington can do to actually bring a halt to China's quest for de facto control of the Spratly Islands. This weakens the central premise of the rebalance strategy, which rests on a foundation of ensuring that common legally based standards of behavior are followed throughout the region. Thomas Donilon, President Obama's former National Security Advisor, put it succinctly in the *Financial Times*: "Security in the region requires that international law and norms be respected, that commerce and freedom of navigation are not impeded, that emerging powers build trust with their neighbors, and that disagreements are resolved peacefully without threats or coercion."[63] Can Washington do anything to improve the situation? It makes a great deal of sense for Washington to make the focus of U.S. policy on international law in general and UNCLOS in particular because it has no direct leverage when it comes to resolution of the sovereignty disputes. But the unhappy reality is that UNCLOS has no provisions on how to determine sovereignty over offshore islands. As there is no treaty that governs the issue of sovereignty, the rules of customary international law and relevant case law on the acquisition and loss of territory pertain. Territorial sovereignty disputes cannot be resolved unless the claimant states reach agreement among themselves or mutually agree to refer the disputes to the International Court of Justice, the International Tribunal for the Law of the Sea (ITLOS), or an international arbitral tribunal.[64] Given the sensitivity and complexity of the disputes, this is not likely to happen, even though lack of "surety of title" will stand in the way of incenting private investors—especially in the oil and gas field—to make investments in projects that are located in disputed region. Obtaining such surety of title was one of the underlying reasons why Bangladesh and Myanmar agreed to refer their long-standing boundary disputes to ITLOS for adjudication.[65]

Furthermore, there are still unresolved legal interpretations, based on case law, that make some of the claims and activities open to question, such as differentiating between an "island" and a "rock." This is important because an "island" rates a twelve-nautical-mile territorial sea and a two-hundred-nautical-mile EEZ, whereas a "rock" rates a territorial sea, but no EEZ. There is no legal agreements as to which features meet the criteria of UNCLOS article 121(3) to be considered an island; to wit, can it sustain human habitation or have an economic life its own? A few courts could have provided clarity on these questions but have declined to do so. Because there is no legal agreement on differentiating between rocks and islands in order to determine maritime zones, most states with features that might be considered rocks have gone ahead and claimed EEZs from them.

Some legal ambiguity seems to remain regarding low-tide elevations (LTEs). LTEs are naturally formed areas of land, surrounded by and above water at low tide, *but submerged at high tide.*[66] An LTE cannot be appropriated.[67] *Sovereignty claims to such features are invalid.* But China and other claimants have ignored this very recent International Court of Justice decision and are busy building on LTEs to make sure they are above water at high tide—turning them into features that might justify a maritime entitlement. (The Beckman article cited in note 14 pertains.)

Australian scholar Greg Austin correctly concludes that Chinese claims are motivated by the unshakable conviction that the land features in the SCS legitimately belong to China according to commonly accepted standards of international law. He argues that resources are important, but are not the primary motivation.[68] The most powerful motivation seems to be a belief—unanimous among China's elites and widespread among its citizens—that an SCS under China's sway is "inherent" to a just international system.

This belief helps explain why in practice China has not been scrupulous in following the rules associated with maritime zones and features that are spelled out in UNCLOS. Not only have the Chinese been "fast and lose" with a strict interpretation of UNCLOS,[69] they have also embarked on an effort to rewrite what is "commonly accepted" international law when it comes to attempting to generate a Chinese claim to resources far beyond those associated with land features because they are within the NDL. Chinese experts argue, unofficially, it has "historic rights," which are circumscribed by the NDL, to justify access to resources that are on the continental shelf and within the EEZs of Vietnam, Indonesia, Malaysia, Brunei, and the Philippines.[70]

Assistant Secretary of State Russel has focused on the problem caused by the NDL and the notion that "historic rights" are important per se. A first step in providing a critique of the NDL and historical rights approach was the issuance on December 5, 2014, of an authoritative and very critical assessment of the legal merits of the NDL regarding broad maritime claims in the SCS.[71] Ultimately, the ruling by the PCA in The Hague in July 2016 set out the guidelines for resolving the status of China's claims. However, China has repeatedly stated it will reject the ruling by the PCA. Jakarta has become increasingly concerned that China's NDL includes some of the waters surrounding its Natuna gas field in Indonesia's Riau Islands province.[72] The inauguration of President Joko Widodo provides a new opportunity for an increase in Indonesian SCS activism. In comments since the election in July, he has called for the establishment of a maritime ministry and has said that his government would be willing to mediate maritime territorial disputes in the region (i.e., in the SCS).[73] Washington should encourage this predilection.

If Jakarta were willing to assume a more open leadership role in dealing with China regarding the Spratlys and the NDL, it could shift the primary voice regarding a rules-based solution from Washington to Jakarta. If ASEAN's most influential member were to become more actively involved in trying to reconcile the disputes, that could be decisive in finally reaching closure on the long-hoped-for Code of Conduct. It seems to have demonstrated to Beijing that its NDL causes problems with states that do not have a territorial claim in the Spratly Islands.

In the meantime continuing press for a rigorous Sino-ASEAN Code of Conduct remains very important. It embodies the policy approach of following the rules of behavior and international law in order to prevent conflict in the maritime domain.

If Washington wants to go further than policy statements focused on international law and become more diplomatically proactive, one approach might be direct U.S. mediation—for example, active involvement in trying to reconcile the competing claims of the Philippines, Vietnam, and Malaysia. By negotiating a resolution to these differences, the United States would set a positive example for subsequent resolution with China, make it easier for ASEAN to speak with one voice to China, and create useful legal precedents that could more broadly apply to other maritime disputes in East Asia.[74]

Shaping policy to advance U.S. interests is a challenge because only one aspect of the SCS set of issues is a direct bilateral Sino-U.S. security issue—the question of military operations in China's EEZ, which Washington and Beijing seem destined to continue to disagree about.

The other main SCS U.S. interests, alliance reassurance and American credibility, need to constantly be addressed through the full range of engagement techniques—engagement in the broadest sense, including diplomatic, economic, and security that continue to focus on the broader question of America's role in East Asia and how that can be accommodated within the context of a rising China. The Obama trip to Asia in April 2014 to three U.S. allies and one "comprehensive partner,"[75] without a stopover in Beijing, is a prime example of how the administration will need to keep addressing this issue. Beijing was not on the agenda again in November 2015 when President Obama was again in Manila, this time for APEC and then Kuala Lumpur for the EAS. As one Southeast Asia expert wrote following these meetings,

> The Obama trip revealed that, despite ASEAN's continuing internal divisions about how to approach South China Sea disputes, the overall level of fear of China within the organization's members is rising. At the summit in Kuala Lumpur, the United States and ASEAN signed an agreement to create a new "strategic partnership." Although for now the U.S.-ASEAN strategic partnership is mostly a symbolic document, it sends a signal to Beijing that not only the most aggrieved Southeast Asian nations, like Vietnam and the Philippines, but all of the Southeast Asian nations, are seeking more assertive ways to hedge against China's rising maritime power.[76]

Washington should also ensure that the planned U.S. military posture and capability improvements in East Asia are portrayed as symbols of reassurance and stability and are not characterized as attempts to directly confront China. The United States must emphasize that the objective of the military portion of the administration's rebalance strategy is to ensure that the United States can fulfill its security responsibilities to its allies and friends.

There is also another context at work—the broader context of the over-all Sino-U.S. relationship, including very important global interests involving climate change, North Korea, Syria, Iran, and Russian behavior in its European near abroad. These are all issues that depend upon Chinese co-operation. In formulating policy, these important U.S. interests have to be taken into account and weighed against U.S. interests in the SCS. Similarly, the fact that the economies of the United States and China are deeply in-tertwined and mutually dependent is very important to Washington. This means that U.S. policy in the SCS cannot be overwhelmingly anti-Chinese. When it comes to the SCS the United States must keep the importance of the area in perspective when it comes to the full menu of bilateral U.S.-China relations.[77]

Over the past seven years the Obama administration has invested more American diplomatic, economic, and security efforts in Southeast Asia than at any time since the end of the Vietnam War. As a result, Washington has created a new normal that includes being more deeply engaged in security relations with all the ASEAN claimants to features in the SCS.

In the realm of military capacity the United States has been helping with a Philippine military and naval modernization program. The reality is that a Philippine defense buildup adequate enough for the Philippines to be able to deter Chinese assertiveness would be a generational effort on the part of the United States, akin to U.S. efforts with South Korea following the Korean War. Given what appears to be the legally questionable basis for most of the Philip-pines' claims in the Spratlys, agreeing that the U.S.-Philippines Mutual De-fense Treaty embraces territory claimed by the Philippines in the SCS would be a very risky attempt at deterrence. Washington certainly does not want a conflict with China over claims that are not legally credible.

For several years Vietnam has been investing in an effort, largely supplied by Russia, to defend its maritime approaches and territory.[78] When Viet-namese plans reach fruition, Vietnam could have in place an effective way to deter a replay in the Spratlys of Beijing's seizure of the Paracel Islands in 1975. Helping Vietnam reach its objectives is now a possibility because of the Oc-tober 2014 decision by Washington to partially lift the arms embargo against Vietnam.[79]

On balance, current U.S. policy is comprehensive, sensible, and well bal-anced. It has been primarily diplomatic, but in 2014–15 hard power played a growing role. Policy remains focuses on creating stability by exhorting all the parties to follow the rules of international law; it explicitly defines how Washington would like conflicts to be solved; and it includes initiatives aimed at redressing some of the power imbalance between the Philippines, Vietnam, and China. Finally, it incorporates an element of deterrence by not ignoring America's security alliance with the Philippines as well as providing for access of U.S. naval and air forces in Singapore and the Philippines. But it also is appropriately modulated through recognition that the SCS is not the most important element of overall U.S. policy with China.

But despite being judged sensible and proportionate, given the U.S. interests involved, the Obama administration has been criticized from both the right and the left for not being "tough" enough with China.[80] The simple reason for the criticism is that U.S. exhortations to follow the rules, to stop pushing other claimants around, and to seek third-party arbitration to resolve claims have largely fallen on deaf ears.

U.S. officials inevitably argue that China needs to recognize that the developments it dislikes in the SCS are not the result of a U.S. effort to contain China or complicate its rise, but rather are the repercussions from its own actions and statements that make many of its neighbors fearful and lead them to seek a strong U.S. presence as a source of reassurance. In short, this lack of self-awareness by Chinese interlocutors leaves observers wondering why China is not acting in its own best interests.

Arguably, China knows exactly what it is doing. The realities of geography are that other claimants to SCS islands are always going to live in the shadow of China. China is already the largest trading partner with all of its Southeast Asian neighbors, and their economies are increasingly interlinked.[81] At a Track II meeting in Southeast Asia, one ASEAN participant captured this reality perfectly: "We are all afraid of China, but we are also afraid of what China might do to our economy if we cross them."[82]

Finally, it is important to recognize the importance that China's domestic issues have in President Xi Jinping's approach to the SCS. Being tough on China's sovereignty claims provides important political cover for Xi's politically difficult attempts to reorient China's economics, stamp out corruption in the Chinese Communist Party, conduct a massive reorganization of the People's Liberation Army, and curb the power of provincial party secretaries who frequently act as regional despots.[83]

So far, China's actions in the SCS have not harmed its economy: its neighbors still line up seeking to improve relations. Beijing does understand that its small neighbors do not want to choose between the United States and China. They all want the best possible relationship with both.[84] Since these small countries will always be China's neighbors, and they will always need China more than it needs them, China can exercise great latitude in how it goes about trying to redress what it believes are historic injustices that a weak China suffered.

When it comes to the SCS, China has asymmetric advantages in terms of its geography, history, military capabilities, and interests. Finally, and most importantly, Beijing believes it has right and history on its side. It really does believe that all the land features and resources belong to China.

On the other hand, by largely ignoring U.S. attempts to encourage a peaceful rules-based approach, Beijing has energized the Obama administration's security relationship with the Philippines and made many of China's neighbors seek closer ties with the United States. It has reawakened Indonesia's concerns about the NDL as well as its maritime frontier, and allowed Malaysia to become a new favorite of the administration, signing it up as a "comprehensive partner." As of this writing, it appears that Beijing may have awakened to the counterproductive impact its hard-nosed approach has had on its near neighbors and embarked on a political-economic-diplomatic campaign intended to assuage regional fears. First evidenced at the November 2014 APEC meeting in Beijing and the subsequent EAS in Myanmar and G-20 meeting in Brisbane, this approach continued throughout 2015.[85]

That said, Beijing fence-mending has so far been more tactical than strategic because SCS issues all involve Chinese sovereignty in one form or another, and as a result, there is scant, if any, room for compromise. Island building has to a large degree undercut this latest iteration of Chinese diplomacy, again an example of how the objective of gaining control of the Spratlys trumps the reaction of its neighbors. None of the other claimants have any doubts that China's ultimate strategic objective remains ultimately exercising de facto sovereignty over all the Chinese claimed features in the SCS currently occupied by others. It is not likely there is any policy approach that Washington could take that would cause China to change its sovereignty aspirations. What is still in doubt, however, is whether or not Beijing will ultimately decide the NDL is a "sovereignty" issue. "Erasing" the NDL would go a long way toward bringing long-term stability to the SCS, since it could provide an incentive to littoral states to make a deal with Beijing over overlapping claims to land features. Perhaps by mid-2016 the PCA will find that the NDL has no basis in international law, thereby providing an incentive for China to do so.

NOTES

1 China has occupied the "rocks" Fiery Cross Reef, Cuarteron Reef, and Johnson Reef South, along with the features Gaven Reef, Subi Reef, and Hughes Reef. These latter features are submerged at high tide and known as low-tide elevations. China seized Mischief Reef, another low-tide elevation, in 1995. Roach, "China's Shifting Sands."

2 The best source for learning more about China's island building activities is CSIS's website, Asia's Maritime Transparency Initiative (AMTI). The site includes satellite photographs and specific data on each feature that China has enhanced. See http://amti.csis.org.

3 Assistant Secretary of State for East Asia Daniel Russel was blunt in his February 5, 2014, testimony, stating, "I want to emphasize the point that under international law, maritime claims in the South China Sea must be derived from land features. *Any use of the 'nine-dash line' by China to claim maritime rights not based on land features would be inconsistent with international law.*" Russel, "Maritime Disputes in East Asia," emphasis added. For a detailed and authoritative legal analysis of the nine-dash line, see U.S. Department of State, Bureau of Oceans and International Environmental and Scientific Affairs, *Limits in the Seas*.

4 The Philippines raised three central issues. The most important is whether China can lawfully make any maritime claim based on its nine-dash line, either to sovereignty over the waters or to sovereign rights to the natural resources within the waters. The Philippines requested the arbitral panel to rule that China can claim rights to maritime space only in maritime zones measured from naturally formed land territory, and that claims based on the nine-dash line are not consistent with Law of the Sea (UNCLOS). The main purpose of the case is to challenge the legality of China's claim to historic rights and jurisdiction inside the nine-dash line.

The second major issue raised is a Philippine request for ruling that all of the "islands" occupied by China (the naturally formed areas of land above water at high tide) are really only "rocks" entitled only to a twelve-nautical-mile territorial sea because they cannot "sustain human habitation or economic life of their own," as set out in Article 121(3) of UNCLOS. The Philippines also requested the tribunal to declare that China has unlawfully claimed maritime entitlements beyond twelve nautical miles from these features.

The third major issue addresses the geographic features currently occupied by China that do not meet the definition of an island as set out in Article 121(1) because they are not naturally formed areas of land above water at high tide (these being Mischief Reef, McKennan Reef, Gaven Reef, and Subi Reef). The Philippines argues that such features are not subject to a claim of sovereignty and that China's occupation of them is illegal because they are part of the continental shelf of the Philippines. Beckman, "Philippine v. China Case."

5 Ministry of Foreign Affairs of the People's Republic of China, "Position Paper on the Matter of Jurisdiction."

6 Permanent Court of Arbitration Press Release, "Arbitration between the Republic of the Philippines and the People's Republic of China."

7 Kraska, "Legal Analysis."

8 Kerry, "Joint Press Availability."

9 Russel, "Maritime Disputes in East Asia."

10 In 1995, a statement read by State Department Press Spokesman Christine Shelly declared, "The United States takes no position on the legal merits of the competing claims to sovereignty over the various island, reefs, atolls, and cays in the South China Sea. The United States would, however, view with serious concern any maritime claim or restriction on maritime activity in the South China Sea that was not consistent with international law, including the 1982 United Nations Convention on the Law of the Sea." U.S. Department of State, "Daily Press Briefing."

11 Okinawa Reversion Hearings, 11, cited in Manyin, "Senkaku (Diaoyu/Diaoyutai) Islands Dispute."

12 The most authoritative unofficial (there is no official Chinese statement) Chinese source on the "nine-dash line" was coauthored by China's representative on the International Tribunal for the Law of the Sea (ITLOS), Judge Guo Zhiguo, and Professor Jia Bing Bing from Tsinghua University Law School, "The Nine Dash Line in the South China Sea.". They conclude the "nine-dash line" has three meanings. First, it represents the title to the islands it encloses, and the UNCLOS appropriates water and seabeds generated by sovereignty over all the land features. Second, it preserves historic rights in fishing, navigation, and such other maritime activities as oil and gas development in the waters and continental shelf surrounded by the line. And third, it is likely to serve as a potential maritime delimitation line.

13 U.S. Energy Information Administration, "South China Sea."

14 Ghosh, "Artificial Islands in the South China Sea."http://thediplomat.com For legal implications, see Beckman, "Large Scale Reclamation Projects." According to Beckman China cannot use reclamation to convert submerged reefs into islands capable of supporting human habitation or economic life of their own that are entitled to maritime zones of their own, because an "island" is defined as a "naturally formed" area of land surrounded by and above water at high tide. If a feature is above water at high tide because of reclamation works, it is an "artificial island." Under UNCLOS, an artificial island is not entitled to any maritime zones of its own, not even a twelve-nautical-mile territorial sea. Therefore, the reclamation works on features that are submerged at high tide do not change their legal status. However, determining the maritime zone is not as clear if China converts any of the three "rocks" it occupies into islands.

15 Wong, "Xi Defends China's Claim."

16 Carter, "Regional Security Architecture."

17 White House, Office of the Press Secretary, "National Security Advisor."

18 White House, Office of the Press Secretary, "Remarks by President Obama and President Xi."

19 Kerry, "Remarks at the US-ASEAN Ministerial Meeting."

20 Russel, "Maritime Disputes in East Asia."

21 Ibid.

22 Ibid., emphasis added.

23 It takes sixty-seven of the one hundred senators to ratify a treaty. In the summer of 2012 the Obama administration mounted a comprehensive push for ratification that many observers, including this author, thought was very well conceived. However, Republican Senator Jim DeMint of South Carolina managed to get thirty-four Republican senators to pledge to oppose ratification, meaning the Obama attempt would fail. Cover, "GOP Senators Sink Law of Sea Treaty."

24 Katigbok, "Obama Calls on US Senate to Ratify UNCLOS."

25 Reagan, "United States Ocean Policy."

26 Ibid.

27 Harf, "Philippines: South China Sea Arbitration Case Filing."

28 Thayer, "Vietnam Files Statement of Interest."

29 Kerry, "Joint Press Availability."

30 Kerry, "Remarks by Secretary of State John Kerry."

31 U.S. Mission to ASEAN, "States Russel on ASEAN Senior Officials Meeting."

32 Mehta, "Carter Announces $425M in Pacific Partnership Funding."

33 "It is my belief that the consistent presence of the Seventh Fleet and our recent force posture movements have been significant factors in deterring conflict between claimants in recent years . . . a strong and sustained US military presence . . . is welcomed by the overwhelming majority of countries in the region . . . [however] . . . diplomacy will continue to be our instrument of first resort." See Russel, "Maritime Disputes in East Asia." See Chatmas, "USS Lassen Promotes Maritime Security."

34 The Obama administration established comprehensive or strategic partnerships with Indonesia in November 2010 and October 2015, Vietnam in July 2013, Malaysia in April 2014, and ASEAN in November 2015. The United States has been a formal treaty ally of the Philippines since 1951. It has been a "Strategic Partner" with Singapore since 2005.

35 This is also true for Singapore. In April 2014, President Obama and President Aquino signed an agreement that will improve U.S. military access to the Philippines. Press Briefing by Deputy National Security Advisor.

36 Clinton, "Testimony before the Senate Committee on Foreign Relations."

37 U.S. Energy Information Administration, "South China Sea."

38 One alternative route would be to leave the Indian Ocean via Indonesia's Sunda or Lomback Straits and then travel north through the Makassar Strait, transiting the Celebes Sea, passing south of the Philippine island of Mindanao into the Pacific and then north to East Asian ports. Another alternative is to proceed all the way around Australia to enter the South Pacific and then head north to East Asia via the Coral Sea and then via either the Solomon Sea or the Bismarck Sea.

39 Yang "Freedom of Navigation."

40 Pedrozo, "Close Encounters at Sea," 102.

41 Pedrozo, "Preserving Navigational Rights and Freedoms."

42 Dutton, "Three Disputes and Three Objectives," 54.

43 For Chinese views on military activities in their EEZ, see the four essays in Dutton, *Military Activities in the EEZ.*

44 Dutton, "MOU's"; and Glaser, "U.S.-China Summit's Big Accomplishment."

45 Bader, *Obama and China's Rise*, 9–17. Bader writes, "During its transition and opening days, the Obama administration looked for ways to demonstrate that from the beginning it intended to place much greater emphasis on U.S. relations with Asia. . . . The U.S. needed to rebuild its presence and relations in parts of the world where it appeared distracted, which first of all meant East Asia" (9).

46 Clinton, "Remarks at Press Availability."

47 Chang, "Hillary Clinton Changes America's China Policy."

48 The best analysis of Chinese assertiveness in the 2009–11 time frame is by Michael Swaine of the Carnegie Endowment and M. Taylor Fravel of MIT. See Swaine and Fravel, "China's Assertive Behavior."

49 The incident took place seventy-five miles south of the island of Hainan in China's EEZ. Pedrozo, "Close Encounters at Sea," 102.

50 McDevitt, "America's New Security Strategy."

51 During his November 2011 trip to Asia, President Obama announced the creation of a U.S. Marine Corps presence in Australia. Today that presence is only 250 strong, but is planned to grow to 2,500—a full Marine Expeditionary Unit (MEU). This is likely to trigger an increase in the number of amphibious ships based permanently in the Western Pacific, so that these Marines will have the necessary means to be deployed within the region. The Obama announcement built upon the announcement that then Secretary of Defense Robert Gates made earlier in 2011, at the Shangri-La Dialogue in Singapore, that several of the U.S. Navy's newest surface combatants, known as the littoral combat ships (LCSs), would be permanently stationed in Singapore. Finally, the idea of reestablishing some sort of rotation presence in the Philippines has now apparently been realized with the signing of the Enhanced Defense Cooperation Agreement (EDCA) with Manila in April 2014. Collectively, these posture announcements were intended to signal that the rebalance strategy includes improving the U.S. presence in Southeast Asia—which, in terms of U.S. presence, had been neglected when compared to Northeast Asia.

52 Kaplan, *Asia's Cauldron*, passim; and Kim, "Territorial Disputes in the South China Sea."www.au.af.mil

53 Rice, "America's Future in Asia."

54 Ibid.

55 Ibid.

56 A good recounting of the incident is provided by Ratner, "Learning the Lessons of Scarborough Reef."

57 Mutual Defense Treaty between the United States and the Republic of the Philippines.

58 Ibid., Article II.

59 For a recent analysis of the Philippine claims, see, Rosen, *Philippine Claims in the South China Sea*. The Philippine claims to the Spratlys originated in 1956 when the Philippine owner of a fishing company and director of the Philippine Maritime Institute named Tomas Cloma claimed he had "discovered" the Spratlys in 1947. Wanting to establish a cannery and develop the guano deposits in the islands, he decided in 1956 to take formal possession first on behalf of the government of the Philippines and then, when they equivocated, as a separate government of the Free Territory of Kalayaan (Freedomland), with Cloma as the "Chairman, Supreme Council of State." He posted a document in English, titled "Notice to the Whole World," listing all features he claimed. His claim comprises about fifty features among the Spratly group. Not surprisingly, his declaration was strongly protested by the Republic of China (Taiwan), the PRC, South Vietnam, as well as the European countries of France, the United Kingdom, and the Netherlands, who were representing their colonies in Southeast Asia. Cloma eventually "sold" Freedomland to the Marcos government for one Philippine peso, and in July 1971 the government of the Philippines made an official claim to the fifty-three islands of the Cloma claim, asserting they were terra nullius. See Samuels, *Contest for the South China Sea*, 81–85; and Yorac, "Philippine Claim to the Spratly Island Group."

60 USNI News, "Document: SECDEF Carter Letter to McCain." The letter itself was dated December 22, 2015. The reason that the operation triggered many public questions is best spelled out in the article by Glaser and Dutton, "U.S. Navy's Freedom of Navigation Operation."

61 Webster, "How China Maintains Strategic Ambiguity."

62 Ibid. In the last sentence of the letter, Carter writes, "We will continue to demonstrate as much by exercising the rights, freedoms and lawful uses of the seas all around the world, and the South China Sea will be no exception."

63 Donilon, "America Is Back in the Pacific."

64 For a short summary of the "rules" regarding the establishment of sovereignty, see Michael McDevitt, *South China Sea*.

65 Rosen, "Myanmar vs Bangladesh."

66 United Nations Law of the Sea Convention (UNCLOS), art. 13(1), www.un.org.

67 *Nicaragua v. Colombia*, ICJ judgment, para. 37, citing *Qatar v. Bahrain*, ICJ Reports 2001, p. 99, para. 197. See *American Journal of International Law* 107, no. 4 (October 2013): 396–403.

68 Austin, *China's Ocean Frontier*, 4.

69 Kraska, "What Would Reagan Do About China's Violations of the Law of the Sea?" Kraska characterizes China as a "recidivist offender of UNCLOS," and then goes on to specifically make his case.

70 See note 12.

71 U.S. Department of State, Bureau of Oceans and International Environmental and Scientific Affairs, "China: Maritime Claims," 4. It finds that China has not clarified its maritime claims associated with the dashed-line maps in a manner

consistent with international law. China's laws, declarations, official acts, and official statements present conflicting evidence regarding the nature and scope of China's claims.

72 Heru, "Indonesia." For more detail on this issue, see Keck, "China's Newest Maritime Dispute." For an excellent overview of Indonesia's concerns regarding China's SCS claims, see Parameswaran, "Indonesia Avoids Open Territorial Dispute."

73 Harding, "Jokowi's Big Maritime Plans."

74 A discussion of how this might unfold is found in McDevitt, "Modest Proposal to Help ASEAN."

75 Japan, South Korea, the Philippines, and Malaysia.

76 Kurlantzick, "Lessons from Obama's Southeast Asia Trip."

77 Bader, Lieberthal, and McDevitt, "Keeping the South China Sea in Perspective."

78 McDevitt, Fravel, and Stern, *Long Littoral Project*, 68–69. In addition, during his December 2013 visit to Vietnam and the Philippines, Secretary Kerry announced US$32.5 million in new U.S. assistance for maritime law enforcement in Southeast Asian states. This assistance will include, among other things, training and new fast patrol vessels for coast guards. Building on existing efforts like the Gulf of Thailand initiative, this assistance will foster greater regional cooperation on maritime issues and ultimately provide the ability of Southeast Asian nations to carry out humanitarian activities and to police and monitor their waters more effectively. See Kerry, "Joint Press Availability."

79 Panda, "United States Lifts Vietnam Arms Embargo."

80 See for example, Colby and Ratner, "Roiling the Waters."

81 Kausikan, "ASEAN-China Relations." In an excellent speech on the topic of China and ASEAN, the former Singapore permanent secretary of foreign affairs notes, "Chinese investments in infrastructure are binding Southwestern China and Southeast Asia into one economic and hence one strategic and political space."

82 Not-for-attribution conference in Southeast Asia, September 14, 2014.

83 Off-the-record discussion with U.S. Embassy Beijing official, September 26, 2014. See also Sun, "China's New Calculations," and Zheng Wang, "Bad Memories, Good Dream," 13.

84 Kausikan, "ASEAN-China Relations."

85 According to Ben Blanchard, "China has gone out of its way to set minds at ease as Xi hosted the Asia Pacific Economic Cooperation (APEC) summit. China made conciliatory gestures to Vietnam, the Philippines and Japan, and, with U.S. President Barack Obama, agreed to a climate deal and to lower the risk of misunderstandings during military encounters. 'We still have to observe what happens in the next six to 12 months or even longer. But I think that now we stand at the beginning of a substantive change in Chinese foreign policy,' said Shi Yinhong, head of the Centre for American Studies at Beijing's Renmin University who has also advised the government on diplomatic issues. Reliance on the military has been replaced by money to guide China's diplomacy, Shi added,

pointing to the US$40 billion New Silk Road fund and US$50 billion China-backed Asian Infrastructure Investment Bank announced before APEC." "Hard Diplomacy Ahead." See also Chen, "After APEC."

BIBLIOGRAPHY

Books and Bound Reports and Analyses

Austin, Greg. *China's Ocean Frontier: International Law, Military Force and National Development*. Sydney: Allen & Unwin Australia, 1998.

Bader, Jeffery A. *Obama and China's Rise: An Insiders Account of America's Asia Strategy*. Washington, DC: Brookings Institution Press, 2012.

Hayton, Bill. *The South China Sea: The Struggle for Power in Asia*. New Haven: Yale University Press, 2014.

Kaplan, Robert D. *Asia's Cauldron: The South China Sea and the End of a Stable Pacific*. New York: Random House, 2014.

Manyin, Mark E. "Senkaku (Diaoyu/Diaoyutai) Islands Dispute: U.S. Treaty Obligations." Congressional Research Service, R42761, January 22, 2013. www.fas.org.

McDevitt, Michael, M. Taylor Fravel, and Lewis M. Stern. *The Long Littoral Project: South China Sea: A Maritime Perspective on Indo-Pacific Security*. CNA Research Memorandum IRP-2012-U-002321-Final. March 2013. www.cna.org.

———. *The South China Sea: Assessing U.S. Policy and Options for the Future*. CNA Occasional Paper, November 14, 2014.

Rosen, Mark E. *Philippine Claims in the South China Sea: A Legal Analysis*. CNA Occasional Paper, August 2014. www.cna.org.

Samuels, Marwyn S. *Contest for the South China Sea*. New York: Methuen, 1982.

Zheng Wang. "Bad Memories, Good Dream: The Legacy of Historical Memory and China's Foreign Policy." *Special Forum, ASAN Forum* 3, no. 5 (2014). www.theasanforum.org.

Articles

Bader, Jeffery, Kenneth Lieberthal, and Michael McDevitt. "Keeping the South China Sea in Perspective." Brookings Foreign Policy Brief, September 2, 2014. www.brookings.edu.

Beckman, Robert. "Large Scale Reclamation Projects in the South China Sea: China and International Law." RSIS Commentary 213/2014, October 29, 2014.

———. "The Philippine v. China Case and the South China Sea Disputes." Asia Society/Lee Kwan Yew SPP Conference, March 13–15, 2013. http://cil.nus.edu.sg.

Chang, Gordon. "Hillary Clinton Changes America's China Policy: The Secretary of State Pulls a 180 on Beijing." *Forbes*, July 28, 2010. www.forbes.com.

Chen, Dingding. "After APEC, East Asia Summit and G 20, China Emerges as a Global Leader." *Diplomat*, November 17, 2014. http://thediplomat.com.

Colby, Elbridge, and Ely Ratner. "Roiling the Waters." *Foreign Policy*, January/February 2014. www.foreignpolicy.com.

Cover, Matt. "GOP Senators Sink Law of Sea Treaty: This Threat to Sovereignty." *CNSNews*. http://cnsnews.com.

Donilon, Tom. "America Is Back in the Pacific and Will Uphold the Rules." *Financial Times*, November 27, 2011. www.ft.com.

Dutton, Peter, ed. *Military Activities in the EEZ: A U.S.-China Dialogue on Security and International Law*. Naval War College, China Maritime Studies Institute, no. 7, December 2010. www.usnwc.edu.

———. "MOU's: The Secret Sauce to Avoiding a U.S.-China Disaster?" *National Interest*, January 30, 2015. http://nationalinterest.org.

———. "Three Disputes and Three Objectives: China and the South China Sea." *Naval War College Review* 64, no. 4 (Autumn 2011).

Ghosh, P. K. "Artificial Islands in the South China Sea." *Diplomat*, September 23, 2014. http://thediplomat.com.

Glaser, Bonnie. "The U.S.-China Summit's Big Accomplishment: 'Rules' in the Sky?" *National Interest*, September 29, 2015. http://nationalinterest.org

Glaser, Bonnie S., and Peter A. Dutton. "The U.S. Navy's Freedom of Navigation Operation around Subi Reef: Deciphering U.S. Signaling." *National Interest*, November 6, 2015. http://nationalinterest.org.

Guo, Zhiguo, and Bing Bing Jia. "The Nine Dash Line in the South China Sea: History, Status, and Implications." *American Journal of International Law* 107, no. 1 (January 2013): 98–124.

"Hard Diplomacy Ahead Despite China Showing Softer Side." Reuters, November 18, 2014. http://uk.reuters.com.

Harding, Brian. "Jokowi's Big Maritime Plans for Indonesia Need International Support." *World Politics Review*, September 3, 2014. www.worldpoliticsreview.com.

Heru. "Indonesia: China Includes Part of Natuna Waters in Its Map." *Jakarta ANTRA Online*, March 13, 2014. http://www.antaranews.com.

Katigbok, Jose. "Obama Calls on US Senate to Ratify UNCLOS." *Philippine Star*, May 30, 2014. www.philstar.com.

Kausikan, Bilihari. "ASEAN-China Relations: Building a Common Destiny." *American Interest*, September 23, 2014. www.the-american-interest.com.

Keck, Zachary. "China's Newest Maritime Dispute." *Diplomat*, March 20, 2014. http://thediplomat.com.

Kim, Jihyun. "Territorial Disputes in the South China Sea: Implications for Security in Asia and Beyond." *Strategic Studies Quarterly*, Summer 2015, 107–49. www.au.af.mil.

Kraska, James. "A Legal Analysis of the Philippine-China Arbitration Ruling." *Diplomat*, November 2, 2015. http://thediplomat.com.

———. "What Would Reagan Do about China's Violations of the Law of the Sea?" *Diplomat*, October 19, 2015. http://thediplomat.com.

Kurlantzick, Joshua. "Lessons from Obama's Southeast Asia Trip." *Diplomat*, December 5, 2015. http://thediplomat.com.

McDevitt, Michael. "America's New Security Strategy and Its Military Dimensions." *Global Asia* 7, no. 4 (Winter 2012). www.globalasia.org.

————. "A Modest Proposal to Help ASEAN Reconcile Their Overlapping Claims in the Spratly's." *Pacific Forum/CSIS, PACNET*, no. 40, July 9, 2015. http://csis.org.

Mehta, Aaron. "Carter Announces $425M in Pacific Partnership Funding." *Defense News*, May 30, 2015. www.defensenews.com.

Panda, Ankit. "United States Lifts Vietnam Arms Embargo (with a Catch)." *Diplomat*, October 3, 2014. http://thediplomat.com.

Parameswaran, Prashanth. "Indonesia Avoids Open Territorial Dispute with China, Despite Concerns." *China Brief, Jamestown Foundation* 14, no. 13 (July 3, 2014). www.jamestown.org.

Pedrozo, Raul. "Close Encounters at Sea: The USNS Impeccable Incident." *Naval War College Review* 62, no. 3 (Summer 2009).

————. "Preserving Navigational Rights and Freedoms: The Right to Conduct Military Activities in China's Exclusive Economic Zone." *Chinese Journal of International Law* 9 (2010): 9–29.

Ratner, Ely. "Learning the Lessons of Scarborough Reef." *National Interest*, November 21, 2013. http://nationalinterest.org.

Roach, J. Ashley. "China's Shifting Sands in the Spratly's." *Insights* 19, no. 54 (May 2015). www.asil.org.

Rosen, Mark. "Myanmar vs Bangladesh: The International Tribunal for the Law of the Sea; Implications of the Case for the Bay of Bengal and Elsewhere." April 2013.

Sun, Yun. "China's New Calculations in the South China Sea." *Asia-Pacific Bulletin*, no. 267 (June 10, 2014). www.eastwestcenter.org.

Swaine, Michael D., and M. Taylor Fravel. "China's Assertive Behavior: Part Two: The Maritime Periphery." *China Leadership Monitor* 35 (Summer 2011). www.hoover.org.

Thayer, Carl. "Vietnam Files Statement of Interest with the Permanent Court of Arbitration." *CogitASIA*, December 15, 2014. http://cogitasia.com.

Webster, Graham. "How China Maintains Strategic Ambiguity in the South China Sea." *Diplomat*, October 29, 2015. http://thediplomat.com.

Wong, Edward. "Xi Defends China's Claim to South China Sea Islands." *New York Times*, November 7, 2015. www.nytimes.com.

Yang, Zewei. "The Freedom of Navigation in the South China Sea: An Ideal or a Reality." *Beijing Law Review* 3 (2012): 137–44.

Yorac, Haydee B. "The Philippine Claim to the Spratly Island Group." *Philippine Law Journal* 58 (1983).

Official Statements and Documents, Press Releases, Congressional Testimony

Carter, Ashton. "A Regional Security Architecture Where Everyone Rises." Presentation, IISS, Shangri-La Dialogue, Singapore, May 30, 2015. www.defense.gov.

Chatmas, Lauren. "USS Lassen Promotes Maritime Security in the South China Sea." *U.S. Navy News Service*, July 9, 2015. www.navy.mil.

Clinton, Hillary. "Remarks at Press Availability." Hanoi, Vietnam, July 23, 2010. www.state.gov.

———. "Testimony before the Senate Committee on Foreign Relations on Ratification of the Law of the Sea." May 23, 2012. www.cfr.org.

Harf, Marie. "Philippines: South China Sea Arbitration Case Filing." March 30, 2014. www.state.gov.

Kerry, John. "Joint Press Availability with Vietnamese Deputy Prime Minister and Foreign Minister Pham Binh Minh." December 12, 2013. www.state.gov.

———. "Remarks at the US-ASEAN Ministerial Meeting." Bandar Seri Begawan, Brunei, July 1, 2013. www.state.gov.

———. "Remarks by Secretary of State John Kerry and Philippine Foreign Secretary Albert del Rosario." Manila, Philippines, December 17, 2013. http://translations. state.gov.

Ministry of Foreign Affairs of the People's Republic of China. "Position Paper on the Matter of Jurisdiction in the South China Sea Arbitration." December 7, 2014. www. cfr.org.

Mutual Defense Treaty between the United States and the Republic of the Philippines. August 30, 1951. http://avalon.law.yale.edu.

Permanent Court of Arbitration Press Release. "Arbitration between the Republic of the Philippines and the People's Republic of China." The Hague, October 29, 2015. www.pcacases.com.

Press Briefing by Deputy National Security Advisor for Strategic Communication Ben Rhodes and NSC Senior Director for Asian Affairs Evan Medeiros. Grand Millennium Hotel, Kuala Lumpur, Malaysia, April 27, 2014. www. whitehouse.gov.

Read Out of Secretary Kerry's Meeting with Chinese Foreign Minister Wang Yi. September 26, 2013. www.state.gov.

Reagan, Ronald. "United States Ocean Policy." March 19, 1983. www.oceanlaw.org.

Rice, Susan B. "America's Future in Asia." Georgetown University, November 20, 2013. www.whitehouse.gov.

Russel, Daniel. "Maritime Disputes in East Asia." Testimony before the House Committee on Foreign Affairs Subcommittee on Asia and the Pacific, February 5, 2014. www.state.gov.

U.S. Department of State. "Daily Press Briefing." May 10, 2005. http://dosfan.lib.uic. edu.

U.S. Department of State, Bureau of Oceans and International Environmental and Scientific Affairs. "China: Maritime Claims in the South China Sea." *Limits in the Seas*, no. 143, December 5, 2014. www.state.gov.

U.S. Energy Information Administration. "South China Sea." February 7, 2013. www. eia.gov.

U.S. Mission to ASEAN. "States Russel on ASEAN Senior Officials Meeting." Regional Telephone Conference in Rangoon, Burma, June 11, 2014. http://asean.usmission. gov.

USNI News. "Document: SECDEF Carter Letter to McCain on South China Sea Freedom of Navigation Operation." January 5, 2016. http://news.usni.org.

United Nations Law of the Sea Convention. www.un.org.

White House, Office of the Press Secretary. "National Security Advisor Susan E. Rice's As Prepared Remarks on the U.S.-China Relationship at George Washington University." September 21, 2015. www.whitehouse.gov.

———. "Remarks by President Obama and President Xi of the People's Republic of China in Joint Press Conference." September 25, 2015. www.whitehouse.gov.

Conclusion

DAVID B. H. DENOON

Background

As noted in the introduction, the purpose of the U.S.-China Relations series is to compare the roles that China and the United States play in different regions of the world, where neither state is completely dominant. In the first volume of the series, on Central Asia (CA), there was a broad consensus among the contributors that China and the United States have very different goals and operating styles in the five states of CA. There, the focus of the United States is on security issues, and China's concerns are overwhelmingly economic. Moreover, in the one Central Asian arena where China and the United States have overlapping interests, limiting the spread of radical Islamic movements, the interests of Beijing are similar and generally compatible with those of Washington.

In Southeast Asia we see a very different set of patterns. China and the United States are competitive across the board: in the political, economic, and strategic arenas. What the CA volume demonstrates is that China can dominate that area economically because it has no major competitor. The shale gas revolution means that CA is no longer important to the United States for energy supplies, so Washington is willing to cede economic dominance there to China, and allow Russia and China together to dominate CA politically.

Southeast Asia, however, is a totally different situation. Of the world's oil supplies, 40 percent go through the Straits of Malacca; Southeast Asia has a population of over four hundred million, so it is a major consumer market; and Southeast Asian states are increasingly linked to global production networks as parts suppliers and assemblers of consumer products.

Thus, both China and the United States see Southeast Asia as important in its own right, and both Beijing and Washington are willing to exert considerable effort there to promote their interests. Also, both China and the United States have a long history of involvement in Southeast Asia. Chinese migrants have been doing manual labor and setting up businesses within the region for centuries, and the United States began its regional links with overtures to Thailand in the 1860s. Then, the United States established dominance in the

Philippines in 1898 and gradually broadened its connections within Southeast Asia during the twentieth century.

So, China and the United States both want access to and influence in Southeast Asia, and have enough invested, economically and strategically, to be true competitors there. What we have seen in this volume is analysis of the linkages into Southeast Asia that both China and the United States have developed. These linkages are deep and central to the Southeast Asian states, so they are likely to continue as long as the United States and China see it as in their interest.

There are three structural features of Southeast Asia that affect how outside powers deal with the region:

1. Although all the states in the region are members of the Association of Southeast Asian Nations (ASEAN), this grouping represents a political compromise, and the country leaders are not committed to real integration.
2. Religious differences within the region have a profound effect on how the member states interact with each other.[1]
3. The North-South split within ASEAN is growing more pronounced.

For *real integration* to occur, the ASEAN states would need to be willing to give up some elements of sovereignty and to make economic adjustments to accommodate substantially greater intraregional trade. Neither of these developments is likely. All of the region's states (except Brunei) became independent of their colonial rulers by 1962; and, even though that was more than fifty years ago, it is still too soon for Southeast Asian political leaders to be confident enough to cede any significant control to regional supranational organizations. This means that most ASEAN agreements on trade, environmental standards, and migration are, essentially, voluntary pledges, not enforceable commitments. So unlike the leaders of nations that are part of the European Union or the Andean Pact in Latin America, the leaders of the ASEAN states see little need to move toward common standards. This perpetuates their links with outside powers rather than forging ties with their closest neighbors.

Also, the lack of commitment to regional integration means that much of the talk about the "ASEAN Way" and assorted ASEAN initiatives is, frequently, hollow talk meant for public relations purposes. So, if a government knows that an ASEAN agreement on, say, climate change is not going to be enforced, there is little incentive to rely on ASEAN for some prospective new proposals, like defense cooperation.

Religious differences are important because they accentuate regional variations among the states. Myanmar, Thailand, Laos, and Cambodia all have
a strong Buddhist tradition, while Vietnam has a diverse mixture of Buddhists, Catholics, Cao Dai, and Hwa Hao. The northern and central regions
of the Philippines are almost entirely Catholic, but the south is predominantly
Muslim. Singapore's Chinese majority is strongly secular, while its Malay and
Indian minorities are split between Islam and Hinduism. Then, the Southern
Tier of ASEAN (Brunei, Malaysia, and Indonesia) is overwhelmingly Muslim.

Why do these religious variations matter? They are significant because
religious leaders often have widespread followings that translate into political power. Although Marxist states generally suppress religion and Indonesia started as a predominantly secular state, religious consciousness has been
growing, especially in Islamic regions. This means that, for example, leaders
in the Philippines feel the need to defer to the Cardinal of Manila and politicians in both Malaysia and Indonesia need to be attentive to local imams.

For our purposes here, it is also important that a committed minority
in both Malaysia and Indonesia has favored the establishment of a caliphate throughout Southeast Asia.[2] Obviously, a religious state, as these groups
support, is incompatible with a secular form of regional integration. Also,
economic integration implies openness to competition from neighboring
states and can lead to job losses, which accentuate friction between states that
already are aware of their religious differences.

These comments are not meant to imply that Southeast Asia is about to
become a grouping of religious states. However, the secular tradition of the
region's independence leaders in the 1940s to the 1960s is being replaced by
a heightened deference to religion as a motivating factor in Southeast Asian
political life.

Yet, the most fundamental problem facing ASEAN, as an organization,
and the Southeast Asian countries, individually, is what to do about the growing split between the *Northern and Southern states* of ASEAN. This split has
not led to formal blocs. Rather, there are two informal groupings of countries: one that is informally aligned with China and the other that presses for
ASEAN autonomy. In general, the Northern Tier (Myanmar, Thailand, Laos,
Cambodia, and Vietnam) cooperates with and takes its lead from China. The
Southern Tier (Malaysia, the Philippines, Brunei, Singapore, and Indonesia)
either seeks nonalignment or has informal links with outside major powers.

This division within ASEAN has not been promoted by the region's governments. Instead, these splits have developed as a result of China's desire to
have a group of pliant states on its border. As we will see below, each state

in the Northern Tier has a slightly different relationship with Beijing; but, only Vietnam and the Philippines are bold enough to directly challenge China (for the former, only when leaders in Hanoi think their interests are threatened).[3] Also, in the Southern Tier, Singapore is unwilling to get involved in an ASEAN attempt to limit Chinese influence. Yet, because it is small and vulnerable, Singapore's leaders are willing to seek, in a low-keyed manner, signs of interest, and potential support, from both the United States and India—as a possible hedge against Chinese power.

Thus, the ASEAN countries have enormous potential: a large population, a major market, and an established set of institutions on which to build. However, the foundation is not solid: there is ambivalence about true integration, plus the structural differences among the states limit the chances of mutually supportive behavior. Also, none of the ASEAN states is willing to make any significant concessions to improve group cohesion. This means that, in the ASEAN area, there is a great deal of congeniality on the surface but few ties that will produce a solid front if there is an outside challenge to the region.

We will now turn to some specific issues raised by our authors to further illustrate the dilemmas facing the ASEAN states. The ASEAN states are a bundle of contradictions. Although there is a widening split, on a North-South basis, between those countries that are acquiescent to China and those that would like to keep their distance from Beijing, all ten ASEAN states are drawing closer to China economically. What we will do below is, first, look at the patterns of tighter economic integration with China and then turn to four arenas where one sees a very disparate set of patterns in Southeast Asia: (1) economic ties with China, (2) domestic politics, (3) support for ASEAN institutions, and (4) security issues.

Economic Linkages between China and ASEAN

Trade between China and the ASEAN states has soared in the past fifteen years. Between 2000 and 2012 alone, the sum of China's exports and imports with ASEAN went from US$50 billion annually to about US$400 billion.[4] Likewise, foreign direct investment in both directions has surged upward. Interestingly, in addition to investment flows from China to the ASEAN states of about US$6 billion per year, by 2011 the ASEAN states were investing in China at an annual rate of US$6.2 billion.[5] Japan and the European Union are still a slightly larger source of FDI for ASEAN, but China's new FDI in Southeast Asia is roughly equivalent to new inflows from the United States.[6]

Two other features of the economic links between ASEAN and China are important. A China-ASEAN Fund on Investment Cooperation has been established with a target of US$10 billion in lending, and the ASEAN states could well be the recipient of funds from the new BRICS Development Bank and the Asian Infrastructure Investment Bank (AIIB).[7] The BRICS Bank was formally launched in March 2013, and the AIIB is in the process of establishing its procedures now. All of these efforts will focus on infrastructure investments. Since the ASEAN states will all want improved infrastructure and China will want to expand its overseas construction activity (funded by these institutions), these ventures are likely to strengthen China's economic ties with ASEAN at the expense of European, Japanese, and American contractors.[8]

So, on balance, the trade, FDI, and financial ties between the ASEAN states and China are likely to grow in the years ahead. In addition, multinational corporations are likely to continue to diversify risk by spreading the locations for the design, parts manufacture, and assembly of manufactured products. Now, for example, many computers are designed in the United States or Taiwan, their parts are fabricated in Southeast Asia, and final assembly is done in China.

In the future, China hopes to be more involved in design, so the direction of these "supply chain management flows" may become more varied. Nevertheless, unless China's growth rate slows much more than at present, the economic ties between China and the ASEAN states will remain close. This has foreign policy implications: interest groups in both China and ASEAN states will want to maintain good relations. Thus, there will be conflicting objectives between the economic imperatives of cooperation and China's territorial and major power ambitions. This dilemma for China and the Southeast Asian countries will be covered, in various settings, below.

Political Trends inside Southeast Asia

There is no single dominant pattern in domestic politics in Southeast Asia. Two states (Indonesia and the Philippines) have remained vigorous democracies.[9] They have freedom of speech, limitations on the power of the executive, and fair elections. Nevertheless, both states have widespread corruption, and their court systems are weak.

At the other end of the spectrum, Vietnam, Cambodia, and Laos have authoritarian political systems with no signs of democracy on the horizon.[10] Communist parties rule in Vietnam and Cambodia; but, as in China, there is no longer a commitment to Marxist goals, and market-oriented economics is used to guide the private sector. The internal political choices do affect foreign policy, however, because neither state wants to endorse Western values or allow an open political system. Likewise, the Laotian state does not endorse any doctrinaire ideology and is just trying to avoid pressure from larger and wealthier neighbors.

The other Southeast Asian nations have a mix of democratic and authoritarian features. Malaysia and Singapore are "quasi-democracies" with open elections but limitations on free speech and lack of true independence for their court systems.[11] Brunei is still, essentially, a princely state ruled by a sultan, but it has some protections for civil liberties and its hydrocarbon wealth permits a generous welfare state.

Thailand and Myanmar are also mixed cases with one (Myanmar) moving, basically, in a democratic direction and the other (Thailand) increasingly under military control. Both countries have elections, but neither is fully open to a true opposition.[12] Thailand is torn between two deeply antagonistic groups, and Myanmar has a combination of ethnic, religious, and civil-military tensions. Thailand was a flourishing democracy a decade ago but cannot seem to find an acceptable middle ground between populist and royalist groups. Myanmar looked as if it was making great strides toward democracy in 2012–13, but has provided mixed messages on civil liberties since then.[13]

Hence, there are no overarching trends in internal political developments in Southeast Asia. The region displays an exceptional variety of regime types but is not moving toward a common form of political organization. Also, because the regimes vary from vibrant democracies to rigid authoritarian states, there is limited prospect of deep cooperation because the political leaders do not trust the motives and values of their peers in neighboring countries. Thus, the vision of 1997, of a cohesive "ASEAN 10" based on political and economic integration, has not come to pass and is unlikely in the near future.

ASEAN Institutions

Because of the long history of friction among the states in Southeast Asia, ASEAN's initial goals were to foster stability within the region by facilitating a nonconfrontational style of interaction. This meant a commitment to avoid interference in the affairs of neighboring states. In the late 1960s and early 1970s, under President Suharto, Indonesia, the region's largest state, played a low-keyed role in ASEAN and worked closely with Thailand to set the tone for early ASEAN deliberations. This approach was successful at setting a conciliatory tone for ASEAN meetings and led to a style of diplomacy known as "the ASEAN Way." Nevertheless, as ASEAN increased the number of member states and raised expectations regarding its programs and activities, ASEAN rapidly expanded the number of institutions dedicated to carrying out its growing mandates.

There are three types of ASEAN institutions that are relevant for this volume: (1) those designed to implement economic agreements, (2) those handling security ties, and (3) those attempting to shape a "regional architecture."

The economic institutions have concentrated primarily on efforts to liberalize trade within ASEAN. The principal method, to date, for liberalizing trade has been the ASEAN Free Trade Agreement (AFTA). In effect for over a decade, AFTA has had a modest impact, but advocates of free trade have pushed it to go further. Their next objective is the creation of the ASEAN Economic Community (AEC), which went into effect on December 31, 2015. The AEC intends to permit free movement of goods, services, and skilled labor throughout Southeast Asia. The problem is that there are stark differences between the ASEAN states on education, income, and skill levels. Also, all but the most advanced ASEAN states are worried about the competition that would ensue if the AEC were fully implemented. There is an AEC Blueprint 2025 and the ASEAN region has a major market of 622 million people, but the disparities in income make an integrated market difficult to achieve. Thus, at the time of this drafting, many observers think a true AEC is a long way off and certainly will not be fully implemented anytime soon.

There are other "regional" economic institutions that affect Southeast Asia and operate in the ASEAN states but are not specifically ASEAN institutions. The Asia-Pacific Economic Cooperation (APEC) organization has been operating since the 1970s, and there are two new trade forums being negotiated now: the U.S.-led Trans-Pacific Partnership (TPP) and the entity supported by the ASEAN states and China, the Regional Comprehensive Economic Partnership (RCEP).[14]

At present, both TPP and RCEP are in the formative stages. Although the Obama administration was, ultimately, able to get approval for "fast-track" negotiating authority on TPP, the Democrats in the U.S. House of Representatives abandoned him and he was able to get the legislation passed only with Republican support. This means that the final approval of TPP may be delayed and the legislation heavily modified when it comes up for final passage. Except for Singapore, Vietnam, and Brunei, the ASEAN states have little interest in TPP because they don't want to commit to unfettered free trade.

The most significant security-related institution within ASEAN is the ASEAN Defense Ministers Meeting (ADMM). It is important in two regards: for its initial three decades, ASEAN avoided any formal discussion of defense issues; and now, with China challenging many Southeast Asian states on sovereignty issues in the South China Sea, ADMM provides a forum where joint positions and actions can be discussed.[15]

ASEAN and cooperating states also support some purely environmental institutions like Reducing Emissions from Deforestation and Forest Degradation (REDD). Although REDD, like ADMM, cannot enforce compliance, it can review grievances. It is notable that both Singapore and Malaysia have been using the REDD mechanism to pressure Indonesia into living up to its commitments to reduce deforestation and burning of peat bogs. Indonesia's weak environmental regime means not only additions to global carbon emissions but also massive smog for Malaysia and Singapore. Thus, REDD is in its early stages but illustrates the growing set of nontraditional links between the ASEAN states and some outside donors.

"Regional Architecture" is the final topic that has spawned a broad range of institutions, some of them originating in ASEAN, others being launched mostly by China but including the Southeast Asian states. ASEAN+3 comprises the Southeast Asian states plus China, Japan, and South Korea. This is China's preferred forum for engaging Southeast Asia because Japan and South Korea have played a somewhat passive role and it allows China to dominate the discussion. China generally sets the agenda and deflects topics that it doesn't want discussed. A more lively regional forum is the East Asia Summit (EAS), which meets on an annual basis and includes a broader range of participants.[16] EAS comes closest to being a truly regional organization, but then, by definition, it cannot concentrate on Southeast Asian issues. Also, because it now includes the United States, policy makers in Beijing are unwilling to bring key issues to the EAS. Therefore, the EAS is inclusive and nonthreatening but, so far, ineffective.

A new entrant in the regional architecture discussions was created in 2014 by China: Conference on Interaction and Confidence-Building Measures in Asia (CICA). CICA was first showcased at a Shanghai Cooperation Organization (SCO) meeting.[17] Although the launch gave it a Central Asian focus, Chinese leaders claim CICA could be an Asia-wide dispute resolution mechanism. CICA is too new to judge its effectiveness, but it is one of many organizations started by China in the past few years that are designed to strengthen Beijing's position and weaken Western influence in Asia.

On balance, then, we see the ASEAN states creating, joining, and affiliating with a plethora of institutions. Yet, ASEAN has still not created a cohesive Southeast Asian grouping as originally envisaged. This grows out of ASEAN's wide variety of regime types and is indicative of the region's conflicted history. At present, ASEAN's economic institutions are not strong enough to ensure a common approach to economic policy making; most ASEAN states depend on outside powers to supplement their defense; and there is insufficient agreement on a regional architecture for Southeast Asia to commit itself to an integrated, supranational set of political ties. Nevertheless, Southeast Asia has an emerging set of political norms that have shaped the character of interaction within the group. Hence, we do not know if the region's institutions are the beginning of closer ties or whether they are just trial balloons that will, ultimately, fall into disuse.

Security Issues

Some of the ASEAN states have serious internal ethnic, religious, and regional insurgencies. However, none of the insurgencies threatens the basic viability of another ASEAN government. Likewise, none of the ASEAN states is currently a military threat to any other ASEAN member.[18] Only China has used force against an ASEAN state in the past two decades; so, when talking about "security," the ASEAN governments are, essentially, referring to China. Thus, the principal security concerns in Southeast Asia at present relate to China's aggressive pursuit of its territorial claims in the South China Sea (SCS).

There are two fundamental problems limiting ASEAN's effectiveness in the security arena: (1) the North-South split in ASEAN means that it cannot operate as a cohesive unit to show solidarity in dealing with China, and (2) China has ratified the United Nations Convention on the Law of the Sea (UNCLOS) and has signed the 2002 Declaration on Conduct of Parties in the South China Sea but has ignored the substance and details of both in its actions.[19]

China's behavior in the SCS is part of a broader pattern during the past seven years where Beijing has taken actions to aggressively assert its territorial claims. In addition, China has antagonized South Korea by disputing the borders and historical legacy of the Koryo dynasty and has harassed Japanese ships and aircraft in the dispute over territory in the East China Sea. China has also declined an Air Defense Identification Zone (ADIZ) that overlaps with territories currently occupied by the South Korean and Japanese governments. Moreover, China has made clear that it intends to project power beyond its current sphere of influence. For example, the One Belt, One Road initiative (linking China with land and sea lanes to Central and South Asia and the Middle East) is claimed to involve sixty-five countries with 4.4 billion people and to be "China's most important strategic initiative."[20] When this is combined with the new commitment by President Xi Jinping, on April 20, 2015, for China to provide US$46 billion of aid to Pakistan for the China-Pakistan Economic Corridor, the scope of China's ambitions is sweeping.[21]

This poses a real dilemma for the ASEAN states that want to protect their claims of sovereignty in the SCS. These governments know that China has not adhered to its prior signed commitments and is planning on expanding its power projection capability. This dilemma is compounded because China has not repudiated its commitment to abide by the UNCLOS and the 2002 Declaration on Conduct of Parties in the SCS; clearly Beijing's actions undercut those agreements. (See the discussion on this in the chapters by Tran Truong Thuy and Chu Shulong.)

Three examples are notable: (1) China has repeatedly claimed that it has "indisputable sovereignty" over the islands, formations, and waters inside its "nine-dash line," (2) China has refused to participate in the arbitration effort that the government of the Philippines has triggered by filing at the International Tribunal for the Law of the Sea (ITLOS), and (3) China undertook a massive dredging and construction effort on seven of the islands it controls, which will give China's military both ports and airfields in the middle of the SCS.[22]

China's actions cannot be supported under international law. Its nine-dash line is merely a statement of Beijing's claims (based mostly on the eleven-dash line asserted by the pre-1949 Kuomintang government) and the Chinese government has never demarcated the precise limits of its claims.[23] Signatory governments to UNCLOS have the right not to participate in ITLOS arbitration; but, if ITLOS supports the Philippine claims, then China would have no internationally recognized basis for continuing its occupation of islands that belong to the Philippines.

Why are these SCS islands so important?[24] If a feature (rock, cay, island) is above sea level at all times, has its own source of fresh water, and can sustain human habitation, then it may be the basis for a particular country's claim of sovereignty. Once sovereignty is established, then the feature is entitled to a twelve-mile territorial sea, an exclusive economic zone under UNCLOS, and possibly even further economic benefits if there is a continental shelf near the feature.

China's tactics are unclear, but it appears that leaders in Beijing are hoping other countries will recognize the dredged islands as sovereign territory even though many of them are below sea level at high tide and, without supplies, cannot sustain human life. Given the dispersed location of the rocks/islets that China has occupied, if other countries were to recognize these features as Chinese sovereign territory, then China would get both the economic and the military advantages of controlling much of the SCS.

Also, once sovereignty is established, a country has the right to control the airspace over its territory. China has already indicated, in international forums, that it may declare an ADIZ over the SCS.[25] The U.S. government has already rejected China's claims to an SCS ADIZ, arguing that sovereignty is disputed and that China has no right to control airspace over features that are not internationally recognized as theirs. In addition, the United States has taken two actions that strongly assert the right to freedom of navigation: (1) in a similar controversy between China and Japan in the East China Sea, the United States has flown bombers into an ADIZ that China claims, and (2) the United States has flown surveillance aircraft inside the twelve-mile limit that China claims for its artificial islands being constructed.[26]

At the time of this drafting, ITLOS has not yet released its decision on the Philippine claim against China. Moreover, the SCS controversies are ongoing and changing rapidly, so it is premature to say how these issues will be resolved. Nevertheless, there is no question that China's actions have created a deep resentment among many ASEAN states and changed the security environment from a calm to a tense one.

Yet, there are other, related security issues facing the ASEAN countries: Will they have to choose between aligning with the United States or China? Are China's expanding military capabilities a threat? Will Russia's renewed interest in Southeast Asia help to "balance" China, or will Russia be joining with China against the Western countries? And will India be a serious strategic actor in Southeast Asia?

China's growing capabilities are formidable. In the SCS alone, China now has more Coast Guard vessels than Japan, Vietnam, Indonesia, Malaysia, and the Philippines combined.[27] Despite China's slowing economy, the Chinese Communist Party leadership has decided to keep expanding the Chinese military budget at an annual rate of about 10 percent per year. Moreover, the PLA Navy is receiving special priority with plans to launch multiple aircraft carriers and increase ballistic missile submarines, amphibious ships, destroyers, frigates, and conventional attack submarines. Now that China has ambitious plans for expanding ties and dual-use ports and airfields in South Asia (including with Sri Lanka, Bangladesh, and Pakistan), how will that affect the calculations of the Southeast Asian states?

The "Asian Pivot," announced by President Obama in the fall of 2011 was designed to let the countries of Asia know that the United States was making a long-term commitment to the security of East Asia and the Pacific.[28] The United States pledged to deploy 60 percent of its naval assets in the Pacific Command and to maintain its long-standing alliance relationships. Some in China tried to portray the Pivot as the start of an anti-China alliance. Nevertheless, its impact was limited because developments in the Middle East (particularly in Syria and Iraq) went so badly that it was hard for the Obama administration to shift its attention to Asia as it wished. The Obama administration subsequently changed the name of this new policy from "Pivot" to "Rebalancing" but left the basic goals the same. Also, with budgetary constraints on new military spending, it was difficult for the United States to show an enhanced presence in Asia. Regardless, the continuing bilateral security treaties with Japan, South Korea, the Philippines, and Thailand plus defense arrangements with Taiwan, Singapore, and Malaysia all indicated a strong U.S. presence in Asia. Other than China and North Korea, most of the countries in the region wanted close security and economic ties with the United States. However, it is important to note that, other than Japan, none of the Asian states has shown any enthusiasm for "balancing" against China's growing military strength.

Shifting focus, the role of India could be a crucial one, as well, because of its ability to provide outside economic and strategic resources that are not currently readily available in Southeast Asia. As discussed above, China is already devoting substantial diplomatic and financial largesse to its pursuit of allies on India's periphery. If the US$46 billion that Beijing has promised to Pakistan is actually disbursed, China will have financed much of Islamabad's new infrastructure investments and cemented its links with India's most implacable opponent. If this is combined with completion of China's past commitments to make a dual-use port on Pakistan's Gwadar Island, India will need to respond in some way that indicates New Delhi's displeasure. Enhancing ties with the ASEAN states would be a subtle way to put pressure on China's sea lines of communication. Prime Minister Modi has replaced his predecessor's policy (of "Looking East") with the new slogan of "Act East." We will see if a substantial Indian program goes with the slogan.[29]

It is also worth noting Russia's increased interest in projecting power in East Asia. Russia has negotiated plans with Vietnam to have its ships return to the port at Cam Ranh Bay. In addition, Russia is participating in the Shanghai Cooperation Organization (with its focus on CA) and has signed a natural gas sales agreement with China worth more than US$40 billion. It is unclear if these Russian moves mean that Moscow will be cooperating closely with China or if they are just meant to counter Western sanctions (because of the Russian occupation of Crimea and support for separatists in Eastern Ukraine).[30] Yet, if China and Russia were to forge a truly close working relationship, that would surely affect the overall strategic balance in Asia.

Hence, the ASEAN states face a number of deep, structural problems in designing their future economic and foreign policies. Most importantly, the ASEAN states are divided between those willing to accommodate China (Myanmar, Thailand, Laos, and Cambodia) and the other states that want to keep Beijing's newfound power at some distance. Nevertheless, each ASEAN state now has greater economic ties with China than it does with any other ASEAN member. So, there is ambivalence toward China: an aversion toward much of Beijing's foreign and defense policies but a hesitancy to give up the lucrative export market.

Moreover, since the ASEAN institutions are weak and there is little compatibility among the member states' political styles, there is only a limited chance that they will be able to form the type of unified bloc that was anticipated when the ASEAN 10 was created in 1997.

Patterns in China-U.S. Interaction in Southeast Asia

In CA, we found that China and the United States operated in very different arenas. There, China's efforts were and are overwhelmingly directed to trade, investment, and resource extraction. Since September 11, 2001, in CA, the United States has been concentrating on the war in Afghanistan and ensuring access to airbases and supply routes necessary to sustain the Afghan and Iraq wars.

In Southeast Asia, the picture is much more complex. Both the United States and China have a long history of involvement in the region; both have diverse interests including economic, security, and personal ties; and these links are likely to grow over time.

Both the United States and China have a desire to avoid conflict in Southeast Asia, but the two states have strikingly different operating styles. The United States prefers market-oriented economic policies, while China is most comfortable relying on state-owned or state-controlled enterprises to carry out its plans. The United States places a very high premium on freedom of naval and air navigation, while China prefers establishing spheres of influence in which a particular state is dominant. These different preferences are also reflected in the type of institutions that Beijing and Washington support. China has supported ASEAN+3, SCO, AIIB, and CICA, all of which Beijing expects to dominate. The United States supports EAS, APEC, and TPP, all of which have more open membership and are open, transparent organizations.[31]

These differences between China and the United States reflect deeply held convictions and are likely to be indicative of their respective operating styles for the foreseeable future. Given the extent of these differences, we can anticipate friction and tension between the United States and China in Southeast Asia—unless one of these states decides to change or there is an agreement to create semipermanent spheres of interest.

NOTES

1   D. Weatherbee, *The International Relations of Southeast Asia* (New York: Rowan & Littlefield, 2014), chap. 1.

2   The movement for a Southeast Asian caliphate began long before the Islamic State launched its efforts to form a caliphate in the Middle East. The Darul Islam movement was strong in Indonesia in the 1950s, created a violent insurgency, and almost led to the breakup of the country.

3   Vietnam's political elite is split between those who are committed to authoritarian rule, who generally favor closer ties with China, and those who are more pro-Western, preferring links with Europe, India, and the United States.

4   China, National Bureau of Statistics, *China Statistical Yearbook 2012*, www.stats. gov.cn.

5   Ibid.

6   The United States is still considered the largest net foreign investor in ASEAN, but this reflects the stock of past investments, which have been massive, in the hydrocarbon and minerals industries.

7   The BRICS Bank is an outgrowth of the Brazil, Russia, India, and China, South Africa grouping, while the AIIB was founded by China and may well have as many as sixty member states.

8   Some of the European states intend to join the AIIB, so they may get some of their funds back in contracts won by their firms.

9   See Evan Laksmana's chapter on Indonesia.

10 See Catharin Dalpino's chapter analyzing Myanmar, Thailand, Cambodia, and Laos.

11 See Zakaria Ahmad's chapter on Malaysia.

12 Myanmar's constitution and long history of military rule mean that the armed forces have both a formal and informal role in governing the society.

13 Myanmar received a great deal of international criticism in 2015 for its harsh treatment of Bengladeshi migrants, the Rohingas. Thousands fled Myanmar in 2014–15, with some going to Bangladesh and other taking boats to southern Thailand, Malaysia, and Indonesia.

14 TPP includes the upper-income states in the Pacific Basin and intends to set high standards for free trade and transparency, while RCEP is more inclusive (comprising the ASEAN states plus Australia, China, India, Japan, South Korea, and New Zealand) but will permit many exceptions and "excluded items," thus is less of a free trade zone.

15 Since ASEAN meetings are handled on a consensus basis, it is unlikely that a South China Sea matter could produce unanimity for an ADMM statement or action, but an open airing of China's actions lets outsiders know of the ASEAN member states' concerns.

16 EAS includes all of ASEAN+3 and the United States, Russia, and Australia plus India as an observer.

17 The SCO members are China, Russia, Kazakhstan, Kyrgyzstan, Tajikistan, and Uzbekistan.

18 Vietnam did invade and occupy part of Cambodia during the 1970s and 1980s, but that expedition ended so badly it is not likely to be repeated.

19 C. Thayer, "Review of the Implementation of the 2002 ASEAN-China DOC and COC and Challenges" (mimeo, May 14, 2015).

20 Wu Jianmin, "One Belt and One Road" (mimeo, Foreign Policy Advisory Committee, Chinese Foreign Ministry, March 26, 2015).

21 R. Hardy, *The Geostrat Advisor*, April 23, 2015, thegeostrat.com.

22 D. Sanger and R. Gladstone, "Piling Sand in a Disputed Sea, China Literally Gains Ground," *New York Times*, April 9, 2015, A-1.

23 The U.S. government has done an exhaustive review of China's position regarding the nine-dash line and found it has little support under international law. See *Limits in the Seas, no. 143, China: Maritime Claims in the South China Sea* (Washington, DC: U.S. Department of State, December 4, 2014).

24 For more detailed analysis of the significance of the SCS islands, see D. Denoon and S. Brams, "Fair Division: A New Approach to the Spratly Islands Controversy," *International Negotiation* 2, no. 2 (1997): 303–29.

25 E. Wong, "China Says It Could Add Defense Zone over Disputed Waters," *New York Times*, June 1, 2015, A-8.

26 It should be noted that the exact procedures for establishing an ADIZ are subject to question and have not been codified by the International Civil Aviation Organization (ICAO). See J. Charbonneau, K. Heelis, and J. Piereder, "Putting Air Defense Identification Zones on the Radar" (PacNet no. 36, June 22, 2015).

27 "China Is Rapidly Adding Coast Guard Ships, U.S. Navy Says," *New York Times*, April 11, 2015.

28 Several months after the original announcement of the "Asian Pivot," the Obama administration decided to change the name of the initiative to a "rebalancing" instead of a pivot.

29 S. Ashraf, "India' Dual Dilemma" (China-India Brief no. 53, National University of Singapore, June 24, 2015).

30 C. Thayer, "Vietnamese Diplomacy 1975–2015" (mimeo, presented at Thu Dau Mot University, Vietnam, April 25, 2015).

31 The United States does dominate the World Bank, the European Union controls the International Monetary Fund, and Japan leads the Asian Development Bank. Though all are "Western" institutions, there are often significant differences in approach among these three.

ABOUT THE CONTRIBUTORS

Zakaria Ahmad is Deputy Vice-Chancellor (Research) and Professor at the Help University, Kuala Lumpur, Malaysia. He has published extensively on politics and international affairs of Malaysia, ASEAN, and the Asia-Pacific. He has a BA from the National University of Singapore and a PhD from MIT.

Chen Shaofeng is Associate Professor of International Political Economy at the School of International Studies at Peking University (PKU). His work has been published in journals such as *China Quarterly*, *Policy and Society*, *Journal of Chinese Political Science*, *Copenhagen Journal of Asian Studies*, *International Politics Quarterly*, and the *International Journal of China Studies*, among others.

Chu Shulong is Professor of Political Science and International Relations at the School of Public Policy and Management and is the Deputy Director of the Institute of International Strategic and Development Studies at Tsinghua University in Beijing, China. His most recent publications include *The Sino-US Relations in the Post–Cold War Era*, *Basic Theories of International Relations*, and *China's Foreign Strategy and Policy*.

Catharin Dalpino is a Sharkey Scholar at the John C. Whitehead School of Diplomacy and International Affairs at Seton Hall University. From 1993 to 1997 she was Deputy Assistant Secretary of State for Democracy in the State Department's Bureau of Democracy, Human Rights and Labor. Her publications include *Deferring Democracy: Promoting Openness in Authoritarian Regimes*.

David B. H. Denoon is Professor of Politics and Economics at New York University and Director of the NYU Center on U.S.-China Relations. He has a BA from Harvard, an MPA from Princeton, and a PhD from MIT. He has served the federal government in three positions: Program Economist for USAID in Jakarta, Vice President of the U.S. Export-Import Bank, and Deputy Assistant Secretary of Defense. He is the author and editor of seven books, including *Real Reciprocity: Balancing U.S. Economic and Security Policy in the Pacific*

Basin, The Economic and Strategic Rise of China and India, and *China, the United States, and the Future of Central Asia.*

Amy Freedman is Professor and Department Chair of Political Science and International Studies at LIU-Post. She is also an Adjunct Associate Research Scholar at Columbia's Weatherhead East Asian Institute, and an editor with the journal *Asian Security.* She has published articles in a diverse array of journals, including *Asian Affairs, World Affairs, Orbis, Journal of Global Affairs, Religion and Politics,* and *Journal of Civil Society.*

Heng Yee-Kuang is Associate Professor of International Relations and Assistant Dean (Research) at the Lee Kuan Yew School of Public Policy, National University of Singapore. He holds a PhD in international relations from the London School of Economics and Political Science (LSE), UK where he also taught from 2002 to 2003.

Evan A. Laksmana is a doctoral candidate at the Maxwell School of Citizenship and Public Affairs of Syracuse University, where he is a Fulbright Presidential Scholar. He is also a researcher with the Centre for Strategic and International Studies in Jakarta. His writings have appeared in *Defence Studies, Journal of Strategic Studies, Asian Security, Contemporary Southeast Asia, Harvard Asia Quarterly, Journal of the Indian Ocean Region,* and others.

Edward J. Lincoln is Professor at The George Washington University. He is former Director of the Center for Japan-U.S. Business and Economic Studies and Professor of Economics at New York University Stern School of Business. He is the author of eight books and monographs, including *East Asian Economic Regionalism, Arthritic Japan: The Slow Pace of Economic Reform,* and *Troubled Times: U.S.-Japan Economic Relations in the 1990s.*

Michael McDevitt, Rear Admiral, U.S. Navy (ret), is a Senior Fellow associated with CNA Strategic Studies, a division of the Center for Naval Analyses (CNA), a nonprofit federally funded research center in Washington, D.C. He was the Director of the East Asia Policy office for the Secretary of Defense during the George H. W. Bush Administration. He also served for two years as the Director for Strategy, War Plans and Policy (J-5) for U.S. CINCPAC.

Ann Marie Murphy is Associate Professor at the John C. Whitehead School of Diplomacy and International Relations, Seton Hall University; Senior Research Scholar at the Weatherhead East Asian Institute, Columbia University; and Associate Fellow, The Asia Society. She is co-editor of *Legacies of Engagement in Southeast Asia* (2008), and her articles have appeared in journals such as *Asian Security, Contemporary Southeast Asia, Orbis, Asia Policy, World Politics Review*, and *PS: Political Science & Politics*.

G. V. C. Naidu is Professor of Southeast Asian Studies and Chairperson at the Centre for South, Central, and Southeast Asian & Southwest Pacific Studies, School of International Studies, Jawaharlal Nehru University New Delhi. He is the author of three books, several monographs, and articles within and outside of India.

Vikram Nehru is Senior Associate in the Asia Program and Bakrie Chair in Southeast Asian Studies at the Carnegie Endowment. From 1981 to 2011, he served at the World Bank, including in a number of senior management positions. Most recently, he was Chief Economist and Director for poverty reduction, economic management, and private and financial sector development for East Asia and the Pacific. He has written numerous journal articles and contributed to several books.

Marvin C. Ott is a professorial lecturer and Visiting Scholar in Southeast Asia Studies at the Paul H. Nitze School of Advanced International Studies, Lecturer in East Asian Studies at Johns Hopkins University, and Public Policy Scholar at the Woodrow Wilson International Center for Scholars. He has authored more than one hundred chapters, articles, and monographs primarily on East Asian, intelligence, and technology assessment topics. He has been a regular commentator on Business Asia (CNN), and, most recently, a commentator on National Public Radio and Radio Free Asia. He received the Meritorious Civilian Service and Meritorious Joint Unit Service awards from the U.S. Department of Defense.

Gulshan Sachdeva is Professor in the School of International Studies, Jawaharlal Nehru University (JNU), New Delhi. His publications include *Economy of the Northeast*.

Tran Truong Thuy is Director of the Center for East Sea (South China Sea) Studies at the Diplomatic Academy of Vietnam (DAV). Before joining DAV, he worked at the European Department in the Ministry of Foreign Affairs of Vietnam. He is editor and co-author of *Disputes in the South China Sea: History, Present and Prospects* and editor of *The South China Sea: Cooperation for Regional Security and Development* and *The South China Sea: Towards a Region of Peace, Security and Cooperation*.